# Amsterdam



"All you've got to do is decide to go and the hardest part is over.

**So go!**"

TONY WHEELER, COFOUNDER – LONELY PLANET

THIS EDITION WRITTEN AND RESEARCHED BY

Karla Zimmerman, Sarah Chandler

# Contents

## Plan Your Trip 4



## Explore Amsterdam 54



## Understand Amsterdam 219



## Survival Guide 253



## Amsterdam Maps 284

WIBOWO RUSLI / LONELY PLANET IMAGES ©

ELLIOT DANIEL / LONELY PLANET IMAGES ©

Left: Canalside houses (p242)

Top: Cannabis College (p69)

Right: House on the Prinsengracht (p105)

JEAN-PIERRE LESCOURRET / LONELY PLANET IMAGES ©

# Welcome to Amsterdam

*Seventeenth-century buildings. Joint-smoking alien sculptures. Few cities meld history with modern urban flair like Amsterdam.*

## Admire Art

You can't walk a kilometre without bumping into a masterpiece in the city. The Van Gogh Museum hangs the world's largest collection by tortured native son Vincent. A few blocks away, Vermeer's *Kitchen Maid,* Rembrandt's *Night Watch* and other Golden Age treasures fill the Rijksmuseum. The Museum het Rembrandthuis offers more of Rembrandt via his atmospheric, etching-packed studio and the Stedelijk pulls out Mondrian among its modern stock. And when the urge strikes for something blockbuster, the Hermitage Amsterdam delivers: the outpost of Russia's State Hermitage Museum picks from its three-million-piece home trove to mount mega exhibits.

## Bike & Boat

Two wheeling is a way of life here. It's how Amsterdammers commute to work, go to the shop and meet a date for dinner. With all the bike rental shops around, it's easy to gear up and take a spin. If locals aren't on a bike, they may well be in a boat. With its canals and its massive harbour, this city reclaimed from the sea offers countless opportunities to drift. Hop in a canal boat (preferably an open-air one) or one of the free ferries behind Centraal Station for a wind-in-your-hair ride.

## Feel Gezellig

Amsterdam is famously *gezellig,* a Dutch quality that translates as convivial or cosy. It's more easily experienced than defined. There's a sense of time stopping, an intimacy of the here and now that leaves all your troubles behind, at least until tomorrow. You can get that warm, fuzzy feeling in many situations, but the easiest place is a traditional brown cafe. Named for their wood panelling and walls stained by smoke over the centuries, brown cafes practically have *gezelligheid* on tap, alongside good beer. You can also feel *gezellig* at any restaurant after dinner, when you're welcome to linger and chat after your meal while the candles burn low.

## Wander into the Past

Amsterdam is ripe for rambling, its compact core laced by atmospheric lanes and quarters. You never know what you'll find: a hidden garden, a shop selling velvet ribbon, a *jenever* (Dutch gin) distillery, an old monastery turned classical music venue. Wherever you end up, it's probably by a canal. And a cafe. And a gabled building that looks like a Golden Age painting.

## Why I Love Amsterdam

By Karla Zimmerman, Author

I love walking around Prinsengracht in the morning. Houseboats bob, bike bells *cling cling*, flower sellers lay out their wares. The old merchants houses tilt at impossible angles, and it's easy to imagine an era when boats unloaded spices out front.

I love that the beer in Amsterdam is perfectly frothed, and you can drink under a windmill without affectation in the city. I love that even the smallest sandwich shop takes exquisite care with their product, and it tastes richer because of it. I love that the Red Light District is by the Oude Kerk (Old Church). Amsterdam is one of a kind!

**For more about our authors, see p312.**

Above: Bicycles, Red Light District

# Amsterdam's Top 10

## Van Gogh Museum *(p155)*

1 Housing the world's largest collection by artist Vincent van Gogh, the museum is as much a tour through the driven painter's troubled mind as it is a tour through his body of work. More than 200 canvases are arranged chronologically, starting with his early career in Holland and ending less than a decade later in sunny France, where he produced his best-known work with its characteristic giddy colour. Works by contemporaries Gauguin, Toulouse-Lautrec, Monet and Bernard round out the retrospective.

***Old South***

## Brown Cafes

2 For the quintessential bite of Amsterdam, pull up a stool in one of the city's famed *bruin cafés* (brown cafes; traditional Dutch pubs). The true specimen has been in business awhile and gets its name from centuries' worth of smoke stains on the walls. Brown cafes have candle-topped tables, sandy wooden floors and sometimes a house cat that sidles up for a scratch. Most importantly, brown cafes induce a cosy vibe that prompts friends to linger and chat for hours over drinks – the same enchantment the cafes have cast for 300 years.

***Drinking & Nightlife***

1

2

5

## Rijksmuseum *(p158)*

**3** The Netherlands' top treasure house bursts with Rembrandts, Vermeers and blue-and-white Delft pottery. More than a million objects of art make up the stash, including 5000 paintings, the most famous by Dutch and Flemish masters from the Golden Age. Feast your eyes on meaty still lifes, dreamy milkmaids, gentlemen in ruffed collars and vintage landscapes bathed in pale yellow light. While the monumental building continues to be renovated, a 'best of' group of masterpieces, including Rembrandt's humongous *Night Watch,* shows in a side wing.

***Old South***

## Jordaan *(p130)*

**4** If Amsterdam's neighbourhoods held a 'best personality' contest, the Jordaan (once the workers quarter) would win. Its intimacy is contagious, with modest old homes, offbeat galleries and vintage shops peppering a grid of tiny lanes. This is the place for jovial bar sing-alongs and beery brown cafes, the neighbourhood where you could spend a week wandering the narrow streets and still not discover all the hidden courtyards and tucked-away eateries. By now you know the Dutch propensity for *gezelligheid* (conviviality); the Jordaan is a font of it.

***Jordaan & the West***

## Vondelpark *(p150)*

**5** On a sunny day it seems the whole city converges on this sprawling equivalent of New York City's Central Park. Couples kiss on the grass, friends cradle beers at the outdoor cafes, while others trade songs on beat-up guitars. Street performers work the crowds, and kids rush the playgrounds. It's all very democratic, and sublime for people watching. The English-style layout offers an abundance of ponds, lawns, thickets and winding footpaths that encourage visitors to get out and explore the free-wheeling scene.

***Vondelpark & Around***

## Outdoor Markets

**6** Amsterdam is market-mad, and its streets hold spreads from silks and coins to organic cheeses and bike locks. The Albert Cuypmarkt is king of the lot. Here Surinamese and Indonesian immigrants mix with locals at stalls hawking rice cookers, spices and Dutch snacks, such as sweet *stroopwafels* (syrup waffles). Flowers fill the Bloemenmarkt, while porcelain teapots and other bric-a-brac tempt at Waterlooplein Flea Market. The Oudemanhuis Book Market has been selling tomes for a few centuries. Then there's the antiques market, stamp market, art market... (BLOEMENMARKT, P117)

***Shopping***

## Queen's Day *(p21)*

**7** On April 30, more than one million revellers descend on Amsterdam for the freakingest street party in Europe. Queen's Day (Koninginnedag) celebrates the monarch's birthday, but that's really just the excuse for a gigantic drinking fest, and for everyone to wear ridiculous outfits in orange, the country's national colour. It's quite a sight to see the city awash in orange fake afros, orange beer, orange balloon animals and orange clogs. There's also a giant free market citywide (where anyone can sell anything), as well as rollicking free concerts.

***Month by Month***

6

## Canal Trips *(p35)*

8 Amsterdam has more canals than Venice, and getting on the water is one of the best ways to feel the pulse of the city. You could catch the vibe by sitting canalside and watching boats glide by: myriad cafes seem purpose-built for this sport. Or you could stroll alongside the canals and check out some of the city's 3300 houseboats. Better yet, hop on a tour boat and cruise the curved passages. From this angle, you'll understand why Unesco recently named the waterways a World Heritage site.

**_Canals_**

## Anne Frank Huis *(p97)*

**9** Seeing Anne Frank's melancholy bedroom and her actual diary, sitting alone in its glass case, is a powerful experience that draws a million visitors annually. Step through the revolving bookcase of the 'Secret Annexe' and up the steep stairs into the living quarters. It was in this dark and airless space that the Franks observed complete silence during the day, outgrew their clothes, pasted photos of Hollywood stars on the walls and read Dickens, before being mysteriously betrayed. (STATUE OF ANNE FRANK)

***Western Canal Ring***

## Cycling *(p32)*

**10** Bicycles are more common than cars in Amsterdam. Everyone cycles: young, old, club-goers in high heels, cops on duty, bankers in suits with ties flapping in the breeze. It's how people commute to work, go to the shop or meet a date for dinner. Renting a bike not only puts you shoulder to shoulder with locals, it gives you easy access to the city's outer neighbourhoods and their cool architecture and museums, as well the windmill-dotted countryside and its time-warped villages.

***By Bike***

## Day Three

### Western Canal Ring (p95)

Visiting the **Anne Frank Huis** is a must. The claustrophobic rooms, their windows still covered with blackout screens, give a real-deal feel for Anne's life in hiding. Seeing the red-plaid diary itself – filled with her sunny writing tempered by quiet despair – is moving, plain and simple.

**Lunch** Grab a canalside table at Spanjer en van Twist (p103).

### Western Canal Ring (p95)

Immerse yourself in the **Negen Straatjes** (Nine Streets), a tic-tac-toe board of oddball specialty shops. Everything from velvet ribbons to toothbrushes to antique eyeglass frames gets its due in the wee stores. Afterward walk along the Herengracht and ogle the Golden Age manors rising up along the canal. No wonder the entire area is a Unesco World Heritage site.

**Dinner** Hostaria (p136) is one of the Jordaan's best Italian restaurants.

### Jordaan (p130)

Charming brown cafes speckle the Jordaan, the chummy district touted as the Amsterdam of yore. Watch the sunset on a canalside terrace at **Café t'Smalle**, join the drunken singalong at **De Twee Zwaantjes** or quaff beers at heaps of other *gezellig* (cosy) haunts.

## Day Four

### Medieval Centre (p63)

Explore the secret courtyard and gardens at the **Begijnhof**. Walk up the street to the Dam, where the **Royal Palace** (Koninklijk Paleis), **Nieuwe Kerk** and **Nationaal Monument** huddle and provide a dose of Dutch history. Rent a bicycle and fuel up for pedalling.

**Lunch** Gartine (p71) grows many ingredients in its garden.

### Plantage, Eastern Islands & Eastern Docklands (p175)

Turn your wheels towards the Eastern Islands and Docklands, strewn with mod architecture such as the shiny **Centrale Bibliotheek Amsterdam** and sparkling **Muziekgebouw aan 't IJ**. Head south to snap a few photos at classic **De Gooyer Windmill**; the bonus here is that organic beermaker **Brouwerij 't IJ** sits at the big spinner's foot.

**Dinner** Dine in the glass greenhouse at De Kas (p189).

### Oosterpark (p184)

You've been a cycling and sightseeing trooper, zipping through most of Amsterdam's neighbourhoods over the past four days. An evening spent plopped on the terrace at **De Ysbreeker**, looking out over the gleaming, houseboat-dotted Amstel river, is a well-deserved treat.

# If You Like...

## Art

**Van Gogh Museum** It has the world's largest collection of the tortured artist's paintings, from his early years to later ones. (p155)

**Rijksmuseum** To master the old masters, visit the Netherlands' top treasure house, bursting with Rembrandts, Vermeers, Delftware and more. (p158)

**Stedelijk Museum** Has paintings by Monet, Picasso and Chagall; De Stijl landmarks by Mondrian; and pop art from Warhol and Lichtenstein. (p161)

**Museum het Rembrandthuis** You almost expect to find the master himself still nipping around his old paint-spattered studio and handsome home. (p87)

**Hermitage Amsterdam** This satellite of Russia's Hermitage Museum features one-off, blockbuster exhibits showing everything from Matisse cut outs to Byzantine treasures. (p112)

**FOAM (Fotografie Museum Amsterdam)** Changing exhibitions feature world-renowned photographers such as Sir Cecil Beaton, Annie Leibovitz and Henri Cartier-Bresson. (p113)

## Markets

**Albert Cuypmarkt** Amsterdam's largest and busiest market has been selling flowers, clothing, household goods and food of every description for 100 years. (p168)

**Waterlooplein Flea Market** The city's famous flea market piles

WILL SALTER / LONELY PLANET IMAGES ©

Bloemenmarkt (p117)

up curios, used footwear, ageing electronic gear, New Age gifts and cheap bicycle parts for bargain hunters. (p89)

**Oudemanhuis Book Market** Located in a moody, old, covered alleyway, this place is lined with second-hand booksellers and is a favourite with academics. (p81)

**Noordermarkt** The Noorderkerk's front plaza has been a market since the early 1600s; antiques and organic fare are the offerings these days. (p132)

**Bloemenmarkt** The 'floating' flower market (it actually sits on pilings) is the place to bag your beautiful bloomin' bulbs. (p117)

## Beer

**Cafe Belgique** Pouring the best lambic beers, Trappist brews and golden ales, this atmospheric beer cafe is the next best thing to being in Belgium. (p75)

**Brouwerij 't IJ** The tasting room of Amsterdam's leading organic microbrewery has a cosy, down-and-dirty beer-hall feel. Bonus: it sits under a windmill. (p182)

**De Bierkoning** They don't call this shop the 'beer king' for nothing; it stocks 950 brews, plus beer glasses and beer guidebooks. (p82)

**Gollem** The pioneer of Amsterdam's beer cafes still pours a bountiful selection in its tiny, brew-paraphernalia-covered space. (p76)

**Brouwerij de Prael** This laudable local brewery employs people overcoming mental illness challenges. Its organic beers are named after famous Dutch singers. (p82)

## Hedonistic Pursuits

**Dampkring** This coffeeshop stalwart has a comprehensive, well-explained menu; a Cannabis Cup winning product; and a George Clooney Hollywood pedigree. (p75)

**Condomerie Het Gulden Vlies** Puts the 'pro' back in prophylactic with its tasteful setting and huge array of condoms for sale. (p83)

**Kokopelli** Life gets a whole lot more colourful (literally) with a serving of magic truffles from this classy smart shop. (p83)

**Prostitution Information Centre** Get frank information about the women in the windows on the centre's tour. (p75)

**Casa Rosso** Jaw-dropping tricks with lit candles and more at the city's most popular sex show (a hen's-night favourite). (p79)

**Webers** When you need a PVC catsuit with whip holster, this little shop can do the fitting. (p94)

## Windmills

**De Gooyer** It's hard to beat drinking freshly made organic beers at the foot of an 18th-century spinner. (p177)

**Riekermolen** Rembrandt used to sketch by this windmill, south of the city at Amstelpark's edge. (p187)

**Zaanse Schans** A whole village of blades turns in the North Sea breeze, a 20-minute train ride from the city. (p204)

**National Windmill Day** Here 's your chance to peek inside the country's 600 twirlers; held the second Saturday in May. (p22)

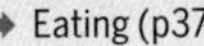
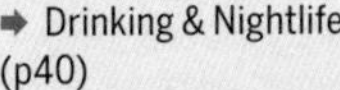

**For more top Amsterdam spots, see**
- Eating (p37)
- Drinking & Nightlife (p40)
- Entertainment (p48)
- Shopping (p50)

## Parks & Gardens

**Vondelpark** A mash-up of ponds, lawns, thickets and winding footpaths beloved by picnickers, dope smokers, kissing couples and frolicking children. (p150)

**Museumplein** The festive green space between the Rijksmuseum, Van Gogh Museum and Stedelijk Museum packs a crowd for winter ice skating and summer lollygagging. (p162)

**Oosterpark** Political monuments and grey herons dot the sweeping expanse of this park, built for *nouveau riche* diamond traders a century ago. (p186)

**Hortus Botanicus** When Dutch ships sailed afar in the 1600s, the tropical seeds they brought back were grown in this wonderful garden. (p177)

**Amsterdamse Bos** The Amsterdam Woods sprawls with thick trees and open fields, cut through with cycling and walking paths, rowing ponds and a goat farm. (p187)

**Westerpark** Abutting a former gasworks-building-turned-edgy-cultural-centre, the west side's rambling, reedy wilderness has become a hipster hangout. (p134)

**Frankendael Park**This formal garden with gushing fountain and Greek-god statues sits behind a Louis XIV-style mansion. (p186)

## Active Endeavours

**Cycling in Amsterdam-Noord** It's surprisingly easy to ride into the countryside and spin by time-warped villages and cow-dotted pastures. (p81)

**Walking Tours** The city has a slew of options for lacing up your shoes and seeing the sights. (p257)

**Canal Bikes** Explore the city from a different perspective with a pedal around the canals. (p36)

**Ice Skating** Museumplein's pond turns into Amsterdam's favourite rink come winter, looking like the top of a wind-up jewellery box. (p162)

## Sustainable Options

**De Ridammerhoeve** Feed the kids (both kinds) at the organic goat farm and cafe in Amsterdamse Bos. (p187)

**De Kas** Sit in a greenhouse and fork into meals whose components were grown just a few steps away. (p189)

**Recycled Bicycles** Rent wheels that have been rescued from the trash and refurbished for economical use. (p32)

**Boerenmarkt** This organic farmers market sets up on Saturdays at Noordermarkt, and Nieuwmarkt at the Waag. (p132 & p88)

**Roots** Ingredients for the rustic dishes come from small Dutch farms, and everything is made from scratch on site (even the condiments). (p170)

**Hempworks** All the clothing and bags are made with organic fibres, plus there's an exclusive label of Dutch-made wares. (p80)

## Architecture

**Rijksmuseum** Pierre Cuypers' magnificent, iconic design from 1875 harks back to earlier times, with Renaissance ornaments carved in stone around the facade. (p158)

**ARCAM** The Amsterdam's Centre for Architecture is a one-stop shop for architectural exhibits, guidebooks and maps. (p179)

**NEMO** Renzo Piano's green-copper, ship-shaped science museum is a modern classic. (p179)

**Scheepvaarthuis** This grand 1916 building is the first true Amsterdam School example, encrusted with nautical detailing and stained glass. (p89)

**Eastern Docklands** If you're looking for one place to see the cutting edge of Dutch architecture, the Docklands is the place. (p178)

**Beurs van Berlage** The 1903 financial exchange building is a temple to capitalism, with tile murals and other decor that venerates labour. (p64)

**Het Schip** A pilgrimage site for design buffs, this 1920 housing project is the pinnacle of Amsterdam School style. (p134)

## Offbeat Museums

**Kattenkabinet** A creaky old canal house filled with kitty-cat art from the likes of Picasso, Steinlen and Rembrandt. (p114)

**Houseboat Museum** Get a feel for the compact, watery lifestyle aboard a 23m-long sailing barge. (p133)

**Tassenmuseum Hendrikje** This entire museum is devoted to handbags, from 16th-century pouches to Madonna's modern arm candy. (p113)

**Pianola Museum** Bursting with musical keys from the early 1900s, this little place is an extraordinary paean to the player piano. (p132)

**Electric Lady Land** Prepare for a trippy time at the world's first museum of fluorescent art, glowing with psychedelic rocks, rice and rabbits. (p133)

## History Lessons

**Anne Frank Huis** The secret annexe, Anne's melancholy bedroom and her actual diary are all here, serving as chilling reminders of WWII. (p97)

**Oude Kerk** The senior citizen of Amsterdam's structures, now more than 700 years old, with many famous Amsterdamers buried under the floor. (p62)

**Amsterdam Museum** Intriguing multimedia exhibits take you through the twists and turns of Amsterdam's convoluted history. (p64)

**Verzetsmuseum** Learn about WWII Dutch Resistance fighters during the German occupation. Learn too about the minority who went along with the Nazis. (p177)

**Stadsarchief** The city's rich archives offer remarkable displays, like Anne Frank's stolen bike report from 1942. (p113)

# Month by Month

**TOP EVENTS**

**Queen's Day,** April

**New Year's Eve,** December

**Museum Night,** November

**Jordaan Festival,** September

**Amsterdam Pride Festival,** August

## January

**Yes, it's cold and dark. Luckily the museum queue was nonexistent, and now you're in a cosy cafe in front of a fireplace.**

### Amsterdam International Fashion Week

Amsterdam's fledgling fashion scene takes flight biannually during Fashion Week (www.amsterdam fashionweek.com), with catwalk, parties, lectures and films around the city. Many events – both free and ticketed – are open to the public. There's a June festival, too.

### Jumping Amsterdam

This is one of the top equestrian sports events (www.jumpingamsterdam.nl) in Europe; it's held at the Amsterdam RAI in late January.

## March

**If the weather complies, you can get a jump-start on tulip viewing in March, and since the season is still off-peak, you won't have to fight the crowds to enjoy them.**

### 5 Days Off

Electronic music festival (www.5daysoff.nl, in Dutch) with dance parties at the Melkweg and Paradiso towards the beginning of the month.

## April

**April is host to Queen's Day, the show-stopping highlight of Amsterdam's jam-packed calendar. You should be there.**

### Queen's Day (Koninginnedag)

The biggest – and possibly the best – street party (www.koninginnedag amsterdam.nl) in Europe celebrates the birthday of Juliana, mother of Queen Beatrix. Expect plenty of uproarious boozing, live music and merriment, plus a giant free market where everything under the sun is for sale.

### World Press Photo

Stunning, moving, jaw-dropping: just a few words to describe this annual show (www.worldpress photo.org) of pictures shot by the best photojournalists on the planet. On display at the Oude Kerk from late April to late June.

## May

**Alternating rainy and gorgeous weather and plenty of historic events make post-Queen's Day May a perfect time to linger in Amsterdam.**

### Art Amsterdam

The Netherland's largest contemporary art fair (www.artamsterdam.nl) is a four-day international event, held mid-month at the Amsterdam RAI. Over 130 galleries from Europe and abroad attract a sophisticated audience.

### National Windmill Day

On the second Saturday in May, 600 windmills throughout the country unfurl their sails and welcome the public into their innards. Look for windmills flying a blue pennant.

## June

**Live music, theatre, and dance take to the outdoors, as well as to the city's most celebrated spaces.**

### Holland Festival

For all of June the country's biggest music, drama and dance extravaganza (www.hollandfestival.nl) practically takes over Amsterdam. Highbrow and pretentious meet lowbrow and silly, with something for everyone.

### Vondelpark Open-Air Theatre

A popular Amsterdam tradition (www.openluchttheater.nl, in Dutch) featuring classical music, dance, musical theatre, cabaret and children's shows in a wonderful park setting. Early June through August.

### Roots Festival

A week-long extravaganza (www.amsterdamroots.nl) of world music, theatre, dance and film held at the Oosterpark, Paradiso and other key venues in late June. Past artists include Robbie Williams, Kelis and Sheryl Crow.

## July

**The days are long, the sun is shining, so who cares if the crowds are flocking to Amsterdam?**

### Over Het IJ Festival

Large-scale theatre, music and fine-arts (www.overhetij.nl) in off-beat venues at the NDSM shipyards in Amsterdam-Noord; for 10 days in early July. Always fresh and exciting.

## August

**August is a surprisingly pleasant time to visit, with temperatures that are far milder than in many other European cultural capitals.**

### Amsterdam Pride Festival

The rainbow flag blankets Amsterdam on the first weekend of the month, with oodles of parties and special events (www.amsterdampride.nl). The climax, the Gay Pride Parade, is the world's only waterborne spectacle of its flesh-baring kind.

### Grachtenfestival (Canal Festival)

This music festival (www.grachtenfestival.nl) delights, with classical concerts around the Canal Ring in the second half of August. The Prinsengracht Concert takes place on barges in front of the Hotel Pulitzer.

## September

**September is one of the best months to visit Amsterdam: mild, summer-like weather and fewer crowds.**

### Jordaan Festival

Music, amateur contests and other festivities (www.jordaanfestival.nl, in Dutch) are held around the Westerkerk and elsewhere in the charming Jordaan district, while hundreds of small boats take to the canals. It's on the third weekend of September.

## October

**While the mild weather may still persist, low-season prices kick in and queues thin out.**

### Amsterdam Dance Event

A club music powwow (www.amsterdam-dance-event.nl), with 700 DJs and more than 80,000 avid dancers attending parties all over the city – all on one long, sweaty weekend late in the month.

## November

**A handful of fun cultural events make up for the possible cold and rain, although November is less cold than you'd expect. You'll find cheaper off-season rates everywhere.**

### Museum Night

Some 40 museums stay open late (www.n8.nl/english), with live music, DJs and a dizzying array of art-fuelled parties.

### International Documentary Film Festival

Ten days in late November are dedicated to screening fascinating true stories (www.idfa.nl) from all over the world.

Top: Revellers, Amsterdam Pride Festival

Bottom: Spend Museum Night at NEMO (p179; architect Renzo Piano)

PAUL BEINSSEN / LONELY PLANET IMAGES ©

WILL SALTER / LONELY PLANET IMAGES ©

### Sinterklaas Parade

St Nicholas literally sails into town (www.sintinamsterdam.nl, in Dutch), arriving by boat from Spain in mid- to late November and parading on his white horse to the Dam and Leidseplein.

### Cannabis Cup

Hosted by *High Times* magazine, this far-out festival (www.hightimes.com) doles out awards for the nicest grass, biggest reefer and best 'pot comedian'.

## December

**Holiday magic blankets the city, even if snow does not (although a few recent white Christmases have given the city much to cheer about).**

### Winter Magic Amsterdam

This ahh-inspiring event (www.wintermagicamsterdam.com) features a parade of beautifully decorated, illuminated boats floating down the canals.

### New Year's Eve

Features fireworks displays over the Amstel and elsewhere around town (try Nieuwmarkt). The Dutch are absolutely mad about pyrotechnics, making even the most informal celebrations a spark-showering spectacle. Big stages on the Museumplein host live bands and plentiful beer tents for a giant party.

# With Kids

*Breathe easy: you've landed in one of Europe's most kid-friendly cities, with an atmosphere that's cheerfully accommodating to children. In fact, most areas – except the Red Light District, of course – are fair game for the younger set.*

WILL SALTER / LONELY PLANET IMAGES ©

Royal Palace (p60)

## Outdoor Fun

Green spaces, parks, and canals galore add up to plenty of fresh-air fun with the little (and not so little) ones.

### Parks & Playgrounds

A hot favourite with kids of all ages is the vast play space of the Vondelpark (p150): it's replete with leafy picnic spots and duck ponds, plus cool space age slides at its western end and a playground in the middle of the park. Westerpark (p134) has a great playground with wooden drawbridges, while Sarphatipark (p167) and Oosterpark (p186) should not be overlooked as great open spaces to let the kids run free.

Amsterdamse Bos (p187) is a huge, forested area with kayaking, a tree-climbing park and a goat farm full of animals to pet and ice cream to eat.

### Winter Magic

Kids will dig the skating rinks and outdoor merriment at the winter carnivals that spring up in Rembrandtplein and Leidseplein come holiday season. Don't miss the unique holiday treats, like *poffertjes* (tiny Dutch pancakes), that the markets serve up from their rustic food stalls.

### Canal Bike

Take to the canals – by bike! – on a unique pedal-powered ride (p36) through the city's beautiful canals.

### Artis Royal Zoo

The extrovert monkeys, the big cats, the shimmying fish and the planetarium will keep those young eyes shining for hours, while teenagers and adults will love the beautifully landscaped, historical grounds.

## Sand & Surf

### BovenNEMO

We've never seen this concept before, but we're sold: the most space-age beach in town has got to be BovenNEMO (translation: on top of NEMO), a man-made beach that's perched on NEMO's dramatic roof, offering a tremendous city view. Expect olive trees, an ice-cream stand, lawn chairs and even sand. As this is a rooftop beach (read: not on the water) don't expect to be able to swim. The good news? It's completely free – no NEMO entrance fee required. Just bring cash for ice cream for the kids (and cocktails for the grown-ups!). Oh, and some sunscreen.

### City Beaches

There are 10 'urban beaches' in Amsterdam. While most cater to adults and emphasise sun and socialising (complete with cocktails and DJs spinning), the most family-friendly is Strand West (Stavangerweg 900), Amsterdam's newest beach on the IJ. Enjoy the river views, but don't hope to swim.

### Scheveningen

Want an actual beach, with ocean waves and salt water? Sure, the Netherlands is not really known for its beaches, but the kids won't be the wiser if you take them to the long sandy coast at Scheveningen (p205), near Den Haag, where plenty of hotels and restaurants cater to families.

## Kid Cuisine

While Amsterdam's foodie scene explodes with adventurous and sophisticated offerings, you can still find plenty of simple, tasty meals that are both toddler-tantrum- and adolescent-proof.

### Pancakes

Even picky eaters tend to say a resounding yes to pancakes. Luckily, the city's full of this kid-pleasing delight. Two of our favourites are Pancakes! (p102) and Pancake Bakery (p103).

For true pancake aficionadas, **De Pannenkoekenboot** (Pancake Boat; www.pannenkoekenboot.nl, in Dutch; Ms van Riemsdijkweg; adult/child from €19.50/14.50; ⏲11am-1pm first Sun of every month, 8pm-11pm Sat) is definitely in order. Morning brunch cruises and evening dinner cruises depart from the NDSM-werf in Amsterdam-Noord; take the free 10 minute ferry ride (⏲9:15am to midnight, every 30 minutes) from Water Square West (behind Centraal Station) to the NDSM-werf.

### Markets

School-age kids love browsing the markets for both familiar and exotic treats. Try the Albert Cuypmarkt for *stroopwafel* (syrup waffle), fruit smoothies, outlandishly topped waffles, chocolate, candy and fresh fruit.

### Ice Cream

Amsterdam's ice-cream shops tend to be seasonal. Come April or May, look out for them in droves in most high-foot traffic areas. Try the chocolate-dipped waffle cones at Jordino (p138).

## Rainy Day Fun

It's prudent to have a rainy day plan in your back pocket. In fact, you might have so much fun that kids will hope the sun doesn't come back out all day.

### TunFun

Set 'em loose for a romp in this underground, all-round pleasure centre (p90).

### Cinema

Going to the art-deco Pathé Tuschinskitheater (p126) or the intimate, atmospheric The Movies (p142) is a perfect

### NEED TO KNOW

- 'Child' is defined as under 18 years. However, at many tourist sites, the cut-off age for receiving free or reduced rates is 12. Some sights may only provide free admittance to children under six.
- Most bike rental shops rent bikes with baby or child seats.
- The I Amsterdam website (www.iamsterdam.com/en/visiting/spotlight/family-kids) has a good page on visiting with children.
- Many upscale hotels provide babysitting services for a fee.

MARTIN MOOS / LONELY PLANET IMAGES ©

Het Scheepvaartmuseum (p178)

compromise: the adults get to revel in the historic environs, while the kids get to eat popcorn and watch the latest new release.

### Indoor Pools

More of a recreation pool than an exercise pool, Zuiderbad (p163) is a good place to take the kids swimming on a rainy day. Adults will enjoy the palatial vintage interior.

### Central Bibliotheek Amsterdam

Yep, the good old library (p179). Only in this case, it's new and stunning, with a whole floor dedicated to children's activities, including comfy reading lounges and plenty of books in English. Check out the weekly story times (some in English) for the younger set. Teenagers will want to make a beeline towards the computer terminals to post their 'I'm in the coolest library on earth' Facebook status update.

## Kid (& Teen) Friendly Museums

While dragging museum-resistant kids through an exhibit on the notoriously sombre paintings of the Dutch Masters might give any parent nightmares, there are plenty of museums that are accessible, educational and fun.

### NEMO

A tailor-made, hands-on science museum (p179) useful for answering all those 'how' and 'why' questions.

### Tropenmuseum

The children's section devoted to exotic locations at this museum (p186) is a hit in any language.

### Joods Historisch Museum

The kids' section on Jewish life in Amsterdam at this historical museum (p88) is accessible and fun.

# Like a Local

*Get on your bike, head to the nearest bruin café and take a free course in Dutch culture by simply observing what goes on around you. It's one thing to witness local life and another to actually immerse yourself in it.*

YADID LEVY / ALAMY ©

Diners at Wolvenstraat 23 (p106)

## Neighbourhood Buzz

### Get Lost in the Jordaan

Even locals get lost in the Jordaan, a neighbourhood of seemingly endless little *grachten* (canals) and streets that change names every block or two. It's one of the best ways to discover the carefree magic of this neighbourhood – without a plan, and with plenty of time…and, of course, beer money.

### Cafe Hop & Shop De Pijp

When the locals are seeking a lazy day of shopping and lunch, they skip the centre and head to De Pijp. It's bursting with cosy cafes and unique locally owned boutiques, and don't forget to hit the Albert Cuypmarkt for the city's best bargains.

## Eat Like a Local

### Hit the Markets

Nothing says 'Amsterdam' quite like a picnic assembled from cheeses, bread, sausages, fruit and bakery goods bought from one of the city's street markets. Good places to hunt for fresh produce, locally made cheeses and baked goods are the De Pijp neighbourhood, where the Albert Cuypmarkt reins as Europe's biggest daily street market, and the Jordaan neighbourhood, home to a Saturday organic farmers market and many tempting specialty food shops.

### Explore With Your Fork

Amsterdam has so many Surinamese and Indonesian restaurants, cafes and takeaway joints, you could eat *rijstaffel* (Indonesian banquet) or *roti kip* every night at a different one for weeks. Want to know what's good? Follow the locals. The Albert Cuypmarkt area is one of the best places to start your foodie quest.

## Celebration Days

### Soak Up Dutch History

One of the best ways to experience Amsterdam's unique history – from the highs of the Golden Age to the tragic years of German occupation – is to join the crowds

Top: De Kaaskamer cheese shop (p106)

Left: Locals commuting across the canals

at one of the city's many history-oriented celebrations. On Liberation Day, Amsterdammers join together to celebrate the end of German occupation way back in 1945; it's jubilantly commemorated with speeches, concerts and street parties. The Dam, Vondelpark and Museumplein are often the centre of festivities.

Another interesting, if more sombre, local experience is to trek down to the Dam on Remembrance Day, when Queen Beatrix lays a wreath for the victims of WWII at the Nationaal Monument on the Dam. At 8pm sharp, the city solemnly observes two minutes' silence.

### Burning of the Christmas Trees

It's a strange Dutch tradition that never fails to make even normally jaded adults positively wide-eyed: the burning of the Christmas trees. Think of it as the pagan version of Sinterklaas – a time when people of all ages take to the streets to create massive bonfires of holiday trees that are past their prime, to usher in the New Year without 'dead wood,' so to speak. The event usually takes place about a week after New Year's. Museumplein is a good spot to check out the madness.

## Outdoor Rituals

### Bike Like a Local

It takes spending all of five minutes in Amsterdam to realise that locals bike everywhere. Literally everywhere. They bike to the dentist, to work, to the opera and to brunch; they bike in snow, rain, sunshine and fog. So don't just rent a bike for a quick tour of the Vondelpark – get onto the beaten path by conducting your sightseeing, dining and nightlife activities by bike. Dressing up to bike to dinner and a show, or to drinks and a club, is a typical Dutch pastime that locals shrug off but visitors marvel over. Put on a suit – or a pair of four-inch heels – and pedal away. No matter what you wear or where you're going, you'll blend in (and have fun doing it).

Another great way to join the locals is on National Cycling Day, which celebrates Holland's most beloved form of transportation. It's held in mid- to late May, and includes family cycling trips along special routes.

### Hang Out in the Neighbours' Gardens

On the third weekend in June, the public has a unique opportunity to view some 30 gardens of private homes and institutions (www.opentuinendagen.nl) along the canals.

## Party Like a Local

### Neighbourhood & Ethnic Festivals

Explore the unique character of Amsterdam's diverse neighbourhoods – each with a different blend of cultures and history – by partying with the locals at a neighbourhood festival. Kwakoe (www.kwakoefestival.com, in Dutch) takes place in Bijlmer Park on weekends in July and early August, and celebrates the city's prominent Surinamese and African heritage.

Or grab your platinum blonde wig and platform shoes for the raucously fun Hartjesdagen Zeedijk festival (Days of Hearts; www.zeedijk.nl), held on the third weekend of August. Dating back to medieval times, it features street theatre, a transvestite parade and all kinds of costumed extroverts on Zeedijk and Nieuwmarkt.

Locals party like it's Queen's Day at the Uitmarkt Festival (www.uitmarkt.nl; late August) in the Eastern Docklands.

### Borrel

*Borrel* in Dutch means, quite simply, 'drink' – as in a glass of spirits, traditionally *jenever* (Dutch gin). But in social parlance, to be invited to *borrel* means to take part in an informal gathering for drinks, conversation and fun – and quite possibly food as well. Any occasion can be a reason for *borrel*: a birthday, the end of a work day, a beautiful sunset that invites patio sitting. When you see a group of locals spilling out of a brown cafe onto the street with a glass of beer in hand? That's *borrel*. Grab a beer (or buy someone one) and join the party. The famously tolerant and open Dutch rarely mind an addition to the party.

# For Free

*While many travellers may bemoan the high cost of Amsterdam's lodging and dining, look on the bright (and cheap) side. Not only is the entire Canal Ring a Unesco Heritage site (read: free living museum), but nearly every day there is something to do that is fabulous and free (or nearly free).*

## Be Entertained

While high culture in Amsterdam can be expensive, you can laugh, applaud and *bravo* your way through town for the price of a beer (or less).

### Student Wednesday at Chicago Social Club & Boom Chicago

Hope you brought your student ID: on Wednesday, Amsterdam's comedy queens and kings present improv (in English; p126), and up to four students can see the show for the price of one (about €6 per person).

### Sunday Jazz at Badcuyp

This funky all-ages event (p173) brings everyone in the neighbourhood out to jam or to listen to jazz. It's totally free, though it's customary to buy a drink or two.

### Irish Music at Mulligans

Our fave Irish bar (p122) in town is known for its no-cover live music. Buy a Guinness for the pleasure of perching at the bar and enjoying everything from traditional Irish music to Scottish ballads to rock and roll.

### Open Air Theatre

The Vondelpark Openluchttheater (p152) brings in some of the city's most diverse programming, from modern dance to classical music to theatre. Entrance is free (or reserve a seat online for €2.50).

### Tuesday Jam Sessions at Bimhuis

Get jazzy on Tuesday nights at Amsterdam's most revered jazz venue (p182). Free admission; sessions start at 8pm.

## Secret Spots

### Rijksmuseum Gardens

Most people (even locals) don't know that the Renaissance and Baroque Gardens (p159) are free and open to the public during the museum's renovation. So let your pre-Raphaelite spirit run free as you explore the rose bushes, hedges and statues.

### Begijnhof

Okay, so the Begijnhof (p61), Amsterdam's most breathtaking courtyard, is hardly a secret. Then why does it still feel so deliciously like one? This garden has a way of instantly transporting visitors to the 14th century: wander the gardens, peek in the medieval church, and drink in the blissful silence. Everyone (except large groups) is welcome here – no matter if you have just an alm (or a euro) to your name.

## Go Outdoors

### Queen's Night & Day

One of the best things about Queen's Day (and night; p21) is that, in addition to being Europe's biggest street party, it's totally free. (Well, you might want to bring some euros for beer and a cheap orange wig.)

### St Nicolaas Boat Tours

Support the St Nicolaas Boat Club (www.amsterdamboatclub.com; Leidseplein 12) – a non-profit group that renovates and preserves historic boats – by taking a free (donations are welcome) 1½-hour boat trip down the city's storied canals.

# Museum Top Tips

*Amsterdam's world-class museums draw millions of visitors each year, and queues at the Van Gogh Museum, Rijksmuseum, Anne Frank Huis and Hermitage Amsterdam can be outrageous, particularly in summer. Want to beat the crowds and save money? Here's how.*

## Be an Early Bird

You've heard it ad nauseam, but it's true – if you go to the big attractions first thing in the morning, as soon as they open, you're going to get in quicker (plus the crowds won't have amassed yet inside, so you'll have less elbowing to do to get close to exhibits). Better yet, go during evening hours. The Van Gogh Museum is open late on Friday, the Hermitage Amsterdam on Wednesday and the Anne Frank Huis every night in summer.

## Take Advantage of E-Tickets

Buy your tickets online. Most sights sell e-tickets (you'll need to be able to print them out) and there's little to no surcharge. Online ticket holders then get to enter via a separate, faster queue (usually) than everyone else.

## Try Tourist Offices

You can also buy advance tickets at tourist offices (p263), but often the queues there are as lengthy as the ones at the sights.

## Buy a Discount Card

There are three main options. For details on purchasing the cards, see p259.

### Museumkaart

The Museum Card (€40) works well if you plan to be in the Netherlands a while. It provides free entry to some 400 museums nationwide for a year. After five or six museums the card will have paid for itself, plus cardholders typically get to jump queues at museums and enter via a special 'fast lane'.

### I Amsterdam Card

If you are making just one quick trip to Amsterdam, consider the I Amsterdam Card (per 24/48/72 hours €39/49/59). It includes admission to many of the same venues as the Museumkaart, plus a GVB transit pass, a canal cruise and discounts at restaurants and shops. You'll need to move fast (ie be able to visit three or so museums per day) to make it pay for itself. Note that I Amsterdam Card holders typically do not get fast-track entry to sights.

### Holland Pass

Holland Pass is like the I Amsterdam Card but without the rush for usage; you can visit sights over a prolonged period. It gets a bit tricky to figure out how much money you're saving because you pick from 'tiers' of attractions (the most popular/expensive sights are top-tier). It does provide fast-track entry.

## Additional Tips

- Many hotels sell surcharge-free tickets to the big museums as a service to guests; be sure to ask your front-desk staff.
- Weekends tend to be the busiest times, along with Wednesday afternoons when school groups often visit museums.
- The most common museum closing day is Monday.

# By Bike

*Bicycles are more common than cars in Amsterdam, and to roll like a local you'll need a two-wheeler. Rent one from the myriad shops in town and the whole city becomes your playground. It is the quintessential thing to do while visiting, and it's remarkably easy to get moving.*

DENNIS COX / ALAMY ©

Bicycle parking lot near Centraal Station

## Hiring a Bike

Many visitors rent a bike towards the end of their stay and wish they had done so sooner. Rental shops are everywhere; most are open from 9am to 6pm (at least). You'll have to show a passport or European national ID card, and leave a credit card imprint or pay a deposit (usually €50). Prices for basic 'coaster-brake' bikes average €12.50 per 24-hour period. Bikes with gears and handbrakes, and especially insurance, cost more.

**Bike City** (☎626 37 21; www.bikecity.nl; Bloemgracht 68-70) There's no advertising on the bikes, so you can pretend you're a local.

**Black Bikes** (☎670 85 31; www.black-bikes.com; Nieuwezijds Voorburgwal 146) Another signless company, with cargo bikes for toting kids.

**Damstraat Rent-a-Bike** (☎625 50 29; www.rentabike.nl; Damstraat 20-22) Has lots of tandem bikes.

**MacBike** (☎620 09 85; www.macbike.nl) The most touristy (and the bikes are equipped with big signs that say 'LOOK OUT!' to locals), but it has the most locations (Centraal Station, Nieuwe Uilenburgerstraat 116 and Weteringschans 2) and sells great maps.

**Mike's Bike Tours** (☎622 79 70; www.mikesbiketours.com; Kerkstraat 134) Has no signs, for those who want to blend in.

**Recycled Bicycles** (☎06 5468 1429; Spuistraat 84a; www.recycledbicycles.org; ⏲closed Sun) Rents bikes rebuilt from scrap parts; the price is right at €5 per day.

## Bike Tours

A bike tour is an exceptional way to get to know Amsterdam. Bike rental is included in prices. There are countless great options, but these are our favourites:

**Orange Bike** (☎528 99 90; www.orangebike.nl; tours €25-33) In addition to traditional city tours, it offers themed options like the Snack Tour, where you sample Dutch *bitterballen* (small croquettes) and *jenever* (gin); a Beer Bike Tour, where you sample four local brews in time-honoured cafes; and an Eastern Harbour architecture tour. Branches at Geldersekade 37 and Singel 233; reserve in advance.

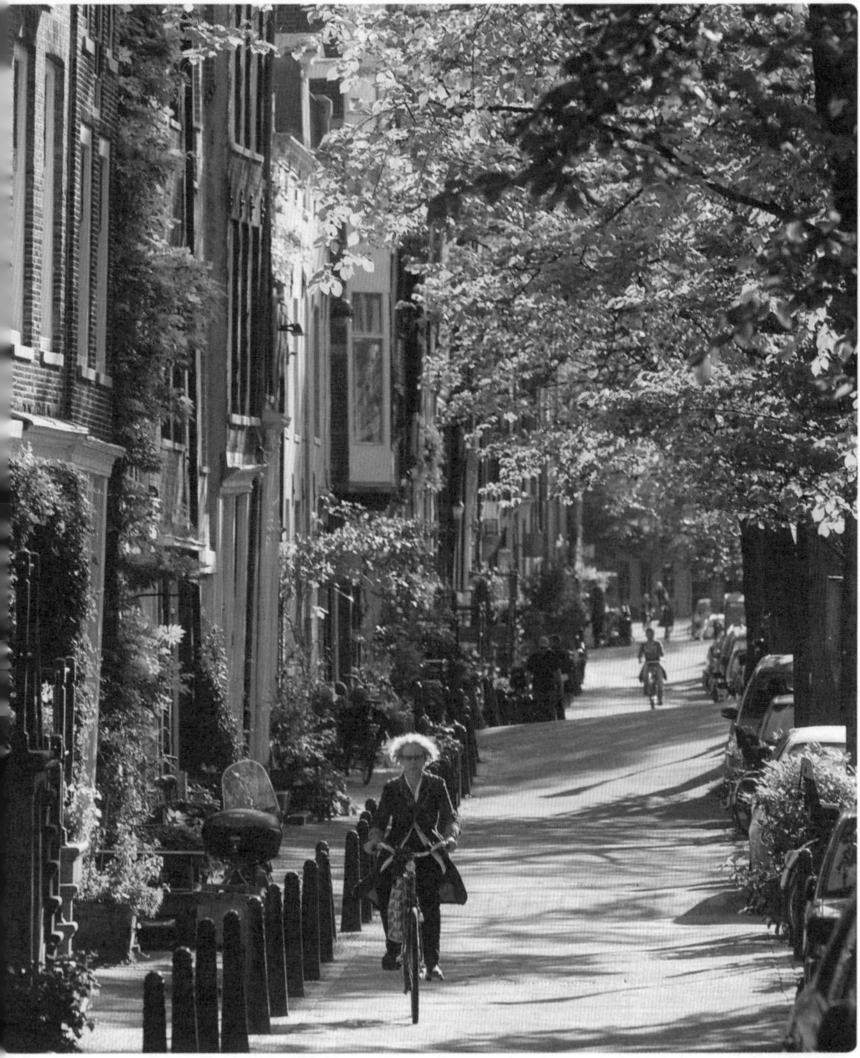

Top: Cycling in the Jordaan

Right: Cyclists heading to a festival

TONY BURNS / LONELY PLANET IMAGES ©

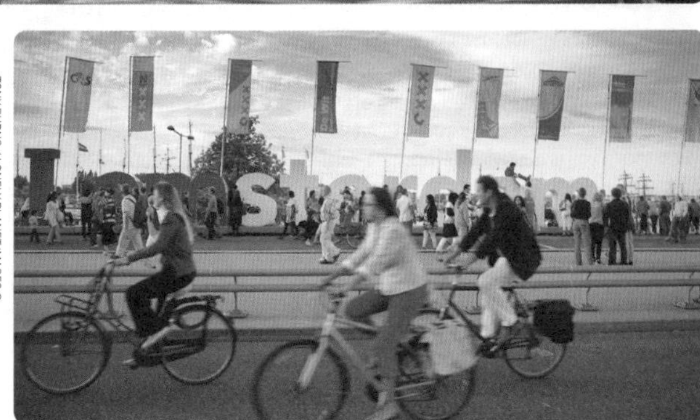

**Mike's Bike Tours** (☎622 79 70; www.mikesbiketours.com; Kerkstraat 134; tours €22) Fantastic four-hour tours take you around the centre of town and south along the Amstel river, past dairy farms and windmills.

**Yellow Bike** (☎620 69 40; www.yellowbike.nl; Nieuwezijds Kolk 29; 2hr city tours €19.50, 4hr countryside tours €29.50) Yellow Bike offered the original Amsterdam bike tour, so it's got it down pat. Choose from city tours or the longer countryside tour through the pretty Waterland district to the north. Tours are less youth-oriented than Mike's. Reservations recommended.

## Road Rules

- Helmets are not required. Most Dutch don't use them, and they don't come standard with rental.
- Use the bicycle lane on the road's right-hand side; white lines and bike symbols mark the spot.
- Cycle in the same direction as traffic, and adhere to all traffic lights and signs.
- Make sure you signal when turning by putting out your hand.
- Use a white headlight and a red tail light after dark.
- Near train and tram stations, on the Dam and in certain public squares, park only in bicycle racks (or risk removal by the police).

## Cycling Tips

- Chain your bike securely. Most bikes come with two locks, one for the front wheel (attach it to the frame) and the other for the back. One lock should also be attached to something stationary (preferably a bike rack).
- Be careful not to get your wheels stuck in the tram rails – cross the rails at a steep angle.
- It's polite to give a quick ring of your bell as a warning. If someone's about to hit you, a good sharp yell is highly effective.

## Buying a Bike

A basic used bicycle (no gears, with coaster brakes, maybe a bit rickety) costs around €80 from bicycle shops or classified ads. New models start at around €200 (on sale). Add another €40 for two good locks.

Fietsfabriek (p173) is an awesome, outrageous shop in De Pijp if you're looking for one-of-a-kind wheels.

## Cycling Beyond the City

Feeling adventurous? You don't have to pedal far from Amsterdam to reach idyllic, windmill-dotted landscapes. LF routes (*landelijke fietsroutes*, or long-distance routes) criss-cross the country, sort of like bike highways. For instance, you could cycle from Amsterdam to Haarlem on LF20 over a distance of 25km – a very manageable day trip. For maps, look for the widely available Falk/VVV *Fietskaart met Knooppuntennetwerk* (cycling network) series, with keys in English.

## Resources

- For route planning, see www.routecraft.nl, which calculates the best bike paths; for English click on 'Bikeplanner' then the British flag. The iPhone app version costs €2.
- MacBike has fun city bike maps covering themes such as Rembrandt sites, gay hot spots, Amsterdam Noord's countryside and more. They cost a euro or two and are available at VVV offices, as well as MacBike shops. The company also distributes a free city map.
- If your bike has been stolen, call the police on ☎0900 88 44 or go to www.politie.nl/aangifte and fill out the declaration form.

## Fun Facts

- Total number of bikes in Amsterdam: 555,000
- Total number of cars: 220,000
- Total number of bike racks: 225,000
- Number of spaces at Centraal Station's bike-parking garage: 2500
- Number of bikes stolen in Amsterdam each year: 150,000

# Canals

*Amsterdammers have always known their Canal Ring, built during the Golden Age, is extraordinary. Unesco made it official in 2010, when it dubbed the waterways a World Heritage site. Today more canals flow in Amsterdam than in Venice.*

CAROL WILEY / LONELY PLANET IMAGES ©

Canalside houses on Prinsengracht

## Names & Layout

In Dutch a canal is a *gracht* (*'khrakht'*), and the main canals form the central *grachtengordel* (canal ring). These beauties came to life in the early 1600s, after Amsterdam's population grew beyond its medieval walls, and city planners put together an ambitious design for expansion. The concentric waterways they built are the same ones you see today.

### Core Canals

Starting from the core, the major semicircular canals are the Singel, Herengracht, Keizersgracht and Prinsengracht. An easy way to remember them is that, apart from the singular **Singel** (which originally was a moat that defended Amsterdam's outer limits), these canals are in alphabetical order.

The **Herengracht** is where Amsterdam's wealthiest residents moved once the canals were completed. They named the waterway after the Heeren XVII (17 Gentlemen) of the Dutch East India Company, and built their mansions alongside it.

Almost as swanky was the **Keizersgracht** (Emperor's Canal), a nod to Holy Roman Emperor Maximilian I.

The **Prinsengracht** – named after William the Silent, Prince of Orange and the first Dutch royal – was designed as a slightly cheaper canal with smaller residences and warehouses. It also acted as a barrier against the crusty working-class quarter beyond, aka the Jordaan. Today the Prinsengracht is the liveliest of Amsterdam's inner canals, with cafes, shops and houseboats lining the quays.

### Radial Canals

From west to east, the major radial canals are Brouwersgracht, Leidsegracht and Reguliersgracht, also in alphabetical order. They cut across the core canals like spokes on a bicycle.

The **Brouwersgracht** (Brewers Canal) is one of Amsterdam's most beautiful waterways. It takes its name from the many breweries that lined the banks in the 16th and 17th centuries.

The **Leidsegracht** was named after the city of Leiden, to which it was the main water route.

Peaceful **Reguliersgracht** was named after an order of monks whose monastery was located nearby. It's pretty, too, and through a quirk of construction you can peer through the arches of at least seven bridges (a fact not lost on canal-boat operators).

## Bridges

Several striking bridges cross the waterways. The **Torensluis**, spanning the Singel, was built in the mid-1600s and is Amsterdam's oldest bridge. The **Blauwbrug** (Blue Bridge) crosses the Amstel river, with fish sculptures and imperial-crowned street lamps dotting the way. And you've probably seen the iconic **Magere Brug** (Skinny Bridge) in photos. It, too, reaches over the Amstel and twinkles under the glow of 1200 tiny lights.

## Houseboats

Some 3300 houseboats line Amsterdam's canals. Living on the water became popular after WWII, when a surplus of old cargo ships helped fill the gap of a housing shortage on land. The Prinsengracht displays a particularly groovy mix. You can climb aboard one and explore the cramped, er, cosy interior at the Houseboat Museum (p133). The Brouwersgracht also has several vessels, including Frederic's (p211), where you can stay overnight on the water.

## Boat Tours

Sure they're touristy, but canal tours are also a delightful way to see the city. Several operators depart from moorings at Centraal Station, Damrak, Rokin and opposite the Rijksmuseum. Costs are similar (around €13 per adult). To avoid the steamed-up glass window effect, look for a boat with an open seating area. On a night tour, there's the bonus of seeing the bridges lit up (though these tours usually cost a few euros more).

**St Nicolaas Boat Club** (www.amsterdamboatclub.com; Leidseplein 12) By far the best boat tour in the city. The open-air, 10-seat boats can manoeuvre into the narrowest canals. Patrons are allowed to smoke dope and drink beer on board, while the captains tell stories about alternative Amsterdam. Rides last 60 to 90 minutes. There is no set fee, just a suggested donation of €10. Departure times vary according to numbers; sign up after noon at the bar at Boom Chicago (p126).

**Canal Bus** (www.canal.nl; day pass adult/child €22/11) Offers a unique hop-on, hop-off service; has 20 docks around the city near the big museums.

**Blue Boat Company** (www.blueboat.nl; Stadhouderskade 30; ⏲every 30min 10am-7pm) Blue Boat's main tour (adult/child €13/7) clocks in at 75 minutes. Evening cruises are offered hourly from 7pm to 9pm from April to September, and at 8pm the rest of the year. The dock is near the Max Euweplein.

**Wetlands Safari** (☎686 11 66; www.wetlandssafari.com; per person incl transport & picnic €43; ⏲9.30am Mon-Fri, 10am Sun) OK, so it's not a canal tour, but it is an exceptional 5½-hour boat trip. Participants meet in town and get bussed to just north of the centre, then canoe through boggy, froggy wetlands, and on past windmills and 17th-century villages. Departure is from the VVV tourist office opposite Centraal Station.

## Canal Bikes & Motorboats

**Canal Bike** (www.canal.nl; per hr per person €8; ⏲10am-6pm Apr-Oct, to 10pm in summer) These pedal boats allow you to splash around the canals at your own speed. Landing stages are by the Rijksmuseum, Leidseplein, Anne Frank Huis, and the corner of Keizersgracht and Leidsestraat. Deposit of €20 required. Affiliated with Canal Bus.

**Canal Motorboats** (☎422 70 07; www.canalmotorboats.com; Zandhoek 10a; per hr €50; ⏲9am-sunset) Has small aluminium boats (maximum six passengers) that are easy to drive. Staff give you a map and plenty of advice, and will come and rescue you if need be. Credit card imprint or €150 cash deposit required. Located in the Western Islands, about 2km northwest of Centraal Station.

*Haring* – a traditional Dutch snack of salted or pickled herring, onion and gherkin

RICHARD NEBESKY / LONELY PLANET IMAGES ©

# Eating

*True, no one sighs over Dutch food the way they do over, say, French fare (mayo-slathered fries after multiple beers notwithstanding). So we'll just call Amsterdam's hot global eats, from Indonesian rice tables to mod Moroccan plates to Basque-inspired pintxos, our little secret. Whatever you choose, meals here are something to linger over as the candle burns low on the tabletop.*

## Specialties

The Netherlands' former colonies spice up the local fare. Dutch chefs fly the flag highest at nouvelle cuisine restaurants, and restaurants serving fish.

### DUTCH

Traditional Dutch cuisine revolves around meat, potatoes and vegetables. Typical dishes include *stamppot* (mashed pot) – potatoes mashed with vegies (usually kale or endive) and served with smoked sausage or strips of pork. *Erwtensoep* is a thick pea soup with smoked sausage and bacon.

*Pannenkoeken* translates as 'pancakes', although North Americans will be in for a surprise – the Dutch variety is huge and a little stretchy, served one to a plate and topped with sweet or savoury ingredients.

### INDONESIAN

The most famous dish is *rijsttafel* (Indonesian banquet): a dozen or more tiny dishes such as braised beef, pork satay and ribs served with white rice. Smaller *nasi rames* (mixed rice) is similar in concept but is served on one plate. *Bami rames* is the same dish but with thick noodles in place of rice.

## NEED TO KNOW

### Price Ranges

In our listings we've used the following price ranges to represent the cost of a main dish at dinner:

| | |
|---|---|
| **€** | less than €12 |
| **€€** | €12–25 |
| **€€€** | more than €25 |

### Opening Hours

➡ Most restaurants: 11am-2.30pm for lunch, 6-10pm for dinner.

### Reservations

➡ It never hurts to phone ahead and make a reservation for eateries in the upper price bracket.

### Service

➡ If you're from a 'service with a smile' kind of society, service in Amsterdam may be impersonal, off-putting and just plain slow. Don't take it personally; it's not directed at you.

### Tipping

➡ Diners do tip, but modestly. Round up to the next euro, or around 5%; a 10% tip is considered generous. If your bill comes to €9.50, you might leave €10.

➡ If you're paying by credit card, state the amount you want to pay, including tip, as you hand your payment to your server.

### Cash Rules

➡ Many restaurants don't accept credit cards, even top-end places. If they do, some levy a 5% surcharge: check first.

### Saving Money

➡ *Dagschotel* is dish of the day; heartier appetites might go for a *dagmenu* (a set menu of three or more courses).

➡ Cafe breakfasts tend to be overpriced. Consider hitting a bakery instead.

### Websites

➡ IENS (www.iens.nl, in Dutch) Everyday eaters give their restaurant opinions.

Indonesian food is usually served mild for Western palates. If you want it *pedis* (hot), say so but be prepared for the ride of a lifetime.

### SURINAMESE

This Caribbean-style cuisine features curries (chicken, lamb or beef) prominently. Roti are burrito-like flatbread wraps stuffed with curried meat or veg; they're delicious, filling and cheap.

## Snacks

**Vlaamse frites** The iconic French fries smothered in mayonnaise or myriad other gooey sauces.

**Kroketten** Croquettes are dough balls with various fillings that are crumbed and deep-fried; the variety called *bitterballen* are a popular meat-filled snack served with mustard.

**Haring** Herring is a Dutch institution, sold at stalls around the city. It's prepared with salt or pickled but never cooked, and served with diced onion and sometimes sweet-pickle chips.

## Eating by Neighbourhood

➡ **Medieval Centre & Red Light District** (p71) Name your price: from elegant Dutch to Zeedijk's Asian restaurants to alley-side sandwich shops.

➡ **Nieuwmarkt** (p91) The lively main square brims with locals digging in at outdoor terraces.

➡ **Western Canal Ring** (p102) Ridiculously cute cafes and small restaurants surround the Negen Straatjes.

➡ **Southern Canal Ring** (p118) Cheap and cheerful around Leidseplein; diverse, quality options on Utrechtsestraat.

➡ **Jordaan & the West** (p134) Convivial little spots (including many Italian restaurants) are the Jordaan's hallmark; scenester-eats dot Westerpark.

➡ **Vondelpark & Around** (p149) The streets north of the park are a real find for lovers of world food.

➡ **Old South** (p163) A scattering of chichi restaurants feeds the genteel neighbourhood.

➡ **De Pijp** (p167) Grazing galore in the Albert Cuypmarket; exotic ethnic places west on Albert Cuypstraat and Ferdinand Bolstraat.

➡ **Plantage, Eastern Islands & Eastern Docklands** (p179) Options can be a trek to reach, but are worth it for the dramatic food/location combo.

➡ **Oosterpark & South Amsterdam** (p189) Indonesian, Moroccan, Turkish and Surinamese takeaways abound.

## Lonely Planet's Top Choices

**Piet de Leeuw** (p118) Tender steak since the 1940s.

**Eetwinkel Het Magazijn** (p168) Gather around the farmhouse table at this magical cafe.

**Tujuh Maret** (p118) Try an Indonesian rice table.

**Gartine** (p71) Slow-food-style sandwiches, salads and a dazzling high tea.

**De Kas** (p189) Dine in the greenhouse where the ingredients for your meal were grown.

## Best by Budget

### €
'Skek (p74)

Latei (p91)

Winkel (p137)

Small World Catering (p136)

Pancakes! (p102)

### €€
Balthazar's Keuken (p134)

Pastini (p120)

Café Touissant (p149)

Stout (p102)

Buffet Van Odette (p102)

### €€€
Blauw aan de Wal (p73)

Fifteen (p180)

De Belhamel (p102)

d'Vijff Vlieghen (p71)

Bordewijk (p138)

## Best Water Views

De Belhamel (p102)

Spanjer en Van Twist (p103)

Odessa (p180)

Van Vlaanderen (p119)

## Best by Cuisine

### Traditional Dutch
La Falote (p163)

Moeders (p137)

Van Dobben (p120)

Haesje Claes (p71)

### Contemporary Dutch
Hemelse Modder (p91)

d'Vijff Vlieghen (p71)

Wilde Zwijnen (p189)

Greetje (p181)

### Indonesian
Blue Pepper (p149)

Tempo Doeloe (p119)

Cilubang (p102)

Café Kadijk (p180)

### Surinamese
Roopram Roti (p189)

Tokoman (p91)

Albina (p170)

Kam Yin (p74)

### Turkish, Moroccan & Middle Eastern
Paloma Blanca (p149)

Raïnaraï (p139)

Mamouche (p168)

Bazar Amsterdam (p169)

### French
Café Touissant (p149)

Le Zinc...et Les Autres (p119)

Van Vlaanderen (p119)

Lastage (p91)

### Italian
Ponte Arcari (p118)

Hostaria (p136)

Fa Pekelhaaring (p167)

Toscanini (p137)

## Best Bakeries & Sweets

Lanskroon (p71)

Jordino (p138)

Bakken Met Passie (p170)

Gebr Niemeijer (p71)

## Best Late Night

Maoz (p121)

Bojo (p121)

Wok to Walk (p121)

Van Dobben (p120)

## Best for Foodies

Marius (p139)

Bordewijk (p138)

Fifteen (p180)

Japanese Pancake World (p136)

## Best Vegetarian

De Waaghals (p168)

De Vliegende Schotel (p139)

De Peper (p151)

Golden Temple (p120)

## Best for Kids

Pancake Bakery (p103)

Moeders (p137)

Burgermeester (p170)

Taart van m'n Tante (p170)

NEL (p122)

## Best Sandwiches

Broodje Bert (p103)

Loekie (p118)

Small World Catering (p136)

Rob Wigboldus Vishandel (p71)

Edgy designer bars abound in the city

# Drinking & Nightlife

*The testosterone-fuelled stag parties of young chaps roaming the Red Light District know exactly what they're doing here: Amsterdam is one of the wildest nightlife cities in Europe, if not the world. Yet given this city's reputation as a commune of rabid party animals, Amsterdam remains a cafe society, where the pursuit of pleasure is more about cosiness and charm than decadence or hedonism.*

Open for business

## NEED TO KNOW

### Opening Hours

➡ Cafes serving breakfast tend to open around 9am or 10am, while others – notably the cosy brown cafes – are late risers, opening around noon. Bars tend to open between 5pm and 6pm. Closing time at all drinking and smoking establishments tends to be late – between midnight and 2am (as late as 3am at weekends).

➡ Most nightclubs close at 2am or 3am Sunday to Thursday and at 4am or 5am on Friday and Saturday. Most places are dead until after midnight on weeknights, or until 1am or 2am on weekends. Looking for an after-party? Keep an eye out for flyers at record shops and clubwear stores. Otherwise, head to an after-hours *nachtcafe* (night cafe).

## Coffeeshop vs Cafe

First things first: the most common mistake of any freshly minted expat or first-time visitor to Amsterdam is calling a cafe a coffeeshop. Cafe culture should not be mistaken for coffeeshop (marijuana-smoking cafe) culture, which is one of Amsterdam's most famous attributes. Remember, there's a big difference between a cafe – occasionally called a *koffiehuis* (esspresso bar) – and a coffeeshop. The latter probably serves coffee but it has a lot to do with cannabis. There are a few cafes that don't mind if you light up a joint, but this is not the norm – don't do it before asking the waiter if it's OK.

## Where to Drink

### CAFES

When the Dutch say 'cafe' they mean a pub, and there are more than 1000 of them in Amsterdam. In a city that values socialising and conversation even more than the art of drinking itself, cafes aren't just places to drink: they're places to hang out for literally hours of contemplation or camaraderie. Amsterdam has a variety of glorious cafes that regular customers or a certain type of clientele have considered a 'second home' for years, if not generations.

Many cafes have outside seating on a *terras* (terrace), which are glorious in summer, and sometimes covered and heated in winter. These are fetching places to relax and people-watch, soak up the sun, read a paper or write postcards. Most of these cafes serve food as well, ranging from sandwiches and fried snacks like traditional Dutch *bitterballen* (small, round meat croquettes) to surprisingly excellent full meals.

Of course, Amsterdam will go down in cafe history for its historic *bruin cafés* (brown cafes). The name comes from the smoke stains from centuries of use (although recent aspirants slap on brown paint to catch up). You may find sand on the wooden floor or Persian rugs on the tables to soak up spilled beer. Most importantly, they provide an atmosphere conducive to deep, meaningful conversation – and inducing the nirvana of *gezelligheid* (conviviality, cosiness).

Grand cafes are spacious, have comfortable furniture and are, well, just grand. A good tradition in many is an indoor reading table stacked with the day's papers and news magazines, usually with one or two in English. Another difference: they all have food menus, some quite elaborate. They're perfect for a lazy brunch or pre-theatre supper.

Theatre cafes are often similar to grand cafes, and are normally attached or adjacent to theatres, serving meals before and drinks after performances. Generally they're good places to catch performers after the show, though they're lovely any time of day.

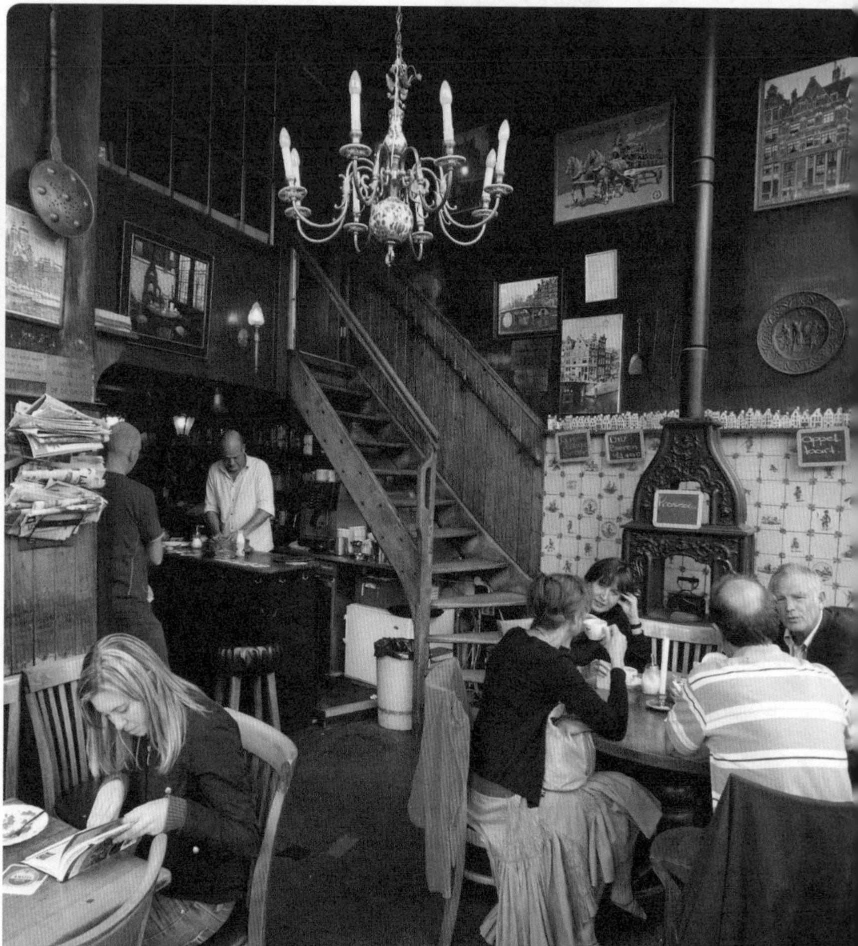

MARTIN MOOS / LONELY PLANET IMAGES ©

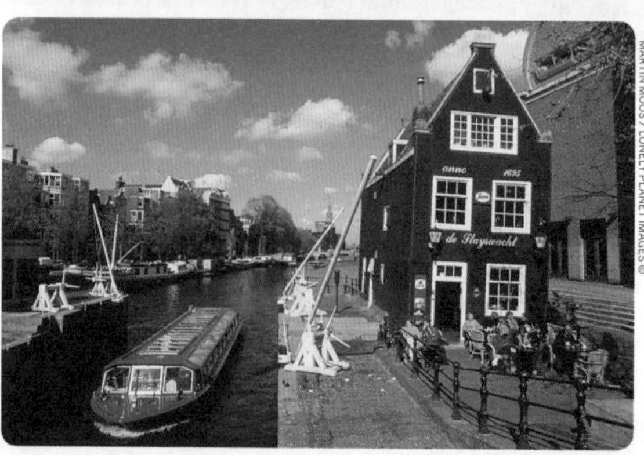

Top: Het Papeneiland (p141)
Left: De Sluyswacht (p92)

# Drinking & Nightlife by Neighbourhood

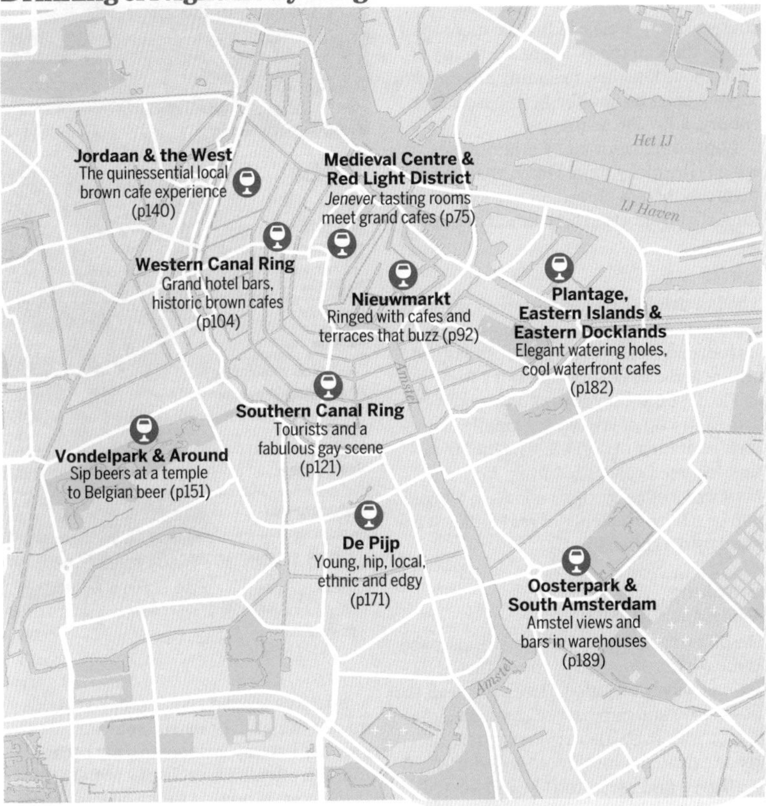

## Drinks

### BEER

In stiff competition with a few of their European cohorts – the Belgians, English, Irish, Czechs and Germans – the Dutch take their beer quite seriously (although they drink less per capita than any of them).

Lager beer is the staple, served cool and topped by a two-finger-thick head of froth, supposedly to trap the flavour. Requests of 'no head please' will meet with a steely response. (The Dutch have their beer drinking rituals, and any Dutch bartender knows that a proper pour is a foamy one, sealed with a spatula.) *Een bier, een pils* or *een vaas* will get you a normal glass of beer; *een kleintje pils* is a small glass and *een fluitje* is a small, thin, Cologne-style glass. Many places also serve *een grote pils (*half-litre mugs) to please tourists, but somehow draught lager doesn't taste the same in a mug and goes flat if you don't drink quickly.

Popular brands include Heineken, Amstel, Grolsch, Oranjeboom, Dommelsch and Bavaria. Tasty and stronger Belgian beers, such as Duvel and Westmalle Triple, are also very popular. *Witbier* (white beer) is a somewhat murky, crisp and citrusy blonde beer that's drunk in summer with a slice of lemon. The dark, sweet *bokbier* comes out in the autumn.

### WINE & SPIRITS

It's not all beer here: the Dutch also make the hard stuff. *Jenever* (ya-nay-ver; Dutch gin; also spelled *genever*) is made from juniper berries and is drunk chilled from a tiny glass filled to the brim. Most people prefer *jonge* (young) *jenever*, which is smooth and relatively easy to drink; *oude* (old) *jenever* has a strong juniper flavour and can be an acquired taste. A common combination, known as a *kopstoot* (head butt), is a glass of *jenever* with a beer chaser – few people can handle more than two or three of these. There are plenty of indigenous liqueurs, including *advocaat* (a kind of eggnog) and the herb-based Beerenburg, a Frisian schnapps.

Long overshadowed by other tipples, wine is drunk by more Dutch than ever before, although almost all of the wine is imported from elsewhere in Europe and abroad.

#### COFFEE

The hot drink of choice is coffee – after all, it was Amsterdam's merchants who introduced coffee to Europe. It should be strong and can be excellent if it's freshly made. If you simply order *koffie* you'll get a sizeable cup of java with a small, airline-style container of *koffiemelk,* similar to unsweetened condensed milk. *Koffie verkeerd* (coffee 'wrong') comes in a bigger cup or mug with plenty of real milk – it's similar to a caffe latte.

### Smoking

#### MARIJUANA & HASHISH

Despite what you may have heard, cannabis is not *technically* legal in the Netherlands – yet it is widely tolerated. Here's the deal: the possession and purchase of small amounts (5g) of 'soft drugs' (ie marijuana, hashish, space cakes, and mushroom-based truffles) is allowed and users won't be prosecuted for smoking or carrying this amount. This means that coffeeshops are actually conducting an illegal business – but again, this is tolerated to a certain extent.

Most cannabis products sold in the Netherlands used to be imported, but today the country has high-grade home produce, so-called *nederwiet*, developed by horticulturists. It's also a particularly strong product – some of the most potent variations contain approximately 20% tetrahydrocannabinol (THC), the active substance that gets people high. To put it in simpler terms, Dutch weed will literally blow your mind – perhaps to an extent that isn't altogether pleasant, which is why many regular native smokers have sworn off the native product in favour of marijuana or hashish imported from Morocco or other regions. Newbies to smoking pot and hash should exercise caution; even many regular smokers can't stomach the home-grown stuff.

Drugs for sale

Space cakes and cookies (baked goods made with hash or marijuana) are sold in a rather low-key fashion, mainly because tourists often have problems with them. If someone is unused to the effects, or the time they can take to kick in and run their course, they could be in for a rather intense (and long-lasting) experience.

#### THE DEATH OF AMSTERDAM COFFEESHOPS?

To the amazement and alarm of tourists and locals alike, the looming threat of coffeeshop restrictions, bans and outright closures has been the talk of the town since 2008, when the Dutch government announced that it would be closing all coffeeshops within 350m of schools. This news effectively condemned the majority of Amsterdam coffeeshops to their imminent demise.

The outlook became even grimmer in June 2011 when the Dutch government proposed a new law that would ban foreigners from cafes that sell cannabis. In legislation initiated by Holland's far-right political figures, even Dutch residents would have to sign up for a one-year pass to purchase 'soft drugs' at a coffeeshop.

Yet to the relief of many – and the dismay of others – the top Dutch court declared that such legislation was unlawful. Yet despite this so-called victory for coffeeshop proponents, the future of coffeeshops and the freedom for foreigners to purchase and consume cannabis remains ambivalent: the courts also issued a statement indicating that in the future, restricting tourists and foreigners from entering coffeeshops would not necessarily be considered unconstitutional.

It's a lot to hash out – pardon the pun. Since decriminalising soft drugs in the 1970s, never has the 'right to smoke' been so threatened in Amsterdam. In the end, many Amsterdammers swear that as long as the city's tolerant population and government resist such restrictive proposals, they'll never happen. The 'coffeeshop issue' remains a wait-and-see situation. For now, the coffeeshops are open to anyone aged 18 and above.

**SMOKING & SOFT DRUGS DOS & DON'TS**

➡ If it's your first coffeeshop experience, do tell the coffeeshop counterperson – they're usually happy to give first-timers advice on how and what to consume.

➡ Don't ask for hard (illegal) drugs.

➡ Whether it is grass or hash, and smoked, eaten or inhaled through a vaporiser, most visitors admit it's much stronger than what they are accustomed to. Ask staff how much to take and heed their advice, even if nothing happens after an hour.

➡ Ask at the bar for the menu of goods on offer, usually packaged in small bags. You can also buy ready-made joints (€3 to €7) in nifty, reusable packaging. Most shops also offer rolling papers, pipes or even bongs to use.

➡ Don't drink alcohol or smoke tobacco in a coffeeshop – it's technically illegal.

➡ Herbal ecstasy – usually a mix of herbs, vitamins, and caffeine – is legal in the Netherlands and sold in smart shops. Ask the smart shop employees what they recommend, as some varieties can have unpleasant speed-like side effects.

➡ Psilocybin mushrooms (aka 'magic mushrooms') are now illegal in the Netherlands, but many smart shops sell mushroom truffles, which have a similar effect.

Grey Area (p105)

### The Art of Being Gezellig

This particularly Dutch quality, which is most widely found in old brown cafes, is one of the best reasons to visit Amsterdam. It's variously translated as snug, friendly, cosy, informal, companionable and convivial, but *gezelligheid* – the state of being *gezellig* – is something more easily experienced than defined. There's a sense of time stopping, an intimacy of the here and now that leaves all your troubles behind, at least until tomorrow. You can get that warm and fuzzy feeling in many places and situations, often while nursing a brew with friends. And nearly any cosy establishment lit by candles probably qualifies.

## Drinking & Nightlife by Neighbourhood

➡ **Medieval Centre & Red Light District** (p75) The prime neighbourhood for 17th-century *jenever* tasting rooms, plus brown cafes and grand cafes galore.

➡ **Nieuwmarkt** (p92) Ringed with cafes and terraces, Nieuwmarkt square is a local favourite for downing a beverage.

➡ **Western Canal Ring** (p104) Full of grand places to tipple, from hotel bars to historic brown cafes.

➡ **Southern Canal Ring** (p121) Where club kids, backpackers and well-heeled tourists somehow happily coexist with a flamboyantly fabulous gay scene.

➡ **Jordaan & the West** (p140) The most convivial place to booze on Queen's Day also boasts the cosiest local drinking scene year-round.

➡ **Vondelpark & Around** (p151) One of the more serene nightlife scenes is also home to some interesting choices: sip beers in a thatched hut or at a temple to Belgian beer.

➡ **De Pijp** (p171) Young, hip, ethnic and edgy, all in the glow of the old Heineken factory.

➡ **Plantage, Eastern Docklands & Eastern Islands** (p182) With student bars and elegant old watering holes in the Plantage, and hot up-and-coming waterfront bars in the Eastern Docklands and Eastern Islands.

➡ **Oosterpark** (p189) Take your pick: waterfront cafes along the Amstel river or urban-cool bars in old newspaper warehouses.

Top: De Drie Fleschjes (p77)
Middle: Enjoying Amsterdam's cafe culture
Bottom: Coffee time, Sarphatipark (p167)

## Lonely Planet's Top Choices

**Café Schiller** (p121) Relive the 1920s with the avant-garde crowd in this sublime art deco theatre cafe.

**Café 't Smalle** (p140) The city's most intimate canalside drinking: you can't get closer to the water without jumping in. Stunning historic interior, too.

**Cafe Belgique** (p75) Belgium's best brews flow from the glinting brass taps.

**Proeflokaal Wynand Fockink** (p78) A 1679 tasting house pouring glorious *jenevers* for the dedicated tippler.

**Luxembourg** (p75) The quintessential European sidewalk cafe to read the newspaper by morning or drink a nightcap alongside an eclectic clientele by night.

**Westergasterras** (p142) A lovely patio and a cosy fireplace draw a fun local crowd to this atmospheric former gasworks.

## Best Brown Cafes

Hoppe (p75)

De Pieper (p140)

Café Berkhout (p171)

De Sluyswacht (p92)

Oosterling (p123)

## Best Cafes

Café Tabac (p104)

Kingfisher (p171)

Café Het Molenpad (p104)

Golden Brown Bar (p151)

De Huyschkaemer (p123)

KHL (p182)

## Best Coffeeshops

Dampkring (p75)

Abraxas (p76)

Greenhouse (p78)

La Tertulia (p141)

Katsu (p173)

## Best Designer Bars

Weber (p122)

Finch (p140)

Canvas Bar (p189)

Bo Cinq (p122)

Kamer 401 (p124)

Bar Barbou (p105)

## Best Cocktail Bars

Vesper Bar (p141)

N'Joy Cocktail Cafe (p124)

Odeon (p125)

Jet Lounge (p142)

## Best Clubs

Trouw (p189)

Sugar Factory (p123)

Bitterzoet (p79)

Club Air (p123)

Café Pakhuis Wilhelmina (p182)

## Best Coffee & Tea Houses

Two for Joy (p123)

De Koffie Salon (p123)

Il Tramezzino (p105)

Patisserie Pompadour (p105)

Koffiehuis 'De Hoek' (p106)

## Best Grand Cafes

De Kroon (p122)

Café Dante (p77)

Café de Jaren (p76)

Café Restaurant Van Puffelen (p104)

Café Americain (p124)

## Best Theatre Cafes

Café Vertigo (p151)

Stanislavski (p124)

Grand Café De La Mar (p126)

De Balie (p127)

The Movies cafe (p142)

Felix Meritis Café (p106)

## Best Beer Cafes

Gollem's Proeflokaal (p151)

't Arendsnest (p104)

Café de Spuyt (p122)

Brouwerij 't IJ (p182)

## Best Outdoor Terraces

Westergasterras (p142)

't Blauwe Theehuis (p152)

Café Binnen Buiten (p171)

Crea Café (p75)

Café-Restaurant Dantzig (p93)

NEL (p122)

## Best Local Scenes

De Tuin (p141)

Café Brecht (p123)

De Twee Zwaantjes (p141)

In 't Aepjen (p78)

Café de Wetering (p122)

De Ysbreeker (p189)

# Entertainment

*Generous subsidies help support a flourishing arts scene in Amsterdam, with loads of big concert halls, theatres, cinemas and other performance venues filled on a regular basis. Music geeks will be in their element, as there's a fervent subculture for just about every genre, especially jazz, classical and avant-garde beats.*

## Music

### JAZZ

Jazz is extremely popular, from far-out, improvisational stylings to more traditional notes. The grand Bimhuis is the big game in town, drawing visiting musicians from around the globe, though its vibe is more that of a funky little club. Smaller jazz cafes abound, and you could easily see a live combo every night of the week.

### CLASSICAL

Amsterdam's classical music scene, with top international orchestras, conductors and soloists crowding the agenda, is the envy of many European cities. Choose between the flawless Concertgebouw or dramatic Muziekgebouw aan 't IJ for the main shows.

### ROCK & DANCE MUSIC

Amsterdam's dance music scene thrives, with DJs catering to all tastes. Many clubs also host live rock bands. Huge touring names often play smallish venues such as the Melkweg and Paradiso; it's a real treat to catch one of your favourites here.

## Comedy & Theatre

Given that the Dutch are fine linguists and have a keen sense of humour, it's natural that English-language comedy would thrive in Amsterdam, especially around the Leidseplein area. Local theatre tends toward the edgy and experimental.

## Cinema

Go to the movies on holiday? Actually, Amsterdam's weather is fickle and let's face it: even art-lovers can overdose on museums. Luckily, this town is a cinephile's mecca, with oodles of art-house cinemas.

## Entertainment by Neighbourhood

- **Medieval Centre & Red Light District** (p79) Several young rock/DJ clubs thrash throughout the 'hood, while avant-garde theatres line Nes.
- **Nieuwmarkt** (p93) A good place to get your classical fix.
- **Southern Canal Ring** (p126) Amsterdam's top spot for comedy clubs, live music venues and jazz cafes, all around Leidseplein.
- **Jordaan & the West** (p142) Venues for blues, punk and cult films, plus Westergasfabriek.
- **Vondelpark & Around** (p152) Free theatre in the park; an alternative scene at the squats.
- **Old South** (p164) Home to the world-renowned, acoustically awesome Concertgebouw.
- **De Pijp** (p173) Vibrant, buzzy little music cafes hold court here.
- **Plantage, Eastern Islands & Eastern Docklands** (p182) The Muziekgebouw aan 't IJ, Bimhuis and Conservatorium show off their style.
- **Oosterpark & South Amsterdam** (p190) The Tropentheater brings the world to the Oost; megavenues lie further south.

## Lonely Planet's Top Choices

**Melkweg** (p126) Housed in a former dairy, this is Amsterdam's coolest club-gallery-cinema-concert hall.

**Paradiso** (p126) One-time church that preaches a gospel of rock.

**Chicago Social Club & Boom Chicago** (p126) Improv comedy for laughs and getting the pulse of local politics.

**Muziekgebouw aan 't IJ** (p178) Stunning high-tech temple of the performing arts.

**Pathé Tuschinskitheater** (p126) Dazzling art deco jewel with a silver screen.

## Best Jazz & Blues

Jazz Café Alto (p126)

Badcuyp (p173)

Bimhuis (p182)

Bourbon Street Jazz & Blues Club (p126)

Maloe Melo (p143)

## Best Rock & Funk

De Nieuwe Anita (p143)

Pacific Parc (p143)

De Heeren van Aemstel (p126)

OCCII (p152)

Winston Kingdom (p79)

Bitterzoet (p79)

## Best Cinemas

Movies (p142)

Het Ketelhuis (p143)

Rialto Cinema (p173)

De Uitkijk (p126)

## Best Classical & Opera

Concertgebouw (p164)

Muziektheater (p93)

Beurs van Berlage (p64)

Bethaniënklooster (p93)

Conservatorium van Amsterdam (p183)

## Best Theatre & Comedy

De Balie (p127)

De La Mar (p126)

Amsterdamse Bos Theatre (p190)

Comedy Café Amsterdam (p127)

De Kleine Komedie (p127)

## Best Experimental Theatre

Frascati (p80)

de Brakke Grond (p80)

Felix Meritis Café (p106)

Theater Bellevue (p127)

Westergasfabriek (p143)

## Best Free or Low Cost

Openluchttheater (p152)

CC Muziekcafe (p173)

Jazz Café Alto (p126)

Bourbon Street Jazz & Blues Club (p126)

Winston Kingdom (p79)

OCCII (p152)

Tropentheater (p190)

Casablanca Variété (p80)

Westergasfabriek (p143)

EYE Film Institute (p177)

## Best for Kids

Amsterdams Marionetten Theater (p93)

Kriterion (p183)

## NEED TO KNOW

### Ticket Shops

➡ You can buy tickets (with a surcharge) via the Uitburo (www.aub.nl, in Dutch; Leidseplein 26; ⊙10am-7.30pm Mon-Fri, 10am-6pm Sat, noon-6pm Sun), a ticket shop run by the tourist office. The last-minute ticket desk (⊙noon to 6pm) sells half-price seats on the day of performance. Comedy, dance and concerts are all potentially available – and marked 'LNP' (language no problem) if the event doesn't hinge on understanding Dutch to have fun.

➡ The Uitboro has another last-minute ticket desk at the Centrale Bibliotheek Amsterdam (Oosterdokskade 143; ⊙noon-7.30pm Mon-Fri, to 6pm Sat & Sun).

### Websites

➡ Last Minute Tickets (www.lastminuteticketshop.nl) Half-price offers start posting online at 8am, though you can buy them only at Uitboro shops or the main tourist office starting at noon.

➡ I Amsterdam (www.iamsterdam.com/whats-on) Events listings.

➡ Film Ladder (www.amsterdam.filmladder.nl, in Dutch) Movie listings.

# Shopping

*During the Golden Age, Amsterdam was the world's warehouse, stuffed with riches from the far corners of the earth. The capital's cupboards are still stocked with all kinds of exotica (just look at that Red Light gear!), but the real pleasure here is finding some odd, tiny shop selling something you'd find nowhere else.*

## Specialities

Dutch fashion is all about cool, practical designs that don't get caught in bike spokes. Dutch-designed homewares bring a stylish touch to everyday objects. Antiques, art and vintage goodies also rank high on the list.

## Markets

In addition to our Best Markets list (see p51), these markets are worth a browse:

### ANTIQUES MARKETS

**Nieuwmarkt** (Map p292; Nieuwmarkt Sq; ⌚9am-5pm Sun May-Sep) Genuine articles, plus books and bric-a-brac. It's held on the square fronting the Waag.

**De Looier Antiques Market** (Map p296; Elandsgracht 109; ⌚11am-5pm Sat-Thu) Mini-mall selling jewellery, furniture and collectibles.

### ART MARKETS

**Spui** (Map p290; ⌚10am-5pm Sun Mar-Oct) Modest wares, mostly modern pictorial art.

**Thorbeckeplein** (Map p302; ⌚10am-5pm Sun Mar-Oct) For paintings and prints.

### FARMERS MARKETS

**Boerenmarkt** (Farmers Market; www.boerenmarktamsterdam.nl, in Dutch; ⌚9am-4pm Sat) Nieuwmarkt (p88); Noordermarkt (p132) Organic foods, picnic provisions.

### OTHER MARKETS

**Lindengracht market** (Map p294; Lindengracht; ⌚9am-4pm Sat) A local affair.

**Postezegelmarkt** (Stamp & Coin Market; Map p290; Nieuwezijds Voorburgwal 280; ⌚10am-4pm Wed & Sat) Streetside area with stamps, coins and medals.

**Westermarkt** (Map p294; Westerstraat; ⌚9am-1pm Mon) Clothes and textiles.

## Shopping By Neighbourhood

- ➡ **Medieval Centre & Red Light District** (p80) Red Light's vibrator shops, Spui's bookstores: there's something for everyone!
- ➡ **Nieuwmarkt** (p93) Beside Waterlooplein Flea Market, with sweetly eccentric local stores.
- ➡ **Western Canal Ring** (p106) The Negen Straatjes (Nine Streets) hold the mother lode of teensy, quirky speciality shops.
- ➡ **Southern Canal Ring** (p127) Hunt for art and antiques in the Spiegel quarter, and fashion, music and housewares in the surrounding lanes.
- ➡ **Jordaan & the West** (p143) Jordaan shops have an artsy, eclectic, homemade feel; Haarlemmerdijk has the newest, coolest boutiques.
- ➡ **Vondelpark & Around** (p152) Outdoors and travel shops fill the streets around the Vondelpark.
- ➡ **Old South** (p164) Ground zero for Van Gogh and Vermeer gear, plus shops on PC Hooftstraat.
- ➡ **De Pijp** (p173) Beyond the Albert Cuypmarkt are galleries and women's fashion boutiques.
- ➡ **Oosterpark & South Amsterdam** (p186) Trawl the ethnically diverse Dappermarkt.

## Lonely Planet's Top Choices

**Condomerie Het Gulden Vlies** (p83) Tasteful setting with a wild array of condoms for sale.

**Albert Cuypmarkt** (p168) Soak up local colour, snap up exotic goods.

**Rock Archive** (p143) Sweet prints of rock and rollers from AC/DC to the White Stripes.

**Frozen Fountain** (p106) The cleverest, coolest home design wares you'll ever see.

**De Kaaskamer** (p106) Hunky goodness stacks the 'cheese room' to the rafters.

## Best Markets

Waterlooplein Flea Market (p89)

Bloemenmarkt (p117)

Dappermarkt (p186)

Noordermarkt (p132)

## Best for Books

Boekie Woekie (p106)

American Book Center (p80)

Pied á Terre (p152)

Mendo (p108)

Oudemanhuis Book Market (p81)

## Best Music

Discostars (p145)

Broekmans & Van Poppel (p164)

Concerto (p129)

## Best Fashion

Young Designers United (p127)

Scotch & Soda (p107)

Phillipa K (p127)

Concrete (p81)

## Best for Kids

De Beestenwinkel (p93)

Joe's Vliegerwinkel (p93)

De Winkel van Nijntje (p164)

Mechanisch Speelgoed (p144)

Tinkerbell (p128)

## Best Antiques & Vintage

Eduard Kramer (p128)

Amsterdam Watch Company (p107)

Boutique Petticoat (p144)

## Best Souvenirs

Museum Shop at the Museumplein (p164)

Nieuws (p107)

Het is Liefde (p173)

't Klompenhuisje (p94)

Kitsch Kitchen (p143)

## Best Dutch-Design Housewares

Droog (p93)

Wonen 2000 (p143)

Hema (p81)

& klevering (p94)

Ook (p144)

## Best Food & Drink

Kaas Huis Tromp (p127)

Puccini Bomboni (p93)

De Bierkoning (p82)

Unlimited Delicious (p107)

Het Oud-Hollandsch Snoepwinkeltje (p144)

## NEED TO KNOW

### Opening Hours

➡ Department stores and large shops: 9am or 10am to 6pm Mon-Sat, noon-6pm Sun.

➡ Smaller shops: 11am or noon to 6pm Tue-Sat; from 1pm Sun & Mon (if open at all).

➡ Many shops stay open late (to 9pm) Thursday.

### Taxes

➡ The Dutch value-added tax (BTW) is 19%; it's reduced to 6% for groceries and books.

➡ Non-EU residents are entitled to a tax refund on purchases, as long as the store has the proper paperwork and you've spent €50 or more. Request a Tax Refund Cheque when paying.

➡ At the airport, present your goods, receipt and passport to customs and get your Refund Cheque stamped. Take it to the Global Refund office in Terminal 3 for cash or credit.

### Cash Rules

➡ A surprising number of stores do not accept credit cards.

### Words to Know

➡ *Kassa* – cashier

➡ *Korting* – discount

➡ *Uitverkoop* – clearance sale

## Best Sex Shops

Female & Partners (p82)

Absolute Danny (p83)

Nana (p84)

Webers (p94)

# Gay & Lesbian Amsterdam

*To call Amsterdam a gay capital still doesn't express just how welcoming and open the scene is here. After all, this is the city that gave the world Butt magazine. It's also the city that claims to have founded the world's first gay and lesbian bar, and hosts one of the world's largest and most flamboyant Pride parades.*

## Scene

The Netherlands was the first country to legalise same-sex marriage (in 2001), so it's no surprise that Amsterdam's gay scene is among the world's largest.

Five hubs party hardest. **Warmoesstraat** in the Red Light District (between the Dam and Centraal Station) hosts the infamous, kink-filled leather and fetish bars. Nearby on the upper end of the **Zeedijk**, crowds spill onto laid-back bar terraces.

In the Southern Canal Ring, the area around **Rembrandtplein** (aka the 'Amstel area') has traditional pubs and brown cafes, some with a campy bent. Leidseplein has a smattering of trendy venues along **Kerkstraat**. And **Reguliersdwarsstraat**, located one street down from the flower market, draws the beautiful crowd (though financial and legal problems have taken a toll on many venues here recently).

## Festivals

The biggest single party is the Roze Wester (www.rozewester.nl) thrown at the Homomonument on Queen's Day on 30 April, with bands and street dancing. The Amsterdam Pride Festival (p22) is the only water-borne gay parade in the world, with lots of pride showing on the outlandish floats.

## Sleeping

Most hotels in town are gay and lesbian friendly, but some cater specifically to queer clientele. Gay Amsterdam (www.gayamsterdam.com) has good listings; it also catalogues hotels it considers non-gay-friendly.

## Gay & Lesbian by Neighbourhood

- **Medieval Centre & Red Light District** (p75) In the Red Light District: Warmoesstraat hosts the leather and kink bars, while Zeedijk has mellower bars and cafes with terraces.
- **Southern Canal Ring** (p121) The action here centres on Kerkstraat (near Leidseplein), on Reguliersdwarsstraat (near the flower market) and on Amstel and Halvemaansteeg (near Rembrandtplein).
- **Jordaan & the West** (p140) Jordaan's low-key scene has a few lesbian cafes in the neighbourhood's southern reaches.

## Lonely Planet's Top Choices

**'t Mandje** (p78) Amsterdam's, and perhaps the world's, oldest gay bar; a *gezellig* (convivial, cosy) beauty.

**Getto** (p79) Island of taste in Warmoesstraat's sea of testosterone.

**Montmartre** (p125) Campy Bohemian bar where the '80s never die.

**Saarein** (p142) The original sisters' cafe, democratised for one and all.

**The Other Side** (p124) House and lounge music provide this trendy coffeeshop's soundtrack.

**Mr B** (p84) For all your jaw-dropping leather, fetish and dungeon wear.

## Best for Fun

Montmartre (p125)

De Huyschkaemer (p123)

Lellebel (p125)

Getto (p79)

Prik (p78)

## Best Cafes

't Mandje (p78)

Café 't Leeuwtje (p125)

Saarein (p142)

Taboo Bar (p125)

## Best Drinking & Nightlife for Lesbians

Saarein (p140)

't Mandje (p78)

De Trut (p141)

Vivelavie (p124)

Prik (p78)

## Best Hardcore & Leather

Church (p125)

Web (p80)

Cuckoo's Nest (p78)

Argos (p80)

## Best Campy & Drag

Lellebel (p125)

Montmartre (p125)

De Engel van Amsterdam (p79)

Queen's Head (p79)

## Best Sleeps

Amistad Hotel (p213)

Golden Bear (p213)

Hotel Orlando (p213)

Xaviera Hollander Bed & Breakfast (p216)

## Best Shops

Vrolijk (p83)

Mr B (p84)

Shirt Shop (p129)

RoB (p84)

## Best Bars & Cafes in the Centre

't Mandje (p78)

Getto (p79)

Café de Barderij (p79)

Prik (p78)

## Best Bars in the Southern Canal Ring

Montmartre (p125)

De Huyschkaemer (p123)

The Other Side (p124)

Taboo Bar (p125)

## NEED TO KNOW

### Websites

➡ **Gay Amsterdam** (www.gayamsterdam.com) The most comprehensive site, with listings for hotels, shops, restaurants and clubs, plus interactive maps.

➡ **Reguliers** (www.reguliers.net) Info on the Reguliersdwarsstraat scene, including current club openings and closings.

➡ **Gay NL** (www.gay.nl, in Dutch) Directory to pretty much anything in town.

➡ **Time Out Amsterdam** (www.timeout.com/amsterdam) The monthly magazine's website has a decent gay and lesbian section.

### Other Resources

➡ **Pink Point** (www.pinkpoint.org; Westermarkt; ⏲noon-6pm Mar-Aug, limited hours Sep-Feb) Located behind the Westerkerk, this is part information kiosk, part souvenir shop. Get details on myriad gay and lesbian hangouts and social groups, and pick up a copy of the candid *Bent Guide*.

➡ **Gay News Amsterdam** (www.gay-news.com) Free monthly listings magazine available around town.

➡ **Gay & Lesbian Switchboard** (☎623 65 65; www.switchboard.nl, in Dutch; ⏲2-6pm Mon-Fri) Provides advice on an anonymous basis.

# Explore Amsterdam

# AMSTERDAM'S TOP SIGHTS

# Neighbourhoods at a Glance

## 1 Medieval Centre & Red Light District (p58)

Amsterdam's oldest quarter is remarkably preserved, looking much as it did in its Golden Age heyday. It's also the busiest part of town for visitors. Some come to see the Royal Palace and Oude Kerk. Others barely get out of the train station before hitting the coffeeshops and Red Light District.

## 2 Nieuwmarkt (p85)

Apart from its turreted Waag (Weigh House) and cafe-lined square, Nieuwmarkt holds the keys to the Rembrandthuis – the master painter's studio – as well as to centuries-old synagogues, diamond factories and the daily Waterlooplein Flea Market in the old Jewish quarter.

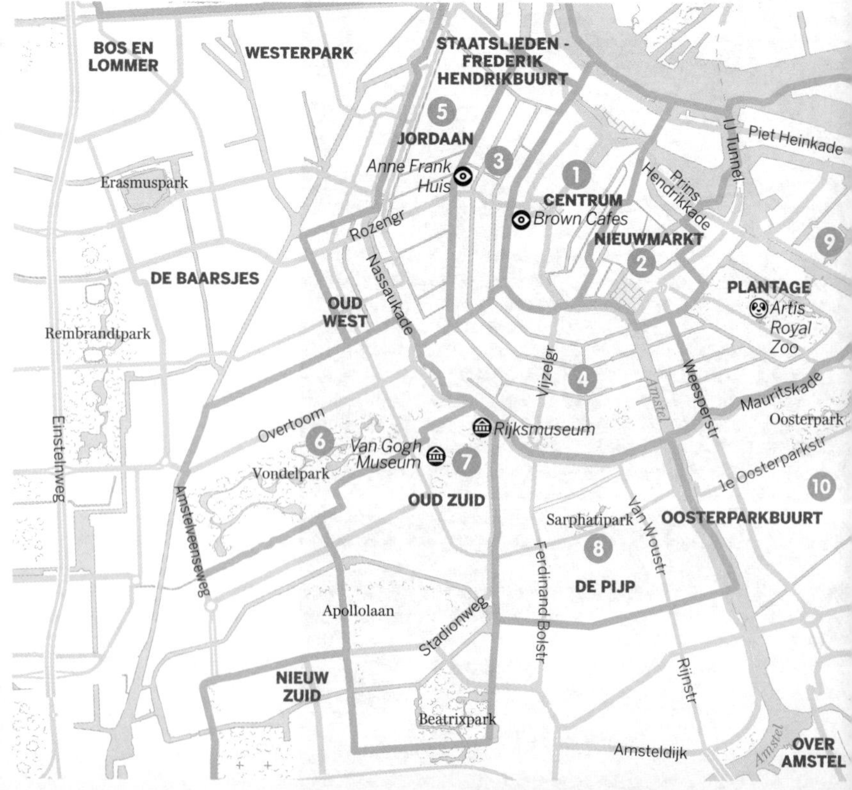

## 3 Western Canal Ring (p95)

This is one of Amsterdam's most gorgeous areas, filled with grand old mansions and quirky little speciality shops, and wandering around the glinting waterways can cause days to just seem to vanish. But most people come here for a singular reason: to visit Anne Frank's house and see the famous diary.

## 4 Southern Canal Ring (p110)

If the Western Canal Ring is upmarket and refined, its southern counterpart is more diverse and populist. Two key nightlife districts – Leidseplein and Rembrandtplein – anchor the scene. In between are the art and antique shops of the Spiegel quarter and the eat street of Utrechtsestraat.

## 5 Jordaan & the West (p130)

A former workers' quarter, the Jordaan teems with cosy pubs, cafes and galleries squashed into a grid of tiny lanes. It's short on conventional sights, yes, but there's no better place to lose yourself for an afternoon's stroll.

## 6 Vondelpark & Around (p146)

Amsterdam's equivalent of New York City's Central Park, Vondelpark unfurls ponds, lawns, thickets and winding footpaths. A festive atmosphere prevails, with picnickers, dope smokers, kissing couples and frolicking children all in on the action.

## 7 Old South (p153)

Often called the Museum Quarter, the Old South holds the top-draw Van Gogh, Stedelijk and Rijksmuseum collections, as well as the Concertgebouw music hall. It's also one of Amsterdam's richest neighbourhoods, and impressive manors line the leafy streets.

## 8 De Pijp (p165)

Ethnic meets trendy in De Pijp, a recently gentrified area that mixes labourers, intellectuals, new immigrants, prostitutes and young urbanites. The best place to marvel at the scene is the colourful Albert Cuypmarkt and the ethnic eateries that surround it.

## 9 Plantage, Eastern Islands & Eastern Docklands (p175)

Once a district of parks and gardens, the Plantage now hosts the city's sprawling zoo, as well as a beery windmill. It segues into the Eastern Islands and Eastern Docklands; old warehouse hubs that have morphed into the cutting edge of Dutch architecture.

## 10 Oosterpark & South Amsterdam (p184)

The Oost is another culturally diverse neighbourhood, with Moroccan and Turkish enclaves. South Amsterdam extends well beyond, offering wild art, lush greenery and goats in the forest.

# Medieval Centre & Red Light District

MEDIEVAL CENTRE | RED LIGHT DISTRICT

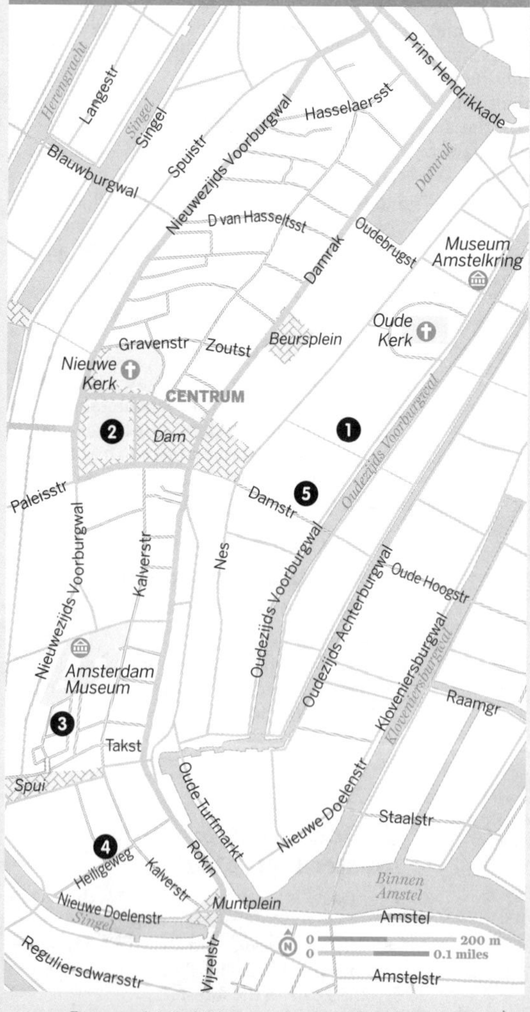


For more detail of this area, see Map p286 and Map p290

## Neighbourhood Top Five

❶ Wandering through the **Red Light District** (p68), which will make your jaw go limp, even if near-naked women beckoning from back-lit windows is the oldest Amsterdam cliché.

❷ Ogling the chandeliered opulence and getting a Dutch history lesson in the **Royal Palace** (p60).

❸ Pushing open the door to the **Begijnhof** (p61) and beholding the hidden gardens and churches.

❹ Biting into a crisp golden spud slathered in mayo, curry or peanut sauce at **Vleminckx** (p71).

❺ Bowling up to a 17th-century tasting house such as **Proeflokaal Wynand Fockink** (p78), to knock back a *jenever* (Dutch gin).

## Explore: Medieval Centre & Red Light District

Amsterdam's heart beats in its medieval core, as well as in the centuries-old Red Light District. All visitors end up here at some point. Centraal Station is the main landmark – indeed, it is the first thing most visitors see as they arrive by train from the airport or elsewhere in Europe. Damrak slices south from the station to the Dam – Amsterdam's central square and home to the Royal Palace.

A tourist-heavy crowd packs the neighbourhood day and night. While there are several intriguing sights, the big-ticket museums lie elsewhere. The main thing to do here is wander. The compact area is laced with atmospheric lanes, and 17th-century tasting rooms, brown cafes, hidden courtyards and wee specialty shops are the prizes for those who venture off the main drags.

As for the infamous Red Light District, far from being a no-go area, it has some beautiful historic bars, as well as the stunning Oude Kerk, the city's oldest church. You'll probably find yourself on Warmoesstraat and Zeedijk while you're here, both commercial thoroughfares chock-a-block with shops and restaurants.

The charming thing about Amsterdam's core is its remarkable state of preservation. The overall layout has changed little since the 17th century. The happy result? The district has the air of a living museum, and certain vistas look like they belong in a Golden Age landscape. You could easily spend your entire trip here, especially when factoring in the quick-ferry-ride-away northern region, so remember: there are more neighbourhoods beyond.

## Local Life

- **Cafe Hangouts** Inviting cafes and brainy bookstores ring the Spui (p64), a favoured haunt of academics and journalists.
- **Shopping Strip** With its designer jeans and leather boots and fancy chain stores, Kalverstraat (p67) buzzes all day long with package-laden locals.
- **Dam Bikes** A fair, a protest, a speech by the Queen – there's always something drawing people to Amsterdam's main square (p63), evident by the sea of cycles locked up in the middle.

## Getting There & Away

- **Tram** Eleven of the city's 16 tram lines go through the neighbourhood en route to Centraal Station.
- **Boat** Free ferries run to NDSM-werf and elsewhere in Amsterdam-Noord, departing from the piers behind Centraal Station.

### Lonely Planet's Top Tip

You're at the local tasting house, and you've ordered a *jenever*. It arrives filled to the brim. You can't pick it up without spilling it. What to do? Bend over the bar, with your hands behind your back, and take a deep sip. That's what tradition dictates.

### Best Places to Eat

- Gartine (p71)
- Blauw aan de Wal (p73)
- Vleminckx (p71)
- Thais Snackbar Bird (p74)
- 'Skek (p74)

### Best Places to Drink

- Proeflokaal Wynand Fockink (p78)
- Hoppe (p75)
- In 't Aepjen (p78)
- Crea Café (p75)
- Cafe Belgique (p75)

### Best Places to Shop

- Condomerie Het Gulden Vlies (p83)
- American Book Center (p80)
- PGC Hajenius (p80)
- Hempworks (p80)
- Kokopelli (p83)

For reviews, see p80

TOP SIGHTS
# ROYAL PALACE (KONINKLIJK PALEIS)

**Welcome to the Queen's house. If she's away, you're welcome to come in and wander around. Today's Royal Palace began life as a glorified *stadhuis* (town hall), and was completed in 1665. The architect, Jacob van Campen, spared no expense to display Amsterdam's wealth in a way that rivalled the grandest European buildings of the day. The result is opulence on a grand scale.**

## The Halls' Treasures

The great *burgerzaal* (citizens hall) that occupies the heart of the building was envisioned as schematic of the world, with Amsterdam as its centre. Look carefully and you'll see motifs representing the four elements: birds (air), fish (water), fruit (earth) and fire.

## King Louis' Gifts

In 1808 the building became the palace of King Louis, Napoleon Bonaparte's brother. In a classic slip-up in the new lingo, French-born Louis told his subjects here that he was the 'rabbit *(konijn)* of Holland', whereas he meant 'king' *(konink)*. Napoleon dismissed him two years later. Louis left behind about 1000 pieces of Empire-style furniture and decorative artworks. As a result, the palace now holds one of the world's largest collections from the period.

## Today's Palace

Officially Queen Beatrix lives here and pays a symbolic rent, though she really lives in Den Haag. State functions are still held in the palace.

### DON'T MISS

- Chandeliers (all 51 of them)
- The *burgerzaal* (citizens hall) and its elemental motifs
- Paintings by Ferdinand Bol and Jacob de Wit
- Empire-style furniture

### PRACTICALITIES

- Map p290
- ☎620 40 60
- www.paleisamsterdam.nl
- The Dam
- adult/child €7.50/6.50
- 11am-5pm daily Jul & Aug, noon-5pm Tue-Sun Sep-Jun

TOP SIGHTS
# BEGIJNHOF

WILL SALTER / LONELY PLANET IMAGES ©

**It feels like something out of a storybook. You walk up to the unassuming door, push it open and voila – a hidden courtyard of tiny houses and gardens opens up before you. The 14th-century Begijnhof is not really a secret these days, but somehow it remains a surreal oasis of peace in the city's midst. The Beguines were a Catholic order of unmarried or widowed women who cared for the elderly and lived a religious life without taking monastic vows. The last true Beguines died in the 1970s.**

### DON'T MISS

- Taking a quiet seat in the garden
- Begijnhof Kapel
- Engelse Kerk
- House at No 34
- Mondrian panels

### PRACTICALITIES

- Map p290
- 622 19 18
- www.begijnhofamsterdam.nl
- main entrance off Gedempte Begijnensloot
- admission free
- 8am-5pm

## Begijnhof Kapel

Contained within the *hof* (courtyard) is the Begijnhof Kapel (1671), a 'clandestine' chapel where the Beguines were forced to worship after the Calvinists took away their Gothic church. Go through the dogleg entrance to find marble columns, paintings and stained-glass windows commemorating the Miracle of Amsterdam (see the boxed text, p63).

## Engelse Kerk

The other church in the Begijnhof is known as the Engelse Kerk (English Church), built around 1392. It was eventually rented out to the local community of English and Scottish Presbyterian refugees – the Pilgrim Fathers worshipped here – and it still serves as the city's Presbyterian church. Look for pulpit panels by Piet Mondrian, in a figurative phase.

## House at No 34

The house at No 34, aka the Houten Huis (Wooden House), dates from around 1465, making it the oldest preserved wooden house in the Netherlands.

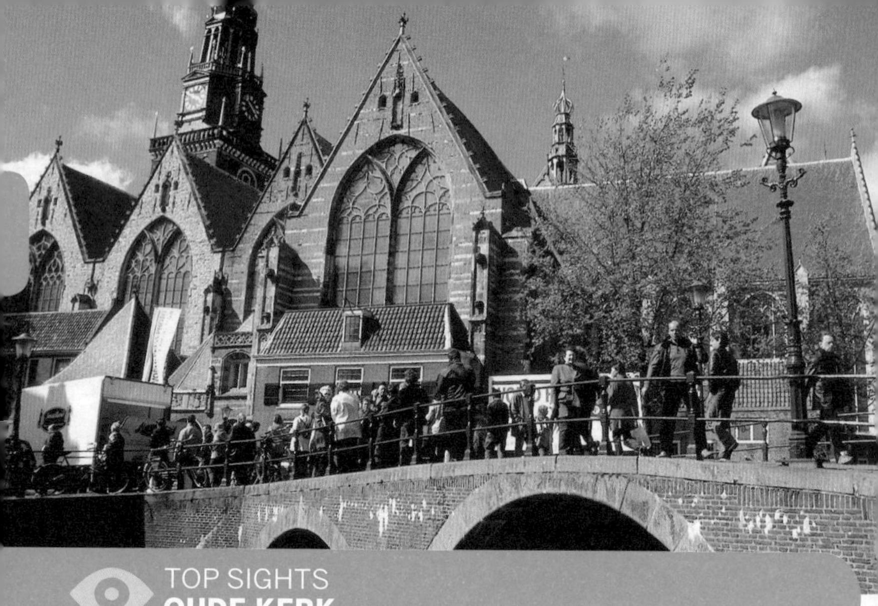

TOP SIGHTS
# OUDE KERK

**The Oude Kerk (Old Church) is Amsterdam's oldest building, dating back to around 1306. It embodies a huge moral contradiction, as it's in full view of the Red Light District, with passers-by getting chatted up a stone's throw from the holy walls. The Gothic-style church has one of the nation's finest carillons, a Müller organ (1724) and 15th-century choir stalls with carvings that are cheekier than you'd imagine. Many famous Amsterdammers lie buried under the worn tombstones set in the floor.**

## Photos & Concerts
The biggest crowds come between April and June for the World Press Photo exhibition (p21). Carillon concerts, often on Tuesday and Thursday afternoons, also draw locals.

## Belle & the Golden Torso
Outside the church on Oudekerksplein is the statue of Belle, erected in 2007 as a nod to sex-industry workers worldwide. The cobblestones nearby (by the church's main entrance) contain another bold statement: a golden torso of a naked woman held by a padlocked hand. The torso mysteriously appeared one day, was removed by police and then put back as most people seemed to like it.

## Trompettersteeg: the Tiny Alley
The Trompettersteeg (by the church) is only 1m wide, but is busy as there are red-light windows lining it. It's worth a shuffle through for the unique, compressed experience.

## DON'T MISS
- World Press Photo exhibit (late April to late June)
- Floor tombstones, including Rembrandt's wife Saskia
- Choir stall carvings
- Golden Torso
- Trompettersteeg's Red Light ambience

## PRACTICALITIES
- Map p286
- ☎625 82 84
- www.oudekerk.nl
- Oudekerksplein 23
- church adult/child €7.50/5.50, tower per person €7
- ⊙church 10.30am-5pm Mon-Sat & 1-5pm Sun, tower every 30min 1-5pm Thu-Sat Apr-Sep

# SIGHTS

## Medieval Centre

**ROYAL PALACE** PALACE

See p60.

**BEGIJNHOF** GARDENS & CHURCH

See p61.

**FREE CIVIC GUARD GALLERY** MUSEUM

Map p286 (☎523 18 22; Kalverstraat 92; ⏱10am-5pm Mon-Fri, 11am-5pm Sat & Sun) The gallery is part of the Amsterdam Museum, located in the alley on its southern side. Traditionally it has displayed enormous tableaux of medieval guards in group portraits, a captivating subgenre of Dutch painting. Divisions such as *voetboog* (foot-bow) and *kloveniers* (hackbut) protected the city and played a large part in deposing the Spanish government. The size of the paintings was determined by the wall space in the guardhouses where the portraits were to be hung. At press time, the museum was making changes to the gallery, and moving many of the paintings into the main building. Supposedly some will remain, along with other free displays from the museum's vast collection.

**DAM** SQUARE

Map p290 The southern part of this famous square was the divine spot where Amsterdam was founded around 1270, and the rest is chequered history. But few people know that long before it hosted fun fairs, the square was split into sections called Vissersdam, a fish market where the Bijenkorf department store now stands, and Vijgendam, probably named for the figs and other exotic fruits unloaded from ships. Markets and events have been held here through the ages, including executions – you can still see holes on the front of the Royal Palace where the wooden gallows were affixed. From the 19th century onwards the Dam became a sort of national square, meaning that when there's a major speech or demonstration, it's held here.

**NATIONAAL MONUMENT** MONUMENT

Map p290 (Dam) This is the Netherlands' best-known memorial to its fallen of WWII, a 22m pylon of concrete and travertine unveiled in 1956. Fronted by two lions, its pedestal has a number of symbolic statues: four males (war), a woman with child (peace) and men with dogs (resistance). The 12 urns at the rear hold earth from war cemeteries of the 11 provinces and the Dutch East Indies. The war dead are still honoured here at a ceremony every 4 May.

**SEXMUSEUM AMSTERDAM** MUSEUM

Map p286 (www.sexmuseumamsterdam.nl; Damrak 18; admission €4, 16yr & over only; ⏱9.30am-11.30pm) Even if it seems rather tame in this environment, the Sexmuseum gets loads of visitors and if you're in the right mood it's good for a giggle. You'll find replicas of pornographic Pompeian plates, erotic 14th-century Viennese bronzes, some of the world's earliest nude photographs, a music box that plays 'Edelweiss' and purports to show a couple *in flagrante delicto,* and an eerie mannequin of Marilyn Monroe re-enacting the pavement-grate scene from *The Seven Year Itch.*

With its farting and flashing (as in nude-guy-in-trench-coat) exhibits, the Sexmuseum ends up being sillier and more fun than its Red Light District neighbour, the Erotic Museum.

### VOMITING THE HOST

The Miracle of Amsterdam had a rather unappetising start.

In 1345 the final sacrament was administered to a dying man, but he was unable to keep down the Host (communion wafer) and – there's no way to put this delicately – vomited it up. Here's the miracle part: when the vomit was thrown on the fire, the Host would not burn. Shortly thereafter, a chapel (demolished in 1908) was built on the site across Kalverstraat from what's now the historical museum, and it soon became a pilgrimage area; the final approach was along the street now known as Heiligeweg.

In the Amsterdam Museum is a wooden chest reported to have once contained the Host. In 1578, when Catholic property was parcelled out, the chest ended up in an orphanage, and several children are said to have been cured of illnesses by sitting on it. You can see it in Room 3.

## TOP SIGHTS AMSTERDAM MUSEUM

Housed in the old civic orphanage, the Amsterdam Museum takes you through all the fascinating twists and turns in the city's convoluted history. Begin with 'Growth Chart,' a large-screen TV depicting an aerial view of the city's evolution, from tiny settlement on the mouth of the Amstel to teeming metropolis. Check out Rembrandt's *Anatomy Lesson of Dr Deijman*, a macabre painting showing the good doctor cutting into a corpse's brain.

You'll find models of old homes, religious objects (including a wooden chest related to the Miracle of Amsterdam; see the boxed text, p63) and a detailed history of Dutch commerce. Later sections cover the world wars, the spread of bicycle use and even a re-creation of the original Café 't Mandje, a touchstone in the gay-rights movement.

At press time the museum was being renovated, and many of the paintings from the free, attached Civic Guard Gallery were being moved into the museum, while more modern exhibits were being added to the free gallery. While you're in the courtyard, note the cupboards in which the orphans stored their possessions (now filled with art).

The museum is a good choice during soggy weather, since there rarely is a queue that requires you to wait outside, as at most other venues.

### DON'T MISS

- *Anatomy Lesson of Dr Deijman*
- Growth Chart
- Café 't Mandje
- Civic Guard paintings
- Miracle of Amsterdam wooden chest

### PRACTICALITIES

- Map p290
- ☎523 18 22
- www.amsterdammuseum.nl
- Kalverstraat 92
- adult/child €10/5
- ⏰10am-5pm Mon-Fri, 11am-5pm Sat & Sun

**MADAME TUSSAUDS AMSTERDAM** MUSEUM

Map p290 (www.madametussauds.nl; Dam 20; adult/child €21/16; ⏰10am-5.30pm Sep-Jun, to 8.30pm Jul & Aug; 👪) Sure, Madame Tussauds wax museum is overpriced and cheesy, but its focus on local culture makes it fun: 'meet' the Dutch royals, politicians, painters and pop stars, along with global celebs (Bieber!). Kids love it. Buying tickets online will save you a few euros and get you into the fast-track queue. Going after 3pm also nets discounts.

**SPUI** SQUARE

Map p290 Flanked by bookshops and cafes, this broad square split by tramlines is an intellectual hub for the city. The statue in the middle is of a playful urchin called *Lieverdje* (Little Darling), a gift from a cigarette company. The Spui was a body of water until the 1880s, and is now the site of Friday book and Sunday art markets. And so you know: it's pronounced 'spow' (rhymes with 'now'). Lots of professors and students spill over from the University of Amsterdam.

**BEURS VAN BERLAGE** ARCHITECTURE

Map p286 (☎530 41 41; Damrak 243) Named after architect HP Berlage (see p249), this landmark building from 1903 was once the leading stock and commodities exchange. The plans show Berlage's humour and an almost perverse willingness to show the guts of a building, such as the exposed steel struts and giant screws of the main hall. Trading quickly outgrew the *beurs,* however, and moved to the nearby Effectenbeurs less than two decades later.

The Beurs van Berlage is now home to the Netherlands Philharmonic Orchestra and hosts museum exhibitions. In the Beurs' B van B Café, stop to ponder the 1903 murals by Jan Toorop, representing past, present and future.

**ROKIN** STREET

Map p290 South of the Dam, this street is part of the route most visitors take from Centraal Station into town, the name being a corruption of *rak-in*, or inward reach. In the early 16th century, the northern part was the site of the first Amsterdam stock exchange, which played a big part in spinning Golden Age riches. The Rokin is now in the grip of the underground construction of a new metro line, which has brought forth a number of archaeological finds from the Amstel's old river bed. At the intersection of Rokin and Grimburgwal stands a **statue of Queen Wilhelmina** on horseback, a reminder of the monarch's trots through Amsterdam during official processions.

### FREE NOORD/ZUIDLIJN VIEWPOINT — LOOKOUT

Map p290 (www.noordzuidlijn.amsterdam.nl; across from Rokin 96; ⌚1-6pm Tue-Sun) Descend the stairs across from Rokin 96 and behold the North–South Metro line excavation in action. The massive engineering project is like a sci-fi movie: an abyss filled with muck and pipes and colossal digging machines. The whole place rumbles when a tram passes overhead. The displays and signage are in Dutch, but English-speaking guides are on hand between 1.30pm and 2.30pm Wednesday to Friday and on Sunday. Look for the big red 'M' next to the bike path.

### DAMRAK — WATERFRONT

Map p286 The Damrak is the original mouth of the Amstel river – *rak* being a reach, or straight stretch of water. The river flowed from a lock in the Dam into the IJ. In the 19th century the canal was filled in, except for the canal-boat docks on the east side. The gabled houses backing onto the water are among the town's most picturesque. The west side of Damrak is like a giant stretch of flypaper, with cheap tourist hotels, fast-food restaurants and souvenir shops ready to catch visitors arriving at Centraal Station. In 2002 the city removed some of the gaudiest signs for the royal wedding of Princess Maxima and Prince Willem-Alexander.

### CENTRAAL STATION — ARCHITECTURE

Map p286 (Stationsplein) Built on an artificial island in 1889, Centraal Station (Amsterdam CS to train travellers) was designed as a neo-Renaissance 'curtain', a controversial plan that effectively cut off Amsterdam from the IJ river. One of the architects, PJ Cuypers, also designed the Rijksmuseum, and you can see the similarities – in the square faux-Gothic towers, the fine red brick and the



WORTH A DETOUR

## NDSM-WERF

Hop on the ferry behind Centraal Station and set sail for a different world. **NDSM-werf** (www.ndsm.nl, in Dutch) looks like the set from a postapocalyptic film – abandoned boats and trams rust by the water's edge, graffiti scrawls across every surface, smoke stacks belch in the distance, and a huge carved wooden tiki head gazes over it all.

The area is actually a city-sponsored art community called **Kinetisch Noord** that has taken over a derelict shipyard. Participants converted a huge old warehouse to hold more than 100 studios, theatres and a thundering **skateboard hall** (www.skateparkamsterdam.com; admission €5.50, rentals €5; ⌚3-10pm Tue-Fri, noon-8pm Sat & Sun), and it has quickly become a centre for underground culture and events, such as the Over het IJ Festival in July (see p22). MTV thought the area was so cutting-edge that it, too, revamped one of the old industrial buildings and made it its European headquarters.

It's true that unless an event is going on, there's not much to do besides wander around and ogle the recycled-junk street-art (which is pretty damn cool). **Café Noorderlicht** (www.noorderlichtcafe.nl; TT Neveritaweg 33; ⌚11am-late), in a colourful-flag-draped greenhouse, provides food and drinks and a funky ambience. To find it, head back past MTV and look for signs posted that point the way.

If you happen to be in town the first weekend of the month, the whopping **IJ Hallen** (www.ij-hallen.nl; admission €4; ⌚9am-4.30pm) flea market takes over the shipyard. Lace up your walking shoes, because there is a *lot* to browse.

The free **NDSM-werf ferry** leaves from Platform 1 behind Centraal Station from 7am (from 9am Saturday and Sunday) to midnight, at 15 minutes and 45 minutes past the hour. The trip takes 15 minutes and you can bring your bike (also free).

abundant reliefs (for sailing, trade and industry). The garage in the right-hand wing was built to shelter the Dutch royal carriage, but it's rarely there (read: never).

As for all that construction, it's for another Amsterdam master traffic plan. Eventually the inner harbour will be enlarged, the station square pedestrianised, and buses and trams rerouted to a new terminal in the rear.

FREE **ST NICOLAASKERK** CHURCH

Map p286 (www.nicolaas-parochie.nl; Prins Hendrikkade 73; ⏲noon-3pm Mon, 11am-4pm Tue-Fri, noon-3pm Sat) In plain view from Centraal Station, the magnificent cupola and neo-Renaissance towers belong to the city's main Catholic church, the first built after Catholic worship became legal again in the 19th century. The interior is notable for its high altar, the theatrical crown of Emperor Maximilian I and depictions of the Stations of the Cross, on which tireless painter Jan Dunselman laboured for 40 years. St Nicholas is the patron saint of seafarers, so the church became an important symbol for Amsterdam. Worship services take place daily at 12.30pm, except on Sunday (10.30am and 1pm).

**SCHREIERSTOREN** HISTORIC BUILDING

Map p286 (www.schreierstoren.nl, in Dutch; Prins Hendrikkade 94-95) This prominent brick tower dating from around 1480 – the oldest of its kind still standing – was once part of the city's defences. Its name comes from an old Dutch word for 'sharp', for this sharp corner jutted out into the IJ. Tourist literature prefers to call it the 'wailing tower' (from *schreien,* to weep or wail) and claims that sailors' wives stood here and cried their lungs out when ships set off for distant lands. There's a fake plaque dedicated to the women inside, in the attractive **VOC Cafe**. Outside, a plaque commemorates Henry Hudson's sailing from here to the New World (see the boxed text, p67).

**MAGNA PLAZA** ARCHITECTURE

Map p290 (www.magnaplaza.nl; Nieuwezijds Voorburgwal 182; ⏲11am-7pm Mon, 10am-7pm Tue-Sat, to 9pm Thu, noon-7pm Sun) This shimmering orange-and-white edifice was the General Post Office, built from 1895 to 1899 by the government architect CH Peters, a pupil of Pierre Cuypers. It has since been converted into a multilevel shopping mall with chain boutiques, but the hall remains



## TOP SIGHTS
## NIEUWE KERK

Don't let the 'New Church' name fool you – the structure dates from 1408 (though it *is* a good century fresher than its neighbour, the Oude Kerk). Located smack on the Dam, the basilica is the historic stage of Dutch coronations and royal weddings. The stained glass over the main entrance recalls Queen Wilhelmina, who ascended the throne in 1898, aged 18. Other than such ceremonies, the building no longer functions as a church, but rather a hall for multimedia exhibitions and organ concerts.

The interior is plain, but several key furnishings – the magnificent oak chancel, the bronze choir screen and the massive gilded organ (1645) – justify a look. Naval hero Admiral Michiel de Ruijter, as well as poets Joost van den Vondel and Pieter Cornelisz Hooft, are among the luminaries buried here.

It's possible to walk in and take a free peek, but you'll have to pay the admission to get up close. Pick up a 'welcome' brochure at the entrance, which maps out the highlights. For more details, go up the stairway leading from the museum's shop, and you'll find an exhibit on the church's history and architecture.

### DON'T MISS

- The window for Queen Wilhelmina's inauguration
- Main organ
- Monuments to de Ruijter, Vondel and Hooft
- Oak chancel

### PRACTICALITIES

- Map p286
- ☎638 69 09
- www.nieuwekerk.nl
- The Dam
- adult/child €8/free
- ⏲10am-5pm

## FROM OUD AMSTERDAM TO NIEUW AMSTERDAM

Among the wall plaques on the Schreierstoren, one explains that the English captain Henry Hudson set sail from here in 1609 in his ship, the *Halve Maen (Half Moon)*. The Dutch East India Company had enlisted him to find a northern passage to the East Indies, but instead he ended up exploring the North American river that now bears his name. On the return voyage his ship was seized in England and he was forbidden to sail again to a foreign nation.

The maverick Hudson disregarded the order. Commissioned by powerful private investors from Britain and Russia, he sailed to America in search of the elusive Northwest Passage. Though an accomplished navigator, the headstrong Hudson hardly endeared himself to his crew, who mutinied in the summer of 1611. The hapless Englishman and a handful of others were set adrift in a rowboat in what's now known as Hudson Bay, where they are presumed to have died.

In any event, Hudson's reports about the island at the mouth of the Hudson River made it back to base. The Dutch soon established a fort on an island called Manhattan that flowered into a settlement called Nieuw Amsterdam; in 1626 an agent of the recently established Dutch West India Company purchased the island from Native Americans for 60 guilders (often cited as the equivalent of US$24!). In 1664 the Dutch West India Company's local governor, the imperious, fanatically Calvinist Pieter Stuyvesant, surrendered the town to the British, who promptly renamed it New York. Stuyvesant retired to the Lower Manhattan market garden called Bouwerij, now known as the Bowery.

Fun fact: Manhattan's Wall St, one of the centres of world finance, was originally the site of a fortified wall erected by the Dutch to keep out the British.

impressive: three storeys of colonnades and an airy, skylit atrium.

### FREE RONDE LUTHERSE KERK — CHURCH

Map p286 (Round Lutheran Church; Singel 11; ⌚hours vary) This domed church, built from 1668 to 1671, has the curious distinction of being the only round Protestant church in the country. Falling attendances forced its closure in 1936, and it now serves as a conference centre for the nearby Renaissance Hotel. Ironically, the old church on the Spui that it was designed to replace is still in use.

Next door along the east side of Singel, the house at No 7 appears to be no wider than its door – except that this is actually the rear entrance of a house of normal proportions.

### KALVERSTRAAT — STREET

Map p290 You're sure to end up on this crowded street at some point. Named after the livestock markets held here in the 17th century, Kalverstraat is now a place where shoppers are often at fever pitch over the latest sales. (The Dutch Monopoly game has Kalverstraat as its most expensive street.) An unexpected oasis in this sea of consumerism is the curious Petrus en Pauluskerk, aka **Papagaai** (Kalverstraat 58; ⌚10am-4pm), a Catholic church from the 17th century that was a clandestine house of worship. Note the parrot over the door that gave the church its funny name. The slogan you'll see upon entering: '15 minutes for God'.

### HEILIGEWEG — STREET

Map p290 Leading west from Kalverstraat, the Heiligeweg (Holy Way) was once part of a route that pilgrims took to the spot where the Miracle of Amsterdam occurred (see the boxed text, p63). It's now a shopping street, but slightly less frenetic than Kalverstraat. Halfway along, and directly opposite Voetboogstraat, you'll see the **Rasphuis Gate**, which led to a correctional institute in medieval times. The pedestal bears the sculpture of a woman with two criminals chained at her side, under the Latin word *castigatio* (punishment). Below, wolves and lions shrink before her whip.

### ALLARD PIERSON MUSEUM — MUSEUM

Map p290 (www.allardpiersonmuseum.nl; Oude Turfmarkt 127; adult/child €6.50/3.25; ⌚10am-5pm Tue-Fri, 1-5pm Sat & Sun) Run by the University of Amsterdam, this museum boasts one of the world's richest archaeological collections. You'll find an actual mummy, vases from ancient Greece and

Mesopotamia, a very cool wagon from the royal tombs at Salamis (Cyprus) and galleries full of other items providing insight into daily life in ancient times. Each section is explained in a detailed overview via English signage, although most individual items are labelled in Dutch only.

It may not be in the same league as the British Museum or the Louvre, but the manageable scale of this museum makes it far more accessible.

**UNIVERSITY LIBRARY** HISTORIC BUILDING

Map p290 (www.uba.uva.nl; Singel 421-425; ⏲8.30am-midnight Mon-Fri, 10am-5pm Sat & Sun) Today's library is a concrete hulk, not nearly the beautiful building you'd expect from such a historic site, but its background is fascinating. Citizen militias used to meet here: the 'hand-bow' *(handboog)* militia in No 421, and the 'foot-bow' *(voetboog)* militia in No 425, which also served as headquarters for the Dutch West India Company. Now you know where the names of the nearby streets Handboogstraat and Voetboogstraat come from. Their firing ranges at the back reached to Kalverstraat.

## Red Light District

**OUDE KERK** CHURCH

See p62.

**PROSTITUTION INFORMATION CENTRE** INFORMATION CENTRE

Map p286 (☎420 73 28; www.pic-amsterdam.com; Enge Kerksteeg 3; ⏲3-8pm Sat or by appointment) Established by a former prostitute and staffed by sex workers, the centre provides frank information and advice about prostitution to anyone who wants it – those in the business, those buying its services and those who are just visiting. The centre's small shop sells enlightening reading material and tasteful souvenirs, but best of all is its excellent hour-long walking tour (5pm Saturday, €15 per person, no reservations needed), which takes you around the neighbourhood and into a prostitute's working room. Proceeds go to the centre.

**ZEEDIJK** STREET

Map p286 The curvy lane called Zeedijk is one of Amsterdam's oldest and its most notorious. Initially a shipping district, it was a respectable place to be until the 17th

### TOP SIGHTS MUSEUM AMSTELKRING

It's another one of those 'secret' Amsterdam places. What looks like an ordinary canal house in the Red Light District turns out to have an entire Catholic church stashed inside, with room for 150 worshippers. Ons' Lieve Heer op Solder (Our Dear Lord in the Attic) was founded in the mid-1600s, when local merchant Jan Hartman decided to build a covert church in his house so his son could study to be a priest. At the time, the country's Calvinist rulers had outlawed public worship of Catholicism.

So, as you wander through, you not only get to see the city's richest collection of Catholic art, but also period pieces from 17th-century canal-house life. There is a fantastic labyrinth of staircases, cubbyhole quarters, heavy oak furniture and a porcelain-tiled kitchen. Once upstairs – in the attic, so to speak – you'll see that the church itself is unexpectedly grand, with a marble-columned altar and a painting by Jacob de Wit, a steep gallery and a surprisingly good organ.

The museum is undergoing restoration until 2012 or 2013. It's open during construction, but many of the artefacts have been put away until work is completed.

**DON'T MISS**

- The altar
- Religious paintings and vessels
- Kitchen and other 17th-century restored rooms

**PRACTICALITIES**

- Map p286
- ☎624 66 04
- www.museumamstelkring.nl
- Oudezijds Voorburgwal 40
- adult/child €8/4
- ⏲10am-5pm Mon-Sat, 1-5pm Sun, longer hours for special exhibits

## RED LIGHT DISTRICT FAQS

- Year prostitution was legalised in the Netherlands: 1810
- Year brothels were legalised: 2000
- Percentage of the Dutch public that claims to have 'no problems whatsoever with prostitution': 78%
- Percentage of working prostitutes born in the Netherlands: 5%
- Estimated percentage of prostitutes working illegally in the Netherlands: less than 5%
- Average rental cost per window (paid by prostitute): €75 to €150 per eight-hour shift, depending on location
- Typical base cost for sex (aka 'a quickie'): €50
- Typical duration of encounter with prostitute: 15 minutes
- Nation that provides the most clients: Great Britain
- Most likely time to see prostitutes with Dutch patrons: Monday morning (when many businesses and most shops are closed)
- Do prostitutes pay taxes? Yes
- Are condoms required by law? No, but it's virtually impossible to find a prostitute who'll work without one
- Is there a union? Yes
- Are medical check-ups required? No
- Is pimping legal? No
- Is trafficking in prostitutes legal? No
- Penalty for either of the above: maximum six years
- Are accommodations made if a patron can't perform? No
- What happens if a patron gets violent? Prostitutes' quarters are equipped with a button that, when pressed, activates a light outside. The offender had better hope that the police get there before the Hell's Angels do.
- Why red light? Because it's flattering. Especially when used in combination with black light, it makes teeth sparkle. Even as early as the 1300s, women carrying red lanterns met sailors near the port. Try it for yourself sometime.

century, when the richer folk moved to fancy homes along newly dug canals such as Herengracht. After that it turned to come-hither entertainment for sailors, and things went rapidly downhill. In the 1960s and '70s the Zeedijk was riddled with drug dealers and street crime, but a clean-up campaign has left the street much safer than it was, with lively cafes, bars and eateries and a very mixed crowd of visitors bumping over the storied cobblestones. It's also the core of Amsterdam's Chinatown.

### FREE GUAN YIN SHRINE — RELIGIOUS

Map p286 (Fo Guang Shan He Hua Temple; www.ibps.nl; Zeedijk 106-118; ⏲noon-5pm Tue-Sat, 10am-5pm Sun, plus noon-5pm Mon Jun-Aug) Europe's first Chinese-Imperial-style Buddhist temple (2000) is dedicated to Guan Yin, the Buddhist prophet. The ornate 'mountain gate' – an intriguing concept in the narrow confines of the Zeedijk, let alone in horizontal Holland – refers to the traditional setting of Buddhist monasteries. The middle section set back from the street was designed along principles of feng shui. Make a donation, light an incense stick and ponder the thousand eyes and hands of the Bodhisattva statue. Traditional Chinese-style recitations of the Sutras (sayings of the Buddha) are held every Sunday at 10.30am and are open to the public.

### FREE CANNABIS COLLEGE — INFORMATION CENTRE

Map p290 (☎423 44 20; www.cannabiscollege.com; Oudezijds Achterburgwal 124; ⏲11am-7pm; ☎) This nonprofit information centre educates visitors on recreational cannabis use. Staff know their stuff: they're the ones who train coffeeshop workers. Get advice on where to find coffeeshops that sell organic weed, tips and tricks to having a positive smoking experience, and the lowdown on local laws and regulations. You can also try out a vaporiser (bring your own smoking material), as well as visit the plants growing sky-high in the basement garden (€3 to see them; photos permitted).

### HASH, MARIJUANA & HEMP MUSEUM — MUSEUM

Map p290 (☎623 59 61; www.hashmuseum.com; Oudezijds Achterburgwal 148; admission €9; ⏰10am-11pm) Did you know that the first recorded use of marijuana was in ancient China? Or that Queen Victoria is said to have used marijuana for menstrual cramps? These are just a couple of essential facts we learned at this simple exhibit, which feels like the back annexe of a devoted user. Admission also includes the **Hemp Gallery**, filled with hemp art and historical items, in a separate building a few doors down.

The Sensi Seed company (conveniently located down the block) owns the whole thing, so it's no surprise you get to peek at a roomful of growing plants as part of the deal. Staff also give vaporiser demonstrations (from 1pm to 6pm Tuesday to Saturday). At press time, the museum was being renovated, and so some exhibits were closed. Visitors on a budget might prefer the Cannabis College, where you can see pretty much the same sights for less money.

### EROTIC MUSEUM — MUSEUM

Map p286 (Oudezijds Achterburgwal 54; admission €7; ⏰11am-1am) Ho hum. Your usual assortment of bondage exhibits, erotic photos and cartoons. Although this museum has the advantage of location, it's less entertaining, not as well laid out, more expensive and a little seedy when compared with the Sexmuseum Amsterdam on the Damrak.

### WARMOESSTRAAT — STREET

Map p286 Amsterdam's earliest canals grew out from the IJ river like the roots of a tree, and Warmoesstraat was one of the first streets to follow. Like Zeedijk, by the 1980s Warmoesstraat was caught in a downward spiral of drugs and petty crime but has since gotten its act together, thanks to frequent policing (note the CCTVs). Some people think things have gone too far: the leather bars, coffeeshops and fetish shops here now have a squeaky-clean 'safe sex' look to them, and any sign that blocks a historic gable is likely to be removed.

### FREE W139 — ARTS CENTRE

Map p286 (www.w139.nl; Warmoesstraat 139; ⏰noon-6pm) Duck into this contemporary arts centre and ponder the multimedia exhibits, which often have an edgy political angle. Check the website for frequent artists talks.

### PUT OUT THE RED LIGHT?

They say it's not about morals but about crime. In early 2008 Amsterdam's city officials announced the launch of Project 1012 to clean up the Red Light District (1012 is the area's postcode).

The first component is to cut the number of prostitution windows in half over the next few years (exact dates are fuzzy in the plan). The city wants to move prostitution away from Oudekerksplein and zone it only to Oude Nieuwstraat and Oudezijds Achterburgwal and its side streets. The empty windows will become fashion and art galleries, and indeed this has already happened to many sites. Coffeeshops are the other big target, with many slated for closure or subjected to new policies restricting foreigners.

Officials claim the two vices attract elements of organised crime. Pimps, traffickers and money launderers have entered the scene and set the neighbourhood on a downward spiral. Opponents say the government is using crime as an excuse, because it doesn't like Amsterdam's current reputation for sin. They also point to a growing local conservatism, which prompted the city to ban tobacco smoking and magic mushrooms, too, over the past few years. In response, groups with slogans like 'Let Amsterdam be Amsterdam' have formed to fight against various rules, and this sums up the opposition's argument.

How far the city will take its clean-up efforts, and how serious it will be about enforcement, remains to be seen. For more detailed information on coffeeshop closures, see the boxed text (p63); for the mushroom lowdown, see p83.

**OUDEMANHUISPOORT** BUILDING

Map p290 (Btwn Oudezijds Achterburgwal & Kloveniersburgwal) On the corner of Oudezijds Achterburgwal stands a distinctive gateway with spectacles over the pedestal. This indicated its role as an almshouse for the elderly, built here in 1601 from the proceeds of a public lottery. It's now the seat of the University of Amsterdam and closed to the public, although you can wander the courtyard. Note the bust of the learned Roman goddess Minerva over the courtyard entrance. A secondhand **book market** (11am-4pm Mon-Fri) has operated in the passage since the mid-1700s.

**NES** STREET

Map p290 Beyond the glare of the Red Light District runs this dark, narrow lane, home to theatres for over 150 years. In 1614 Amsterdam's first bank opened in a pawnshop here, at No 57. One of the more sizzling performance stages in town is Frascati (p80).

## EATING

### Medieval Centre

**TOP CHOICE GARTINE** CAFE €€

Map p290 (320 41 32; www.gartine.nl; Taksteeg 7; mains €6-12, high tea €11-20; 10am-6pm Wed-Sun) Gartine makes delectable breakfast pastries, sandwiches and salads from produce grown in its own garden plot. Throw in slow-food credentials and gorgeous antique plates and it's a winner – a rare bright spot in the dull Kalverstraat area. The full, sweet-and-savoury high tea is a scrumptious bonus.

**TOP CHOICE VLEMINCKX** FRITES €

Map p290 (Voetboogstraat 31; small/large €2/2.50, sauces €0.80; 11am-6pm Tue-Sat, to 7pm Thu, noon-6pm Sun & Mon) This hole-in-the-wall takeaway has drawn the hordes for its monumental *frites* since 1887. The standard is smothered in mayonnaise, though you can ask for ketchup, peanut sauce or a variety of spicy mayos.

**ROB WIGBOLDUS VISHANDEL** SANDWICH SHOP €

Map p286 (626 33 88; Zoutsteeg 6; sandwiches €2.50-4.50; breakfast & lunch) A wee three-table oasis in the midst of surrounding tourist tat, this fish shop in a tiny alley serves excellent herring sandwiches on a choice of crusty white or brown rolls. Don't like fish? **Van den Berg's Broodjesbar** (similar prices and hours), right next door, prepares a variety of other sandwiches, from a humble cheese-filled roll to *gehakt* (thin meatball slices served warm with killer-hot mustard).

**D'VIJFF VLIEGHEN** CONTEMPORARY DUTCH €€€

Map p290 (530 40 60; www.vijffvlieghen.nl; Spuistraat 294-302; mains €26-33, set menus from €35.50; dinner) So what if every tourist and business visitor eats here? Sometimes the herd gets it right. 'The Five Flies' is a classic, spread out over five 17th-century canal houses. Old-wood dining rooms are full of character, featuring Delft tiles and works by Rembrandt and Breitner. Some chairs have brass plates for the celebrities who have sat in them.

**GEBR NIEMEIJER** CAFE €

Map p286 (www.gebroedersniemeijer.nl, in Dutch; Nieuwendijk 35; mains €4-8; 8.15am-6.30pm Tue-Fri, to 5pm Sat, 9am-5pm Sun) This French bakery is a real find amid the Nieuwendijk's head shops. Grab a newspaper and plop down at one of the sturdy wood tables to linger over flaky croissants for breakfast or fantastic sandwiches made with walnut bread and lamb sausage (or gruyére cheese, or fig jam…) for lunch.

**LANSKROON** BAKERY & SWEETS €

Map p290 (623 74 43; www.lanskroon.nl; Singel 385; items from €2; 8am-5.30pm Mon-Fri, 9am-5.30pm Sat, 10am-5.30pm Sun) Other historic bakeries have prettier fixtures and daintier cakes, but only humble Lanskroon has such a remarkable *stroopwafel* – crispy, big as a dessert plate and slathered with caramel, honey or a deceptively healthy-tasting fig paste. In winter, locals come for spicy *speculaas* cookies and other holiday treats, and in summer there's thick nut- or fruit-swirled ice cream.

**HAESJE CLAES** TRADITIONAL DUTCH €€

Map p290 (624 99 98; www.haesjeclaes.nl; Spuistraat 273-275; mains €16-23, set menus from €23.50; noon-midnight; ) Haesje Claes' warm surrounds, a tad touristy but with lots of dark wood and antique knick-knacks, are just the place to sample comforting pea soup and *stamppot* (mashed pot with potatoes). The fish starter has a great sampling of different Dutch fish.

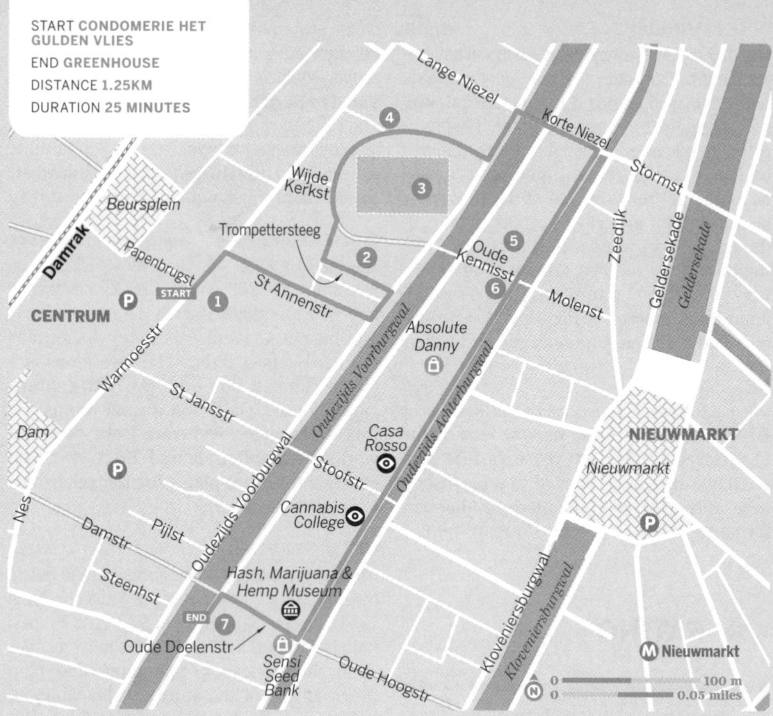


## Neighbourhood Walk

# Red Light Quickie

The typical 'quickie', according to Red Light District workers, is 15 minutes, and our walk shouldn't take you much longer.

What better way to set the mood than at 1 **Condomerie Het Gulden Vlies**? Cherry red, cobalt blue, hypoallergenic, cartoon character embodiments – the shop sells sheathes in all sizes and colours. It's a shrine to condom art!

It's easy to walk right by the teeny alley 2 **Trompettersteeg**. To help you find it: after turning onto Oudezijds Voorburgwal from St Annenstraat, it'll be the second little street you come to en route to the church. Claustrophobes beware: the medieval alley is only 1m wide, but it's plenty busy since there are red-light windows inside.

A contradiction if ever there was one: the 14th-century 3 **Oude Kerk** is Amsterdam's oldest building, but the surrounding square has long been ground-zero for prostitution. Look near the entrance for the 'golden torso' pavement plaque, with a hand groping a breast.

The 4 **Prostitution Information Centre** dispenses forthright facts to sex workers and visitors alike. Next door is a room-rental shop, where workers book their Red Light quarters. As you move onwards, see if can you tell the separate zones for African, Asian and European women.

Bondage exhibits and dildo bikes educate visitors in the 5 **Erotic Museum**. For further browsing, multiple shops around here offer 'nonstop hard porno' and trinkets such as whips, masks and spiked collars.

It's rapid-fire vice as you continue down 6 **Oudezijds Achterburgwal**: fetish gear at Absolute Danny, live sex shows at Casa Rosso, smoky vaporisers at the Cannabis College, botany lessons at the Hash, Marijuana & Hemp Museum and 'Big Bud' at the Sensi Seed Bank.

Take a load off at 7 **Greenhouse**, a Cannabis-Cup-worthy coffeeshop that serves up food and funky music in a surprisingly classy atmosphere. Or choose among the many other coffee joints (pardon the pun!) in the district.

**TOMAZ** FRENCH, DUTCH €€

Map p290 (www.tomaz.nl; Begijnensteeg 6-8; mains €16-25; ⊙lunch & dinner; ☑) Charming little Tomaz hides near the Begijnhof, and is a fine spot for a light lunch or informal dinner, accompanied by a bottle of wine, of course. A vegetarian special is always available. Linger for a while over a game of chess.

**DE KEUKEN VAN 1870** TRADITIONAL DUTCH €€

Map p286 (☎620 40 18; Spuistraat 4; mains €9.50-15.50, 3-course menu €10; ⊙dinner Mon-Sat) You'd never guess that this smart-looking place was once a restaurant for the poor. It still keeps up that heritage, though, with decent cooking (think *stamppot* or couscous) at exceedingly decent prices. Arrive early if you want the set menu, as sometimes they run out of food. The service can be a bit surly – just consider it part of the cultural experience.

**LUCIUS** SEAFOOD €€€

Map p290 (☎624 18 31; www.lucius.nl; Spuistraat 247; mains €18.50-28, set menu €39.50; ⊙dinner) Simple, delicious and consistently full, Lucius is known for both fresh ingredients and not mucking them up with lots of sauce and spice. The interior, all fish tanks and tiles, is workmanlike and professional, just like the service.

**PANNENKOEKENHUIS UPSTAIRS** CONTEMPORARY DUTCH €

Map p290 (☎626 56 03; Grimburgwal 2; mains €5-10; ⊙noon-6pm Fri & Sat, to 5pm Sun) Climb some of the steepest stairs in town to reach this small-as-a-stamp restaurant. The lure? Pancakes that are flavoursome, inexpensive (most under €8) and filling. We like the one with bacon, cheese and ginger. It's a one-man show, so service operates at its own pace. Opening hours can be erratic.

**MORNING STAR** CAFE €

Map p290 (☎625 65 42; Nieuwezijds Voorburgwal; mains €5-8.50; ⊙11am-6pm Tue-Sat, to 8pm Thu, noon-6pm Sun & Mon) *Biologische* (organic) is the name of the game at this tiny shop, which resembles a kiddie train station in the traffic island. Try organic burgers, *tostis* (grilled sandwiches), *frites* and soy lattes while watching the world go by at the picnic-table seating outdoors. It is on Nieuwezijds Voorburgwal, opposite No 289.

**DOP** SANDWICH SHOP €

Map p290 (☎624 75 51; Taksteeg 6; sandwiches €2-4; ⊙11am-4.30pm Mon-Fri) Sandwiches at Dop may look simple, but they're certainly not skimpy – your white roll comes slathered with plenty of butter and an ample portion of ingredients such as leg of lamb, roast beef or liverwurst. With a side of the noteworthy *frites*, you have a real workhorse Dutch lunch.

**SUPPERCLUB** CONTEMPORARY DUTCH €€€

Map p290 (☎638 05 13; www.supperclub.com; Jonge Roelensteeg 21; 5-course menu €65-70; ⊙dinner) If you're looking for a scene, you've found one. Enter the theatrical, white room, snuggle on the mattresses and snack on victuals as DJs spin house music. Shows are provocative and entertaining – if it's lamb night, live sheep may be led through to the kitchen. If it's hospital night, look out.

**VILLA ZEEZICHT** CAFE €

Map p286 (☎626 74 33; Torensteeg 7; mains €5-12; ⊙9am-9.30pm) Although you *could* try sandwiches and pastas here, half the patrons seem to be eating the famous apple pie. For €5 you get a mountain of apples dusted in cinnamon, surrounded by warm pastry and fresh cream. In warm weather, tables are set up on the bridge over the Singel.

**FROZZ** DESSERTS €

Map p290 (www.frozz.com; Rokin 30; cup €3-4; ⊙noon-10pm) Looking for a sweet, healthy pit stop among the sea of fast-food outlets along Rokin? Frozz's creamy frozen yoghurt topped with fresh strawberries, blueberries or nuts is the answer. There's usually a big queue to get at it on warm days.

## Red Light District

**BLAUW AAN DE WAL** INTERNATIONAL €€€

Map p290 (☎330 22 57; www.blauwaandewal.com; Oudezijds Achterburgwal 99; mains from €27, set menu €55; ⊙lunch Thu-Sat, dinner Tue-Sat) Definitely a rose among thorns: a long, often graffiti-covered hallway in the middle of the Red Light District leads to this garden of Eden. Originally a 17th-century herb warehouse, the whitewashed, exposed-brick, multilevel space still features old steel weights and measures, plus friendly, knowledgeable service and refined French- and Italian-inspired cooking. In summer, grab a table in the romantic garden.

## ON YOUR BIKE IN THE CITY

See p32 for information on bicycling in Amsterdam. For bike rentals and bike tours in the Medieval Centre and Red Light District, try one of the following:

**Damstraat Rent-a-Bike** (Map p290; ☎625 50 29; www.rentabike.nl; Damstraat 20-22)

**Black Bikes** (☎670 85 31; www.black-bikes.com; Nieuwezijds Voorburgwal 146)

**MacBike** (☎620 09 85; www.macbike.nl) Centraal Station (Map p286); Nieuwe Uilenburgerstraat 116

**Recycled Bicycles** (Map p286; ☎06 5468 1429; Spuistraat 84a; www.recycledbicycles.org; ⊙closed Sun)

**Orange Bike** (☎528 99 90; www.orangebike.nl; tours €25-33) Geldersekade 37; Singel 233 (Map p290)

**Yellow Bike** (Map p286; ☎620 69 40; www.yellowbike.nl; Nieuwezijds Kolk 29; 2hr city tours €19.50, 4hr countryside tours €29.50)

### THAIS SNACKBAR BIRD — THAI €€

Map p286 (☎420 62 89; www.thai-bird.nl; Zeedijk 77; mains €8-14; ⊙1-10pm) Don't tell the Chinese neighbours, but this is some of the best Asian food on the Zeedijk – the cooks, wedged in a tiny kitchen, don't skimp on lemongrass, fish sauce or chilli. The resulting curries and basil-laden meat and seafood dishes will knock your socks off. There's a bit more room to spread out in the (slightly pricier) restaurant across the street at No 72.

### 'SKEK — CAFE €

Map p286 (☎427 05 51; www.skek.nl; Zeedijk 4-8; sandwiches €3-7, mains €12-14; ⊙noon-10pm; ) Run by students for students (flashing your ID gets you one-third off), this friendly cafe-bar is an excellent place to get fat sandwiches on thick slices of multigrain bread, and healthy main dishes with chicken, fish or pasta. Bands occasionally perform at night (the bar stays open to 1am weekdays, and 3am on weekends).

### DWAZE ZAKEN — CAFE €€

Map p286 (☎612 41 75; www.dwazezaken.nl; Prins Hendrikkade 50; mains €6.50-17; ⊙noon-midnight Mon-Wed, to 1am Thu-Sat, kitchen to 9pm) A refuge from red-light madness, this mosaic-trimmed corner cafe has big windows and a menu of spicy sandwiches, vegie-rich soups and creative fondue. A fine selection of beer (emphasis on Belgian elixirs) helps wash it down, and jazzy live music adds to the vibe, typically on Mondays and the first Thursday of the month. The bathrooms are by far the nicest in the city centre.

### HOFJE VAN WIJS — CAFE €

Map p286 (☎624 04 36; www.hofjevanwijs.nl; Zeedijk 43; mains €8.50-10.50; ⊙noon-6pm Tue-Fri & Sun, 10am-6pm Sat, closed Mon) The 200-year-old coffee and tea vendor Wijs & Zonen (the Queen's purveyor) maintains this pretty courtyard cafe. In addition to the usual offerings (cakes!), it serves inexpensive Dutch stews plus local beers and liqueurs.

### DE BAKKERSWINKEL — CAFE €

Map p286 (☎489 80 00; www.debakkerswinkel.nl; Zeedijk 37; mains €5-10; ⊙8am-6pm Tue-Fri, 8am-5pm Sat, 10am-5pm Sun; ) Family-friendly De Bakkerswinkel offers excellent baked goods (especially scones), sandwiches, soups, and breakfast fare like quiche, French toast and omelettes. A smaller outlet pops up nearby at Warmoesstraat 133, serving sandwiches on wonderfully crusty bread and fresh-squeezed juices for takeaway. The Zeedijk location is temporary until renovation is completed on the bakery's original building at Warmoesstraat 69.

### NAM KEE — CHINESE €€

Map p286 (☎624 34 70; www.namkee.net; Zeedijk 111-113; mains €8.50-18.50; ⊙noon-10pm) It won't win any design awards, but year in, year out, Nam Kee's the most popular Chinese spot in town. And why not: there's good roast anything, and service is snappy. A fancier branch serves in Nieuwmarkt at Geldersekade 117.

### KAM YIN — SURINAMESE €

Map p286 (☎625 31 15; Warmoesstraat 8; mains €7-10; ⊙noon-midnight) It's nothing much to look at, but this plastic and fluorescent operation nonetheless dispenses excellent versions of Surinamese standards like roti and *tjauw min* (thick noodles with assorted meats). Its *broodje pom* (a chicken-casserole sandwich) ranks as one of the city's best.

# DRINKING & NIGHTLIFE

## Medieval Centre

**TOP CHOICE HOPPE** BROWN CAFE

Map p290 (www.cafe-hoppe.nl, in Dutch; Spui 18-20) Go on. Do your bit to ensure Hoppe maintains one of the highest beer turnovers in the city. The gritty brown cafe has been filling glasses for more than 300 years. Journalists, bums, socialites and raconteurs toss back brews amid the ancient wood panelling. Most months the energetic crowd spews out from the dark interior and onto the Spui. Note the entrance is to the right of the pub-with-terrace of the same name.

**TOP CHOICE CAFE BELGIQUE** BEER CAFE

Map p286 (www.cafe-belgique.nl; Gravenstraat 2; ⊙from 2pm) Pull up a stool at the carved wooden bar and make your pick from the glinting brass taps. It's all about Belgian beers here, as you may have surmised. Eight flow from the spouts, and 30 or so are available in bottles. The ambience is quintessential *gezellig* (cosy) and draws lots of chilled-out locals. There's live music and DJs some nights.

**CREA CAFÉ** CAFE

Map p290 (www.crea.uva.nl; Turfdraagsterpad 17) Walking along Grimburgwal, you can't help but notice the prime cafe chairs across the canal. They're part of the University of Amsterdam's cultural centre, a laid-back spot that's superb for sipping well-priced beers while watching boats manoeuvre under the nearby bridge.

**DAMPKRING** COFFEESHOP

Map p290 (www.dampkring.nl; Handboogstraat 29; 📶) You saw it in *Ocean's Twelve;* now see it up close. Consistently a winner of the Cannabis Cup, Dampkring is darkish, youngish with rather hobbitish decor. Its name means the ring of the Earth's atmosphere where smaller items combust. Dampkring is known for having the most comprehensive menu in town, including details about smell, taste and effect.

**LUXEMBOURG** GRAND CAFE

Map p290 (www.cafeluxembourg.nl, in Dutch; Spui 24) Join gaggles of glam locals and tourists at this permanently busy cafe. Grab a paper (from the reading table or the Athenaeum newsagency across the square), procure a sunny seat on the terrace, order the

### WALKING TOURS IN THE 'HOOD

Several walking tours meander around the Centre and Red Light District and can help you get acquainted with the neighbourhood (see p257 for listings). These are some of our favourites:

**Randy Roy's Redlight Tours** (www.randyroysredlighttours.com; tours €12.50; ⊙8pm Sun-Thu, 8pm & 10pm Fri & Sat) Quirky evening trek through the Red Light District, with celebrity trivia thrown in for good measure. Meet in front of the Victoria Hotel (Damrak 1-5), opposite Centraal Station.

**Prostitution Information Centre Tour** (www.pic-amsterdam.com; tours €15; ⊙5pm Sat) Gives the nitty-gritty of the window business, including going into one of the rooms.

**Sandeman's New Amsterdam Tours** (www.newamsterdamtours.com; by donation; ⊙11am & 1pm) Slick young guides take you on a three-hour jaunt through the Centre and Red Light District, rain or shine. Meet at the VVV office.

**Mee in Mokum** (www.gildeamsterdam.nl; tours €5; ⊙11am Tue-Sun) Senior-citizen volunteers lead you around, starting from the Amsterdam Museum cafe (Kalverstraat 92).

**Drugs FAQ** (www.drugsfaq.nl; by donation; ⊙1.30 Mon, Tue, Thu & Fri) An informative look at Amsterdam's drug culture, both its myths and reality. Tours depart by the Oude Kerk.

## STAYING ON TRACK

It's only 9.7km long, but the new Noord/Zuidlijn (north–south metro line) has stretched into a challenge of far greater size. Begun in 2003 and originally targeted for completion in 2011, the project deadline has now been pushed back to 2017.

It's no wonder, given the massive task at hand. To build the metro's route between Amsterdam-Noord and the World Trade Centre in the south, engineers must tunnel under the IJ river and the centuries-old buildings of Amsterdam's city centre. The first part went OK, but when some of the historic monuments in the centre started to shift off their foundations, engineers halted construction.

Debates flared over what to do. Continue, even though the budget was running sky-high? Quit, and lose the millions of euros already spent? How much longer would residents tolerate the inconvenience of their main streets being torn to bits?

The city ultimately decided to proceed. Engineers added additional support beams beneath the affected buildings. And so far, so good. Take a peek at the epic project at the subterranean Noord/Zuidlijn Viewpoint (p65).

'Royale' snack platter (bread, cured meats, Dutch cheese and deep-fried croquettes) and watch the world go by. Inside are parquet floors, a marble bar and an art deco stained-glass skylight.

### CAFÉ DE JAREN — GRAND CAFE

Map p290 (www.diningcity.nl/cafedejaren; Nieuwe Doelenstraat 20) Watch the Amstel flow by from the balcony and waterside terraces of this soaring, bright and *very* grand cafe, one of our favourites. The great reading table has loads of foreign publications for whiling away hours over beers. If you're feeling peckish, hit the fabulous buffet salad bar (a rarity in Amsterdam).

### DE ZWART — BROWN CAFE

Map p290 (☎624 65 11; Spuistraat 334) 'Not everyone has knowledge of beer, but those who have it drink it here' is the translation of the slogan on a panel above this atmospheric bar, which has an original tiled floor from 1921. Just across the alley from Hoppe, De Zwart gets a different (though amicable) crowd of left-wing journalists and writers, as well as local-government people.

### IN DE WILDEMAN — BEER CAFE

Map p286 (www.indewildeman.nl; Kolksteeg 3; ⏲from noon Mon-Sat) This former distillery house has been transformed into an atmospheric yet quiet beer cafe with more than 200 bottled beers, 17 varieties on tap and a smoke-free area. Locals rave about the choice of Trappist ales, the huge selection from Belgium and the Netherlands, and the potent French Belzebuth (13% alcohol!).

### B VAN B CAFÉ — CAFE

Map p286 (☎638 39 14; Beursplein 1; ⏲10am-6pm Mon-Sat, 11am-6pm Sun) The cafe in the Beurs van Berlage, one of the city's most spectacular buildings, boasts original brick and tilework, and murals by Jan Toorop (1903) representing past, present and future. Food includes lasagne, croquettes and the usual assortment of sandwiches and salads. Unless the main building happens to be open to the public (eg for a concert), this is your only sure way to get inside.

### DE SCHUTTER — BROWN CAFE

Map p290 (www.deschutter.nl; Voetboogstraat 13-15) This large student *eetcafé* has a brown-cafe look, a relaxed vibe and inexpensive, tasty *dagschotels* (dishes of the day). It's open for lunch and dinner, and is a good place to fortify yourself on the cheap before a night on the town.

### GOLLEM — BEER CAFE

Map p290 (www.cafegollem.nl; Raamsteeg 4; ⏲from 4pm Mon-Fri, from 2pm Sat & Sun) The pioneer of Amsterdam's beer cafes is a minuscule space covered all over in beer paraphernalia. The 200 beers on tap and in the bottle attract lots of drinkers.

### ABRAXAS — COFFEESHOP

Map p290 (www.abraxas.tv; Jonge Roelensteeg 12; 📶) Hands down the most beautiful coffeeshop in town. Choose from southwest USA, Middle Eastern and other styles of decor, spread over three floors. There are live DJs, extra-friendly staff and free internet usage.

**CAFÉ HET SCHUIM** BAR

Map p290 (☎638 93 57; Spuistraat 189) *Schuim* means 'foam' (on beer) and this grungy, arty bar is extraordinarily popular with beer-swilling locals – it gets packed any time of day or night. While the people-watching can be distracting, it's wise to keep one eye on your belongings.

**TARA** IRISH PUB

Map p290 (www.thetara.com; Rokin 85-89) This expat meeting place combines Irish folksiness with Amsterdam chic. In its maze of rooms (the one-time home of German expressionist Max Beckmann) you'll find warm fireplaces, a cool bar, gorgeous wall carvings and seats salvaged from an old Irish church. Catch frequent musical happenings and sports on the telly. Meals include a full Irish breakfast, and burgers (mains €13.50 to €18.50).

**DE BLAUWE PARADE** TASTING HOUSE

Map p286 (☎624 48 60; Nieuwezijds Voorburgwal 176-180; ⏰5pm-midnight Thu-Sat) The building, now the Hotel Die Poort van Cleve, was the site of the original Heineken brewery, so it seems an appropriate place for tastings (of *jenevers* though, not beers). While there, feast your eyes on the Delft-blue tile mural (1870s) of a parade of children bearing gifts to an emperor.

**DE DRIE FLESCHJES** TASTING HOUSE

Map p286 (☎624 84 43; Gravenstraat 18) Behind the Nieuwe Kerk, the distiller Bootz' tasting room dates from 1650. It is dominated by 52 vats that are rented out to businesses that entertain clients here. It specialises in liqueurs (although you can also get *jenever*) – the macaroon liqueur is quite nice. Take a peek at the collection of *kalkoentjes,* small bottles with hand-painted portraits of former mayors.

**PILSENER CLUB** BROWN CAFE

Map p290 (☎623 17 77; Begijnensteeg 4; ⏰Mon-Sat) Also known as Engelse Reet (ask the bartender for a translation), this small, narrow and ramshackle place doesn't allow you to do anything but drink and talk, which is what a 'real' brown cafe is all about. It opened in 1893 and has hardly changed since.

**CAFÉ THE MINDS** BAR

Map p290 (www.theminds.nl; Spuistraat 245; ⏰9pm-3am Sun-Thu, to 4am Fri & Sat) Don't let the word cafe in the name fool you – this is a hard-core (but very friendly) punk bar where the beer's cheap, the music's loud and the party's rockin', man. It's smack in the middle of a little strip of the Spui that's home to a few squats and plenty of graffiti.

**CAFÉ VAN ZUYLEN** BROWN CAFE

Map p286 (www.cafevanzuylen.nl, in Dutch; Torensteeg 4) Although the sun terrace is one of the prettiest spots for a drink on the Singel, the interior – with its cosy rooms featuring lots of wood and old leather banquettes – is just as appealing in the cooler months.

**OPORTO** BROWN CAFE

Map p286 (☎638 07 02; Zoutsteeg 1) This tiny brown cafe is worth visiting just for the inlaid woodwork behind the bar (check out the Zodiac signs). Its wrought-iron-and-parchment lighting fixtures are said to have been the same for 60 years.

**TWEEDE KAMER** COFFEESHOP

Map p290 (☎422 22 36; Heisteeg 6) The small, original location of the Dampkring chain of coffeeshops feels more like a brown cafe than a coffeeshop. But weed there is, and the selection is vast (the chain is known for its detailed, informative menus). The Sativa is highly recommended for a special happy high.

**DUTCH FLOWERS** COFFEESHOP

Map p290 (☎624 76 24; Singel 387) Were it not for this shop's main wares, you'd be hard pressed to distinguish it from a brown cafe, with the game on TV and a lovely view of the Singel. It all means that you needn't slum it with the college kids or feel as if you've gone to Jamaica or India in order to enjoy a toke.

**CAFÉ DANTE** GRAND CAFE

Map p290 (☎638 88 39; Spuistraat 320; 📶) This huge art deco space is quiet as auntie's back garden during the day, but after 5pm weeknights it transforms into a lively bar for the downtown business crowd. Plus, you get your choice of outside views: the busy Spui out front or the lovely Singel in the back.

**HOMEGROWN FANTASY** COFFEESHOP

Map p286 (www.homegrown-fantaseeds.com; Nieuwezijds Voorburgwal 87a; 📶) Organic Dutch-grown product, 3m-long glass bongs, vaporisers, rotating artwork on the walls and famous space cakes attract a good mixed crowd.

**AKHNATON** CLUB

Map p286 (www.akhnaton.nl, in Dutch; Nieuwezijds Kolk 25) A young, multicultural crowd jams this club to dance to hip hop, Latin and Afrocentric acts. It's been going strong for 50 years.

**PRIK** GAY BAR

Map p286 (www.prikamsterdam.nl; Spuistraat 109) 'Sexy snacks and liquids' is the motto of this peppy retro bar with an 'I've just redone my loft' clientele of 20- to 30-year-olds. Live DJs spin pop, house and dance discs.

**CUCKOO'S NEST** GAY BAR

Map p286 (www.cuckoosnest.gaynl.net; Nieuwezijds Kolk 6) A small, busy bar said to have the largest 'playroom' in Europe. You could spend a whole night exploring the labyrinth of cubicles and glory holes.

## Red Light District

**TOP CHOICE PROEFLOKAAL WYNAND FOCKINK** TASTING HOUSE

Map p290 (www.wynand-fockink.nl; Pijlsteeg 31; ⏲3-9pm) This small tasting house (dating from 1679) serves scores of *jenever* and liqueurs in an arcade behind Grand Hotel Krasnapolsky. Although there are no seats or stools, it is an intimate place to knock back a taste or two with a friend. We particularly enjoy the house speciality *boswandeling* (secret of the forest), a vivacious combination of young *jenever,* herb bitters and orange liqueur – the effect is like cloves. Guides give a free, English-language tour of the distillery every Saturday at 12.30pm (reservations not required).

**IN 'T AEPJEN** BROWN CAFE

Map p286 (☎626 84 01; www.cafeintaepjen.nl, in Dutch; Zeedijk 1) Candles burn even during the day at this bar based in a mid-16th-century house, which is one of two remaining wooden buildings in the city. The name allegedly comes from the bar's role in the 16th and 17th centuries as a crash pad for sailors from the Far East, who often toted *aapjes* (monkeys) with them. The place is stuffed with advertising signs and plenty of locals.

**GREENHOUSE** COFFEESHOP

Map p290 (www.greenhouse.org; Oudezijds Voorburgwal 191; 📶) One of the most popular coffeeshops in town. Smokers love the funky music, multicoloured mosaics, psychedelic stained-glass windows, and high-quality weed and hash. It also serves a breakfast, lunch and dinner to suit all levels of the munchies.

**PROEFLOKAAL DE OOIEVAAR** TASTING HOUSE

Map p286 (www.proeflokaaldeooievaar.nl; St Olofspoort 1; ⏲Mon-Sat) Not much bigger than a vat of *jenever,* this magnificent little tasting house has been going since 1782. On offer are spirits of the De Ooievaar distillery, still located in the Jordaan. The house was built leaning over and has not subsided, as many people wrongly assume even before a shot of Old Dutch.

**'T MANDJE** BROWN CAFE

Map p286 (www.cafetmandje.nl; Zeedijk 63; ⏲closed Mon) Amsterdam's oldest gay bar opened in 1927, then shut in 1982, when the Zeedijk grew too seedy. But its trinket-covered interior was lovingly dusted every week until it reopened in 2008. The devoted bartenders can tell you stories about the bar's brassy lesbian founder. It's one of the most *gezellig* places in the centre, gay or straight.

**CAFÉ-RESTAURANT KAPITEIN ZEPPO'S** CAFE

Map p290 (☎624 20 57; www.zeppos.nl, in Dutch; Gebed Zonder End 5) This site, off Grimburgwal, has assumed many guises over the centuries: a cloister during the 15th, a horse-carriage storehouse in the 17th and a cigar factory in the 19th. These days it's festive, attractive and almost romantic, with a beautiful garden and Belgian beers. Between October and April there's live music on Sundays from 4pm (cover groups and big bands).

**MOLLY MALONE'S** IRISH PUB

Map p286 (☎624 11 50; www.mollyinamsterdam.com; Oudezijds Kolk 9) Regularly packed with Irish folk, this dark, woody pub holds spontaneous folk-music sessions. Bring your own guitar and let loose with the other Eireophiles. The mainly Irish pub grub is decent and on Mondays there's curry and a pint for €12.50.

**BUBBLES & WINES CHAMPAGNE BAR** WINE BAR

Map p290 (☎422 33 18; www.bubblesandwines.com; Nes 37; ⊙3.30pm-1am Mon-Sat) Ignore the silly name; this stylish wine bar is a rarity in Amsterdam. There are more than 50 quality wines by the glass, tasting flights (several different wines to try) and the city's most scrumptious bar food: caviar blinis, cheese plates and our favourite, 'bee stings' (parmesan drizzled with white-truffle-infused honey).

**QUEEN'S HEAD** GAY BAR

Map p286 (www.queenshead.nl; Zeedijk 20) This beautifully decorated, canal-view, old-world-style cafe was once run by legendary drag queen Dusty. The place has toned down a bit: the crowd is more mixed, and straight people are welcome. Drag bingo nights and clubby DJ nights are some of the events that pop up throughout the week.

**BABA** COFFEESHOP

Map p286 (www.babashops.nl; Warmoesstraat 64) The teak-and-Ganesha decor transport you to India – and that's before you indulge. It's not the cheapest weed in town, but it packs a punch. Pick up a bag of Silver Haze, plant yourself at the front window and watch the colourful types all run together along Warmoesstraat.

**BRASSERIE HARKEMA** THEATRE CAFE

Map p290 (☎428 22 22; www.brasserieharkema.nl; Nes 67; 📶) At the rear of the Frascati theatre, technicolour-walled Brasserie Harkema gets crammed with a young student crowd having a pre-theatre meal or post-theatre drinks.

**DE BUURVROUW** BAR

Map p290 (www.debuurvrouw.nl, in Dutch; St Pieterspoortsteeg 29; ⊙9pm-2am Mon-Thu, to 3am Fri & Sat) This grungy late-night bar is where you inevitably end up when there's nowhere else to go. Take it easy because someone's watching: above the entrance is a painting of *De Buurvrouw* (the woman next door). And yes, everyone *is* probably as drunk as you. Febo, anyone?

**GETTO** GAY BAR

Map p286 (www.getto.nl; Warmoesstraat 51; ⊙Tue-Sun) This groovy, long restaurant-bar is loved for its open, welcoming attitude, great people-watching from the front, and a rear lounge where you can chill. It draws a cross-section of the gay community. The owners also rent out a swanky apartment.

**DURTY NELLY'S** IRISH PUB

Map p286 (www.durtynellys.nl; Warmoesstraat 117; 📶) Huge, dark and always busy, Nelly's attracts foreign visitors from the cheap hotels in the area with fun, drinks, darts and pool. It serves a first-rate Irish breakfast.

**CAFÉ DE BARDERIJ** BAR

Map p286 (www.barderij.com, in Dutch; Zeedijk 14) This very friendly beer bar draws a mixture of local gay regulars and tourists. It has killer views of the canal out back and Zeedijk in front, making it a must on Queen's Day.

**DE ENGEL VAN AMSTERDAM** GAY BAR

Map p286 (www.engelamsterdam.nl; Zeedijk 21; ⊙from 1pm) The 'Angel' draws a cruisey terrace crowd who toast the evening's promise with a flute of blended juice or champagne. On Sundays there's a meet and greet with a sing-along party, and the TGIF drink night sees action.

## ☆ ENTERTAINMENT

**BITTERZOET** CLUB

Map p286 (www.bitterzoet.com, in Dutch; Spuistraat 2) Always full, always changing, this is one of the friendliest venues in town. One night it might be full of skater dudes; the next, relaxed 30-somethings. Music (sometimes live, sometimes a DJ) can be funk, roots, drum'n'bass, Latin, Afro-beat, old-school jazz or hip-hop groove.

**WINSTON KINGDOM** CLUB

Map p286 (www.winston.nl; Hotel Winston, Warmoesstraat 127) This is a club that even non-clubbers will love for its indie-alternative music beats, smiling DJs and solid, stiff drinks. No matter what's on – from 'dubstep mayhem' to Elvis Costello cover bands – the scene can get pretty wild in this goodtime little space.

**CASA ROSSO** SEX SHOW

Map p290 (www.casarosso.nl; Oudezijds Achterburgwal 106-108; admission with/without drinks €50/35; ⊙8pm-2am) Casa Rosso's claim to fame: live sex on stage – or, as we once heard a Casa Rosso barker put it, 'Quality sleaze and filth!' Acts can be male, female, both or lesbian (although not gay...sorry boys!). Performers demonstrate everything from positions of the Kama Sutra to pole dances, incredible tricks with lit candles, and moves readily associated with competitive figure skating. You may even catch a good old-fashioned striptease. It isn't exactly classy, but it is clean and comfortable and always packed with couples and hen's-night parties.

**FRASCATI** THEATRE

Map p290 (☎626 68 66; www.theaterfrascati.nl; Nes 63; ⏲closed Aug) This experimental theatre is a draw for young Dutch directors, choreographers and producers. You can expect multicultural dance and music performances, as well as hip hop, rap and breakdancing. It hosts a theatre, dance, art and music festival, **Breakin'Walls** (www.breakinwalls.nl/bw/english), in both November (main festival) and April (mini-festival).

**CASABLANCA** LIVE MUSIC

Map p286 (www.cafecasablanca.nl; Zeedijk 24) Casablanca once had a hot reputation for jazz (combos still take the stage early in the week), but now it's better known as a karaoke madhouse on the weekends.

**CASABLANCA VARIÉTÉ** THEATRE

Map p286 (www.casablanca-amsterdam.nl, in Dutch; Zeedijk 26; dinner & show €36.50, show only €7) Next door to Casablanca is the Netherlands' only theatre devoted to the art of circus performance, where magicians and more take the stage. There's a special kids' show on the last Saturday of the month at 4pm (€7, including one nonalcoholic beverage).

**DE BRAKKE GROND** THEATRE

Map p290 (☎626 68 66; www.brakkegrond.nl; Flemish Cultural Centre, Nes 45) A fantastic array of music, experimental video, modern dance and exciting young theatre is performed here.

**ARGOS** LEATHER BAR

Map p286 (Warmoesstraat 95; ⏲11pm-3am Sun-Thu, to 4am Fri & Sat) Amsterdam's oldest leather bar hosts leather boys of all ages in its famous darkrooms. The regular 'Sex on Sunday' party and other events were undergoing some changes as new owners took over in 2011

**WEB** LEATHER BAR

Map p286 (www.thewebamsterdam.com; St Jacobsstraat 6; ⏲noon-1am Sun-Thu, to 2am Fri & Sat) Cruisey, well-established leather and clone bar with darkrooms and 'bear nights'. No, the pit below the grate in the floor is not a real loo.

# SHOPPING

## Medieval Centre

**AMERICAN BOOK CENTER** BOOKS

Map p290 (www.abc.nl; Spui 12; ⏲11am-6.30pm Sun, 11am-8pm Mon, 10am-8pm Tue, Wed, Fri & Sat, 10am-9pm Thu) This excellent three-storey shop is the biggest source of English-language books in Amsterdam. Its greatest strengths are in the artsy ground-floor department, but on the upper floors there's fiction and oodles of special-interest titles, plus a good travel section. It also stocks foreign periodicals such as the *New York Times*.

**PGC HAJENIUS** SPECIALTY SHOP

Map p290 (www.hajenius.com; Roken 96) Even if you're not a cigar connoisseur, this tobacco emporium is worth a browse. Inside is all art deco stained glass, gilt trim and soaring ceilings. Regular customers, including members of the Dutch royal family, have private humidors here. Note to Americans hoping to take home a Cuban cigar: ask the helpful staff, as they may have an idea for you...

**HEMPWORKS** CLOTHING, ACCESSORIES

Map p286 (www.hempworks.nl; Nieuwendijk 13) Hempworks carries a big selection of eco-friendly clothing and bags, all made with organic hemp, cotton and bamboo. The locally made Dutch items sell under the label Hemp Hoodlamb. Some of the clothes have special touches like hidden pockets for your stash.

**MAGIC MUSHROOM GALLERY** SMART DRUGS

Map p290 (www.magicmushroom.com; Spuistraat 249; ⏲10am-10pm) This outlet of the local chain has an excellent choice of truffles, pipes and bongs. Feel free to wobble the garden swing while you nurse a smart drink, or check out the trippy mood lighting while you wait for the herbal ecstasy to kick in. Even non 'shroomers will appreciate the 3D shark playing cards, mushroom banks and other novelty toys for sale.

**LAUNDRY INDUSTRY** CLOTHING

Map p290 (www.laundryindustry.com; Spui 1) Hip, urban types head here for well-cut, well-designed women's clothes by this Dutch design house. There's another branch at Magna Plaza, but the Spui location is the main shop.

**CONCRETE** ART, CLOTHING

Map p290 (www.concrete.nl; Spuistraat 250) This is part exhibition space showing rotating exhibitions of adventurous photography, graphics and illustration, and part cool clothes store floating racks of zany T-shirts, jeans and trendy trainers.

**DE BIJENKORF** DEPARTMENT STORE

Map p290 (www.debijenkorf.nl, in Dutch; Dam 1) The city's most fashionable department store is in the highest-profile location, facing the Royal Palace. Design-conscious shoppers will enjoy the well-chosen clothing, toys, household accessories and books. It has a small restaurant or snack bar and a bathroom (€0.50) on each floor. The very snazzy cafe on the 5th floor has a terrace with steeple views.

**HEMA** DEPARTMENT STORE

Map p286 (www.hema.nl, in Dutch; Nieuwendijk 174) What used to be the nation's equivalent of Marks & Spencer, Woolworths or Target now attracts as many design aficionados as bargain hunters. Expect low prices, reliable quality and a wide range of products, including good-value wines and delicatessen goods.

**ATHENAEUM** BOOKS

Map p290 (www.athenaeum.nl, in Dutch; Spui 14-15) Amsterdam's savviest bookshop is a bit of an intellectual and style hub. Its adjoining newsagency has a selection of cutting-edge international magazines, newspapers and guidebooks.

**MARK RAVEN GRAFIEK** SOUVENIRS

Map p286 (www.markraven.nl; Nieuwezijds Voorburgwal 174) Artist Raven's distinctive vision of Amsterdam is available as posters and on T-shirts – they make genuinely tasteful souvenirs. He also has a stand on Museumplein.

**TIBETWINKEL** SPECIALTY SHOP

Map p290 (www.tibetwinkel.nl, in Dutch; Spuistraat 185a) Volunteers staff this tiny shop that sells fair-trade items from Tibet, including incense, prayer flags, yak-bone jewellery and spinning prayer wheels. Proceeds go to a non-profit group that supports Tibet's liberation 'through peaceful actions'.

**OUDEMANHUIS BOOK MARKET** BOOKS

Map p290 (Oudemanhuispoort; ⏲11am-4pm Mon-Fri) Second-hand books weigh down the tables in the atmospheric covered alleyway between Oudezijds Achterburgwal and Kloveniersburgwal, where you'll rub tweed-patched elbows with professors thumbing through 19th-century copies of *Das Kapital* and Icelandic sagas. Much of the material is in Dutch.

**IK** CLOTHING, ACCESSORIES

Map p290 (Voetboogstraat 16a; ⏲11am-6pm Wed-Sat, 1-6pm Sun) It's an indie designer shop with unique, creative flight bags, T-shirts, dresses, skirts, jewellery and crafts.

**MAISON DE BONNETERIE** DEPARTMENT STORE

Map p286 (www.debonneterie.nl, in Dutch; Rokin 140) Exclusive and classic clothes for the whole family are featured here. Men are particularly well catered for with labels like Ralph Lauren and Armani, best purchased during the brilliant 50%-off sales,

### CYCLING IN AMSTERDAM-NOORD

Travel 20 minutes north from central Amsterdam, and the landscape morphs to windmills, cows and wee farming communities. Talk about culture shock! It's easy to access via an afternoon bicycle ride. Take your wheels onto the free **Buiksloterweg ferry** behind Centraal Station, and cross the IJ river. The ride takes about five minutes, and boats depart continuously throughout the day. Then pedal north along the **Noordhollands Kanaal**. Within a few kilometres you're in the countryside.

You can buy cycling maps at the VVV office by Centraal Station. Many bike rental companies (see p32) also sell maps, as well as offer guided tours that cover this very area.

but there is still plenty for the ladies. Note the amazing chandeliers and beautiful glass cupola.

**VROOM & DREESMANN** DEPARTMENT STORE

Map p290 (www.vd.nl, in Dutch; Kalverstraat 201) Slightly more upmarket than Hema, this national chain is popular for its clothing and cosmetics. Its fabulous cafeteria, La Place, serves well-priced, freshly prepared salads, hot dishes and pastries.

**FEMALE & PARTNERS** EROTICA, CLOTHING

Map p286 (www.femaleandpartners.nl, in Dutch; Spuistraat 100) Everything you need for your inner dominatrix…or the one who's waiting for you at home. Female & Partners is filled with clothing, undies, leather and toys for women and those who love them.

**ANDRIES DE JONG BV** SPECIALTY SHOP

Map p290 (www.andriesdejong.nl; Muntplein 8) When seafarers need ship fittings, rope or brass lamps, they sail to Andries de Jong. Traditional clocks, bells, boats in bottles and other quaint maritime gifts fill the crowded shelves among the workers' items. It's perhaps best known as a supplier of strong, vividly coloured flags.

**BROUWERIJ DE PRAEL** FOOD & DRINK

Map p286 (www.deprael.nl; Oudezijds Voorburgwal 30; ⌚9am-4.30pm Mon-Fri) This noteworthy brewery employs more than 60 people with a history of mental illness, and names its beers (all organic) after famous Dutch singers. The shop sells all seven of its beer varieties (four are seasonal), like the bitter, spicy and amber-coloured Johnny (named after the late folk singer Johnny Jordaan). If you just can't wait to slurp it down, the brewery has a tasting room conveniently located around the corner at Oudezijds Armsteeg 26.

**DE BIERKONING** FOOD & DRINK

Map p290 (www.bierkoning.nl; Paleisstraat 125; ⌚from 11am Tue-Sat, from 1pm Sun & Mon) Come here for beer – it stocks some 950 varieties (with an emphasis on Belgian, German, British and, of course, Dutch brews), the largest beer-glass selection we've ever seen, beer-logoed T-shirts and beer guidebooks to the region. It also carries a small selection of wines.

**HANS APPENZELLER** JEWELLERY

Map p290 (www.appenzeller.nl; Grimburgwal 1; ⌚Tue-Sat) Appenzeller is one of Amsterdam's leading designers in gold and stone, known for the simplicity and strength of his designs. If his sparse work is not to your taste, along the same street is a row of jewellery shops of all kinds.

**3-D HOLOGRAMMEN** JEWELLERY, ART

Map p290 (www.3-dhologrammen.com; Grimburgwal 2) This fascinating (and trippy) collection of holographic pictures, jewellery and stickers will delight even the most jaded peepers. You can even get a hologram custom-made of yourself.

**BOLS LE CELLIER** FOOD & DRINK

Map p286 (☎638 65 73; Spuistraat 116; ⌚closed Sun) You'll find a splendid selection of Dutch *jenever,* absinthe, spirits and liqueurs, a super range of Old and New World wines and around a hundred beers.

**MAGNA PLAZA** SHOPPING CENTRE

Map p290 (www.magnaplaza.nl; Nieuwezijds Voorburgwal 182) This grand 19th-century landmark building, once the main post office, is now home to a marvellous upmarket shopping mall with more than 40 shops stocking fashion, gifts and jewellery – everything from Mango and Sissy Boy to a cashmere shop.

**CHILLS & THRILLS** SMART DRUGS

Map p286 (www.chillsandthrills.com; Nieuwendijk 17; ⌚10am-10pm) Always packed with tourists straining to hear each other over thumping techno music, busy Chills & Thrills sells truffles, herbal trips, E-testing kits, psychoactive cacti, amino-acid and vitamin drinks, novelty bongs and life-sized alien sculptures.

**KALVERTOREN SHOPPING CENTRE** SHOPPING CENTRE

Map p290 (www.kalvertoren.nl; Kalverstraat 212-220) This popular, modern shopping centre contains a Vroom & Dreesmann, a small Hema, and big-brand fashion stores like Replay, Quiksilver, Levi's, Timberland and DKNY.

**INNERSPACE** SMART DRUGS

Map p286 (www.innerspace.nl; Spuistraat 108; ⌚11am-10pm) Known for good service and information, this big shop started as a

LOCAL KNOWLEDGE

## MUSHROOMS, TRUFFLES & SMART SHOPS

Raoul Koning, manager at Kokopelli (p83), gave us the lowdown on smart shops and their wares.

First, a bit of background: smart shops have always been known for selling magic mushrooms. Then, in 2007 and 2008, the fungi were blamed for a series of high-profile incidents, including the death of a French schoolgirl who jumped from an Amsterdam bridge after allegedly eating the plants. Subsequently, the government enacted a ban on nearly 200 varieties of hallucinogenic mushrooms. But missing from the list were magic truffles...

**What is the difference between magic mushrooms and truffles?** Truffles come from a different part of the plant, but they contain the same active ingredients as mushrooms.

**Why were truffles excluded from the ban?** Technically and scientifically, truffles are not mushrooms.

**How does a truffle trip compare to a mushroom trip?** It's a little more like a body high than a visual experience, though this varies according to where you are when you trip, as well as how you are feeling mentally and physically.

**What is the best advice you can give to those seeking a pleasant trip?** Ask lots of questions. If you aren't satisfied with the answers, or the salesperson won't give you the answers, go to another shop. Once you've purchased the truffles, have the experience in an outdoor space, ideally a park. Avoid bars and other enclosed spaces. Don't drink alcohol during your trip and don't mix truffles with other drugs. Take the trip with friends, or better yet, do it accompanied by a friend who is not taking the truffles.

*Interview by Caroline Sieg*

supplier to large parties; it now sells truffles, herbal ecstasy, psychoactive plants and cacti. True to its origins, it's also a good place for party info and tickets.

**VROLIJK** BOOKS

Map p286 (www.vrolijk.nu; Paleisstraat 135) The Netherlands' largest gay and lesbian bookshop carries the major mags as well as novels, guidebooks and postcards. Upstairs you'll find art, poetry and DVDs.

**CRACKED KETTLE** FOOD & DRINK

Map p290 (www.crackedkettle.nl; Raamsteeg 3; ⏲noon-8pm) *Proost!* This delightful shop stocks more than 500 international beers as well as a healthy selection of wines and sprits. It ships worldwide.

**FAME MUSIC** MUSIC

Map p290 (www.fame.nl, in Dutch; Kalverstraat 2-4) This megastore has an enormous number of titles, with broad (and mainstream) collections of pop, jazz and classical CDs, DVDs and videos. Sale prices can be quite reasonable.

## Red Light District

**TOP CHOICE CONDOMERIE HET GULDEN VLIES** SPECIALTY SHOP

Map p286 (www.condomerie.nl; Warmoesstraat 141) This is where the well-dressed Johnson shops for variety. Perfectly positioned for the Red Light District, the boutique stocks hundreds of types of condoms (including the Coripa brand, which comes in 55 sizes), lubricants and saucy gifts. Some of the novelty condoms may remind you of your favourite cartoon character.

**KOKOPELLI** SMART DRUGS

Map p286 (Warmoesstraat 12; ⏲11am-10pm) Were it not for its truffles trade you might swear this large, beautiful space was a fashionable clothing or homewares store. In addition to smart drugs, there's a coffee and juice bar and a chill-out lounge area overlooking Damrak.

**ABSOLUTE DANNY** EROTICA

Map p290 (www.absolutedanny.com; Oudezijds Achterburgwal 78; ⏲11am-9pm Mon-Sat, from noon Sun) Named by Dutch *Playboy* as

Amsterdam's classiest sex shop, Absolute Danny specialises in fetish clothing, lingerie and leather, along with hard-core videos and dildos just for fun.

### COCA LEAF EXPERIENCE FOOD & DRINK

Map p286 (www.agwabuzz.com; Warmoesstraat 32; ⏲1.30-8.30pm daily) Here's a one-of-a-kind shop for a browse. It's the retail outlet for a company that processes Bolivian coca leaves into liquor and energy drinks. Learn about the plant's traditional uses (and less savoury uses as an element of cocaine) in the 'museum' and sample the wares.

### NANA EROTICA

Map p286 (www.happy-shops.com; Warmoesstraat 62; ⏲11am-midnight) The 'most vibrating shop in town' is actually pretty classy. Choose from a massive assortment of devices that can battery-power your happiness.

### GEELS & CO FOOD & DRINK

Map p286 (www.geels.nl, in Dutch; Warmoesstraat 155) A distinguished, 140-year-old tea-and-coffee merchant, Geels also sells chocolate, teapots and coffee plungers. The shop at Warmoesstraat 155 is temporary while its real home up the street at No 67 is being renovated.

### HIMALAYA NEW AGE

Map p286 (www.himalaya.nl; Warmoesstraat 56) What a surprise: a peaceful, New Age oasis in the Red Light District. Stock up on crystals, incense and oils, ambient CDs and books on the healing arts, then visit the lovely tearoom.

### MR B EROTICA

Map p286 (www.misterb.com; Warmoesstraat 89; ⏲10am-6.30pm Mon-Wed & Fri, 10am-9pm Thu, 11am-6pm Sat, 1-6pm Sun) Kinky! The tamer wares at this renowned Red Light District shop include leather and rubber suits, hoods and bondage equipment, all made to measure if you want. It also pierces and tattoos.

### ROB EROTICA

Map p286 (www.rob.eu; Warmoesstraat 71) RoB sells anything and everything for one's bondage and rough-sex fantasy: army gear, leather and rubber are just the start. Oh my!

### WONDERWOOD DESIGN, HOMEWARES

Map p290 (www.wonderwood.nl; Rusland 3; ⏲noon-6pm Wed-Sat & by appointment) As much a museum as a shop, here you can ogle the sensuous, delicate, moulded-plywood creations of George Nelson, Marcel Breuer and more – some of the vintage furniture pieces are for sale and some are available in reissue (ie old designs re-made). If the furniture's impractical, smaller art objects (made of wood, naturally) are also available.

### MCCARTHY'S FOOD & DRINK

Map p286 (Zeedijk 27a; ⏲noon-10pm, closed Tue) McCarthy's is a run-of-the-mill liquor shop, but it has good prices on absinthe in decorative bottles.

# Nieuwmarkt

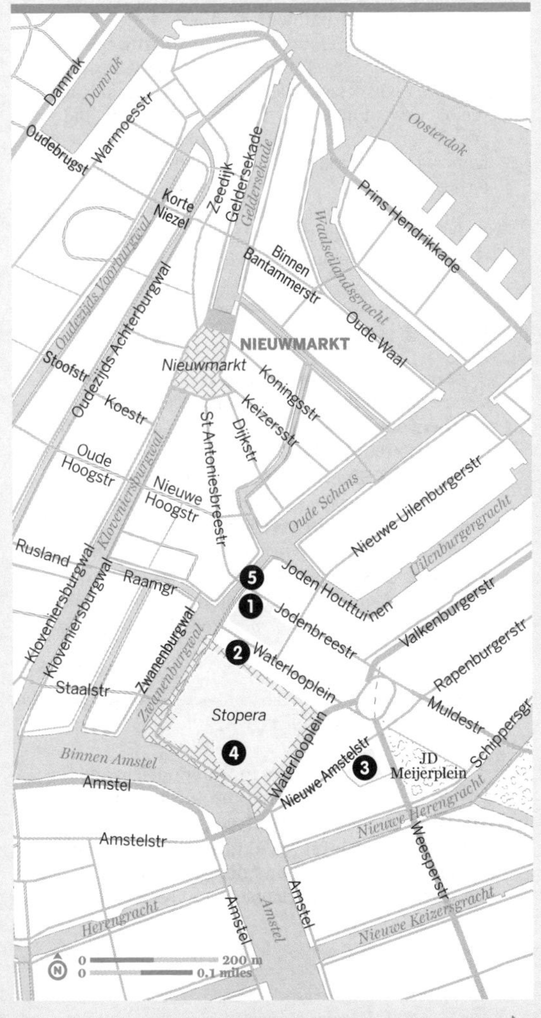


For more detail of this area, see Map p292

## Neighbourhood Top Five

1. View the inner sanctum of a master painter at **Museum het Rembrandthuis** (p87), where you can immerse yourself in the Dutch icon's studio and see his brushes, sketches and cabinet stuffed with seashells and Roman busts.
2. Browse the **Waterlooplein Flea Market** (p89), where porcelain teapots, Buddha statues and other bric-a-brac tempt.
3. Explore the **Joods Historisch Museum** (p88) for a look at life in Amsterdam's old Jewish quarter.
4. Get a taste of classical music during Tuesday's free lunchtime concert at the **Muziektheater** (p93).
5. Down a Dommelsch beer in the old lock-keeper's house at **De Sluyswacht** (p92).

## Lonely Planet's Top Tip

Nieuwmarkt holds heaps of intriguing architecture, from the imposing Scheepvaarthuis (a classic example of the Amsterdam School style) to the odd, mod Stopera. Several unique buildings cluster near where Kloveniersburgwal and Oude Hoogstraat intersect, including Amsterdam's narrowest house and the mighty Oostindisch Huis, office of the 17-century, world-dominating Dutch East India Company. Keep an eye out as you wander the neighbourhood!

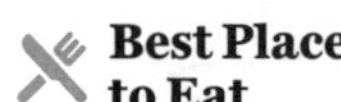

### Best Places to Eat

- Latei (p91)
- Tokoman (p91)
- Hemelse Modder (p91)
- Café Bern (p91)
- Toko Joyce (p92)

For reviews, see p91

### Best Places to Drink

- De Sluyswacht (p92)
- Café de Doelen (p92)
- De Bekeerde Suster (p92)
- Lokaal 't Loosje (p93)
- Café-Restaurant Dantzig (p93)

For reviews, see p92

### Best Places to Shop

- Puccini Bomboni (p93)
- Droog (p93)
- De Beestenwinkel (p93)
- Jacob Hooy & Co (p94)
- Juggle (p94)

For reviews, see p93

## Explore: Nieuwmarkt

Nieuwmarkt (New Market) is a district as historic as anything you'll find in Amsterdam. Rembrandt painted canalscapes in Nieuwmarkt, and Jewish merchants generated a fair share of the city's wealth with diamonds and other ventures here.

The area's focal point is Nieuwmarkt square, just east of the Red Light District. This bright, relaxed place – ringed with cafes, shops and restaurants – is arguably the grandest spot in town after the Dam. When the weather warms, the outdoor terraces boom with locals enjoying food and drink well into the evening.

The neighbourhood's top sight is Museum het Rembrandthuis, the master's impressive home/studio where he sketched and painted his finest works. It can get crowded, but never obnoxiously so. Nearby, the open-air Waterlooplein Flea Market provides fertile ground for treasure and bargain quests. Jodenbreestraat leads into the old Jewish quarter, which has a museum and synagogue worth checking out. The famed Gassan Diamond factory is also here, displaying its shiny baubles and offering free tours.

The neighbourhood is compact and its sights can easily be seen in a day, though the moody brown cafes and classical music venues may keep you longer.

## Local Life

- **Party at the Plaza** The cafes ringing Nieuwmarkt square buzz in the afternoon and evening. When the weather cooperates, everyone sits outside in the shadow of the turreted Waag.
- **Markets & Shops** Fill your bag with juggling balls, chilli-spiced chocolates or old film posters at the neighbourhood favourites along Staalstraat. Then plunge into the Saturday farmers market at Nieuwmarkt square.
- **Best Broodjes** Queue with folks getting their Surinamese spice on at Tokoman; chowhounds agree it makes the best *broodje pom* (chicken-and-tuber-mash sandwich).

## Getting There & Away

- **Tram** Trams 9 and 14 go to Waterlooplein and the Jewish sights; there are no trams to Nieuwmarkt square, but it's a short walk from Waterlooplein.
- **Metro** It's doubtful you'll travel using the subway (which mainly runs to outer districts), but just in case: there are stops at Waterlooplein and Nieuwmarkt.

TOP SIGHTS
# MUSEUM HET REMBRANDTHUIS



**Rembrandt van Rijn lived and worked here between 1639 and 1656. The years spent here were at the high point of his career, when he was regarded as a star and ran the largest painting studio in Holland. Thanks to an itemised list drawn up by a debt collector, as well as Rembrandt's original drawings and paintings, the interior looks almost identical as to when the master lived here. You'll get a real-deal feel for how Rembrandt painted his days away.**

## Riches

The house dates from 1606. Rembrandt bought it for a fortune in 1639, made possible by his wealthy wife, Saskia van Uylenburgh. (Later, chronic debt forced him to move to cheaper digs in the Jordaan.) In addition to the studio, you'll see Rembrandt's living room/bedroom and the anteroom where he entertained business clients. The collection of objects in his 'cabinet' alone is mind-boggling: seashells, glassware, Roman busts and stuffed alligators. No wonder he went bankrupt!

## Etchings

The museum has a near-complete collection of Rembrandt's famous etchings (about 250), although they are not all on display at once. Expect to see between 20 and 100 etchings at any one time, depending on the exhibition. Demonstrations of etching techniques take place several times daily.

## Tickets & Tours

Ask for the free audio guide at the entrance. You can buy advance tickets online, though it's not as vital here as at some of the other big museums. Note that the crowds are lightest right at opening time.

### DON'T MISS

- The large studio
- The cabinet stuffed with exotica
- Etchings collection
- Etching demonstrations
- Free audio tour

### PRACTICALITIES

- Map p292
- 520 04 00
- www.rembrandthuis.nl
- Jodenbreestraat 4-6
- adult/child €10/3
- 10am-5pm

# SIGHTS

### MUSEUM HET REMBRANDTHUIS — MUSEUM

See p87.

### WAAG — HISTORIC BUILDING

Map p292 (www.indewaag.nl; Nieuwmarkt 4; ⏲10am-1am) The multi-turreted, very grand Waag (Weigh House) dates from 1488, when it was part of the city's fortifications. It looked more like a castle in those days, fronted by a moat-like canal and built into the old city walls. From the 17th century onwards it was the main weigh house.

The surgeons guild, which occupied the upper floor, commissioned Rembrandt's famous *The Anatomy Lesson of Dr Tulp* (displayed in the Mauritshuis museum in Den Haag). The masons guild was based in the tower facing the Zeedijk; note the superfine brickwork.

Public executions took place at the Waag, but more recently it served as a fire station and a vault for the city's archives. A bar-restaurant occupies it today, lit by medieval candle-wheels to great effect. Out front, Nieuwmarkt square is a venue for markets – the big ones are the **Boerenmarkt** (farmers market) on Saturday and **Antiques Market** on Sunday– as well as other events.

### PORTUGUESE-ISRAELITE SYNAGOGUE — RELIGIOUS

Map p292 (www.esnoga.com; Mr Visserplein 3; adult/child €6.50/4; ⏲10am-4pm Sun-Fri Apr-Oct, 10am-4pm Sun-Thu, to 2pm Fri Nov-Mar) Built between 1671 and 1675 by Amsterdam's Sephardic community, this edifice was the largest synagogue in Europe at the time. The architect, Elias Bouman, was inspired by the Temple of Solomon, but the building's classical lines are typical of the Dutch capital. It was restored after the war and remains in use today.

The interior features massive pillars and some two dozen brass candelabra, suspended from the ceiling and lit for evening services. The large library belonging to the Ets Haim seminary is one of the oldest and most important Jewish book collections in Europe.

Pick up a free audio tour in the gift shop. You'll need it, as there are limited placards and other explanatory text around.

## TOP SIGHTS
## JOODS HISTORISCH MUSEUM

Impressive in scale and scope, the Jewish Historical Museum is housed in a beautifully restored complex of four Ashkenazic synagogues from the 17th and 18th centuries. The enormous Great Synagogue is home to two exhibitions: the 'History of the Jews in the Netherlands, 1600–1890' and 'Religion,' about Judaism and Jewish traditions. Exhibits start with the pillars of Jewish identity and gradually give way to an engaging portrait of Jewish life in the city, with profiles of key figures and displays of religious items.

Even more enlightening is the New Synagogue and its 'History of Jews in the Netherlands, 1900–Present Day'. The WWII exhibits cover how 25,000 Dutch Jews went into hiding (18,000 survived) and what life was like after the war as they tried to repatriate.

The complex also has a children's museum set up as a Jewish home. Kids can bake challah bread in the kitchen and play tunes in the music room while learning about Jewish traditions.

The free, English-language audio tour that guides you through the collection is excellent, as is the bright cafe serving kosher dishes. If you plan on also visiting the Portuguese-Israelite Synagogue, ask about the discounted combination ticket.

### DON'T MISS

- WWII exhibits
- Children's Museum
- Free audio tour
- Kosher cafe
- Combo ticket with Portuguese-Israelite Synagogue

### PRACTICALITIES

- Map p292
- ☎626 99 45
- www.jhm.nl
- Nieuwe Amstelstraat 1
- adult/child €7.50/3
- ⏲11am-5pm, closed Yom Kippur

LOCAL KNOWLEDGE

## DOCKWORKER STATUE

Beside the Portuguese-Israelite Synagogue, in triangular JD Meijerplein, Mari Andriessen's **Dockworker statue** (1952; Map p292) commemorates the general strike that began among dockworkers on 25 February 1941 to protest against the treatment of Jews. The first deportation round-up had occurred here a few days earlier. The anniversary of the strike is still an occasion for wreath-laying, but has become a low-key affair with the demise of the Communist Party.

Those also planning to visit the Joods Historisch Museum should ask about the discounted combination ticket.

### FREE GASSAN DIAMONDS — GUIDED TOUR

Map p292 (www.gassandiamonds.com; Nieuwe Uilenburgerstraat 173-175; ⏲9am-5pm) This vast workshop, a short walk from Waterlooplein, demonstrates how a rough, ungainly clump of rock is transformed into a girl's best friend. You'll get a quick primer in assessing the gems for quality, and see diamond cutters and polishers in action. The one-hour tour is the best of its kind in town, which is why so many tour buses stop here. Don't worry: the line moves quickly.

The factory sits on Uilenburg, one of the rectangular islands reclaimed in the 1580s during a sudden influx of Sephardic Jews from Spain and Portugal. In the 1880s Gassan became the first diamond factory to use steam power.

### WATERLOOPLEIN FLEA MARKET — MARKET

Map p292 (www.waterloopleinmarkt.nl; ⏲9am-5pm Mon-Sat) This square was once known as Vlooienburg (Flea Town), a good description for the curios, secondhand clothing, tools and other items on offer here today. The street market started in 1880 when two canals were filled in, and Jewish traders living in the neighbouring Jodenbreestraat were allowed to vend their wares here. It was so successful that in 1893 it became a daily market, apart from on the Sabbath (it's now closed on Sunday only). These days it is usually packed with sharp-eyed customers seeking antique knick-knacks, imitation Diesel jeans and cheap bicycle locks (a highly recommended place to find them!).

### STOPERA — ARCHITECTURE & THEATRE

Map p292 (Waterlooplein 22) The hulking white pile between Waterlooplein and the Amstel houses both the town hall *(stadhuis)* and the opera hall (the Muziektheater), hence the name 'Stopera'. The 1986 building design was highly controversial, and protest delayed construction for two decades. When it was finally completed, one critic derided the Stopera as having 'all the charm of an IKEA chair'. Our view: yea on the music theatre, nay on the town hall.

For details of performances in the Muziektheater, see p93. There are usually free lunchtime concerts (12.30pm to 1pm) on Tuesdays from September to June. In the arcade between the town hall and the theatre, you'll find a display on NAP water levels (see the boxed text, p92).

### SCHEEPVAARTHUIS — ARCHITECTURE

Map p292 (Shipping House; Prins Hendrikkade 108) The imposing Scheepvaarthuis was built in 1916 for a consortium of shipping companies. Utilising the street layout to resemble a ship's bow, this remarkable building was the first true example of Amsterdam School style. A statue of Neptune, his wife and four female figures that represent the points of the compass crown the building's prow-like front. The window frames, entrances and interior walls display nautical imagery such as anchors and sailing ships. The building is now refurbished as a luxury hotel. Step inside to admire the intricate wrought ironwork and stained glass of the majestic central stairwell (staff are used to visitors wandering in for a look).

### TRIPPENHUIS — ARCHITECTURE

Map p292 (Kloveniersburgwal 29) After making their fortune in arms-dealing, the Trip brothers commissioned a young Dutch architect, Justus Vingboons, to build the Trippenhuis in 1660. It's a greystone mansion with eight Corinthian columns across two houses, one for each brother. In a nod to their ignoble profession, the chimneys are shaped like mortars. It's closed to the public.

LOCAL KNOWLEDGE

## TOWER TOURS

Amsterdam has three church towers to get high in: the Zuiderkerk (p90), the Westerkerk (p99) and the Oude Kerk (p62). The Westerkerk tour takes you highest and provides the best view of the canals. However, it's also the most crowded since it gets traffic from the next-door Anne Frank Huis, and tours are limited to only seven people at a time. The Zuiderkerk is quite similar looking (Hendrick de Keyser designed both), but the crowds are fewer and 15 people at a time can go up. The Oude Kerk tower is the same height as the Zuiderkerk, but its design is distinct from the other two.

### TUNFUN — PLAYGROUND

Map p292 (www.tunfun.nl; Mr Visserplein 7; adult/child free/€7.50; ⏲10am-6pm, last entry 5pm; 🚸) This cool indoor playground is located in a former traffic underpass, an unused eyesore for over a decade. These days kids can build, climb, roll, draw, jump on trampolines and play on a soccer pitch. There's even a children's disco – this *is* Amsterdam – and a cafe serving *poffertjes* (little pancakes). Kids must be accompanied by an adult. It gets busy when the weather's bad.

### PINTOHUIS (OPENBARE BIBLIOTHEEK) — ARCHITECTURE

Map p292 (www.oba.nl; St Antoniesbreestraat 69; ⏲2-8pm Mon & Wed, 2-5pm Fri, 11am-4pm Sat) The street that runs from Nieuwmarkt square towards Waterlooplein is St Antoniesbreestraat, once a busy street that lost its old buildings during the construction of the metro line. One of the original buildings still standing is the Pintohuis, once owned by a wealthy Sephardic Jew, Isaac de Pinto, who had it remodelled with Italianate pilasters in the 1680s. It's now a *bibliotheek* (library) – pop inside to admire the beautiful ceiling frescos.

### ZUIDERKERK — CHURCH

Map p292 (www.zuiderkerk.amsterdam.nl, in Dutch; Zuiderkerkhof 72; church admission free, tower adult/child €7/3.50; ⏲church 10am-5pm Mon-Fri, noon-4pm Sat, tower 1-5pm Mon-Sat Apr-Sep) A passageway through the modern **Pentagon housing estate** leads to the Zuiderkerk, the 'Southern Church' built by famed Dutch Renaissance architect Hendrick de Keyser. His tower, 1m off plumb, dates from 1614. This was the first custom-built Protestant church in Amsterdam – still Catholic in design but with no choir. The final church service was held here in 1929. During the 'Hunger Winter' of WWII it served as a morgue. It is now used as an office.

To really get a feel for the structure, take a tower tour. Guides lead visitors up lots of stairs every 30 minutes, past the bells and to a lookout area for a sky-high city view. The same folk also run tours at Westerkerk in the Western Canal Belt.

### OOSTINDISCH HUIS — ARCHITECTURE

Map p292 (East Indies House; Oude Hoogstraat 24) This is the former office of the mighty Dutch East India Company (VOC), which was the globe's very first multinational corporation. You could easily walk past it, as there's no sign or plaque to identify it. The sweeping complex, built between 1551 and 1643, was attributed in part to Hendrick de Keyser, the busy city architect. On the Kloveniersburgwal side you can see that the gables defy convention by tilting backwards, making them seem much larger. The mighty VOC sailed into rough waters and was dissolved in 1798.

### MOZES EN AÄRONKERK — CHURCH

Map p292 (Moses & Aaron Church; www.mozeshuis.nl, in Dutch; Waterlooplein 205) This neoclassical Catholic church, built in 1841 on the northeastern corner of Waterlooplein, shows that this wasn't exclusively a Jewish area. It replaced the 'clandestine' Catholic church that occupied two houses named Mozes and Aäron in what is now the rear of the church along Jodenbreestraat (note the wall tablet of Moses above the street corner). Despite its impressive organ, it is no longer used as a church, but rather by social, cultural and educational organisations, which often hold exhibitions. Otherwise, the church is generally closed to the public.

**MONTELBAANSTOREN** HISTORIC BUILDING

Map p292 (Montelbaan Tower; Oude Schans 2) The lower part of this striking tower was built to strengthen Amsterdam's eastern defences in 1512. It's positioned on the old city wall, and gave sentries a good view of suspicious characters on the wharves along Oude Schans. The octagonal base and open wooden steeple were added in 1606 to dampen the bells on the clock after the neighbours complained. Just a few years later the tower began to list under the weight, but residents attached cables and pulled it upright. The elegant tower has two sets of bellworks, four clock faces and a nautical vane like the one on top of the Oude Kerk.

## EATING

TOP CHOICE **LATEI** CAFE €

Map p292 (www.latei.net, in Dutch; Zeedijk 143; mains €4-10; ⏲8am-6pm Mon-Wed, to 10pm Thu & Fri, 9am-10pm Sat, 11am-6pm Sun; ☑) Young locals throng groovy Latei, where you can buy the lamps right off the wall (or the vintage chandeliers, or the tables, or any of the other mod decor – it's all for sale). The cafe goes ethnic (usually Ethiopian or Indian) for dinner Thursday through Saturday. Otherwise it serves sandwiches, apple pie and *koffie verkeerd* (milky coffee).

**TOKOMAN** SURINAMESE €

Map p292 (Waterlooplein 327; sandwiches €3-4, mains €7-9; ⏲11am-8pm Mon-Sat) We have it on good authority that this is the place to get the city's best *broodje pom* (a sandwich filled with a tasty mash of chicken and a starchy Surinamese tuber). You'll want the *zuur* (pickled-cabbage relish) and *peper* (chilli) on it, plus a cold can of coconut water to wash it down.

**HEMELSE MODDER** CONTEMPORARY DUTCH €€

Map p292 (☎624 32 03; www.hemelsemodder.nl, in Dutch; Oude Waal 11; mains €23-27, 3-course menu €29.50; ⏲dinner) Celery-green walls and blond-wood tables are the backdrop for equally light and unpretentious food, which emphasises North Sea fish and farm-fresh produce. If there's no berry pudding for dessert, the namesake *hemelse modder* (heavenly mud) chocolate mousse is a good fallback. The back terrace makes for lovely al fresco dining. The restaurant is a bit out of the way, but worth it.

**CAFÉ BERN** SWISS €€

Map p292 (☎622 00 34; Nieuwmarkt 9; mains €11-17; ⏲dinner) Indulge in a fondue frenzy at this delightfully well-worn brown cafe. People have been flocking here for more than 30 years for the gruyère fondue as well as the entrecôte. Note: it's generally closed for a large part of the summer, but do you really want fondue in hot weather anyway? Reservations advised.

**LASTAGE** FRENCH €€€

Map p292 (☎737 08 11; www.restaurantlastage.nl, in Dutch; Geldersekade 29; set menus from €36; ⏲dinner Wed-Sun) Small, cosy Lastage is another one of those rose-among-thorns places. The changing menu might start with, say, stuffed guinea fowl atop red cabbage, followed by halibut with nutty Camargue wild rice, beetroot puree and saffron sauce. It's all beautifully presented, and the elegant wine list matches to a tee. It's located at the seedy edge of the Red Light District.



### IN A TIGHT SPOT

Amsterdam is chock-full of slender homes because property used to be taxed on frontage. So the narrower your facade, the less you paid.

Witness the narrow house at Oude Hoogstraat 22 (Map p292). It's 2.02m wide, 6m deep and several storeys tall, occupying a mere 12 sq metres per storey. This could well be the tiniest (self-contained) house in Europe.

Nearby, the Kleine Trippenhuis (Map p292) at Kloveniersburgwal 26 is 2.44m wide. It stands opposite the mansion once owned by the wealthy Trip Brothers and, so the story goes, their coachman exclaimed: 'If only I could have a house as wide as my masters' door!' Webers fetish shop now occupies the skinny building.

### TOKO JOYCE INDONESIAN €

Map p292 (www.tokojoyce.nl, in Dutch; Nieuwmarkt 38; mains €5-9.50; ⏲11am-8pm Tue-Sat, 4-8pm Sun & Mon) Pick and mix a platter of Indonesian-Surinamese food from the glass case; start with spiced yellow rice and add various spicy, coconutty stews. The 'lunch box' (you choose noodles or rice, plus two toppings) is good value. To finish, get a wedge of *spekkoek* (moist, layered gingerbread). Take your meal upstairs to the handful of tables, or outside, where canalside benches beckon a few steps from the door.

### NYONYA ASIAN €€

Map p292 (Kloveniersburgwal 38; mains €11-17; ⏲1-9pm, closed Tue) Humble little Nyonya makes a mean bowl of *laksa* (spicy noodle soup), a complex *rendang* curry (spicy and coconutty) and several other Malaysian specialities. There's no alcohol, but you can sip milky tea or Sarsae (a Chinese root beer).

## DRINKING & NIGHTLIFE

### TOP CHOICE DE SLUYSWACHT BROWN CAFE

Map p292 (www.sluyswacht.nl, in Dutch; Jodenbreestraat 1) Listing like a ship in a high wind, this tiny black building was once a lock-keeper's house on the Oude Schans. Today the canalside terrace is one of the nicest spots we know in town to relax and down a beer (Dommelsch is the house speciality), and it has gorgeous views of the Montelbaanstoren.

### CAFÉ DE DOELEN BROWN CAFE

Map p292 (Kloveniersburgwal 125) This cafe (on a busy canalside crossroads between the Amstel and the Red Light District) dates back to 1895 and looks it: carved wooden goat's head, leaded stained-glass lamps and sand on the floor. Still, it's far from stuffy. There's a fun, youthful atmosphere, and in fine weather the tables spill across the street for picture-perfect canal views. It sometimes screens movies during the week.

### DE ENGELBEWAARDER BROWN CAFE

Map p292 (www.cafe-de-engelbewaarder.nl, in Dutch; Kloveniersburgwal 59) Jazz-heads will want to settle in at this little cafe on Sunday afternoon (from 4.30pm), which is when an open session takes place that has earned quite a following. The rest of the week, it's a tranquil place to sip a beer by the sunny windows.

### CAFÉ CUBA CAFE

Map p292 (Nieuwmarkt 3) If a brown cafe was beamed to the tropical Atlantic, it would probably have Café Cuba's air of faded elegance. Slouch behind a table with names etched into it, and quaff blender drinks like mai tais, Planter's Punch and the legendary mojito. It may remind you of Hemingway or the Buena Vista Social Club.

### DE BEKEERDE SUSTER BEER CAFE

Map p292 (www.debekeerdesuster.nl, in Dutch; Kloveniersburgwal 6-8) It's got the brew tanks, it's got the beautiful hardwood interior,

### TAKING A NAP

It is widely known that Amsterdam (and indeed more than half of the Netherlands) lies a couple of metres below sea level, but when's the last time you heard anyone ask 'which sea level'? In fact, sea levels vary around the globe and even around the Netherlands. The average level of the former Zuiderzee, in the lee of Holland, was slightly lower than that of the North Sea along Holland's exposed west coast.

A display in the arcade of the Stopera shows the ins and outs of Normaal Amsterdams Peil (NAP; Normal Amsterdam Level), established in the 17th century as the average high-water mark of the Zuiderzee. This still forms the zero reference for elevation anywhere in the country and is also used in Germany and several other European countries.

Water in the canals is kept at 40cm below NAP, and many parts of the city lie lower still. The Stopera display has water columns representing different sea levels, as well as the highest level of disastrous floods in 1953 (4.55m above NAP). Information sheets explain the details. A paid-admission exhibit (€4) delves further into the subject.

it's even got the history – a 16th-century brewery-cloister run by nuns. Stop in for a meal of pub grub, or make it the start of an evening on Nieuwmarkt.

**HILL STREET BLUES** COFFEESHOP

Map p292 (Nieuwmarkt 14) It feels more like a lounge bar than a coffeeshop, with jazzy music, an in-the-groove vibe and an international swath of visitors. Firm beanbag stools and comfy benches make great stations for watching the life forms on busy Nieuwmarkt while sipping a blended fruit-and-yogurt smoothie or one of the phenomenal shakes. For a grungier vibe, check out its other location at Warmoesstraat 52 (Map p286), where graffiti covers every inch of the space and furniture.

**LOKAAL 'T LOOSJE** BROWN CAFE

Map p292 (Nieuwmarkt 32-34) With its beautiful etched-glass windows and tile tableaux on the walls, this is one of the oldest and prettiest cafes in the Nieuwmarkt area. It attracts a vibrant mix of students, locals and tourists.

**CAFÉ-RESTAURANT DANTZIG** GRAND CAFE

Map p292 (Zwanenburgwal 15) Located in the Stopera building, Dantzig doesn't have the history of some of the other cafes in town, but that doesn't make it any less appealing. The great Amstel-side terrace is always busy in summer, with excellent views over the water and lots of sunlight.

## ENTERTAINMENT

**MUZIEKTHEATER** CLASSICAL MUSIC

Map p292 (☎625 54 55; www.hetmuziektheater.nl; Waterlooplein 22; ⊙closed Aug) The swanky Stopera theatre is home to the Netherlands Opera and the National Ballet. Big-name performers and international dance troupes also take the stage here. Visitors aged under 30 can get tickets for €10 to €15 by showing up 90 minutes before show time. Free lunchtime concerts (12.30pm to 1pm) are usually held on Tuesdays from September to June in the Boekmanzaal.

**AMSTERDAMS MARIONETTEN THEATER** THEATRE

Map p292 (☎620 80 27; www.marionettentheater.nl; Nieuwe Jonkerstraat 8; adult/child €16/7.50) In a former blacksmith's shop near Nieuwmarkt, the marionette theatre has a limited repertoire (mainly Mozart operas such as *The Magic Flute*), but kids and adults alike are enthralled by the fairy-tale stage sets, period costumes and beautiful singing voices that bring the diminutive cast to life. From June to August the theatre only performs for groups; at other times, check the website for a schedule.

**BETHANIËNKLOOSTER** CLASSICAL MUSIC

Map p292 (☎625 00 78; www.bethanienklooster.nl; Barndesteeg 6b; ⊙closed Aug) This former monastery near Nieuwmarkt has a glorious ballroom, and is the perfect place to take in some exceptional chamber music.

## SHOPPING

**PUCCINI BOMBONI** FOOD & DRINK

Map p292 (www.puccinibomboni.com; Staalstraat 17; ⊙9am-6pm Tue-Sat, noon-6pm Sun & Mon) We're not the only ones who go gaga over Puccini's large, handmade chocolate bonbons with rich fillings and distinctive flavours like anise, tamarind or calvados. There is another branch at Singel 184 (Map p300). Note: these shops have been known to close in warm weather – for the sake of the chocolates, of course.

**DROOG** DESIGN, HOMEWARES

Map p292 (www.droog.nl; Staalstraat 7b; ⊙closed Mon) This slick Amsterdam-based firm is a market leader, with inventions such as the 85-lamp chandelier, the cow chair, and curtains with dress patterns. There are more than 180 products by 100-plus designers.

**DE BEESTENWINKEL** TOYS

Map p292 (www.beestenwinkel.nl, in Dutch; Staalstraat 11) From teeny-tiny teddy bears to pink plastic pig snouts, this pleasantly crowded shop sells *de best* (the best) of *de beesten* (animals). Other bests: plush toys from great toy makers, lamps in animal shapes, and lots of plastic reptiles.

**JOE'S VLIEGERWINKEL** KITES

Map p292 (www.joesvliegerwinkel.nl; Nieuwe Hoogstraat 19; ⊙Tue-Sat, plus Mon in summer) Whether you're after a kite that flies in nice patterns for the kids, or you're looking for something more exotic, head to this specialised kite shop. You can also buy build-it-yourself kits.

LOCAL KNOWLEDGE

## SPARKLING OPTIONS

Two diamond factories in town offer free guided tours. Gassan Diamonds (p89) offers the slicker version. Coster Diamonds' (p162) perk is its convenient location at the Museumplein. You'll see lots of gems, and workers shining them, at both places.

For those in the market to buy, note that diamonds aren't necessarily cheaper in Amsterdam than elsewhere, but between the tours and extensive descriptions and factory offers, you'll know what you're buying.

And a bit of local diamond trivia: Amsterdam has been a diamond centre since Sephardic Jews introduced the cutting industry in the 1580s. The Cullinan, the largest diamond ever found (3106 carats), was split into more than 100 stones here in 1908, after which the master cutter spent three months recovering from stress.

### JACOB HOOY & CO — ALTERNATIVE MEDICINE

Map p292 (www.jacobhooy.nl, in Dutch; Kloveniersburgwal 12) This charming chemist's shop – with its walls of massive wooden drawers – has been selling medicinal herbs, homeopathic remedies and natural cosmetics since 1743.

### 'T KLOMPENHUISJE — SOUVENIRS

Map p292 (www.klompenhuisje.com, in Dutch; Nieuwe Hoogstraat 9a; ⏲closed Sun) Reasonably priced and finely crafted, traditional Dutch clogs are just the thing to potter around the garden in, away from prying eyes. Good ones are surprisingly comfortable. There are also handmade leather goods and cute kids' galoshes.

### HENXS — CLOTHING

Map p292 (http://shop.henxs.com; St Antoniesbreestraat 136) The two tiny floors of this indie clothes store are crammed with fave labels of skaters and graffiti artists, such as Hardcore, Bombers Best, Evisu and G-Star. Graffiti supplies and edgy accessories are available in Henxs' space next door.

### FILMANTIQUARIAAT CINE QUA NON — ART, BOOKS

Map p292 (www.cinequanonline.com; Staalstraat 14; ⏲Tue-Sat) An encyclopedic collection of film posters, arthouse DVDs and books on films fills this dusty, crammed space. Amazingly, if you ask for something specific, the staff will know exactly where it is in the organised chaos.

### JUGGLE — SPECIALITY SHOP

Map p292 (www.juggle-store.com; Staalstraat 3; ⏲closed Sun & Mon) Wee Juggle puts more than just balls in the air: it also sells circus supplies, from unicycles to fire hoops to magic tricks.

### KNUFFELS — TOYS, SHOES

Map p292 (www.knuffels.com; St Antoniesbreestraat 39-51) Kids will be drawn to the bobbing mobiles hanging from the ceiling of this busy corner shop. Adults, too, may be drawn in by the clogs, soft toys, puppets, teddies and jigsaw puzzles.

### & KLEVERING — HOMEWARES

Map p292 (www.klevering.nl, in Dutch; Staalstraat 11) This fun home-accessories shop is a great place to pick up examples of Dutch-designed cleverness without blowing your budget. Funky glasses, lamps, clocks and children's toys fill the shelves.

### BOOK EXCHANGE — BOOKS

Map p292 (www.bookexchange.nl; Kloveniersburgwal 58) This rabbit warren specialises in secondhand English books, with temptingly priced literary titles as well as volumes on the social sciences and more. It's near the university.

### WEBERS — EROTICA

Map p292 (www.webersholland.nl; Kloveniersburgwal 26; ⏲1-7pm, from 11am Sat) Indulge in top-end versions of every kind of fetish-wear imaginable (and unimaginable).

### BOERENMARKT — MARKET

Map p292 (Farmers Market; Nieuwmarkt square; ⏲9am-4pm Sat) Organic foods and produce.

### ANTIQUES MARKET — MARKET

Map p292 (Nieuwmarkt square; ⏲9am-5pm Sun May-Sep) Good for old books and bric-a-brac.

### WATERLOOPLEIN FLEA MARKET — MARKET

Map p292 (www.waterloopleinmarkt.nl; ⏲9am-5pm Mon-Sat) The best of the Nieuwmarkt bunch for browsing; see p89 for details.

# Western Canal Ring

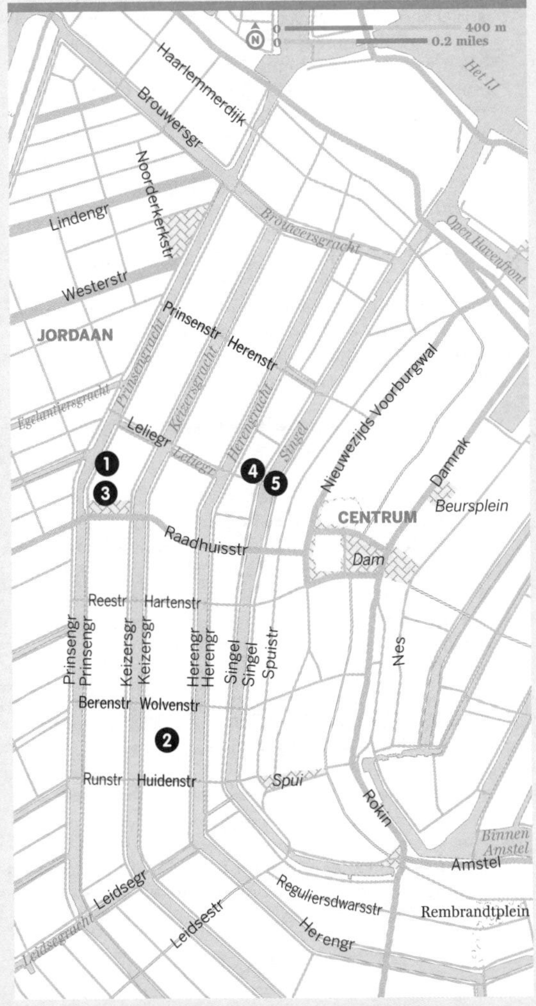


For more detail of this area, see Map p299 and Map p300

## Neighbourhood Top Five

1. Contemplate the amazing life and tragic death of the most famous Dutch girl in history at **Anne Frank Huis** (p97).
2. Shop along the compact, captivating **Negen Straatjes** (Nine Streets; p99).
3. Visit the grand **Westerkerk** (p99), home to the largest nave in the Netherlands.
4. Learn to distinguish an aged Gouda from a creamy young *boerenkaas* at the **Reypenaer Cheese Tasting** (p99).
5. Explore the city's canals on a **Western Canal Ring walking tour** (p100).

## Lonely Planet's Top Tip

In the spring and summer, we recommend taking advantage of the later evening hours of the Anne Frank Huis. Go to an early dinner at one of the many excellent nearby cafes, and then spend the rest of the evening hours in Amsterdam's most moving sight – with no crowds, and plenty of time to contemplate this remarkable Dutch girl's life and legacy.

## Best Places to Eat

- Buffet Van Odette (p102)
- De Belhamel (p102)
- Stout (p102)
- Pancakes! (p102)
- Cilubang (p102)

For reviews, see p102

## Best Places to Drink

- Café Restaurant Van Puffelen (p104)
- Café Tabac (p104)
- Café het Molenpad (p104)
- Café de Vergulde Gaper (p104)
- De Doffer (p104)

For reviews, see p104

## Best Places to Shop

- De Kaaskamer (p106)
- Frozen Fountain (p106)
- Scotch & Soda (p107)
- Unlimited Delicious (p107)
- Boekie Woekie (p106)

For reviews, see p106

## Explore: Western Canal Ring

Before you start out, remember that this whole area is a Unesco World Heritage site; you could spend an entire day admiring the architecture down one canal alone. Although this area is indeed loaded with sights (and in high season attracts the amount of tourists you'd expect), half of the charm is simply soaking up the atmosphere: from the street, from a boat, from a backyard garden or rooftop balcony, or from the terrace of a canalside cafe.

Don't expect to see the entire district in one day. It's easiest to start at the northern end of the neighbourhood, on Haarlemmerdijk, and work your way towards Westerkerk and Anne Frank Huis the first day. Browse through the trendy Haarlemmerdijk and Haarlemmerstraat shops, eat lunch at one of the nearby cafes, stroll the lovely Brouwersgracht, and then spend the afternoon weaving in and out of the lanes and canals until you wind up at Anne Frank Huis in the early evening, when the crowds are thinnest.

On the south side of the neighbourhood, the Negen Straatjes (Nine Streets) comprise a tic-tac-toe board of perhaps Amsterdam's most enjoyable shopping. The *straatjes* (streets) are full of quirky little shops dealing in antiques, vintage fashions, housewares and one-offs including everything from toothbrushes to antique eyeglass frames. It's all peppered with pubs, cafes and informal dining that spills out into the streets in warmer weather. Fair warning: many a traveller has happened upon the Nine Streets and inadvertently spent the whole day wandering the shops, eating and drinking.

## Local Life

- **Ad perfect** As you mosey down the Singel and the Herengracht canal, glance into the windows of some of the posh advertising agencies and design firms that line the streets, where the artistically designed interiors might cause serious job envy.
- **Felix Merits House** Get cultured with the neighbourhood intelligentsia at this community gathering place.
- **Happy hour** Want to hobnob (or network) with the local young professionals? Come early evening – they congregate at stylish Werck (p104).

## Getting There & Away

- **Trams** Trams 13, 14 and 17 drop off near the main attractions, and any tram or bus that stops near the Dam is just a short walk away.

TOP SIGHTS
# ANNE FRANK HUIS

**It is one of the 20th century's most compelling stories: a young Jewish girl forced into hiding with her family and their friends to escape deportation by the Nazis. The house they used as a hideaway should be a highlight of any visit to Amsterdam; indeed, it gets nearly a million visitors a year. Stepping through the revolving bookcase of the 'Secret Annexe' and up the steep stairs into the living quarters – where the family lived for over two years before they were betrayed to the Gestapo – is to step back into a time that seems both distant and tragically real. Perhaps nowhere else in Europe does the brutal legacy of the Nazi rise to power – and the beauty and humanity that stubbornly persisted in spite of it – seem more palpable.**

It seems impossible now, but it's true: it took the German army just five days to occupy all of the Netherlands, along with Belgium and much of France. And once Hitler's forces had swept across the country, many Jews – like Anne Frank and her family – eventually went into hiding. Anne's famous diary describes how restrictions were gradually imposed on Dutch Jews: from being forbidden to ride streetcars to being forced to turn in their bicycles and not being allowed to visit Christian friends. Ultimately, most of Holland's Jewish population – more, in fact, than that of any other European country – perished in the Holocaust.

The Franks moved into the upper floors of the specially prepared rear of the building, along with another couple, the Van Daans, and their son Peter, and were joined later by a Mr van Dussel. Here they survived until they were betrayed to the Gestapo in August 1944.

## DON'T MISS

- Anne Frank's diary
- Anne's old bedroom
- WWII news reels
- Peter van Pels' room
- The video of Anne's old schoolmate Hannah Gisler

## PRACTICALITIES

- Map p300
- ☎556 71 00
- www.annefrank.org
- Prinsengracht 276
- adult/child under 10yr/10-17 yr €8.50/free/4
- ⏰9am-7pm Sun-Fri, to 10pm Sat Jan–mid-Mar, 9am-9pm Sun-Fri, to 10pm Sat mid-Mar–Jun, 9am-10pm daily Jul & Aug, 9am-9pm daily Sep 1-14, 9am-7pm daily mid-Sep–Dec

### DID YOU KNOW?

The Franks were among the last Jews to be deported and Anne died in the Bergen-Belsen concentration camp in March 1945, only weeks before it was liberated. Otto was the only member of the family to survive, and after the war he published Anne's diary, which was found among the litter in the annexe (the furniture had been carted away by the Nazis). Addressed to the fictitious Kitty, the diary – written in Dutch – traces the young teenager's development through puberty and persecution, and displays all the signs of a gifted writer in the making. The diary, meanwhile, has taken on a life of its own. It's been translated into some 60 languages and was made into a stage play performed in 34 countries, a 1959 Hollywood movie and a 2001 British movie. The diary has been reissued in recent years, complete with controversial passages deleted by Otto that serve to remind us that she was, among other things, an ordinary girl, unable to swim against the tide of extraordinary times.

## Ground Floor

After several renovations, the house itself is now contained within a modern, square shell that attempts to retain the original feel of the building (it was used during WWII as offices and a warehouse).

On this floor, be sure to watch the multilingual news reels of WWII footage narrated using segments of Anne's diary: it inextricably links the rise of Hitler with the Frank family's personal saga.

### Offices

View the former offices of Victor Kugler, Otto Frank's business partner; his identity card, and the film magazines he bought for Anne, are on display. The other office area belonged to Miep Gies, Bep Voskuijl and Jo Kleiman, three women who worked in the office by day and provided food, clothing, school supplies and other goods – often purchased on the Black Market or with ration cards – for the eight members of the Secret Annexe. You can see some of their personal documents here.

## Secret Annexe

While the lower levels are painstakingly curated in a way that boldly presents history with interactive modern technology, the former living quarters of the Frank family in the *achterhuis* (rear house) retain their stark, haunting austerity. It's as if visitors are stepping back into 1942. Notice how windows of the annexe were blacked out to prevent suspicion among people who might see it from surrounding houses (blackouts were common practice to disorient bombers at night).

Take a moment to observe the ingenious set-up of the Secret Annexe as you walk through. You then enter two floors of the dark and airless space where the Franks and their friends observed complete silence during the daytime, outgrew their clothes and read Dickens, before being mysteriously betrayed and sent to their deaths.

### Anne's Bedroom

As you enter Anne's simple, small bedroom, which she shared with Fritz Pfeffer (called Mr Van Dussel in the diary), you can still sense the remnants of a young girl's dreams: the physical evidence of her interests and longings is on the wall with her photos of Hollywood stars and postcards of the Dutch Royal family.

## SIGHTS

### ANNE FRANK HUIS — MUSEUM

See p97.

### WESTERKERK — CHURCH

Map p300 (Western Church; ☎624 77 66; www.westerkerk.nl; Prinsengracht 281; church admission free, tower €6 (by tour only); ⊙church 11am-3pm Mon-Fri Apr-Jun & Sep, 11am-3pm Mon-Sat Jul & Aug, tower 10am-5.30pm Mon-Sat Apr-Sep) The main gathering place for Amsterdam's Dutch Reformed community, this church was built for rich Protestants to a 1620 design by Hendrick de Keyser. The nave is the largest in the Netherlands and is covered by a wooden barrel vault. The huge main **organ** dates from 1686, with panels decorated with instruments and biblical scenes. Rembrandt (1606–69), who died bankrupt at nearby Rozengracht, was buried in a pauper's grave somewhere in the church.

Another highlight is the **bell tower**, topped by the blue imperial crown that Habsburg emperor Maximilian I bestowed to the city for its coat of arms in 1489. The climb of the 85m tower can be strenuous and claustrophobic (it's inside a tower, after all), but the guide takes breaks on the landings while describing the bells.

Carillon recitals take place on Fridays at 1pm (though check the schedule posted by the entrance, as this can vary); best listening is from the nearby Bloemgracht. The bells also chime mechanically every 15 minutes.

### NEGEN STRAATJES — STREETS

Map p299 (Nine Streets; www.de9straatjes.nl) In a city packed with countless shopping opportunities, each seemingly more alluring than the next, the Negen Straatjes represent the very densest concentration of consumer pleasures. These nine streets are indeed small, each just a block long. They form a grid bounded by Reestraat, Hartenstraat and Gasthuismolensteeg to the north, Prinsengracht to the west, Singel to the east and Runstraat, Huidenstraat and Wijde Heisteeg to the south. The shops are tiny, too, and many are highly specialised. Eyeglasses? Cheese? Toothbrushes? Single-edition art books? Each has its own dedicated boutique. Many are closed entirely on Monday, and sometimes Tuesday. For details on specific shops in the area, see p106.

### REYPENAER CHEESE TASTING — CULINARY

Map p300 (☎320 63 33; www.reypenaer.com; Singel 182; tasting with/without wine pairings €10/7.50; ⊙2pm & 4pm Wed-Sun) Here's your chance to become a *kaas* connoisseur. The 100-plus-year-old Dutch cheese maker Reypenaer offers tastings in a rustic classroom under its shop. The hour-long session includes six cheeses – two made from goat's milk and four from cow's milk – plus optional wine and port pairings. The staff leads you through them from young to old, helping you to appreciate each hunk's look, smell and taste.

It's best to call ahead, as the tastings only occur if a small group partakes; also, make your English or Dutch language preference known. Afterwards, tasters get a 15% discount on all shop merchandise.

### FELIX MERITIS BUILDING — CULTURAL BUILDING

Map p299 (www.felix.meritis.nl; Keizersgracht 324; ⊙box office 9am-7pm) This centre for the performing arts was built in 1787 by Jacob Otten Husly for an organisation called Felix Meritis (Latin for 'Happiness through Achievement'), a society of wealthy residents who promoted the ideals of the Enlightenment through the study of science, arts and commerce. The colonnaded facade served as a model for that of the Concertgebouw, and its oval concert hall (where Brahms, Grieg and Saint Saëns performed) was copied as the Concertgebouw's Kleine Zaal (Small Hall) for chamber music.

Nowadays the reconstituted Felix Meritis Foundation promotes European performing arts and literature. On a sunny morning the cafe's huge windows make a comfy reading spot (see p106).

### NETHERLANDS MEDIA ART INSTITUTE — CULTURAL BUILDING

Map p299 (www.nimk.nl; Keizersgracht 264; adult/student €4.50/2.50; ⊙gallery 1-6pm Tue-Sat & 1st Sun of month) From the hilarious and the ridiculous to the deep and the experimental, there's always something interesting in this gallery's changing exhibits. Don't expect to see works by the hit makers or TV directors of tomorrow, though. The institute is specifically about video as art; there's an artist-in-residence program if you get inspired. The collection numbers some 1500 works, assembled since the institute was established in 1978. The **mediatheek** (admission free; ⊙1-5pm Mon-Fri) works

START SINGEL/TORENSLUIS
END NINE STREETS
DISTANCE 3 KM
DURATION 1¼ HOURS

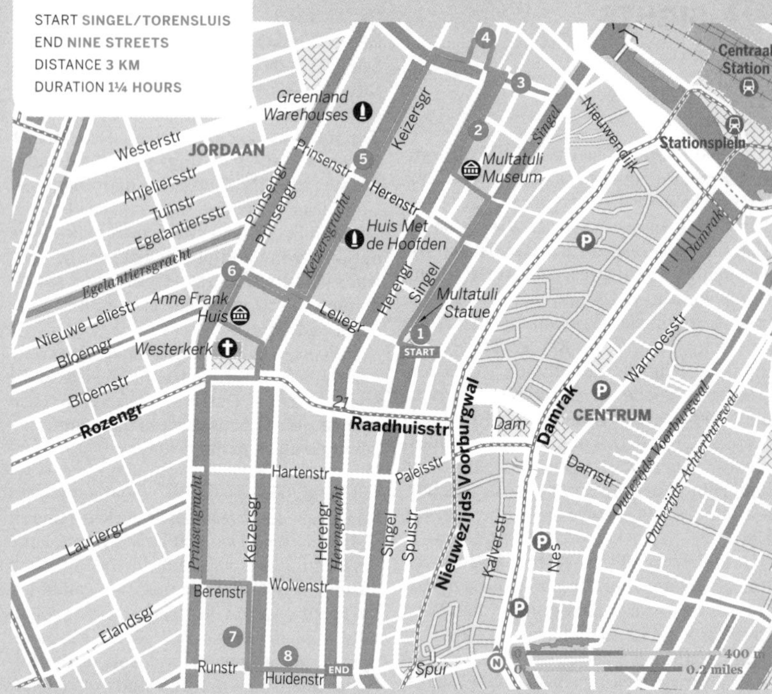




Neighbourhood Walk

## Western Canal Ring Walking Tour

Amsterdam has more canals than Venice. Get to know the Canal Ring's 17th-century beauties with this jaunt.

Originally a moat that defended Amsterdam's outer limits, the 1 **Singel** is the first canal from the centre. Torensluis, Amsterdam's oldest bridge (built in the mid-1600s), crosses it. Before embarking, give the Multatuli statue a pinch; the Dutch literary giant's museum is a few blocks north.

Amsterdam's wealthiest residents once lived along the 2 **Herengracht**, named after the Heeren XVII (17 Gentlemen) of the Dutch East India Company. Note how some buildings lean forward and have hoists in the gables. Given the narrowness of interior staircases, this is how folks hauled large goods to upper floors.

The Herengracht soon intersects with the pretty 3 **Brouwersgracht** (Brewer's Canal), which took its name from the many suds makers located here in the 16th and 17th centuries. To the north is Herenmarkt, with the 17th-century 4 **Westindisch Huis**, the former head office of the Dutch West India Company. It was here that the booty of Admiral Piet Heyn, the great naval hero, was stored after his men captured the Spanish silver fleet off the coast of Cuba.

Turning south, cross the Brouwersgracht into the 5 **Keizersgracht** (Emperor's Canal). You'll soon spot the imposing, red-shuttered Greenland Warehouses and, further on, the Huis Met de Hoofden, with carvings of Apollo, Ceres and Mars. At peaceful Leliegracht, turn west into 6 **Prinsengracht**. You'll pass the Anne Frank Huis and the soaring towers of the Westerkerk. Back on Keizersgracht, you can't miss the quirky 7 **Felix Meritis Building**, a one-time Enlightenment society venue turned alternative theatre. Since you're probably hungry, thirsty, or both by this point, make haste to one of the fetching little cafes that line the nearby 8 **Negen Straatjes** (Nine Streets).

like a library, complete with librarians to advise you.

### HOMOMONUMENT MONUMENT

Map p300 (cnr Keizersgracht & Raadhuisstraat) Behind the Westerkerk, this 1987 cluster of three 10m x 10m x 10m granite triangles recalls persecution by the Nazis, who forced gay men to wear a pink triangle patch. One of the triangles actually steps down into the Keizersgracht, and is said to represent a jetty from which gays were sent to the concentration camps. Others interpret the step-up from the canal as a rising symbol of hope. Note the monuments are flush to the ground, and can be easy to miss at first glance.

Just south of the Homomonument is the **Pink Point** (www.pinkpoint.org; Westermarkt; ⌚10am-6pm). Part information kiosk, part souvenir shop, it's a good place to pick up gay and lesbian publications, and news about parties, events and social groups.

### HUIS MARSEILLE MUSEUM

Map p299 (www.huismarseille.nl; Keizersgracht 401; adult/under 18yr €5/free; ⌚11am-6pm Tue-Sun) This well-curated photography museum stages large-scale, temporary exhibitions, drawing from its own collection as well as hosting travelling shows. Themes might include portraiture, nature or regional photography, spread out over several floors and a 'summer house' behind the main house.

Huis Marseille also has a noteworthy building. The name refers to its original owner, a French merchant in 1665, and the original structure has remained largely intact. It retains some antique touches such as the 18th-century fountain in the library, and a painting of Apollo, Minerva and the muses in the garden room.

### MULTATULI MUSEUM MUSEUM

Map p300 (www.multatuli-museum.nl; Korsjespoortsteeg 20; admission free; ⌚10am-5pm Tue, noon-5pm Sat & Sun) Better known by the pen name Multatuli – Latin for 'I have suffered greatly' – novelist Eduard Douwes Dekker was best known for *Max Havelaar* (1860), about corrupt colonialists in the Dutch East Indies. Dekker himself worked in colonial administration in Batavia (now Jakarta), and the book made him something of a social conscience for the Netherlands. This small but fascinating museum-home chronicles his life and works, and shows furniture and artefacts from his period in Indonesia.

### HET GRACHTENHUIS MUSEUM

Map p299 (The Canal House; www.hetgrachtenhuis.nl; Keizersgracht 123; adult/child €8/4; ⌚10am-5pm Tue-Sun) If you're the kind of person who walks through the Canal Ring and marvels over what a true feat of engineering this area is, you won't want to miss the Canal House, which explains how the canals and the houses that line them became an integral part of Amsterdam city planning. Call ahead and book a spot on a small group tour as tickets are limited; unlike most Amsterdam museums, it's not the kind of place you simply wander through.

### HUIS MET DE HOOFDEN MUSEUM

Map p300 (House with the Heads; Keizersgracht 123) A shining example of Dutch Renaissance style, this whimsical structure has a beautiful step gable with six heads at door level representing the classical muses. Folklore has it that the heads depict burglars, decapitated in quick succession by a fearless maid as they tried to break in. The facade drips with decorations – lion masks, obelisks and vases – as well as the famous heads (match 'em up): Apollo, Diana, Ceres, Bacchus, Minerva and Mars. The building now houses the Bureau Monumentenzorg, the city office of monument preservation.

### BIJBELS MUSEUM MUSEUM

Map p299 (Bible Museum; www.bijbelsmuseum.nl; Herengracht 366-368; adult/under 13yr/13-17yr €7.50/free/3.75; ⌚10am-5pm Mon-Sat, 11am-5pm Sun) This place first gained notoriety thanks to a dedicated minister, Leendert Schouten, who built a scale model of the Jewish Tabernacle described in Exodus. Now on the museum's 3rd floor, the model is said to have attracted thousands of visitors even before it was completed in 1851. Another large exhibit examines the Temple Mount/Haram al-Sharif in Jerusalem from Christian, Jewish and Muslim perspectives. A collection of Dutch Bibles includes a **Delft Bible** printed in 1477. On the ground floor you can sniff scents mentioned in the Good Book and stroll through a garden of biblical trees.

### POEZENBOOT BOAT

Map p300 (Cat Boat; www.poezenboot.nl; Singel 38; admission free, but donations encouraged; ⌚1-3pm, closed Wed & Sun) This boat on the

Singel is a must for cat lovers. It was founded in 1966 by an eccentric woman who became legendary for looking after several hundred stray cats at a time. The boat has since been taken over by a foundation and holds a mere few dozen kitties in proper pens, ready to be spayed or neutered, implanted with an identifying computer chip (as per Dutch law) and, hopefully, adopted out.

**VAN BRIENENHOFJE** COURTYARD

Map p300 (Prinsengracht 85-133; admission free; ⏲6am-6pm Mon-Fri, to 2pm Sat) This charming courtyard was named in the late 18th century for Jan van Brienen, who bought the Star Brewery located here, one of 13 breweries in town at the time. (The place is still called De Star *hofje* by many.) It was turned into an almshouse for older residents, who had a clear division of labour: the women cleaned house for the single men, who in turn toted water buckets from the outside pump (topped by a curious lantern). There's also a manicured garden. If *hofjes* grab you, be sure to visit the Jordaan (see the boxed text, p133).

**DE RODE HOED** CULTURAL BUILDING

Map p300 (The Red Hat; www.rodehoed.nl; Keizersgracht 102; admission free; ⏲8.30am-5.30pm, except during special events) De Rode Hoed is a cultural centre that occupies three glorious 17th-century canal houses. Its line-up includes lectures by world-renowned authors and debates on the topics of the day, sometimes in English. It's worth a visit, even when nothing's on, to view the three-storey main auditorium, which was once the largest clandestine church in the Netherlands. The centre was named for the hat shop once located here (spot the tile on the facade that identified the place).

## EATING

It may not have the ethnic dining diversity of other parts of town, but the Western Canal Ring makes up for it with sheer charm and a fashion-forward swagger. The Negen Straatjes (Nine Streets) are filled with cute cafes and small restaurants to match their lovely boutiques.

**DE BELHAMEL** FRENCH €€€

Map p300 (☎622 10 95; www.debelhamel.nl; Brouwersgracht 60; mains €20-25, set menu €35; ⏲lunch & dinner) In warm weather the canalside tables at the head of the Herengracht are an aphrodisiac, and the sumptuous art nouveau interior provides the perfect backdrop for excellent French- and Italian-inspired dishes like silky roast beef.

**CILUBANG** INDONESIAN €€

Map p299 (☎626 97 55; www.cilubang.com; Runstraat 10; mains from €21, rijsttafel from €23; ⏲dinner Tue-Sun) Cute, cosy and slightly romantic, celadon-hued Cilubang soothes the stomach and soul with *rijsttafel* (Indonesian banquet) and attentive, personal service. Located in the Negen Straatjes, it's been at it for 2½ decades. The food is west Javanese, and with any luck you'll hear gamelan music, too.

**BUFFET VAN ODETTE** CAFE €€

Map p299 (www.buffet-amsterdam.nl; Herengracht 309; mains €5-15; ⏲8.30am-5.30pm Mon & Wed-Fri, 10am-5.30pm Sat & Sun) This is not a buffet but a sit-down cafe, where Odette and Yvette show how good simple cooking can taste when you start with great ingredients and a dash of creativity. Soups, sandwiches, pastas and quiches are mostly organic, and you might find smart little extras like pine nuts in your quiche. Sit by the window for one of the city's loveliest canal views.

**PANCAKES!** CONTEMPORARY DUTCH €

Map p299 (www.pancakesamsterdam.com; Berenstraat 38; mains €6-10; ⏲10am-7pm; 👪) Just as many locals as tourists grace the blue-tile tables at snug little Pancakes!, carving into all the usual options, plus daily creations like ham, chicory and cheese or chicken curry pancakes. The batter is made with flour sourced from a local mill.

**STOUT** INTERNATIONAL €€

Map p300 (www.stout.nl; Haarlemmerstraat 73; mains €6-24; ⏲lunch & dinner) Architects and designers on their lunch break join hip couples to congregate at this airy cafe to air-kiss, read design magazines, gossip and share imaginative fusion dishes (pumpkin soup with coriander crème fraiche; mushroom ravioli with tarragon butter) under sexy black and white photos. In warm weather, sip a fresh fruit shake on the outdoor benches and watch the world go by. Ask about special themed Sunday-night menus, like sushi night.

**MOKKA** CAFE €

Map p299 (Berenstraat 37; mains €5-10; ⌚10am-6pm) Lasagne fanatics, look no further for your lunch of choice in the Nine Streets. Yes, there are perfectly lovely sandwiches and soups, but we come to agonise over ordering the mozzarella aubergine (eggplant) or the spinach and basil varieties.

**LUNCHCAFE NIELSEN** CAFE €

Map p299 (☎330 60 06; Berenstraat 19; mains €5-10; ⌚8am-4pm Mon-Fri, to 6pm Sat, to 5pm Sun) Looking for where the locals go to lunch and brunch in the Negen Straatjes? Well, here it is. Under leafy murals, munch on the speciality quiches, salads, and fresh lemon and apple cakes that disappear as quickly as they're put out.

**CASA PERÚ** PERUVIAN €€

Map p299 (www.casaperu.nl; Leidsegracht 68; mains €16-20; ⌚dinner daily, plus lunch Apr-Sep) When the weather's good, there's nothing quite like enjoying a *crema de ajo* (cream of garlic) soup or *lomo saltado* (beef with onion, tomato and French fries) while looking out over the Leidsegracht and the Prinsengracht. Indoors, it's busy and homelike.

**BROODJE BERT** SANDWICH SHOP €

Map p299 (☎423 38 17; Singel 321; sandwiches €4-7; ⌚breakfast, lunch & dinner) This is one of our favourite sandwich shops in town, with an attentive, friendly staff and winning canalside location. So how come it remains off the radar? Probably because the locals want to make sure they can grab a seat in the sun (or at the window seats inside) to nosh on made-to-order fresh omelettes, tomato-pesto-mozzarella sandwiches, and more.

**DE STRUISVOGEL** FRENCH €€

Map p299 (www.restaurantdestruisvogel.nl; Keizersgracht 312; 3-course menu €23; ⌚dinner) This former kitchen to some large canal houses is in the basement and offers good value. True to its name, it does serve the bird (*struisvogel* means 'ostrich'), along with a nightly rotating menu with more-conventional French-inspired choices. It gets crowded; book ahead.

**SINGEL 404** CAFE €

Map p300 (Singel 404; mains €5-9; ⌚lunch Mon-Sat) It's easy to miss this sweet tucked-away spot, despite its bustling location near the Spui. Sure, the menu is simple as can be – smoked salmon sandwiches, pumpkin soup – but we've heard locals whisper that this is one of their fave lunch cafes.

**KOH-I-NOOR** INDIAN €€

Map p300 (☎623 31 33; Westermarkt 29; mains €12.50-20; ⌚dinner; 🌶) Tandoori meats, coconutty curries, three-alarm vindaloos and other subcontinent classics fill plates at this long-standing Indian restaurant close to Anne Frank Huis. A lengthy list of lentil, pea, eggplant and spinach dishes will please vegetarians.

**SPANJER EN VAN TWIST** CAFE €€

Map p300 (www.spanjerenvantwist.nl; Leliegracht 60; mains €7-15; ⌚10am-10pm) Just north of the Anne Frank Huis, Spanjer en van Twist's tables on Leliegracht are great for watching the boats cruise by. The eclectic lunch and dinner menu is good – say shrimp croquettes on pumpkin bread or roasted vegies with saffron aioli – but a highlight is the divine apple tart.

**FOODISM** CAFE €€

Map p300 (☎427 51 03; Oude Leliestraat 8; mains €5-15; ⌚11.30am-10pm Mon-Fri, to 6pm Sat & Sun) A hip, colourful little joint run by a fun, relaxed crew. All-day breakfasts (€9.50) and sandwiches like chicken mango and salads make up the day menu. Nighttime sees patrons tucking into platefuls of pasta. Try the 'Kung Funghi' (with three kinds of mushrooms, parsley, walnuts and cream).

**PANCAKE BAKERY** CONTEMPORARY DUTCH €

Map p300 (www.pancake.nl; Prinsengracht 191; mains €5.50-13; ⌚lunch & dinner; 👪) This basement restaurant in a restored warehouse features a dizzying 79 varieties of pancakes, from sweet (chocolate) to savoury (the 'Egyptian', topped with lamb, sweet peppers and garlic sauce). There are also omelettes, soups, desserts and lots of tourists, given its proximity to Anne Frank Huis.

**WIL GRAANSTRA FRITESHUIS** FRITES €

Map p300 (☎624 40 71; Westermarkt 11; frites €2-3.75; ⌚11am-6pm Mon-Sat) This little stall near Anne Frank Huis has been serving up crispy fries with delectable mayo since 1956. Legions of Amsterdammers swear by them. Fork into a golden, crispy coneful, and you'll see why.

**LEF** CAFE €

Map p299 (Wijde Heisteeg 1; mains €4-9; ⌚daily) By going for the delish homemade soups, daily specials and sandwiches at the Negen Straatjes' most inexpensive little cafe, you might be able to swing *both* lunch and a shopping spree. Sit at the counter and watch the shoppers go by in a post-spending daze.

# DRINKING & NIGHTLIFE

Most cafes in this refined district tend to have a touch more polish than elsewhere – the interiors are slicker, the brass fittings shinier, the menus more elaborate. The rest of the places just steep themselves in half-lit atmosphere and hope no one notices.

**TOP CHOICE 'T ARENDSNEST** BEER CAFE

Map p300 (www.arendsnest.nl; Herengracht 90) This gorgeous, restyled brown cafe, with its glowing copper *jenever* (Dutch gin) boilers behind the bar, only serves Dutch beer – but with more than 300 varieties (many from small breweries), including 23 on tap, you'll need to move here to try them all.

**TOP CHOICE CAFÉ TABAC** CAFE

Map p300 (www.cafetabac.eu; 2e Brouwersgracht 101; from 11am Sat-Mon, from 4pm Tue-Fri) Is Café Tabac a brown cafe, a designer bar, or simply an effortlessly cool place to while away a few blissful hours at the intersection of two of Amsterdam's most stunning canals? The regulars don't seem concerned about definitions, so just enjoy the graceful views and kick back under the high-beamed ceilings to cool rock tunes. The light menu offers dim sum and Indonesian flair.

**TOP CHOICE CAFÉ RESTAURANT VAN PUFFELEN** GRAND CAFE

Map p299 (www.restaurantvanpuffelen.com; Prinsengracht 377) This large cafe-restaurant, popular among cashed-up professionals and intellectual types, has lots of nooks and crannies for nice, cosy drinks and big, communal tables for sharing meals like antipasto and large salads.

**CAFÉ DE VERGULDE GAPER** BROWN CAFE

Map p300 (www.goodfoodgroup.nl; Prinsenstraat 30; ) Decorated with old chemists' bottles and vintage posters, this former pharmacy has amiable staff and a terrace with afternoon sun. It's popular with locals, and gets busy with 20- and 30-something media types meeting for after-work drinks. The name translates as the 'Golden Gaper', for the open-mouthed bust of a Moor traditionally posted at Dutch apothecaries.

**CAFÉ HET MOLENPAD** CAFE €

Map p299 (www.goodfoodgroup.nl; Prinsengracht 653; ) By day, this gem of a canalside cafe is full of folks poring over newspapers on the terrace, perhaps in homage to the days when a beloved library was next door. By night the atmosphere turns offhandedly romantic, with the right mix of low slung lamps and candlelight illuminating little tables where an after-work crowd, along with students and a sprinkling of tourists, munch on house-made carrot cake and calamari under pressed tin ceilings. It's our favourite spot on the Prinsengracht for a glass of wine and a light sunset meal (mains €12 to €18).

**WERCK** DESIGNER BAR

Map p300 (www.werck.nl; Prinsengracht 277) See and be seen (or exchange business cards) with the nattily dressed young professionals – and their admirers – who congregate at this buzzing bar next to the Westerkerk. Thankfully it's more about pleasure than business. In summer, there's a big courtyard complete with a tiki bar that couldn't be in a more bizarre location: between a historic church and the Anne Frank Huis.

**DE DOFFER** BROWN CAFE

Map p299 (www.doffer.com; Runstraat 12-14) Writers, students and artists congregate at this popular cafe (with adjoining bar) for affordable food and good conversation. The dining room, with its old Heineken posters, large wooden tables and, occasionally, fresh flowers, is particularly atmospheric at night.

**DAMPKRING** COFFEESHOP

Map p300 (www.dampkring.nl; Haarlemmerstraat 44; ) Duck into this cosy, industrial, multi-storied stoner paradise, which is about as photogenic as these places get, with lush ferns, comfy seats and wide-open windows in warm weather. Even non-smokers might want to hang out for a coffee or a fresh fruit shake here and dig the 1960s mod atmosphere. The knowl-

LOCAL KNOWLEDGE

## PRINSENGRACHT

Sure, the Keizersgracht and Herengracht are grander, but why is it that locals flock to hang out on the Prinsengracht? By the look of the lively crowds that spill out of bars with their beer, it's clear that the Prinsengracht is the liveliest of Amsterdam's inner canals these days. In summertime, you could spend a whole weekend just enjoying its warm-weather charms – exploring the shops and kicking back on its cafe terraces – as boats glide by and houseboats sway in the breeze against the quays.

edgeable staff are more than happy to educate coffeeshop neophytes.

### CAFÉ DE PELS — BROWN CAFE

Map p299 (www.cafedepels.nl; Huidenstraat 25) The action at this appealingly shabby traditional brown cafe is focused on drinking, and attracts a mix of students, academics and creative types. It's also a Sunday morning breakfast fave, with plenty of international newspapers to pore over as you sip your *koffie verkeerd* (milky coffee).

### GREENHOUSE — COFFEESHOP

Map p300 (www.greenhouse.org; Haarlemmerstraat 64; ) Nope, the pot hasn't gone to your head (yet) – that stretch of the floor is glass and there really are koi swimming underfoot in this modern lounge-cum-coffeeshop. Once you tire of the fish action, peer into the microscope to see THC crystals or contemplate one of the pies spinning in the display case.

### GREY AREA — COFFEESHOP

Map p300 (www.greyarea.nl; Oude Leliestraat 2; noon-8pm) Owned by a couple of laid-back American guys, this tiny shop introduced the extra-sticky, flavoursome 'Double Bubble Gum' weed to the city's smokers. It also keeps up the wonderful American tradition of free coffee refills (it's organic). It keeps shorter hours than most coffeeshops.

### BAR BARBOU — DESIGNER BAR

Map p299 (www.dylanamsterdam.com; Dylan, Keizersgracht 384) Like the hotel surrounding it, the Dylan's lobby bar is superposh – sleek black and white with Indonesian influences, and a great place to pose...if you can get in. Restaurant patrons get seating priority. You might swear that all the beautiful people surrounding you stepped out of the pages of the fashion magazines on the coffee tables.

### IL TRAMEZZINO — CAFE

Map p300 (www.iltramezzino.nl; Haarlemmerstraat 79; 9.30am-6pm, to 5.30pm Sun) A perfect Haarlemmerstraat shopping break for those in pursuit of *la dolce vita*, this little slice of Milan in Amsterdam serves steaming hot espresso from a magnificent silver contraption imported from Italy. The white lacquer and red-cushioned interior invites nibbling on creative paninis and savoury *torte salate* while browsing through a glossy fashion mag.

### DE II PRINSEN — BROWN CAFE

Map p300 (624 97 22; Prinsenstraat 27) With its large windows, chandelier, mosaic floor and big terrace, this cafe looks suitably restrained. You may be surprised then by the pumping music inside; all those students munching on tasty sandwiches don't seem to mind.

### PÂTISSERIE POMPADOUR — CAFE

Map p299 (623 95 54; Huidenstraat 12; 10am-6pm Mon-Fri, to 5pm Sat) Join society ladies sipping top-notch tea and nibbling away at homemade Belgian-style chocolates and pastries at this chichi little tearoom in the Negen Straatjes. Note: it's not open on Sundays, but a second branch is: **Kerkstraat 148** (Map p302; 330 09 81; 9am-6pm).

### SIBERIË — COFFEESHOP

Map p300 (www.siberie.nl; Brouwersgracht 11; ) Popular among locals, Siberië's inviting setting goes beyond marijuana – its owners regularly schedule cultural events like art exhibits, poetry slams, acoustic concerts, DJ nights and even horoscope readings. It also features a tobacco-friendly lounge.

### BRIX FOOD 'N' DRINX — DESIGNER BAR

Map p299 (www.cafebrix.nl; Wolvenstraat 16) The mod jazz lounge setting makes this a great place to chill over a cocktail and enjoy nibbles from the starters-only menu, like raw oysters, gravlax and mini Peking duck.

There's live jazz on Sunday and Monday nights from about 9pm.

**WOLVENSTRAAT 23** DESIGNER BAR

Map p299 (☎320 08 43; Wolvenstraat 23; ⊙9am-1am Sun-Thu, to 3am Fri & Sat) This funky bar with no name – we dare you to find a sign anywhere – is especially popular with locals, who come for the good wines by the glass, great music and tasty Asian snacks. If this is your kind of place, check out their other bar, Finch (p140).

**KOFFIEHUIS 'DE HOEK'** CAFE

Map p299 (☎625 38 72; Prinsengracht 341) This is a *koffiehuis* (espresso bar), not a coffeeshop, and one of the best places in the city to experience an old fashioned coffee house experience of Amsterdam. Come for *lekker* (tasty) breakfasts, sandwiches, and cakes in a charming old-school atmosphere.

**DULAC** GRAND CAFE

Map p300 (☎624 42 65; Haarlemmerstraat 118) This former bank building is outrageously decked out in a kooky, but kind of spooky, mixture of styles (think Turkish, art nouveau and Amsterdam School, with a few Gothic accents). It has a pool table and an amiable mix of students, older folks and Americans. Come for the decor and the drinks.

**DE ADMIRAAL** TASTING HOUSE

Map p299 (www.deadmiraal.nl; Herengracht 319; ⊙5pm-midnight Mon-Sat) The grandest and largest of Amsterdam's tasting houses, De Admiraal is also a restaurant and party venue. Although some grumble that they pour only their own house brands (16 *jenevers* and 60 liqueurs), it's hard to quibble over the lovely setting and pleasant staff.

**FELIX MERITIS CAFÉ** THEATRE CAFE

Map p299 (www.felix.meritis.nl; Felix Meritis Bldg, Keizersgracht 324) Join the city's cultural cognoscenti imbibing in this high-ceilinged, quietly refined (think theatrical lighting) cafe in the Felix Meritis Building. Huge windows and clever outdoor seating (you'll see) overlooking the canal make it a stylish spot for a coffee or cocktail. Sit and ponder the society's motto carved above the entrance: 'Happiness through Achievement'.

**VYNE** WINE BAR

Map p299 (www.vyne.nl, in Dutch; Prinsengracht 411; ⊙6pm-midnight Mon-Thu, 5pm-1am Fri & Sat, 5-10pm Sun) The slickest wine bar in town employs knowledgeable staff who'll guide you in the right direction, no matter your price point.

## ENTERTAINMENT

**FELIX MERITIS** CULTURAL BUILDING

Map p299 (☎623 13 11; www.felix.meritis.nl; Felix Meritis Bldg, Keizersgracht 324) Amsterdam's centre for arts, culture and science puts on innovative modern theatre, music and dance, as well as special talks on politics, diversity, art, technology and literature. Its adjoining cafe (p106) is exceptional.

## SHOPPING

You could easily spend all of your shopping time in the Negen Straatjes (Nine Streets) in the Canal Ring just east of the Jordaan. The selection is arty, worthwhile and constantly changing, and lots of cafes means plenty of break time.

TOP CHOICE **FROZEN FOUNTAIN** DESIGN, HOMEWARES

Map p299 (www.frozenfountain.nl; Prinsengracht 629) The city's best-known showcase of furniture and interior design. Prices are not cheap, but the daring designs are offbeat and very memorable (designer pen-knives, kitchen gadgets, and that birthday gift for the impossible-to-wow friend).

TOP CHOICE **DE KAASKAMER** CHEESE SHOP

Map p299 (www.dekaaskamer.nl; Runstraat 7; ⊙noon-6pm Mon, 9am-6pm Tue-Fri, 9am-5pm Sat, noon-5pm Sun) The name means 'cheese room' and it is indeed stacked to the rafters with Dutch and organic varieties, as well as olives, tapenades, salads and other picnic ingredients. You try before you buy, and if it's too much to take home a mondo wheel of Gouda you can at least procure a cheese and/or meat sandwich or a baguette to take away.

TOP CHOICE **BOEKIE WOEKIE** BOOKS

Map p299 (www.boekiewoekie.nl; Berenstraat 16) While other shops handle art books, this artist-run bookstore sells books *as* art, created by artists specifically for this medium. Some tell stories (elegantly illustrated, naturally); others are riffs on graphic motifs. You may want to browse around for a long time.

TOP CHOICE **SCOTCH & SODA** CLOTHING

Map p299 (www.scotch-soda.com; Huidenstraat 5) The Nine Streets exude high style, but if forced to go on a shopping spree, we might head here first. Couples shopping together can compare the sleek outfits now that Maison Scotch, the new women's line, has made its debut. We especially love the chic outerwear here, guaranteed to keep you looking impossibly cool even during the most tempestuous Dutch weather.

**DE SPEIGELBEELD** CLOTHING

Map p299 (☎630 53 64; Huidenstaat 24b) Girls who like dresses, or anyone who digs a mix of vintage and vintage-inspired new clothes, will love browsing through this friendly boutique. You're as likely to discover a vintage special occasion dress by Diane von Furstenbuerg or Chanel as you are to find a casual sundress by your favourite new Dutch dress designer.

**NIEUWS** GIFTS, KITSCH

Map p300 (Prinsengracht 297) A mind-boggling array of kooky trinkets crams this entertaining store – from quirky action figures (we love the Crazy Cat Lady, the Obsessive Compulsive, Rosie the Riveter and Albino Bowler!) to mini patron saints, foreplay dice and voodoo dolls. Travellers love the Wash Away Your Sins soap.

**UNLIMITED DELICIOUS** FOOD & DRINK

Map p300 (www.unlimiteddelicious.nl; Haarlemmerstraat 122) Is it ever! It's tempting to dive into the sculptural cakes and tarts, but – if you can – walk past them to the dozens of varieties of chocolates made in-house. Some of the more outlandish combinations (that somehow work) are rosemary sea salt, caramel cayenne and citron *witbier*. Also on offer are tastings, and bonbon and patisserie workshops.

**LADY DAY** VINTAGE CLOTHING

Map p299 (www.ladydayvintage.com; Hartenstraat 9) This is the premier location for unearthing spotless vintage clothes from Holland and elsewhere. The leather jackets, swingin' 1960s and '70s wear, and woollen sailors' coats are well-priced winners. There are also some men's suits and new shoes.

**GAMEKEEPER** GAMES

Map p299 (www.gamekeeper.nl, in Dutch; Hartenstraat 14) The selection of board games is dizzying, as is the imagination that went into making them. Start with chequers, chess and mah jong, and move on to Cathedral (build a city in the style of the Great Wall of China or the souk in Marrakech) or Rush Hour (help a car get out of traffic). 'Co-operative' games encourage players to play with, not against, each other.

**FASHION FLAIRS** CLOTHING

Map p299 (www.fashionflairs.nl; Berenstraat 18) One generic name, sure, but two cool stores. Here you'll find the most affordable yet fashion-forward collection of women's clothing on the Nine Streets; come here expecting genuinely friendly service, fetching costume jewellery, and party-worthy frocks.

**MARLIES DEKKERS** CLOTHING

Map p299 (www.marliesdekkers.com; Berenstraat 18) The pre-eminent Dutch lingerie designer Marlies Dekkers is known for her subtle hints to bondage, detailed on exquisite undergarments. Summer sees an equally enticing range of swimwear. The shop itself is a sultry bastion of decadence, with hand-painted wallpaper and a titillating lounge area with a fireplace.

**BAKKERIJ ANNEE** BAKERY

Map p299 (☎623 53 22; Runstraat 25) Once you've tasted the signature apple cake – moist, divine and totally addictive – it's almost impossible to walk by this bakery without buying one. So why not pick up some bread for your Vondelpark picnic and some other goodies while you're at it? At least it's all good for you.

**AMSTERDAM WATCH COMPANY** ACCESSORIES

Map p299 (www.awco.nl, in Dutch; Reestraat 3; ⊙Tue-Sat) An intimate team of watchmakers restores old watches (postwar to mid-1970s). The company is also the exclusive Amsterdam dealer of such brands as Germany's D Dornblüth and the Dutch Christiaan van der Klaauw, who makes fewer than 200 watches a year.

**BRILMUSEUM** ACCESSORIES

Map p299 (www.brilmuseumamsterdam.nl; Gasthuismolensteeg 7; ⊙Wed-Sat) This spectacles shop is an institution, both for its wares and for its presentation. You can take in the 700-year history of eyeglasses as well as a very 21st-century collection, some of which is pretty outlandish.

**FATES** ACCESSORIES

Map p300 (www.fates.nl; Herenstraat 19; ⊙Wed-Mon) Fates offers modern fashion accessories made of natural materials, from fair-trade studios in India and Southeast Asia. We were particularly taken with the groovy tulip-shaped bags from Bali, diaphanous silk shawls and fresh-water pearl necklaces.

**DARLING** ACCESSORIES & CLOTHING

Map p299 (www.thedarling.nl; Runstraat 4) Funky, affordable, locally designed clothes. Whimsical accessories. And cupcakes! Shops like these are why the Nine Streets continue to delight and surprise.

**NIC NIC** ANTIQUES, KITSCH

Map p299 (www.nicnicdesign.com; Gasthuismolensteeg 5) A trip here is like a visit to a gallery of 20th-century design. Cramped shelves take you from art deco to Bauhaus, Googie, the '70s, *The Simpsons* and heaven knows what else.

**ARCHITECTURA & NATURA** BOOKS

Map p300 (www.architectura.nl; Leliegracht 22) This charming canalside shop has art, architecture, design, landscape and coffee-table books. Upstairs, **Architectuurantiquariat Opbouw** (Architecture Antique Shop; ☎638 70 18) has a selection of its namesake.

**LOCAL SERVICE** CLOTHING

Map p299 (☎626 68 40; Keizersgracht 400-402) Media types (male at 400, female at 402) hunt here for the latest Paul Smith (it's Amsterdam's exclusive dealer for his main line), and the Ghost, Stone Island and Drykorn collections.

**ANTONIA BY YVETTE** SHOES

Map p299 (www.antoniabyyvette.nl; Gasthuismolensteeg 18) Shoes, boots, sandals and espadrilles here run from supremely classy to just plain fun. The sales pack in gals with an eye for style. There's also a small section for guys.

**EXOTA** CLOTHING, ACCESSORIES

Map p299 (www.exota.com; Hartenstraat 10 & 13) Exota sells its own hip King Louie label plus global brands such as Kookai and French Connection. Number 10 sells sporty women's casual gear and kids' threads; men's and women's clothing is across the street at number 13.

### SHOPPING THE NINE STREETS

Pick up a copy of *The Nine Streets* shopping guide, available at many tourist offices as well as in many of the Nine Streets shops themselves. Or check out www.9straatjesonline.com.

**MENDO** BOOKS

Map p299 (www.mendo.nl; Berenstraat 11) The Mendo graphic-design agency runs this smart, black-walled bookshop specialising in books in the creative realm: art, design, architecture, fashion and photography.

**NUKUHIVA** CLOTHING, ACCESSORIES

Map p300 (www.nukuhiva.nl, in Dutch; Haarlemmerstraat 36) This eco-boutique stocks only ethical and fair-trade clothing and accessories, by brands such as Veja (vegan shoes) and Dutch designer Kuyishi (organic denim).

**VAN RAVENSTEIN** CLOTHING

Map p299 (www.van-ravenstein.nl; Keizersgracht 359) Chic men and women shop here for upmarket Dutch and Belgian designers, including Dries van Noten, Ann Demeulemeester and Viktor & Rolf.

**ZIPPER** CLOTHING, ACCESSORIES

Map p299 (www.zipperstore.nl; Huidenstraat 7) Amsterdam hipsters head here for seriously nostalgic, retro secondhand gear – wacky printed shirts, stovepipe jeans, '40s zoot suits, pork-pie hats and the like.

**SKINS COSMETICS** COSMETICS

Map p299 (www.skins.nl; Runstraat 9) This is the Netherlands' exclusive importer of special brands of fragrances, cosmetics and skincare and beauty products: think Aesop, Dyptique, Etro, Laura Mercier and the Art of Shaving. Makeup sessions and facials are also available.

**DE WITTE TANDEN WINKEL** DENTAL HYGIENE

Map p299 (☎623 34 43; Runstraat 5) We love shops that are obsessed, and 'The White-Teeth Shop' certainly is – with dental hygiene. There's a huge selection of toothbrushes, toothpastes from around the world, brushing accessories you never knew you needed, and friendly advice.

### LAURA DOLS — VINTAGE CLOTHING

Map p299 (www.lauradols.com, in Dutch; Wolvenstraat 6 & 7) Compulsive style watchers head to this vintage-clothing store for fur coats, 1920s beaded dresses, lace blouses and '40s movie-star accessories like hand-stitched leather gloves.

### MEEUWIG & ZN — FOOD & DRINK

Map p300 (www.meeuwig.nl, in Dutch; Haarlemmerstraat 70) Fill your own bottle from metal crocks containing more than 50 types of olive oil from around the world. You'll also find bottles of gourmet vinegar, mustard, chutney and fresh olives.

### BEADIES — JEWELLERY

Map p299 (www.beadies.com; Huidenstraat 6) Once the funky jewellery in the window draws you in, you'll find yourself here for hours, selecting gorgeous beads, gems, charms and trinkets to design your own necklaces and bracelets. Our advice: don't start from scratch; opt for a variation on Beadies' fab designs.

### HESTER VAN EEGHEN — SHOES, ACCESSORIES

Map p299 (www.hestervaneeghen.com; Hartenstraat 1; ⏲Tue-Sat) Designed in Amsterdam and handcrafted in Italy from fine leather, internationally renowned Hester van Eeghen's unique shoes are for those who dare to dress their feet dramatically in bright colours, fur, suede, and geometric patterns and prints. Her handbags (available down the street at Hartenstraat 37) are just as attention-grabbing.

### EPISODE — VINTAGE CLOTHING

Map p299 (www.episode.eu; Berenstraat 1) Visiting rock stars head to Episode to trawl through two floors of fabulous vintage and secondhand gear. Most impressive when we last dropped in were the seemingly endless racks of 1970s suede coats, folky peasant blouses, '80s jewellery and big, bright plastic sunglasses.

# Southern Canal Ring

## Neighbourhood Top Five

❶ Enjoying an awe-inspiring, *ahh*-inducing starry night or sunset on the **Seven Bridges** (p116), which never fails to wow with its canals-in-every-direction view.

❷ Shopping, eating and drinking your way down **Utrechtsestraat** (p118).

❸ People-watching on **Rembrandtplein** (p114) at night.

❹ Partying on **Leidseplein** (p112) is straight-up decadent fun.

❺ Meandering through the **Hermitage** (p112), Amsterdam's impressive branch of the St Petersburg original.

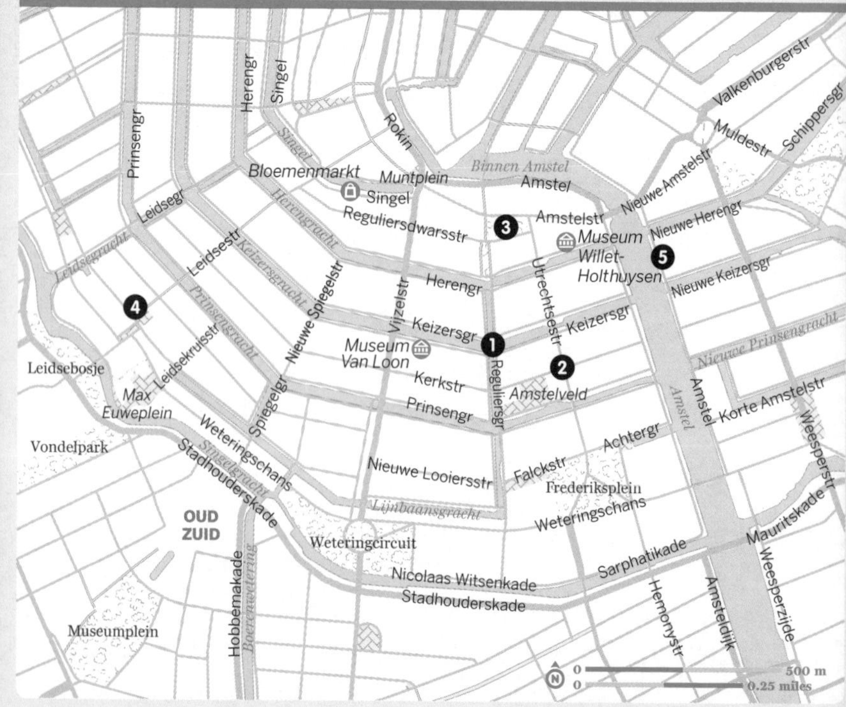


For more detail of this area, see Map p302

## Explore: Southern Canal Ring

If the Western Canal Ring is upmarket and refined, the Southern Canal Ring is more diverse and populist, though no less stately. Like its western neighbour, it's possible to see – though not fully explore – in one day.

The Southern Canal Ring spans the area from the radial Leidsegracht in the west to the Amstel in the east, anchored by two key nightlife districts: Leidseplein and Rembrandtplein. In between are the elegant antique and art shops of the Spiegel Quarter, the gay nightlife hub on the Reguliersdwarsstraat, and the Golden Bend, a stretch along the Herengracht that makes some Western Canal Ring houses look like servants' quarters.

With museums, restaurants, cafes and shops galore, not to mention miles of gorgeous canal photo-ops, it's best to give yourself some time here, exploring the areas around Rembrandtplein and Utrechtsestraat one day, and the areas from the Spiegelgracht to Leidseplein the next.

All the sightseeing is sure to make you hungry, so it's lucky Utrechtsestraat is in the 'hood – it's arguably the city's best restaurant strip thanks to its diverse, quality options. If you prefer more action, Rembrandtplein and Leidseplein buzz with visitors eating, drinking and watching the crowds roll by.

## Local Life

➡ **Serene Stroll** Sure, the Southern Canal Ring parties all night long, but it's also home to one of Amsterdam's loveliest, stroll-worthy canals, Reguliersgracht.

➡ **Smooth Jazz** Locals pack lovable Jazz Café Alto every night of the week to chill out to smooth jazz by local and international musicians.

➡ **Weteringstraat** This tiny street off the Prinsengracht feels like a secret passage that's still undiscovered, anchored by favourite local brown cafe, Café de Wetering.

➡ **Eating Cheap in Party Central** In search of a budget meal? Skip Leidseplein at dinner time and head to adjacent Lange Leidwarssestraat, a corridor chock-full of budget pizza and pasta joints that offer meals for around €5.

## Getting There & Away

➡ **Tram** This area is well-served by trams. To the Leidesplein area, take tram 1, 2, 5, 7 or 10. To Rembrandtplein, take tram 4, which travels down Utrechtsestraat. Trams 16, 24 and 25 cut through the centre of the neighbourhood down busy Vijzelstraat.

### Lonely Planet's Top Tip

Don't discount the areas around Leidseplein or Rembrandtplein as simply tourist traps for either the tour bus set or cheerfully drunk hooligans on pub crawls (although indeed they are both that). They can be serious (or not-so-serious) fun, with plenty of local, authentic bars and cafes just waiting to be discovered.

### Best Places to Eat

➡ Ponte Arcari (p118)
➡ Tujeh Maret (p118)
➡ Piet de Leeuw (p118)
➡ Van Vlaanderen (p119)
➡ Loekie (p118)

For reviews, see p118 ➡

### Best Places to Drink

➡ Café Schiller (p121)
➡ Café de Spuyt (p122)
➡ Bo Cinq (p122)
➡ De Kroon (p122)
➡ Weber (p122)

For reviews, see p121 ➡

### Best Places to Shop

➡ Young Designers United (p127)
➡ Reflex Modern Art Gallery (p127)
➡ Kaas Huis Tromp (p127)
➡ Phillipa K (p127)
➡ Cora Kemperman (p127)

For reviews, see p127 

## SIGHTS

**LEIDSEPLEIN** SQUARE

Map p302 Take one part historic architecture, one part neon, one part beer; add plenty of tourists, and shake. Welcome to Leidseplein! A one-stop shop for party-goers, this hyperactive square is a major tram intersection and a litmus test for nightlife at any given time. On its eastern side the Leidsepoort (Leiden Gate) once stood, where farmers would leave their horses and carts before entering town. This was demolished in 1870. The strip of greenery with large chestnut trees on the other side of the Singelgracht is sweetly called Leidsebosje (Leiden Wood).

There's something here for everyone. The pavement cafes at the northern end of the square are perfect for watching street artists and eccentric passers-by. There are countless pubs and clubs, and a smorgasbord of restaurants. Entertainment venues radiate from its centre, and nearby Kerkstraat pulses with trendy gay establishments. For more intimate (but not necessarily more serene) bars and restaurants, explore the festive streets of Lange Leidwaarsestraat and Korte Leidwaarsestraat, as well as the streets behind the Stadsschouwburg.

**STADSSCHOUWBURG** HISTORIC BUILDING

Map p302 (City Theatre; ☎624 23 11; www.stadsschouwburgamsterdam.nl, in Dutch; Leidseplein 26; ⊙box office noon-6pm Mon-Sat) In 1894, when this theatre with the grand balcony arcade was completed, public criticism was so fierce that funds for the exterior decorations never materialised. The architect, Jan Springer, couldn't handle this and promptly retired. The theatre is used for large-scale plays, operettas and festivals such as the Holland Festival and Julidans.

**AMSTERDAM AMERICAN HOTEL** HISTORIC BUILDING

Map p302 (☎556 30 00; www.amsterdamamerican.com; Leidsekade 97) The only reason this gorgeous hotel got its Yankee Doodle label is because the architect, CAA Steineweg, studied hotel design in the USA. Steineweg made sure that the style (mostly Viennese Renaissance actually) was adorned with abundant Americana –

## TOP SIGHTS
## HERMITAGE AMSTERDAM

The long-standing ties between Russia and Holland – remember Tsar Peter the Great learned shipbuilding and Dutch cursing here in 1697 – led to the establishment of an Amsterdam branch of the State Hermitage Museum of St Petersburg. You'll experience prestigious exhibits on loan from the St Petersburg museum's amazing collection of over three million art objects, such as treasures from the Russian palace or masterworks by Matisse and Picasso. Exhibits change about twice a year, and they're as stately (and wildly popular) as you'd expect.

The Hermitage is housed in the Amstelhof, a 17th-century former almshouse set around a sweeping courtyard. Facing the Amstel river, it offers breathtaking views from the west-side galleries.

Bear in mind that the museum has fast become one of the city's most popular attractions since its 2009 opening, and waiting times to enter can stretch to 30 to 60 minutes during peak periods. To avoid the worst of it, arrive before 11am daily or after 5pm on Wednesday (the museum's late night, perfect for art-loving night owls). To get here, take tram 9 or the Metro to Waterlooplein.

### DON'T MISS

- The permanent collection
- The lovely courtyard
- River views from the west-side galleries
- The dazzling temporary exhibits from St Petersburg

### PRACTICALITIES

- Map p302
- ☎530 74 88
- www.hermitage.nl
- Amstel 51
- adult/under 16yr €15/free
- ⊙10am-5pm Thu-Tue, to 8pm Wed

### ON YOUR BIKE IN THE SOUTHERN CANAL RING

See p32 for information on bicycling in Amsterdam. For bike rentals and bike tours in the Southern Canal Ring:

**MacBike** (Map p302; ☎620 09 85; www.macbike.nl; Weteringschans 2)

**Mike's Bike Tours** (Map p302; ☎622 79 70; www.mikesbiketours.com; Kerkstraat 134, tours €22)

life-sized Native American chiefs and their squaws as well as a 4m heraldic eagle over the entrance. That building was demolished in 1900, but the magnificent structure you see today is broadly similar, if less bombastic. The brilliant Café Americain, in art deco style, was added in 1927 and still looks much like it did then, save for the fedora hats and the Marlene Dietrich lookalikes.

#### METZ DEPARTMENT STORE — HISTORIC BUILDING

Map p302 (☎520 70 36; www.metz.nl; cnr Keizersgracht & Leidsestraat) This building opened in 1891 to house the New York Life Insurance Company (hence the eagles inside and out), but soon passed to Metz, a purveyor of luxury furnishings, which still owns it today. The functionalist designer and architect Gerrit Rietveld added the gallery on the top floor at the **M Café** (☎520 78 48; Keizersgracht 455; mains €8-13; ⏲10am-6pm Mon-Sat, to 5pm Sun) where you can have lunch or tea and cakes.

#### FOAM (FOTOGRAFIE MUSEUM AMSTERDAM) — MUSEUM

Map p302 (☎551 65 00; www.foam.nl; Keizersgracht 609; adult/under 12yr €8/free; ⏲10am-6pm Sat-Wed, to 9pm Thu & Fri) Simple, functional but roomy galleries, some with skylights or grand windows for natural light, make this museum an excellent space for all genres of photography. Two storeys of exhibition space create a great setting for admiring the changing exhibits from photographers of world renown, including Sir Cecil Beaton, Annie Leibovitz and Henri Cartier-Bresson.

#### TASSENMUSEUM HENDRIKJE — MUSEUM

Map p302 (Museum of Bags & Purses; ☎524 64 52; www.tassenmuseum.nl; Herengracht 573; adult/under 12yr €7.50/free; ⏲10am-5pm) Here you'll find half a millennium's worth of arm candy, the largest collection of handbags in the Western world. You'll find everything from a crumpled 16th-century pouch to dainty art deco and design classics by Chanel, Gucci and Versace, as well as Madonna's tasteful ivy-strewn 'Evita' bag from the film premiere. Even if you don't see the '80s touch-tone phone bag, the 17th-century interiors alone are worth the entrance price.

#### GOLDEN BEND — ARCHITECTURE

Map p302 (Gouden Bocht; Herengracht, btwn Leidsestraat & Vijzelstraat) One of the ultimate places to mutter 'if only my family had bought that property way back then,' the Golden Bend is about the most prestigious stretch of real estate in Amsterdam, a monument to the Golden Age, when precious goods swelled in cellars of homes already stuffed with valuables. The earliest mansions date from the 1660s, when the Canal Ring was expanded south. Thanks to some lobbying at city hall, the gables here were twice as wide as the standard Amsterdam model, and the rear gardens were deeper. The richest Amsterdammers lived, loved and ruled their affairs from here. Apart from the museum Kattenkabinet (p114), the homes are opened to the public only on Open Monument Day (Open Monumentendag).

#### STADSARCHIEF — HISTORICAL ARCHIVE

Map p302 (Municipal Archives; ☎251 15 11; www.stadsarchief.amsterdam.nl; Vijzelstraat 32; admission free; ⏲10am-5pm Tue-Fri, 11am-5pm Sat & Sun) The Amsterdam archives occupy a monumental bank building that dates from 1923. When you step inside, head to the left to the enormous tiled basement vault and displays of archive gems such as the 1942 police report on the theft of Anne Frank's bike. A small cinema at the back shows vintage films about the city. Upstairs, a gallery space is dedicated to temporary exhibits (for a small entry fee), and the fantastic **Stadsboekwinkel** (p128) sells city-oriented tomes. Building tours (€6) run at 2pm from Tuesday to Sunday and must be reserved in advance.

**KATTENKABINET** MUSEUM

Map p302 (Cats Cabinet; ☎626 53 78; www.kattenkabinet.nl, in Dutch; Herengracht 497; adult/under 4yr/4-12yr €6/free/3; ⊙10am-4pm Tue-Fri, noon-5pm Sat & Sun) One Golden Bend house that's open to the public is this offbeat museum, devoted to, of all things, the feline presence in art. It was founded by a wealthy financier, John Pierpont Morgan III, in memory of his red tomcat. The collection includes works largely from Dutch and French artists – Theopile-Alexandre Steinlen (1859–1923) figures prominently – as well as a small Rembrandt (a Madonna and Child with cat and snake) and Picasso's *Le Chat*.

**GEELVINCK HINLOPEN HUIS** MUSEUM

Map p302 (☎639 07 47; www.museumgeelvinck.nl, in Dutch; Keizersgracht 633; adult/child €8/4; ⊙11am-5pm Wed-Mon) Though not quite as impressive as Museum Van Loon or Museum Willet-Holthuysen, this 17th-century house is more serene, and definitely worth a look. Guides are on hand to show you the rooms. Chamber music concerts using the estate's vintage instruments take place on Sundays.

**REMBRANDTPLEIN** SQUARE

Map p302 Originally called Reguliersplein and then Botermarkt, after the butter markets held here until the mid-19th century, this square now takes its name from the statue of the painter erected in 1876. He's gazing pensively towards the Jewish quarter, where he lived until circumstances forced him to the Jordaan.

Now-notorious Rembrandtplein soon evolved into a nightlife hub as various cafes, restaurants and clubs opened their doors. It's almost genteel during the day, though often heaving with visitors. On the northern side of the square, De Kroon (opened 1898) is one of the grandest cafes in town. Opposite, Café Schiller (1892) is renowned for its theatrical crowd and fabulous art deco interior, including leadlight glass windows. Come midnight, the Rembrandtplein club crowd gets down to the serious business of partying: it provides fascinating people-watching, even if you don't want to let loose.

**GIJSBERT DOMMER HUIS** HISTORIC BUILDING

Map p302 (Amstel 216) Look closely, ladies and gentlemen, at the facade of this sober residence known locally as the 'House

## TOP SIGHTS MUSEUM VAN LOON

Our favourite house museum in town is the only complete replica of a canal house with its back coach house. It has a luscious courtyard garden, opulent furniture and countless family portraits that seem to whisper family secrets as you pass from room to gorgeous room.

There's certainly no better way to instantly whisk yourself back to 19th-century Amsterdam than by spending an hour or two here. Built in 1672, it was first home to acclaimed painter Ferdinand Bol. By the late 1800s the Van Loons, a prominent patrician family, moved in and have lived here (they still occupy the building's upper floors) ever since.

Make sure you take your time soaking up the quiet, calm atmosphere of each room, which are notable for the feeling of history, wealth and artistry they exude. Among some 150 portraits of the Van Loon family, you'll spy important paintings such as *Wedding Portrait* by Jan Miense Molenaer. But the main exhibit is the house itself. Don't miss the intricate wedding-cake plasterwork on the ceilings, and the most fascinating room: the old-fashioned basement kitchen, where cook Leida presided for almost 40 years. Some of the family's favourite recipes are displayed.

### DON'T MISS

- The coach house
- The gorgeous brass Rococo banisters on the open staircase
- The 19th-century basement kitchen
- The dramatic red bedroom

### PRACTICALITIES

- Map p302
- ☎624 52 55
- www.museumvanloon.nl
- Keizersgracht 672
- adult/under 6yr/6-18yr €6/free/4
- ⊙11am-5pm Wed-Mon

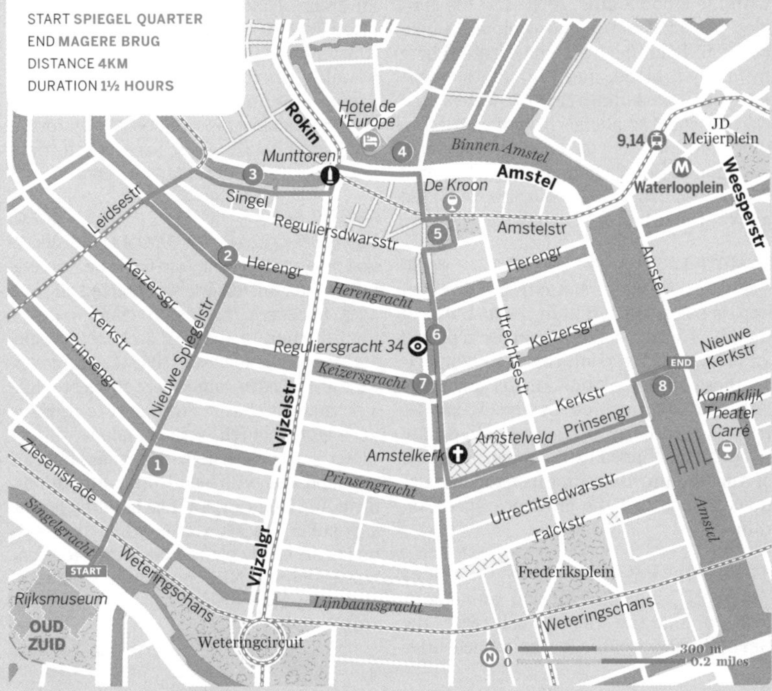


Neighbourhood Walk

## Southern Canal Ring Walking Tour

Set off at the Singelgracht and head north into the nexus of art and antique shops, the 1 **Spiegel Quarter**, along the Nieuwe Spiegelstraat.

One of Amsterdam's swankiest patches of real estate, the aptly named 2 **Golden Bend** on Herengracht is awash with classical French flourishes. No other part of Amsterdam exudes more Golden Age wealth.

Stop by the bustling 3 **Bloemenmarkt** (Flower Market) and from the eastern end you'll see one of Amsterdam's most enduring emblems, the striking Munttoren (Mint Tower), which turned out precious little cash before falling into French hands.

From the tower, head east along the 4 **Amstel river** to take in the grand Hotel de l'Europe, where polished skiffs moor at the terrace restaurant. At the bridge, turn south into tiny Halvemaansteeg (Half-Moon Lane) and the beating heart of the entertainment district around 5 **Rembrandtplein**. As you cross the square, stop to admire the statue of master painter Rembrandt, then make a beeline to De Kroon, one of the most stylish 'grand cafes'.

Saunter over shady Thorbeckeplein to the Herengracht, lean on the bridge and sigh over the gooey postcard vista of 6 **Reguliersgracht**, aka the canal of the seven bridges. The house at Reguliersgracht 34 has an unusual twin entrance and an eagle gable for the original owner, Arent van den Bergh (*arend* is a Dutch word for eagle).

Where the Keizersgracht and Reguliersgracht join up, there's a scene to outdo the mere seven bridges before: here you can count a whopping 7 **15 Bridges** as you peer east–west and north–south. A few steps further south you'll come to the Amstelkerk, the curious wooden church with a belfry that still looks quite makeshift.

Head east down a quiet section of the Prinsengracht until you reach the shores of the Amstel river. From this vantage point you can admire the comely 8 **Magere Brug** and, beyond the *sluizen* (locks), the neon-lit roof of the Koninklijk Theater Carré.

with the Blood Stains'. As he lost his marbles, six-time mayor and diplomat Coenraad van Beuningen scribbled graffiti here in his own blood, and his unfathomable message – including Hebrew letters and obscure cabal symbols – from the 17th century is still faintly visible. Well-to-do businessman Gijsbert Dommer commissioned this house from 1671, but it's the mad mayor who is better known today.

**BLAUWBRUG** BRIDGE

Map p302 (Blue Bridge; Amstel river, btwn Waterlooplein & Amstelstraat) Built in 1884, one of the city's most striking bridges replaced an old wooden version that had connected these shores of the Amstel since the 17th century. Inspired by the Alexander III bridge in Paris, it features tall, ornate street lamps topped by the imperial crown of Amsterdam, fish sculptures and foundations shaped like the prow of a medieval ship.

**REGULIERSGRACHT** CANAL

Map p302 This peaceful canal was dug in 1658 to link the Herengracht with the canals further south. It was named after an order of monks whose monastery was located nearby. It rates right up there with Amsterdam's prettiest canals, and through a quirk of construction you can peer through the arches of at least seven bridges, a fact not lost on canal-boat operators. A number of houses along here have intriguing gables, tablets and fancy decorations.

**AMSTELKERK** CHURCH

Map p302 (☎520 00 70; Amstelveld 10; admission free; ⏰9am-5pm Mon-Fri) The unique pinewood Amstelkerk was erected in 1668 as a *noodkerk* (makeshift church) under the direction of the city architect, Daniël Stalpaert. The idea was that the congregation would have somewhere to meet while a permanent church arose next to it. Plans for a stone church were abandoned in the 1840s, and the Amstelkerk's square interior was updated with neo-Gothic alterations, including a pipe organ. The building is now a popular concert venue, while the seats under the shady plane trees at the adjacent bar-restaurant NEL provide a wonderful place to nurse a drink.



## TOP SIGHTS
## MUSEUM WILLET-HOLTHUYSEN

This sumptuous residence, now part of the Amsterdam Museum, is named after the widow who bequeathed the property to the city in the late 19th century. It's now a shining star in Amsterdam's vast architectural treasure trove.

As you stroll through the elegant house, you'll be surrounded by former resident's Abraham Willet's inspiring art, design, and furniture collection, including paintings by Jacob de Wit. Also look for the *place de milieu* (centrepiece) that was part of the family's 275-piece Meissen table service, and the intimate French-style garden with sundial – you can also peek at the garden through the iron fence at the Amstelstraat end. Be sure to borrow the notebook from the front desk, with details that make the house (and indeed, an entire era) come alive, such as the tedious, back-breaking ways in which servants went about their domestic tasks, such as roasting the meat and cleaning the windows. It's fascinating to see the house through the eyes of the servants.

To get to the museum, take tram 9 or 14 to Rembrandtplein, or the Metro to Waterlooplein.

**DON'T MISS**

- Jacob de Wit paintings
- The French garden
- The notebook
- The Louis XVI-style ground floor

**PRACTICALITIES**

- Map p302
- ☎523 18 22
- www.willetholthuysen.nl
- Herengracht 605
- adult/under 6yr/6-18yr €8/free/4
- ⏰10am-5pm Mon-Fri, 11am-5pm Sat & Sun

TOP SIGHTS
# BLOEMENMARKT

One of the world's most famous flower markets, the Bloemenmarkt boasts some serious historical credibility. Since 1860, it's been located at the spot where nurserymen, having sailed up the Amstel from their smallholdings, would moor their barges for direct selling to customers.

No longer floating (it's now perched on piles), the market here is a colourful sight and the place is packed with tourists (and pickpockets). Prices are steep by Amsterdam standards but the quality is top notch. Before you buy a 10lb bag of Burning Heart or Queen of Night bulbs, check if you can take it back home – regulations vary by country, so ask the vendors or do your research before you buy. Look out for bulbs destined for the USA, which are marked with a special label.

A few tips: don't wait for a perfect sunny day to indulge in floral heaven – the Bloemenmarkt is lovely even in fog or cold weather, when the flowers only seem brighter against grey skies. Why not pick up a bunch of crimson tulips to brighten up your hotel room? There's no better way to feel like a local than navigating Amsterdam's streets with flowers under the crook of your arm...

## DON'T MISS

- Tulips, tulips and more tulips
- Christmas trees in winter
- Colourful wooden clogs and other only-in-Holland souvenirs
- Seeds, bulbs and garden tools to take home

## PRACTICALITIES

- Singel, btwn Muntplein & Koningsplein
- admission free
- 9am-5.30pm Mon-Sat, 11am-5.30pm Sun

### DE DUIF — CHURCH

Map p302 (The Dove; 520 00 70; Prinsengracht 756; services 10am Sun) In 1796, shortly after the French-installed government proclaimed freedom of religion, De Duif was the first Catholic church to be built with a public entrance for over two centuries. These days De Duif is no longer Catholic but Ecumenical, and it's also a venue for concerts, opera and private events. If you're able to peek inside, check out the clay friezes of the Stations of the Cross on the right-hand wall. The pulpit carvings are of St Willebrordus of Utrecht, and the organ is a sight in its own right, reaching clear to the vaulted ceiling.

### MAGERE BRUG — BRIDGE

Map p302 (Skinny Bridge; Amstel river, btwn Kerkstraat & Nieuwe Kerkstraat) Ah, the iconic 'Skinny Bridge:' this undeniably picturesque spot is the site of many a Dutch wedding photo. Dating from the 1670s, the nine-arched structure has been rebuilt several times in both concrete and timber. It's still operated by hand and remains photogenic even at night, when 1200 tiny lights make the bridge look like a Christmas confection. You can spot it in many films, including the 1971 James Bond thriller *Diamonds are Forever*. Stand in the middle and feel it sway under the passing traffic.

### AMSTELSLUIZEN — ARCHITECTURE

Map p302 (Amstel Locks; Amstel river, near Koninklijk Theater Carré) These impressive sluices, or locks, date from 1674 and allowed the canals to be flushed with fresh water from lakes north of the city, rather than salt water from the IJ, an innovation that made the city more liveable. They were still operated by hand until recently. Four times a week in summer, and twice a week in winter, the locks are shut while fresh water flows in. The sluices on the west side of the city are left open as the stagnant water is pumped out to sea.

### KONINKLIJK THEATER CARRÉ — HISTORIC BUILDING

Map p302 (524 94 52, 0900 252 52 55; www.theatercarre.nl; Amstel 115-125; box office 4-8pm) This esteemed theatre was built in 1887 by the Carré family, who had started their career years earlier with a horse act at the annual fair. The first structure was of wood, but it was eventually rebuilt in concrete because of the fire hazard (early performances for 2000 spectators were lit by gas lamps). The classical facade is richly decorated with faces of jesters, dancers and theatre folk. Today the Carré hosts high-calibre musicals, theatre and dance events, and its Christmas circus is regarded as a seasonal highlight.

**KRIJTBERG** CHURCH

Map p302 (☎623 19 23; www.krijtberg.nl, in Dutch; Singel 446; ⊙1-5pm Tue-Thu, Sat & Sun) The soaring turrets of this neo-Gothic church are an odd sight in this row of sedate Singel homes. Officially known as the St Franciscus Xaveriuskerk, it replaced a clandestine Jesuit chapel on the same site; these days it's still Jesuit. The lavish paintings and statuary make this one of the most beautiful church interiors in the city.

**MAX EUWE CENTRUM** SQUARE

Map p302 (☎625 70 17; www.maxeuwe.nl; Max Euweplein 30a-1; admission free; ⊙noon-4pm Tue-Fri, limited hours Jul & Aug) Max Euwe (1901–81) was the Netherlands' only world chess champion (in the 1930s) and here you'll find a permanent exhibition devoted to the history of the game. You can play against live or digital opponents. The pavement of the square out the front is often crowded with players and onlookers raptly watching games on the outsized chessboard.

**UTRECHTSESTRAAT** STREET

Map p302 The southern end of the street used to terminate at the Utrechtse Poort, a gate to the nearby city of Utrecht, hence the name. This popular artery, stocked with enticing shops, designer bars and cosy eateries, seems a world away from the gaudy lights of Rembrandtplein, a stone's throw to the north. Lack of space becomes a charm as the trams, confined to a single line apart from passing points on the bridges, play a game of stop and go, and passers-by marvel at the choreography of it all. Many stores on Utrechtsestraat stay open even on Sunday, making this a prime Sunday shopping-eating-drinking trinity of fun.

## EATING

All roads in Amsterdam seem to lead to Leidseplein, but we don't really recommend eating there – it's best to poke around the adjacent side streets or nearby canals.

Much the same could be said for Rembrandtplein. Instead of eating there, walk a few steps to Utrechtsestraat, the finest restaurant row in town.

**TOP CHOICE TUJUH MARET** INDONESIAN €€

Map p302 (www.tujuhmaret.nl; Utrechtsestraat 73; mains €7-22, rijsttafel veg/nonveg €22/27; ⊙lunch Mon-Sat, dinner nightly; ✍) Dare we say it? Tujuh Maret, next door to Tempo Doeloe, is just as good, but with a more casual atmosphere. Grab a wicker chair and tuck into spicy Sulawesi-style dishes like dried, fried beef or chicken in red-pepper sauce. The *rijsttafel* (Indonesian banquet) is laid out according to spice intensity; *makanan kecil* is a mini-*rijsttafel* for €15.

**TOP CHOICE PIET DE LEEUW** STEAKHOUSE €€

Map p302 (www.pietdeleeuw.nl; Noorderstraat 11; mains €12.50-19; ⊙lunch Mon-Fri, dinner nightly) The building dates from 1900, it's been a steakhouse and hang-out since the 1940s, and the dark and cosy atmosphere has barely changed since. If you don't get your own table, you may meet folks from all over at a common table, eating well-priced steaks with toppings like onions, mushrooms or bacon, served with salad and piping-hot *frites*.

**TOP CHOICE PONTE ARCARI** ITALIAN €€

Map p302 (☎625 0853; Herengracht 534; mains €12-28; ⊙dinner nightly, lunch Tue-Sat) When you can't jet off to Venice for the weekend, Ponte Arcari will have to suffice. We've found ourselves dreaming about nightly dinner specials long after we had them, like an eggplant rollatini *au gratin* that was the best we'd eaten anywhere (yes, even in Italy). While there are many intimate, canalside restaurants, few are this cosy. It's a stone's throw away from Rembrandtplein yet a world away.

**LOEKIE** SANDWICH SHOP €

Map p302 (www.loekie.net; Utrechtsestraat 57; sandwiches €5-9; ⊙9am-6pm Mon-Sat, to 1pm Wed) This delicatessen piles fresh, delicious ingredients into its takeaway sandwiches, such as smoked beef with egg and salt, or warm goat's cheese with pine nuts and honey. Ask for the English menu if it's not on the counter already.

### VAN VLAANDEREN FRENCH €€€

Map p302 (☎622 82 92; www.restaurant-vanvlaanderen.nl; Weteringschans 175; 3-course menu €42.50; ⊙dinner Tue-Sat) One of our favourite French restaurants in town, Van Vlaanderen has lovely canal views from the raised deck. The fine nuances of dishes are always surprising – think tuna carpaccio with avocado, chicken with bacon mousse or langoustines done three ways. Owner Bas Verstift will come out to chat and advise on your wine.

### TEMPO DOELOE INDONESIAN €€€

Map p302 (☎625 67 18; www.tempodoeloe.nl; Utrechtsestraat 75; mains €19.50-23.50, rijsttafel & set menus €27.50-37.50; ⊙dinner Mon-Sat; ✓) One of the best Indonesian restaurants in the city, Tempo Doeloe's setting and service are pleasant and decorous without being overdone. The same applies to the *rijsttafel:* a ridiculously overblown affair at many places, here it's a fine sampling of the range of flavours found in the country. Warning: dishes marked 'very hot' are indeed like napalm. An excellent wine list and options for vegetarians round out the scene.

### ULIVETO ITALIAN €

Map p302 (www.uliveto.net; Weteringschans 118; mains €6-8.50; ⊙11am-8pm Mon-Fri, noon-6pm Sat & Sun) In a capacious, spare atmosphere of understated luxury, this shop is lined with huge crocks of olive oil and splendid displays of Italian specialities. If you prefer to dine in, munch on a creative panini at the long white marble table.

### SEGUGIO ITALIAN €€€

Map p302 (☎330 15 03; www.segugio.nl; Utrechtsestraat 96; pastas €17-20, mains €22-36; ⊙dinner Mon-Sat) This fashionably minimalist storefront with two levels of seating is the sort of place other chefs go for a good dinner. It's known for risotto and high-quality ingredients combined with a sure hand. Book ahead – it's almost always busy.

### IN DE KEUKEN INTERNATIONAL €€€

Map p302 (☎616 74 14; www.indekeuken.com; Utrechtsestraat 114; mains €16-28, tasting menu €60; ⊙dinner Tue-Sat) With cookbooks lining the front walls and spices and culinary implements lining the back, this open pantry of a restaurant practically screams 'Foodie!' Striking an appealing balance between elegance and whimsy, the seasonal menu makes this a dinnertime destination for folks who know their tarragon from their thyme. The tasting menus are full of delightful surprises and the service is attentive – the waiters know their stuff.

### LOS PILONES MEXICAN €€

Map p302 (www.lospilones.nl; Kerkstraat 63; mains €13-20; ⊙4-10.30pm Tue-Sun) Owners Hector and Pedro consistently set the standard among Amsterdam's handful of Mexican restaurants. If you're looking for grilled *bistek* (beefsteak), crispy chicken rolls and fruity mango margaritas in a colourful, social environment, you're definitely in the right place. A few shots from the 60-plus tequila list (they even make their own brand), and you'll be feeling brave enough to ask for the extra-hot salsa.

### SLUIZER INTERNATIONAL €€

Map p302 (☎622 63 76; www.sluizer.nl; Utrechtsestraat 43-45; mains €15.50-25, 3-course menu €21.50; ⊙5-11pm) This old-line institution, with its romantic, enclosed garden terrace, historically comprises two restaurants – a Parisian-style 'meat' restaurant (No 43) and a fish restaurant (No 45) – though both menus are available in both restaurants. Spare ribs are the speciality of the former and bouillabaisse the speciality of the latter.

### LE ZINC…ET LES AUTRES FRENCH €€

Map p302 (☎622 90 44; www.lezinc.nl; Prinsengracht 999; mains €14.50-24.50, 3-course menu €34.50; ⊙5.30-11pm Mon-Sat) This cosy old canal-house restaurant is an unapologetically old-fashioned affair, with candlelight, wine and romance to spare. The menu matches the vibe, with rustic dishes like pigeon and rabbit, and an option of matched reds and whites alongside each course. Vegetarians can fill up, too – maybe a dish with beetroot and goat's cheese or an oven-roasted tomato tart.

### RISTORANTE D'ANTICA ITALIAN €€€

Map p302 (☎623 38 62; www.dantica.nl; Reguliersdwarsstraat 80-82; mains €17-30, 4-course menu €49; ⊙6-11pm Mon-Thu, to midnight Fri & Sat) Although d'Antica's three dining rooms get their share of celebrities, you'd be hard pressed to find a more welcoming restaurant in town. There's a familiar selection of pastas and meats, but cognoscenti order *spaghetti al parmigiano* – and everyone may watch as waiters turn steaming pasta inside a wheel of cheese.

### LA RIVE FRENCH €€€

Map p302 (☎520 32 64; www.restaurantlarive.com; InterContinental Amstel Amsterdam, Professor Tulpplein 1; mains €48-55, 5-course menu €85; ⊙lunch Tue-Fri, dinner Tue-Sat) A Michelin star and a formal dining room with graciously spaced tables and views over the Amstel make La Rive the perfect venue for an out-to-impress lunch or dinner. The menu changes frequently, but standbys include turbot and truffle in potato pasta and, as you'd expect, a starter of caviar.

### PASTINI ITALIAN €€

Map p302 (☎622 17 01; www.pastini.nl; Leidsegracht 29; mains €13.50-21.50; ⊙dinner) With a *gezellig,* rustic-Renaissance interior and a can't-beat-it location facing two canals, Pastini wins praise for its looks, pastas and prices. A speciality is the three-choice antipasto starter, but save room for dessert.

### CAFÉ MORLANG CAFE €€

Map p302 (www.morlang.nl; Keizersgracht 451; mains €14-20; ⊙lunch & dinner) Grab a fashion magazine and order tomato soup or tarte tatin, or choose from a rotating menu with influences from Italy to Thailand. The canalside terrace is fab in warm weather; indoors, enjoy the high ceilings and gigantic portraits of staff members painted on the back wall. On Friday nights it's a low-key gay hang-out – so low-key that you may not realise it.

### COFFEE & JAZZ INDONESIAN €€

Map p302 (☎624 58 51; Utrechtsestraat 113; mains €14-18; ⊙10.30am-11pm Tue-Fri) This tiny eatery, with just a handful of tables and mellow jazz playing in the background, is run by an eccentric Dutchman and his Indonesian wife. She does most of the cooking – except for the house speciality sates, which he prepares. It's a must for jazz freaks and anyone who loves a snug place with a passionate owner.

### NA SIAM THAI €€

Map p302 (www.nasiam.nl; Kerkstraat 332; mains €11-21; ⊙dinner) Get transported to Thailand amid the serenity of this wood-panelled dining room, an evening oasis near Utrechtsestraat – but don't underestimate the spicy dishes. Local shopkeepers like to head here to unwind at dinner after their stores close.

### CAFÉ WALEM CAFE €€

Map p302 (www.walen.nl; Keizersgracht 449; sandwiches €6-9, mains €11-19; ⊙10am-10.30pm) The industrial-mod building by Gerrit Rietveld, two terraces, friendly service and a changing menu keep this place busy and perennially popular.

### LO STIVALE D'ORO ITALIAN €€

Map p302 (www.lostivaledoro.nl; Amstelstraat 49; mains €10-17; ⊙dinner Wed-Mon) Loosen the belt for awesome pizzas and straightforward pastas at this trattoria's chummy tables. The gregarious Italian owner occasionally pulls out his guitar and starts strumming for the crowd when he's in a good mood.

### VAN DOBBEN SANDWICH SHOP €

Map p302 (☎624 42 00; Korte Reguliersdwarsstraat 5; items €2.50-7.50; ⊙9.30am-1am Mon-Thu, 9.30am-2am Fri & Sat, 11am-8pm Sun) Open since the 1940s, the venerable Van Dobben has white-tile walls and white-coated counter men who specialise in snappy banter. Traditional meaty Dutch fare is its forte: try the *pekelvlees* (something close to corned beef), or make it a *halfom* (if you're keen on that being mixed with liver). The *kroketten* are the best in town and compulsory after a late-night Rembrandtplein booze-up. There is also a sparkling new branch in the De Pijp neighbourhood.

### GOLDEN TEMPLE VEGETARIAN €€

Map p302 (www.restaurantgoldentemple.com; Utrechtsestraat 126; mains €8.50-17; ⊙dinner nightly; 🅥) Golden Temple has a quietly upmarket setting and a good, inexpensive international menu of Indian thali, Italian pizzas and Middle Eastern and Mexican platters.

### BOUCHON DU CENTRE FRENCH €€

Map p302 (☎616 74 14; www.bouchonducentreamsterdam.com; Falkstraat 3; ⊙noon-3pm, 5pm-8pm Wed-Sat) Practically a secret for meat fanatics and Francophiles in the know, this little restaurant isn't for everyone – and it doesn't want to be. There's a changing, daily menu of a few dishes only: bet on it being French, meat-oriented and divine.

**BOJO** INDONESIAN €

Map p302 (www.bojo.nl; Lange Leidsedwarsstraat 51; mains €8.50-14; lunch Mon-Fri, dinner nightly until 1am or so) After a night on the town, there's nothing like a little Indonesian. Bojo is a late-night institution that's surprisingly serene, given the location. Clubbers come for sizzling sates, filling fried rice and steaming bowls of noodle soup, and generally leave smiling.

**JAPANS** SUSHI €€

Map p302 (616 74 14; www.japansrestaurantan.nl; Weteringschans 76; rolls €3-8; dinner Tue-Sat) The hardest choice at Japans isn't which sushi rolls to pick, it's where to sit: the intimate back patio opening up to a backyard garden reverie, or the serene, Zen-like front room? The streamlined menu of sushi and a handful of Japanese dishes are perfectly good (though service can be a bit slow), but we really come for the atmosphere.

**MAOZ** MIDDLE EASTERN €

Map p302 (420 74 35; Muntplein 1; mains €3.70-7.40; 11am-1am Sun-Thu, to 3am Fri & Sat; ) Falafel, saviour of vegetarians the world over, is perfected at this minichain, which has now expanded beyond the Netherlands. Just €4.40 gets you a falafel with unlimited access to a fresh, massive salad bar – a true test of your pita's strength. Other outlets are popping up like wildfire all over town.

**VILLAGE BAGELS** SANDWICH SHOP €

Map p302 (www.villagebagels.nl; Vijzelstraat 137; bagel sandwiches €4-7; 7.30am-6pm Mon-Fri, 9am-6pm Sat & Sun) The people who gave Amsterdam bagel-chic are going gangbusters. You may feel like a New Yorker as you dive into a bagel with salmon, chive cream cheese and capers, especially if you grab the newspaper. Then again, what Manhattan bagel shop sports stained-glass windows and picturesque views of boats docked alongside lovely 17th-century canal houses?

**WOK TO WALK** CHINESE €

Map p302 (www.woktowalk.com; Leidsestraat 96; mains €5-8; 11.30am-1am Sun-Thu, to 3am Fri & Sat) Many fast-food joints in Amsterdam assume you're too drunk or stoned to care what you're eating. Wok to Walk, however, serves fast food fresh. Choose noodles or rice, meat or veg, and a sauce; add to a wok and stir. There are other branches, but the culinary wasteland of Leidsestraat is where you'll need one most.

## DRINKING & NIGHTLIFE

Drinking in this area requires a serious strategy. With coffeeshops, theatre cafes, brown cafes and gay bars galore, it helps to know exactly what kind of atmosphere you want. Want to trade tales with other travellers? Head to the bars of Leidesplein. Want to dance? Rembrandtplein's the ticket. For one of the city's best concentrations of brown cafes, Utrechtestraat practically begs a *bruin café* pub crawl. For some serious partying, head for the gay scene on Reguliersdwarsstraat.

TOP CHOICE **CAFÉ SCHILLER** THEATRE CAFE

Map p302 (www.cafeschiller.nl, in Dutch; Rembrandtplein 26; 3pm-midnight) Most cafes would pay a fortune to recreate Schiller's fabulous art-deco interior, but this is original. Walls are lined with portraits of Dutch actors and cabaret artists from the 1920s and '30s. Bar stools and booths are often occupied by tippling journalists and artists, and folks tucking into pre- and post-theatre menus.

### THE GAY SCENE

For the best gay action in the 'hood, head to Reguliersdwarsstraat or Kerkstraat and cruise around for what strikes your fancy. Do keep in mind that many bars on Reguliersdwarsstraat, as of press time, had been closed for several months – due to financial problems and, sadly, a suicide of one of the biggest club impresarios in town – but are slated to reopen during 2011. Keep your eyes open for new bars and clubs as this area regains its former glory.

TOP CHOICE **CAFÉ DE SPUYT** BEER CAFE

Map p302 (www.despuyt.nl, in Dutch; Korte Leidsedwarsstraat 86) Steps away from the bustling Leidseplein, the bar staff at this mellow, friendly cafe will happily guide you through the massive chalkboard menu of more than 100 beers, from Belgian Trappist ales to American Sierra Nevada.

TOP CHOICE **DE KROON** GRAND CAFE

Map p302 (www.dekroon.nl, in Dutch; Rembrandtplein 17-1) A popular venue for media events and movie-premiere parties that's been restored to its original 1898 splendour, expect high ceilings, velvet chairs, and the chance to wave at the Little People below on Rembrandtplein. There is a lift to get up the two storeys, but climb the two flights instead and you'll be rewarded with an art-deco tiled staircase. Be sure to sit at the atmospheric English-library-themed bar and be mesmerised by the curious display of 19th-century medical and scientific equipment.

**WEBER** DESIGNER BAR

Map p302 (Marnixstraat 397; ⌚8pm-3am Mon-Thu, to 4am Fri-Sun) We love this buzzy bar for its indie and Brit rock, retro decor and unpretentious local vibe. Cheap drinks and friendly service are added incentives to head here on a Saturday night. As you sip your beer, ponder how the themes of American astronauts, elk heads and vaguely Asian decor all somehow make sense together, at least to the slightly intoxicated.

**CAFÉ LANGEREIS** BROWN CAFE

Map p302 (http://cafelangereis.com; Amstel 202; ⌚5pm-around midnight Mon-Sat) A lovely brown cafe along the Amstel river near Rembrandtplein, Café Langereis feels like it has been around forever. That's because the friendly young owner scoured the city for antique fixtures and furniture to recreate the lived-in feel of the vintage brown cafes she had long admired. Freshly ground coffee, fresh flowers on the tables, an upright piano and a classic rock soundtrack keep things fresh.

**MULLIGANS** IRISH PUB

Map p302 (www.mulligans.nl; Amstel 100; ⌚4pm-1am Sun-Thu, 4pm-3am Fri & Sat; 📶) This is probably the most 'authentic' Irish pub, at least music-wise. There's a congenial atmosphere, Guinness and Magners cider on tap, live Irish music most nights from 9.30pm or 10pm (no cover charge) and a tobacco-smoking room (which usually closes about an hour before last call). Sunday *sesiùns* let you participate: BYOI (instrument) and T (talent). Wednesdays, sing along to Irish tunes in the back room.

**BO CINQ** DESIGNER BAR

Map p302 (www.bocinq.nl; Lange Leidsedwarsstraat 53-59) Beautiful people and their admirers flock to this ultra-long, gleaming bar after work and on into the wee hours. We dig that on any given night, there's a healthy balance of expats and Dutch locals. Grab a mojito and strike your best languid pose on one of the couches as you try to decipher the multiple languages being spoken around you.

**CAFÉ DE WETERING** BROWN CAFE

Map p302 (Weteringstraat 37) Bursting with locals of all ages, local secret Café de Wetering isn't hard to miss. Tucked into one of central Amsterdam's hidden streets, it's not far from the famed antiques corridor of Nieuwe Spiegelstraat. Perch on the upper level by the fireplace, or sit at the bar to chat with the wisecracking bartenders. On chilly days, it's an ideal refuge.

**AMSTEL BAR & BRASSERIE** BAR

Map p302 (☎520 32 69; InterContinental Amstel Amsterdam, Professor Tulpplein 1) So you need to entertain a client. She's very high powered and you can't leave things to chance. The bar at the InterContinental Amstel Amsterdam is dignified and appropriately clubby, and its river-view location is the power spot in town. We expect you'll get that contract you wanted and you may even rub elbows with famous financiers for your next deal.

**WHISKEY CAFÉ L&B** WHISKEY BAR

Map p302 (Korte Leidsedwarsstraat 92) Is whiskey your poison? If so, skip the beer cafes and head straight to this utterly convivial (and usually packed) bar near Café de Spuyt. It's an intense party fuelled by the hard stuff, and a fitting homage to one of humankind's more potent elixirs.

**NEL** CAFE

Map p302 (www.nelamstelveld.nl, in Dutch; Amstelveld 12) Inside there's a mellow brasserie on one side and a stylish bar on the other, but on a sunny afternoon there's nothing better than to sit under the lush canopy of trees and lazily contemplate the quiet surrounding the brick, canalside square beyond. Full of beautiful people with nary a pose.

**EIJLDERS** BROWN CAFE

Map p302 (www.eijlders.nl; Korte Leidsedwarsstraat 47) During WWII Eijlders was a meeting place for artists who refused to toe the cultural line imposed by the Nazis, and the spirit lingers on. It's still an artists cafe with poetry readings the third Sunday of every month (sometimes in English – call to be sure).

**OOSTERLING** BROWN CAFE

Map p302 (Utrechtsestraat 140) Opened in the 1700s as a tea and coffee outlet for the Dutch East India Company, Oosterling is as authentic as it gets – run by the same family since 1877. These days it's packed with the after-work-drinks crowd and is one of the very few cafes that has a bottle-shop (liquor-store) permit.

**PATA NEGRA** COCKTAIL BAR

Map p302 (www.pata-negra.nl, in Dutch; Utrechtsestraat 124) Some come for the hit-or-miss tapas, but we come for the sangria and the fresh-squeezed margaritas. The alluringly tiled exterior is matched by a vibrant crowd inside, especially on weekends, downing sangria with the garlic-fried shrimps and grilled sardines. It gets packed, and that's half the fun.

**CAFÉ KALE** CAFE

Map p302 (www.cafekale.nl, in Dutch; Weteringshans 267) A bright place that's good for a beer and a tasty sandwich or salad. Stained glass, creative light fixtures and soft jazz make this a tad more elegant than the average brown cafe.

**DE KOFFIE SALON** CAFE

Map p302 (www.dekoffiesalon.nl; Utrechtsestraat 130) While this place may possibly serve the city's best latte, it's definitely the most effortlessly stylish coffeehouse. The airy, sophisticated vibe here is genuine, not a put-on affair, with communal tables that invite conversation, magazine sharing, and gazing at that cute stranger who's lost in a novel. With Sophia Loren sipping coffee and Gina Lollobrigida winking coquettishly down from the walls, we swore we were in Milan—and one sip of the devilishly strong espresso nearly convinced us.

**CAFÉ BRECHT** CAFE

Map p302 (www.cafebrecht.nl; Weteringschans 79) Named after the renowned German dramatist and poet, Bertolt Brecht, the Café Brecht may be the only establishment in Amsterdam with German poetry inscribed on the walls. The young and gorgeously rumpled dig the funky, elegant vibe – think mismatched velvet chairs, vintage lamps, and plenty of books and games – along with the chance to feel like an intellectual for the price of a beer.

**TWO FOR JOY** CAFE

Map p302 (www.twoforjoy.nl; Fredericksplein 29) Full of French-speaking customers drinking wickedly strong espresso on the umbrella-shaded sidewalk terrace, this skylit cafe on lush Fredericksplein is a hit with the international crowd. They take coffee seriously here: pick your poison from among French press, lovingly crafted lattes, or several connoisseur styles of drip coffee (try the high-tech, Japanese-style 'Syphon' method) along with the home-made banana bread.

**DE HUYSCHKAEMER** DESIGNER BAR

Map p302 (www.huyschkaemer.nl, in Dutch; Utrechtsestraat 137) With conversation-piece art – like a giant photo of a Dutch football team drinking beer in the buff – there's always plenty of buzzing chatter at De Huyschkaemer. Inside, the rock 'n' roll soundtrack veers from classic to indie. Nursing a beer next to the big windows on Utrechtsestraat is tempting, but the real action spills out on the street, where a mixed crowd – gay and straight, expat and local, old and young – shakes off the workday with serious fun.

**SUGAR FACTORY** CLUB

Map p302 (www.sugarfactory.nl; Lijnbaansgracht 238) A cool vibe, an excellent location and a varied line-up are the hallmarks here. But this ain't your average club – most nights start with music, cinema, or a dance or spoken-word performance, followed by late-night DJs and dancing.

**CLUB AIR** CLUB

Map p302 (www.air.nl; Amstelstraat 24) Not far from Rembrandtplein, but worlds away in terms of its cool quotient, this is one of Amsterdam's It clubs. It's an environmentally friendly design with features we appreciate, like the free mini lockers and refillable drink cards that preclude fussing with change at the bar. There's also a retro '80s-feel light show and a unique tiered dance floor. Though the place gets packed, it has ultra-high ceilings and it feels like there's still plenty of room to get funky.

**N'JOY COCKTAIL CAFÉ** COCKTAIL BAR

Map p302 (www.cocktailclubnjoy.nl; Korte Leidsedwarsstraat 93; ⌚Thu-Sat) A perfect place to kick off, or cap off, a night of bar hopping, N-Joy takes its saucily named, frilly cocktails seriously. One of the only bars in the area where women far outnumber men, this little vixen of a bar generates a chilled-out, stylish vibe that's a refreshing break from the madness of the street outside. Try the delish vanilla sour or the blackberry bramble.

**ROKERIJ** COFFEESHOP

Map p302 (www.rokerij.net; Lange Leidsedwarsstraat 41) Behind the black hole of an entrance you'll find Eastern decor and candlelight. Staff at this Rokerij flagship branch have a reputation for friendliness, which explains why outlets have shot up like weed(s), but this is the cosiest location by far.

**CAFÉ AMERICAIN** GRAND CAFE

Map p302 (www.edenamsterdamamericanhotel.com; Eden Amsterdam American Hotel, Leidsekade 97) This art-deco monument, opened in 1902, was a grand cafe before the concept even existed, with huge stained-glass windows overlooking Leidseplein, a lovely, library-like reading table and a great terrace.

**BULLDOG** COFFEESHOP

Map p302 (www.bulldog.nl; Leidseplein 13-17; 📶) Amsterdam's most famous coffeeshop chain has evolved into its own empire, with multiple locations (some double as cafes), a hotel, bike rental and even its own brand of energy drink. At press time this flagship location on the Leidseplein was under threat of closure due to its proximity to a school. Not just an outlet for weed, Bulldog's a full-fledged Amsterdam entertainment empire these days. The brawny, brassy Leidesplein flagship has two sides for its brand-name debauchery: one for smoking, one for drinking. The crowds on either side are pretty much the same: a mix of stag parties, corporate travellers blowing off steam, and backpackers. The gaudy decor only makes sense to the stoned.

**STANISLAVSKI** THEATRE CAFE

Map p302 (www.stanislavski.nl; Stadschouwberg) This drama queen of a bar, named after famed Russian theatre practitioner Constantin Stanislavski (the original father of 'method' acting), is full of chandeliered splendour, actors, and well-dressed cultural types deconstructing the avant-garde play they just watched in the attached Stadsschouwburg.

**KAMER 401** DESIGNER BAR

Map p302 (www.kamer401.nl; Marnixstraat 401) One of several happening bars along this street, attracting gorgeous-looking, cocktail-drinking young locals who pack the place till late. With DJs providing a funky soundtrack, it's perfect for preclubbing drinks. If you can't breathe or move, see if you can snag a corner at **Lux** (☎422 14 12; Marnixstraat 403) next door – it's a similar scene, and equally popular.

**SUZY WONG** DESIGNER BAR

Map p302 (Korte Leidsedwarsstraat 45; ⌚7pm-1am Sun, Wed & Thu, 5pm-3am Fri, 7pm-3am Sat) Riding a thin line between cheesy and cool, Suzy Wong packs a visual punch nonetheless. The look? Victorian-drawing-room-on-speed, with red velveteen wallpaper and a bamboo garden; a photo of Andy Warhol observes. It's a worthy place to fortify yourself before heading across to Jimmy Woo. Grab a fresh fruit mojito and nab a seat in the back by the bamboo with the Dutch trendies and actors.

**DE SMOESHAAN** THEATRE CAFE

Map p302 (www.desmoeshaan.nl; Leidsekade 90) Theater Bellevue's cafe gets pretty lively, both before and after the shows, with theatre visitors and performers. During the day it's a nice place to relax by the Singelgracht and there's a good restaurant upstairs too (closed Sunday year-round and all of July and August).

**VIVELAVIE** LESBIAN CAFE

Map p302 (www.vivelavie.net; Amstelstraat 7; ⌚4pm-1am Sun-Thu, to 4am Fri & Sat; 📶) Just off Rembrandtplein, this lively place is probably Amsterdam's most popular lesbian cafe for its flirty girls, with good-natured staff, loud music and large windows. In summer the outdoor terrace buzzes.

**THE OTHER SIDE** GAY COFFEESHOP

Map p302 (www.theotherside.nl; Reguliersdwarsstraat 6) House and lounge music, sometimes spun by a DJ, make this a hopping and trendy coffeeshop – straights are most welcome, too.

**LELLEBEL** DRAG BAR

Map p302 (www.lellebel.nl; Utrechtsestraat 4; ⏲9pm-3am Mon-Thu, 8pm-4am Fri & Sat, 3pm-3am Sun) This hole-in-the wall just off Rembrandtplein has karaoke, singing and comedy shows that bring out the best in any girl's wardrobe. It can get bitchy, but always in the funniest possible way.

**MONTMARTRE** GAY BAR

Map p302 (www.cafemontmartre.nl; Halvemaansteeg 17) Regarded by many as the best gay bar in the Benelux, and a busy weekend will show why. Patrons sing along (or scream along) to recordings of Dutch ballads and old top-40 hits.

**MINIBAR** DESIGNER BAR

Map p302 (www.minibaronline.com; Prinsengracht 478) If Homer Simpson went glam, this would be his palace. Present an ID at the counter; choose a fully stocked beer, champagne or mixed fridge; and grab your key to your own self-service minibar (more maxi than mini, actually). Select your tipple and sip in the mod-lounge setting, zoning out on the computerised light show; on our visit, plump white raindrops cascaded down a solid black wall. DJs spin a few nights a week, too.

**CAFÉ 'T LEEUWTJE** GAY BAR

Map p302 (www.cafehetleeuwtje.nl; Reguliersdwarsstraat 105) 'The Little Lion' stands out from the rest of the venues on this street – snazzy it ain't, the music doesn't thump loudly and the interior feels a bit like a brown cafe. A fairly extensive beer selection makes it a prime place to chat or chill with a newspaper.

**COFFEESHOP FREE** COFFEESHOP

Map p302 (Reguliersdwarsstraat 670; ⏲9.30am-1am) Little Coffeeshop Free has been sporting its lazy tiki bar vibe in the centre of the around-Rembrandtplein action for over 25 years. It's perfect for getting spaced out before seeing that new Guillermo del Toro film playing around the corner at Pathe Tuschinski: munch on a space cake under the South Seas mural for a trip to paradise, regardless of the weather outside.

**TABOO BAR** GAY CAFE

Map p302 (www.taboobar.nl; Reguliersdwarsstraat 45; ⏲9am-8pm; 📶) While many Reguliersdwarsstraat regulars are still mourning the closing of Downtown – the oldest and most beloved kid on the block for 40 years – everyone's figured out that the wicked two-for-one happy hours at Taboo (6pm to 7pm and midnight to 1am, plus 6pm to 8pm Sunday) offer the most delicious way to drown one's sorrow.

**ESCAPE** CLUB

Map p302 (www.escape.nl, in Dutch; Rembrandtplein 11) A fixture of Amsterdam nightlife for two decades, this cavernous club is the city's slickest, with several dance floors, two smoking lounges, a video-screen-filled studio and an adjoining cafe. Dress to impress on weekends, or you may not get in.

**ODEON** COCKTAIL BAR

Map p302 (www.odeonamsterdam.nl, in Dutch; Singel 460) This historic venue from the 1660s includes a classy restaurant, a swanky cocktail bar and a canalside terrace to give those ears a rest. Massive murals of models adorn the walls. Club nights rarely rise above a €15 entry fee.

**CHURCH** GAY CLUB

Map p302 (www.clubchurch.nl; Kerkstraat 52) This hardcore gay nightclub gives a whole new meaning to the phrase 'I'm going to church'. Unless you come dressed appropriately for the evening (S&M, leather…check the website for events) or with super hot boys (or happen to be one yourself) you probably won't get in to this high-action cruise spot, but they'll be terribly nice about it.

**JIMMY WOO** CLUB

Map p302 (☎626 31 50; www.jimmywoo.com; Korte Leidsedwarsstraat 18) For a long time this club was the hottest thing in town, with zero serious competition. It's still a platform for the young and beautiful, with fab light-and-sound shows. And really long queues: be patient, or call ahead to get on the list.

**STACEY'S PENNYWELL** CAFE

Map p302 (www.staceys.nl; Herengracht 558) While the food is undeniably so-so, you can't beat the canalside, many-windowed ambience for a late afternoon coffee or early evening cocktail. Lovely crown mouldings and wrought ironwork chandeliers woo diners up to the second level, a perfect place to curl up on the comfy white leather chairs with a fresh mint tea on a snowy day. Cocktails taste best on the lower level, with pillow-strewn couches overlooking the Herengracht canal.

## ENTERTAINMENT

Shrill and obnoxious, or perfectly thrilling? Whatever your opinion, it's true that much of the after-dark action gravitates towards two of Amsterdam's busy pleasure centres, Leidseplein and Rembrandtplein. Lest you mistake these squares for Dutch versions of Disneyland, do a little exploring and you'll find that many locales here feel surprisingly authentic despite the somewhat tacky surrounds. A more discriminating crowd hits Utrechtsestraat, where you'll find some of the city's most enticing cafes and bars.

**TOP CHOICE JAZZ CAFÉ ALTO** JAZZ

Map p302 (www.jazz-cafe-alto.nl; Korte Leidsedwarsstraat 115; ⊙9pm-3am Sun-Thu, to 4am Fri & Sat) You'll enjoy serious jazz and blues at this respected cafe near Leidseplein. Tuesdays mean salsa and Latin jazz. Doors open at 9pm but music starts around 10pm – get there early if you want to snag a seat.

**PARADISO** ROCK

Map p302 (www.paradiso.nl; Weteringsshans 6) Worship rock 'n' roll in a gorgeous old church where the Beatles once played. Opened in 1968 as 'Cosmic Relaxation Center Paradiso', this historic, multi-storeyed club exudes an anything-goes, relaxed vibe. Midweek club nights with low cover charges lure the young and the restless, while the Small Hall upstairs provides an intimate venue to see up-and-coming bands from around the world. The real attraction, of course, is the chance to hear artists like the White Stripes and Lady Gaga rock the Main Hall as you wonder if the stained-glass windows just might shatter.

**MELKWEG** JAZZ & BLUES

Map p302 (www.melkweg.nl; Lijnbaansgracht 234a) The 'Milky Way' is a dazzling galaxy of diverse music. One night it's reggae or punk, the next night heavy-metal legend Zach Wilde lures in the leather-jacketed biker crowd. We dig the Kill All Hipsters and Adult Swimming dance nights, which might place electronica in one room and '80s and '90s rock and hip hop in the other. Check out its website for cutting-edge cinema and theatre offerings, too.

**BOURBON STREET JAZZ & BLUES CLUB** JAZZ & BLUES

Map p302 (www.bourbonstreet.nl; Leidsekruisstraat 6-8; ⊙10pm-4am Sun-Thu, to 5am Fri & Sat) Catch blues, funk, soul and rock and roll in this intimate venue, with everyone's-welcome open jam sessions on Tuesdays. Free entrance before 11pm.

**DE HEEREN VAN AEMSTEL** LIVE MUSIC

Map p302 (www.deheerenvanaemstel.nl, in Dutch; Thorbeckeplein 5) Office workers and students cram into this grand-cafe-style club to enjoy the roster of live big bands and pop and rock cover bands.

**CINECENTER** CINEMA

Map p302 (www.cinecenter.nl, in Dutch; Lijnbaansgracht 236) Euro and American art-house films are the standard fare. Don't miss the hip bar with white padded walls.

**DE UITKIJK** CINEMA

Map p302 (www.uitkijk.nl, in Dutch; Prinsengracht 452) This fun art-house stalwart, located in an old canal house (1913), is the city's second-oldest surviving cinema (the oldest is Movies). For film buffs who know their Fuller from their Fellini.

**PATHÉ TUSCHINSKITHEATER** CINEMA

Map p302 (www.pathe.nl/tuschinski, in Dutch; Reguliersbreestraat 26-34) Extensively refurbished, Amsterdam's most famous cinema is worth visiting for its sumptuous art deco/Amsterdam School interior. The *grote zaal* (main auditorium) is the most stunning and generally screens blockbusters; the smaller theatres play art-house and indie films.

**CHICAGO SOCIAL CLUB & BOOM CHICAGO** COMEDY, CLUB

Map p302 (☎423 01 01; www.chicagosocialclub.nl; Leidseplein Theater, Leidseplein 12, ⊙bar noon-3am, to 4am Sat & Sun, club 11pm-3am Thu, to 4am Sat & Sun) In 2011, Boom Chicago upped its ante to become the holy trinity of Leidesplein entertainment (okay, save for a coffeeshop): it's a comedy club, a late night bar, and a nightclub. Add to that the fact you can enjoy Amsterdam's leading English-language improv comedy show over dinner and a few drinks, and you'll have to add 'dinner theatre' to the list, too. What do these multi-talented and seriously funny folks *not* do well?

**DE LA MAR** THEATRE

Map p302 (www.delamar.nl; Leidsekade 90; ⊙closed Aug) Big-name blockbuster musicals and crowd-pleasing plays shine in the most impressive venue to hit the theatre district in years. After the curtain comes down, head to the **Grand Café De La Mar** for a post-theatre glass of champagne in decadent elegance.

### COMEDY CAFÉ AMSTERDAM COMEDY

Map p302 (www.comedycafe.nl; Max Euweplein 43-45) The Comedy Café books Dutch and international stand-up comics. Sundays are reserved for *Hole in the Boat!*, a two-man improv show.

### DE KLEINE KOMEDIE THEATRE

Map p302 (www.dekleinekomedie.nl, in Dutch; Amstel 56-58) This renowned little theatre, founded in 1786, puts on concerts, dance, comedy and cabaret, sometimes in English.

### DE BALIE THEATRE

Map p302 (☎553 51 51; www.debalie.nl, in Dutch; Kleine Gartmanplantsoen 10) The focus here is multicultural and political, with big international productions. De Balie also conducts short-film festivals and debates, and has new-media facilities. In the stylish bar, there's a breezily bohemian vibe and a pre-theatre buzz, as actors, students and artsy types unfurl magazines or just knowing glances.

### THEATER BELLEVUE THEATRE

Map p302 (☎530 53 01; www.theaterbellevue.nl; Leidsekade 90; ⏲closed Aug) Come here for experimental theatre, international cabaret and modern dance, mainly in Dutch.

## SHOPPING

From sleek Dutch fashion and design to colourful bouquets and rare Dutch *jenever*, the variety of goods on offer in the Southern Canal Ring is nothing short of staggering. The Nieuwe Spiegelstraat (aka the Spiegel Quarter) is celebrated for its antique stores, bric-a-brac collectibles, tribal and oriental art, and commercial art galleries.

### TOP CHOICE YOUNG DESIGNERS UNITED CLOTHING

Map p302 (www.ydu.nl; Keizersgracht 447) Angelika Groenendijk Wasylewski's boutique is a showcase for young designers (mainly Dutch). They regularly rotate the racks but on our visit we spotted Monique Poolman's strong, designed cuts; Letke de Roos' fun, feminine pieces; Heidi Long's striking collection; and Susa Plaza's sporty, comfortable look.

### TOP CHOICE REFLEX MODERN ART GALLERY ART

Map p302 (www.reflex-art.nl, in Dutch; Weteringschans 79a; ⏲Tue-Sat) This prominent gallery, opposite the Rijksmuseum, is filled with contemporary art and photography, including works by members of the CoBrA and Nouveau Réaliste movements.

### TOP CHOICE KAAS HUIS TROMP CHEESE

Map p302 (www.cheesebymail.nl; Utrechtsestraat 90) Perhaps a more fitting name for this 'cheese house' would be a temple, for it's a wonderful place to come if you want to worship fermented dairy products from all over Holland and the world. Fortunately, Henk, the affable proprietor, knows that this is best done with plenty of free samples – a concept that most other cheese shops in Amsterdam miss.

### PHILLIPA K CLOTHING

Map p302 (www.phillipa-k.com; Leidsestraat 53) Dutch film luminary, Carice van Houten, has been spotted shopping here, so why shouldn't you? A favourite of local designers, Phillipa K is one of the top Scandinavian designers worldwide; wearing one of her glam-yet-functional dresses or ensembles guarantees compliments as well as comfort.

### CORA KEMPERMAN CLOTHING

Map p302 (☎625 12 84; www.corakemperman.nl; Leidsestraat 72) Kemperman was once a designer with large Dutch fashion houses, but since 1995 she's been working on her own empire – now encompassing nine stores, including three in Belgium. Her well-priced creations feature mainly solid colours, floaty, layered separates and dresses in linen, cotton and wool.

### SHOEBALOO SHOES

Map p302 (www.shoebaloo.nl; Leidsestraat 10) We like the chic shoes here – imports include Fendi, Jimmy Choo, Miu Miu and Prada Sport, along with the less expensive but just as wearable house label. This branch is more central, but the one at PC Hooftstraat 80 has one of our favourite interiors in town: imagine a giant white spaceship tinged with green and lined with shoe shelves and eggs for you to sit on.

### HEINEN DELFTWARE
SOUVENIRS

Map p302 (www.heinen-delftware.nl; Prinsengracht 440) With four floors of Delftware, all the major factories are represented and all budgets catered for (you can spend about €6 for a spoon, or €2000-plus for a replica 17th-century tulip vase).

### WHEN NATURE CALLS
SMART DRUGS

Map p302 (www.whennaturecalls.nl; Keizersgracht 508; ⌚10am-10pm Mon-Sat, from 11am Sun) Despite its curious name, this smart shop dispenses serious, informative, helpful and no-nonsense advice about its wares, which include the usual offerings – magic truffles, herbal ecstasy, energisers, cannabis seeds and sex stimulants.

### MARAÑON HANGMATTEN
OUTDOORS

Map p302 (www.maranon.com; Singel 488) Anyone who loves hanging around should come here and explore Europe's largest selection of hammocks. The colourful creations, made of everything from cotton to pineapple fibres, are made by many producers, from indigenous weavers to large manufacturers. It ships worldwide.

### TINKERBELL
CHILDREN'S

Map p302 (www.tinkerbelltoys.nl, in Dutch; Spiegelgracht 10) The mechanical bear blowing bubbles outside this shop fascinates kids, as do the intriguing technical and scientific toys inside. You'll also find historical costumes, plush toys and an entire section for babies.

### JASKI
ART

Map p302 (www.jaski.nl; Nieuwe Spiegelstraat 27-29; ⌚noon-8pm Tue-Sat) This large commercial gallery sells paintings, prints, ceramics and sculptures by some of the most famous members of the CoBrA movement.

### LIEVE HEMEL
ART

Map p302 (www.lievehemel.nl; Nieuwe Spiegelstraat 3; ⌚Tue-Sat) You'll find magnificent contemporary Dutch realist painting and sculpture at this smart gallery. It shows works by Dutch painters Ben Snijders and Theo Voorzaat, and astounding, lifelike representations of clothing – hewn from wood – by Italian Livio de Marchi.

### REFLEX NEW ART GALLERY
ART

Map p302 (www.reflex-art.nl, in Dutch; Weteringschans 83; ⌚Tue-Sat) This exhibition space across the street from the original Reflex specialises in new art. There's an emphasis on photography, and artists include young up-and-comers like David La Chapelle, Phyllis Gallembo and Miles Aldridge.

### EDUARD KRAMER
ART, ANTIQUES

Map p302 (www.antique-tileshop.nl; Nieuwe Spiegelstraat 64; ⌚Tue-Sun) Specialising in antique Dutch wall and floor tiles, Eduard Kramer has an extensive tile collection that sits alongside books, jewellery and vintage homewares including glassware and Delft pottery. Stroll a few doors down to browse the expanded selection of art and tiles at its new addition at Prinsengracht 807, a gorgeously refurbished old grocery store.

### INTERNATIONAL THEATRE & FILM BOOKS
BOOKS

Map p302 (www.theatreandfilmbooks.com; Leidseplein 26) In the Stadsschouwburg building, this excellent shop is crammed with books on its namesake subjects, as well as speciality sections on musicals and famous directors. The majority of titles are in English.

### EH ARIËNS KAPPERS
ART, ANTIQUES

Map p302 (www.masterprints.nl; Nieuwe Spiegelstraat 32; ⌚Tue-Sat) This pretty gallery stocks original prints, etchings, engravings, lithographs, maps (primarily of the Netherlands) from the 15th to 20th centuries, and Japanese woodblock prints.

### CITYBOEK
ART, BOOKS

Map p302 (www.cityboek.nl; Kerkstraat 211; ⌚by appointment) We normally wouldn't include shops selling souvenir posters, but this small publishing house is an exception, with precisely drawn, multicoloured, architecturally faithful prints, books and postcards of Amsterdam's canalscapes (such as images of the entire Herengracht or Singel).

### SELEXYZ SCHELTEMA
BOOKS

Map p302 (www.selexyz.nl; Koningsplein 20) The largest bookshop in town is a true department store, with many foreign titles, New Age and multimedia sections, and a large travel-guide selection. It can be dizzying. Readings and book launches take place next to the upstairs cafe.

### STADSBOEKWINKEL
BOOKS

Map p302 (www.stadsboekwinkel.nl; Vijzelstraat 32; ⌚Tue-Sun) Run by the city printer, this is the best source for books about Amster-

LOCAL KNOWLEDGE

## THE CURIOUS HISTORY OF STREET NAMES

Ever wonder where these streets and squares and canals get their notoriously long, difficult-to-pronounce names, made even more confusing by the fact that many names are nearly identical to one another?

The history of street names in the Southern Canal Ring may shed some light on that enigma. Before the construction of the Canal Ring, the monks of the Regulier (Regular) order had a monastery outside the city walls roughly where Utrechtsestraat now crosses Keizersgracht. This explains the frequent use of the name in the area (Reguliersbreestraat, Reguliersdwarsstraat, Reguliersgracht). And Thorbeckeplein, the cafe zone southwest of Rembrandtplein, is named after Jan Rudolf Thorbecke, the Liberal politician who created the Dutch parliamentary system in 1848. His statue faces outwards from the square, although he might have enjoyed watching over its leafy car-free atmosphere.

In a more straightforward naming convention, Lange Leidwarsestraat simply means 'long' Leidwarsestraat, while Korte Leidwarsestraat ('short,' in Dutch) is the shorter version of the street.

dam's history, urban development, ecology and politics. Most titles are in Dutch (you can always look at the pictures), but you'll also find some in English. It's in the Stadsarchief (Municipal Archives) building.

**GONE WITH THE WIND** CHILDREN'S, GIFTS

Map p302 (www.gonewind-mobiles.com, in Dutch; Vijzelstraat 22) A delight for the kid in all of us, most of the items – toys, train sets, mobiles and games – are made from high-quality wood. Finger puppets, whimsical gifts and jewellery round out the selection.

**VLIEGER** STATIONERY

Map p302 (www.vliegerpapier.nl; Amstel 34) Since 1869 this well-organised two-storey shop has been supplying upmarket paper to Amsterdam: Egyptian papyrus; lush handmade papers from Asia and Central America; papers inlaid with flower petals or bamboo; and paper with a texture that looks like snake skin. It also sells indestructible Freitag messenger bags (to safely tote away all that paper on your bike?).

**LOOK OUT** CLOTHING

Map p302 (www.lookoutmode.com; Utrechtsestraat 91 & 93) Searching through the racks at these wonderful neighbouring men's and women's stores is a real delight. Look out for superstylish labels such as Paul Smith, Philosophy, Etro, Kenzo, Bruuns Bazaar and Annemie Verbeke.

**HART'S WIJNHANDEL** FOOD & DRINK

Map p302 (www.hartswijn.nl, in Dutch; Vijzelgracht 27) Listen to classical music as you peruse the large selection of *jenever* and French and Italian wines at this peaceful shop. It's been around since 1880, and supplies many a local restaurant with top tipples.

**CONCERTO** MUSIC

Map p302 (www.concerto.nl, in Dutch; Utrechtsestraat 52-60) Most excellent. This rambling shop, spread over several buildings, has Amsterdam's best selection of new and secondhand CDs and records; you could spend hours on end browsing in here. It's often cheap and always interesting, and has good listening facilities.

**CARL DENIG** OUTDOORS

Map p302 (www.denig.nl, in Dutch; Weteringschans 113-115; ⏲Tue-Sat) Opened in 1912, this is Amsterdam's oldest and best outdoor retailer, though you pay for the quality. There are five floors of packs, tents, hiking and camping accessories, snowboards and skis.

**KOM** HOMEWARES

Map p302 (www.kom.nl; Utrechtsestraat 129) Alluring kitchen stuff on the Utrechtsestraat, including Delftware, pretty dishes, cake knives, and glasses, all wrapped up in pretty blue paper.

**SHIRT SHOP** CLOTHING

Map p302 (www.shirtshopamsterdam.com; Reguliersdwarsstraat 64) On gay Amsterdam's main street, this funky, two-storey shop sells tight-fitting men's shirts to make you look fabulous. Look for sale items around €20.

# Jordaan & the West

JORDAAN | WESTERPARK | WESTERN ISLANDS

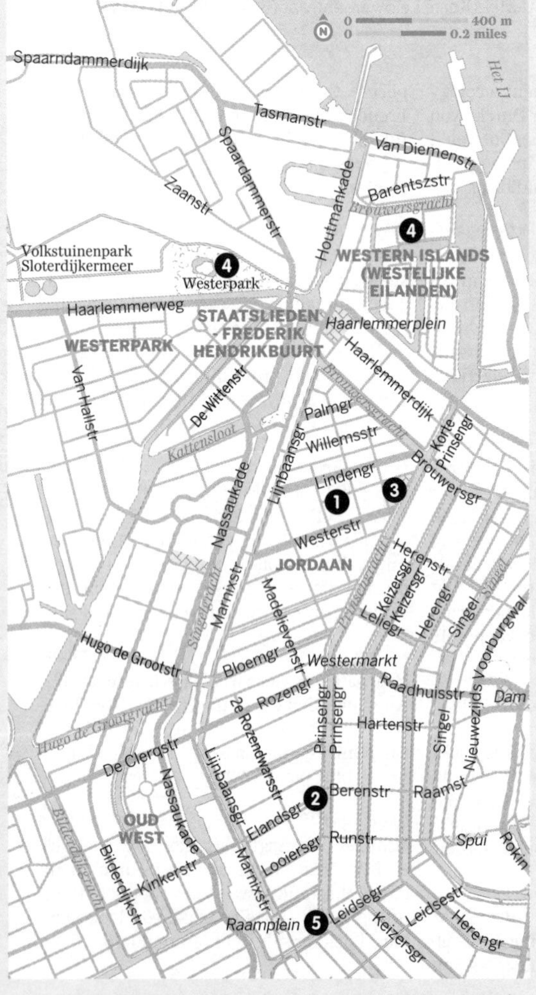


For more detail of this area, see Map p294 and Map p296

## Neighbourhood Top Five

❶ There's really nothing more quintessentially Amsterdam than simply getting lost in the **Jordaan** (p132), as you wander the cosy labyrinth of streets and canals in Holland's most beloved neighbourhood.

❷ Head to **Johnny Jordaanplein** (p133) to find the epicentre of the Queen's Day party.

❸ Morning bliss in the Jordaan means cruising the weekly outdoor markets, including the **Noordermarkt** (p132), for organic food, bargain clothes and funky flea market treasures.

❹ A gorgeous city park, a post-industrial culture complex and an island adventure await those who go exploring around the **Westerpark** (p134) and **Western Islands** (p136).

❺ There are many ways to experience the 'real' Amsterdam, but little equals an evening drinking beer in one of the Jordaan's famed brown cafes, such as **De Pieper** (p140).

## Explore: Jordaan & the West

Though gentrified today, the Jordaan was a rough working-class district in the early 17th century, and that history still shows. You'll soon discover that this neighbourhood is a curiously enchanting mix of traditionally gritty, hard-drinking, leftist character (you can't throw a rock without hitting a sociable old *bruin café*) and its revitalised, trend-conscious sheen.

The area doesn't hold many traditional sights, but that's not the point. The Jordaan is about taking your time wandering the narrow lanes and not worrying if you get lost.

We like to start the day at the northern end of the Jordaan and crisscross our way towards the southern part. If it's a Saturday or Monday, start your day browsing one of the street markets such as the Noordmarkt; if it's not, start off exploring Haarlemmerdijk's up-and-coming shopping scene. Take a coffee break at one of the many brown cafes on the Prinsengrachtl.

On day two, go west. Hop on a bike and cruise the Western Islands for shopping and lunch, before a pre-dinner spin around verdant Westerpark. In the evening, revel in the exciting possibilities that any evening in the Westergasfabriek presents, from an arthouse film at Het Ketelhuis to rock and roll at Pacific Parc.

## Local Life

➡ **The Movies** The perfect antidote to the age of the soulless cineplex, this is the oldest – and most charming – cinema in a town of great cinemas.

➡ **Off the Beaten Canal** To get the feeling that you have a canal (practically) all to yourself, amble down the elegant and serene Eglantiersgracht.

➡ **Brouwersgracht Beauty** Among some seriously tough competition, Amsterdammers still swear that this is their fair city's most beautiful canal.

➡ **Haarlemmerdijk** This street is fast becoming a culinary destination; not just for restaurants but for gourmet provisions and kitchen shops.

## Getting There & Away

➡ **Tram** Tram 10 along Marnixstraat is your best bet for the neighbourhood's western edge; trams 13 and 14 along Rozengracht go through the centre.

➡ **Car** Whatever you do, don't try to drive through the Jordaan's narrow streets. We're not kidding.

### Lonely Planet's Top Tip

To experience the Jordaan's famous (or infamous) tradition of drunken sing-alongs, duck into De Twee Zwaantjes (p141), to witness a rollicking cabaret-meets-karaoke evening. You'll hear a mix of classics and traditional Dutch tunes that everyone from the piano player to the patrons sing with ebullient relish, so don't be afraid to join in.

### Best Places to Eat

➡ Balthazar's Keuken (p134)

➡ Hostaria (p136)

➡ Small World Catering (p136)

➡ Japanese Pancake World (p136)

➡ Winkel (p137)

For reviews, see p134 ➡

### Best Places to Drink

➡ Café 't Smalle (p140)

➡ Finch (p140)

➡ Westergasterras (p142)

For reviews, see p140 ➡

### Best Places to Shop

➡ Kitsch Kitchen (p143)

➡ Petsalon (p143)

➡ Wonen 2000 (p143)

➡ Boutique Petticoat (p144)

➡ Mooi Gallery (p144)

For reviews, see p143 

# SIGHTS

## Jordaan

### BROUWERSGRACHT — CANAL

Map p296 Pretty as a Golden Age painting, the Brewers Canal took its name from the many breweries located here in the 16th and 17th centuries. Goods such as leather, coffee, whale oil and spices were stored and processed here in giant warehouses, such as those with the row of spout gables that still stand at 188-194. De Ooievaar, Amsterdam's last *jenever* (Dutch gin) distillery, was located on the corner of Driehoekstraat. A few years ago, the Brouwersgracht was voted 'most beautiful street' in Amsterdam by newspaper *Het Parool,* and it even has its own Facebook page. In short, it's a great a place to stroll, and to see the waterborne action on Queen's Day.

### NOORDERKERK — CHURCH

Map p294 (Northern Church; www.noorderkerk.org; Noordermarkt 48; admission free; 10.30am-12:30pm Mon, 11am-1pm Sat, 1.30-5.30pm Sun) Near the northern end of the Prinsengracht, this imposing Calvinist church was completed in 1623 for the 'common' people in the Jordaan. (The upper classes attended the Westerkerk further south.) It was built in the shape of a broad Greek cross (four arms of equal length) around a central pulpit, giving the entire congregation unimpeded access to the word of God in suitably sober surroundings. This design, unusual at the time, would become common for Protestant churches throughout the country.

Noorderkerk hosts a well-regarded **Saturday afternoon concert series** (620 45 56; www.nooderkerkconcerten.nl; tickets from €15; 2pm Sat mid-Sep–mid-Jun).

> **ON YOUR BIKE IN THE JORDAAN**
>
> See p32 for information on bicycling in Amsterdam. For bike rentals and bike tours in the Jordaan:
>
> **Bike City** (Map p294; 626 37 21; www.bikecity.nl; Bloemgracht 68-70)

### NOORDERMARKT — MARKET

Map p294 (Northern Market; Noorderkerkplein; www.boerenmarktamsterdam.nl, in Dutch; 8am-2pm Mon, 9am-4pm Sat) A market square since the early 1600s, the plaza in front of the Noorderkerk now hosts several lively markets every week. On Monday morning there's a flea market with wonderful bargains; early on Saturday morning there's a bird market (with birds in cages, a holdover from the former livestock market), followed by a *boerenmarkt* (farmers market) with herbs and organic produce until early/mid-afternoon. There's a nice selection of cafes surrounding the square, including Winkel on the southwest corner, home of some of the city's best apple pie.

### PIANOLA MUSEUM — MUSEUM

Map p294 (627 96 24; www.pianola.nl; Westerstraat 106; adult/child under 12yr €5/3; 2-5pm Sun) This is a very special place, crammed with pianolas from the early 1900s. The museum has a stock of 50 pianolas, although only a dozen are on display at any given time, as well as nearly 20,000 music rolls. There's even a player pipe organ. Every month player-piano concerts are held, featuring anything from Mozart to Fats Waller and rare classical or jazz tunes composed especially for the instrument. The curator gives demonstrations with great zest. Lately the museum is also home to more eclectic musical offerings, such as a popular tango series.

### AMSTERDAM TULIP MUSEUM — MUSEUM

Map p294 (421 00 95; www.amsterdamtulipmuseum.com; Prinsengracht 112; adult/child €4/2; 10am-6pm) Ah, the noble history of the tulip, pride and joy of the Netherlands. While less exciting than wandering through a colourful field of what the museum calls 'the world's most dangerous flower,' this small, rather clinical exhibit does offer a chance to trace the prince of petals from its beginnings in Turkey to Dutch 'Tulipmania', bulbs as food in the war years, and present-day scientific methods of growing and harvesting. A highlight is the tulip paintings by 17th-century painter Judith Leijster, a student of Frans Hals. The gift shop offers one-stop shopping for all your tulip souvenirs.

### EGELANTIERSGRACHT — CANAL

Map p296 Many parts of the Jordaan are named after trees and flowers, and this canal takes its name from the eglantine

LOCAL KNOWLEDGE

## HOFJES

A charming legacy of the Jordaan is its many *hofjes*, the courtyard homes built by wealthy benefactors to house elderly people and widows – a noble act in the days before social security. Some *hofjes* are real gems, set back from the street with lovely prim gardens and beautifully restored houses. Unfortunately, many courtyards became such tourist magnets that residents complained and they were closed to the public (an exception being the Begijnhof, p61).

However, if you should find any of the following open, try to take a discreet peek.

**Karthuizerhofje** (Map p294; Karthuizersstraat 89-171) This *hofje* for widows, dating from 1650, is on the site of a former Carthusian monastery.

**Claes Claeszhofje** (Map p294; 1e Egelantiersdwarsstraat 3) Also known as Anslo's Hofje; has three pretty courtyards dating from around 1630.

**St Andrieshofje** (Map p296; Egelantiersgracht 107-141) The second-oldest surviving *hofje;* it was founded by cattle farmer Jeff Gerritzoon and finished in 1617.

**Suyckerhofje** (Map p294; Lindengracht 149-163) A charming courtyard founded in 1670.

**Lindenhofje** (Map p294; Lindengracht 94-112) The city's oldest *hofje*, dating from 1614; you'll have to admire it from outside only as the building is now a children's hospice and is closed to the public.

rose, or sweetbrier. (You can see its dainty pink petals and hooked prickles in many a Jordaan garden.) Built for artisans and skilled tradesmen, the houses here are scaled-down, yet thoroughly lovely, versions of those in the Western Canal Ring.

At Egelantiersgracht 107-141 you'll find the St Andrieshofje (see p133).

### BLOEMGRACHT — CANAL

Map p296 In the 17th century the 'Herengracht of the Jordaan', as the gorgeous Bloemgracht was called, was home to paint and sugar factories, and boasted a large number of fine gabled houses. A striking example is **De Drie Hendricken** (Bloemgracht 87-91), built in a sober Renaissance style. The gable stones above the ground floor depict a townsman, a farmer and a seafarer. Many artists also lived on Bloemgracht, including Jurriaen Andriessen, whose work is displayed in the Rijksmuseum.

### HOUSEBOAT MUSEUM — MUSEUM

Map p296 (☎427 07 50; www.houseboatmuseum.nl; Prinsengracht, opposite 296; adult/child under 152cm €3.50/2.75; ⏰11am-5pm Tue-Sun Mar-Oct, 11am-5pm Fri-Sun Nov-Feb, closed most of Jan) This quirky museum, a 23m-long sailing barge from 1914, offers a good sense of how *gezellig* (convivial, cosy) life can be on the water. The actual displays are minimal, but you can watch a slide show of houseboats (some pretty and some ghastly), and inspect the sleeping, living, cooking and dining quarters with all mod cons. In case you were wondering, houseboat toilets used to drain directly into the canals, but now most have sewerage hook-ups.

### JOHNNY JORDAANPLEIN — SQUARE

Map p296 (cnr Prinsengracht & Elandsgracht) This shady little square is named for Johnny Jordaan (a pseudonym), a popular musician in the mid-1900s who sang the romantic music known as *levenslied,* or tears-in-your-beer-style ballads. The colourfully painted hut – a municipal transformer station – proudly displays the lyric '*Amsterdam, wat bent je mooi*' (Amsterdam, how beautiful you are) from a song by Johnny, the greatest expression of the Jordaan's ethos since the last riots. Behind the hut you'll find Johnny and members of the Jordaan musical hall of fame, cast in bronze. On Queen's Day, this is where many Jordaanians head to rock out to live music.

### ELECTRIC LADY LAND — MUSEUM

Map p296 (www.electric-lady-land.com; 2e Leliedwarsstraat 5; adult/child under 12 €5/free; ⏰1-6pm Tue-Sat) Even if you didn't eat a space cake before visiting Electric Lady Land – the world's first museum of fluorescent art – you're gonna feel like you have. Grey-ponytailed owner Nick Padalino has his art gallery/shop upstairs, and the glow-in-the-dark 'museum' is in the basement. It's really just a small room with Nick's psychedelic sculpture on one side, and cases of naturally luminescent rocks and man-made glowing objects (money, government ID cards etc) on the other side. Jimi Hendrix, the Beatles' 'Lucy in the Sky with Diamonds' and other trippy tunes play on the stereo while Nick lovingly describes each item in the collection. Check out the mind-blowing info on the fluorescent rabbit, and wow your friends with the fact that the most naturally fluorescent place on earth is…drum roll…New Jersey, USA (lots of incandescent minerals in the ground there). Allow a good hour to visit.

**FREE STEDELIJK MUSEUM BUREAU AMSTERDAM** MUSEUM
Map p296 (Municipal Museum Office; ☎422 04 71; www.smba.nl; Rozenstraat 59; ⊙11am-5pm Tue-Sun) Don't blink or you might walk right past this unobtrusive outpost, a 'project space' of the leading Stedelijk Museum; it's in a one-time clothing workshop on a very quiet block. Exhibits here – from painting and sculpture to new media and installation pieces – present contemporary artists whose work reflects Amsterdam culture. Shows change about every two weeks; ring to make sure it's not closed while exhibitions are being changed.

**HAARLEMMERPOORT** GATE
Map p294 (Haarlem Gate; Haarlemmerplein) Once a defensive gateway to the city, the Haarlemmerpoort marked the start of the busy route to Haarlem, which was a major trading route. The structure was finished just in time for King William II's staged entry for his 1840 coronation, hence its little-known official name of Willemspoort (see the plaque inside). Traffic no longer runs through the gate since a bypass was built over the Westerkanaal. Today this grand archway is home to apartments with an alluring view of the canal and Westerpark beyond.

## The West

The sights here are closer than you think! (About a 20-minute walk from Centraal Station, in fact.)

**WESTERGASFABRIEK** CULTURAL BUILDING
Map p298 (☎586 07 10; www.westergasfabriek.nl; Haarlemmerweg 8-10) A stone's throw northwest of the Jordaan, this late-19th century Dutch Renaissance complex was the city gasworks until it was all but abandoned in the 1960s, with its soil contaminated. The *fabriek* has re-emerged, thankfully, as a cultural and recreational park, with lush lawns, a long pool suitable for wading, sports facilities and even child care. The aesthetic around public green space **Westerpark** (which lends the surrounding neighbourhood its name) goes from urban plan to reedy wilderness, with marshes and shallow waterfalls.

Inside the main buildings you'll find cinemas, cafes, restaurants, nightspots and creative office spaces. Watch for events in the Westergasterras (p142), a slick, post-industrial party venue.

If you're coming by public transport, take tram 10 to the end of the line.

**MUSEUM HET SCHIP** ARCHITECTURE, MUSEUM
Map p298 (☎418 28 85; www.hetschip.nl; Spaarndammerplantsoen 140; admission €7.50; ⊙1-5pm Wed-Fri, 11am-5pm Sat & Sun) This remarkable housing project (1920) is a flagship of the Amsterdam School of architecture. The triangular block, loosely resembling a ship, was designed by Michel de Klerk for railway employees. The rocketlike tower has no purpose apart from linking the wings of the complex.

It's located just north of Westerpark over the train tracks. Bus 22 ends its route right at the front door.

# EATING

The restaurants here exude the conviviality that has long been a hallmark of the Jordaan. The Haarlemmerstraat and Haarlemmerdijk are trendy, but many people still gravitate to the eateries along Westerstraat. You may want to lose your way in the narrow backstreets, where the next hot spot may be opening up. Craving Italian? The Jordaan is chock full of some of the city's best pasta, pizza and *la dolce vita* (the good life).

## Jordaan

**TOP CHOICE BALTHAZAR'S KEUKEN** FRENCH, MEDITERRANEAN €€
Map p296 (☎420 21 14; Elandsgracht 108; 3-course menu €29; ⊙dinner Wed-Fri) This is

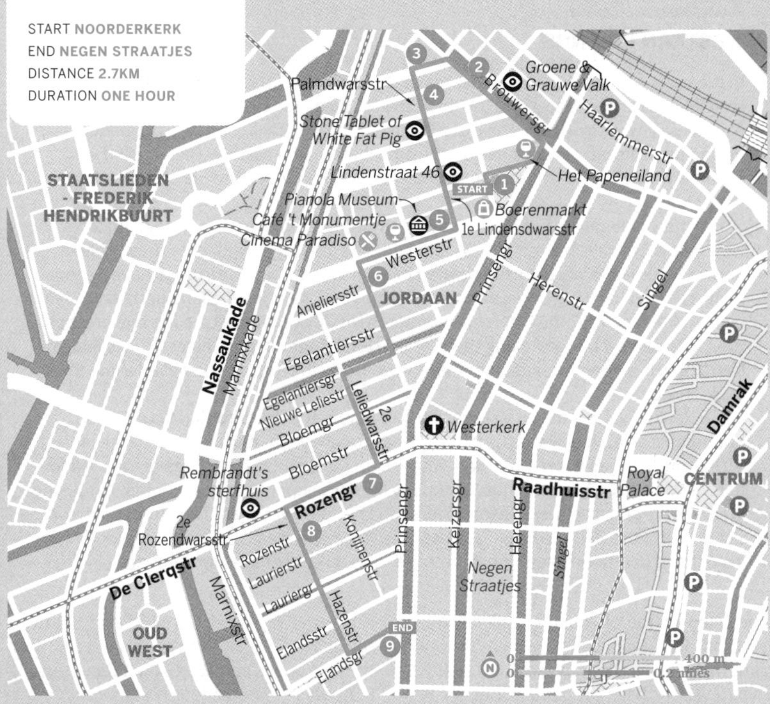


Neighbourhood Walk

## Lost in the Jordaan

Begin at the 1 **Noorderkerk**, site of Amsterdam's most attractive *boerenmarkt*. The impressive, cross-shaped church was revolutionary at the time, providing the working-class congregation of the Jordaan with alter views from four transepts.

Make your way north to 2 **Brouwersgracht**. Fall into a chair at Het Papeneiland and order a coffee. As you move west along Brouwersgracht, you'll spy the old warehouses Groene & Grauwe Valk (Green & Grey Falcon). At the second drawbridge, turn left into Palmgracht, and look out for the red door to the 3 **Rapenhofje** (at 28-38). This little courtyard was home to one of Amsterdam's oldest almshouses (1648).

South along 4 **Palmdwarsstraat** you'll pass tiny food shops frequented by the locals. Note the stone tablet of the 'white fat pig' over the butcher/deli at 2e Goudsbloemdwarsstraat 26. Soon you'll reach 5 **Westerstraat**, a main drag of the Jordaan, with the Pianola Museum and alluring places for a bite or drink, including Café 't Monumentje and Cinema Paradiso. At the 2e Anjeliersdwarsstraat, turn left to enter what locals call the 6 **'garden quarter'** of ivy-clad lanes and diminutive squares.

On busy 7 **Rozengracht**, speciality shops sell silk pillows and beaded saris, among other wares.Rembrandt's *sterfhuis* (death house) is at 184, where the master painter died in 1669 (look upwards for a plaque marking the spot, atop the ground-floor Japanese gallery). The part of the Jordaan on 8 **2e Rozendwarsstraat** and around is a mad jumble of styles, and though the winch beams may appear decorative, they still see plenty of active duty. Secondhand stores, fancy boutiques and art shops pop up along the way.

The 9 **Johnny Jordaanplein** is dedicated to the local hero and singer of schmaltzy tunes such as 'Bij ons in de Jordaan' (We in the Jordaan). There are bronze busts of Johnny and his band, but the real star here is the colourful utility hut splashed with nostalgic lyrics.

WORTH A DETOUR

## WESTERN ISLANDS

In the early 17th century, the wharves and warehouses of the **Western Islands** (Westelijke Eilanden; Map p298), north of the Jordaan, were abuzz with activity . The Golden Age was taking off, the Dutch still dominated the sea trade, and money flowed into this old harbour like beer from a barrel. The wealthy Bicker brothers, both mayors of Amsterdam, even built their own Bickerseiland here to cater for their ships.

Few tourists make it out here today, partly because the district is shielded from view by the railway line, but it's a wonderful area to explore, with cute drawbridges and handsome old warehouses nestled in quiet lanes. Many addresses have been converted to charming homes and artists studios. The Prinseneiland and Realeneiland (named after the 17th-century merchant Reynier Reael) are the two prettiest isles. The narrow bridge linking them, the **Drieharingenbrug** (Three Herrings Bridge; Map p298), is a quaint replacement for the pontoon that used to be pulled aside to let ships through.

On Realeneiland's eastern shore, be sure to visit the **Zandhoek** (Map p298), a photogenic stretch of waterfront. It's now a modern yacht harbour, but back in the 17th century it was a 'sand market', where ships would purchase bags of the stuff for ballast. Many a Dutch East India Company (VOC) skipper lived hereabouts, carousing in local bars and enjoying the view over the IJ between voyages. The street south of Zandhoek is the Galgenstraat (Gallows St), which on a clear day afforded a look at the executions in Amsterdam-Noord. In those days it was called entertainment.



consistently one of Amsterdam's top-rated restaurants, but don't expect a wide-ranging menu. The byword is basically 'whatever we have on hand' – but it's usually absolutely delectable. Plus, there's a modern-rustic look and attentive service. Reservations recommended.

### TOP CHOICE JAPANESE PANCAKE WORLD — JAPANESE €€

Map p294 (320 44 47; www.japanesepancakeworld.com; 2e Egelantiersdwarsstraat 24a; mains €8-20; lunch & dinner) This little restaurant has a worthy global mission: to spread the addictive taste of Japanese pancakes outside Japan. At the continent's only shop specialising in *okonomiyaki* (literally 'cook as you like'), you'll get your pancakes in a hot iron dish with your choice of fillings (meat, seafood, vegies, cheese) topped with flakes of dried fish. There are barely two dozen seats: we love to perch at the back counter and watch the chef work his magic. Reservations recommended.

### TOP CHOICE LA OLIVA — SPANISH €€

Map p294 (www.laoliva.nl, in Dutch; Egelantierstraat 122-124; mains €21-26; lunch Thu-Sun, dinner nightly) The Jordaan's hottest new restaurant offers its most visually stunning food, inspired by the Basque region. Stroll by and you can see the colourful *pintxos* (a version of tapas with a northern Spanish/southern French twist) skewered with wooden sticks and stacked on the gleaming bar, where hungry foodies sip cava (Spanish sparkling wine) and gaze lustfully at the stuffed figs, mushroom Manchego tartlets, and *Pata Negra* ham with pear. (Yes, there are perfectly lovely meat and fish mains, but it's the *pintxos* that everyone's raving about.) In summer, the party spills out into the street like an impromptu dinner among friends.

### HOSTARIA — ITALIAN €€

Map p294 (420 21 14; 2e Egelantiersdwarsstraat 9; mains €13-26; dinner Tue-Sun) On a street bursting with excellent Italian food – Tuscan classics, fresh stuffed pastas, sublime yet simple desserts – this is our favourite. We witnessed a diner so thrilled with her ravioli that she asked to kiss the chef; he graciously complied.

### SMALL WORLD CATERING — INTERNATIONAL, SANDWICHES €

Map p294 (www.smallworldcatering.nl; Binnen Oranjestraat 14; mains €6-9; 10:30am-8pm Tue-Sat, noon-8pm Sun; ) It's no secret that the carrot cake here has been known to spawn serious addictions, leading to impulsive bike rides across town to score a fix before closing time. If the cake isn't reason enough to come, the friendly international staff serves up daily specials like Aussie beef pie and ricotta cannelloni, along with possibly the most killer sandwiches in town. (To make your choice less agonising, the owner confessed his fave remains the pesto melt with grilled vegies and taleggio.)

### WINKEL CAFE €

Map p294 (www.winkel43.nl; Noordermarkt 43; mains €4-14; ⊙breakfast, lunch & dinner; ) This sprawling, indoor-outdoor space is great for people-watching, popular for coffees and small meals, and out-of-the-park for its tall, cakey apple pie. On market days (Monday and Saturday) there's almost always a queue out the door.

### TOSCANINI ITALIAN €€

Map p294 (☎623 28 13; Lindengracht 75; mains €13-23, 6-course menu €45; ⊙dinner Mon-Sat) It's easy to see why locals clamour for simple, classy Toscanini: it bakes its own bread, rolls its own pasta and pours a lengthy list of Italian wines. The ever-changing dishes that hit the white tablecloths might include seared beef with tarragon or lamb shoulder stewed with white wine and rosemary. The desserts, such as salt caramel pannacotta, promise to undo even the fiercest dietary resolves. Book ahead; even on weeknights it can be packed.

### BRASSERIE BLAZER FRENCH €€

Map p296 (www.brasserieblazer.nl; Lijnbaansgracht 190;€13-15; ⊙lunch & dinner, closed Tue) Amsterdam's simplest French brasserie is also its most effortlessly sexy. Fancy it's not, but it gets bohemian street cred for its winning combo of well-priced classic dishes – including *confit de canard* (preserved duck), and rib eye Béarnaise – outgoing staff, and a certain *je ne sais quoi*.

### FESTINA LENTE CAFE €

Map p296 (www.cafefestinalente.nl, in Dutch; Looiersgracht 40b; sandwiches €3-6, small plates €4-10; ⊙noon-1am Sun & Mon, 10.30am-1am Tue-Thu, 10.30am-3am Fri & Sat; ) This canalside neighbourhood hang-out is typical Jordaan *gezelligheid* (conviviality/cosiness), packed with regulars playing board games, reading poetry and snacking on small-portion Mediterranean dishes and big sandwiches.

### BURGER'S PATIO MEDITERRANEAN €€

Map p294 (www.burgerspatio.nl; 2e Tuindwarsstraat 12; mains €14-23; ⊙dinner) Despite its name, this is no hamburger joint. Rather, an air of easy-going cool permeates the modern interior, and the namesake patio is a fun hideout. A seasonally changing menu features free-range meats and poultry, creative vegie dishes and daily pasta specials, with touches like crudités, aioli and tapenade that make the prices seem more reasonable than they already are.

### MOEDERS TRADITIONAL DUTCH €€

Map p296 (☎626 79 57; www.moeders.com; Rozengracht 251; mains €15-19, 3-course menus €25-30; ⊙5pm-midnight Mon-Fri; noon-midnight Sat & Sun; ) Mum's the word at 'Mothers'. When this friendly place opened over 20 years ago, staff asked customers to bring their own plates and photos of their mums as donations, and the result is still a delightful hotchpotch. So is the food, including pumpkin *stamppot* (mashed pot with potatoes and smoked sausage), seafood, Moroccan dishes and a vegetarian frittata. Book ahead.



## JORDAAN GENTRIFICATION

The Jordaan of the late 19th century was a densely populated district, with large families in tiny, run-down homes living in deplorable conditions. In the 1960s and '70s the Jordaan lost much of its working-class character as residents moved to more spacious digs in the suburbs. In came the students, artists and well-heeled professionals which caused some growing pains.

It's been said that the Jordaan is no longer the *volksbuurt* (a district for the common people) it once was. But this talk is exaggerated. If you look at the city's figures you'll see that the overwhelming majority of Jordaan residents have quite average incomes. Wealthy people have also moved in, but it's a limited group. In other parts of the city there are more tourist attractions, but it's the little things that are nice here – the lanes, the old facades, the funny little shops. Visitors like all of this and think it's *gezellig*. The Jordaan is certainly not spectacular, but it has charm. Meanwhile, rents keep climbing...

### LITTLE ITALY

The area on and around Eglantier-dwarstraat and Angeliersdwarstraat is packed with so many Italian restaurants, it should be called Little Italy, even though it's not (well, as far as we know). Here are just two of our favourites:

- ➡ Hostaria (p136)
- ➡ Koevoet (p138)

**DIVAN** TURKISH €€

Map p296 (☎626 82 39; Elandsgracht 14; mains €14-19; ⏰dinner, closed Mon) In a town where 'Turkish' usually means 'takeaway' (or 'pizza'), Divan offers an authentic and enjoyable sit-down alternative. The meze combo starter provides 10 assorted dips, skewers and salads. We loved the *ali nazik* (minced lamb with aubergines in yoghurt garlic sauce) and the gracious, sweet service.

**JORDINO** BAKERY, SWEETS €

Map p294 (☎420 32 35; Haarlemmerdijk 25; ice cream 1 scoop €1.25; ⏰1-7pm Sun & Mon, 10am-7pm Tue-Sat) It's the best of both worlds: Jordino makes rich chocolates and velvety ice cream, and combines the two by scooping the ice cream atop cones dipped in the house's chocolate or caramel. Having a hard time choosing? Splurge on a double scoop of hazelnut and pistachio.

**DE PIZZA BAKKERS** ITALIAN €

Map p294 (www.depizzabakkers.nl, in Dutch; Haarlemmerdijk 128; mains €7-13; ⏰5-10pm Sun-Thu, 5-11pm Fri, noon-11pm Sat) 'Pizza and Prosecco' is the motto at this arty eatery, which means you sip the bubbly latter while waiting for the wood-oven-fired former. Generous toppings range from pancetta and mascarpone to ham and truffle sauce, though we're partial to the vegetarian with taleggio, aubergine and courgette. Look for locations in the Plantage and near Vondelpark, but be sure to take your ATM or credit card; strangely, it doesn't accept cash.

**BORDEWIJK** FRENCH, ITALIAN €€€

Map p294 (☎624 38 99; www.bordewijk.nl; Noordermarkt 7; mains €20-32, set menus €39-57; ⏰dinner Tue-Sat) Other places have grander reputations, but some critics dub Bordewijk the king of the hill. The interior is so minimal that there's little to do but appreciate the spectacular French/Italian cooking. The chefs are not afraid to take risks and the skilled staff take your wishes with aplomb. Book ahead on weekends.

**KOEVOET** ITALIAN €€

Map p294 (☎624 08 46; Lindenstraat 17; mains €12-23; ⏰dinner Tue-Sun 🖉) The congenial Italian owners of Koevoet took over a former cafe on a quiet side street, left the *gezellig* decor untouched and started cooking up their home-country staples. Don't miss its signature, drinkable dessert, *sgroppino limone* (€7): sorbet, vodka and prosecco whisked at your table and poured into a champagne flute.

**SEMHAR** ETHIOPIAN €€

Map p296 (www.semhar.nl, in Dutch; Marnixstraat 259-261; mains €11-17; ⏰4-10pm Tue-Sun) Owner Yohannes gives his customers a warm welcome, and is a fanatic about the quality of his *injera* bread (like a thick, spongy pancake) – all the better to sop up richly spiced stews and vegetable combos. Feel free to skip the menu and just ask for a mixed platter.

**CINEMA PARADISO** ITALIAN €€

Map p294 (Westerstraat 184-186; mains €11-18; ⏰dinner Wed-Sun) Action! Located in a former movie theatre, this spirited Italian restaurant still pays homage to its cinematic roots with black and white movie stills, the visages of iconic directors on the walls, and plenty of glitterati to appreciate them. Direct yourself to a booth or table near the open kitchen and enjoy pastas, pizzas, lots of antipasti and stargazing. Go for cocktails and drink in the atmosphere.

**PAZZI** PIZZA €

Map p296 (www.pazzislowfood.nl, in Dutch; Looiersdwarsstraat 4; pizzas €7-14, panini €4-6; ⏰breakfast, lunch & dinner daily, dinner only Sun) The moniker 'Italian slow food' doesn't seem to be simply hype here. Seating consists of a single high banquette, and there's one wood-burning oven. Each pizza – dripping with fresh buffalo mozzarella on a perfectly charred crust – is made with serious care. (Which gives you plenty of time to sip your Peroni and chat with your seatmates). A good spot to grab a fresh lunch panini, too.

**DUENDE** TAPAS €

Map p294 (www.cafe-duende.nl, in Dutch; Lindengracht 62; tapas €4-6; dinner) This long-running tapas cafe is the kind of place that ex-Jordaanese return to when visiting the city. The casual nightlife buzz in the evenings is enlivened by sultry flamenco performances on many Saturday nights and lessons during the week.

**DE VLIEGENDE SCHOTEL** VEGETARIAN €

Map p296 (Nieuwe Leliestraat 162-168; mains €11-14; 4pm-10:45pm) Service can be spotty at the 'Flying Saucer', but if you're prepared to take your time in the summer-camp-chic dining room, you'll enjoy some of the city's favourite vegie gratins, lasagnes and Indian-inflected meals.

**RIAZ** SURINAMESE, INDIAN €

Map p296 (www.riaz.nl, in Dutch; Bilderdijkstraat 193; mains €6-12; 11.30am-9pm, closed Sat) No-frills Riaz cooks up excellent rotis and an addictive, spicy peanut soup, as well as several Indian vegie dishes (the *saag*, aka spinach, earns special commendation). Note that the restaurant does not serve alcohol.

**BROODJE MOKUM** SANDWICHES €

Map p296 (623 19 66; Rozengracht 26; sandwiches from €2; 6.30am-6pm Mon-Fri, 8am-6pm Sat) This humble vintage lunchroom serves great sandwiches – just point and they'll tell you the price. More so than at most other *broodje* shops, there's room to sit down and spread out on one of the many window-facing seats.

**MANZANO** SPANISH €€

Map p296 (www.manzano.nl; Rozengracht 106; tapas €3-12, mains €15-21; dinner nightly, lunch Fri-Sun) The Dutch Golden Age remains palpable in this historic restaurant – never mind that the cuisine is Spanish. In a wood-beamed, enchanting 1648 building (once the private club for Bols employees who worked across the street), well-dressed folks sip on *vinos blancos* while nibbling on paella and a wide selection of tapas and regional specialties. Take your Catalan crème and Spanish coffee in the charming courtyard after dinner.

**DE BOLHOED** VEGETARIAN €€

Map p294 (626 18 03; Prinsengracht 60-62; mains €13-15, 3-course menu €22; lunch & dinner) The interior here is a nice setting to tuck into enormous, organic Mexican-, Asian- and Italian-inspired dishes; in warm weather, there's a verdant little canalside terrace. Remember to leave some room for the banana-cream pie. Vegetarians swear by it.

## The West

Those in the mood for nouveau, scenester eats will strike it rich around Westerpark.

TOP CHOICE **MARIUS** INTERNATIONAL €€

Map p298 (422 78 80; Barentszstraat 243; mains €13-28, set menu €45; dinner Tue-Sat) Foodies swoon over pocket-sized Marius, which is tucked in amid artists studios in the Western Islands. Chef Kees, an alumnus of California's Chez Panisse, shops daily at local markets, then creates his menu from what he finds. The result might be grilled prawns with fava bean purée, or beef rib with polenta and ratatouille. You can also choose from a few house-speciality standbys, such as bouillabaisse.

**RESTAURANT PS** INTERNATIONAL €€

Map p298 (421 52 18; www.restaurantps.nl; Planciusstraat 49; mains €14-19, 3-course menu €30; dinner Tue-Sat) Run by an unlikely yet vastly experienced pair – an English chef and a Colombian maître d' – this restaurant in the Western Islands has an army of devoted fans. You can expect reasonable prices, an excellent wine menu and attentive service, plus an artsy interior with mosaics of Venetian glass. The set meals change weekly and feature seasonal ingredients.

**RAÏNARAÏ** MEDITERRANEAN €€

Map p298 (486 71 09; Polonceaukade 40; 4-course menu €38; 11am-1am Tue-Sun) The menu at this Algerian restaurant might offer seared salmon on chickpea-pumpkin-spiced couscous, or grilled sardines with asparagus, broad beans and tomatoes. The menu changes all the time, but rest assured it usually wows the palate. The old industrial building, decked out with Arabian-style cushions and copper fixtures, is in the Westergasfabriek.

# DRINKING & NIGHTLIFE

## Jordaan

Visitors who seek a typical cafe experience 'with the locals' will love the Jordaan, a chummy district still touted as the Amsterdam of yore. Of course, the locals may bag a remote table away from curious foreigners, but in this jolly part of town it's just as likely they'll toast your good health and break out in song (and invite you to join in, too).

**TOP CHOICE CAFÉ 'T SMALLE** BROWN CAFE

Map p294 (www.t-smalle.nl, in Dutch; Egelantiersgracht 12) It's hard to pick favourites among the scores of charming *bruin cafés*, but we'll admit it: this is one of our not-so-secret faves. Take your boat and dock right on 't Smalle's pretty stone terrace – there's hardly a more convivial setting in the daytime or a more romantic one at night. It's equally charming inside, dating back to 1786 as a *jenever* (Dutch gin) distillery and tasting house, and restored during the 1970s with antique porcelain beer pumps and lead-framed windows. It's so gorgeous, so authentic and so Dutch *gezellig* that there's a reproduction of it in Japan.

**TOP CHOICE DE PIEPER** BROWN CAFE

Map p296 (Prinsengracht 424) Considered by some customers to be the king of the brown cafes, De Pieper is small, unassuming and unmistakably old (1665). The interior features stained-glass windows, fresh sand on the floors, antique Delft beer mugs hanging from the bar and a working Belgian beer pump (1875). It's a friendly, sweet place for sipping a late-night Wieckse Witte as you marvel at the lovable claustrophobia of this low-ceilinged bar (after all, people were shorter back in the 17th century – even the famously tall Dutch).

**FINCH** DESIGNER BAR

Map p294 (☎626 24 61; Noordermarkt 5) This funkalicious bar with its retro decor (deliberately mismatched yet somehow harmonious) is just the spot to hang out and knock back a few beers after a visit to the market. It's known for an arty-designy clientele and is always packed on the weekends.

**LOCAL KNOWLEDGE**

### DRINK LIKE A JORDAANIAN

While we're not promoting drinking to excess, there's a certain hard-drinking, hard-living spirit left over from the Jordaan's working-class days – imagine a neigbourhood bursting with 80,000 people compared to today's 20,000 – when the *bruin cafés* functioned as a refuge from the slings and arrows of workaday life. Some of our favourites:

- De Reiger (p141)
- Café 't Monumentje (p141)
- Café de Jordaan (p142)

**CAFÉ P 96** BROWN CAFE

Map p294 (www.p96.nl, in Dutch; Prinsengracht 96; ⏲8pm-3am Mon-Thu, 8pm-4am Fri, 11am-4am Sat, 11am-3am Sun) If you don't want the night to end, P *96* is an amiable spot to land. When most other cafes in the Jordaan shut down for the night, this is where everyone ends up, rehashing their evening, striking up conversations with strangers and grinning into their beers. In summertime, head to the terrace, which is on an actual houseboat – perfect for a photo op.

**CAFÉ DE KOE** BAR

Map p296 (www.cafedekoe.nl, in Dutch; Marnixstraat 381) 'The Cow' is loved for its homey *gezellig* atmosphere, fun pop quizzes, darts tournaments, good (cheap) restaurant and free performances by local rock bands. A down-to-earth neighbourhood crowd swills beers upstairs by the funky cow mosaic, while diners below gather around worn wooden tables and order comfort food. Come for Sunday movie nights, or just to play board games.

**CAFÉ SOUNDGARDEN** BAR

Map p296 (www.cafesoundgarden.nl; Marnixstraat 164-166) In this grungy dive bar, the 'Old Masters' are the Ramones and Black Sabbath rather than Rembrandt and Vermeer. Somehow a handful of pool tables, 1980s pinball machines, unkempt DJs and lovably surly bartenders all add up to an ineffable magic that lures people from all over the world. Bands occasionally make an appearance and the waterfront terrace scene is more like an impromptu party in someone's backyard. All walks of life swig here: the common denominator isn't fashion, age or politics, it's a diehard love of rock and roll.

### CAFÉ 'T MONUMENTJE
BROWN CAFE

Map p294 (624 35 41; Westerstraat 120) This slightly scruffy yet likable cafe with sand on the floor is always heaving with local barflies. It's a good spot for a beer and a snack after shopping at the Westermarkt.

### DE PRINS
BROWN CAFE

Map p294 (624 93 82; www.deprins.nl; Prinsengracht 124) Close to the Anne Frank Huis, this pleasant, popular brown cafe prepares good lunchtime sandwiches, a terrific blue-cheese fondue at night, and international dishes like vegetarian wraps to eat on the sunny terrace or inside at the friendly bar.

### DE BLAFFENDE VIS
BROWN CAFE

Map p294 (625 17 21; Westerstraat 118) Home to cute lawyers and real estate agents who chill out after work at this affable corner, the 'Barking Fish' is Westerstraat's unofficial people-watching epicentre. It seems the entire world walks or cycles past this place, and the tall windows that open onto the pavement tables ensure that the outside chatter flows into the interior. It dishes up killer *bitterballen* (small meat croquettes) made with Oma's (Grandma's) recipe.

### VESPER BAR
DESIGNER BAR

Map p294 (420 45 92; www.vesperbar.nl; Vinkenstraat 57; 8pm-1am Tue-Thu, to 3am Fri & Sat) Rather than feeling totally out of place in the Jordaan, this luxe cocktail bar only gains a certain ineffable mystique by its location on a low-key stretch of Jordaanian shops and businesses. The cocktails will coax out your inner James Bond – or Vesper Lynd.

### DE REIGER
BROWN CAFE

Map p294 (624 74 26; Nieuwe Leliestraat 34) Assiduously local but very atmospheric, this cafe has a quiet front bar and a noisy, more spacious dining section at the back serving a short menu (including steaks, and duck with peppercorns).

### DE TUIN
BROWN CAFE

Map p294 (624 45 59; 2e Tuindwarsstraat 13) Always a good place to start the evening – join the youngish clientele enjoying the wide selection of Belgian beers, good food and funky soul music.

### DE TWEE ZWAANTJES
BROWN CAFE

Map p294 (www.detweezwaantjes.nl; Prinsengracht 114; 3pm-1am Sun-Thu, to 3am Fri & Sat) The small, authentic 'Two Swans' is at its hilarious best on weekend nights, when you can join some 100 people belting out torch songs and pop standards. It's a typically Dutch experience that's totally unforgettable. The fact that singers are often fuelled by liquid-courage only adds to the spirited fun. Feeling bold? Ask for the microphone.

### HET PAPENEILAND
BROWN CAFE

Map p294 (www.papeneiland.nl, in Dutch; Prinsengracht 2) You won't be the only tourist visiting this cafe, but that doesn't make it any less worthwhile. It's a 1642 gem with Delft-blue tiles and a central stove. The name, 'Papists' Island', goes back to the Reformation, when there was a clandestine Catholic church on the north side of the canal. By some accounts you got there via a secret tunnel from the top of the stairs.

### CAFÉ DE LAURIERBOOM
BROWN CAFE, CHESS CAFE

Map p296 (www.laurierboom.nl, in Dutch; Laurierstraat 76) The hub of the Jordaan chess circuit is one of its oldest cafes, still bearing a stone tablet labelled *tapperij en slijterij* (ask the bartender to explain what this is). From 3pm the local masters test their wits over a drink or three.

### CAFÉ THIJSSEN
CAFE

Map p294 (623 89 94; Brouwersgracht 107) The glowing umber, art deco–inspired interior with stained-glass windows and big tables is a crowd-puller. It's busy on weekends with groups of neo-Jordaanese yuppies meeting up for a late brunch and staying on until dinner.

### LA TERTULIA
COFFEESHOP

Map p296 (www.coffeeshopamsterdam.com; Prinsengracht 312; 11am-7pm Tue-Sat) A backpackers' favourite, this mother-and-daughter-run coffeeshop has a greenhouse feel. You can sit outside by the Van Gogh-inspired murals, play some board games, or take in those Jurassic-sized crystals by the counter.

### DE TRUT
LESBIAN CLUB

Map p296 (612 35 24; www.trutfonds.nl; Bilderdijkstraat 165e; 11pm-4am Sun) Just west of the Jordaan, this Sunday night club is a lesbian institution held in the basement of a former squat. Its name means 'the tart' and it comes with an attitude; arrive well before 11pm (the space only fits 220 people), and know that heteros are definitely not welcome.

**SANEMENTERENG** COFFEESHOP

Map p296 (624 19 07; 2e Laurierdwarsstraat 44; hours vary) Way back when, Amsterdam coffeeshops were merely regular shops that also sold marijuana alongside their other wares. Bursting to the brim with secondhand everything (part junk, part antique), the dusty old Sanementereng is one of the last of these. Don't expect friendly service but do come for the stillness and to experience an old-school original.

**G-SPOT** DESIGNER BAR

Map p296 (Prinsengracht 422; 11am-1am) This contemporary minimalist bar-restaurant, with its bright light-filled interior, couldn't be more different from De Pieper, its brown-cafe neighbour, but it's equally as appealing. While the interior is stylish, the canalside terrace with pretty views will keep you outside. It's sleek without being overly slick, but with an old canal house ambience. The food is fresh and straightforward, and the service is polished and friendly.

**CAFÉ DE JORDAAN** BAR

Map p296 (627 58 63; Elandsgracht 45) The epitome of an old-style Jordaan cafe, this place is where the original Jordaanese (ie not the current students, artists and professionals) would sing oompah ballads with drunken abandon. After midnight, merry and drunk crooners link arms and sing along to classic Dutch tunes in this quintessentially local haunt. The lyrics playing on the TV screens are a hoot and grins are a guarantee. Earlier in the evening it's less vocal, and a more relaxed spot for a *biertje* (glass of beer).

**DI'VINO WIJNBAR** WINE BAR

Map p294 (www.wijnbardivino.nl; Boomstraat 41a; 6pm-midnight Mon-Fri, 3pm-1am Sat, 3-9pm Sun) This wine bar serves only quality Italian wines (glasses €4 to €6, bottles €19 to €55), plus divine charcuterie and cheese plates (€6.50 to €17.50). The polished wood bar, flickering candles and lofty corner windows beckon you in – though the snuggle-into-me blankets strewn about the tables and chairs outside are equally inviting.

**THERMOS DAY SAUNA** GAY SAUNA

Map p296 (www.thermos.nl; Raamstraat 33; under 26yr/26yr & over €10/19; noon-8pm) Thermos is a sprawling, popular place for sexual contacts, with porn movies, private (or not so private) darkrooms, a roof deck, a hair salon and a restaurant.

**SAAREIN** LESBIAN CAFE

Map p296 (Elandsstraat 119; Tue-Sun) This onetime feminist stronghold is still a meeting place for lesbians, although these days gay men are welcome too. The cafe dates from the 1600s and vestiges remain. There's a small menu with tapas, soups and specials.

## The West

It's off the tourist's radar, but that doesn't mean it's not cool: in fact, some of our favourite places to socialise are in the West. Expect to see artsy, alternative types attracted to the cultural amenities.

TOP CHOICE **WESTERGASTERRAS** BAR, CAFE

Map p298 (www.westergasterras.nl, in Dutch; Klönneplein 4) This cool, post-industrial, indoor-outdoor cafe next to the 1903 Gasometer (which now hosts cultural events and club nights) is screamingly popular every day of the week. Locals flock to the massive outdoor terrace (and one coveted comfy swing) on sunny afternoons.

**JET LOUNGE** BAR, CLUB

Map p298) www.jetlounge.nl; Pazzanistraat 1) A cool, but not too cool, rock and roll hangout where bartenders sling drinks with a vengeance. Tired of Dutch folk music or techno? Head here for the antidote.

**MEDIA CAFÉ** BAR, RESTAURANT

(Map p298; 486 21 23; Pazzanistraat 1) Media types (this is a TV production studio by day) and glam professionals naturally congregate to this airy, dramatic space that's a perfect place to grab drinks and a light meal before a film at Het Ketelhuis, which is next door.

# ENTERTAINMENT

TOP CHOICE **MOVIES** CINEMA, CAFE

Map p294 (638 60 16; www.themovies.nl, in Dutch; Haarlemmerdijk 161) This *gezellig* art deco cinema (the oldest in Amsterdam, dating from 1912) features indie films alongside mainstream flicks. From Monday to Thursday you can treat yourself to a meal in the restaurant (a two- or three-course 'dinner and movie ticket' goes for €29/31) or grab a premovie tipple at its equally inviting cafe-bar.

TOP CHOICE **DE NIEUWE ANITA** LIVE MUSIC, CAFE

Map p296 (☎415 35 12; www.denieuweanita.nl, in Dutch; Frederik Hendrikstraat 111) Living-room venue expanded for noise rockers, with a great cafe.

TOP CHOICE **WESTERGASFABRIEK** CULTURAL BUILDING, CAFE

Map p298 (☎586 07 10; www.westergasfabriek.nl; Haarlemmerweg 8-10) This cultural complex has it all: festivals, theatre, music, and a fantastic restaurant and bar with one of the most soothing terraces in town.

**HET KETELHUIS** CINEMA, CAFE

Map p298 (☎684 00 90; www.ketelhuis.nl, in Dutch; Westergasfabriek, Haarlemmerweg 8-10) In the old gasworks, the three screening rooms have a chic post-industrial vibe and comfy seats; it's a great platform for art-house films. It also has a cosy cafe.

**KORSAKOFF** LIVE MUSIC, BAR

Map p296 (☎625 78 54; www.korsakoffamsterdam.nl; Lijnbaansgracht 161; ⊙from 10pm) It's dark. It's a little dirty. And the punk rock chick in the corner is wearing an outfit you haven't seen since Kurt Cobain was alive. Welcome to the heavy metal/punk/industrial heartbeat of the Jordaan, a fun spot since the 1980s for anyone who likes to punk out every now and then. Two levels of dancing, a diverse crowd, a pole if you're feeling saucy, and a video screen projecting everything from '90s grunge to '70s new wave to techno, depending on the night.

**MALOE MELO** LIVE MUSIC, BAR

Map p296 (☎420 45 92; www.maloemelo.com; Lijnbaansgracht 163) This is the free-wheeling, fun-loving altar of Amsterdam's tiny blues scene, just a few blocks from Leidseplein. Music ranges from garage and Irish punk to Texas blues and rockabilly.

**FILMHUIS CAVIA** CINEMA

Map p298 (www.filmhuiscavia.nl, in Dutch; Van Hallstraat 52) If it's cult, queer, alternative, politically charged or an edgy classic, it will fit in well at the tiny Cavia, housed in a former school and squat.

TOP CHOICE **PACIFIC PARC** BAR, RESTAURANT, LIVE MUSIC

Map p298 (☎420 45 92; Lijnbaansgracht 163) A favourite of the indie-rock set, Pacific Parc is home to live music, DJ sets, and plenty of rock and roll spirit to go along with the stiff drinks and hearty food in a tropical pirate ship setting.

## SHOPPING

Shops here have an artsy, eclectic, homemade feel. The area around Elandsgracht is the place for art, particularly photography, and speciality shops covering everything from hats to cats. Haarlemmerdijk, the extension of Haarlemmerstraat, is exploding with small boutiques – it's shopping central for anyone in the know.

TOP CHOICE **PETSALON** ACCESSORIES

Map p296 (www.petsalon.nl; Hazenstraat 3; ⊙Wed-Sat) In Dutch a *pet* is a cap, and lifelong milliner Ans Wesseling has been designing hats from this shop for over 20 years. Step into his workshop and gasp.

TOP CHOICE **ROCK ARCHIVE** ART

Map p294 (☎423 04 89; www.rockarchive.com; Prinsengracht 110; ⊙Wed-Sat 2pm-6pm, Sat noon-6pm & by appointment) The whites are white and the blacks are black at this professional shop of limited-edition rock 'n' roll prints. Robert Plant, Debbie Harry, Sting and tons of others are all here to be had for small change, in a format of your choice.

TOP CHOICE **KITSCH KITCHEN** KITSCH

Map p296 (☎622 82 61; www.kitschkitchen.nl, in Dutch; Rozengracht 8-12) You want it flowered, frilly, colourful, over the top or just made from plastic? The chances are you'll find it here – it's got handbags, homewares, toys, doll gowns, lamps, Mexican tablecloths, pink plastic chandeliers from India and, of course, bouquets of plastic flowers.

**WONEN 2000** HOME FURNISHINGS

Map p296 (☎521 87 10; www.dekasstoor.nl, in Dutch; Rozengracht 219-221; ⊙Tue-Sat) Begun over a century ago, this home furnishings shop has been at the forefront of Dutch design ever since, boasting names such as Gispen, Edra and Artifoort, and some foreign designers as well. Its affiliates, De Kasstoor (across the street at 202-210) and Wonen 2000 Bed & Bad (next door at 215-217), apply the same design concept to kitchens and lighting, and bed linens and bath, respectively.

### OOK — HOMEWARES

Map p294 (☎427 32 87; Haarlemmerdijk 147) How does Dutch design manage to be so chic and functional all at once? We're at a loss, but this well-priced shop has a zillion bowls, cups, trivets and more to bring some modern (and useful) style into your home.

### MOOOI GALLERY — DESIGN, HOMEWARES

Map p294 (☎528 77 60; www.moooi-gallery.com; Westerstraat 187; ⊙Tue-Sun) Dutch design at its most over-the-top, from the life-sized black horse lamp to the 'blow away vase' (a whimsical twist on the classic Delft vase) and the 'killing of the piggy bank' ceramic pig (with a gold hammer).

### BOUTIQUE PETTICOAT — CLOTHING

Map p294 (Lindengracht 99; ⊙closed Sun) This is our favourite vintage and second-hand shop in the Jordaan, with a posh yet approachable collection of men's and women's fashions.

### HET OUD-HOLLANDSCH SNOEPWINKELTJE — FOOD & DRINK

Map p294 (☎420 73 90; www.snoepwinkeltje.com; Egelantiersdwarsstraat 2) This corner shop is lined with jar after apothecary jar of Dutch penny sweets with flavours from chocolate to coffee, all manner of fruit and the salty Dutch liquorice known as *drop*.

### A SPACE ODDITY — TOYS, GIFTS

(www.spaceoddity.nl; Prinsengracht 204) This geekalicious shop will sate even the most hardcore Star Wars fanatic, DC comics collector or Stanley Kubrick obsessionist. Get lost in the memorabilia, action figures, comics, books, and loads of other pop culture ephemera.

### CELLARRICH — ART

Map p294 (www.cellarrich.nl; Haarlemmerdijk 98) Got accessories fever? Cellarrich is the perfect place to sate your craving for creative wallets, bags, jewellery, and fabric and leather goods.

### DE KUNSTFABRIEK — ART

Map p298 (www.dekunstfabriek.com, in Dutch; Polonceaukade 20; ⊙Tue-Sun) Realistic oil paintings in every genre imaginable rule here. You can also custom order a piece – if you want a portrait of yourself bring in a photo and they'll commission their select artists in China to paint it.

### ENGLISH BOOKSHOP — BOOKS

Map p296 (www.englishbookshop.nl; Lauriergracht 71; ⊙Tue-Sun) This attractive canalside shop has a well-chosen selection of English-language biographies, novels and translations of the works of Dutch writers.

### JOSINE BOKHOVEN — ART, ANTIQUES

Map p296 (www.galeriejosinebokhoven.nl; Prinsengracht 154; ⊙Tue-Sat & 1st Sun of every month) Across the canal from the Anne Frank Huis, this friendly gallery features contemporary art and the work of emerging young artists, including German artist Ralph Fleck.

### BROER & ZUS — CHILDREN'S CLOTHING

Map p296 (www.broerenzus.nl; Rozengracht 94; ⊙Tue-Sat) Cosy little 'Bro & Sis' specialises in Dutch designers and fabrics for kids, from birth to six years. You can get brands like Kidscase, tiny tops emblazoned with slogans like 'Mr Charming' and 'Ladykiller', and wild prints (think Hawaiian shirts).

### OLIVARIA — FOOD

Map p296 (Hazenstraat 2A; ⊙Tue-Sat) Is this the most divine olive oil shop in Holland? Yes. Pretty glass containers provided, or bring your own.

### MECHANISCH SPEELGOED — TOYS

Map p294 (Westerstraat 67; ⊙closed Wed & Sun) This fun shop is crammed full of nostalgic toys, including snow domes, glow lamps, masks, finger puppets and wind-up toys. And who doesn't need a good rubber chicken every once in a while?

### BROWN CLOTHES — CLOTHING

Map p296 (www.brownclothes.eu; Hazenstraat 28; ⊙Wed-Sat) Englishwoman Melanie Brown designs women's clothing with elegant lines and whimsical twists, such as feminine flowing tops with gathered sleeves and figure-hugging coats featuring unexpected, sexy accents. Her studio is adjacent to the shop, so you may see her stitching a new skirt as you contemplate the designs.

### EVA DAMAVE — CLOTHING

Map p296 (☎627 73 25; www.evadamave.nl; 2e Laurierdwarsstraat 51c; ⊙Wed-Sat) Eva Damave creates funky woollen sweaters and zip jackets with her signature front patchwork panels made up of graphic cotton, silk and wool squares. She only produces one-offs or small series, so you're unlikely to see anyone else wearing your woolly knit.

### JEFFERSON HOTEL CLOTHING

Map p296 (www.jeffersonhotel.nl; Elandsgracht 57; ⌚Wed-Sat) Sure to wow men with a discerning taste for edgy designers like Vintage 66 and Girls love DJs, this shop feels like a museum of men's clothing. Can't decide between quality shirts and rare denim? You can mull it over while sipping a cappuccino at the in-store espresso bar.

### CHOCOLATL CHOCOLATE

Map p296 (Hazenstraat 25A; ⌚Wed-Sat) Eclectic chocolate gifts for the serious chocoholic or connoisseur.

### YOUR CUP OF T CLOTHING

Map p294 (www.yourcupoft.com; Westerstraat 77; ⌚10am-2pm Mon, 2-7pm Wed-Fri, noon-6pm Sat) A T-shirt proclaiming 'Pacman has a stiffie' in swirling purple font flanked by a video-game machine will brighten any grey day, right? Sisters Petra and Gitta decorate and print on nearly anything, based on your design. Bring your own bag, underpants, sweatshirt etc (or buy a blank top or sweatshirt in the shop). They donate €0.25 per piece to an orthopaedic training centre in Ghana.

### LAB 13 CLOTHING, ACCESSORIES

Map p294 (Haarlemmerplein 13) Want a shop where soft T-shirts, handmade bags and jewellery, casual cotton blouses, bath products, floral dresses, spiffy retro pieces and Guatemalan worry dolls co-exist? If so, Lab 13 is your spot.

### SPRMRKT CLOTHING, DESIGN

Map p296 (☎330 56 01; www.sprmrkt.nl, in Dutch; Rozengracht 191-193; ⌚Wed-Sat) Whether you want a supertight pair of Acne jeans, a vintage Thor Larson Pod chair or the latest copy of *Butt* magazine, it's all here at this lofty industrial concept store, a major player in Amsterdam's fashion scene.

### NOU MOE STRIPWINKEL COMICS, GIFTS

Map p294 (☎693 63 45; Lindenstraat 1) This tiny corner shop features everything from Asterix to Garfield, Tintin to *24* (yes, that *24*). More importantly, it sells the merchandise: soft toys, notebooks, stickers, games, coffee mugs and bedroom slippers.

### ARNOLD CORNELIS FOOD & DRINK

Map p296 (www.cornelis.nl, in Dutch; Elandsgracht 78) Your dinner hosts will think you're in the know if you present them with something from this long-standing shop, such as fruitcake, cheesecake, chocolate-stuffed cookies or blue sphere biscuits made with Malaga wine. At lunchtime, grab a flaky pastry filled with cheese, meat or vegetables. There is another branch at Van Baerlestraat 93.

### 'T ZONNETJE FOOD & DRINK

Map p294 (www.t-zonnetje.nl, in Dutch; Haarlemmerdijk 45; ⌚Tue-Sat) This space has been a teashop since 1642. You can find teas from all over the world, coffees and implements, and be waited on by a cheerful owner.

### CHRISTODOULOU & LAMÉ HOME FURNISHINGS

Map p296 (Rozengracht 42; ⌚Tue-Sat) Handwoven Tibetan silk pillows, velvet throws and hand-beaded saris from this treasure-trove of soft furnishings will transform your home into a plush sanctuary.

### DISCOSTARS MUSIC

Map p294 (☎626 11 77; www.discostars-recordstore.nl; Haarlemmerdijk 86) Both the disco generation and the 'disco sucks' generation will enjoy this repository of the music of yesteryear. If the names Olivia Newton-John, Engelbert Humperdinck, Paul Young, Celia Cruz, Candy Dulfer, Buddy Holly, Yves Montand, Doris Day or Roy Rogers mean anything to you, you'll find lots more to like.

### LA SAVONNERIE SKINCARE, COSMETICS

Map p296 (☎428 11 39; www.savonnerie.nl; Prinsengracht 294; ⌚Tue-Sun) Aromatic La Savonnerie makes more than 80 natural soaps on the premises, as well as stocking some wonderful varieties from around the world – from rustic Aleppan olive-oil soap to gentle Belgian donkey-milk soap. There's also an enormous range of loofahs, sponges, backscrubbers and gift packs.

### GALLERIA D'ARTE RINASCIMENTO SOUVENIRS

Map p296 (☎622 75 09; www.delft-art-gallery.com; Prinsengracht 170) This pretty shop sells Royal Delftware ceramics (both antique and new), all manner of vases, platters, brooches, Christmas ornaments and interesting 19th-century wall tiles and plaques.

### CALLAS 43 VINTAGE CLOTHING, ACCESSORIES

Map p294 (☎427 37 90; Haarlemmerdijk 86) Dig through tightly packed vintage designer garments, creative secondhand finds, good-as-new samples and a large assortment of leather bags (some new, some not) for your next favourite outfit.

# Vondelpark & Around

## Neighbourhood Top Five

❶ Find your bliss in the **Vondelpark** (p150), where joggers, picnickers, dope smokers, kissing couples, accordion players and frolicking children all cheerfully coexist.

❷ Get cultured under the stars with some modern dance or classical music at the **Openluchttheater** (p152).

❸ Watch as horses are put through their paces at the grand 1882 **Hollandsche Manege** (p149).

❹ Travel around the world without leaving your chair at **Pied à Terre** (p152), Europe's largest travel bookshop and a tempting place to while away a rainy afternoon.

❺ Chill out in bucolic splendour in any one of the Vondelpark cafes, like **Café Vertigo** (p151); in a city of gorgeous terraces, these are among the most relaxing.

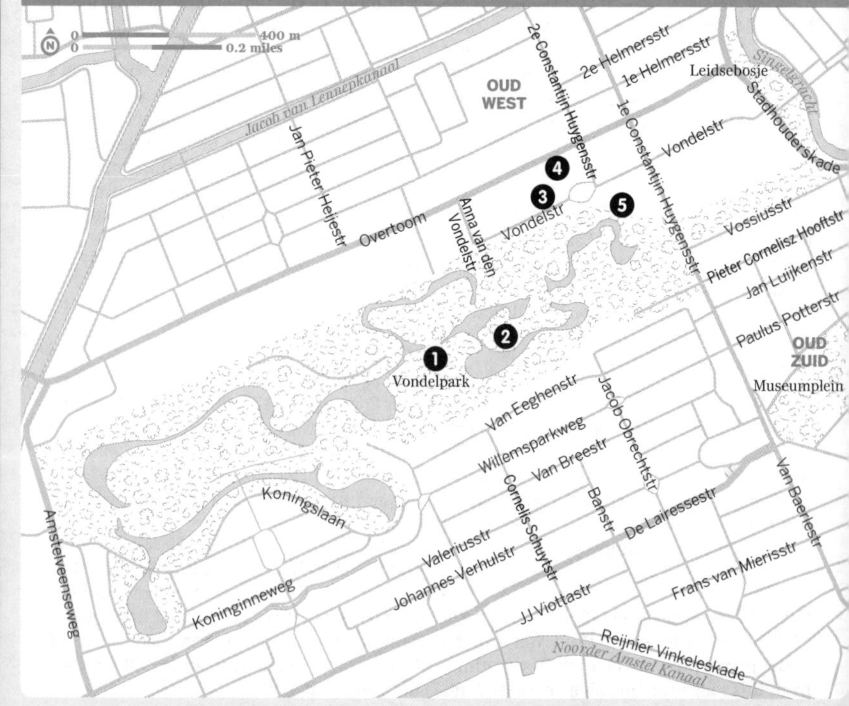


For more detail of this area, see Map p307

## Explore: Vondelpark & Around

Though it's big enough to get lost in – at least metaphysically – Vondelpark is more epic for its near-pastoral beauty than it is for its actual size. Long and thin (about 1.5km long and 300m wide) the park itself can be easily explored in an afternoon. The easiest entry point is at the top (northeast) of the park. As you walk southwest, the path splits off to the left or right and makes a complete circle in either direction.

Outside of the park, the streets around Overtoom burst with stylish ethnic eateries and some excellent shops. Step out of the park through one of its several exits (you'll spot the telltale iron gates) in order to soak up the gorgeous 19th century houses of the many moneyed residents.

## Local Life

- **Crash Course** Need a quick tutorial in the art of Dutch biking? This is the perfect place to practise spinning your wheels like a local.
- **Picture-Perfect Streetscape** Is Bosboom Toussaintstraat Amsterdam's prettiest sans-canal street? It's certainly a contender.
- **Natural High** If the scenery doesn't quite cut it, keep in mind that no one will bat an eye if you light up your, um, coffeeshop booty here.
- **Best People Watching** On a summer day, the hottest people-watching action takes place from the upper terrace of Cwafé Vertigo.
- **Outdoor Drama** Locals know that one of the best summer evenings out is the Openluchttheater. Bring a blanket, a picnic and a bottle of wine: entertainment provided.

## Getting There & Away

- **Tram** Trams 2 and 5 stop at the front entrance of the park, on Hobbemastraat near Leidseplein.

### Lonely Planet's Top Tip

Why not spend a whole day in the Vondelpark? Laze over morning coffee at 't Blauwe Theehuis, pack a lunchtime picnic, and stay for an evening of open-air theatre, followed by cocktails and dinner at Café Vertigo. No wonder the locals look so relaxed.

### Best Places to Eat

- Café Touissant (p149)
- Lalibela (p149)
- Blue Pepper (p149)
- Paloma Blanca (p149)
- De Italiaan (p151)

For reviews, see p149

### Best Places to Drink

- Café Vertigo (p151)
- Gollem's Proeflokaal (p151)
- Parck (p152)
- 't Blauwe Theehuis (p152)
- Golden Brown Bar (p151)

For reviews, see p151

### Best Experiences Out of the Park

- Vondelkerk (p149)
- Orgelpark (p149)
- Squat Buildings (p149)
- Pied à Terre (p152)
- Sauna Fenomeen (p152)

For reviews, see p149

TOP SIGHTS
# VONDELPARK

**New York has its Central Park. London has its Hyde Park. But there's really nothing on earth quite like the lush urban idyll of the Vondelpark, where tourists, lovers, cyclists, backpackers, cartwheeling children, soccer-playing teenagers and champagne-swilling revellers all come out to play. It's as vital to Amsterdam as Rembrandt, canals and coffeeshops, and on a sunny day there's no place better than the Vondelpark. On warm weekends, an open-air party atmosphere ensues: some kick back by reading a book, others hook up with friends to share a spliff or cradle a beer at one of the cafes, while others trade songs on beat-up guitars. In short, it's pure magic.**

The Vondelpark is named after the Shakespeare of the Netherlands, poet and playwright Joost van den Vondel (1587–1679). If it feels like a picture-perfect playground for the bourgeois set, that's because it was designed to be exactly that. In fact, this pleasant, English-style park with ponds, lawns, and winding footpaths was laid out on marshland – a typically Dutch feat of drainage and landscaping – in the 1860s and '70s as a park for the bourgeoisie. City planners hoped it would soften the loss of the Plantage, a city park that became residential around this time.

During the late 1960s and early 1970s, Dutch authorities turned the park into a temporary open-air dormitory for the droves of hippies who descended on Amsterdam. The sleeping bags are long gone (although you might spy a lone neo-hippie chilling out on one) and the park is now used by one and all, from inline skaters to families with prams and, if you're lucky, performing acrobats. Amazingly, although the park receives over 10 million visitors per year, it never feels too crowded to enjoy.

## DON'T MISS

- The swoon-worthy rose gardens
- Picnicking at pond's edge
- Renting a bike and taking a spin through the park
- The Openluchttheater
- Getting lost on the serpentine paths and footbridges...is this *really* the middle of the city?

## PRACTICALITIES

- Map p307
- www.vondelpark.nl
- Admission free
- ⌚dawn-midnight

## SIGHTS

**VONDELPARK** PARK
See p148.

**HOLLANDSCHE MANEGE** RIDING SCHOOL
Map p307 (www.dehollandschemanege.nl, in Dutch; Vondelstraat 140; admission free; ⏲2-11pm Mon, Tue, Thu & Fri, 9am-11pm Wed, 9am-6pm Sat, 9am-5pm Sun) Just outside the Vondelpark is the neoclassical Hollandsche Manege, an indoor riding school inspired by the famous Spanish Riding School in Vienna. Designed by AL van Gendt and built in 1882, the building has been fully restored, but has thankfully kept its charming horse-head facade. Sip a beer or coffee in the cafe as you watch the instructors put the horses through their paces.

**ORGELPARK** CONCERT HALL
Map p307 (www.orgelpark.nl, in Dutch; Gerard Brandtstraat 26; tickets adult/student from €15/9) This is not a park as we know it, but a renowned stage for organ music located in a lovely restored church on the edge of the Vondelpark. It has four big organs, and there are more than 100 events every year, including concerts of classical, jazz and improvised music.

**VONDELKERK** CHURCH
Map p307 Vondelstraat 77; ⏲8am-6pm) Architect Pierre Cuypers' favourite church (designed and built 1870–80) suffered from a lack of funds during construction and a fire in 1904. It was marked for demolition in 1978, but a group of architecture enthusiasts saved it. It's a charming steepled church featuring a fascinating series of shapes with an octagon at its base. People in the offices inside are happy to let you in for a peek.

**SQUAT BUILDINGS** CULTURAL BUILDINGS
Given its hippie past, it's probably no surprise that Vondelpark is fringed by squats (ie abandoned buildings that people move into and occupy for free). Graffiti-covered **OT301** (Map p307; www.ot301.nl; Overtoom 301) hosts an eclectic roster of bands, international films, parties, dance workshops, and DJs. With two bars, the vegan restaurant De Peper and a fun Tuesday ping-pong night, it's the most fun alternative destination in town. **Occii** (off Map p307; www.occii.org, in Dutch; Amstelveenseweg 134), a 19th-century stable that was squatted in 1984, also serves up alternative music and arts, plus vegie fare at the Eetcafé MKZ.

## EATING

TOP CHOICE **CAFÉ TOUISSANT** FRENCH €€
Map p307 (www.bosboom-toussaint.nl; Bosboom Touissantstraat 26; mains €5-19; ⏲9am-10pm) On one of Amsterdam's prettiest streets, this casual neighbourhood gem feels like it's straight out of an Edith Piaf song. Come to sip cappuccino under the trees, or for creative twists on French classics in the candlelit evenings: it's carelessly sexy from noon to night.

TOP CHOICE **PALOMA BLANCA** MOROCCAN €€
Map p307 (www.palomablanca.nl; Jan Pieter Heijestraat 145; mains €16-24; ⏲dinner Tue-Sun) The name is Spanish, but the lanterns, dishware and mosaic-topped tables are straight out of a Marrakesh souk. Start with a gorgeous *mezze* platter before moving on to savoury mains of couscous and *tajine* (Moroccan stew) dishes featuring an array of meats, vegetables and fish.

**LALIBELA** ETHIOPIAN €€
Map p307 (www.lalibela.nl, in Dutch; 1e Helmersstraat 249; mains €8-12; ⏲dinner) This shop, just north of the Overtoom, was the Netherlands' first Ethiopian restaurant, and it's still our favourite. You can drink Ethiopian beer from a half-gourd, and taste your stews, egg and vegetable dishes using *injera* (a spongy pancake) instead of utensils. Trippy African music rounds out the experience.

**BLUE PEPPER** INDONESIAN €€€
Map p307 (☎489 70 39; www.restaurantbluepepper.com; Nassaukade 366; set menus €53-70; ⏲10am-5pm Mon-Wed, 10am-9pm Thu-Sun) Chef Sonja Pereira elevates Indonesian cuisine to art in her dramatic blue dining room. The exquisite *rijsttafel* (Indonesian banquet) includes an array of Pacific Rim-influenced dishes such as crackly crab, lamb sate, grilled scallops with tropical fruit, blue pears and coconut flan. Vegetarians options abound, too.

**FONDUE & FONDUE** FRENCH €€
Map p307 (www.restaurantfondue.nl, in Dutch; Overtoom 415; fondues €15-17; ⏲dinner 6pm-1am)

START VONDELPARK MAIN ENTRANCE
END CAFÉ VERTIGO
DISTANCE LESS THAN 1 KM
DURATION 1½ TO 2 HOURS

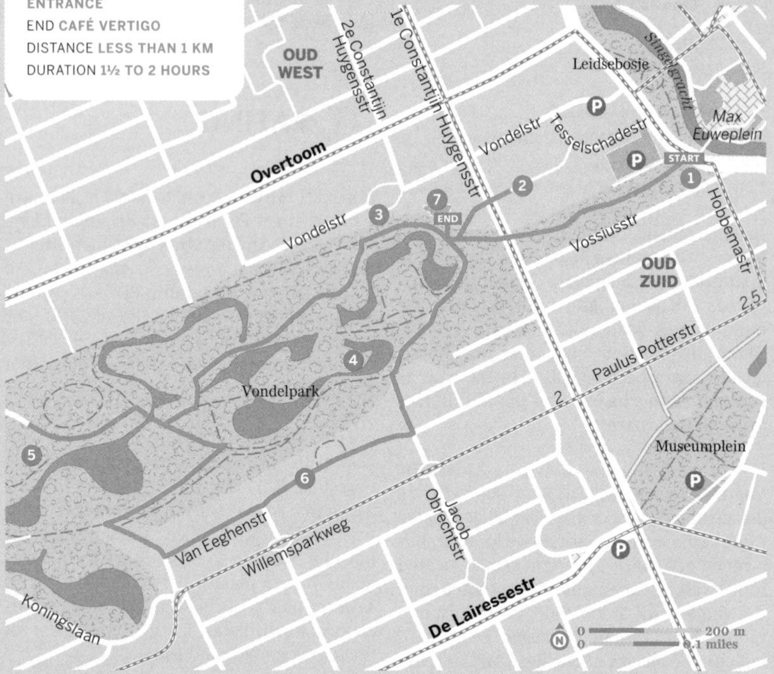

Neighbourhood Walk

## Vondelpark

While an unstructured stroll through the Vondelpark is perfectly wonderful, this tour ensures that you'll hit several highlights both in and around the park, from a fragrant rose garden to a Moorish manor to hidden treasures of Art Nouveau architecture.

Enter the park through the 1 **main entrance** and walk straight; veer to the right when the path diverges into a loop. Exit the park by walking down pretty 2 **Roemer Visscherstraat**, where you'll come upon a row of several themed houses whose architecture is inspired by different European cultures: Russian, French, English, German, and our favourite, a Moorish-style Spanish house.

Head back to the park, continuing on the southwest loop, and exit the part again to check out the lovely 3 **Vondelkerk**. Now home to offices rather than used as a church, the folks working inside generally don't mind if you ask to take a peek at the inspiring interior. Back in the park, stay on the same path until you reach a footbridge on your left; cross it and walk over to 4 **'t Blauwe Theehuis**, for a relaxing lunch or coffee break. Continue deeper into the park and take time to smell the roses in the 5 **rose garden**; it's seldom crowded even in high season. Take the other side of the path loop back towards the park entrance, taking a detour down 6 **Van Eeghenstraat**, where you'll spy some of the city's most enchanting Art Nouveau-inspired architectural details; the highlight is definitely the ornate Atlas Hotel. Pop back into the park through the entrance gates, stopping for a beer on the patio at 7 **Café Vertigo** for the park's best people watching.

It's cosy, reasonably priced, and serves the most wickedly delicious comfort food to ever come out of the Alps. Cheese worship aside, the fact that Lady Gaga and her entourage have recently eaten here twice may be endorsement enough.

### DE ITALIAAN PIZZA €€

Map p307 (www.deitaliaan.com; Bosboom Touissantstraat 29; mains €13-18; ⊙dinner) The owners of across-the-street Café Touissant, who had vacationed in France for years, finally went to Italy. They fell in love with the country, and the result is this charming homage to *la dolce vita*. The wood-burning oven turns out pizzas with exotic ingredients – black truffles, red-fin tuna, taleggio – in a warm, social atmosphere. Excellent bruschetta and entree specials will woo even those for whom pizza is not a weakness.

### DE PEPER VEGAN €

Map p307 (☎412 29 54; www.depeper.org; Overtoom 301; meals €7-10; ⊙7pm-8.30pm Tue, Thu, Fri & Sun; ✍) This friendly restaurant at the graffiti-covered OT301 squat serves cheap, organic, vegan meals in a lovable dive bar atmosphere. Sit at the communal table to connect with like-minded folk. Same-day reservations are required; call between 4pm and 6:30pm.

### LUNCHROOM WILHELMINA CAFE €

Map p307 (www.lunchroomwilhelmina.nl; 1e Helmersstraat 83-A; ⊙10am-5pm Mon-Wed, 10am-9pm Thu-Sun.) This sunny, corner spot is the perfect place near Vondelpark to while away an afternoon with a novel over a simple lunch, brunch or *borrel* (drink) when the Dutch weather turns out to be a bit more tempestuous than you'd hoped.

### CAFÉ WESTERS CAFE €

Map p307 (www.cafewesters.nl, in Dutch; 1e Constantijn Huygensstraat 35-37; mains €5-12; ⊙11am-1am Sun-Thu, 11am-2am Fri & Sat) This friendly, brightly painted sidewalk terrace is a perfect place to head for a post-Vondelpark lunch or beer.

### HAP HMM TRADITIONAL DUTCH €

Map p307 (www.hap-hmm.nl; 1e Helmersstraat 33; mains €7-11; ⊙4.30-8pm Mon-Fri) Elsewhere €7.50 might buy you a bowl of soup, but at this wood-panelled neighbourhood place, it might buy an entire dinner: simple Dutch cooking (soup, plus meat, vegies and potatoes), served on stainless-steel dishes.

### EETCAFÉ MKZ VEGAN €

off Map p307 (☎679 07 12; 1e Schinkelstraat 16; meals from €6; ⊙from 7pm Tue, Wed & Fri, closed Tue in summer; ✍) Eetcafé MKZ is a collectively run, no-frills squat restaurant on Vondelpark's southern edge. Call between 2.30pm and 6pm to reserve your spot for the three-course vegan meals.

### OVERTOOM GROENTE EN FRUIT TURKISH €

Map p307 (Overtoom 129; mains €3-5; ⊙10am-6pm) Along with fruit and vegies, this Turkish grocery has a range of pre-made salads and snacks, including kebabs, and cheese-and-tomato-filled pitas – perfect for picnics in the park.

## DRINKING & NIGHTLIFE

### TOP CHOICE CAFÉ VERTIGO THEATRE CAFE

Map p307 (www.vertigo.nl; Vondelpark 3; ⊙11am-1am) This cinematic cafe is a film fanatic's paradise, with headshots of everyone from Ingrid Bergman to Dutch film star Carice van Houton striking femme fatale poses on the wall. We love how silent movies play in the dining area, a concept we've never seen before. In nice weather, there's a leafy terrace to linger for hours outdoors watching the goings-on in the Vondelpark.

### TOP CHOICE GOLLEM'S PROEFLOKAAL BEER CAFE

Map p307 (www.cafegollem.nl; Overtoom 160-162; ⊙4pm-1am Mon-Thu, 2pm-2am Fri-Sun) Take a day trip to Belgium without leaving Holland. Sip a cherry Kriek or a Trappist ale amid vintage beer signs and paintings of tippling monks at this relaxed temple to all things Belgian. Bartenders offer guidance to beer neophytes and fanatics alike. Dishes (€14 to €18), including Trappist cheese fondue, croquettes, and Flemish stew, tempt beer drinkers who work up an appetite.

### GOLDEN BROWN BAR CAFE, DESIGNER BAR

Map p307 (www.goldenbrownbar.nl, in Dutch; Jan Pieter Heijestraat 146) This totally hip, two-level bar attracts a young professional crowd that spills out onto the sidewalk. In winter, the cream-and-brown interior with its mod woodwork offers stylish respite from the chill, especially if you snag a seat on the faux velvet couch. The tasty bistro menu offers three courses for €25.

**PARCK** CAFE

Map p307 (www.cafeparck.nl, in Dutch; Overtoom 428; 3pm-1am Mon-Fri, from noon-3am Sat & Sun) Ah, the simple concepts in life: cold beer on tap and crave-worthy burgers (vegie ones, too!) in a friendly corner pub stocked with oodles of magazines, a pool table, and plenty of outdoor tables and couch space for lounging.

**HET GROOT MELKHUIS** CAFE

Map p307 (www.grootmelkhuis.nl; Vondelpark 2) Kind of a Goldilocks apparition, this huge thatched house at the forest's edge invites you in. The vast drinking and dining forecourt and playground cater to families and all kidlike guests.

**'T BLAUWE THEEHUIS** CAFE

Map p307 (www.blauwetheehuis.nl, in Dutch; Vondelpark 5) Did a flying saucer land in the park? That's what you might think as you approach this wacky structure, but it's simply a fabulous cafe surrounded by greenery. In summer the terrace is packed with seemingly everyone in town enjoying coffee and cake or cocktails and dinner.

## ENTERTAINMENT

**OCCII** CULTURAL BUILDING

off Map p307 (671 77 78; www.occii.org, in Dutch; Amstelveenseweg 134; closed mid-Jul–Aug) This former squat maintains a thriving alternative scene, and books underground bands, many from Amsterdam. There's also an anarchist library, a children's theatre and Sauna Fenomeen.

**SAUNA FENOMEEN** SAUNA

off Map p307 (589 14 00; www.saunafenomeen.nl; Eerste Schinkelstraat 14-16; 1pm-11pm, women only Mon; entry €4-9) One of Amsterdam's favourite – and most relaxed – saunas is run by the alternative folks at Occii. It boasts a Turkish steam bath, Finnish sauna and quality massages, along with a relaxing room and a vegetarian cafe where you can play games or read in your blissed-out state.

FREE **OPENLUCHTTHEATER** THEATRE

Map p307 (Vondelpark Open-Air Theatre; www.openluchttheater.nl, in Dutch; Vondelpark; Jun-Aug) Each summer the Vondelpark hosts free concerts in its intimate open-air theatre. It's a fantastic experience to share with others. Expect world music, dance, theatre and more. You can make a reservation (€2.50 per seat) on the website up to two hours in advance of showtime.

## SHOPPING

The winding paths of the Vondelpark must inspire a certain wanderlust, as the nearby streets are full of outdoor and travel shops.

TOP CHOICE **PIED À TERRE** BOOKS

Map p307 (www.jvw.nl, in Dutch; Overtoom 135-137) The galleried, sky-lit interior of this enormous yet elegant travel-book shop feels like a Renaissance centre of learning. If it's travel or outdoor-related, its likely got it: hiking and cycling tomes, gorgeous globes, travel guides and over 600,000 maps. Order a cappuccino and dream up your next trip at the cafe tables.

**MARQT** FOOD & DRINK

Map p307 (422 62 11; www.marqt.com, in Dutch; Overtoom 21-25; 9am-8pm Mon-Sat, 10am-7pm Sun) Need to stock up for your picnic in nearby Vondelpark? Pick up prepared gourmet food (often organic) like pastas or salads, cheese, fresh bread and a bottle of wine and you're set for a lazy, delicious afternoon. No cash; card only.

**WOMEN'S OUTDOOR WORLD** OUTDOORS

Map p307 (412 28 79; Overtoom 51-53) Owned by Bever, one of the city's leading sporting-equipment shops, the WOW had to open a separate shop due to overwhelming demand. It also sells nongender-specific equipment such as tents.

# Old South

## Neighbourhood Top Five

1. You'll wait in line outside and jostle the crowds inside, but seeing those vivid brushstrokes of yellow sunflowers and purple-blue irises makes it all worthwhile at the **Van Gogh Museum** (p155).

2. Plunge into the Golden Age trove of Dutch master paintings, Delft tiles, gold goblets and gilded dollhouses at the **Rijksmuseum** (p158).

3. Admire the abstractions of Mondrian, Matisse and all their modern compadres at the **Stedelijk Museum** (p161).

4. Listen to music soar in pristine acoustics at the **Concertgebouw** (p164).

5. Wander past genteel homes and Amsterdam School **architecture** on streets throughout the Old South, such as Johannes Vermeerstraat.

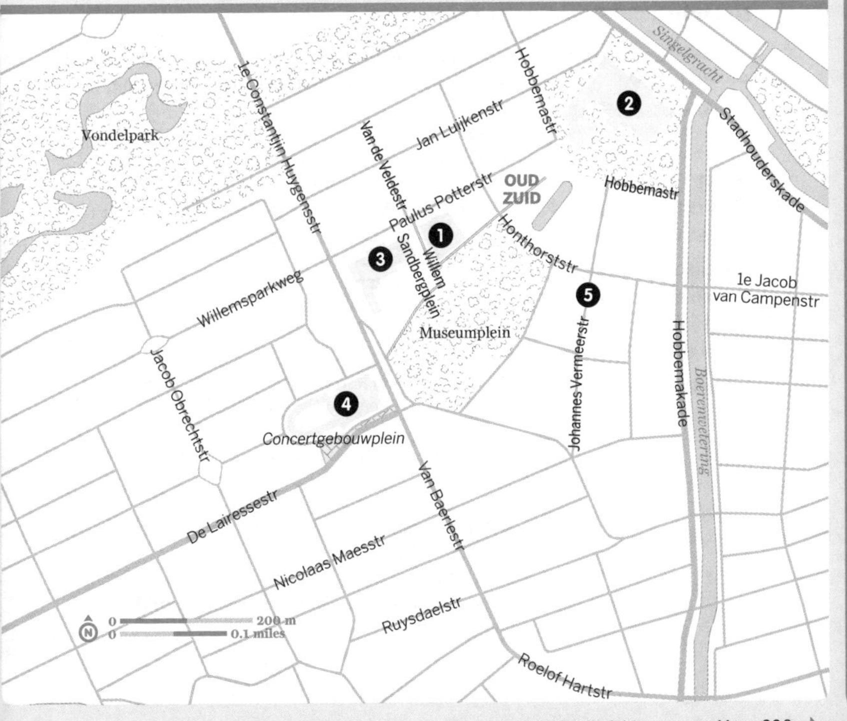


For more detail of this area, see Map p306

## Lonely Planet's Top Tip

Yes, the Van Gogh and Stedelijk museums have cafes, and snack vendors pave the way to the Rijksmuseum, but we prefer submerging into the Albert Heijn at the Museumplein's foot on Van Baerlestraat. The supermarket has prepared salads and sandwiches, or you can buy cheese and a bottle of wine to take out for picnic on the lawn.

### Best Places to Eat

- Loetje (p163)
- La Falote (p163)
- Renzo's (p163)

For reviews, see p163

### Best Places to Drink

- Welling (p163)
- Wildschut (p163)

For reviews, see p163

### Best Places Beyond the Art Museums

- Concertgebouw (p162)
- Museumplein (p162)
- Coster Diamonds (p162)
- House of Bols (p162)

For reviews, see p162

## Explore: Old South

The Old South is home to the city's big three art museums, all lined up all in a walkable row. The Rijksmuseum, an 1885 Dutch Renaissance-style behemoth stuffed with Rembrandts, Vermeers and other Golden Age treasures, is the granddaddy. The Van Gogh Museum is the fan favourite, evidenced by the queues winding around the block. The Stedelijk is the triumvirate's third member, open once again to show off its vast modern art collection after a multi-year renovation. No wonder they call it the Museum Quarter. Count on spending a full day here to see the sights.

The big patch of grass behind the museums is called Museumplein, handy for footsore tourists and well used by locals, too, especially in winter, when an ice-skating rink is installed.

While most visitors clear out by late afternoon, there are plenty of reasons to linger. The Old South is one of Amsterdam's most gracious – and richest – neighbourhoods. Impressive manors rise on the leafy streets, and it's fun to wander around and see the cool architecture.

In the evening, the action shifts to the Concertgebouw, the grand music hall built in conjunction with the Rijksmuseum. Well-dressed locals flock to the neighbourhood, and several genteel cafes spring to life.

## Local Life

- **Plan for the Plein** Yes, the Museumplein is tourist-packed, but locals are out there, too, picnicking, smooching and tossing a frisbee.
- **Go Dutch** For eats, the eastern part of Van Baerlestraat leads to several traditional Dutch restaurants and cafes, such as Wildschut.
- **Style Tips** Paulus Potterstraat, the street that runs by the museums, turns into Willemsparkweg as you move southeast. Continue along it and you'll pass cafes and local designers' shops where stylish locals sip coffee and get more, er, stylish.
- **Go Gliding** In winter, Museumplein's pond becomes a popular ice-skating rink, and the scene looks like the top of a wind-up jewellery box. In warmer weather, skateboarders head to the park's half-pipe.

## Getting There & Away

- **Trams** Trams 2 and 5 are handy for getting to/from the city centre.
- **Bus** Bus 197 zips to the Museumplein from the airport, which is handy if you're staying in the neighbourhood.

JEAN-PIERRE LESCOURRET / LONELY PLANET IMAGES ©

TOP SIGHTS
# VAN GOGH MUSEUM

**The Van Gogh Museum is Amsterdam's top-dog sight. Opened in 1973 to house the collection of Vincent's younger brother Theo, it is home to 200 paintings and 500 drawings by Vincent and his contemporaries, such as Gauguin, Monet, Toulouse-Lautrec and Bernard. Through Van Gogh's paintings, the museum chronicles his journey from Holland, where his work was dark and sombre, to Paris, where, under the influence of the Impressionists, he discovered vivid colour. Get ready for all the swirls and sunflowers you can handle.**

### DON'T MISS

- *The Potato Eaters*
- *The Yellow House*
- *The Bedroom*
- *Wheatfield with Crows*
- *Sunflowers*
- Special exhibits

### PRACTICALITIES

- Map p306
- ☎570 52 00
- www.vangoghmuseum.nl
- Paulus Potterstraat 7
- adult/child €14/free, audio tour €5
- ⊙10am-6pm Sat-Thu, to 10pm Fri

## Floor 1

Let's cut to the quick: the museum's best stuff is on Floor 1 (not to be confused with Floor 0, aka the ground floor, which is where you enter). Floor 1 hangs Van Gogh's greatest hits, and it does so chronologically as you move clockwise from the main stairs.

### Earliest Works (1883–86)

The first room you enter is filled with Van Gogh's earliest works – shadowy, sombre and crude – from his time in the Dutch countryside and in Antwerp between 1883 and 1886. He was particularly obsessed with peasants and 'painting dark that is nevertheless light'. *The Potato Eaters* (1885) is his most famous painting from this period. *Still Life with Bible* (1885) shows his religious inclination. The burnt-out candle is said to represent the recent death of his father, who was a Protestant minister. *Skeleton with Burning Cigarette* (1886) – the print all the stoners are buying in the downstairs gift shop – was painted when Van Gogh was a student at Antwerp's art academy.

### QUEUES & TICKETS

Entrance queues can be long, as only so many visitors are allowed inside at a time. Come right at opening time, or else wait until after 2pm. I Amsterdam Card and Holland Pass holders have a separate 'fast' lane for entry. Advance ticket holders and Museumkaart owners fare the best in their quick-moving lane. Advance tickets are available online or at tourist information offices, with no surcharge.

**While Van Gogh would come to be regarded as a giant among artists, he sold only one painting during his lifetime ('Red Vineyard at Arles', in case you're wondering; it hangs at Moscow's Puskin Museum).**

### FRIDAY NIGHT

The museum stays open late on Friday, when it also hosts special cultural events and opens a bar downstairs for patrons. Register at the information desk for the free tours at 5.30pm and 8pm.

**Van Gogh was a prolific letter writer. The museum has categorised all of his missives online at www.vangoghletters.org.**

### Paris Self Portraits (1886–87)

In March 1886 Van Gogh moved to Paris, where his brother Theo was working as an art dealer. There, his palette changed under the influence of the Impressionists he met. Dip into the museum's Paris room and check out all of Van Gogh self-portraits from the period. He wanted to master the art of portraiture, but was too poor to pay for models.

### Sunflowers in Arles (1888–89)

In 1888 Van Gogh left for Arles in Provence to delve into its colourful landscapes. The room devoted to this period hangs an awesome line-up of *Sunflowers* (1889) and other blossoms. Also here is *The Yellow House* (1888), the abode that Van Gogh rented, intending to start an artists colony with Paul Gaugin. *The Bedroom* (1888) depicts Van Gogh's bedroom at the Yellow House. But 1888 is perhaps most notorious as the year Van Gogh sliced off part of his ear.

### The Final Years (1889–90)

The museum's last room on Floor 1 has paintings from Van Gogh's final years. He had himself committed to an asylum in St Remy in 1889. While there he painted several landscapes with cypress and olive trees, and he went wild with *Irises*. In 1890 he left the clinic and went north to Auvers-sur-Oise. One of his last paintings, *Wheatfield with Crows* (1890), is an ominous work finished shortly before his suicide.

## Other Floors

The ground floor shows paintings mostly by Van Gogh's precursors, such as Millet and Courbet, though Vincent's work is sprinkled in. Floor 2 houses temporary educational exhibits and works on paper. Floor 3 hangs Van Gogh's contemporaries and those he influenced. This is another bountiful level, where you might spy landscapes by Monet and Gaugin, or a room full of French fauvists; works from the permanent collection rotate through here.

The museum's main building was designed by Gerrit Rietveld, the seminal Dutch architect. Behind it, reaching onto the Museumplein, is a separate exhibition wing (1999) designed by Kisho Kurokawa and commonly referred to as 'the Mussel'. It typically hosts a blockbuster exhibition.

The **library** (Museumplein 4; ⏲10am-12.30pm & 1.30-5pm Mon-Fri) has a wealth of reference material – 24,000 books to be exact – for serious study.

At the time of research, it was announced that the Van Gogh Museum will be closed from October 2012 to March 2013 for renovations. During that time, much of the collection will be at the Hermitage Amsterdam (p112).

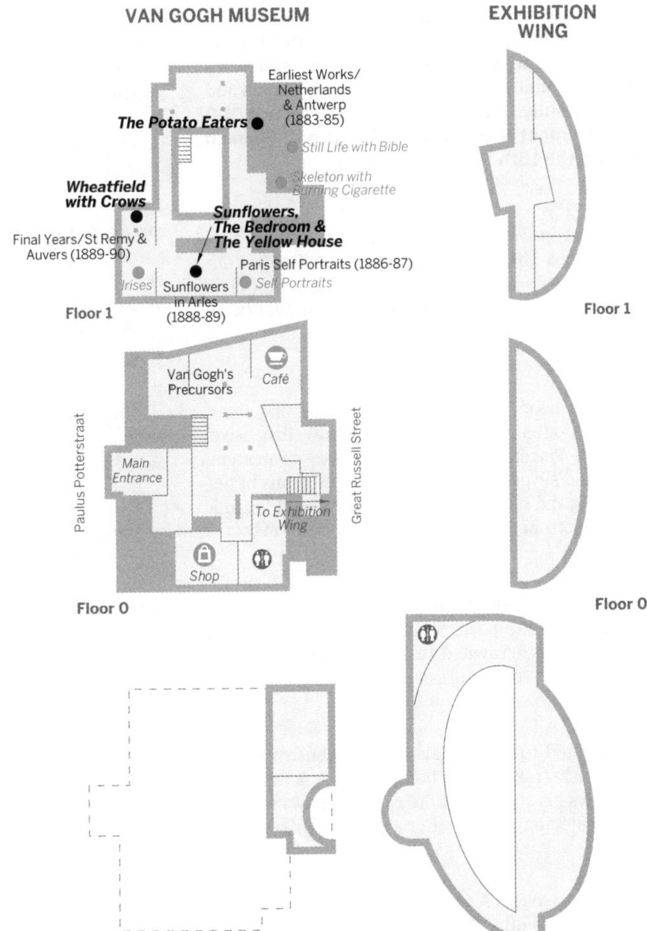
VAN GOGH MUSEUM
EXHIBITION WING
Earliest Works/ Netherlands & Antwerp (1883-85)
The Potato Eaters
Still Life with Bible
Skeleton with Burning Cigarette
Wheatfield with Crows
Sunflowers, The Bedroom & The Yellow House
Final Years/St Remy & Auvers (1889-90)
Paris Self Portraits (1886-87)
Irises
Sunflowers in Arles (1888-89)
Self Portraits
Floor 1
Van Gogh's Precursors
Café
Paulus Potterstraat
Great Russell Street
Main Entrance
To Exhibition Wing
Shop
Floor 0
Floor -1
Floor 1
Floor 0
Floor -1

# TOP SIGHTS RIJKSMUSEUM



**The Rijksmuseum (National Museum) is the premier art museum of the Netherlands, and no self-respecting visitor to Amsterdam can afford to miss it. Though most of the building is closed for renovations until 2013, there is an excellent collection of around 200 masterpieces exhibited in a side section, the Philips Wing. The museum was conceived as a repository for several national collections, including art owned by the royal family. The group includes some 5000 paintings, the most important by Dutch and Flemish masters from the 15th to 19th centuries.**

### DON'T MISS

- Rembrandt's *Night Watch*
- Frans Hals' *The Merry Drinker*
- Vermeer's *Kitchen Maid*
- Delftware pottery
- The museum's facade

### PRACTICALITIES

- Map p306
- ☎674 70 00
- www.rijksmuseum.nl
- Stadhouderskade 42
- adult/child €12.50/free
- ⊙9am-6pm

## Civic Guards

The first room you walk into whets your appetite with a *Night Watch* look-alike. Titled *Banquet in Celebration of the Treaty of Munster* (1648), it shows a group of civic guards partying at the end of the Eighty Years War (with Spain). Remember those white-lace ruffs...

## Dollhouses

Now before you pooh-pooh the concept, know that these are expensive dollhouses in Room 3. Really expensive. Merchant's wife Petronella Oortman employed carpenters, glassblowers and silversmiths to make the 700 items in her dollhouse, using the same materials as they would for full-scale versions. Petronella's miniature house ended up costing more than a true canal house.

## Delftware

Delftware was the Dutch attempt to reproduce Chinese porcelain in the late 1600s. The delicate blue-and-white pottery packs Room 5. Many pieces are painted with images of royalty. Queen Mary (crowned in England in 1689) was an avid collector. Many of her pieces are now in the museum's collection.

## Frans Hals

Room 7 is devoted to Frans Hals and his contemporaries from Haarlem. Hals painted with broad brushstrokes and a fluidity that was unique for the time. *The Merry Drinker* (1628–30) shows his style in action. No one knows who the gent with the beer glass is, but it's clear he's enjoying himself after a hard day of civic guarding.

## Rembrandt

Rembrandt is the Golden Age's most famous and inexhaustible brush-man, and his works dominate Rooms 8 and 9. *The Jewish Bride* (1665), showing a couple's intimate caress, made Van Gogh giddy. 'I would give 10 years of my life to be allowed to sit before this painting for 14 days with just a crust of bread to eat,' he said to a friend.

## Jan Vermeer

Vermeer has the run of Room 10. Check out the dreamy *Kitchen Maid* (1658) for his famed attention to detail. See the holes in the wall? The nail with shadow? The broken pane of glass? In *Woman in Blue Reading a Letter* (1663) Vermeer uses a different style. He shows only parts of objects, such as the tables, chairs and map, leaving the viewer to figure out the rest.

### Jan Steen

Jan Steen became renowned for painting chaotic households, such as the one in *The Merry Family* (1668). Everyone is having such a good time in the picture, no one notices the little boy sneaking a taste of wine. Steen's images made quite an impression: in the 18th century, the expression 'a Jan Steen household' entered the local lexicon to mean a crazy state of affairs. Room 11 hangs several of his works.

### Rembrandt's Night Watch

Rembrandt's *Night Watch* (1650) engulfs Room 12. It shows the militia led by Frans Banning Cocq, a future mayor of Amsterdam. The work is actually titled *Archers Under the Command of Captain Frans Banning Cocq*, or *Company of Frans Banning Cocq and Willem van Ruytenburch*. The *Night Watch* name was bestowed years later, thanks to a layer of grime that gave the impression it was evening. The image you see now is clean, in the colours that Rembrandt intended.

As was tradition, the 16 guards in the painting had to pay to be portrayed. Hand over a little more, and Rembrandt put you in a more prominent position in the foreground. Rembrandt earned 1600 guilders for *Night Watch*. The painting was commissioned for the civic guard hall that used to stand at the corner of Amstel and Kloveniersburgwal (now the Hotel Doelen).

### Other Highlights

When the museum is open at full capacity, other good sections include Dutch History and Asiatic Art, including the famous 12th-century *Dancing Shiva*. The museum's famous print archives have some 800,000 prints and drawings.

### Building Facade

Pierre Cuypers designed the museum, which was completed in 1885. He planned Centraal Station four years later. Both buildings are a mixture of neo-Gothic and Dutch Renaissance. The neo-Gothic elements (towers, stained-glass windows) brought a hailstorm of criticism from Protestants, including the king, who dubbed the building 'the archbishop's palace' (Cuypers was Catholic, and proudly so in his approach to architecture).

### Gardens

Most people don't even realise the Rijksmuseum has gardens. But it does, and they're free. Sculptures and odd fragments of architectural detail pop up amid the rose bushes and hedges in the Renaissance and Baroque Gardens.

#### QUEUES & TICKETS

More than a million people visit the Rijksmuseum every year, so be prepared for queues. Come right at opening time, or else wait until after 2pm. I Amsterdam Card holders must wait in the regular queue. Advance ticket holders and Holland Pass and Museumkaart owners can jump into the separate 'fast lane' (look for the sign northeast of the Philips Wing entrance). Advance tickets are available online or at tourist information offices, with no surcharge.

**Kids can explore with their own audio tour focusing on the paintings' food and drink (€3.50); adults learn about the masterpieces (€5).**

#### AIRPORT ART

The Rijksmuseum has a free branch at Schiphol Airport. The mini-museum hangs 10 Golden Age paintings that change every few months. It's located after passport control between the E and F Pier, and is open from 7am to 8pm daily.

**Captain Cocq, the main ruffed gentleman in Night Watch, once lived in the house at Singel 140-142.**

**The Merry Drinker (Hals)**
Room 7
Room 8
Room 6
**Kitchen Maid (Vermeer)**
*Woman in Blue Reading a Letter (Vermeer)*
Room 10
Room 14
Room 9
*Museum Shop*
*The Jewish Bride (Rembrandt)*
Room 11
Room 12
*The Merry Family (Steen)*
Room 13
**Night Watch (Rembrandt)**

**First Floor**

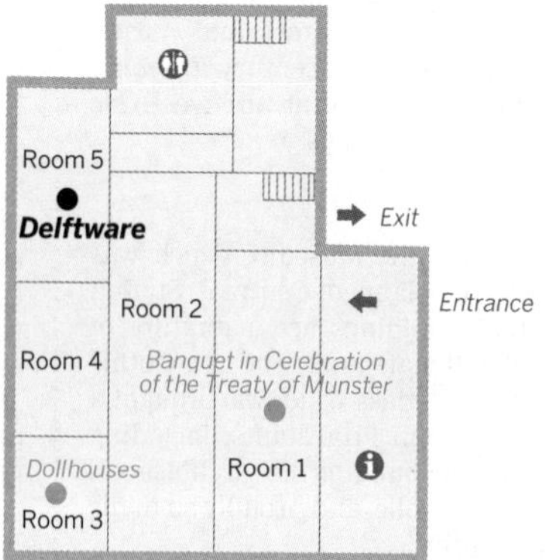


**Ground Floor**

TOP SIGHTS
# STEDELIJK MUSEUM

**The Stedelijk is the permanent home of the National Museum of Modern Art. Its modern classics, amassed with great skill by postwar curator Willem Sandber, are among the world's most admired. The permanent collection includes all the blue chips of 19th- and 20th-century painting. Alas, the building has been undergoing an expansion and renovation that has taken forever. It's been closed for seven years, and re-opened in part in 2010 as the 'Temporary Stedelijk,' showcasing some of the prize pieces.**

## Matisse to Wonder Woman

AM Weissman designed the 1895 main building. It's hard to say what you'll see from the 90,000-works collection, as building construction means the galleries keep changing. At press time, one could wander through and see Henri Matisse masterpieces and paintings by Dutch homeboys Piet Mondrian, Willem de Kooning, Charlie Toorop and Karel Appel.

## Freebies

Stop by the front desk when you enter to enquire about free gallery talks, guided tours, smartphone-enabled tours and children's painting workshops. Also note that while the Stedelijk is free for Museumkaart holders, it is *not* gratis for I Amsterdam Card holders (who get 25% off admission).

## The Future

So when will 'the Bathtub,' as locals have dubbed the new wing, be finished, allowing the Stedelijk to re-open in its entirety? At press time, the museum didn't know.

### DON'T MISS

- Karel Appel mural in the Temporary Cafe
- Piet Mondrian grid paintings
- Henri Matisse paper cut outs
- Willem de Kooning abstract works
- Museum highlights tour (3.30 to 4.30 Sun, in English)

### PRACTICALITIES

- Map p306
- ☎573 29 11
- www.stedelijk.nl
- Paulus Potterstraat 13
- Admission €10
- ⏲10am-5pm Tue-Sun

# SIGHTS

**VAN GOGH MUSEUM** MUSEUM
See p155.

**RIJKSMUSEUM** MUSEUM
See p158.

**STEDELIJK MUSEUM** MUSEUM
See p161.

**MUSEUMPLEIN** SQUARE
Map p306 (Paulus Potterstraat) Museumplein was laid out to host the World Exhibition in 1883, but gained its lasting title only when the Rijksmuseum was opened two years later. One of many facelifts raised a triangle of turf at the southern end, dubbed the 'ass's ear' for its shape; it's now a popular spot for sun worshippers. There's a large supermarket, Albert Heijn, concealed below.

For as long as anyone can remember, the square has been used for concerts, special events and political demonstrations. At other times it's a relaxing place to hang out, play hacky-sack, skateboard (ramp provided), toss a frisbee or enjoy a picnic. In winter the long concrete pond is transformed into a festive skating rink.

**CONCERTGEBOUW** ARCHITECTURE
Map p306 (www.concertgebouw.nl, in Dutch; Concertgebouwplein 2-6; ticket prices vary; ⏲box office 10am-8.15pm) The literal name 'Concert Building' scarcely does justice to this amazing facility, which attracts some 850,000 visitors a year to 800 shows. This makes it the busiest concert hall in the world, but refreshingly it hasn't lost its common touch.

The Concertgebouw was completed in 1888 to a neo-Renaissance design by AL van Gendt. In spite of his limited musical knowledge, he managed to give the two-tiered Grote Zaal (Main Hall) near-perfect acoustics that are the envy of sound designers worldwide. Add in baroque trim, panels inscribed with the names of classical composers, a massive pipe organ and a grand staircase via which conductors and soloists descend to the stage, and you have a venue where the best performers are honoured to appear.

In the 1980s the Concertgebouw threatened to collapse because its 2000 wooden piles were rotting. Thanks to new technology, the piles made way for a concrete foundation, and the building was thoroughly restored to mark its 100th anniversary. The architect Pi de Bruin added a glass foyer along the southern side that raised a few eyebrows, though everyone agrees it's effective.

The facility offers one-hour **tours** (per person €10; ⏲12.15pm Sunday and 5pm Monday) that cover the hall's design in more detail; buy tickets at the box office.

For information on getting show tickets or attending the free lunchtime concerts, see p164.

**PHOTO OP**

You can't leave the Museumplein without stopping by the **I Amsterdam sculpture** for a photo. Feel free to climb in, around or on top of the 2m-high letters. It's located in the square's northwest corner, by the Rijksmuseum.

**DIAMOND MUSEUM** MUSEUM
Map p306 (www.diamantmuseum.nl; Paulus Potterstraat 8; adult/child €7.50/5; ⏲9am-5pm) Amsterdam's Diamond Museum explores the history of the trade and the sparkling creations that have adorned the world's rich and powerful. You'll learn how Amsterdam was the globe's diamond trade epicentre for many centuries, where local Jews dominated the cutting and polishing business, and how that trade moved to Antwerp after WWII, once Amsterdam lost its Jewish population. Almost all of the exhibits are clever re-creations, glinting in glass cases.

The museum is fairly small and low-tech. Those who are economically minded might want to save money by just going next door to **Coster Diamonds** (the company owns the museum and is attached to it) and taking a free factory tour, where you can see gem cutters and polishers at work and hear about the process.

**HOUSE OF BOLS** MUSEUM
Map p306 (www.houseofbols.com; Paulus Potterstraat 14; admission €11.50, 18yr & over only; ⏲noon-6pm, to 10pm Fri, closed Tue) Want to know what was slipped into your drink? This *jenever* (Dutch gin) museum is the place to find out. An hour's self-guided tour takes you on a journey that will leave you stirred but not shaken – that is, until you try the Tom Cruise moves on a TV monitor

here for your friends. The visit includes a confusing sniff test, a distilled history of the Bols company and a cocktail made by one of its formidable bartenders, who train at the academy upstairs. Ladies get a €5 discount when visiting after 5pm on Friday.

**ZUIDERBAD** SWIMMING POOL

Map p306 (☎678 13 90; Hobbemastraat 26; adult/child €4/2; ) If you're looking for something offbeat to do on a rainy day or to entertain the kids, consider this pool. The 1912 edifice behind the Rijksmuseum has been restored to its original glory, full of tiles, character and appreciative paddlers. Call for opening hours.

## EATING

Several snack vendors line the sidewalk between the Rijksmuseum and Van Gogh Museum, serving burgers, sandwiches, ice cream and drinks.

**LOETJE** TRADITIONAL DUTCH €€

Map p306 (www.cafeloetje.nl/index.html, in Dutch; Johannes Vermeerstraat 52; mains €15-25; ⏲lunch Mon-Fri, dinner Mon-Sat) This cafe's short menu may be written on the chalkboard, but everyone just orders thick steak, served medium-rare and swimming in delicious brown gravy. The staff are surprisingly good humoured, particularly considering the loud, meat-drunken mobs they typically serve.

**LA FALOTE** TRADITIONAL DUTCH €€

Map p306 (☎622 54 54; www.lafalote.nl; Roelof Hartstraat 26; mains €13-19; ⏲dinner Mon-Sat) Wee chequered-tablecloth La Falote is about Dutch home-style cooking, such as calf liver, meatballs with endives, and stewed fish with beets and mustard sauce. The prices are a bargain in an otherwise ritzy neighbourhood. And wait till the owner brings out the accordion.

**RENZO'S** ITALIAN €

Map p306 (☎673 16 73; www.renzos.nl, in Dutch; Van Baerlestraat 67; items per 100g €1.50-3.25; ⏲11am-9pm) Renzo's deli dishes out most of its pesto-y pastas, thickly cut sandwiches and omelettes for takeaway, though don't be shy about tucking in at the white-wood tables and benches on the mini terrace.

**RESTAURANT ELEMENTS** INTERNATIONAL €€

Map p306 (☎579 17 17; www.heerlijkamsterdam.nl; Roelof Hartstraat 6-8; 4-course set menu €24.50; ⏲5.30-10pm Mon-Fri) Students – the same ones who run the nearby College Hotel – prepare and serve contemporary international dishes at this mod restaurant. The result is white-glove service at an excellent price. There are usually two seatings per night (5.30pm and 7pm).

**SAMA SEBO** INDONESIAN €€

Map p306 (☎662 81 46; www.samasebo.com; PC Hooftstraat 27; rijsttafel per person €29.50, mains from €16.50; ⏲lunch & dinner Mon-Sat) Sama Sebo looks more like a brown cafe than a trip to the South Seas, and that's OK. The *rijsttafel* (Indonesian banquet) is 17 dishes (four to seven at lunchtime), but you can get individual plates if that's too much. It's had the same formula since 1970, so who are we to question?

**COBRA CAFE-RESTAURANT** CAFE €€

Map p306 (☎470 01 11; www.cobracafe.nl; Hobbemastraat 18; mains €7-13; ⏲lunch & dinner) This arty glass cube of a restaurant, which is full of original works by Corneille and Appel, sure is touristy. But when you're all museumed out and need a salad, a massive club sandwich or a slice of 'Karel Appel taart', you'll hardly notice.

## DRINKING & NIGHTLIFE

**WELLING** BROWN CAFE

Map p306 (www.cafewelling.nl, in Dutch; Jan Willem Brouwersstraat 32; ⏲4pm-1am Mon-Fri, 3pm-1am Sat & Sun) Tucked away behind the Concertgebouw, this is a relaxed spot to unwind with a newspaper, sip a frothy, cold *biertje* (glass of beer) and mingle with intellectuals and artists. Don't be surprised if the cafe's friendly cat hops onto your lap.

**WILDSCHUT** CAFE

Map p306 (Roelof Hartplein 1) This is a real gathering place for the Old South. When the weather's warm, pretty much everyone heads to the terrace for views of the Amsterdam School buildings. When the weather's not great, soak up the atmosphere in the art deco interior.

**MUSEUM SOUVENIRS**

If you're running short on time, and the Van Gogh Museum shop is packed to the rafters as usual, dash out instead to the **Museum Shop at the Museumplein.** The Van Gogh Museum and Rijksmuseum operate it jointly, so you can pick up posters, note cards and other art souvenirs from both museums in one fell swoop. While the selection is not as vast as the in-museum stores, the shop has enough iconic wares to satisfy most needs.

# ENTERTAINMENT

**CONCERTGEBOUW** CLASSICAL MUSIC

Map p306 (671 83 45; www.concertgebouw.nl, in Dutch; Concertgebouwplein 2-6; box office 1-7pm Mon-Fri, 10am-7pm Sat & Sun) One of the world's great concert halls, the Concertgebouw has near-perfect acoustics that flatter the already esteemed Royal Concertgebouw Orchestra. Bernard Haitink, the celebrated conductor, once remarked that the hall was the best instrument the orchestra ever had.

Every Wednesday at 12.30pm from September till the end of June, the Concertgebouw holds free half-hour concerts, traditionally of chamber music or public rehearsals of an evening event. The conductors and musicians often have an international pedigree so, unsurprisingly, the events are exceedingly popular.

Visitors aged up to 27 can purchase last-minute tickets costing a mere €10 (when available) from 45 minutes before the curtain goes up. All tickets function as free transit passes before and after concerts (just show it to the driver).

# SHOPPING

The biggest concentration of shops is around PC Hooftstraat, which teems with brands that need no introduction: Chanel, Burberry, Hugo Boss, Cartier, Gucci, Armani, Hermes, Tommy Hilfiger and Lacoste, to name just a few.

**BROEKMANS & VAN POPPEL** MUSIC

Map p306 (www.broekmans.com; Van Baerlestraat 92-94; closed Sun) Near the Concertgebouw (surprise!), this is the city's top choice for classical and popular sheet music, as well as music books. Head to the 1st floor for a comprehensive selection from the Middle Ages through to classical and contemporary.

**DE WINKEL VAN NIJNTJE** CHILDREN'S TOYS, MERCHANDISE

Map p306 (www.dewinkelvannijntje.nl; Beethovenstraat 71; ) Dutch illustrator Dick Bruna's most famous character, Miffy (Nijntje in Dutch), is celebrated in toys and kids' merchandise. Items range from pencils and soap bubbles to note pads, mouse pads, books, plush toys, clothing, playhouses, and even Royal Delftware plates. It's a good 1km south of the Museumplein via Beethovenstraat en route to Beatrixpark.

**VAN AVEZAATH BEUNE** FOOD & DRINK

Map p306 (www.vanavezaath-beune.nl, in Dutch; Johannes Verhulststraat 98; closed Sun & Mon) Counter-staff in serious-looking black aprons box up your chocolate-shaped *amsterdammertjes* (the bollards along city sidewalks) – a great gift, if you can keep from eating them yourself. And if you do, well, there's plenty more chocolatey goodness beckoning from the glass cases.

# De Pijp

## Neighbourhood Top Five

❶ Feast your senses on the international free-for-all of fresh produce, cheese, fish, clothing and quirky Dutch souvenirs at the **Albert Cuypmarkt** (p168), Europe's largest daily street market.

❷ Chill out, De Pijp style, at the lush **Sarphatipark** (p167), an urban oasis of rolling lawns, statues and fountains.

❸ Diverge from the well-trodden tourist pub crawls with a **bar hop** (p172) through the exuberantly friendly watering holes of De Pijp.

❹ Get treated *like* a beer, and then get treated to a beer, at the boisterously fun **Heineken Experience** (p167).

❺ Dive into the adventurous culinary terrain, from Surinamese to Kurdish, at an **ethnic eatery** (p167) where even globe-trotting foodies will find surprising delights.

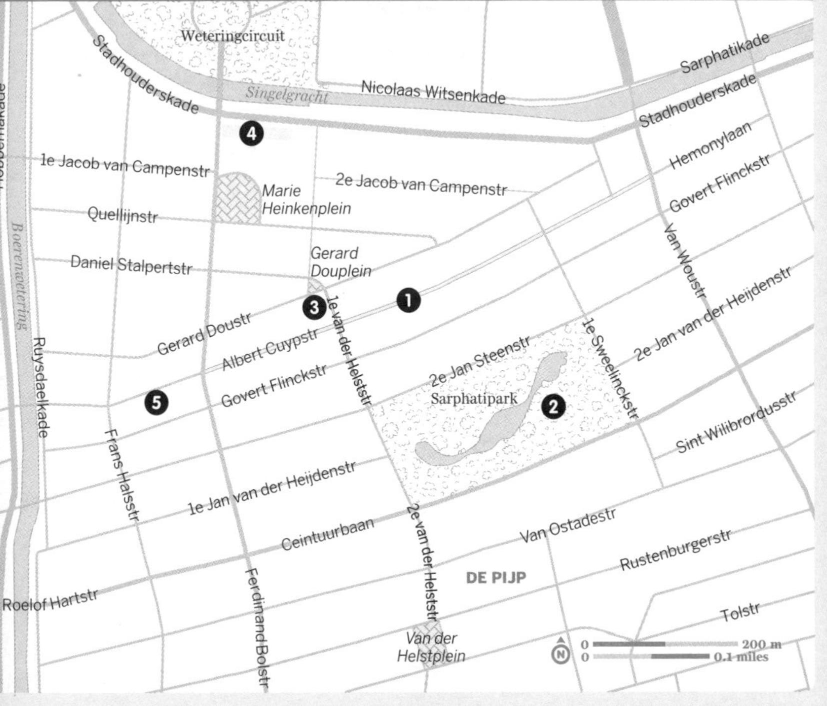


For more detail of this area, see Map p308 ➡

## Lonely Planet's Top Tip

Assemble an eclectic picnic from the Albert Cuypmarkt, then head two blocks to the gorgeous Sarphatipark.

### Best Places to Eat

- Op de Tuin (p168)
- Fa Pekelhaaring (p167)
- Orontes (p169)
- Mamouche (p168)

For reviews, see p167

### Best Places to Drink

- Café Berkhout (p171)
- Kingfisher (p171)
- Café Binnen Buiten (p171)
- Café Sarphaat (p171)
- Café de Greene Vlinder (p171)

For reviews, see p171

### Best Places to Shop

- Albert Cuypmarkt (p168)
- Het is Liefde (p173)
- Bleecker (p174)
- De Vredespijp (p174)
- Stenelux (p174)

For reviews, see p173

## Explore: De Pijp

No wonder locals say that De Pijp feels like a village smack in the centre of Amsterdam: the district is actually a large island connected to the rest of the city by 16 bridges.

It was Amsterdam's first 19th-century slum, and the district's name, 'the Pipe' (originally the 'YY neighbourhood'), is said to reflect its straight, narrow streets that supposedly resemble the stems of old clay pipes. It's very straightforward to explore. Start at the Albert Cuypmarkt with an open mind and keen eyes: deals and unique finds, from stiletto heels to fresh salmon fillets, abound. Give yourself an hour to soak up the sprawling market. Head to the lush Sarphatipark for a stroll before chilling out in one of the nearby brown cafes for an afternoon coffee.

De Pijp's streets are full of unique boutiques and speciality shops, so take some time exploring them (and be sure to stake out your dinner destination from the overwhelming options) before heading to the Heineken Experience. If you go in the late afternoon, the tasting at the end provides a built-in happy hour. Of course in fun-loving De Pijp it almost always feels like happy hour. Hobnob with the friendly locals by doing a neighbourhood bar crawl (p172), and you'll see how this district earns its moniker as Amsterdam's Latin Quarter.

## Local Life

- **The Other Red Light District** On the western border of De Pijp, and within view of the Rijksmuseum, there's a little red-light district along Ruysdaelkade, opposite Hobbemakade. For a glimpse of the world's oldest profession, minus stag parties and drunken crowds, this is the place to sate your curiosity.
- **Get Fishy** This is one Dutch delicacy you can smell from a block away: locals love to hit up De Pijp's raw herring stands on and around Albert Cuypmarkt. A tip: if you're feeling timid, order it in a bread roll, sans tail.
- **Budget Fashionista** In addition to the bargain clothing sold at the Albert Cuypmarkt, local fashion mavens know that the streets surrounding the market are home to some of the best budget clothing stores in town.

## Getting There & Away

- **Tram** Trams 16 and 24 roll down Ferdinand Bolstraat right by De Pijp's main sights; they come all the way from Centraal Station.

# SIGHTS

**SARPHATIPARK** PARK

Map p308 (Ceintuurbaan; ⌚24hr) While the Vondelpark is bigger and far more famous, this tranquil English-style park delivers an equally potent shot of pastoral summertime relaxation, with far fewer crowds. Named after Samuel Sarphati (1813–66), a Jewish doctor, businessman and urban innovator, the grounds are a mix of ponds, gently rolling meadows and wooded fringes. In the centre you'll see the **Sarphati memorial** (1886), a bombastic temple with a fountain, gargoyles and a bust of the great man himself.

**DE DAGERAAD** ARCHITECTURE

Map p308 (Dawn Housing Project; Pieter Lodewijk Takstraat) Following the key Housing Act of 1901, which forced the city to rethink neighbourhood planning and to condemn slums, de Dageraad housing estate was developed between 1918 and 1923 for poorer families. One of the most original architects of the expressionist Amsterdam School, Piet Kramer, drew up plans for this idiosyncratic complex in collaboration with Michel de Klerk. The swirling contours of the main tower have been compared to a butter churn.

# EATING

Come hungry, in every sense of the word. Anything and everything – funky, frilly, and fashionable – is fair game on De Pijp's cuisine scene. It's multi-ethnic yet also quintessentially Dutch, with plenty of old brown cafes churning out hearty lunch specials and bakeries selling lunchtime *broodjes* (breadrolls with fillings). Albert Cuypstraat, Ferdinand Bolstraat and Ceintuurbaan are all lined with unique ethnic spots.

TOP CHOICE **FA PEKELHAARING** ITALIAN €€

off Map p308 (www.pekelhaaring.nl, in Dutch; Van Woustraat 127-129; mains €5-10 lunch, €10-23 dinner; ⌚10am-midnight, closed Sun) Full of graphic designer types having long lunches with wine, this joint offers an arty industrial vibe with loads of fun and little pretence. Social touches – like the communal table,



## TOP SIGHTS HEINEKEN EXPERIENCE

Heineken, the Netherlands' famous beer brewery, wants you to know that this is not a museum – it's an experience. So you've tasted beer before: but have you experienced it with your five senses? Heineken has been going strong since 1864, and isn't shy about celebrating its place in the history of Dutch beer, and the 'Experience' is an appropriately immodest celebration. Welcome to Valhalla for beer lovers: we hope you're thirsty.

Right on the site of the company's old brewery, the state-of-the-art Heineken Experience is a rollicking self-guided tour that's tantamount to brew-worship. Learn the storied history of the Heineken family, find out how the logo has evolved, and follow the brewing process from water and hops all the way through to bottling. Along the way you can watch Heineken commercials from around the world, sniff the mash in copper tanks, visit the horse stables and make your own music video to send to folks back home. The Experience's crowning glory is Brew U – a 4-dimensional multimedia exhibit where you actually 'become' a beer as you get shaken up, heated up, sprayed with water, and 'bottled.' Do you need to love beer to dig this tour? No. (But it certainly helps.)

### DON'T MISS

- Becoming a beer by graduating from Brew U
- Learning to pour a proper frothy pint, Dutch-style

### PRACTICALITIES

- Map p308
- ☎20 523 94 35
- www.heinekenexperience.com
- Stadhouderskade 78
- Adult/child €8-15 €16/12 (under 18 only with adult supervision)
- ⌚11am-7pm

strewn with magazines and board games to play over dessert – belie the focused attention on fresh Italian flavours.

**EETWINKEL HET MAGAZIJN** CAFE €€

Map p308 (670 13 76; www.hetmagazijn.nl, in Dutch; Frans Halsstraat 68; 3-course menu €33; 5pm-9pm Tue-Sat, from 4pm Sun) Don't have any Dutch friends who might invite you over for a lovely three-course meal in their cosy, candlelit dining room? Never fear. That's where this tiny but magical spot comes in. Book ahead and anticipate conversing over antipasti and market-fresh fish at a big wooden farmhouse table with strangers who might become friends by the time the cheesecake arrives.

**MAMOUCHE** MOROCCAN €€

Map p308 (670 07 36; www.restaurantmamouche.nl; Quellijnstraat 104; mains €16-22; dinner, closed Mon) Mamouche gets serious acclaim for its French-accented North African cuisine: think Morocco amid minimalism. The sleek design, with exposed flooring, mottled raw plaster walls and slat-beam ceilings, complement the changing selection of organic, seasonal *tajine* (Moroccan stew) and couscous dishes. One of De Pijp's most posh urban spots.

**OP DE TUIN** MEDITERRANEAN €€

Map p308 (www.opdetuin.nl, in Dutch; Karel du Jardinstraat 47; 3-course menu €26-29; dinner Tue-Sun; ) This is the kind of breezy, informal neighbourhood restaurant where you can while away an evening snacking on an antipasti platter (let the chef decide on a mix of Mediterranean standards) or a beautifully prepared three-course meal, and fantasise that you live across the street.

**MAMBO** CAFE €

Map p308 (679 96 09; Eerste van der Helsstraat 66; mains €4-8; 9am-6pm Mon-Sat; ) Multicolored little wooden tables on the patio speak to the fresh flavours within. Our favourite post-Albert Cuypmarkt lunch stop, charming little Mambo rocks fresh salads, quiches, soups and cakes with whimsical flair.

**DE WAAGHALS** VEGETARIAN €€

Map p308 (679 96 09; www.waaghals.nl; Frans Halsstraat 29; mains €12-20; 5-9.30pm, closed Mon; ) The popular white-walled 'Dare-

## TOP SIGHTS
## ALBERT CUYPMARKT

Want to experience the 'real' Amsterdam at its wonderfully chaotic, multicultural best? Look no further than Europe's most sprawling – and dare we say most fun? – daily street market.

Named after landscape painter Albert Cuyp (1620–91), Albert Cuypmart is Amsterdam's largest and busiest market, and is legendary for its huge variety – including aromatic stalls selling Dutch cheese, fish, olives, herbs and spices, and fresh produce. Need some Saturday night bling or a new cell phone? How about a bike lock, curling iron, or some tulips for your sweetheart? There's also a staggering array of (mostly funky, sometimes junky) clothes and accessories. If you want it, it's likely the market's got it, and it's probably cheaper than anywhere else.

Don't forget to sample the cheese (just ask!), from a four-year-old Gouda to a creamy *boerenkaas* (farmer's cheese), or to blush at the adult chocolates, and indulge in a piping-hot *stroopwafel* (syrup waffle).

Take tram 16 or 24 to get to the market.

### DON'T MISS

- Cheese galore
- X-rated chocolates
- Only-in-Holland gifts (furry clog slippers, anyone?)
- *Stroopwafel* to nibble as you go

### PRACTICALITIES

- Map p308
- www.albertcuypmarkt.com, in Dutch
- Albert Cuypstraat, btw Ferdinand Bolstraat & Van Woustraat
- Admission free
- 9am-5pm, closed Sun

## AMSTERDAM'S LATIN QUARTER

*De Pijp uit gan,* which loosely translates to 'no one leaves De Pijp alive' was an old joke told for years around this historically working-class, close-knit neighbourhood. If the joke once drew upon truth, it now rings hollow: while a distinct (and multi-ethnic) blue collar culture still thrives here, it's tinged with an edge of such unmistakable coolness that De Pijp is sometimes called the 'Latin Quarter' of Amsterdam.

Like most 'hoods that earn the bohemian moniker, De Pijp's roots are humble. Its early shoddy tenement blocks, some of which collapsed even as they were being built in the 1860s, provided cheap housing not just for newly arrived workers drawn by the city's industrial revolution, but also for students, artists, writers and other poverty-stricken individuals. In the 1960s and '70s many of the working-class inhabitants left for greener pastures and the government began refurbishing the tenement blocks for immigrants from Morocco, Turkey, Suriname and the Netherlands Antilles. Many of these immigrants are being pushed out as De Pijp attracts a wealthier breed of professionals who are doing up apartments in grand style and lending the neighbourhood a more gentrified air.

Yet its hipness persists: like many illustrious neighbourhoods with blue-collar roots, De Pijp owes its spark and energy to a lively mix of people: labourers, intellectuals, immigrants and prostitutes, and now gays, lesbians and artists. Hip advertising agencies and funky boutiques line the streets, freelancers with their Mac Books crowd the coffeeshops, and occasional sightings of local resident (and Dutch film star) Carice Van Houten all lend this 'hood an irrepressible appeal, with enough street smarts and grit to keep it authentic. Let's hope it stays that way.



devil' is stylish enough that even non-vegies may re-examine their dining priorities. The menu concentrates on one country each month – say, Thailand or Italy – plus a rotating array of inventive seasonal, organic dishes. Book ahead (it takes online reservations, too).

### BALTI HOUSE — INDIAN €€

Map p308 (www.baltihouse.nl; Albert Cuypstraat 41; mains €12-20; ⊙dinner) One of the best-kept secrets in De Pijp is this friendly spot with its soothing interior. The classics – from a smooth butter chicken masala to fiery tandooris and biryanis – never disappoint, and the three kinds of Indian *rijsttafel* (banquet) present a worthy culinary adventure for the seriously hungry.

### DE SOEPWINKEL — SOUP €

Map p308 (www.soepwinkel.nl; 1e Sweelinckstraat 19; mains €5-8; ⊙11am-8pm Mon-Fri, to 6pm Sat; 🅥) Our favourite soup joint in town? Probably. In a sunny spot near Sarphatipark, rotating house-made soups (Thai fish, vegie harissa) compete with savoury, flaky quiches for lunchtime appetites.

### ZEN — JAPANESE €€

Map p308 (☎627 06 07; Frans Halsstraat 38; mains €8-20; ⊙noon-10pm Tue-Sat) Let's be frank: many Japanese restaurants are lovely, elegant poseurs. Zen, however, offers cooking like *okāsan* (mum) used to make: *domburi* (bowls of rice with various ingredients on top), sushi and *tonkatsu* (deep-fried pork cutlet) are just the start. Decor is minimalist Dutch-meets-Japanese.

### ORONTES — TURKISH €€

Map p308 (www.orontes.nl, in Dutch; Albert Cuypstraat 40; mains €13-17; ⊙dinner) The chef imports many of his ingredients (olives, pomegranate sauce and chickpeas) from his Turkish homeland, and authentic flavours are the result. Charcoal-grilled meat and fish dishes wow in their savoury simplicity; we're still dreaming about the grilled sea bass, lovingly stuffed with lemon, that we feasted upon. Vegetarians can proceed with enthusiasm: fantastically flavoursome hummus and eggplant dishes ensure you won't miss out.

### BAZAR AMSTERDAM — MIDDLE EASTERN €€

Map p308 (www.bazaramsterdam.nl; Albert Cuypstraat 182; mains €8-15; ⊙11am-midnight Mon-Thu, 11am-1am Fri, 9am-1am Sat, 9am-midnight Sun; 👪🅥) Beneath a golden angel in the middle of the Albert Cuypmarkt, this one-time Dutch Reformed church has fab-u-lous tile murals and 10,001 Arabian lights to complement the cuisine: from Moroccan to Turkish, Lebanese and Iranian. Fish and chicken dishes please meat eaters; eggplant and portobello mushroom dishes gratify vegetarians. Come for the gigantic breakfast spread – Amsterdam's best breakfast bargain – or just for a beer and baklava.

**BURGERMEESTER** BURGERS €

Map p308 (www.burgermeester.eu, in Dutch; Albert Cuypstraat 48; burgers €6-9; ⌚noon-11pm) This sleek little bistro – a play on 'mayor' *(burgemeester)* – makes the finest burgers in town, bar none. It uses only organic beef (or lamb, falafel or fish), in huge portions that would pass as a main dish without a bun. Then come the toppings: feta, fresh mint, pesto, pancetta and more. You can also get a killer milkshake, but don't ask for chips or fries.

**TODAY'S** ITALIAN €

Map p308 (www.todaysamsterdam.com; Saenredamstraat 26hs; items €4-8; ⌚1-8pm Tue-Sat) We love that this tiny deli/cafe functions as an impromptu Italian cultural centre, with snatches of Italian heard among the English, Japanese and Dutch being spoken by neighbourhood expats and long-time residents. They all know that chef Davide makes the most wicked focaccia and creative lasagnes (the pumpkin knocked our socks off) around. Take away, eat in or book a private dinner in the lofted dining room. The house-made tiramisu is one of De Pijp's worthier sins.

**CAFÉ VOLLE MAAN** CAFE €€

Map p308 (www.eetcafevollemaan.nl, in Dutch; Sarphatipark 4; mains €5-16; ⌚10am-1am Sun-Thu, to 3am Fri & Sat; 📶) You can't go wrong for lunch or brunch at this airy, bi-level cafe right on Sarphatipark. Play a game of Scrabble near the sunny floor-to-ceiling windows while munching on cheese pancakes, good burgers or homemade soups like sweet potato and thyme. The apple tart rocks.

**ZAGROS** KURDISH €€

Map p308 (www.zagrosrestaurant.nl; Albert Cuypstraat 50; mains €11-15; ⌚5.30-10.30pm Tue-Sat) Never tried Kurdish food? Neither had we, but we're glad we did. Just as Kurdistan straddles Turkey and Iran, so does the cuisine, with grills and stews (mostly lamb and chicken), salads of cucumber, tomato or onion, and starters like hummus and *dumast* (thick, dry yoghurt). Book ahead on weekends.

**ALBINA** SURINAMESE-CHINESE €

Map p308 (☎671 13 96; Albert Cuypstraat 67-71; mains €6-10; ⌚lunch & dinner) If you're looking for stylish surrounds, stop reading now. If, however, you're after quality examples of Surinamese food (skip the rather bland Chinese selections), by all means take a seat. A colossal portion of *roti kip* (chicken curry, flaky roti, potatoes, cabbage and egg) is a fine replenishment after a couple of hours at Albert Cuypmarkt.

**LUNCHROOM HANNIBAL** CAFE €

Map p308 (☎673 54 88; Ferdinand Bolstraat 92; mains €3-9; ⌚9am-5.30pm Mon-Sat) Diners unfurl newspapers over big omelettes, pancakes and coffee at tables by big, bright windows. This quintessentially Dutch workingman's cafe also knocks out burgers and sandwiches.

**BAKKEN MET PASSIE** BAKERY & SWEETS €

Map p308 (☎670 13 76; Albert Cuypstraat 51-53; items €2-7; ⌚7am-6pm Tue-Sat) Say your sweetie hates ethnic food but you desperately want something exotic on the Albert Cuypstraat. This quietly fancy shop bakes the appropriate bribes, like yummy Valrhona chocolate tart and lemon cake.

**TAART VAN M'N TANTE** BAKERY & SWEETS €

Map p308 (www.detaart.com; Ferdinand Bolstraat 10; items €4-7; ⌚10am-6pm; 👪) One of Amsterdam's best-loved cake shops operates from this uber-kitsch parlour, turning out apple pies (Dutch, French or 'tipsy'), pecan pie, and wish your-mother-baked-like-this cakes. Hot-pink walls accent cakes dressed like Barbie dolls – or are they Barbies dressed like cakes?

**ROOTS** DUTCH €€

Map p308 (www.rootsamsterdam.nl; Stadhouderskade 123; mains €17-20; ⌚noon-1am Sun-Thu, to 2am Fri & Sat; 📶) What's not to like when every dish is locally sourced and house-made – even the mayonnaise – and many dishes are baked in a wood-fired oven? The integrity of the chefs shines through in the flavours. Savour the mod-rustic interior as you sample the Dutch cheese plate featuring delicacies.

**WILD MOA PIES** PIES €

Map p308 (www.pies.nu; Marie Van Ostadestraat 147; mains €3-4; ⌚9am-6:30pm Mon-Fri, 10:30am-6pm Sat; 📶) Just because this unassuming corner joint serves the only authentic

New Zealand-Australian-style meat pies in town doesn't mean they aren't the best. It has creative vegie, egg and cheese varieties. Everyone will enjoy heading Down Under come lunchtime.

## DRINKING & NIGHTLIFE

The neighbourhood that houses the old Heineken brewery is appropriately chock-full of watering holes. In particular, the streets around Gerard Douplein heave with a spirited, youngish, local crowd.

### TOP CHOICE CAFÉ BERKHOUT — BROWN CAFE

Map p308 (www.cafeberkhout.nl, in Dutch; Stadhouderskade 77) Once a derelict spot, this beautifully refurbished brown cafe – with its dark wood, mirrored and chandelier-rich splendour, and shabby elegance – is a natural post-Heineken Experience wind-down spot. (No matter how much beer you've swilled at the Experience, you can't miss this cafe: it's right across the street.)

### TOP CHOICE KINGFISHER — DESIGNER BAR/CAFE

Map p308 (www.kingfishercafe.nl; Ferdinand Bolstraat 24) With friendly staff and loyal regulars, Kingfisher is the nexus of De Pijp's signature feel-good vibe. The communal table welcomes laptops, newspapers and lunching by day. By happy hour the place is kicking, disproving any rumours that the Dutch are any less than sociable to strangers.

### CAFÉ DE GREENE VLINDER — BROWN CAFE

Map p308 (www.cafedegroenevlinder.nl; Albert Cuypstraat 130) The Green Butterfly strikes just the right balance between hip and *gezellig* (cosy), meaning it's the perfect spot to go for a *koffie verkeerd* (coffee with lots of milk) in the warm wood interior before meeting up for a *biertje* (glass of beer) on the hopping patio.

### CAFÉ BINNEN BUITEN — BROWN CAFE

Map p308 (Ruysdaelkade 115) The minute there's a sliver of sunshine – or warmth – in the air, this cafe gets packed. Sure the food looks good (and the people even better), and the bar is candlelit and cosy. But what really brings the crowds is simply the best canal-side terrace in De Pijp, offering a terrific way to waste an entire afternoon.

### CAFÉ SARPHAAT — BROWN CAFE

Map p308 (☎675 15 65; Ceintuurbaan 157) Grab an outdoor table along the Sarphatipark, tuck into a *croque monsieur* (grilled ham and cheese sandwich) and a frothy beer, and see if you don't feel like a local. This is one of the neighbourhood's most genial spots, with a lovely old bar that makes sipping a *jenever* (Dutch gin) in broad daylight seem like a good idea.

### PILSVOGEL — BROWN CAFE

Map p308 (www.pilsvogel.nl; Gerard Douplein 14) The kitchen dispenses small plates (€3.50 to €5.50) to a crowd aged 20-something, but that's really secondary when you're sitting on De Pijp's most festive corner. A warm Mediterranean feel reigns at this casual tapas-cum-bar, with one of the neighbourhood's prime people-watching patios.

### GAMBRINUS — BROWN CAFE

Map p308 (www.gambrinus.nl, in Dutch; Ferdinand Bolstraat 180) This congenial bi-level cafe, with its giant windows and sprawling terrace, boasts some of the best 'bar' food in town, from lunchtime *broodjes* to full-on dinner. With a clientele whose ages span from college-age to retirement-age, wise-cracking bartenders and vintage fixtures, it's as cheerful as a candy store – which is exactly what it used to be in the old days.

### CHOCOLATE BAR — DESIGNER BAR

Map p308 (www.chocolate-bar.nl, in Dutch; 1e Jan van der Helststraat 62a) Chocolate isn't the draw here – it's the sleek vibe, bright turquoise walls and Europol soundtrack. The candlelit bar makes this place feel like a night out even at noon: curl up with a cosy blanket on the patio on chilly days and pose with a fashion mag. At night, it's a scene.

### CAFÉ KRULL — BROWN CAFE

Map p308 (☎662 02 14; Sarphatipark 2) This very sophisticated cafe is full of folks either reading thick books or having intense conversations. A communal table, enormous windows, 10 beers on tap, and smiling bartenders spinning eclectic music make this place ooze with effortless charm from morning to night.

### YO-YO — COFFEESHOP

off Map p308 (☎664 71 73; 2e Jan van deer Heijdenstraat 79) The large windows, minimalist furnishings and funky art might make you think you've stumbled upon an airy

START BARÇA
END CHOCOLATE BAR
DISTANCE LESS THAN 1KM
DURATION 2½ TO 3 HOURS

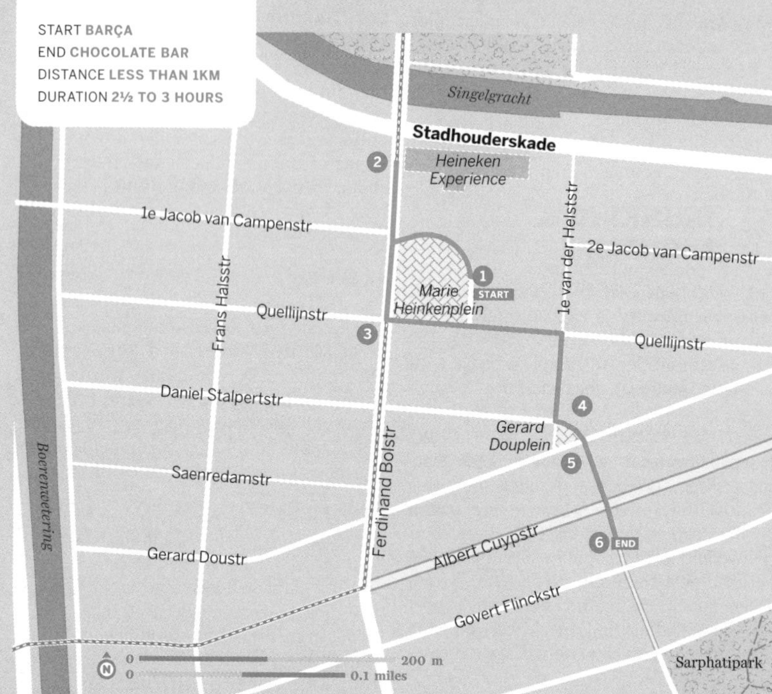




Neighbourhood Walk

## De Pijp Pub Crawl

For a memorable pub crawl worth sending a (hopefully sober) postcard home about, start with the enthusiastic after-work crowd on Marie Heinekenplein and drink your way south towards Sarphatipark, ending the night (if you dare) in a late-night *nachtcafe* (night cafe).

First off, make sure you're properly fortified: order some tapas at 1 **Barça**, along with your first cocktail. Make it sangria or a mojito. After soaking up the Iberian vibe – either on the patio or inside listening to the clubby music – cross the street for a beer with the chatty after-work set at 2 **Café Berkhout**. Admire the furnishings and kick back on the window-side couches before heading down Ferdinand Bolstraat to 3 **Kingfisher**. Sit at the bar, converse with the bright young professionals or the friendly staff, and feel like you own the place. Enjoy yourself with some *bitterballen* (small meat croquettes) before moseying down to 4 **Het Paardje**, the see-and-be-seen nexus of De Pijp's beautiful people. As you leave Het Paardje, marvel at the festive impromptu street party that Gerard Douplein becomes in all kinds of weather. Head south for some sangria at 5 **Pilsvogel** or a nightcap at the 6 **Chocolate Bar**, where the cuddle-worthy blankets will keep you toasty on a chilly night.

museum-cafe. But this coffeeshop on a leafy residential corner of De Pijp is all about organic weed and quiet reflection.

**KATSU** COFFEESHOP

Map p308 (www.katsu.nl; 1e Jan van der Helststraat 70) One of Amsterdam's hidden secrets, flamboyant Katsu will chill you out before you even light up. Like the surrounding neighbourhood, it brims with colourful characters of all ages and dispositions. A front table with newspapers lends a bookish vibe, although the smoke inside probably won't make you feel any smarter.

**BARÇA** DESIGNER BAR

Map p308 (www.bar-ca.nl, in Dutch; Marie Heinekenplein 30-31) One of the hottest bars in the 'hood, this club (themed like 'Barcelona in Amsterdam') is the heartbeat of Marie Heinekenplein. Hang in the posh plush-red and dark-wood interior, or spread out onto the terrace.

**HET PAARDJE** BAR

Map p308 (☎664 35 39; Gerard Douplein 1) Single? Get on 'the horse'. On any given night the neighbourhood's hotties head here, whether fresh from a broken heart or from a football game. Equal opportunity sexiness abounds. In fact, you might spend so much time turning your head that your beer goes warm.

## ENTERTAINMENT

TOP CHOICE **BADCUYP** JAZZ

Map p308 (www.badcuyp.nl, in Dutch; 1e Sweelinckstraat 10) If every neighbourhood were fortunate enough to have a vibrant music cafe like this, the world would be a jazzier place. Combining a community feel with top notch, international performers, Badcuyp brings a shot of pure bohemian energy to the neighbourhood. From Sunday jazz sessions to salsa nights, you can't walk out after an evening here and not feel the love.

**RIALTO CINEMA** CINEMA

Map p308 (www.rialtofilm.nl, in Dutch; Ceintuurbaan 338) This great, old cinema near Sarphatipark focuses on premieres, and shows eclectic art-house fare from around the world. Note that foreign films feature Dutch – not English – subtitles. The bi-level, stylish cafe buzzes with pre- and post-cinema folks dissecting plot, theme and cinematography.

**CC MUZIEKCAFÉ** LIVE MUSIC

Map p308 (www.cccafe.nl; Rustenburgerstraat 384) De Pijp has long needed a place like this: a low-key yet buzzing little nightclub that dishes up interesting live acts – from reggae to soul to rock – along with zero attitude.

## SHOPPING

After you've hit the Albert Cuypmarkt, head to the surrounding small streets. They're less crowded than the market, and dotted with boutiques and galleries – perfect for a quiet browse. You'll find eclectic women's fashion and shoes on Van Woustraat, off Ceintruurbaan.

TOP CHOICE **TILLER GALERIE** ART

Map p308 (www.tillergalerie.com; 1e Jacob van Campenstraat 1; ⏲Thu-Sun) This intimate, friendly gallery has works by George Heidweiller (check out the surreal Amsterdam skyscapes) and Peter Donkersloot (think fuzzy, magnificent portraits of animals and famous actors like Marlon Brando). Prints by the late Herman Brood round out the selection.

TOP CHOICE **FIETSFABRIEK** BICYCLES

Map p308 (www.fietsfabriek.nl, in Dutch; 1e Jacob van Campenstraat 12; ⏲closed Sun) Wessel van den Bosch trained as an architect, and now he makes custom bicycles from this wild and crazy workshop, one of several in Amsterdam. Come in and pick up a *bakfiets* (cargo bike), a *familiefiets* (bike with covered 'pram') or a standard *omafiets* (one-gear city bike). Just browsing is a joy.

TOP CHOICE **HET IS LIEFDE** GIFTS

Map p308 (www.hetisliefde.nl, in Dutch; 1e van der Helststraat 13-15; ⏲Tue-Sat) Come feel the love in this wedding shop, where all forms of romance and general festivity are celebrated. Browse all manner of wedding keepsakes and ephemera, including whimsical cake toppers in boy-girl, boy-boy and girl-girl couplings. Shopping here is a sheer delight – whether you're falling in love or recovering from heartbreak.

**STENELUX** GIFTS

Map p308 (☎662 14 90; 1e Jacob van Campenstraat 2; ⊙Thu-Sat) Find a delightful collection of gems, minerals and stones in this longtime favourite shop, or buy a (surprisingly affordable) old fossil for that old fossil you left back home. Stenelux has a fascinating collection from this world and beyond (including meteorites).

**BLEECKER** CLOTHING

Map p308 (www.bleeckernewvintage.nl; 1e Jan Steenstraat 131; ⊙Tue-Sat) Sleek but not slick, this well-curated store, inspired by shops in New York and Paris, is a vintage lover's heaven, with a thoughtful eye towards men's and women's fashions, fab shoes and helpful staff. No rifling through dusty racks here.

**BLONDE** GIFTS

Map p308 (www.blonde-amsterdam.nl; Gerard Doustraat 69; ⊙Thu-Sat) The friendly blonde owners glaze plates and dishes in designs that are hilarious, adorable and colourful: ladies lunching, beach scenes, cakes and chocolates. Great gifts for anyone who likes modern kitsch with a sense of humour.

**DE EMAILLEKEIZER** HOMEWARES

Map p308 (☎664 18 47; www.emaillekeizer.nl; 1e Sweelinckstraat 15; ⊙closed Sun) This colourful store brims with appealing enamel treasures, including metal tableware decorated in interesting designs from China, Ghana and Poland. The Dutch signs, such as the unmistakeable 'coffeeshop' signs, make interesting souvenirs.

**DE VREDESPIJP** HOMEWARES, FURNITURE

Map p308 (www.vredespijp-artdeco.com, in Dutch; 1e van der Helstraat 11a; ) Art deco home-accessories and furniture shop meets tiny cafe with excellent home-baked goods. It's De Pijp's ideal rainy day refuge.

**RAAK** CLOTHING, GIFTS

Map p308 (www.raakamsterdam.nl, in Dutch; 1e Van der Helstraat 46; ⊙closed Sun) Near the Albert Cuypmarkt, you'll find unique, mid-priced fashion and gifts by Dutch and Scandinavian designers.

**NOOR** CLOTHING, GIFTS

Map p308 (☎670 29 16; Albert Cuypstraat 145) There are so many women's clothing stores on the Albert Cuypmarkt, you could spend a week browsing the bargains. The affordable, modern fashion at Noor may make you want to skip the competition altogether. Don't miss the jam-packed sale rack.

# Plantage, Eastern Islands & Eastern Docklands

PLANTAGE | EASTERN ISLANDS | EASTERN DOCKLANDS

## Neighbourhood Top Five

❶ Lions and tigers and bears, oh my! Frolicking with the animals at the gorgeous **Artis Royal Zoo** (p178) is one of Amsterdam's wildest adventures.

❷ Put yourself in the shoes of courageous WWII Dutch Resistance fighters at the sobering yet inspiring **Verzetsmuseum** (p177).

❸ Imagine a time when the Dutch East India Trading company ruled the seas at the atmospheric **Entrepotdok** (p177).

❹ Experience live classical music or jazz at the acoustically, and visually, stunning **Muziekgebouw Aan 't IJ** (p178).

❺ Glimpse the future of Amsterdam at the **Eastern Docklands** and **Eastern Islands** (p178), where modern architecture and design meet a forward-thinking yet ages-old maritime tradition.

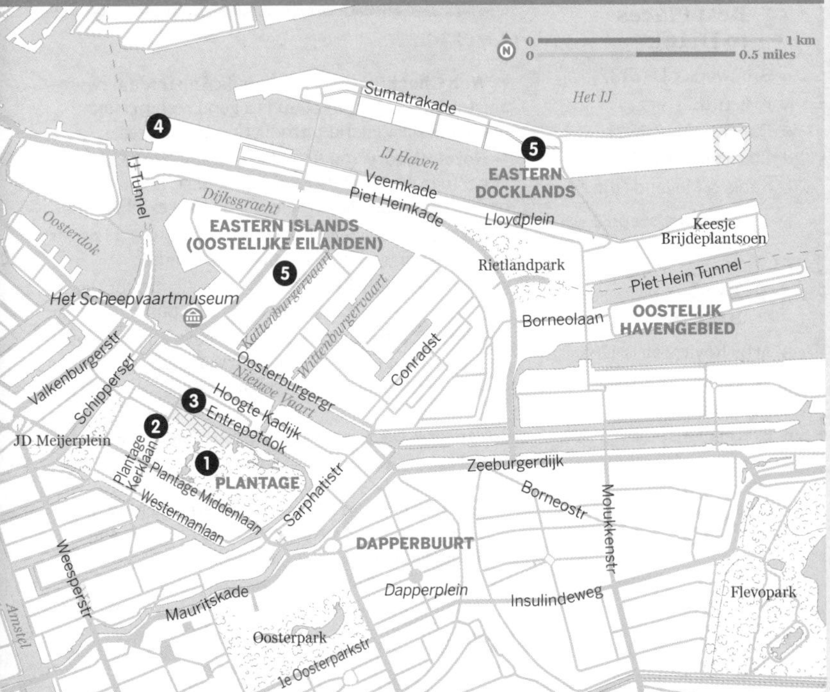


For more detail of this area, see Map p310 ➡

## Lonely Planet's Top Tip

Too many travellers overlook the Eastern Docklands and Eastern Islands, thinking them too far out of the centre (when it's actually less than a 10-minute bike or tram ride). If you're remotely into boats, maritime history or modern architecture, don't even think about skipping this area.

## Best Places to Eat

- Fifteen (p180)
- Koffiehuis van Den Volksbond (p180)
- Odessa (p180)
- Café Kadijk (p180)
- Paerz (p180)

For reviews, see p179

## Best Places to Drink

- Brouwerij 't IJ (p182)
- KHL (p182)
- Café Koosje (p182)
- Star Ferry (p182)
- Kanis & Meiland (p182)

For reviews, see p182

## Best Sights

- Artis Royal Zoo (p178)
- Verzetsmuseum (p177)
- Hortus Botanicus (p177)
- EYE Film Institute (p177)
- Het Scheepvaartsmuseum (p178)

For reviews, see p177

## Explore: Plantage, Eastern Islands & Eastern Docklands

The leafy district known as the Plantage (Plantation) was once a district of parks and gardens, named after the plantations the Dutch tended in their colonies. That legacy lives on, and the neighbourhood is a lovely place to stroll and admire the 19th century architecture.

North and east of the Eastern Islands (the epicenter of Amsterdam's residential and commercial expansion projects), the historic Eastern Docklands, a one-time shipyard and warehouse district, sat derelict for decades. If you're looking for one place to see the cutting edge of Dutch – and indeed European – architecture, this is the place.

Spend the first day in the Plantage, with at least a couple of hours at the Artis Royal Zoo, followed by a walk through the Hortus Botanicus. Have a picnic lunch in the Wertheimpark before you spend your afternoon at the Verzetsmuseum.

The Eastern Docklands and Eastern Islands are literally a breath of fresh air – invigorating to visit as a contrast to the city centre. There are few traditional sights, but mod architecture such as the silver building dubbed 'the Whale', the swooping red footbridge off Borneo, the shiny central library and the sparkling performance halls of the Muziekgebouw aan 't IJ are arresting.

## Local Life

- **Web Check** Eastern Docklands Amsterdam (www.amsterdamdocklands.com) is a good resource for history and a general introduction to the area.
- **Hotel History** You don't have to stay at the Lloyd Hotel to experience its fascinating past. Pop in to wine or dine, and don't skip the hotel history exhibit.
- **Bike It** The Eastern Docklands and Eastern Islands are best seen by bike – so take a bike tour.
- **Dinner & Nightlife** Come for dinner, stay for the DJs, dancing and stargazing onboard the fabulous Odessa.
- **Lights, Camera, Action** Locals have long awaited the opening of the EYE Film Institute, Europe's most innovative homage to the cinematic arts.

## Getting There & Away

- **Tram** Trams 9 and 14 are handy for reaching the Plantage; tram 10 goes to the Eastern Islands and Eastern Docklands.

# SIGHTS

## Plantage

### VERZETSMUSEUM — MUSEUM

Map p310 (Dutch Resistance Museum; ☎620 25 35; www.dutchresistancemuseum.org; Plantage Kerklaan 61; adult/under 7yr/7-15yr €6.50/free/3.50; ⌚10am-5pm Tue-Fri, 11am-5pm Sat-Mon) This museum shows, in no uncertain terms, how much courage it takes to actively resist an adversary so ruthless that you can't trust neighbours, friends or even family. The exhibits give an excellent insight into the difficulties faced by those who fought the German occupation during WWII from within – as well as the minority who went along with the Nazis. Topics include the concepts of active and passive resistance, how the illegal press operated, how 300,000 people were kept in hiding and how all this could be funded. Labels are in Dutch and English. The elegant cafe next door is a perfect refuge for a post-museum discussion of the politics of resistance over coffee and cakes.

### EYE FILM INSTITUTE — MUSEUM

off Map p310 (☎589 14 00; www.eyefilm.nl) The EYE Film Institute opened in late 2011 in a stunning new building in the Eastern Docklands, on the banks of IJ. Not a museum with displays as such, the museum has a large collection of memorabilia including over half a million photos, 20,000 books and a priceless archive of 37,000 films that are screened in four theatres, sometimes with live music. The museum features several cafes with expansive indoor and outdoor seating.

### HORTUS BOTANICUS — GARDEN

Map p310 (☎625 90 21; www.dehortus.nl; Plantage Middenlaan 2a; adult/child 5-14yr €7.50/3.50; ⌚9am-5pm Mon-Fri, 10am-5pm Sat & Sun, to 7pm daily Jul & Aug, to 4pm daily Dec & Jan) Established way back in 1638, this venerable garden became a repository for tropical seeds and plants brought in (read: smuggled out of other countries) by Dutch trading ships. From here, coffee, pineapple, cinnamon and palm-oil plants were distributed throughout the world. The 4000-plus species are kept in wonderful structures, including the colonial-era seed house and a three-climate glasshouse (1993). The butterfly house is a hit with kids and stoned adults. Guided tours (additional €1) are held at 2pm on Sunday year-round.

### WERTHEIMPARK — PARK

Map p310 (Plantage Parklaan; ⌚dawn-dusk) Opposite the Hortus Botanicus, this park is a brilliant, willow-shaded spot for lazing by the Nieuwe Herengracht. Its most significant feature is the Auschwitz Memorial, designed by Dutch writer Jan Wolkers: a panel of broken mirrors installed in the ground reflects the sky.

### HOLLANDSCHE SCHOUWBURG — HISTORIC BUILDING

Map p310 (Dutch Theatre; ☎626 99 45; www.hollandscheschouwburg.nl; Plantage Middenlaan 24; admission free; ⌚11am-4pm, closed Yom Kippur) This historic theatre – first known as the Artis Theatre after its inception in 1892 – quickly became a hub of cultural life in Amsterdam, staging major dramas and operettas. In WWII the occupying Germans turned it into a 'show theatre' for Jews, then a detention centre for Jews awaiting deportation. Up to 80,000 Jews passed through here on their way to the death camps. Glass panels are engraved with the names of all Jewish families deported, and upstairs is a modest exhibit hall with photos and artefacts of Jewish life before and during the war.

### ENTREPOTDOK — ARCHITECTURE

Map p310 The area northeast of the Plantage was the stomping ground of the Dutch East India Company (VOC), which grew rich on sea trade in the 17th century. The VOC owned this 500m row of warehouses, located in a customs-free zone and the largest storage depot in Europe at the time. Some of the original facades have been preserved, and the facility has been converted into desirable offices, apartments and fetching dockside cafes, with tables perfect for lazing away an afternoon at the water's edge.

### DE GOOYER WINDMILL — WINDMILL

Map p310 (Funenkade 5) This 18th-century grain mill is the sole survivor of five windmills that once stood in this part of town. It was moved to its current spot in 1814. The mill was fully renovated in 1925 and is now a private home. The public baths alongside the windmill were converted into the Brouwerij 't IJ in 1985.

TOP SIGHTS
## ARTIS ROYAL ZOO

A zoo, a bourgeois park or a manicured English garden? The Artis Royal Zoo feels like all three wrapped up in one elegant package.

The zoo is the world's third-largest, and the oldest zoo in mainland Europe – but lest you think this is an anachronistic homage to the old days when wildlife was regarded with fear, know that it's a beautifully curated experience, with plenty of room to observe and simply reflect on the wildness and the grandness of the animal kingdom.

In addition to the expected zoo attractions – big cats, apes and gorillas – the African savannah is a highlight. Another must-see is the aquarium, a graceful purpose-built hall with a rainforest, a tropical coral reef and a cross-section of an Amsterdam canal.

Locals as well as tourists visit to stroll the lush, manicured paths, laid out in the former Plantage gardens. The grounds are packed with heritage-listed 19th-century buildings and monuments, making it feel more like a zoological museum than a zoo. It also has a lovely, airy cafe.

Take tram 9 from Centraal Station or tram 14 from Dam Square

### DON'T MISS

- The aquarium
- The lion habitat
- The African savannah
- The planetarium

### PRACTICALITIES

- Map p310
- ☎523 34 00
- www.artis.nl, in Dutch
- Plantage Kerlaan 38-40
- Adult/child 3-9yr €18.95/15.50
- ⏲9am-6pm Apr-Oct, to 5pm Nov-Mar

**KADIJKSPLEIN** SQUARE

Map p310 (cnr Kadijksplein & Hoogte Kadijk) Mention this tranquil square, flanked by some of the best cafe terraces in town, and locals might give you a puzzled look. That's because despite its pretty location and twin views – 17th century canals and cruise ships docking at the Docklands – it somehow remains off the radar. Is this Amsterdam's most underrated square?: enjoy a *koffiee verkeerd* (coffee with lots of milk) at one of its excellent cafes and take your time deciding if you agree.

**MUIDERPOORT** GATE

Map p310 (Alexanderplein) This grand, classical arch was built in 1770 as a gateway to the city. On the south side you'll see the Amsterdam emblem of three St Andreas' crosses, while on the other side there's a cog ship emblem, which appeared on Amsterdam's coat of arms in medieval times. In 1811 Napoleon rode triumphantly through the gate with his royal entourage, and promptly demanded food for his ragged troops.

## Eastern Islands & Eastern Docklands

**HET SCHEEPVAARTMUSEUM** MUSEUM

Map p310 (☎523 22 22; www.scheepvaartmuseum.nl; Kattenburgerplein 1; adult/child 5-17yr €15/7.50; ⏲9am-5pm) After a lengthy renovation, this historic admiralty building is celebrating 30 years as home to one of the world's most extensive collections of maritime memorabilia. Early shipping routes, naval combat, fishing and whaling are all explained in loving detail, and there are some 500 models of boats and ships.

The highlight of your visit may be viewing the full-scale replica of the Dutch East India Company's 700-tonne *Amsterdam*, one of the largest ships of the fleet, moored just outside. Take bus 22 east from Centraal Station to get here.

**MUZIEKGEBOUW AAN 'T IJ** CONCERT HALL

Map p310 (☎tickets 788 20 00; www.muziekgebouw.nl; Piet Heinkade 1; admission to building free, performance prices vary; ⏲ticket office noon-7pm Mon-Sat) Even if you don't catch a show here, the bold and beautiful 'Music Building on the IJ' is a feast for the eyes. The performance complex – with a main hall, Muziekgebouw aan 't IJ, for varying types of shows and the smaller Bimhuis for jazz – was designed by the Danish firm 3xNielsen and was some 20 years in the making.

The venue's Star Ferry cafe makes a great stop for the view alone. On the upper floor you'll find the computerised 'sound garden', a perfect diversion for children. You can visit the concert hall during box office opening hours, or when a show is on.

**NEMO** MUSEUM

Map p310 (☎531 32 33; www.e-nemo.nl; Oosterdok 2; adult/child under 4yr/student €12.50/free/6.50; ⏰10am-5pm Tue-Sun Sep-May, 10am-5pm daily Jun-Aug; 👪) Perched atop the entrance to the IJ Tunnel is NEMO, the largest museum of science and technology in the Netherlands. Italian architect Renzo Piano (whose works also include the Centre Pompidou in Paris) conceived of this design as the inverse of the tunnel below it.

It's really meant for kids, but most grown-ups will enjoy it, too. There are loads of interactive exhibits: drawing with a laser, 'antigravity' trick mirrors and a 'lab' where you can answer such questions as 'How black is black?' and 'How do you make cheese?'. Signage is in English and Dutch. NEMO's stepped roof (admission free) is the city's largest summer terrace, and worth a stair climb for the fantastic view.

**PERSMUSEUM** MUSEUM

Map p310 (Press Museum; ☎692 88 10; www.persmuseum.nl, in Dutch; Zeeburgerkade 10; adult/child under 13yr/13-18yr €4.50/free/3.25; ⏰10am-5pm Tue-Fri, noon-5pm Sun) This museum is the thoughtful and vigilant caretaker of Dutch journalism history, and is loads more interesting to non-Dutch speakers than it may sound. It's housed in sleek new premises, and has a large collection of historic newspapers (going all the way back to 1600), political and editorial cartoons and press photos, and a great stock of amusing old publicity posters.

**CENTRALE BIBLIOTHEEK AMSTERDAM** LIBRARY

Map p310 (Amsterdam Central Library; ☎523 09 00; www.oba.nl; Oosterdokskade 143; admission free; ⏰10am-10pm) Unveiled with great fanfare in 2007, this pleasingly symmetrical, nine-storey 'tower of knowledge' (its self-appointed nickname) is the country's largest library and has claimed a commanding spot in Amsterdam's increasingly modern landscape. Inviting chairs and couches are scattered around every floor, as are loads of free internet terminals and free wi-fi. Relax in the top-floor cafe with its views over the city and water.

LOCAL KNOWLEDGE

### A WILD WWII HIDING PLACE

Local rumour has it that one of the little-known hiding places in Amsterdam for persecuted Jews, and young Dutch men fearing mandatory forced labour in the German war effort, was in the Artis Royal Zoo along with the animals.

**ARCAM** ARCHITECTURE

Map p310 (Stichting Architectuur Centrum Amsterdam; ☎620 48 78; www.arcam.nl; Prins Hendrikkade 600; admission free; ⏰1-5pm Tue-Sat) This showpiece building of the Amsterdam Architecture Foundation is a one-stop shop for all your architectural needs. Exhibits vary, but you are sure to find books, guide maps and suggestions for tours on foot, by bike and by public transport.

**WERFMUSEUM 'T KROMHOUT** MUSEUM

Map p310 (☎627 67 77; www.machinekamer.nl, in Dutch; Hoogte Kadijk 147; adult/child €4.75/2.75; ⏰10am-3pm Tue) On the outer side of the dyke is an 18th-century wharf where boats are still repaired. The eastern hall is a museum devoted to shipbuilding and to the indestructible marine engines that were designed and built here. Anyone with an interest in marine engineering will love the place; others will probably want to move on. Signage is almost entirely in Dutch only.

## EATING

The Plantage may be just steps from Nieuwmarkt, but what a difference those few steps make, taking you to an area that's blissfully quiet yet close to some fascinating sights. In the Eastern Islands and Eastern Docklands, a lot of our favourite eating places are by (or in some cases, literally on) the water.

## Plantage

### TOP CHOICE KOFFIEHUIS VAN DEN VOLKSBOND INTERNATIONAL €€

Map p310 (www.koffiehuisvandenvolksbond.nl, in Dutch; Kadijksplein 4; mains €13-18; ⊙dinner) This laid-back place began life as a charitable coffeehouse for dockworkers, and it still has a fashionably grungy vibe – wood floors, tarnished chandeliers and a giant red-rose mural. The ever-changing menu features huge plates of creative comfort food with dishes like a red onion tart with blue cheese and lamb with artichoke puree. Swoon over the Belgian chocolate terrine as you gaze up and wonder when someone last took a bath in the antique tub perched above your head.

### CAFÉ KADIJK INDONESIAN €€

Map p310 (www.cafekadijk.nl, in Dutch; Kadijksplein 5; mains €10-20; ⊙4-10pm Mon, noon-10pm Tue-Sun) This hip, split-level cafe looks like it can serve no more than coffee from its tiny kitchen, but in fact it does quite good Indonesian food. Go for the *Eitjes van Tante Bea* (a spicy mix of egg, shrimp and beans), as well as a mini version of the normally gigantic *rijstaffel* (Indonesian banquet). At lunchtime, munch on tasty sandwiches and sates on the sunny Kadijksplein terrace.

### PAERZ INTERNATIONAL €€

Map p310 (www.paerz.nl, in Dutch; Entrepotdok 64; mains €6-20; ⊙lunch & dinner, closed Mon) Design types will appreciate this cheery, bi-level cafe along the Entrepotdok. It's ideal for a dockside lunch of creative sandwiches and soups after a trip to the nearby zoo. In the evening, expect simple yet inventive preparations of fish and pasta.

### CAFÉ SMITH EN VOOGT CAFE €€

Map p310 (www.cafesmitenvoogt.nl; Plantage Parklaan 10; mains €4-17; ⊙10am-10pm) This high-ceilinged, high-spirited cafe is equal parts refined and relaxed, and an ideal spot to stop for lunch or a coffee when visiting the adjacent Wertheimpark or its environs. A lovely selection of simple salads and sandwiches is complemented by a handful of dinner selections, like baked aubergine with goat's cheese, and duck breast with black bean sauce.

### AGORA CAFETERIA €

Map p310 (Roetersstraat 11; mains €3-6; ⊙8am-7pm Mon-Fri) When professors in suits are spotted eating in a student cafeteria, it's usually either out of sheer desperation or because the food is actually pretty good. In the case of Agora, it's luckily the latter. Cheap and cheerful meals, like soups and good sandwiches, served with youthful intellectual chatter that just may inspire you to finally read that massive history tome.

## Eastern Islands & Eastern Docklands

### TOP CHOICE FIFTEEN INTERNATIONAL €€€

Map p310 (☎509 50 15; www.fifteen.nl; Jollemanhof 9; mains €17-28; ⊙lunch & dinner daily Sep-May, dinner only Tue-Sat Jun-Aug) 'Naked chef' Jamie Oliver has brought to Amsterdam a concept he began in London: take 15 young people from underprivileged backgrounds and train them for a year in the restaurant biz. Results: noble intention, sometimes spotty execution. The setting, however, is beyond question: Fifteen faces the IJ, and the busy, open-kitchen space is city-cool, with graffitied walls and exposed wood beams.

### TOP CHOICE ODESSA INTERNATIONAL €€€

Map p310 (⊙419 30 10; www.de-odessa.nl; Veemkade 259; mains €12-29, 3-course menu €34; ⊙dinner Wed-Sat) Odessa rocks. Literally. This groovy boat, with indoor and outdoor eating decks and a 1970s-themed 'plush-porno' decor, is just the sort of place where Hugh Hefner would hold a debauched pyjama party. As if to emphasise that fact, DJs take over late at night. The menu changes frequently, with an eye towards simple steaks and fish. Combining a sense of whimsy and humour along with its unique brand of cool, it's a scene for people who normally hate scenes. Book ahead on weekends.

### GARE DE L'EST INTERNATIONAL €€€

Map p310 (www.garedelest.nl, in Dutch; Cruquiusweg 9; 4-course menu €32; ⊙dinner) Gare de l'Est has both the smallest menu in Amsterdam and also the largest. They say that because four chefs (from culinary traditions spanning the globe) take turns nightly in the kitchen, and what their course menus lack in length they make up for in variety over the course of a year. Portuguese tiles and glowing Middle Eastern lamps adorn the interior, and courtyard seating exudes good vibes.

### DE WERELDBOL INTERNATIONAL €€

Map p310 (www.dewereldbol.nl, in Dutch; Piraeusplein 59; mains €16-20; ⏲5-9pm Tue-Sun) A passionate and personable owner-chef, an ever-changing menu and a sweet view of bobbing boats on the water make this small, dark-wood restaurant a fine place to end a day of sightseeing in the area.

### KOMPASZAAL CAFE €€

Map p310 (www.kompaszaal.nl, in Dutch; KNSM-laan 311; mains €14-18; ⏲11.30am-1am Wed-Sun) Set in the century-old Royal Dutch Steamboat Company (KNSM in Dutch) arrivals hall, this airy cafe has a menu featuring Malaysian, Indian and Indonesian flavours. But the groovy green tiles and the water view from the balcony – a great spot for a beer – are even more captivating. On the ground floor, check out the scale models of the Eastern Docklands.

### CAFÉ DE CANTINE CAFE €

Map p310 (www.decantine.nl, in Dutch; Reitlandpark 373; mains €5-14; ⏲11am-1am Sun-Thu, to 2am Fri & Sat) History buffs, come to feast on this cosy cafe's bizarre past: in the 1920s it was a quarantine house for emigrants staying at the nearby Lloyd Hotel who were shipping off to a new life in the Americas. Luckily there's nothing institutional about the eclectic food, from savoury and sweet pancakes to vegie tapas.

### ROOS EN NOOR INTERNATIONAL €

Map p310 (www.roosennoor.nl; Baron GA Tindalstraat 148; mains €9-13; ⏲4-9pm Mon-Fri, 3-8pm Sun, plus 3-8pm Sat in summer) This chic little takeaway shop has a vast buffet, with prepared items like Chinese-spiced duck and roasted beets, as well as full meals and sweets. It's a nice place to grab a late lunch or a sunset picnic while exploring the docklands' architecture. It's located in the Whale building.

### EINDE VAN DE WERELD VEGETARIAN €

Map p310 (www.eindevandewereld.nl; opposite Javakade 4; meals €7-9; ⏲from 6pm Wed & Fri; 🖉) At 'the end of the world', look for the big yellow-and-green boat *Quo Vadis*. The volunteer-run onboard restaurant is cheap and very cheerful. Show up early, because you can't reserve, and when the food's gone, it's gone.

### ÉÉNVISTWÉÉVIS SEAFOOD €€

Map p310 (www.eenvistweevis.nl, in Dutch; Schippersgracht 6; mains €17-22; ⏲dinner Tue-Sun) This unassuming local favourite, with a shell-and-chandelier decor, has a short, handwritten menu of whatever's fresh from the sea. The service is slow and the restaurant gets noisy, but it's all about the great oysters, soup and simply prepared mains, such as sole in butter.

### SEA PALACE CHINESE €€

Map p310 (www.seapalace.nl; Oosterdokskade 8; mains €14-26; ⏲lunch & dinner) It's a funny thing about floating Chinese restaurants: they look like tourist traps and may well be, but from Hong Kong to Holland, many are admired for their good food. The Sea Palace's three floors are busy with all kinds of folk who come not just for the great views of the city from across the IJ. Try the dim sum or the excellent hot pot, a Chinese version of fondue.

### GREETJE CONTEMPORARY DUTCH €€

Map p310 (www.restaurantgreetje.nl; Peperstraat 23-27; mains €21-25; ⏲dinner Tue-Sun) Elegant Greetje will make you reconsider Dutch cuisine. Never mind *stamppot* (mashed pot with potatoes, vegies and bacon) – here you'll see dishes like leek soup, pickled mackerel and Dutch venison, all composed of market-fresh ingredients and beautifully presented. Sweet tooths can finish with the Grand Finale: a combo plate of six creamy, fruity, cakey desserts.

### LANGENDIJK EETCAFE CAFE €€

Map p310 (www.langendijkeetcafe.nl; Zeeburgerstraat 1; mains €5-19; ⏲lunch & dinner; 📶) As you sip a frothy *biertje* (glass of beer) at the foot of the De Gooyer Windmill, it's easy to pretend you're out in rural Holland rather than smack in the city, although the lounge-like, cushion-strewn terrace and stylish after-work crowd nibbling tapas may convince you otherwise. Come for live music on Sundays from 4pm to 7pm, and terrace barbecues on summer weekends when the weather complies.

## DRINKING & NIGHTLIFE

In keeping with all the daring architecture out here, the Plantage, Eastern Islands and Eastern Docklands area has seen an invasion of back-lit designer bars and media-savvy cafes; we've listed those that meld mod style with good ol' Dutch *gezelligheid.*

**BROUWERIJ 'T IJ** BEER CAFE

Map p310 (www.brouwerijhetij.nl; Funenkade 7; ⏲3-8pm, free tours 4pm Fri) The tasting room of Amsterdam's leading organic microbrewery has a cosy, down-and-dirty beer-hall feel (its walls are lined with dried hops and bottles from around the world) and the house brew is on tap. In nice weather you can enjoy your beer on the terrace at the foot of the De Gooyer Windmill. Where better to sample a 9% amber Columbus sweet or an orange-coloured Struis (Ostrich)? Bonus: most of the beer brewed here never leaves the building, so it is fresh *and* eco-friendly.

TOP CHOICE **KHL** CAFE

Map p310 (www.khl.nl, in Dutch; Oostelijke Handelskade 44; ⏲Tue-Sun) Proof of how far this district has come, KHL is a one-time squatter cafe gone legit. It's a historic brick building with great tile work, and the garden is worth a glass or two. There's live music every Sunday evening – everything from Latin to pop to *klezmer* (traditional Jewish music).

**CAFÉ PAKHUIS WILHELMINA** CLUB

Map p310 (www.cafepakhuiswilhelmina.nl, in Dutch; Veemkade 576) Well known for its hilariously fun hard-rock karaoke as well as its alternative dance nights, this is low-key clubbing (singing) at its best.

**STAR FERRY** THEATRE CAFE

Map p310 (www.starferry.nl; Piet Heinkade 1) It's practically a commandment nowadays that any performing space worth its name has to have a flash cafe, and the cafe at the Muziekgebouw aan 't IJ is hard to beat for location and views. Several storeys of glass give you an IJ's-eye perspective.

**KANIS & MEILAND** CAFE

Map p310 (www.kanisenmeiland.nl, in Dutch; Levantkade 127; ⏲daily) A favourite among the 'islanders', this cavernous spot has an inviting wooden reading table, tall windows facing the 'mainland' and a quiet terrace directly on the water.

**CAFÉ ORLOFF** CAFE

Map p310 (www.orloff.nl, in Dutch; Kadijksplein 11) On the picturesque Kadijksplein, this sprawling terrace is one of the most tranquil in town. Inside, folks chat around the magazine-strewn communal table. The kitchen turns out light breakfasts and cornbread sandwiches during the day and light dinners with plenty of French wine in the evening.

**DE GROENE OLIPHANT** BROWN CAFE

Map p310 (www.degroeneolifant.nl, in Dutch; Sarphatistraat 510) Reeking of the kind faded opulence and intricate woodwork that only the Victorian era can muster, the 'Green Elephant' feels stuck in the past – in a totally enchanting way. Sit at the circa-1880 bar with the locals and admire the art deco glass, or retreat to the lofted dining room for dinner and pretend like you're one of the elegant residents of yesteryear's Plantage.

**CAFÉ KOOSJE** BROWN CAFE

Map p310 (Plantage Middenlaan 37) If the three catchwords for real estate are location, location and location, then Koosje – located between the Artis Royal Zoo and the Hollandsche Schouwburggot – has got a lock on the market. Perch yourself at the window or on the terrace to soak up the great corner vibe.

**PANAMA** CLUB

Map p310 (Oostelijke Handelskade 4) A glamorous restaurant/theatre/dance venue. Most come for the club nights spinning Latin, Ibiza vibes, Cuban big bands and more.

## ENTERTAINMENT

**BIMHUIS** JAZZ

Map p310 (☎788 21 88; www.bimhuis.nl; Piet Heinkade 3; ⏲closed Aug) The Bimhuis is the beating jazz heart of the Netherlands, and its stylish digs at the Muziekgebouw aan 't IJ draw international jazz greats.

**MUZIEKGEBOUW AAN 'T IJ** CONCERT VENUE

Map p310 (☎tickets 788 20 00; www.muziekgebouw.nl; Piet Heinkade 1; ⏲box office noon-

6pm Mon-Sat) This dazzling performing-arts venue brings together several agendas under one roof. Behind the high-tech exterior, you'll find a dramatically lit main hall with flexible stage layout and great acoustics. Its jazz stage, Bimhuis, is more intimate. It often offers free lunchtime concerts.

**KRITERION** CINEMA

Map p310 (www.kriterion.nl, in Dutch; Roetersstraat 170) Student-run since 1945, this theatre-cafe has a great array of premieres, themed parties, classics, kids' flicks and more. It also hosts several film festivals throughout the year.

**CONSERVATORIUM VAN AMSTERDAM** CLASSICAL MUSIC

Map p310 (www.cva.ahk.nl; Oosterdokskade 151) Catch a delightful classical recital by students at the Netherlands' largest conservatory of music. It's in a snazzy contemporary building with state-of-the-art acoustics, endless glass walls and light-flooded interiors.

## SHOPPING

**FRANK'S SMOKEHOUSE** FOOD & DRINK

Map p310 (www.smokehouse.nl; Wittenburgergracht 303; ⏲Tue-Sat) Frank is a prime supplier to Amsterdam's restaurants. He learned how to smoke fish from the Swedes, and his excellent Alaskan salmon, halibut and yellowfin tuna can be vacuum-packed for easy passage through airport customs (which works, unlike with meat).

**LOODS 6** SHOPPING CENTRE

Map p310 (www.loods6.nl, in Dutch; KNSM-laan 143) This isn't a shopping centre of the mall variety, but rather a small arcade of shops in a former passenger terminal building. Noteworthy shops include designer pottery and home accessories, two art galleries, a fun children's store and designer fashions.

**JC CREATIONS** CLOTHING

Map p310 (www.jc-creations.com, in Dutch; Baron GA Tindalstraat 150; ⏲Tue-Sat) Take a deep breath when you enter this shop: classy corsets (for males and females) are the speciality. Plenty of ready-made options abound, but custom orders are welcome, too.

**ARRIVAL/DEPARTURE** CLOTHING

Map p310 (www.arrivaldeparture.nl; KNSM-laan 301) This trendy shop, inspired by the world of skateboarding, offers an array of clothes, shoes, books, art and toys that bring out your inner rock and roll daredevil. Look for of-the-moment brands such as Ben Sherman, Stop Staring! and We are the Superlative Conspiracy.

# Oosterpark & South Amsterdam

OOSTERPARK | SOUTH AMSTERDAM

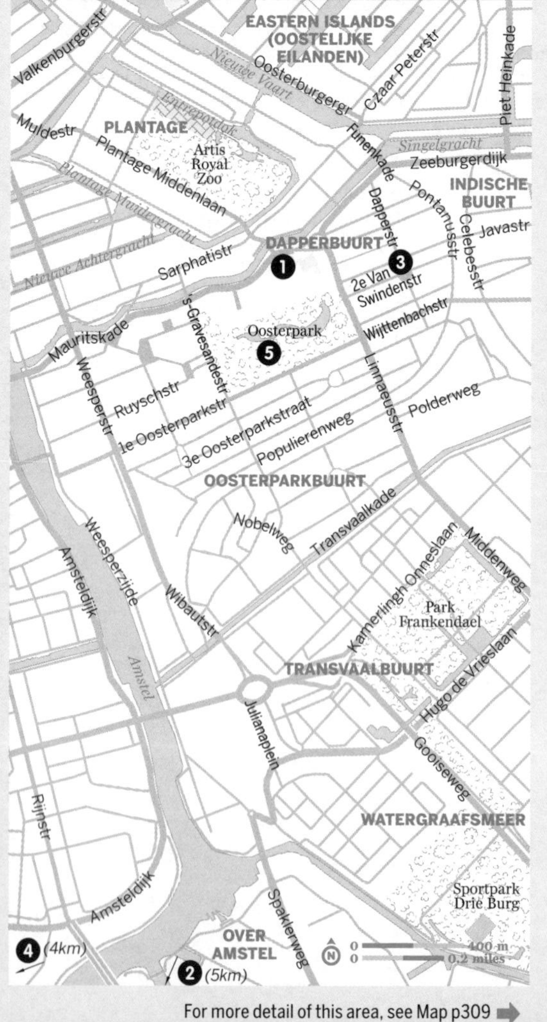


For more detail of this area, see Map p309

## Neighbourhood Top Five

❶ Spend the afternoon yodelling, sitting in a *yurt* and checking out Dutch colonial booty at the **Tropenmuseum** (p186).

❷ Take a trip through the big, bold, avant-garde paintings of Karel Appel and friends at the **Cobra Museum** (p187).

❸ Sniff out the Turkish pide stall amid multipack sock vendors at the lively **Dappermarkt** (p186).

❹ Cycle through **Amsterdamse Bos** (p187) and visit an organic farm cafe for fresh goat's-milk ice cream.

❺ Seek out the political monuments and wild parrots of sublime **Oosterpark** (p186).

## Explore: Oosterpark & South Amsterdam

Oosterpark is one of Amsterdam's most culturally diverse neighbourhoods. Unlike De Pijp, it has seen only the tiniest bit of gentrification and it's not (yet) on any trend-watchers' radar – this is what makes it interesting.

The sights to see are off the everyday tourist path. On the northern fringe you'll find the Tropenmuseum, which gives insights into Dutch colonial activities in the East Indies. The green expanse of Oosterpark itself makes a fine diversion afterwards, with its large pond and several monuments. This is ground zero for big events such as the annual Holland Festival.

A walk east from the museum down 1e Van Swindenstraat leads to the street market on Dapperstraat and eventually into Javastraat, a Moroccan and Turkish enclave. Make your way to the neighbourhood's western edge, home to urban-cool bars Trouw and Canvas, and your day and night are booked.

Amsterdam extends well beyond here. The sights scatter as you head south, but the nuggets you'll find – wild art, lush greenery and goats in the forest – are worth the trip. Reaching them is pretty straightforward by public transport; count on it taking between 30 and 60 minutes.

## Local Life

➡ **Moroccan & Turkish Delights** On Javastraat (which 1e Van Swindenstraat runs into to the east), old Dutch fish shops and working-class bars sit adjacent to Moroccan and Turkish groceries.

➡ **Garden Homes** Toward the northwest side of Park Frankendael lies a whole community of garden plots with teeny houses on them. The owners sit out on sunny days with wine and picnic fixings.

➡ **Market Madness** If you're looking for an authentic place to shop, Dappermarkt is it. If organic fare is more your style, the monthly De Pure Markt in Park Frankendael is where everyone flocks.

## Getting There & Away

➡ **Tram** Tram 9 goes from the city centre to the Tropenmuseum. Take tram 5 to the end of the line for the Cobra Museum.

➡ **Bus** Buses 170 and 172 from Centraal Station go to Amsterdamse Bos and Cobra Museum, but note if you're using a GVB transit pass, it's not valid on these particular routes.

➡ **Metro** Amsterdam ArenA and Amsterdam RAI have their own Metro stops, making them easy to reach from the centre.

## Lonely Planet's Top Tip

With the Amstel river slicing through the area, Oosterpark and South Amsterdam have no shortage of riverside cafes that remind you of the age-old Dutch bond with water. On gorgeous summer evenings many patrons arrive by boat, settle at a terrace table and watch the freight barges, tugs and rowing teams ply the waters.

## Best Places to Eat

➡ De Kas (p189)
➡ Roopram Roti (p189)
➡ Wilde Zwijnen (p189)

For reviews, see p189 ➡

## Best Places to Drink

➡ Canvas (p189)
➡ Trouw (p189)
➡ De Ysbreeker (p189)
➡ Amstel Haven (p190)

For reviews, see p189 ➡

## Best Parks

➡ Oosterpark (p186)
➡ Park Frankendael (p186)
➡ Amsterdamse Bos (p187)
➡ Amstelpark (p187)

For reviews, see p186 ➡

# SIGHTS

## Oosterpark

**OOSTERPARK** PARK

Map p309 (s'-Gravesandestraat; ⌚dawn-dusk) Oosterpark was laid out in 1891 to accommodate the nouveau riche diamond traders who found their fortunes in the South African mines, and it still has an elegant, rambling feel. On the south side, look for two monuments: one commemorates the abolition of slavery in the Netherlands in 1863; the other, **De Schreeuw** (the Scream), honours free speech and, more specifically, filmmaker Theo van Gogh, who was murdered at the southeast corner of the park in 2004. Another (living) monument to Van Gogh is the **Spreeksteen**, a rock podium marking a 'speakers' corner' established on the park's east side in 2005.

When you're in the area near the Spreeksteen, keep an eye out for large grey herons that swoop around the ponds here, as well as wild parrots chattering in the trees. The park is in the process of being expanded, so additional playgrounds and paths may be available by the time you visit.

**DAPPERMARKT** MARKET

Map p309 (Dapperstraat, btwn Mauritskade & Wijttenbachstraat; ⌚9am-5pm Mon-Sat) The larger Albert Cuypmarkt in De Pijp may the king of street bazaars, but the Dappermarkt is a worthy prince. Reflecting the Oost's diverse immigrant population, it's a whirl of people (Africans, Turks, Dutch), foods (apricots, olives, fish) and goods from sports socks to shimmering fabrics to sunflowers, all sold from stalls lining the street.

**FRANKENDAEL HOUSE** HOUSE & GARDENS

Map p309 (www.frankendaelfoundation.nl, in Dutch; Middenweg 72; ⌚dawn-dusk) As early as the 18th century, wealthy Amsterdammers would spend their summers in plush country retreats south of Plantage on a tract of drained land called Watergraafsmeer. The last survivor of this era is Frankendael, an elegant Louis XIV–style mansion that sparkles from its recent restoration. There's a cafe inside, and you can ask there if it's OK to walk around the historic building. On Sunday staff offer one-hour

## TOP SIGHTS TROPENMUSEUM

Completed in 1926 to house the Royal Institute of the Tropics, and still a leading research institute for tropical hygiene and agriculture, the fascinating Tropenmuseum puts out a whopping collection of colonial artefacts. Galleries are spread around a huge central hall over three floors, and present exhibits with insight, imagination and a fair amount of multimedia.

You can visit an African market, a Mexican-style cantina and a life-sized *yurt* (traditional Central Asian felt hut). A particular must-see is the 'Cabinet of Curiosities', a display of exotica found in every good colonialist's home containing ritual masks, spiky spears and dead butterflies. 'Music World' is another fine exhibit, showing how music and instruments travel throughout the world and remix sounds; enter the 'Singing School' to learn to yodel or throat sing like a Mongolian.

The museum is especially great for kids. Ask at the ticket desk for a free audio tour (€5 deposit). The gift shop stocks lots of international goodies. The attached Tropentheater screens films and hosts music, dance, plays and other performances by visiting artists. The slick Soeterijn cafe and Ekeko restaurant serve food if you need a bite after all the activity.

### DON'T MISS

- Cabinet of Curiosities
- Music World & Singing School
- Tropentheater
- Free audio tour

### PRACTICALITIES

- Map p309
- ☎568 82 15
- www.tropenmuseum.nl
- Linnaeusstraat 2
- adult/child €9/5
- ⌚10am-5pm

**guided tours** (per person €5; ⌚11am). The house backs onto a formal garden that's open to the public, but be sure to view the forecourt with its gushing fountain and statues of Bacchus and Ceres. The property is swathed in a larger landscaped garden, Park Frankendael, with walking paths, flapping storks, decorative bridges and the remains of follies.

On the last Sunday of the month **De Pure Markt** (www.puremarkt.nl, in Dutch; ⌚11am-6pm Sun Mar-Jun & Aug-Dec) sets up in the park, with artisanal food and craft producers selling sausages, home-grown grapes and much more.

## South Amsterdam

### AMSTERDAMSE BOS — PARK

(Amsterdam Woods; www.amsterdamsebos.nl; Bosbaanweg 5; ⌚park 24hr, visitors centre noon-5pm; ) The product of a 1930s make-work program, Amsterdamse Bos is a sprawling green area (roughly 2km by 5km) of thick trees and open fields, cut through with cycling and walking paths. In the densest thickets you can forget you're near a city at all (though, actually, you're right by Schiphol airport), and it's a wonderful place to let the kids run free. Get your bearings with a map from the visitors centre by the main entrance.

Perhaps the most delightful attraction is **De Ridammerhoeve** (www.geitenboerderij.nl, in Dutch; admission free; ⌚10am-5pm, closed Tue), an organic, working goat farm where kids can feed bottles of milk to, well, kids (€7.50 for two bottles). The cafeteria sells goat's-milk smoothies and ice cream, as well as cheeses made on the premises. The farm is 4km from the park entrance.

Another old farmhouse, this one on the Bos' northwestern side, has been converted into a kid-friendly pancake restaurant called Boerderij Meerzichtt.

On the park's north side, near the entrance, is the Bosbaan – a long lake used for sculling. You can sit and watch the rowers from yet another busy cafe, or you can rent a **kayak** (per hr €6) just south at Grote Speelweid and paddle through the wetlands yourself. **Bicycles** (per 2hr/day €6/9.50; ⌚10am-6pm, closed Mon) are available at the main entrance. At **Fun Forest** (www.funforest.nl; adult/child €21.50/16.50; ⌚noon-6pm Mon-Fri, 10am-7pm Sat & Sun) climbing park, also by the entrance, families gear up and swing through the trees using ropes, ladders and bridges.

Take bus 170 or 172 from Centraal Station; it's about a 40-minute ride. Keep an eye out for the wild-looking ING Building en route (shining just past Amstelveensweg station). Or ride the historic tram from the Haarlemmermeer Station on summer Sundays (see Electrische Museumtramlijn Amsterdam, below).

### COBRA MUSEUM — MUSEUM

(www.cobra-museum.nl; Sandbergplein 1, Amstelveen; adult/child €9.50/5; ⌚11am-5pm Tue-Sun) Artists from Denmark, Belgium and the Netherlands formed the CoBrA movement after WWII. (The name is derived from their capital cities; see p237 for more details.) Members included Asger Jorn, Anton Rooskens, Corneille, Constant and the great Karel Appel, but the group lasted for just three years (1948–51). The art is less of a unified whole than a philosophy, inspired by Marxism, of using materials at hand to create painting, sculpture and even poetry.

Changing exhibits are on show as well; expect to see bold colours and busy designs.

Take bus 170 or 172 from Centraal Station or tram 5 to the end of the line in Amstelveen. The latter puts you about a half-mile from the museum; follow the 'Cobra' signs through the mall to reach it. The buses arrive right by the museum.

### ELECTRISCHE MUSEUMTRAMLIJN AMSTERDAM — MUSEUM

(Tram Museum Amsterdam; ☎673 75 38; www.museumtramlijn.org; Amstelveenseweg 264; return adult/child €4/2; ⌚11am-6pm Sun mid-Apr–Oct; ) Beyond the southwestern extremities of Vondelpark, just north of the Olympic Stadium, is the former Haarlemmermeer Station, which houses the tram museum. Historic trams sourced from all over Europe run between here and Amstelveen, making a great outing for kids and adults alike. A return trip takes about 1¼ hours and skirts the large Amsterdamse Bos recreational area. It departs two to three times per hour; see the website for details.

Take bus 170 or 172 or tram 16 to get here.

### AMSTELPARK — PARK

(Europaboulevard; ⌚8am-dusk; ) South of the Amsterdam RAI convention centre, in the suburb of Buitenveldert, lies the vast Amstelpark, the grounds of an international flower show that was held in 1972. The park is a paradise for kids, with a petting zoo, minigolf, pony rides and a playground. In summer a miniature train chugs its way around the park. Other attractions include rose and rhododendron gardens, and art exhibitions are held in the Glazen Huis (Glass House), the Orangerie and the Papillon Gallery.

Just outside the park's south edge, on the west side of the Amstel river, you'll see a 1636 windmill called the **Riekermolen** (www.molens.nl, in Dutch). In a field southwest of the mill, you'll find a statue of a sitting Rembrandt, who made sketches here along the riverbank.

To reach Amstelpark, take the metro to Amsterdam RAI or tram 4.

### DE BIJLMER NEIGHBOURHOOD

A decade ago De Bijlmer was Amsterdam's most notorious neighbourhood, known for muggings, junkies and public housing gone wrong. Today it's a playground for some of the Netherlands' most innovative architects.

You can visit by bike, though the 30-minute ride from the city centre isn't particularly scenic. Hop on the metro (you can bring your wheels) to the dramatic Nicholas Grimshaw–designed **Bijlmer station**, opened in 2007. To the west lies Amsterdam ArenA (p190), home of AFC Ajax, Amsterdam's revered football club, and the Heineken Music Hall (p190). In the shopping plaza east of the tracks, look for the **Imagine IC cultural centre** (☎489 48 66; www.imagineic.nl; Bijlmerplein 1006; ⏲11am-5pm Tue-Sat), which has free photography and other audiovisual exhibits highlighting migrant culture and identity. To get here from the train, walk toward the Amsterdamse Poort shopping complex; the centre is about 200m on the right, after the first overpass. From here, you can wind your way east, passing all kinds of novel structures.

Eventually these give way to the few remaining '**honeycomb blocks**' of the original Bijlmer layout, each containing some 400 apartments. The 1960s brochures touted 'a modern city where the people of today can find the residential environment of tomorrow'. But the isolated, austere project rapidly lost its lustre and, in the 1970s, the city began to funnel poor immigrants into the empty apartments. By the 1980s crime was common and the infrastructure crumbling. Former residents lament the trash-filled lawns and broken elevators of those days, but many also wax nostalgic about the tight-knit community and the surrounding greenery.

In 1992 an El Al cargo plane crashed into two of the blocks, killing 43 people, many of them undocumented foreigners – a memorial stands in front of the missing buildings. The tragedy kick-started a re-evaluation of the neighbourhood, which has moved into wholesale rebuilding, and shifted the balance far in favour of privately owned property, rather than publicly managed apartments.

De Bijlmer still holds the city's largest Surinamese population, along with immigrants from west and north Africa, so ethnic eats are available. The neighbourhood's park is the site of the cultural bash **Kwakoe** (www.kwakoefestival.nl, in Dutch), drawing crowds on weekends throughout July and early August.

### AMSTERDAM RAI BUILDING

(www.rai.nl; Europaplein 22) This exhibition and conference centre (featured, by the way, in Jacques Tati's 1971 film *Trafic*) is the largest such complex in the country. The building opened in 1961 and just keeps expanding for the car, fashion, horse-jumping and 50-odd other shows held here every year. RAI stands for Rijwiel en Automobiel Industrie, the bicycle and auto association. To get here, take the metro to the Amsterdam RAI stop or tram 4.

### OLYMPIC STADIUM STADIUM

(www.olympischstadion.nl; Olympisch Stadion 21) The grand Olympic Stadium was designed by Jan Wils, a protégé of famous architect HP Berlage, and is functionalist in style. The arena was built for the 1928 summer Olympic Games, and has a soaring tower from which the Olympic flame burned for the first time during competition. The stadium is classified as a national monument; today it hosts sporting events and concerts.

Much of the housing in southwest Amsterdam originates from the time of the 1928 games. Many of the streets and squares in the area bear Greek names like Olympiaplein and Herculesstraat.

Trams 16 and 24 go from Centraal Station directly to the stadium.

# EATING

### DE KAS — INTERNATIONAL €€€

Map p309 (☎462 45 62; www.restaurantdekas.nl; Kamerlingh Onneslaan 3, Frankendaelpark; lunch menu €37.50, dinner menu €49.50; lunch & dinner Mon-Fri, dinner only Sat; ) Admired by gourmets citywide, De Kas has an organic attitude to match its chic glass greenhouse setting – try to visit during a thunderstorm! It grows most of its own herbs and produce right here (if it's not busy you might be offered a tour), and the result is incredibly pure flavours with innovative combinations. De Kas keeps the selection simple – one set menu each day, based on whatever has been freshly harvested. Reserve in advance.

### ROOPRAM ROTI — SURINAMESE €

Map p309 (1e Van Swindenstraat 4; mains €4-10; 2-9pm Tue-Sat, 3-9pm Sun) There's often a line to the door at this bare-bones Surinamese place, but don't worry – it moves fast. Place your order – lamb roti 'extra' (with egg) and a *barra* (lentil donut) at least – with the man at the bar, and don't forget the fiery hot sauce. It's some of the flakiest roti you'll find anywhere, super-delicious for takeaway or to eat at one of the half-dozen tables.

### WILDE ZWIJNEN — CONTEMPORARY DUTCH €€

off Map p309 (☎463 30 43; www.wildezwijnen.com; Javaplein 23; mains €15-21, 3/4 courses €29.50/35.50; lunch & dinner Tue-Sun; ) The name means 'wild boar' and if it's the right time of year, you may indeed find it on the menu. The rustic, wood-tabled restaurant serves locally sourced, seasonal fare with bold results. There's usually a vegetarian option, and chocolate ganache with juniper berries for dessert. It's not too far from Oosterpark; get here via Eerste van Swindenstraat, which turns into Javastraat, which runs into Javaplein. Tram 14 stops nearby, too.

### PATA NEGRA — SPANISH €€

Map p309 (☎692 25 06; www.pata-negra.nl, in Dutch; Reinwardtstraat 1; tapas €6-12, mains €12-18; noon-11pm Sun-Thu, to 11.30pm Fri & Sat) This is an equally colourful branch of the Utrechtsestraat tapas joint (p123), with the added bonus that it serves a big ol' potful of paella on Sunday.

### CAFE RUYS — ITALIAN €€

Map p309 (☎663 53 66; www.caferuys.nl, in Dutch; Ruyschstraat 15; mains €11-17; lunch & dinner) The Oost is short on stylish eateries, so this grand cafe serving antipasti, risotto and nice glasses of prosecco to wash it down stands out. There's lots of outdoor seating, but then you'd miss out on the gorgeous interior, which glitters with Murano-glass mosaics and other flash details.

# DRINKING & NIGHTLIFE

### CANVAS — BAR

Map p309 (www.canvasopde7e.nl; Wibautstraat 150; from 11am Mon-Fri, from noon Sat & Sun) Take the elevator to the 7th floor for this restaurant-bar-club. It's edgy and improvisational, and is the social centre for all the artists with studios in the building (the former *Volkskrant* newspaper office). The sweet views are heightened by the creative cocktails – perhaps a lemongrass martini or Japanese gin fizz (with lychee liqueur). Music is varied, from vintage voodoo to hippy psychedelic, with jazz and funk thrown in, too. The Wibautstraat metro stop is a stone's throw away; follow signs saying 'Gijsbrecht van Aemstelstraat' as you exit the station.

### TROUW — BAR

Map p309 (463 77 88; www.trouwamsterdam.nl; Wibautstraat 127; closed Sun & Mon; ) Trouw is housed in a former newspaper printing warehouse, where the printing press floor has been transformed into an industrial-chic restaurant serving snack-sized plates of organic, Mediterranean-tinged dishes. You can also have a drink on the sculpture-studded terrace. Beyond the food and drink, Trouw is known for its way-late club nights (with food served til 2am) and its salon series talks on culture, architecture and urban design. It's supposed to be a temporary establishment, so you might want to check that it's open before making your way out here.

### DE YSBREEKER — BROWN CAFE

Map p309 (www.deysbreeker.nl, in Dutch; Weesperzijde 23; ) Pull up a chair on the terrace at this cafe on the Amstel and it's hard to decide whether to face the beautiful buildings or the gleaming river lined with houseboats. Inside used to house a major jazz and avant-garde music club – that institution has become the Muziekgebouw aan 't IJ – leaving more room here for stylish drinkers in the plush booths and along the marble bar. The cafe serves breakfast, lunch and dinner, but go for the organic and local beers (such as de Prael) and bar snacks like lamb meatballs.

**AMSTEL HAVEN** BAR, CAFE

Map p309 (www.amstelhaven.nl, in Dutch; Mauritskade 1) Bike or boat up to where the Amstel meets the Singelgracht, snag a canalside table under an umbrella and have yourself a swell view of the water and skyscrapers. The dining room becomes a dance floor with DJs on Friday ('80s and '90s) and Saturday (house and club classics). Sunday features live music.

## ENTERTAINMENT

**TROPENTHEATER** THEATRE

Map p309 (568 85 00; www.tropentheater.nl; Tropenmuseum, Linnaeusstraat 2; closed Jul & Aug) Adjoining the Tropenmuseum, but with a separate entrance, this is like no place else in Amsterdam, with music, films and performances from South America, India, Turkey, Kurdistan and beyond.

**AMSTERDAMSE BOS THEATRE** THEATRE

(www.bostheater.nl, in Dutch; Amsterdamse Bos, Bosbaanweg 5; Jun-Aug) This large, open-air amphitheatre stages plays (Shakespeare, Brecht, Chekhov) in Dutch. We love it when the actors pause as planes pass overhead.

**AMSTERDAM ARENA** FOOTBALL

(www.amsterdamarena.nl; Arena Blvd 11, Bijlmermeer) Four-times European champion Ajax is the Netherlands' most famous football team. Ajax plays in Amsterdam ArenA, a high-tech complex with a retractable roof and seating for 52,000 spectators. Games usually take place on Saturday evenings and Sunday afternoons between August and May. Fans can take a one-hour 'World of Ajax' **tour** (adult/child €12/10); see website for tour times.

**HEINEKEN MUSIC HALL** LIVE MUSIC

(www.heineken-music-hall.nl, in Dutch; Arena Blvd 590, Bijlmermeer) This midsized venue is praised for its quality acoustics and lighting. Expect rock and pop acts from medium to big names.

# Day Trips from Amsterdam

## Haarlem p192

Ahh, the historic grandeur of Haarlem: the wealth of 17th-century buildings, leafy *hofjes* (courtyard homes) and old-world antique shops, plus loads of pretty bridges and winding alleys that give Amsterdam a run for her money.

## Leiden p196

This pretty, easygoing town is home to the country's oldest university, the alma mater of Descartes. Another claim to fame? It's Rembrandt's birthplace.

## Delft p200

While its hand-painted, quaint, blue-and-white 'Delftware' is recognised and coveted all over the world, the beauty of Delft's Gothic and Renaissance architecture rivals even the most elegant piece of pottery.

## Alkmaar p203

Friesian cows graze under windmills as Gouda fanatics flock to the cheese market at Alkmaar, one of the last bastions of the traditional cheese guilds.

## Zaanse Schans p204

Feed your windmill cravings in Zaanse Schans, an engrossing, open-air museum where you can see the twirling national icons in action and even meet the millers.

# Haarlem

## Explore

If you arrive by train, take a few minutes to bask in Haarlem Centraal's glory before you stroll to the old centre along Kruisstraat. Haarlem's wealth and elegance soon becomes apparent as you pass exclusive stores, art galleries and antique shops. Stop off at the Corrie Ten Boom House to pay homage to one of the Netherland's most admired Resistance figures before heading to the lively Grote Markt for lunch. Give yourself plenty of time to soak up the atmosphere here (it's the town's pulsing centre, whether it's a market day or not) before heading south several blocks to the incomparable Frans Hals Museum. Garden lovers shouldn't miss a peek into one or two of Haarlem's pretty *hofjes*; the most famous among them, the Provenierhuis, is a five-minute walk northwest of the Frans Hals Museum.

It's definitely worth sticking around during the evening, too. Grab a beer or two at one of the Grote Markt's terrace cafes, enjoy some sunset people-watching and check out some live music amid Haarlem's nightlife – a perfect mix of small town chill and big city sophistication.

## The Best...

- **Sight** Frans Hals Museum (p194)
- **Place to Eat** Jacobus Pieck (p195)
- **Place to Drink** Proeflokaal in den Uiver (p195)

## Top Tip

Arrive early on a Monday or Saturday to hit the festive outdoor markets, then unwind with a leisurely lunch at a cafe on the Grote Markt.

## Getting There & Away

**Travel time** 15 to 20 minutes

**Train** Services to Haarlem are frequent (€3.80, up to eight per hour); the Grote Markt is a 500m walk to the south of the station.

**Car** From the ring road west of the city, take the N200, which becomes the A200.

## Need to Know

- **Area Code** ☎023
- **Location** 20km west of Amsterdam
- **Tourist office** (☎0900 616 16 00; www.vvvhaarlem.nl, in Dutch; Verwulft 11; ⏰9.30am-5.30pm Mon-Fri, 10am-5pm Sat, 11am-3pm Sun Apr-Sep, closed Sun Oct-Mar)

## SIGHTS

### HAARLEM CENTRAAL — TRAIN STATION

If you come to Haarlem by train, your first sight will be this glorious art deco masterpiece, hands-down the country's most beautiful train station.

### GROTE MARKT — MARKET

Circled by elegant Renaissance and Gothic buildings and lined with lovely cafes and restaurants, this open-air plaza is the city's beating heart. It's fronted by the 14th-century Town Hall (Stadius), which features a balcony where judgments from the high court were pronounced. The Counts' Hall contains some amazing 15th-century panel paintings, and if it's open you can take a peek. Don't miss the bustling market day each Saturday, when everyone in town floods the square to peruse the market stalls selling everything from *stroopwafel* (syrup waffles) and tulips to locally made cheeses and that quintessential Dutch treat, raw herring. On Mondays you'll find a clothing market.

### TRAVEL TIPS

The fast, efficient Dutch railway network makes it a snap to get around. Cycle paths are everywhere, but don't bother to bring your own bike – most train stations have bike-rental shops charging around €7 per day, though you'll need to book ahead. Don't forget that discounts are available for holders of rail tickets.

All the destinations in this chapter lie within an hour's journey from Amsterdam by train (and if need be, by connecting bus). Get an early start and you might 'do' two locations without feeling rushed.

## Haarlem

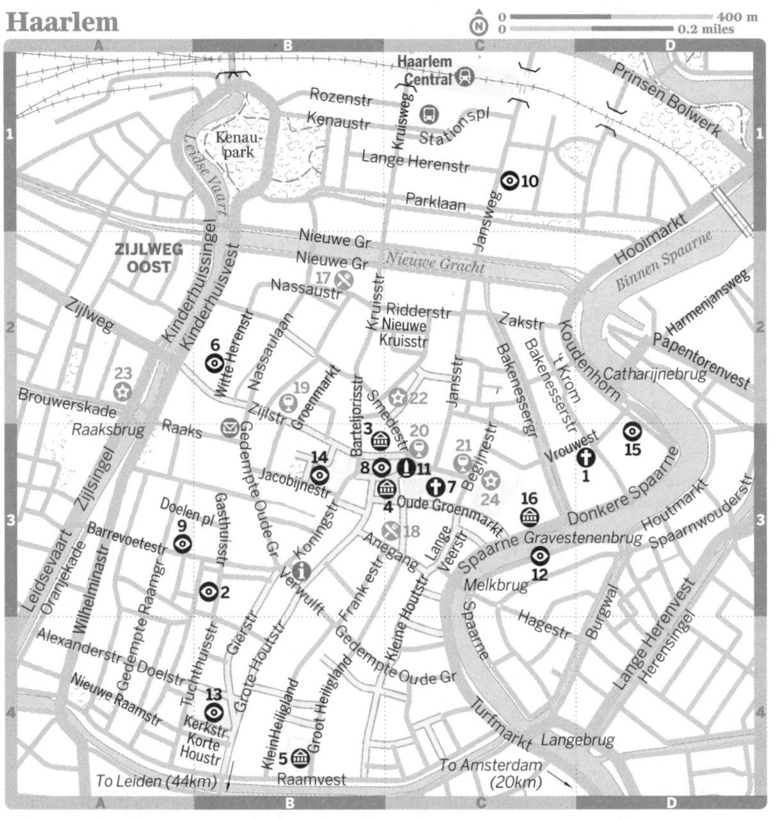


### Haarlem

| **Sights** | **(p192)** |
|---|---|
| 1 Bakenesserkerk | D3 |
| 2 Brouwers Hofje | B3 |
| 3 Corrie Ten Boom House | B3 |
| 4 De Hallen | C3 |
| 5 Frans Hals Museum | B4 |
| 6 Frans Loenen Hofje | B2 |
| 7 Grote Kerk van St Bavo | C3 |
| 8 Grote Markt | B3 |
| 9 Hofje van Loo | A3 |
| 10 Hofje van Staats | C1 |
| 11 Laurens Coster statue | C3 |
| 12 Post Verkade Cruises | C3 |
| 13 Provenierhuis | B4 |
| 14 Stadhuis | B3 |
| 15 Teylers Hofje | D3 |
| 16 Teylers Museum | C3 |

| **Eating** | **(p195)** |
|---|---|
| 17 Complimenti | B2 |
| 18 Jacobus Pieck | C3 |

| **Drinking** | **(p195)** |
|---|---|
| 19 Café Het Melkwoud | B2 |
| 20 Café Studio | C3 |
| 21 Proeflokaal In den Uiver | C3 |

| **Entertainment** | **(p195)** |
|---|---|
| 22 Café Stiels | C2 |
| 23 Patronaat | A2 |
| 24 Philharmonie | C3 |

**GROTE KERK VAN ST BAVO** CHURCH
(www.bavo.nl; Oude Groenmarkt 23; adult/child €2/1.50; ⏲10am-4pm Mon-Sat) Across from the town hall looms this Gothic cathedral with a 50m-high steeple. It contains some fine Renaissance artworks, but the star

attraction is its **Müller organ** – one of the most magnificent in the world, and once played by both Mozart and Handel. There are tours in English on request, and free organ recitals take place at 4pm on Thursday from July to early September, and at 8.15pm on Tuesday from May to October. The organ stands 30m high and has about 5000 pipes, and the acoustics are terrific.

**LAURENS COSTER STATUE** STATUE

On the square north of the Grote Kerk is the Laurens Coster statue. Haarlemmers believe that Coster has a claim, along with Gutenberg, to be called the inventor of moveable type.

**DE HALLEN** MUSEUM

(www.dehallen.nl; Grote Markt 16; adult/child €6/free; ⏲11am-5pm Tue-Sat, noon-5pm Sun) Haarlem's modern and contemporary art museum resides within two historic 'halls': the 17th-century Dutch Renaissance **Vleeshal**, a former meat market and the sole place that meat was allowed to be sold in Haarlem from the 17th through to the 19th century, and the neoclassical **Verweyhal** (fish house). Eclectic exhibits rotate every three months and range from Dutch impressionists and CoBrA artists to innovative video, installation art and photography by cutting-edge international artists.

FREE **PROVENIERSHUIS** HISTORIC BUILDING

(off Grote Houtstraat) To the south of Haarlem stands Proveniershuis, the former headquarters of the Joris Doelen (Civic Guards of St George), which started life as an almshouse. Its wonderful old *hofje* is one of Haarlem's prettiest, and like all *hofjes* it provides clues about the origins of the Dutch social state.

FREE **HOFJES** HISTORIC BUILDINGS

In addition to Proveniershuis, other *hofjes* worth a look include the **Brouwers Hofje** (Tuchthuisstraat 8), which lodged the brewers' guild; the **Frans Loenen Hofje** (Witte Herenstraat 24), pared out of a merchant's estate; the **Hofje van Loo** (Barrevoetestraat 7), a former women's hospital; the **Hofje van Staats** (Jansweg 39), one of the town's largest and still occupied by older women; and the unusually grand **Teylers Hofje** (Koudenhorn 144), built by the founder of the Teylers Museum. Most *hofjes* are open from 10am to 5pm Monday to Saturday.

**FRANS HALS MUSEUM** MUSEUM

(www.franshalsmuseum.nl; Groot Heiligland 62; adult/child €10/free; ⏲11am-5pm Tue-Sat, noon-5pm Sun) A short stroll south of Grote Markt, the Frans Hals Museum is a must for anyone interested in the Dutch Masters. Kept in a poorhouse where Hals spent his final years, the collection focuses on the 17th-century Haarlem School; its pride and joy are eight group portraits of the Civic Guard that reveal Hals' exceptional attention to mood and psychological tone. Look out for works by other greats such as Pieter Bruegel the Younger, and Jacob van Ruysdael. Among the museum's other treasures are the works of Hals' teacher, Flemish artist Carel van Mander: stunning illustrations of the human anatomy, all ceiling-high with biblical and mythological references.

**TEYLERS MUSEUM** MUSEUM

(www.teylersmuseum.eu; Spaarne 16; adult/child €9/2; ⏲10am-5pm Tue-Sat, noon-5pm Sun) This is the oldest museum in the country (open since 1784), and has an eclectic display of everything from drawings by Michelangelo and Raphael to intriguing 18th-century inventions. It also houses an amazing old electrostatic machine that conjures up visions of mad scientists.

**BAKENESSERKERK** CHURCH

(cnr Vrouwestraat & Bakenesserstraat) This striking 15th-century church has a curious steeple of wood and sandstone. In the evening the steeple glows orange from the lamplight within. It's closed to the public.

**CORRIE TEN BOOM HOUSE** MUSEUM

(www.corrietenboom.com; Barteljorisstraat 19; admission free; ⏲10am-3.30pm Tue-Sat) Also known as 'the hiding place', Corrie Ten Boom House is named for the matriarch of a family that lived in the house during WWII. Using a secret compartment in her

## SPANISH INVASION

When the Spanish invaded Harlem in 1572, virtually the entire population was slaughtered after a seven-month siege, but, against the odds, the community recovered quickly. The city then soared into the prosperity of the Golden Age, attracting painters and artists from around Europe.

## BLOEMENVEILING AALSMEER

The world's biggest flower auction is a heady combination of hard-nosed business and sweet-smelling pleasure.

Just 22km from Amsterdam, **Bloemenveiling** (Aalsmeer Flower Auction; www.floraholland.com; Legmeerdijk 313, Aalsmeer; adult/child €5/3; ⏲7-11am Mon-Fri) is fascinating even for those who don't have tulip fever. Make sure you're in the viewing gallery before 9am to catch the best action as the flower-laden carts go to auction. Selling is conducted – surprise! – by Dutch auction, with a huge clock showing the starting price. From the starting bell, the hand keeps dropping until someone takes up the offer and a deal is struck. There's a self-guided audio tour that will let you peek into the auction rooms and see arrangers prepping the blooms for display.

The auction takes place in Europe's largest commercial complex (1 million sq metres), and one look at the car park and truck fleets will tell you why so much space is necessary. Some 90 million flowers and two million plants change hands here every single day, racking up nearly €7 million in business. More and more transactions are taking place online, so catch the action while it's still here. Monday is the busiest time; Thursday the quietest.

bedroom, she hid hundreds of Jews and Dutch resistors until they could be spirited to safety. In 1944 her family was betrayed and sent to concentration camps, where three died. Later, Corrie Ten Boom toured the world preaching peace. Displays cover her work and life.

**POST VERKADE CRUISES** BOAT CRUISE
(☎023-535 77 23; www.postverkadegroep.nl, in Dutch; Spaarne 11a; adult/child €9.50/4.50; ⏲noon-5pm Tue-Sun Apr-Sep) Runs 50-minute canal boat tours in English.

## EATING & DRINKING

TOP CHOICE **JACOBUS PIECK** INTERNATIONAL €€
(www.jacobuspieck.nl, in Dutch; Warmoesstraat 18; mains €11-18; ⏲lunch Mon-Sat, dinner Tue-Sat) Touches like freshly squeezed orange juice put this tidy bistro on a higher plane. The menu bursts with fresh dishes, from salads and sandwiches at lunch to more complex pasta and seafood choices at dinner. Staff are welcoming. Snag a sunny table on the back patio.

**COMPLIMENTI PER VOI** ITALIAN €
(www.complimenti.nl, in Dutch; Nassaustraat 24; snacks from €3; ⏲noon-6pm Wed-Fri, 10am-5pm Sat) Note the scent of garlic wafting over the street from this picnicker's heaven of a deli. Fresh Italian breads, pesto, cheeses and more are arrayed in display cases. Try not to drool.

TOP CHOICE **PROEFLOKAAL IN DEN UIVER** CAFE
(www.indenuiver.nl, in Dutch; Riviervismarkt 13) Housed in an old fishmonger's, this quirky place has shipping doodads and a schooner sailing right over the bar. There's jazz on Thursday and Sunday evenings. It's one of many atmospheric cafes overlooking the Grote Markt.

**CAFÉ STUDIO** CAFE
(www.cafestudio.nl, in Dutch; Grote Markt 25) It's a genteel watering hole during the day, but this grand cafe-bar with cathedral views buzzes after dark and has DJs on weekends.

**CAFÉ HET MELKWOUD** BROWN CAFE
(Zijlstraat 63) This crunchy brown cafe, named after a Dylan Thomas radio play, is a great place to sample a welter of Dutch and Belgian brews.

## ENTERTAINMENT

**CAFÉ STIELS** LIVE MUSIC
(www.stiels.nl, in Dutch; Smedestraat 21) For jazz and R&B, the back stage here hosts bands almost every night from 10pm onwards.

**PATRONAAT** LIVE MUSIC
(www.patronaat.nl, in Dutch; Zijlsingel 2) Haarlem's top music and dance club attracts bands with banging tunes. Events in this cavernous venue usually start around 9pm.

### KEUKENHOF FLOWER GARDENS

Before you visit the Netherlands' most famous flower gardens, a little background on 'tulip fever' is in order. The lovely tulip has been seducing Europeans since the 16th century, when an enterprising Dutch ambassador brought back (read: smuggled out) the first precious bulbs from the Near East. The Netherlands is now a major world supplier of all kinds of colourful and exotic blooms, and most thrive in the cool, wet climate. They're much more than a commodity; the 'flower culture' means you'll see droves of people with a bunch tucked under one arm.

Covering some 32 hectares, the **Keukenhof** (www.keukenhof.nl; adult/child under 11yr €14.50/7; ⌚8am-7.30pm mid-Mar–mid-May, last entry 6pm) is the world's largest bulb-flower garden, attracting nearly 800,000 visitors during a mere eight weeks every year.

The gardens were opened in 1949 with the idea of having a place for European growers to show off their hybrids. This isn't just any old trade show, however. Nature's talents are combined with artificial precision to create a wonder of landscaping where millions of tulips, narcissi and daffodils blossom perfectly in place and exactly on time. You can easily spend half a day here filling your camera's digital memory.

If it has been hot, don't worry about wilting flowers: fresh blooms are planted by helping hands for the duration of the season. Special exhibits are held in the pavilions around the site, and there are cafes and refreshment stands throughout.

Opening dates vary slightly from year to year, so check before setting out. Connexxion bus 54 travels from Leiden Centraal Station to Keukenhof (25 minutes, four times per hour). A combo ticket for the bus and the gardens costs €21/11 per adult/child. All tickets can be purchased online, which helps avoid huge queues.

**PHILHARMONIE** MUSIC

(☎023-512 12 12; www.theater-haarlem.nl, in Dutch; Lange Begijnestraat 11) This venerable concert hall features music from across the spectrum. The orchestra, Philharmonie Haarlem, ranks among the best in the Netherlands.

# Leiden

## Explore

As you walk south from the striking, hypermodern Centraal Station, the city's traditional character unfolds. A five-minute stroll takes you into Leiden's district of historic waterways, the most notable being the Oude Rijn and the Nieuwe Rijn. They meet at Hoogstraat to form a canal, simply called the Rijn. Take time to explore the canals and waterways, which are lined with traditional gabled canal houses that are quintessentially Dutch.

Leiden's 20,000 students make up a big chunk of the population and lend a young, dynamic ambience to the place that is easily experienced in its many cafes and bars. It makes this a fun place to sightsee during the day and to simply hang out in the evening.

Leiden is nicknamed Museumstad (Museum City), and you'll want to allow time to explore at least a few of the city's 14 museums.

## The Best...

- ➡ **Sight** Rijksmuseum van Oudheden (p197)
- ➡ **Place to Eat** Oudt Leyden (p199)
- ➡ **Place to Drink** Cafe L'Esperance (p200)

## Top Tip

Don't skip the chance to absorb Leiden's vibrant student life by exploring the area around the Netherlands' oldest university, where such historic sights as Europe's oldest botanical gardens coexist with lively cafes and a cultural buzz.

## Getting There & Away

**Train** NS runs services from Amsterdam six or seven times per hour (€8).

**Car** From the southwest point of the A10 ring road, take the A4.

### Need to Know

- **Area Code** ☎071
- **Location** 45km southwest of Amsterdam
- **Tourist Office** (☎071-516 60 00; www.vvvleiden.nl; Stationsweg 41; ⊙8am-6pm Mon-Fri, 10am-4pm Sat, 11am-5pm Sun) Across from the station.

## SIGHTS

**TOP CHOICE RIJKSMUSEUM VAN OUDHEDEN** MUSEUM

(National Museum of Antiquities; www.rmo.nl; Rapenburg 28; adult/child 13-17yr/under 13yr €9/5.50/free; ⊙10am-5pm Tue-Sun) This museum has a world-class collection of Greek, Roman and Egyptian artefacts, the pride of which is the extraordinary Temple of Taffeh, a gift from former Egyptian president Anwar Sadat to the Netherlands for helping to save ancient Egyptian monuments from flood.

**FREE DE BURCHT** PARK, MONUMENT

(admission free; ⊙sunrise-sunset) This 11th-century citadel on an artificial hill lost its protective functions as the city grew around it. Now De Burcht is a park with lovely places to view the steeples and rooftops. There's a wonderful cafe at its base.

**FREE LEIDEN UNIVERSITY** UNIVERSITY

(www.leiden.edu) This is the oldest university in Europe, and was a gift to Leiden from William the Silent for withstanding two Spanish sieges in 1574. It was a terrible time, only ending when sea beggars arrived and repelled the invaders. But one-third of the residents starved before the Spaniards retreated on 3 October (the town's big festival day). The campus comprises an interesting mix of modern and antique buildings that are scattered around town.

**MUSEUM VOLKENKUNDE** MUSEUM

(National Museum of Ethnology; www.volkenkunde.nl; Steenstraat 1; adult/child 13-18yr/under 13yr €5.50/3/2; ⊙10am-5pm Tue-Sun) Cultural achievements by civilisations worldwide are on show here. More than 200,000 artefacts span China, South America and Africa, much like Amsterdam's Tropenmuseum. There's also a rich Indonesian collection; watch for performances by the museum's gamelan troupe.

**HORTUS BOTANICUS** GARDEN

(www.hortus.leidenuniv.nl; Rapenburg 73; adult/child €6/3; ⊙10am-6pm daily Apr-Oct, 10am-4pm Tue-Sun Nov-Mar) The lush Hortus Botanicus is Europe's oldest botanical garden (1590), and home to the country's oldest descendants of the Dutch tulips. It's a wonderful place to relax, with explosions of tropical colour and a fascinating steamy greenhouse.

### ART OUTSIDE OF AMSTERDAM

Fine paintings can be found in collections across the Netherlands, and it's worth noting that first-rate galleries even a stone's throw from Amsterdam tend to be less crowded than in the capital. The following cities all have historic quarters and museum treasures that invite you to explore.

- **Haarlem** It's hard to know where to start, but the 17th-century heart of lovely Haarlem, less than 20 minutes away, is always a good bet. At one time the city was more important in the art world than Amsterdam, so it's no surprise that Haarlem's Frans Hals Museum possesses one of the country's finest assemblies of Dutch paintings. There are also examples of the CoBrA art movement in museums nearby. The city will seem bite-sized after the capital, and most sites of interest are within a short stroll of the lively main square, Grote Markt, and its attractive cathedral.
- **Leiden** Rembrandt's birthplace is an easygoing university town with several first-class museums, the world's oldest botanical garden, and a wealth of lively student pubs. In the 17th century the pilgrim fathers settled in Leiden before beginning their epic voyage to the New World. Some of its key artworks stem from the Renaissance era, such as the impressive triptych of *The Last Judgment* at the Lakenhal museum.

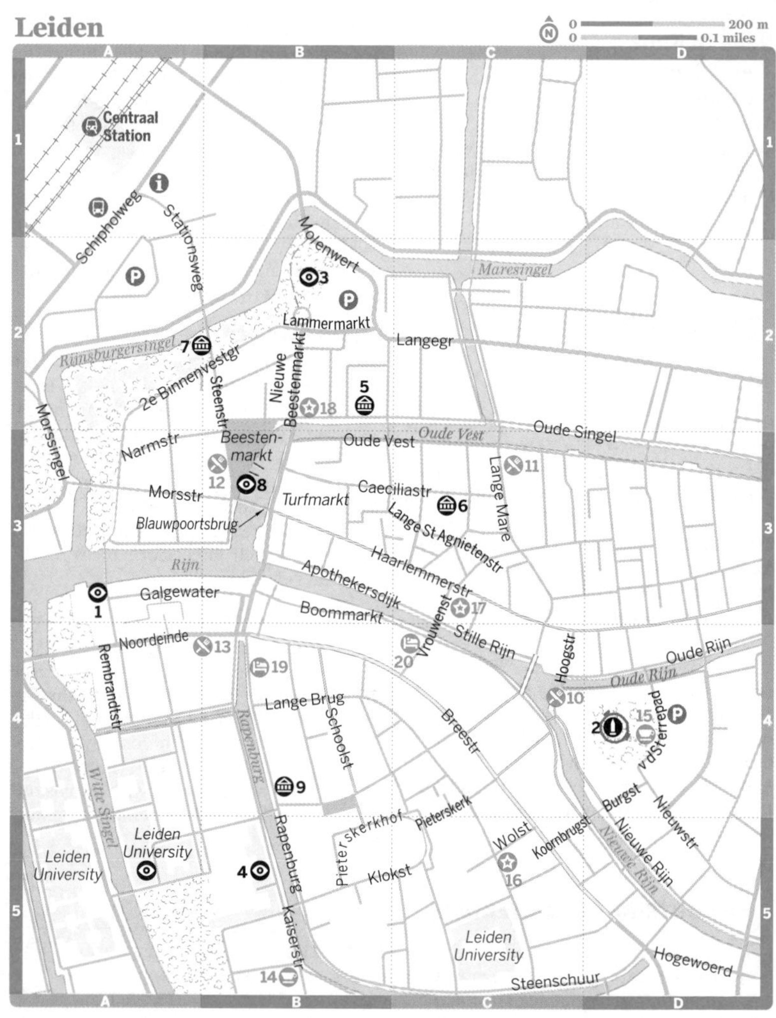


**LAKENHAL** MUSEUM

(www.lakenhal.nl; Oude Singel 28-32; adult/child €7.50/free; ⏲10am-5pm Tue-Fri, noon-5pm Sat & Sun) This 17th-century museum houses the Municipal Museum, with an assortment of works by Old Masters (including Rembrandt), as well as period rooms and temporary exhibits. The 1st floor has been restored to the way it would have looked when Leiden was at the peak of its prosperity.

**DE VALK** MUSEUM

(The Falcon; ☎071-516 53 53; 2e Binnenvestgracht 1; adult/child €3/2; ⏲10am-5pm Tue-Sat, 1-5pm Sun) Leiden's landmark windmill museum has been carefully restored, and many consider it the best example of its kind. Its arms are free to turn 'whenever possible' and can still grind the ol' grain.

**NATURALIS – NATIONAAL NATUURHISTORISCH MUSEUM** MUSEUM

(National Museum of Natural History; www.naturalis.nl; Darwinweg 2; adult/child €11/7; ⏲10am-5pm) A stuffed elephant greets you at this large, well-funded collection. There are all the usual dead critters and the million-year-old Java Man discovered by Dutch anthropologist Eugene Dubois in 1891. The museum is 300m west of the town centre.

## Leiden



**MUSEUM BOERHAAVE** MUSEUM
(www.museumboerhaave.nl; Lange St Agnietenstraat 10; adult/child €7.50/3.50; ⏱10am-5pm Tue-Sat, noon-5pm Sun) Leiden University was an early centre for Dutch medical research and you can see the often-grisly results (five centuries of pickled organs, surgical tools and skeletons) here.

**REDERIJ REMBRANDT** BOAT CRUISE
(☎071-513 49 38; www.rederij-rem brandt.nl; Beestenmarkt; adult/child €10/6.50; ⏱tours 11am-4pm Mar-Oct) Leisurely one-hour canal boat tours of the channel around the old town centre, with commentary (English available).

**BOTENVERHUUR 'T GALGEWATER** BOAT RENTAL
(Boat Hire Galgewater; ☎071-514 97 90; www.galgewater.nl; Galgewater 44a; per hr from €5; ⏱11am-7pm mid-Apr–Sep) For a more intimate canal experience, hire a canoe or kayak and navigate the canals yourself.

### LEIDEN: BIRTHPLACE OF THE ARTS

Wealth from the linen industry helped to make Leiden rich, and provided a fertile atmosphere for artists during the 17th century. The great Dutch painters Rembrandt, Jan Steen and Jan van Goyen were all from Leiden, yet the city has only one Rembrandt painting, even though the master lived here for 26 years.

## EATING & DRINKING

TOP CHOICE **OUDT LEYDEN** DUTCH €
(Steenstrat 49; pancakes €6-13; ⏱11.30am-9.30pm; ) Get ready to meet giant Dutch-style pancakes with creative fillings that make kids and adults alike go wide-eyed and giddy. Whether you're feeling savoury (marinated salmon, sour cream and capers), sweet (warm cherries and vanilla ice cream) or simply adventurous (ginger and bacon, anyone?), this cafe hits the spot every time.

**DE BRASSERIE DE ENGELENBAK** INTERNATIONAL €€
(www.brasseriedeengelenbak.nl, in Dutch; Lange Mare 38; lunch €6-9, 3-course dinner €31; ⏱lunch & dinner, closed Sun) Right in the shadow of the 17th-century octagonal Marekerk, this elegant bistro serves a seasonally changing menu of fresh fare that takes its cues from across the continent. Local organic produce features in many of the dishes. Tables outside enjoy views of the hoi polloi.

**SURAKARTA** INDONESIAN €€
(www.surakarta.nl, in Dutch; Noordeinde 51-53; mains from €13, rijsttafel from €23; ⏱dinner) Javanese art lines the walls at this neighbourhood Indonesian place, which does a busy takeaway service in addition to its elegant *rijsttafel* (Indonesian banquet) service.

**ANNIE'S** CAFE €€
(www.annies.nu, in Dutch; Hoogstraat 1a; mains €6-21; ⏱11am-1am; 👪) At the confluence of

## SLEEPING IN LEIDEN

➡ **Pension Witte Singel** (☎071-512 45 92; www.pension-ws.demon.nl; Witte Singel 80; r €50-95; @📶) Seven bright rooms (some sharing bathrooms) with large windows overlook most agreeable scenery: the perfectly peaceful Singel canal in front and a typically Dutch garden out the back.

➡ **Hotel de Doelen** (☎071-512 05 27; www.dedoelen.com; Rapenburg 2; s/d €85/105; @📶) Has a slightly faded air of classical elegance. Some canalside rooms in this regal building are larger and better appointed. Breakfast costs €7.50.

➡ **Hotel Nieuw Minerva** (☎071-512 63 58; www.hotelleiden.com; Boommarkt 23; r from €72; @📶) Located in six 16th-century canalside houses, this central hotel has a mix of 40 regular and themed rooms, including a room with a bed in which King Lodewijk Bonaparte (aka Louis Bonaparte) slept.

canals and pedestrian zones, Annie's has a prime water-level location with dozens of tables on a floating pontoon. This classy cafe is perfect for a drink or a casual meal.

TOP CHOICE **CAFÉ L'ESPERANCE** CAFE

(www.lesperance.nl, in Dutch; Kaiserstraat 1) This long, dark and handsome cafe is all decked out in nostalgic wood panelling *and* overlooks an evocative bend in the canal. Tables abound outside in summer.

**HET KOETSHUIS** CAFE

(www.koetshuisdeburcht.nl; Burgsteeg 13) On a sunny day, it's hard to beat the terrace tables just outside the grand Burcht gate, where all of humankind gathers for an afternoon coffee or *borrel* (alcoholic drink of your choice).

## ☆ ENTERTAINMENT

**CAFÉ DE WW** LIVE MUSIC

(www.deww.nl, in Dutch; Wolsteeg 4) On Friday and Saturday, live rock in this glossy scarlet bar can expand to an impromptu stage in the alley with crowds trailing up to the main street. On other nights there's a DJ. Though the emphasis is on the music, there's a great beer selection.

**HUNKY DORY** LIVE MUSIC

(☎071-514 63 86; Vrouwensteeg 6) Locals swarm to this cool music bar to see some of the best touring bands from Holland and beyond. Music ranges from jazz to rock 'n' roll.

# Delft

### Explore

After spending the morning at Delft's prime tourist attraction, De Koninklijke Porceleyn Fles, spend the afternoon wandering the city's gorgeous streets and canals. Pick up a copy of the 'Historic Walk Through Delft' brochure (€3.50) from the Tourist Information Pointe and explore the city's riches at your own pace. Be sure to allow time for shopping and wining and dining around the Markt. And since it's about an hour from Amsterdam, it's definitely worth spending a night in this lovely town, whose gracious hotels cater to daytrippers who don't want to go home quite yet.

### The Best...

➡ **Sight** De Koninklijke Porceleyne Fles (p201)

➡ **Place to Eat** Natuurlijk 015 (p201)

➡ **Place to Drink** Belgisch Bier Café Belvédère (p201)

### Top Tip

It's not all pottery, really: take time to wander the streets of what many say is Holland's prettiest city, a veritable treasure trove of Gothic and Renaissance architecture.

### Getting There & Away

**Travel time** One hour

**Train** Services to Delft are frequent (€8, up to six per hour).

**Car** Take the A13/E19, which passes through the Hague en route to Rotterdam.

## Need to Know

- **Area Code** 015
- **Location** 55km southwest of Amsterdam
- **Tourist office** (0900 51 51 555; www.delft.nl; Hippolytusbuurt 4; hours vary)

# SIGHTS

### TOP CHOICE DE KONINKLIJKE PORCELEYNE FLES — MUSEUM, GALLERY, SHOP

(www.royaldelft.com; Rotterdamseweg 196; adult/child €4/free; 9am-5pm) Welcome to china heaven: this is why you came to Delft, isn't it? Pottery fans, and even those new to the iconic blue-and-white earthenware, will enjoy this factory-meets-gallery-meets-shopping experience. The truly Delftware-obsessed will want to take a workshop (€37.50) in which you get to paint your own piece of Delft blue, or indulge in an English-style **high tea** (€25 including entrance ticket; last Sunday of the month) served on (you guessed it) Delftware. Regular tickets include an audio tour which leads you through a painting demonstration, the company museum, and the factory production process. For many, of course, the real thrills begin and end in the gift shop.

### TOP CHOICE VERMEER CENTRUM DELFT — MUSEUM

(www.vermeerdelft.nl; Voldersgracht 21; adult/child €7/3; 10am-5pm) As the place where Vermeer was born, lived, and worked, Delft is 'Vermeer Central' to many art-history and Old Masters enthusiasts. Finally, the town is home to a fitting place to explore the life and works of one of the Dutch Golden Age's greatest painters, otherwise known as the 'Master of Light'. Along with viewing life-sized images of Vermeer's oeuvre, you can tour a replica of Vermeer's studio, which gives insight into the way the artist approached the use of light and colour in his craft. A 'Vermeer's World' exhibit offers biographical insight into his environment and upbringing, while temporary exhibits showcase the ways in which his work continues to inspire other artists.

### GROTE MARKT — MARKET, SQUARE

(Koornmarkt 67) The pedestrian city plaza is worth a stroll for its pleasant collection of galleries, antique stores, clothing boutiques and quirky speciality shops. Come for a Friday night dinner and shopping excursion. Most stores are open to 9pm on Friday, a rarity in small-town Holland. On Thursday you'll find the General Market, while on Saturday from April to September, the Antiques, Bric-a-Brac and Book Market draws in visitors seeking treasures and deals alike.

### OUDE KERK — CHURCH

(www.oudekerk-delft.nl; Heilige Geestkerkhof 25) Nicknamed 'Oude Jan' (Old Jan) by Delft's citizens in homage to its most famous resident (Johannes Vermeer is buried here), this beautiful church was built in 1246. Note the striking white interior and the 27 stained glass windows, which cast their brilliantly coloured lights on the walls on sunny days.

### MUSEUM PAUL TETAR VAN ELVEN — MUSEUM

(Koornmarkt 67; adult/child €3/free; 1-5pm Tue-Sun) This off-the-radar museum has surprising delights within. A former studio and home of the 19th-century Dutch artist Paul Tetar van Elven, the museum features several Rembrandts and a Vermeer, along with many reproductions of notable paintings by the artist himself. Yet the most interesting thing about this museum might be the evocative 17th-century interior, with its original furnishings and lived-in feel.

# EATING & DRINKING

### NATUURLIJK 015 — CAFE €

(Burgwal 11; mains from €5; 10am-6pm Mon-Sat; ) This new organic cafe is already getting accolades from travellers and locals alike, who congregate on the terrace for creative sandwiches, smoothies and salads.

### SPIJSHUIS DE DIS — DUTCH €€

(www.spijshuisdedis.com; Beestenmarkt 36; lunch €5-15, dinner €16-25; lunch & dinner Tue-Sun; ) Foodies, romantics and oenophiles flock to this cosily elegant restaurant, where fresh fish and amazing soups served in bread bowls take centre stage. Meat eaters and vegies are both well catered for. Don't skip the creative, mouth-watering starters or the Dutch pudding served in a wooden shoe.

### TOP CHOICE BELGISCH BIER CAFÉ BELVÉDÈRE — BEER CAFE

(www.bbcbelvedere.nl; Beestenmarkt 8) We dare you to try saying the name of this Belgian beer temple three times after a

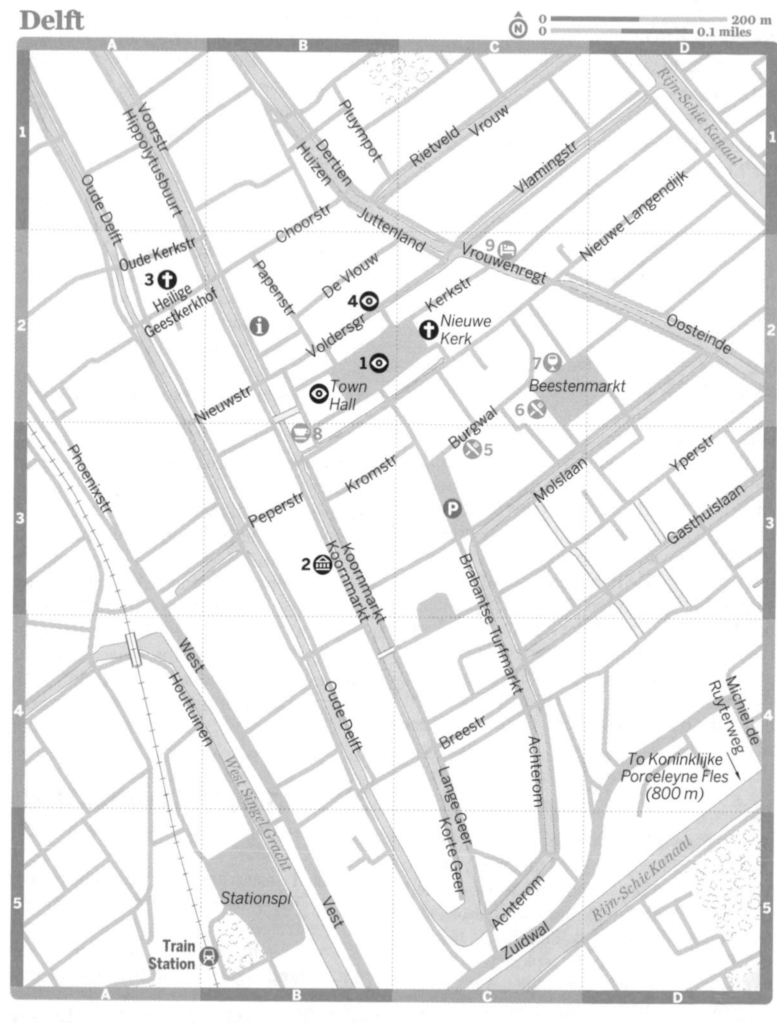


## Delft

| **Sights** | **(p201)** |
|---|---|
| 1 Markt | B2 |
| 2 Museum Paul Tetar van Elven | B3 |
| 3 Oude Kerk | A2 |
| 4 Vermeer Centrum Delft | B2 |

| **Eating** | **(p201)** |
|---|---|
| 5 Natuurlijk 015 | C3 |
| 6 Spijshuis de Dis | C2 |

| **Drinking** | **(p201)** |
|---|---|
| 7 Belgisch Bier Café Belvédère | C2 |
| 8 Stadscafe de Waag | B3 |

| **Sleeping** | **(p203)** |
|---|---|
| 9 Hotel de Emauspoort | C2 |

couple of cold La Chouffes. The cafe is located inside an old historic house, and you can choose from six beers on tap and many more by the bottles. There's food, too, but everyone really comes to worship Belgian brews.

**STADCAFE DE WAAG** CAFE

(www.de-waag.nl, in Dutch; Markt 11; ⊙10am-1am) With a sprawling terrace on the Markt, this is a perfect spot for a post-sightseeing beer or a light meal. There's also a high-end restaurant, De Proeverij, on the premises.

# Alkmaar

## Explore

After spending the morning at the Cheese Market, you'll be understandably hungry. So head to lunch, or make your own Gouda or *boerenkaas* (farmer's cheese) sandwiches at de Kaashuis Tromp. Spend the rest of the afternoon at a museum or two: beer lovers will dig the National Beer Museum. And after that, why not a beer (which, of course, goes perfectly well with more cheese) on one of the laid-back terraces?

## The Best...

- **Sight** Cheese Market (p203)
- **Place to Eat** Café Restaurant De Buren (p204)
- **Place to Drink** Café Lindeboom (p204)

## Top Tip

While most people come for the cheese, it's worth a trip to the Stedelijk Museum, which houses an impressive collection of Dutch Masters.

## Getting There & Away

**Train** Services run at least twice per hour from Amsterdam (€6.70, 45 minutes); the canal-bound centre is 500m southeast of the train station.

**Car** Take the A9 in the west of Amsterdam, which goes directly to Alkmaar.

## Need to Know

- **Area Code** ☎072
- **Location** 35km northwest of Amsterdam
- **Tourist Office** (☎072-511 42 84; www.vvvalkmaar.nl; Waagplein 2; ⊙1-5pm Mon, 10am-5.30pm Tue-Fri, 9.30am-5pm Sat)

## SIGHTS

TOP CHOICE **CHEESE MARKET** MARKET

(Waagplein; ⊙10am-noon Fri Apr-early Sep) If ever there was a cheese town, Alkmaar is it. Most visitors come to this picturesque town for the traditional cheese market dating back to the 17th century.

On Friday mornings, waxed rounds of *kaas* (cheese) are ceremoniously stacked on the main square. Soon, porters appear in colourful hats (denoting the cheese guild), and dealers in white smocks insert a hollow rod to extract a cheese sample, and sniff and crumble to check fat and moisture content. Once deals are struck, the porters whisk the cheeses on wooden sledges to the old cheese scale, accompanied by a zillion camera clicks. It's primarily for show – nowadays the dairy co-ops have a lock on the cheese trade. Still, as living relics go it's a colourful show.

## SLEEPING IN DELFT

- **Soul Inn** (☎071-215 72 46; www.soul-inn.nl; Willemstraat 55; s/d/tr from €60/70/100; @📶) Why doesn't every adorable small town have a hip crash pad like this funky bed and breakfast? It's a cool antidote for those who've experienced an overload of Delft quaintness; rooms play themes and colour schemes like hot pink and retro 1970s, along with several African-themed suites.
- **Hotel de Emauspoort** (☎015-219 02 19; www.emauspoort.nl; Vrouwenregt 9-11; s/d/tr €88/99/138; @📶) Couples, singles, and business travellers alike rave about this sweet, well-priced little hotel near the Markt. Spacious rooms strike a nice balance of old-world antique and totally modern comfort. Extras include a bountiful breakfast, an outdoor terrace and free wi-fi in the lounge. The lofted Vermeer room is a bargain of a splurge.

**STEDELIJK MUSEUM** MUSEUM

(www.stedelijkmuseumalkmaar.nl, in Dutch; Canadaplein 1; adult/child €6/free; ⏰10am-5pm Tue-Sun) This museum is overlooked by many visitors, which is a shame because its collection of oils by the Dutch Masters is first-rate. There are life-sized portraits of Alkmaar nobles and historic scenes of the city in decline after the Golden Age. In the upstairs gallery, Charley Toorop's painting of the cheese bearers with grotesque features still stirs controversy.

**WAAGGEBOUW** HISTORIC BUILDING

The Waaggebouw (Weigh House; 1390) houses the tourist office, where you can pick up a walking tour of Alkmaar's historic buildings (€2) covering historical sights. Inside you'll also find the **Hollands Kaasmuseum** (Dutch Cheese Museum; www.kaasmuseum.nl; adult/concession €3/1.50; ⏰10am-4pm Mon-Sat Apr-Oct), a reverential display of cheese-making utensils, photos and a curious stock of paintings by 16th-century female artists. The mechanical tower **carillon** (⏰6.30pm & 7.30pm Thu, 11am & noon Fri, noon & 1pm Sat mid-Apr–mid-Sep) with jousting knights still springs to life.

**NATIONAAL BIERMUSEUM** MUSEUM

(www.biermuseum.nl, in Dutch; Houttil 1; adult/child €3.50/1.75; ⏰1-4pm Mon-Sat) Across the main square from the Kaasmuseum lies this decent collection of beer-making equipment, plus a series of wax dummies showing how the suds were made. The rare video of Dutch beer commercials since the 1950s is a real howler. Choose from 30 beers (eight on draught) in the friendly bar after your tour.

**GROTE KERK** CHURCH

(Kerkplein; adult/child €5/free; ⏰10am-5pm Tue-Sun Jul & Aug) The Grote Kerk reminds us that Noord Hollanders are organ lovers. The most famous here is the little 'Swallow Organ' (1511) in the north ambulatory. The 17th-century organ built by Jacob van Campen dominates the nave. Organ recitals take place frequently; check the schedule for upcoming dates at www.alkmaarorgelstad.nl. At other times, you may be able to sneak a peek if the doors are open.

**WOLTHEUS CRUISES** BOAT CRUISE

(www.woltheuscruises.nl; adult/child €5.30/3.80; ⏰every 20min from 9.30am Apr-Oct) Tours depart from Mient near the Waaggebouw and last 45 minutes. Offers multilingual commentary.

## EATING & DRINKING

TOP CHOICE **DE TROMP KAASHUIS** CHEESE €

(www.kaashuistromp.nl, in Dutch; Magdalenenstraat 11; ⏰10am-6pm Mon-Sat) If you're looking to grab some cheese after seeing so much of it, check out this quality certified shop with Dutch and French cheeses stacked everywhere you look. Samples abound, and there's fresh bread for sale that's perfect for making impromptu sandwiches with that delish two-year-old Gouda you just bought.

**HET HOF VAN ALKMAAR** INTERNATIONAL €€

(www.hofvanalkmaar.nl, in Dutch; Hof van Sonoy 1; lunch €5-15, dinner €16-22; ⏰lunch & dinner Tue-Sun) This atmospheric place offers creative cuisine in a former 15th-century monastery, with courtyard seating.

**CAFÉ RESTAURANT DE BUREN** INTERNATIONAL €€

(www.restaurant-deburen.nl, in Dutch; Mient 37; mains €6-20; ⏰lunch & dinner) Outside tables at this vintage cafe span the canal and wrap around to the old fish market. The menu is a fresh take on Dutch fare.

**CAFÉ LINDEBOOM** CAFE

(www.lindeboom-alkmaar.nl, in Dutch; Verdronkenoord 114) By the old fish market, this cosy bar is where talkative locals linger on the canal terrace.

# Zaanse Schans

### Explore

Spend your time exploring the six working windmills, which are the undisputed highlight of a visit here. One mill sells fat jars of its freshly ground mustard, while the others turn out oils, meal and sawed planks. Most are open for inspection, and it's a treat to clamber about the creaking works while the mills shake in the North Sea breeze.

## Top Tip

Hire a bike and pedal from Amsterdam to Zaanse Schans. It only takes about 90 minutes, and many travellers claim that the picturesque trip is one of the highlights of their trip.

## Getting There & Away

**Train** Use local trains towards Alkmaar and get off at Koog-Zaandijk (€2.90, 17 minutes, four times hourly), then walk the 1km to Zaanse Schans.

**Car** Travel to the northwestern side of the city on the A10 ring road, and take the A8 turn-off. Exit at Zaandijk.

## Need to Know

- **Area Code** ☎075
- **Location** 10km northwest
- **Tourist Office** (Zaanse Schans Information Desk; ☎681 00 00; www.zaanseschans.nl; reception area, Zaans Museum)

# SIGHTS

**WINDMILLS** WINDMILLS

People come for an hour and stay for several at this working and fully inhabited village, which functions as a kind of open air windmill gallery on the Zaan river. It's *the* place to see windmills operating, although only a few of the formerly more than 1000 windmills in the area have been restored. While the village has a touristy element, the mills are completely authentic and are operated with enthusiasm and love. Visitors can explore the windmills at will, seeing firsthand the vast moving parts that make these devices a combination of sailing ship and Rube Goldberg. As a bonus, the riverbank setting is lovely. While most attractions are free, some (like the Zaans Museum) charge an entrance fee.

The mill selling paint pigments will delight artists, as you see the actual materials used in producing Renaissance masterpieces turned into powders. Ask to see the storeroom of ground pigments for sale.

The other buildings have been brought here from all over the country to re-create a 17th-century community. There is an early Albert Heijn market, a cheese maker and a popular clog factory that turns out wooden shoes as if grinding keys (and which has a surprisingly interesting museum). The engaging pewtersmith will explain the story behind dozens of tiny figures while the soft metal sets in the moulds.

The impressive **Zaans Museum** (☎075-616 28 62; www.zaansmuseum.nl; adult/child €7/4; ⌚10am-5pm) shows how the harnessing of wind and water was done.

Once you've finished poking about the village, take a **boat** (adult/child €3/2; ⌚9am-6pm May-Sep) across the Zaan river. It runs on demand and the cheery volunteers will give you a walking guide of the old town of Zaandijk.

### HIT THE BEACH: SCHEVENINGEN

Surprise! Yes, there are beaches in Holland – and pleasant (if a bit chilly) ones at that. Arguably Holland's most popular beach, and a good family destination, **Scheveningen** (www.scheveningen.com) makes a perfect day trip: it's only a 15-minute tram ride from the Hague. Even if you don't swim, it's a lovely spot to stroll along the beach, shop at the Palace Promenade or grab a bite to eat in a seaside cafe. With its swirling sand dunes and forest, the beach is also popular with walkers who come to hike the 'Dutch Dune' from Scheveningen to Noordwijk.

The beach itself is about 3km long. The Noorderstrand (North Beach) is built up with modern hotel and condo developments, and is home to a pier and a shopping promenade with restaurants and bars that get insanely packed on summer days – the Dutch love their sun however they can get it. Retreat to the Zuiderstrand (South Beach) to find solitude, but mind the current, which is known to be strong.

To reach the Noorderstrand, take tram 1 or 9 from the city centre of Den Hague, or take bus 22 from the Centraal Station. To get to Zuiderstrand take tram 11 from Hollands Spoor, Den Hague's smaller train station.

# Sleeping

*In its typically charming way, Amsterdam has loads of hotels in wild and wonderful spaces: inspired architects have breathed new life into old buildings, from converted schools and industrial lofts to entire rows of canal houses joined at the hip. Many lodgings overlook gorgeous waterways or courtyards. But charm doesn't come cheap...*

## Seasons & Prices

Rates and crowds peak in summer, and on weekends at any time of the year. Book well in advance if you're travelling then. Prices are lowest from October to April (excluding Christmas/New Year and Easter).

## Hotels

Any hotel with more than 20 rooms is considered large, and most rooms themselves are on the snug side. You'll see a 'star' plaque on the front of every hotel, indicating its rating according to the Benelux Hotel Classification. The stars (from one to five) have to do with the existence of certain facilities, rather than quality. This means that a two-star hotel may be in better condition than a hotel of higher rank, though admittedly with fewer facilities.

## B&Bs

Amsterdam has a scattering of B&Bs. Most don't have exterior signage and access is by reservation only, giving an intimate feel.

## Youth Hostels

Hostels are popular in Amsterdam. The Netherlands youth hostel association goes by the name **Stayokay** (www.stayokay.com) and is affiliated with **Hostelling International** (www.hihostels.com).

## Party & Stoner Hotels

A number of hotels in the budget category cater to party guests as well as pot smokers. By and large they're pretty basic affairs. If in doubt whether smoking marijuana is permitted, ask when you make your reservation. Many hotels have strict no-drugs policies.

## Amenities

Wi-fi is nearly universal across the spectrum, but air-conditioning and lifts are not.

### TOP END

Expect lifts (elevators), minibars and room service. At the top end of top end, facilities like air-conditioning and fitness centres are par for the course. Breakfast is rarely included.

### MIDRANGE

Most hotels in this category are big on comfort, low on formality and small enough to offer personal attention. Rooms usually have a toilet and shower, and TV and phone. Not many hotels in this category over two storeys have lifts, and their narrow stairwells can take some getting used to, especially with luggage. Rates typically include breakfast.

### BUDGET

Lodgings in the lowest price bracket, other than hostels, are thin on the ground. Some are nothing short of run-down flophouses. The better options tend to be spick and span with furnishings that are, at best, cheap and cheerful. Rates often include breakfast.

## Accommodation Websites

➡ **Lonely Planet** (hotels.lonelyplanet.com) Find reviews and make bookings.

➡ **I Amsterdam** (www.iamsterdam.com) Options from the city's official website.

## Lonely Planet's Top Choices

**Cocomama** (p212) Only in Amsterdam: a red-curtained boutique hostel in an old brothel.

**Backstage Hotel** (p212) Rock and roll hotel hosting musicians from the cool-cat clubs nearby.

**Bicycle Hotel Amsterdam** (p217) Another Amsterdam speciality: a bed-and-bike with eco-friendly trimmings.

**Collector** (p215) Offbeat B&B with piles of clogs, clocks and backyard chickens.

**Hotel Résidence Le Coin** (p209) Shiny, university-owned apartments in historical buildings, just steps from the Centre's action.

## Best by Budget

### €

Cocomama (p212)

Christian Youth Hostel 'The Shelter Jordaan' (p214)

Bicycle Hotel Amsterdam (p217)

Stadsdoelen Youth Hostel (p210)

Hotel Prinsenhof (p213)

Van Gogh Hostel & Hotel (p216)

### €€

Hotel Fita (p216)

The Toren (p210)

Hotel de Filosoof (p214)

Hotel Aalders (p216)

Hotel Zandbergen (p215)

Hotel Piet Hein (p215)

### €€€

Hotel de L'Euorpe (p209)

Seven One Seven (p211)

InterContinental Amstel Amsterdam (p212)

Hotel Vondel (p214)

Mint Hotel (p218)

## Best Canal Views

Seven Bridges (p212)

Chic & Basic Amsterdam (p211)

Hotel Pulitzer (p211)

Sebastian's (p211)

Seven One Seven (p211)

Hotel Pax (p211)

## Best Only in Amsterdam

Frederic's Rentabike & Houseboats (p211)

Hemp Hotel (p213)

Lloyd Hotel (p218)

Captain's Place (p218)

Xaviera Hollander Bed & Breakfast (p216)

## Best Design Savvy

Lloyd Hotel (p218)

Mint Hotel (p218)

Banks Mansion (p212)

Park Hotel (p215)

Hotel Vondel (p214)

College Hotel (p216)

## Best Small Gems

All Inn the Family B&B (p214)

Sunhead of 1617 (p211)

Miauw Suites (p211)

Between Art & Kitsch B&B (p217)

Maes B&B (p211)

Cake Under my Pillow (p217)

## Best for Romantics

Hotel de Filosoof (p214)

The Toren (p210)

Seven Bridges (p212)

Seven One Seven (p211)

## Best Gay Friendly

Amistad Hotel (p213)

Golden Bear (p213)

Hotel Orlando (p213)

## NEED TO KNOW

### Price Ranges

In our listings we've used the following price codes to represent the cost of an en suite double room in high season (including the 5% city hotel tax and excluding breakfast unless stated otherwise).

| | |
|---|---|
| **€** | less than €80 |
| **€€** | €80–160 |
| **€€€** | more than €160 |

### Reservations

➡ Book as far in advance as possible, especially in summer, and for weekends anytime of the year.

➡ Many hotels offer discounts via their websites, especially for last-minute bookings.

➡ VVV (tourist) offices can make last-minute bookings, but they charge €5 or more to do so.

### Tipping

Tipping is not expected, though at larger hotels, the porter often receives a euro or two for carrying bags, and the room cleaner gets a few euros for a job well done.

### Tax

Properties often include the 5% city hotel tax in quoted rates, but ask before booking. If you're paying by credit card, some hotels add a surcharge of up to 5%.

## Where to Stay

| Neighbourhood | For | Against |
|---|---|---|
| **Medieval Centre & Red Light District** | In the thick of the action; close to sights, nightlife, theatres and transport | Can be noisy, touristy and seedy; not great value for money |
| **Nieuwmarkt** | Still near the action, but with a slightly more laid-back vibe than the Centre | Some parts are close enough to the Red Light District to get rowdy spillover |
| **Western Canal Ring** | Tree-lined canals. Oddball boutiques and the Jordaan's cafes are nearby. Within walking distance of Amsterdam's most popular sights | Given all the positives, rooms book out early and can be pricey |
| **Southern Canal Ring** | Swanky hotels, not far from the dining hub of Utrechtsestraat and Nieuwe Spiegelstraat's antique shops | Can be loud, crowded, pricey, and touristy – especially around the high-traffic areas of Leidseplein and Rembrandtplein |
| **Jordaan & the West** | Cosy cafes, quirky shops and charming village character surround you | Sleeping options are few, due in part to the paucity of big-name sights close by |
| **Vondelpark & Around** | An aura of wealth and history surrounds Vondelpark, and the serene, designer hotels reflect it | High prices reflect the ideal location, which is also near Museumplein and Leidseplein |
| **Old South** | Quiet, leafy streets; walking distance to Museumplein; small, gracious properties; lots of midrange options | Not much nightlife |
| **De Pijp** | Recent explosion of dining/drinking cool in the area; located near Museumplein and Southern Canal Ring | Easy walking distance to Museumplein, Vondelpark and Leidseplein, but a hike from the Centre. Options are fairly limited |
| **Plantage, Eastern Islands & Eastern Docklands** | Abundant greenery, cutting-edge architecture and the rippling expanse of the IJ dotted with riverboats | Not easily walkable to Amsterdam's major sights; you'll need to tram or bike |
| **Oosterpark & South Amsterdam** | Lower prices due to remote location (which is really just a short tram/metro ride away); quiet area amid locals | Fewer options for food and drink |

## Medieval Centre & Red Light District

**TOP CHOICE HOTEL RÉSIDENCE LE COIN** APARTMENTS €€
Map p290 (☎524 68 00; www.lecoin.nl; Nieuwe Doelenstraat 5; s €119, d €139-154, f €230; ) This shiny inn, owned by the University of Amsterdam, offers 42 small, high-class apartments spread over seven historical buildings, all equipped with designer furniture, wood floors and kitchenettes – and all reachable by lift. It's in the thick of things, opposite the popular grand Café de Jaren and just a five-minute stroll to pretty Nieuwmarkt. Breakfast costs €11.50 per person and wi-fi costs €5 per 24 hours.

**HOTEL BROUWER** HOTEL €€
Map p286 (☎624 63 58; www.hotelbrouwer.nl; Singel 83; r incl breakfast €60-100; ) Our favourite hotel in this price range, it has just eight rooms in a house dating back to 1652. Its rooms, named for Dutch painters, are furnished with simplicity, but all have canal views. There's a mix of Delft-blue tiles and early-20th-century furniture and – get this – a tiny lift. Staff dispense friendly advice. Reserve well in advance. No credit cards accepted.

**HOTEL DE L'EUROPE** LUXURY HOTEL €€€
Map p290 (☎531 17 77; www.leurope.nl; Nieuwe Doelenstraat 2-8; r from €330; ) Oozing Victorian elegance, L'Europe welcomes you with a glam chandelier, a marble lobby, 100 gloriously large rooms (some have terraces and all have handsome marble bathrooms) and smart extras like a shoeshine service and boats for canal cruises. The attached restaurant and chichi gym are equally impressive. Due to customer demand, there's now an elegant smoking lounge (with killer water views). Wi-fi costs €15.95 per 24 hours. The hotel has been undergoing an extensive renovation that was due for completion in 2011.

**AIVENGO YOUTH HOSTEL** HOSTEL €
Map p286 (☎421 36 70; www.aivengoyouthhostel.com; Spuistraat 6; dm €15-25, 4-bed r per person €20-35; ) Funky Aivengo, with dorms (some with kitchens and en suite bathrooms) and two private four-bed rooms, is a treat. It has a quiet, respectful vibe and is spread out across two buildings – one with a Middle Eastern interior, the other with exposed wood beams. Rates here include clean bed linen and towels, as well as a safety deposit box, but there's no breakfast or common rooms. Note: there is a 4am to 6am lockout.

**ST CHRISTOPHER'S AT THE WINSTON** PARTY HOTEL, PARTY HOSTEL €€
Map p286 (☎623 13 80; www.winston.nl; Warmoesstraat 123; dm €32-42, r €73-120; ) This place is party central for touring bands, with rock 'n' roll rooms and a busy club, bar, beer garden and smoking deck downstairs; it hops 24/7. Group dorm rooms (all en suite) sleep up to eight. Most rooms are 'art' rooms: local artists were given free rein, with results from super-edgy (entirely stainless steel) and playful to questionably raunchy. Caveat: there's no internet *at all* in the rooms – but the ground-floor (lobby and bar) wi-fi is free. Staff can be less than friendly, but hey, it's rock 'n' roll, man. Deal with it. Rates include breakfast.

**NH GRAND HOTEL KRASNAPOLSKY** HOTEL €€€
Map p290 (☎554 91 11; www.nh-hotels.com; Dam 9; d from €220; ) Pride of place belongs to this 468-room edifice across from the Royal Palace, one of the city's first grand hotels (1866). It has elegant if compact rooms and spectacular public spaces. The 19th-century 'winter garden' dining room, with its soaring steel-and-glass roof, is a national monument (the splendid breakfast buffet costs an extra €28.50), and there are fitness and business centres.

**BELLEVUE HOTEL** HOTEL €€
Map p286 (☎530 95 30; www.bellevuehotel.nl; Martelaarsgracht 10; r €100-170; ) Of the small hotels around Centraal Station, this three-star place is the only one we'd stay at. The 77 rooms are small, white and tidy, and feature mod loos and themes of sand, water and grass. If you're sensitive to noise, get a room in the back. Breakfast costs €12.50.

**HOTEL HOKSBERGEN** BOUTIQUE HOTEL €€
Map p290 (☎626 60 43; www.hotelhoksbergen.nl; Singel 301; r incl breakfast €90-150, apt €165-220; ) You sure can't beat Hoksbergen's fantastic canalside location, and there's a breakfast buffet, but be warned: even sardines would have trouble squishing into the microscopically small rooms (with clean but plain furnishings). If you feel claustrophobic, a self-contained apartment (for up to five people) may be a better option.

### HOTEL LUXER
HOTEL €€

Map p286 (330 32 05; www.hotelluxer.com; Warmoesstraat 11; r €90-150; ) A pleasant surprise if ever there was one, this smart little number is probably the best option for your money in the thick of the Red Light District. Rooms are small but well equipped (air-con!) and at night the breakfast area becomes a chic little bar. Breakfast is €10.

### FLYING PIG DOWNTOWN HOSTEL
STONER HOSTEL €

Map p286 (420 68 22; www.flyingpig.nl; Nieuwendijk 100; dm incl breakfast €30-42; ) Hang out with hundreds of young, dope-smoking backpackers at this very relaxed, massive, 250-bed hostel. It's pretty grungy, but no one seems to mind, especially when there's so much fun to be had in the throbbing lobby bar with pool table and DJs some nights. There's also an indoor smoking area, full-service kitchens and a cushion-lined basement nicknamed the 'happy room'.

### HOTEL THE CROWN
PARTY HOTEL €€

Map p286 (626 96 64; www.hotelthecrown.com; Oudezijds Voorburgwal 21; r €70-160; ) Rooms at this Brit-run hotel are pretty monastic (shared toilet, no TV or phone), and don't even bother asking for breakfast. Although it is priced in our midrange bracket, quality is firmly budget. So what's the draw? Fun. The 1930s art deco bar has sports on TV, a pool table, a dartboard and hordes of celebrating stag-nighters.

## Nieuwmarkt

### TOP CHOICE MISC EAT DRINK SLEEP
BOUTIQUE HOTEL €€€

Map p292 (330 62 41; www.misceatdrinksleep.com; Kloveniersburgwal 20; d €145-235; ) Steps from Nieuwmarkt square, the Misc's six themed rooms range from 'baroque' (quite romantic) to 'the room of wonders' (a modern Moroccan escapade); two rooms contain quirky 'bumble-bee' ceiling fans. Canal View rooms cost more, but the Garden View rooms are equally charming (and bigger). Bonus: all nonalcoholic in-room snacks and beverages (minibar) and coffee (your own Nespresso machine) are free.

### STADSDOELEN YOUTH HOSTEL
HOSTEL €

Map p292 (624 68 32; www.stayokay.com; Kloveniersburgwal 97; dm €20-33, r €60; ) Efficient Stadsdoelen is always bustling with backpackers and we can understand why. Staff are friendly and the 11 ultraclean single-sex and mixed rooms (each with up to 20 beds and free lockers) offer a modicum of privacy. There's a big TV room, a pool table, laundry facilities, free lobby wi-fi, bicycle storage (€2 per day) and free continental breakfast. Laptop rental costs €3 per hour.

### CHRISTIAN YOUTH HOSTEL 'THE SHELTER CITY'
HOSTEL €

Map p292 (625 32 30; www.shelter.nl; Barndesteeg 21; dm incl breakfast €22-34; ) The price is right at this rambling hostel just outside the Red Light District, but only if you can handle enormous 'Jesus loves you' signs and a tough no-drugs-or-alcohol policy. The pros of staying here include large, airy, single-sex dorms, filling breakfasts, a quiet cafe, a garden courtyard with ping-pong table and eternal salvation. Its partner hostel in the Jordaan (p214) has less missionary zeal.

## Western Canal Ring

### TOP CHOICE DYLAN
LUXURY HOTEL €€€

Map p299 (530 20 10; www.dylanamsterdam.com; Keizersgracht 384; d €295-1700; ) With a renovation in 2011, the Dylan continues to prove its reputation as a true temple of style. Slink through the 17th-century canal house's courtyard garden entrance and past the gorgeous staff to ensconce yourself in the restaurant or the black-and-white lobby, where world beats don't so much play as fizz. The 41 sumptuous, themed rooms and suites all enchant, whether you're after flamboyant colours or Zen minimalism. We're partial to the Dylan Thomas – with its silver makeup table and antique wood furniture, along with a fully stocked cocktail cabinet – in honour of the famed Welsh poet who notoriously drank himself to death.

### TOP CHOICE THE TOREN
BOUTIQUE HOTEL €€

Map p300 (622 60 33; www.toren.nl; Keizersgracht 164; s/d/garden patio with Jacuzzi from €100/135/210; ) A title-holder for price, room size and personal service, the Toren's communal areas mix 17th-century decadence – gilded mirrors, fireplaces and magnificent chandeliers – with a sensual, decadent flair that screams (or, rather, whispers) Parisian boudoir. Guest rooms are elegantly furnished with modern facilities (including Nespresso coffee machines).

### SEBASTIAN'S BOUTIQUE HOTEL €€

Map p300 (☎433 23 42; www.hotelsebastians.nl; Keizersgracht 115; s/d from €80/105; ❄@📶) Check out the Toren's new and instantly popular sister property, which magically rocks the same brand of dramatic cool. It's just a few blocks down the same canal.

### HOTEL PULITZER LUXURY HOTEL €€€

Map p300 (☎523 52 35; www.luxurycollection.com/pulitzer; Prinsengracht 315-331; d from €309; ❄@📶) Scoring high on elegance but low on pomposity, the Pulitzer manages to combine big-hotel efficiency with boutique-hotel charm. Spread among 25 historic canal houses, the individually decorated, beautifully restored rooms all have mod touches galore, including sweet and cosy bathrooms. There are loads of extras, too (from the cigar bar and art gallery to a sleek gym and private canal cruises) along with lush garden courtyards and a wonderful restaurant and bar. Wi-fi is €19 for 24 hours.

### MIAUW SUITES BOUTIQUE HOTEL €€€

Map p300 (☎893 29 33; www.miauw.com; Hartenstraat 36; r/ste from €160/260; @📶) Located above the designer fashion shop of the same name, Miauw's spacious quarters are just what the doctor ordered for a weekend's shopping blitz in the Negen Straatjes (Nine Streets) district. The snug rooms mix stylish and vintage interior decor, and have electronic goodies such as wide-screen TVs and DVD/CD players. Minimum two-night stay on weekends.

### SUNHEAD OF 1617 BOUTIQUE HOTEL €€€

Map p300 (☎626 18 09; www.sunhead.com; Herengracht 152; r €119-149, apt €129-179; @📶) The fabulous and funny Carlos is your host at these lovely, cheerful rooms and suites along some of Amsterdam's prettiest stretches of canal. Expect a delightful balance of modern design and traditional Dutch charm, along with an excellent breakfast. Spanish spoken.

### CHIC & BASIC AMSTERDAM BOUTIQUE HOTEL €€

Map p300 (☎522 23 45; www.chicandbasic.com; Herengracht 13-19; s/d from €120/140; @📶) Spread across three canal houses, the all-white, modern rooms here merge minimalism with cosiness and flair. Score a room facing the quaint footbridge across the Herengracht canal. Rates include breakfast.

### MAES B&B B&B €€

Map p300 (☎427 51 65; www.bedandbreakfastamsterdam.com; Herenstraat 26hs; s €85-105, d €105-135, apt €115-285; @📶) If you were designing a traditional home in the western canals, it would probably turn out a lot like this property: oriental carpets, wood floors and exposed brick. It's actually fairly spacious for such an old building. The kitchen (open all day for guests to use) is definitely *gezellig* (convivial, cosy).

### FREDERIC'S RENTABIKE & HOUSEBOATS HOTEL, HOUSEBOAT €€

Map p300 (☎624 55 09; www.frederic.nl; Brouwersgracht 78; s/d from €50/75, apt from €90, houseboats from €115; 📶) Some visitors harbour a Mark Twain fantasy of drifting on the waves all night (sans the nasty steerage) and then find their rustbucket is cold and clammy. Not so with Frederic, whose nicely outfitted houseboats on the more picturesque canals are bona fide floating holiday homes with all the mod cons. We're partial to houseboats 1, 4 and 6. On land, he also offers various accommodation in central locations graced with his signature welcoming touches – complimentary organic weed and *jenever* (Dutch gin).

### HOTEL PAX HOTEL €

Map p300 (☎624 97 35; www.hotelpax.nl; Raadhuisstraat 37; d/tr/q from €50/60/80, s/d/tr without bathroom from €35/40/50; 📶) This budget choice on hotel-lined Raadhuisstraat is run by two friendly, funky brothers –and has an artsy student vibe. All eight rooms have cable TV and each is individually decorated, with pretty views of the Westerkerk and Keizersgracht.

### BUDGET HOTEL CLEMENS AMSTERDAM HOTEL €

Map p300 (☎624 60 89; www.clemenshotel.nl; Raadhuisstraat 39; d/tr €120/150, s/d without bathroom €60-75; @📶) Tidy, steep-staired Clemens gears itself to all budgets. Take your pick from the chic themed rooms (one with a sexy red-gold interior, another with delicate French antiques) or simpler budget rooms.

## Southern Canal Ring

### TOP CHOICE SEVEN ONE SEVEN LUXURY HOTEL €€€

Map p302 (☎427 07 17; www.717hotel.nl; Prinsengracht 717; r €425-680; ❄@📶) This is one of the most wonderful hotels in Amsterdam –

designed, boutiqued and simply breathtaking. Its eight hyperplush, deliciously appointed rooms come with that rare luxury: space. Step into the splashy Picasso suite – with its soaring ceiling, prodigiously long sofa, contemporary and antique decorations, and bathroom as big as some European principalities – and you may never, *ever* want to leave. Rates include breakfast, afternoon tea, house wine and oodles of one-on-one service.

**TOP CHOICE BACKSTAGE HOTEL** HOTEL **€€**

Map p302 (☎624 40 44; www.backstagehotel.com; Leidsegracht 114; d €75-135, tr €90-150, q €110-190, 5-bed r €135-230, without bathroom s €35-60, d €60-100, tr €75-125; @☎) We wanna rock all night at the Backstage. This seriously fun music-themed hotel is a favourite among musicians jamming at nearby Melkweg and Paradiso, as evidenced by the lobby bar's band-signature-covered piano and pool table. Gig posters (many signed) line the corridors, and rooms are done up in mod-retro black and white, with iPod docking stations, and drum kit overhead lights. Late at night, bands (and their fans) hold court in the lively bar.

**TOP CHOICE COCOMAMA** BOUTIQUE HOSTEL **€€**

Map p302 (☎627 24 54; www.cocomama.nl; Westlnde 18; d/r from €36/100; @☎) Rather than hide its tawdry past (the building was once home to a high-end brothel), Amsterdam's first self-proclaimed 'boutique hostel' plays it up with wink-wink humour – from the high-ceilinged, brothel-themed bunk rooms (with red curtains and 1970s porn) to the brothel shrine in the lobby. Luckily the best things about this hostel are hardly X-rated: we love the gorgeous back garden with picnic table, well-equipped kitchen, book exchange and super comfy lounge for movie nights. Private rooms (check out the monarchy-themed room) come equipped with iPod docking stations and flatscreen TVs.

**SEVEN BRIDGES** BOUTIQUE HOTEL **€€€**

Map p302 (☎623 13 29; Reguliersgracht 31; d €110-250; @☎) Private, sophisticated and intimate, the Seven Bridges is one of the city's most exquisite little hotels on one of its loveliest canals. It has eight tastefully decorated rooms (all incorporating lush oriental rugs and elegant antiques). The urge to sightsee may fade once breakfast, served on fine china, is delivered to your room.

**INTERCONTINENTAL AMSTEL AMSTERDAM** HOTEL **€€€**

Map p302 (☎622 60 60; www.amsterdam.intercontinental.com; Professor Tulpplein 1; r from €400; ❄@☎≋) Everything about this five-star edifice is spectacular, from its imposing location overlooking the Amstel to its magnificent colonnaded lobby. Lavishly decorated rooms, reverential service and luxe extras – such as the Michelin-starred La Rive restaurant, heated indoor pool, and fitness centre with all sorts of steam options – delight even the fussiest trans-Atlantic celebrities and Euro royalty. Wi-fi costs €25 per 24 hours.

**HOTEL V** BOUTIQUE HOTEL **€€**

Map p302 (☎623 13 29; www.hotelv.nl; Weteringschans 136; d incl breakfast €80-160; @☎) Facing lush Fredericksplein and minutes away from Utrechtestraat's fab dining, the 48-room Hotel V offers style and location in spades for the price. Artsy rooms done up in charcoal colours feature stone wall bathrooms and to-die-for beds. Grab a cocktail from the bar and curl up in the mod lobby around the gas fireplace with a magazine.

**EDEN AMSTERDAM AMERICAN HOTEL** HOTEL **€€€**

Map p302 (☎556 30 00; www.amsterdamamerican.com; Leidsekade 97; d from €230; ❄@☎) You can't get closer to the action than this, right off Leidseplein and a quick walk to the Museum Quarter. Its ornate facade and tower are filled with a mixture of art deco and '90s contemporary furnishings. Guests have use of a gym with a sauna.

**BANKS MANSION** HOTEL **€€€**

Map p302 (☎420 00 55; www.banksmansion.nl; Herengracht 519-525; d €200-450; ❄@☎) You get far more than a fancy bed here: tipples are complimentary at the self-service wet bar in the Frank Lloyd Wright-designed lobby. When you finally retire to your contemporary room, you'll enjoy a plasma-screen TV, DVD player (with free in-house films), an enormous showerhead *and* complimentary gin, whisky and cognac. The first 50 minutes of wi-fi is free; after that you pay €4 for another 50 minutes or €14 for 24 hours.

**HOTEL FREELAND** HOTEL **€€**

Map p302 (☎622 75 11; www.hotelfreeland.com; Marnixstraat 386; s/d/tr from €70/120/150, s without bathroom from €60; @☎) Freeland has the Leidseplein scene twigged. Think tidy rooms with themes (tulips, roses and sunflowers, and a few with Moroccan details) at an excellent canalside location. Add in a tasty breakfast and it pretty much kills the competition.

**HOTEL ASTERISK** BOUTIQUE HOTEL €€

Map p302 (☎626 23 96; www.asteriskhotel.nl; Den Texstraat 16; s/d from €66/87; ) Sleep like a baby on the plush new mattresses at this family-owned hotel that's notable for its little touches of elegance including crown mouldings, crystal chandeliers and a gorgeous breakfast room.

**HOTEL ORLANDO** BOUTIQUE HOTEL €€

Map p302 (☎638 69 15; www.hotelorlando.nl; Prinsengracht 1099; s/d/tr from €95/115/180; ) Oh Orlando, how do we love thee? Let us count the ways. One: seven biggish, high-ceilinged, canalside rooms at smallish rates. Two: hospitable, gay-friendly hosts. Three: a hearty breakfast. Four: impeccably chic, boutique style with custom-made cabinetry and satin curtains. We could go on…

**HOTEL AMSTELZICHT** HOTEL €€

Map p302 (☎623 66 93; www.hotelamstelzicht.nl; Amstel 104; s/d from €69/109, apt €129-209; ) The view out front is straight from a 17th-century painting, so make sure you get one of the rooms facing the Amstel river and the gabled houses beyond. From the blue tiles in the lobby to the elegant decor, this hotel feels smooth and refined, and it's just a minute's walk from Rembrandtplein.

**HOTEL ADOLESCE** HOTEL €€

Map p302 (☎626 39 59; www.adolesce.nl; Nieuwe Keizersgracht 26; s/d/tr €65/100/120; ) In a lovely nook near Waterlooplein, this little family-owned hotel, based in an old canal house, will put a smile on your face. There are bright art prints in the simple rooms and you can help yourself all day to coffee, tea and snacks, including fruit.

**HOTEL KAP** HOTEL €€

Map p302 (☎624 59 08; www.kaphotel.nl; Den Texstraat 5b; d €83-110, tr €105-153, q €124-168, without bathroom s €51-70, tw €69-95; ) Yes, the rooms are plain. The draw? Affordable rates, a buffet breakfast served in an attractive dining room or courtyard garden, and courteous, gay-friendly owners. Wi-fi costs €5 per stay, and bikes are available for hire.

**HOTEL PRINSENHOF** HOTEL €

Map p302 (☎623 17 72; www.hotelprinsenhof.com; Prinsengracht 810; s/d/tr/q €84/89/119/149, without bathroom €49/69/99/119; ) This good value, 18th-century house features lovely canal views and a breakfast room with some Delft-blue tiles. Staff are affable and the rooms are spacious.

**CITY HOTEL** HOTEL €

Map p302 (☎627 23 23; www.city-hotel.nl; Utrechtsestraat 2; r per person from €30; ) Above the Old Bell pub, and practically on Rembrandtplein, is this unexpectedly fabulous hotel, run by a friendly family. The rooms (sleeping two to five) are decorated with crisp linens and each comes with a TV. The attic annexe has a wonderful view of town.

**HANS BRINKER BUDGET HOTEL** PARTY HOSTEL €

Map p302 (☎622 06 87; www.hans-brinker.com; Kerkstraat 136; dm €25-35, d from €40; ) The lobby is mayhem and spartan rooms have the ambience of a public hospital, but its beds are almost always filled to capacity with school groups and boisterous backpackers, who pack into the bright and happy bar, the pulsating disco and the inexpensive restaurant.

**AMISTAD HOTEL** BOUTIQUE HOTEL €€

Map p302 (☎624 80 74; www.amistad.nl; Kerkstraat 42; s from €100, d €130-150, s/d without bathroom from €75/94; ) Rooms at this bijou hotel are dotted with Philippe Starck chairs, CD players and computers. The breakfast room (with ruby-red walls and communal tables) becomes a hopping internet cafe later, popular with the gay set.

**GOLDEN BEAR** BOUTIQUE HOTEL €€

Map p302 (☎624 47 85; www.goldenbear.nl; Kerkstraat 37; dm from €36, d €102-120; ) The oldest gay hotel in Amsterdam has been operating since 1948. It straddles two 18th-century buildings, and the mod rooms are decorated in bright colours.

**HEMP HOTEL** STONER HOTEL €

Map p302 (☎625 44 25; www.hemp-hotel.com; Frederiksplein 15; d €75, s/d without bathroom €55/70; ) Proof positive that Amsterdam is the capital of the northern 'hempisphere,' this chilled-out hotel serves hemp-flour rolls with your breakfast and the tattooed, appropriately stoned bartenders serve hemp teas and beer as they bop to reggae in the cafe. Yes, they're a little worn, but the colourful, individually themed rooms (Tibetan, Afghani) are nicely decked out with hemp soap and fabrics, exuding a 'just back from Goa' vibe. Rates include breakfast.

## Jordaan & the West

**ALL INN THE FAMILY B&B** B&B €€

Map p294 (☎776 36 36; www.allinnthefamily.nl; Tweede Egelantiersdwarsstraat 10; r €95; @📶) This new B&B, in a charming old Amsterdam canal house, gets rave rviews for embodying the very qualities of the inimitable Jordaan itself. Spirited hosts who speak five languages, a bountiful organic Dutch breakfast, and a quiet location in the heart of the neighbourhood. It's an ideal base for those seeking the *gezellig*, open-minded friendliness that travellers come to Amsterdam for.

**HOTEL AMSTERDAM WIECHMANN** HOTEL €€

Map p296 (☎626 33 21; www.hotelwiechmann.nl; Prinsengracht 328; s/d/tr/2-bed ste from €85/125/195/200; @📶) This family-run hotel occupies three houses in a marvellous canalside location. The cosy, lovingly cared-for rooms are furnished like an antique shop, with country quilts and chintz, and the lobby *tchotchkes* (knick-knacks) have been here for some 60 years.

**CHRISTIAN YOUTH HOSTEL 'THE SHELTER JORDAAN'** HOSTEL €

Map p296 (☎624 47 17; www.shelter.nl; Bloemstraat 179; dm €19-34; @📶) OK, we'll put up with the 'no-everything' (drinkin', partyin', stumblin') policy at this small hostel because it's such a gem. Single-sex dorms are quiet and clean, breakfasts – especially the fluffy pancakes – are beaut and the garden patio is a relaxing retreat. The cafe serves cheap meals the rest of the day. Wi-fi costs €2.50 per hour.

**HOTEL VAN ONNA** HOTEL €€

Map p296 (☎626 58 01; www.hotelvanonna.nl; Bloemgracht 102-108; s/d/tr/q from €50/80/130/175; @) Some of these simple, reasonably priced rooms occupy a lovely circa-1644 canal house in a gorgeous section of the Jordaan. The bells of the Westerkerk are within earshot, which is either charming or not (get a room in the back if you're sensitive to noise). Try to book one of the two attic rooms with their old wooden roof beams and panoramic views over the Bloemgracht (Flower Canal).

**HOTEL ACACIA** HOTEL €€

Map p294 (☎622 14 60; www.hotelacacia.nl; Lindengracht 251; s/d/tr/q €70/90/110/130; @📶) If you simply want to park your bones after a day wandering the canals, the freshly renovated Acacia is just the ticket. It's in a sleepy corner of the Jordaan, and rooms in the angular corner building are larger than the norm. All have a bathroom and toilet attached. Ask about studios with kitchenettes. Rates include breakfast.

**INTERNATIONAL BUDGET HOSTEL** STONER HOSTEL €

Map p296 (☎624 27 84; www.internationalbudgethostel.com; Leidsegracht 76; dm €18-32, tw €65-80; @📶) Reasons to stay: canalside location in a former warehouse; really close to nightlife; four-person limit in rooms; cool mix of backpackers from around the world; clean rooms with lockers; printer access and bike rental; staff who are more pleasant than they need to be.

## Vondelpark & Around

**TOP CHOICE HOTEL DE FILOSOOF** BOUTIQUE HOTEL €€

Map p307 (☎683 30 13; www.hotelfilosoof.nl; Anna van den Vondelstraat 6; s/d/ste from €80/110/170; 📶) It's easy to clear your mind in rooms named after philosophers. Each room has its own theme representing something from its namesake, from Thoreau (with a mural of Walden Pond) to Nietsche (lots of red, representing his book *Morning Red*). We love the breakfast rooms, the elegant bar, and the tranquil English garden that's a pastoral pleasure come summer.

**TOP CHOICE HOTEL VONDEL** BOUTIQUE HOTEL €€€

Map p307 (☎612 01 20; www.vondelhotels.com; Vondelstraat 28-30; r €85-285; @📶) Named after the famed Dutch poet Joost Van den Vondel, who also lent his namesake to the nearby park, this chic hotel is owned by the same attentive people who run Hotel Roemer. Rooms have a dark and subdued calm with comfy decor (lots of plush grey), and guests can lounge next to goldfish and koi ponds in the Zen-like back gardens. Downstairs, Restaurant Joost offers a brief menu of fish, meat and vegie options in a dramatic dining room, or just come to sip on a caipirinha (Brazilian cocktail) at the pretty bar. Wi-fi is €10 per 24 hours.

### TOP CHOICE HOTEL ZANDBERGEN HOTEL €€€

Map p307 (☎676 93 21; www.hotel-zandbergen.com; Willemsparkweg 205; s/d/tr/q/ste from €93/125/165/195/235; @☜) The Zandbergen stands out like sterling silver in a tray of plastic cutlery. The caring staff in this wonderful hotel go overboard, and the rooms are absolutely faultless; those at the rear have balconies overlooking a quiet courtyard.

### HOTEL PIET HEIN BOUTIQUE HOTEL €€

Map p307 (☎662 72 05; www.hotelpiethein.nl; Vossiusstraat 52-53; s/d €92/135; @☜) Overlooking the Vondelpark's fine old arbour, this immaculate hotel offers a startling variety of contemporary rooms (including snug, single 'business' rooms) in a quiet location, a sublime garden and a relaxing bar. Wi-fi costs €12 per 24 hours.

### OWL HOTEL HOTEL €€

Map p307 (☎618 94 84; www.owl-hotel.nl; Roemer Visscherstraat 1; s/d from €80/105; @☜) Some guests love this place so much that they send in owl figurines from all over the world. Staff are warm and welcoming, and rooms are dapper, bright and quiet. Best of all, buffet breakfast is served in a serene, light-filled room overlooking a gorgeous garden. Wi-fi costs €10 per 24 hours.

### FUSION SUITES LUXURY HOTEL €€€

Map p302 (☎618 46 42; www.fusionsuites.com; Roemer Visscherstraat 40; ste €245-275; ❄@☜) Nestled in a quiet, tree-lined street right by Museumplein, these spacious suites go right off the comfort charts. Four-poster beds with Cocomat mattresses, flat-screen computers and TVs, free-standing baths and tasteful decor in Eastern earth tones are just a few reasons you may choose never to go out. We dig the fresh flowers, international newspapers and unlimited drinks.

### CONSCIOUS HOTEL VONDELPARK BOUTIQUE HOTEL €€

off Map p307 (☎820 33 33; www.conscioushotels.com; Overtoom 519; r €100-145; ☜) A hotel with style *and* a conscience? Bring it on. The first officially eco-certified hotel in Europe, the eco-friendly features here are both practical and whimsical: from a growing wall in the stylish lobby and the live plants in the rooms; the recycled materials made into artful furnishings; and the organic breakfast buffet. Guests can swim or work out next door at David Lloyds, Holland's largest gym, for €20 per day.

### FLYNT B&B B&B €€

Map p307 (☎618 46 14; www.flyntbedandbreakfast.nl; 1e Helmersstraat 34; r €70-120; @☜) The spacious slate bathrooms feel more mod boutique hotel than Vondelpark neighbourhood B&B, but the cheerful colours, friendly owner, cosy breakfast nook and pet-friendly policy say otherwise. Single travellers will bliss out in the Buddha room.

### STAYOKAY AMSTERDAM VONDELPARK HOSTEL €

Map p307 (☎589 89 96; www.stayokay.com; Zandpad 5; dm €27-35, tw €50-130; @☜) A blink away from the Vondelpark, this 536-bed hostel attracts over 75,000 guests a year – no wonder the lobby feels like a mini-UN (with a pool table and pinball). The renovated rooms sport lockers, a shower, a toilet and well-spaced bunks. Chill out in the congenial bar/cafe.

### HOTEL ROEMER BOUTIQUE HOTEL €€€

Map p307 (☎589 08 00; www.vondelhotels.com; Roemer Visscherstraat 8-10; d €155-255, ste €295-345; @☜) This cosy, high-design hotel is an oasis of calm. All high-ceilinged, sunny rooms overlook either a quiet, leafy street or the stately back garden. Other extras: flat-screen TVs, an iPod dock, DVD player and Jacuzzis. Wi-fi is €10 per 24 hours.

### PARK HOTEL HOTEL €€€

Map p307 (☎671 12 22; www.parkhotel.nl; Stadhouderskade 25; s/d/ste from €80/110/170) Rooms here are artistically mod, with adjustable mood lighting, incense, and stunning George Heidweiller cityscapes on the walls. Downstairs, curl up with a book and a cappuccino in the 'Living Room' with its changing gallery of modern art. It has a well-equipped fitness room and is within spitting distance from Vondelpark, so there's little excuse to not work out. An Asian-inspired breakfast (€18) is offered in the mornings, while wi-fi is €20.

## Old South

### TOP CHOICE COLLECTOR B&B €€

Map p306 (☎673 67 79; www.the-collector.nl; De Lairessestraat 46hs; r €80-115; @☜) This B&B is a real find. The 1914 building is spotless, with contemporary renovations, and it's furnished with museum-style displays of clocks, wooden shoes, ice skates and shot glasses – things the owner, Karel, *collects*. Each of the three rooms has balcony access and a TV. Karel stocks the kitchen for guests to prepare breakfast at their leisure (the eggs come from his hens in the garden), and the kitchen is open all day if you want to cook your own dinner. He also has a couple of bikes he lends out to guests.

**HOTEL FITA** HOTEL **€€**

Map p306 (679 09 76; www.hotelfita.com; Jan Luijkenstraat 37; r incl breakfast €105-165; ) This tiny, family-owned hotel, on a quiet street off Museumplein and PC Hooftstraat, is one of the best in the Old South. It has 15 handsome rooms with nicely appointed bathrooms; a bountiful breakfast of eggs, pancakes, cheeses and breads; and an elevator. Room rates include free telephone calls to Europe and the USA. Note that Fita tends to book up with older Americans, ever since a popular US guidebook recommended it. A dynamic, new young owner took over recently, and it looks like things might get even better.

**HOTEL AALDERS** HOTEL **€€**

Map p306 (662 01 16; www.hotelaalders.nl; Jan Luijkenstraat 13-15; s/d from €99/136; ) There are fancier hotels in town, but the 28-room, family-owned Aalders is homey and well situated on a quiet street near Museumplein. Each room in its two row homes is different (the old-style room has wood panelling and leaded windows). The breakfast room has a Venetian-glass chandelier, and it bakes its own pastries and rolls for guests each morning (breakfast is included in the rates). It also rent bikes.

**CONSCIOUS HOTELS MUSEUM SQUARE** BOUTIQUE HOTEL **€€**

Map p306 (671 95 96; www.conscioushotels.com; De Lairessestraat 7; r €115-179; ) Conscious hotels are dedicated green hotels. It starts with the living plant wall in the lobby and the organic breakfast (€10 extra). And then come modern rooms – beds made with 100% natural materials, desks constructed from recycled yoghurt containers, carpets woven with 80% Mongolian goat hair, and energy-saving plasma TVs framed by soothing forest murals. A second location is at Overtoom 519 near Vondelpark.

**XAVIERA HOLLANDER BED & BREAKFAST** B&B **€€**

(673 39 34; www.xavierahollander.com; Stadionweg 17; d from €100; ) A living legend of flickering celluloid, and glad to provide all the details, the *Happy Hooker* author has settled down to run this fabulous B&B – that is, when she's not writing columns, producing theatre shows or poring over her next set of memoirs. The interior contains plenty of racy allusions to her past life, in leather, shag and stain-proof formica, but chambers are uniformly luxurious, particularly the princely garden hut. Xaviera is still something of a media star, and if you're lucky enough to meet her during your stay you'll quickly understand her charisma. The B&B is a good 1km south of the Museumpleinen, a stone's throw from Beatrixpark and the RAI convention centre. Two-night minimum stay.

**VAN GOGH HOSTEL & HOTEL** HOSTEL & HOTEL **€**

Map p306 (262 92 00; info@hotelvangogh.nl; Van de Veldestraat 5; dm €20-25, r from €80; ) No false advertising here: it sits about 14 steps from the Van Gogh Museum, and every room has a Van Gogh mural. The set-up at the brand spankin' new property puts the 100-bed hostel on one side, the hotel on the other, and the common area for breakfast (€5) divides them. The hostel dorms have six to 10 beds, en suite bath and flat-screen TV. The hotel rooms have balconies on the higher floors (ask for one when booking).

**COLLEGE HOTEL** BOUTIQUE HOTEL **€€€**

Map p306 (571 15 11; www.thecollegehotel.com; Roelof Hartstraat 1; r from €200; ) A breath of fresh air, this venerable property was originally a 19th-century school. It's now a trendy hotel with stylish accents: flat-screen TVs, silk throw pillows, cordless phones, the occasional stained-glass window and exposed beams on the top floor. Here's the difference, though: it's staffed by hotel-school students. Continental breakfast costs a steep €19.50, but if the dining hall was this cool where we went to college, we'd have figured out a way not to graduate. Wi-fi costs €17 per 24 hours.

**HOTEL ACRO** HOTEL **€€**

Map p306 (662 05 26; www.acrohotel.nl; Jan Luijkenstraat 44; s/d incl breakfast from €102/120; ) The big bed pretty much takes up the whole space in Acro's rooms, and the white-and-black colour scheme is a bit stark, but the plus side is low prices for a leafy location a couple blocks from the museums. Everything has been recently renovated at this 2-star property. The welcoming bar is filled with photos of old Amsterdam, and staff are warm and helpful.

**HOTEL BEMA** HOTEL €€

Map p306 (☎679 13 96; www.bemahotel.com; Concertgebouwplein 19b; s from €45, d with/without bathroom €90/70; @📶) Climb the stairs to this six-room hotel in an old movie theatre: the old velvet seats sit in the halls, and the place is filled with African art. Expect tidy doubles and breakfast in bed but no phone in the room. Staff can also arrange private apartments for up to four people. Rates include breakfast. It's across from the Concertgebouw.

## De Pijp

**TOP CHOICE BICYCLE HOTEL AMSTERDAM** BICYCLE HOTEL €

Map p308 (☎679 34 52; www.bicyclehotel.com; Van Ostadestraat 123; s €35-65, d €70-115, d without bathroom €40-80; @📶) If you're into the bed-and-bike thing, this is the place to go. Run by Marjolein and Clemens, who love pedal power, this casual, friendly, green-minded hotel has rooms that are comfy and familiar. It also rents bikes, and serves a killer organic breakfast (included in the rate).

**HOTEL AALBORG** HOTEL €€

Map p308 (☎676 03 10; www.aalborg.nl; Sarphatipark 106; s €60-99, d €65-110, tr €80-165, q €120-195; @📶) One of the more innovative hotels around, the Aalborg is slowly commissioning artists to redo each room in a unique style. All of the rooms at Aalborg are tidy and newly installed, and the front rooms enjoy a fine view over the lush Sarphatipark. Guests can also enjoy a luxuriant Asian-style back garden, and monthly artist receptions.

**BETWEEN ART & KITSCH B&B** B&B €€

Map p308 (☎679 04 85; www.between-art-and-kitsch.com; Ruysdaelkade 75-2; s/d from €70/100, tr €130; @📶) Mondrian once lived here – that's part of the art – and the kitsch are bits like the crystal chandelier in the baroque room and the smiling brass Buddha nearby. The art deco room, meanwhile, has seriously gorgeous tile work and views of the Rijksmuseum. The husband and wife hosts, Ebo and Irene (and Hartje, their fluffy white cat), couldn't be friendlier.

**CAKE UNDER MY PILLOW** B&B €€

Map p308 (☎751 09 36; http://cakeundermypillow.com; 1e Jacob van Campenstraat 66; d from €170, without bathroom from €140; @📶) Run by the owners of Taart van m'n Tante),

### AIRPORT ACCOMMODATION

If you need a bed by the airport, try these reasonably priced boutique hotels:

➡ **Citizen M** (☎811 70 80; www.citizenmamsterdamairport.com; Plezierweg 2; r €79-139; ❄@📶) A five-minute walk from the terminals, Citizen M's rooms are like the starship *Enterprise*. Check-in and -out is self-service ('ambassadors' are on hand to help) in the Vitra-designed lobby. Rooms are snug but maximise space to the utmost, with plush, wall-to-wall beds, and shower and toilet pods. Each room includes a Philips MoodPad – command central for the lighting (purple, red or white?), blinds, flat-screen TV (free on-demand movies), music, temperature and rain shower. Sushi, sake and self-service snacks and breakfast are on offer in the lobby's canteen. There's a second Citizen M at Prinses Irenestraat 30, not far from the Amsterdam RAI convention centre, with an identical look and feel.

➡ **Yotel** (☎in UK 020-7100 1100; www.yotel.com; Schiphol Airport Plaza; r from €40 per 4hr; @📶) Yotel's Japanese-style capsule hotel at Schiphol is a sleepsaver with style. Prices for the standard 7-sq-metre glam cabins are time-based (four-hour minimum) for short layovers. The standards and twins have bunks and fold-up desks, while the premiums contain regular beds; all are stylish, with crisp white bedspreads and light wood. It's a blessing for travellers who need to catch a red-eye flight.

which is known for its outrageous cakes, this B&B above the cafe is less kitsch and just plain comfy and stylish. A two-night stay is required.

## Plantage, Eastern Islands & Eastern Docklands

**TOP CHOICE** **LLOYD HOTEL** BOUTIQUE HOTEL €€€

Map p310 (☎561 36 36; www.lloydhotel.com; Oostelijke Handelskade 34; r €90-400; @📶) This ultrastylish building used to be a hotel for migrants back in 1921, and many of the original fixtures still exist, combined with triumphs of more contemporary Dutch design. The result is a combination hotel, cultural centre and local gathering place. One-star (bathroom down the hall) to five-star (plush and racquetball-court-sized) rooms are so one-of-a-kind (industrial singles, bathtub in the centre, fold-away bathrooms, a giant bed for eight…) that they'll even impress travellers who think they've seen it all.

**HOTEL ALLURE** HOTEL €€

Map p310 (☎627 27 14; www.hotelallure.com; Sarphatistraat 177-199; r €109-139; @📶) Scarlet drapes, carpets, and a mod scarlet dining room add a dramatic flair to this gleaming new hotel. It's in walking distance of the Hermitage Amsterdam and the Artis Royal Zoo.

**HOTEL REMBRANDT** HOTEL €€

Map p310 (☎627 27 14; www.hotelrembrandt.nl; Plantage Middenlaan 17; s €75, d €95-115, tr/q €140/165; @📶) With its spotless modern rooms, the Rembrandt shines. Most rooms contain pop-art prints of Mr Rembrandt himself, but room 8 is graced with a nearly life-sized mural of *Night Watch*. Breakfast (€7.50) is served in a wood-panelled room with chandeliers and 17th-century paintings on linen-covered walls.

**CAPTAIN'S PLACE** HOUSEBOAT €€

Map p310 (☎419 81 19; www.captainsplace.nl; Levantkade 184; d per person €49.50-69.50; 📶) This charming number is set on a rebuilt ship, the *Pas Meprese,* in the former ore harbour of the Eastern Docklands. There are two rooms, both large and comfortably fitted out, with their own heated bathrooms. As the owner is a bit star-struck, the quarters are dubbed Orion and Cassiopeia. The best part is the on-board garden for grazing (it serves a nice breakfast) and plain lazing, even when the weather is foul as it has a sliding glass roof.

**HOTEL PARKLANE** HOTEL €€

Map p310 (☎622 48 04; www.hotel-parklane.nl; Plantage Parklaan 16; s €78-99, d €115-170, tr from €150, q from €170; @📶) This 12-room, one-time dressmaker's shop features high-ceilinged, comfy rooms equipped with fridges. Two rooms have Jacuzzis, too.

**HOTEL HORTUS** HOTEL €

Map p310 (☎625 99 96; www.hotelhortus.com; Plantage Parklaan 8; s €25-30, d €30-40; @) Facing the botanical garden, this old-shoe, 20-room hotel could use a little facelift, but still, it's terrific value for this area and contains a large common area with a pool table and several TVs. There are only two doubles, with or without shower (luck of the draw); all have a safe and a sink. Large rooms sleep up to 10 people (€30 per person per night).

**MINT HOTEL** HOTEL €€€

Map p310 (☎530 08 00; www.minthotel.com; 4 Oosterdoksstraat; r €127-264; ❄@📶) This sparkling new hotel has already been host to some of Amsterdam's hottest parties and after-hours events, and cultural types seem to gather at all hours of the day to enjoy its contemporary design and riverfront views. After blissing out as the sun goes down on the deck of the breathtaking Skylounge, go back to your hyper-mod digs and play around with your sunset photos on the in-room iMac.

## Oosterpark & South Amsterdam

**HOTEL ARENA** PARTY HOTEL €€

Map p309 (☎850 24 00; www.hotelarena.nl; 's Gravesandestraat 51; d/ste from €109/209; @📶) With more facelifts than a Hollywood star, this building, bordering lush Oosterpark, has morphed from chapel to orphanage to backpackers hostel to, now, a modern, four-star, 116-room hotel with a trendy restaurant, cafe and nightclub. A recent makeover means minimalist rooms have a 'designer industrial' feel, and most of the chic, black-tiled bathrooms were designed by Philippe Starck. Breakfast costs €18.50 and wi-fi is an extra €10 per 24 hours.

# Understand Amsterdam

# Amsterdam Today

**As the architecture on the banks of the IJ river comes into focus as the city's future frontier, this area seems perfectly positioned to embody a metaphor for 21st-century Amsterdam: an ever-shifting blend of Renaissance values emboldened by a visionary hypermodernity. Is the city where the ghosts of Rembrandt and Anne Frank not only endure, but also are enlivened by a multicultural community, still one of the freest communities on earth? Its citizens seem committed to making sure that the answer is yes.**

### Best on Film

**Oorlogswinter** (Winter in Wartime; directed by Martin Koolhoven; 2008) Voted by Dutch critics as the top film of 2008. The film centres on a young boy whose integrity and loyalty is tested when he decides to help the Dutch Resistance who are sheltering a downed British pilot.

**Zwartboek** (Black Book; directed by Paul Verhoeven; 2006) This action-packed story explores some of the less heroic aspects of the Dutch Resistance in WWII. It launched the international career of today's hottest Dutch actor, Carice van Houten.

### Best in Print

**The Diary of Anne Frank** (Anne Frank; 1952) A moving account of a young girl's thoughts and yearnings while in hiding from the Nazis in Amsterdam. The book has been translated into 60 languages.

**Netherland** (Joseph O'Neill; 2008) When a Dutch man faces the breakdown of his marriage in post-September 11 New York City, the game of cricket, memories of the Netherlands and a mysterious friendship complicate his life yet inexplicably repair his spirit in this comically dark novel.

## Culture

Laid-back. Tolerant. Fun-loving. Bilingual (sometimes trilingual). Industrious. Aware. International. Amsterdam's locals embody these qualities in spades for their famously tolerant attitudes towards diversity and differences. Perhaps this is why Amsterdam is celebrated for being a consummately easy and relaxed place to travel.

You'll find that local life goes on in public in Amsterdam: this is not a city that conducts its business behind closed doors. In fact, walk down any street and notice the abundance of open windows – even in the toniest neighbourhoods – where families and couples openly cook, eat, watch TV and play with their children in full view.

Despite recent strain between the Dutch far-right government and Amsterdam's far-left-leaning politics, the city's lasting legacy of tolerance transcends politics and has become part of its character. Eccentric conduct in public might pass without comment, hence the Dutch saying: 'Act normal, that's crazy enough'.

The Dutch also have a moralistic streak (coming from the Calvinists) and a tendency to wag the finger in disapproval. They may seem stunningly blunt, but the impulse comes from the desire to be direct and honest.

## Sex & Drugs Redux

It's like a throwback to the 1960s and '70s, but this time, the radical movement is on the right, not the left.

Most of the ever-practical Dutch argue that vice is not going to disappear, so you might as well control it. Yet a growing faction of voters in the Netherlands, along with the elected officials they support, have come out vocally against several of the civil liberties that Amsterdammers cherish – regardless of whether or not they partake in them. So far, the liberties under fire have been the most obvious forms of vice: the freedom to purchase and consume soft drugs without criminal penalties for possession, and legalised prostitution. Supporters of the more restrictive laws on the drug and sex trade argue that such 'vice' industries encourage everything from organised crime to illegal immigration to drug and sex tourism – and all of these arguments are somewhat true.

With the Dutch making up about 5% of Red Light District customers, and only a slightly larger portion of the coffeeshop denizens, most Amsterdammers (liberal or not) are inclined to leave well enough alone. Yet with the most vocal opposition party – the Party for Freedom (PVV), headed by Geert Wilders – becoming more prominent, even Amsterdam's citizens and its municipal leaders have felt the tension of a politically divided country that threatens to change its famously progressive environment.

Sexual freedom is still strong, however, when it comes to same-sex relationships: gays and lesbians enjoy considerable freedom in Amsterdam. In 2001 the Netherlands became the first country in the world to legalise same-sex marriages; 2011 marked the 10-year anniversary.

## The City Expands

It's best known for its romantic canals (of which the 17th-century Canal Ring, the crowning glory of the city's Golden Age, was recently honoured with a place on Unesco's World Heritage list) and its contemporary architecture has exploded in the past two decades to become some of the most visionary in the world. Yet for many people the dream of a cosy home with a canal view remains just that: a dream. Because Amsterdam is so densely populated (4509 people per sq km), housing is in notoriously short supply.

No wonder Amsterdam's urban planners are constantly looking for extra space. Millions of euros are being invested to renovate housing in older districts such as Amsterdam-Oost, but this alone won't be enough: by 2030 the city's population is expected to swell by 100,000.

Help is on the way. The shores along the IJ river have rapidly become the city's new dormitories. More than 10,000 homes have emerged in the Eastern Docklands, a former industrial area. Northwest of Centraal Station lies the Westerdokseiland, an imposing clutch of flats, offices and cafes embracing a pleasure harbour; to the northeast is Oosterdokseiland, a mixed-use business and residential area, and Overhoeks, a housing estate on the old Shell Oil compound that is now the proud home of the sparkling new EYE Film Institute Netherlands. And it's not just architecture and urban planning that's cutting edge, of course; from mandating bike storage rooms at work to subsidising green roofs and walls, the city remains a visionary world leader in environmental creativity.

## if Amsterdam were 100 people

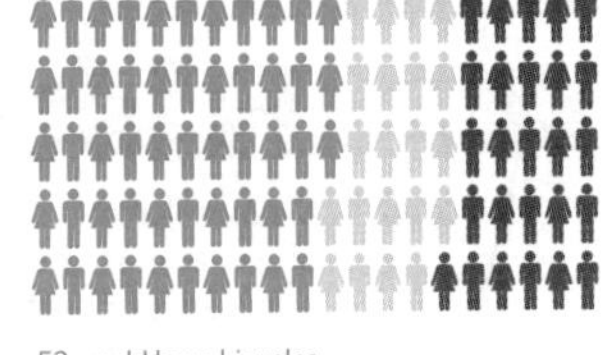

53 would have bicycles
21 would have cars
26 would have neither

## ethnicity

(% of population)

## population per sq km

 ≈ 406 people

# History

**Close your eyes and imagine water everywhere. It may be difficult to picture that the region that spawned a giant trading community was once an inhospitable patchwork of lakes, swamps and peat, at or below sea level; its contours shifted with the autumn storms and floods. The oldest archaeological finds in this area (in what is now Amsterdam) date from Roman times, when the IJ river lay along the northern border of the Roman Empire.**

## FROM THE BEGINNING

Too busy elsewhere, and no doubt put off by the mushy conditions, the mighty Romans – who had conquered the lands now known as the Netherlands in the 1st century – left behind no colosseums or magnificent tombs. In uncharacteristic style, they left practically no evidence, much less any grand gestures, of settlement. While the swampy, sea-level topography made the construction of grand edifices challenging, the Romans had been known to bypass such challenges before in other regions. In the end, they simply had other more important lands south of the Low Countries to inhabit and rule.

*It was commercial trade that would put Holland on the map*

Around 1200, a fishing community known as Aemstelredamme ('the dam built across the Amstel') emerged at what is now the Dam, and the name Amsterdam was coined.

## EARLY TRADE

Farming was tricky on the marshland, and with the sea on the doorstep, early residents turned to fishing. But it was commercial trade that would put Holland on the map. While powerful city-states focused on overland trade with Flanders and northern Italy, Amsterdam shrewdly levelled its sights on the maritime routes. The big prizes? The North and Baltic Seas, which were in the backyard of the powerful Hanseatic League, a group of German trading cities.

**TIMELINE**

**1150–1300**

Dams are built to retain the IJ river between the Zuiderzee and Haarlem. A tiny community of herring fishermen settles on the banks of the Amstel river.

**1275**

Amsterdam is founded after the Count of Holland grants toll-free status to residents along the Amstel. The city gains its first direct access to the ocean via the Zuiderzee, now the IJsselmeer.

**1380**

Canals of the present-day Medieval Centre are dug. Amsterdam flourishes, winning control over the sea trade in Scandinavia and later gaining free access to the Baltic.

Ignoring the league's intimidating reputation, Amsterdam's clever *vrijbuiters* (buccaneers) sailed right into the Baltic, their holds full of cloth and salt to exchange for grain and timber. It was nothing short of a coup. By the late 1400s nearly two-thirds of ships sailing to and from the Baltic Sea were from Holland, mostly based in Amsterdam.

By this time sailors, merchants, artisans and opportunists from the Low Countries (roughly present-day Netherlands, Belgium and Luxembourg) made their living here.

At the time, Amsterdam was unfettered by the key structures of other European societies. With no tradition of Church-sanctioned feudal relationships, no distinction between nobility and serfs, and hardly any taxation, a society of individualism and capitalism slowly took root. The modern idea of Amsterdam – free, open, progressive, and flush with opportunity – was born.



## INDEPENDENT REPUBLIC

The Protestant Reformation wasn't just a matter of religion; it was also a classic power struggle between the 'new money' (an emerging class of merchants and artisans) and the 'old money' (the land-owning, aristocratic order sanctioned by the established Catholic Church).

The Protestantism that took hold in the Low Countries was its most radically moralistic stream, known as Calvinism. It stressed the might of God and treated humans as sinful creatures whose duty in life was sobriety and hard work. The ascetic Calvinists stood for local decision-making and had a disdain for the top-down hierarchy of the Catholic Church.

*The modern idea of Amsterdam – free, open, progressive – was born*

Calvinism was a key to the struggle for independence by King Philip II of Spain. The hugely unpopular Philip, a fanatically devout Catholic, had acquired the Low Countries in something of a horse trade with Austria. His efforts to introduce the Spanish Inquisition, centralise government and levy taxes enraged his subjects and, even worse, awoke a sense of national pride.

With mighty Amsterdam on their side, in 1579 the seven northern provinces declared themselves to be an independent republic, led by William of Orange: the seed that grew into today's royal family. William was famously dubbed 'the Silent' because he wisely refused to enter into religious debate. To this day, he remains the uncontested founder – and father – of Holland.

**1519**

Spain's Charles V is crowned Holy Roman Emperor. Treaties and dynastic marriages make Amsterdam part of the Spanish empire, with Catholicism the main faith.

**1535**

A group of naked Anabaptists (motto: 'Truth is Naked') occupies Amsterdam's city hall, but is defeated by the city watch in fierce battle and brutally executed.

**1543**

Charles V unites the Low Countries (roughly the area of what is now the Netherlands, Belgium, and Luxembourg) and establishes Brussels as the region's capital.

**1578**

Amsterdam is captured in a bloodless coup. A Dutch Republic made up of seven provinces is declared a year later, led by William the Silent.

## GOLDEN AGE (1580–1700)

Amsterdam grew rapidly. By 1600 Dutch ships controlled the sea trade between England, France, Spain and the Baltic, and had a virtual monopoly on North Sea fishing and Arctic whaling. Jewish refugees taught Dutch mariners about trade routes, giving rise to the legendary Dutch East India and Dutch West India Companies. Tiny Holland burned brightly; for a while it ran rings around the fleets of great powers, which were too slow or cumbersome to react. In the absence of an overriding religion, ethnic background or political entity, money reigned supreme.

By 1620 Dutch traders had gone global, exploring the far corners of the earth. By the mid-17th century Dutch had more seagoing merchant vessels than England and France combined. Half of all ships sailing between Europe and Asia belonged to the Hollanders, and exotic products – coffee, tea, spices, tobacco, cotton, silk and porcelain – became commodities. Amsterdam became home to Europe's largest shipbuilding industry, and the city was veritably buzzing with prosperity and innovation.

In 1651, England passed the first of several Navigation Acts that posed a serious threat to Dutch trade, leading to several thorny, inconclusive wars on the seas. Holland's competitors sussed out its trade secrets, regrouped and reconquered the sea routes. In one nasty and historically memorable encounter, the Dutch lost the colony of New Amsterdam (New York City) to the British. Louis XIV of France seized the opportunity to invade the Low Countries two decades later, and the period of prosperity known as Golden Age ended. While the city hardly went into decay or ruin, the embattled economy would take more than a century to regain its full strength. In fact, some might say that it was not until the 1960s and '70s that Amsterdam fully blossomed again, as cultural revolution swept Europe and transformed Dutch society.

**DUTCH POLITICS**

Say the name Geert Wilders and you're bound to get a reaction, whether positive or negative. This parliamentary leader has been a divisive, controversial politician in the Netherlands, comparing the Koran to *Mein Kampf*, calling for immigrants to be deported, and demanding churches preach in Dutch. He's called the 'most famous bleached blond since Marilyn Monroe'.

## WEALTHY DECLINE (1700–1814)

If you can't beat them, pacify them: while the Dutch Republic didn't have the resources to fight France and England head-on, it had Amsterdam's money to buy them off and ensure freedom of the seas.

As the costs mounted, Amsterdam went from being a place where everything (profitable) was possible, to a lethargic community where wealth creation was a matter of interest rates. Gone were the daring sea voyages, the achievements in art, science and technology, and the innovations of government and finance. Ports such as London and Hamburg became powerful rivals.

**1600s**

The Golden Age places Amsterdam firmly on the culture map. While Rembrandt paints in his atelier, the grand inner ring of canals is constructed. The city's population surges to 200,000.

WILL SALTER / LONELY PLANET IMAGES ©

Cycling across one of Amsterdam's many canals

**1602**

Amsterdam becomes the site of the world's first stock exchange when the offices of the Dutch East India Company trade their own shares.

## THE CURIOUS HISTORY OF TULIPMANIA (1636–37)

When it comes to investment frenzy, the Dutch tulip craze of 1636 to 1637 ranks alongside the South Sea Bubble of 1720, the Great Crash of 1929, Enron and the Netherlands' home-grown Ahold scandal.

Tulips originated as wildflowers in Central Asia and were first cultivated by the Turks, who filled their courts with these beautiful spring blooms ('tulip' derives from the Turkish word for turban). In the mid-1500s the Habsburg ambassador to Istanbul brought some bulbs back to Vienna, where the imperial botanist, Carolus Clusius, learned how to propagate them. In 1590 Clusius became director of the Hortus Botanicus in Leiden – Europe's oldest botanical garden – and had great success growing and cross-breeding tulips in Holland's cool, damp climate and fertile delta soil.

The more exotic specimens of tulip featured frilly petals and 'flamed' streaks of colour, which attracted the attention of wealthy merchants, who put them in their living rooms and hallways to impress visitors. Trickle-down wealth and savings stoked the taste for exotica in general, and tulip growers arose to service the demand.

A speculative frenzy ensued, and people paid top florin for the finest bulbs, many of which changed hands time and again before they sprouted. Vast profits were made and speculators fell over themselves to outbid each other. Bidding often took place in taverns and was fuelled by alcohol, which no doubt added to the enthusiasm.

Of course, this bonanza couldn't last, and when several bulb traders in Haarlem failed to fetch their expected prices in February 1637, the bottom fell out of the market. Within weeks many of the country's wealthiest merchants went bankrupt and many more people of humbler origins lost everything.

However, love of the unusual tulip endured, and cooler-headed growers perfected their craft. To this day, the Dutch continue to be the world leaders in tulip cultivation and supply most of the bulbs planted in Europe and North America. They also excel in other bulbs such as daffodils, hyacinths and crocuses.

So what happened to the flamed, frilly tulips of the past? They're still produced but have gone out of fashion, and are now known as Rembrandt tulips because of their depiction in so many 17th-century paintings.

The decline in trade brought poverty, and exceptionally cold winters hampered transport and led to serious food shortages. The winters of 1740 and 1763 were so severe that some residents froze to death.

Amsterdam's support of the American War of Independence (1776) resulted in a British blockade of the Dutch coast, followed by British conquests of Dutch trading posts around the world, forcing the closure of the Dutch West India and Dutch East India Companies.

Enter the French: in 1794 French revolutionary troops invaded the Low Countries. In a convenient act of nepotism, the Dutch Republic

**1618**

The world's first regular newspaper, the *Courante uyt Italien, Duytslandt, &c.*, is printed in Amsterdam. Catholicism is outlawed, though clandestine worship is permitted.

**1688**

William III of Orange repels the French with the help of Austria, Spain and Brandenburg. William then invades England, where he and his wife are proclaimed king and queen.

**1650s**

Oops! Big mistake. The Dutch infamously lose the colony of New York to the British, killing all future likelihood that Broadway musicals will be sung in Dutch.

**1795**

French troops occupy the Netherlands and install the Batavian Republic. The fragmented United Provinces become a centralised state, with Amsterdam as its capital.

became a monarchy in 1806, when Napoleon nominated his brother Louis Napoleon as king.

After Napoleon's defeat in 1813, Amsterdam's trade with the world recovered only slowly; domination of the seas now belonged to the British.



## NEW INFRASTRUCTURE (1814–1918)

Amsterdam in the first half of the 19th century was a gloomy, uninspiring place. Its harbour had been neglected, and the sandbanks in the IJ proved too great a barrier for modern ships. Rotterdam was set to become the country's premier port.

Things began to look up as the country's first railway, between Amsterdam and Haarlem, opened in 1839. Trade with the East Indies was the backbone of Amsterdam's economy, and a canal, later extended to the Rhine, helped the city to benefit from the Industrial Revolution under way in Europe.

*Dockworkers led a protest strike over the treatment of Jews*

Amsterdam again attracted immigrants, and its population doubled in the second half of the 19th century. Speculators hastily erected new housing beyond the Canal Ring – dreary, shoddily built tenement blocks.

The Netherlands remained neutral in WWI, but Amsterdam's trade with the East Indies suffered from naval blockades. Food shortages brought riots, and an attempt to bring the socialist revolution to the Netherlands was put down by loyalist troops.

## BOOM & DEPRESSION (1918–1940)

After WWI, Amsterdam remained the country's industrial centre. The Dutch Shipbuilding Company operated the world's second-largest wharf and helped carry a large steel and diesel-motor industry. The harbour handled tropical produce that was processed locally, such as tobacco and cocoa (today, Amsterdam is still the world's biggest centre for cocoa distribution).

The 1920s were boom years. KLM (Koninklijke Luchtvaart Maatschappij; Royal Aviation Company) began the world's first regular air service in 1920 between Amsterdam and London from an airstrip south of the city, and bought many of its planes from Anthony Fokker's factory north of the IJ. There were two huge breweries, a sizeable clothing industry and even a local car factory. The city hosted the Olympic Games in 1928.

**1813–14**

The French are overthrown and William VI of Orange is crowned as Dutch King William I.

**1830**

With French help, the southern provinces secede to form the Kingdom of Belgium. The country is not formally recognised by the Dutch government until 1839.

**1865–76**

In a period of rapid economic and social change, the North Sea Canal is dug, the Dutch railway system is expanded and socialist principles of government are established.

**1889**

Centraal Station makes its grand debut, and poof – in an instant – Amsterdam is connected by rail to the rest of Europe.

The world Depression in the 1930s hit Amsterdam hard. Make-work projects did little to defuse the mounting tensions between socialists, communists and a small but vocal party of Dutch fascists. The city took in 25,000 Jewish refugees fleeing Germany; a shamefully large number were turned back at the border because of the country's neutrality policy.



## WWII (1940–45)

The Netherlands tried to remain neutral in WWII, but Germany invaded in May 1940. For the first time in almost 400 years, Amsterdammers experienced war firsthand.

Few wanted to believe that things would turn really nasty (the Germans, after all, had trumpeted that the Dutch were of the 'Aryan brotherhood'). But in February 1941, dockworkers led a protest strike over the treatment of Jews, commemorated as the 'February Strike'. By then, however, it was already too late. Only one in every 16 of Amsterdam's 90,000 Jews survived the war (one in seven in the Netherlands), the lowest proportion of anywhere in Western Europe. The Dutch handed over a bigger percentage of the Jewish population than any place else in Europe.

The Dutch Resistance, set up by an unlikely alliance of Calvinists and communists, only became large-scale when the increasingly desperate Germans began to round up able-bodied men to work in Germany.

Towards the end of the war, the situation in Amsterdam was dire. Coal shipments ceased; many men aged between 17 and 50 had gone into hiding or to work in Germany; public utilities were halted; and the Germans began to plunder anything that could assist their war effort. Thousands of lives were lost to severe cold and famine. Canadian troops finally liberated the city in May 1945 in the final days of the war in Europe.

Contrary to what many people assume, the German occupation was actually based in Den Haag.

GERMAN OCCUPATION

## POSTWAR GROWTH (1945–62)

The city's growth resumed after the war, with US aid through the Marshall Plan.

Massive apartment blocks arose in areas annexed west of the city to meet the continued demand for housing, made more acute by the demographic shift away from extended families. The massive Bijlmermeer housing project (now called De Bijlmer) southeast of the city, begun in the mid-1960s and finished in the 1970s, was built in a similar vein.

ANTHONY PIDGEON / LONELY PLANET IMAGES ©

Centraal Station (p65)

**1914–20**

The Netherlands remains neutral in WWI. Food shortages cripple the country leading to strikes, unrest and growing support for the Dutch Communist Party.

**1939**

The Dutch government establishes Westerbork as an internment camp to house Jewish refugees.

## JEWISH AMSTERDAM

It's hard to overstate the role Jews played in the evolution of civic and commercial life in Amsterdam. The first documented Jewish presence goes back to the 12th century, but it was expulsion from Spain and Portugal in the 1580s that brought a flood of Sephardic (Jews of Spanish, Middle Eastern or North African heritage) refugees.

As in much of Europe, Jews in Amsterdam were barred from many professions. Monopolistic guilds kept most trades firmly closed. But some Sephardim were diamond cutters, for which there was no guild. Other Sephardic Jews introduced printing and tobacco processing, or worked in unrestricted trades such as retail, finance, medicine and the garment industry. The majority, however, eked out a meagre living as labourers and small-time traders. They lived in the Nieuwmarkt area, which developed into the Jewish quarter.

Yet Amsterdam's Jews enjoyed freedoms unheard of elsewhere in Europe. They were not confined to a ghetto and, with some restrictions, could buy property. Although the Protestant establishment sought to impose restrictions, civic authorities were reluctant to restrict such productive members of society.

The 17th century saw another influx of Jewish refugees, this time Ashkenazim (Jews from Europe outside of Iberia), fleeing pogroms in Central and Eastern Europe. Amsterdam became the largest Jewish centre in Europe – some 10,000 strong by Napoleonic times. The guilds and all remaining restrictions on Jews were abolished during the French occupation, and Amsterdam's Jewish community thrived in the 19th century.

All that came to an end, however, with WWII. The Nazis brought about the near-complete annihilation of Amsterdam's Jewish community. Before the war, about 140,000 Jews lived in the Netherlands, of which about 90,000 lived in Amsterdam, (comprising 13% of the city's population). Only about 5500 of these Amsterdam Jews survived the war, barely one in 16.

Today there are roughly 41,000 to 45,000 Jews in the Netherlands; nearly half of them live in Amsterdam. Among Dutch Jews, the vast majority identify themselves as Jewish, although only about one-quarter belong to synagogues. More than half are nonpractising.

## CULTURAL REVOLUTION (1962–82)

Over the 80 years leading up to the 1960s, Dutch society had become characterised by *verzuiling* (pillarisation), a social order in which each religion and political persuasion achieved the right to do its own thing, with its own institutions. Each persuasion represented a pillar that supported the status quo in a general 'agreement to disagree'. In the 1960s the old divisions were increasingly irrelevant and the pillars came tumbling down, but not the philosophy that they spawned.

**1940**

Germany invades the Netherlands. Rotterdam is destroyed by the Luftwaffe, but Amsterdam suffers only minor damage before capitulating.

**1944–45**

The Allies liberate the southern Netherlands, but the north and west of the country are cut off from supplies. Thousands of Dutch perish in the bitter 'Hunger Winter'.

**1975**

The Netherlands' drugs laws distinguish soft from hard drugs; possession of small amounts of marijuana is decriminalised.

*Marijuana plant*

Amsterdam became Europe's 'Magic Centre', an exciting place where almost anything was possible. The late 1960s saw an influx of hippies smoking dope on the Dam, sleeping in the Vondelpark and tripping in the nightlife hot spots. The women's movement began a campaign that fuelled the abortion debate.

In the 1970s a housing shortage fuelled speculation. Free-market rents (and purchase prices) shot out of reach of the average citizen. Many young people turned to squatting in buildings left empty by (assumed) speculators.

'Ordinary' Amsterdammers, initially sympathetic towards the housing shortage, became fed up with the squatters, and by the mid-1980s the movement was all but dead. Squatting still takes place now, but the rules are clear and the mood is far less confrontational.



## NEW CONSENSUS (1982–2000)

Twenty years after the cultural revolution began, a new consensus emphasised a decentralised government. Neighbourhood councils were established with the goal of creating a more liveable city, through integration of work, schools and shops within walking or cycling distance; decreased traffic; renovation rather than demolition; friendly neighbourhood police; a practical, nonmoralistic approach towards drugs; and legal recognition of homosexual couples.

By the early 1990s, families and small manufacturers that had dominated inner-city neighbourhoods in the early 1960s had been replaced by professionals and a service industry of pubs, 'coffeeshops', restaurants and hotels. The city's success in attracting large foreign businesses resulted in an influx of higher-income expats.

### Historical Reads

- *The Embarrassment of Riches (Simon Schama)*
- *Amsterdam: The Brief Life of a City (Geert Mak)*
- *Tulip Fever (Deborah Moggach)*
- *Max Havelaar (Eduard Douwes Dekker)*
- *Murder in Amsterdam: Liberal Europe, Islam and the Limits of Tolerance (Ian Buruma)*

## TESTING TIMES (2000–PRESENT)

The first years of the new century have been ones of darkness and light for Amsterdam. After smouldering for years, a noisy debate erupted over the Netherlands' policy towards newcomers, which quickly led to a tightening of immigration laws. The limits of tolerance, a core value of Dutch identity, were called into question. Pim Fortuyn, a right-wing politician, declared the country 'full' before being assassinated in 2002.

Social tensions flared in the wake of the Fortuyn murder, and the atmosphere darkened further as the Netherlands slid into recession following the September 11 attacks in the US. The number of people leaving the country reached a 50-year high, although most departed

**1980**

Queen Beatrix marries German diplomat Claus von Arnsberg; the coronation is disrupted by a smoke bomb and riot on the Dam.

**2001**

Same-sex marriage is legalised in the Netherlands, the first country in the world to do so. In the next few years Belgium, Spain, Canada and South Africa follow suit.

**2002**

Leading politician Pim Fortuyn, a hard-liner on immigration and integration, is assassinated. The ruling Dutch parties shift to the right after suffering major losses in the national election.

**2004**

Activist filmmaker Theo van Gogh, a fierce critic of Islam, is assassinated, touching off intense debate over the limits of Dutch multicultural society.

## SIGHTS FOR HISTORY BUFFS

- **Amsterdam Museum** (p64) Lift the veil on a storied past.
- **Stadsarchief** (p113) Plumb the city's rich archives.
- **Anne Frank Huis** (p97) See the annexe and pages from the diary.
- **Verzetsmuseum** (p177) Learn about Dutch resistance during WWII.
- **Oude Kerk** (p62) Admire Amsterdam's oldest building, still looking fine.

for economic and family reasons. The mood was edgy, like a cauldron about to boil over.

It finally did in the autumn of 2004, when filmmaker Theo van Gogh – known for his anti-Muslim views – was brutally murdered on an Amsterdam street. In a city famous for tolerance of other cultures, what did it mean that a native Amsterdammer, albeit of foreign descent, was behind this crime?

The leading political parties in the Netherlands responded with a big shift to the right. In 2006 the government passed a controversial immigration law requiring newcomers to have competency in Dutch language and culture before they could get a residency permit. While most people agreed with the law's premise – immigrants have a better chance of successfully integrating if they know cultural basics – the contentious bit was in how the law was applied. All EU citizens were exempt due to reciprocal arrangements between EU member states, and immigrants from places such as the USA and Japan were exempted due to pre-existing treaties with the Dutch government. This meant the policy mostly fell on immigrants from non-Western countries, including Morocco and Turkey, traditionally two of the biggest contributors to Amsterdam's cultural mix. Indeed, immigration from these countries has slowed considerably over the past few years – though immigration overall has ticked upwards, thanks to newcomers from Eastern Europe.

In 2008, the Dutch government made waves – both locally and abroad – by announcing its plans to reduce the number of coffeeshops and legal brothels in the Netherlands. Following suit, then-mayor Jeb Cohen reluctantly made public the city's plans to close 43 of its 228 coffeeshops to comply with a 'distance rule' that stated such establishments could not exist within 250m from schools. It was pretty big news for what *De Telegraaf* once deemed 'The Cannabis Capital of the World,' as the ruling essentially meant curtains for 90% of Amsterdam's coffeeshops. At press time, the matter was still being debated.

**2006**
The government passes a law requiring immigrants to have competency in Dutch language and culture in order to get a residency permit.

**2008**
The city announces Project 1012. The goal is to close several prostitution windows and coffeeshops believed to be controlled by 'organised crime'.

**2009**
Amsterdam courts prosecute Dutch parliamentary leader Geert Wilders for 'incitement to hatred and discrimination'.

**2010**
Members of the Dutch government officially apologise to the Jewish community for failing to protect the Jewish population from genocide.

And then there was the global financial crisis of the late 2000s. No one was immune, and while Amsterdam felt the impact – with tourism down and unemployment up – overall it has weathered the storm pretty well. Certainly the huge amount of new construction around town shows that this is a city moving forward fast. A bike ride out to the IJburg, a string of artificial islands in the Eastern Docklands, gives a picture of the way that Amsterdam continues to approach its future with innovation, style, and vision, forever finding ways to defy the limits of its natural surroundings.



**2010**

For the third triumphant time, the Netherlands football team makes it to the World Cup finals – only to lose to Spain by a single point in overtime.

FRANS LEMMENS / LONELY PLANET IMAGES ©

Dutch football supporter

**2011**

Dutch authorities announce that they will implement a rule banning tourists from coffeeshops, while locals will require a registration card.

# Dutch Painting

**They don't call them the Dutch Masters for nothing. The line-up includes Rembrandt, Frans Hals and Jan Vermeer – these iconic artists are some of world's most revered and celebrated painters. And then, of course, there's Vincent van Gogh, the rock star of Impressionism, the jilted lover who cut off his ear, the artist who toiled in ignominy while supported by his loving brother, Theo. Understanding these quintessential Dutch painters requires a bit of history, as the roots of their respective styles go back to a time when Italy was the centre of the art world and painters would retreat there to study.**

## 16TH CENTURY

### Flemish School

Prior to the late 16th century, when Belgium was still part of the Low Countries, art focused on the Flemish cities of Ghent, Bruges and Antwerp. Paintings of the Flemish School featured biblical and allegorical subject matter popular with the Church, the court and to a lesser extent the nobility, who, after all, paid the bills and called the shots.

Among the most famous names of the era are Jan van Eyck (c 1385–1441), the founder of the Flemish School, who was the first to perfect the technique of oil painting; Rogier van der Weyden (1400–64), whose religious portraits showed the personalities of his subjects; and Hieronymus (also known as Jeroen) Bosch (1450–1516), with his macabre allegorical paintings full of religious topics. Pieter Bruegel the Elder (1525–69) used Flemish landscapes and peasant life in his allegorical scenes.

### Dutch School

In the northern Low Countries, artists began to develop a style of their own. Although the artists of the day never achieved the level of recognition of their Flemish counterparts, the Dutch School, as it came to be called, was known for favouring realism over allegory. Haarlem was the centre of this movement, with artists such as Jan Mostaert (1475–1555), Lucas van Leyden (1494–1533) and Jan van Scorel (1494–1562). Painters in the city of Utrecht were famous for using chiaroscuro (deep contrast of light and shade), a technique associated with the Italian master Caravaggio.

*Understanding these quintessential Dutch painters requires a bit of history*

## 17TH CENTURY (GOLDEN AGE)

When the Spanish were expelled from the Low Countries, the character of the art market changed. There was no longer the Church to buy artworks and no court to speak of, so art became a business, and artists were forced to survive in a free market – how very Dutch. In place of Church and court emerged a new, bourgeois society of merchants, artisans and shopkeepers who didn't mind spending money to brighten up their houses and workplaces. The key: they had to be pictures the buyers could relate to.

Painters became entrepreneurs in their own right, churning out banal works, copies and masterpieces in factory-like studios. Paintings were mass-produced and sold at markets alongside furniture and chickens.

Soon the wealthiest households were covered in paintings from top to bottom. Foreign visitors commented that even bakeries and butcher shops seemed to have a painting or two on the wall. Most painters specialised in one of the main genres of the day.

## Rembrandt van Rijn

The 17th century's greatest artist, Rembrandt van Rijn (1606–69), grew up a miller's son in Leiden, but had become an accomplished painter by his early 20s.

In 1631 he came to Amsterdam to run the painting studio of the wealthy art dealer Hendrick van Uylenburgh. Portraits were the studio's cash cow, and Rembrandt and his staff (or 'pupils') churned out scores of them, including group portraits such as *The Anatomy Lesson of Dr Tulp*. In 1634 he married Van Uylenburgh's niece Saskia, who often modelled for him.

Rembrandt fell out with his boss, but his wife's capital helped him buy the sumptuous house next door to Van Uylenburgh's studio (the current Museum Het Rembrandthuis). There Rembrandt set up his own studio, with staff who worked in a warehouse in the Jordaan. These were happy years: his paintings were a success and his studio became the largest in Holland, though his gruff manner and open agnosticism didn't win him dinner-party invitations from the elite.

*Rembrandt's paintings were a success and his studio became the largest in Holland*

Rembrandt became one of the city's biggest art collectors. He was a master manipulator not only of images; the painter was also known to have his own pictures bid up at auctions. He often sketched and painted for himself, urging his staff to do likewise. Residents of the surrounding Jewish quarter provided perfect material for his dramatic biblical scenes.



### Night Watch

In 1642, a year after the birth of their son Titus, Saskia died and business went downhill. Although Rembrandt's majestic group portrait *Night Watch* (1642) was hailed by art critics (it's now the Rijksmuseum's prize exhibit), some of the influential people he depicted were not pleased. Each subject had paid 100 guilders, and some were unhappy at being shoved to the background. In response, Rembrandt told them where they could shove their complaints. Suddenly he received far fewer orders.

Rembrandt began an affair with his son's governess but kicked her out a few years later when he fell for the new maid, Hendrickje Stoffels, who bore him a daughter, Cornelia. The public didn't take kindly to the man's lifestyle and his spiralling debts, and in 1656 he went bankrupt. His house and rich art collection were sold and he moved to the Rozengracht in the Jordaan.

### Etchings

No longer the darling of the wealthy, Rembrandt continued to paint, draw and etch – his etchings on display in the Museum Het Rembrandthuis are some of the finest ever produced. He also received the occasional commission, including the monumental *Conspiracy of Claudius Civilis* (1661) for the city hall, although authorities disliked it and had it removed. In 1662 he completed the *Staalmeesters* (the 'Syndics') for the drapers' guild and ensured that everybody remained clearly visible, though it ended up being his last group portrait.

### Later Works

The works of his later period show that Rembrandt had lost none of his touch. No longer constrained by the wishes of clients, he enjoyed newfound freedom; his works became more unconventional yet showed an ever-stronger empathy with their subject matter, as in *The Jewish Bride* (1667). The many portraits of Titus and Hendrickje, and his ever-gloomier self-portraits, are among the most stirring in the history of art.

A plague epidemic between 1663 and 1666 killed one in seven Amsterdammers, including Hendrickje. Titus died in 1668, aged 27 and just married; Rembrandt died a year later, a broken man.

## Frans Hals

Another great painter of this period, Frans Hals (c 1581–1666), was born in Antwerp but lived in Haarlem, just west of Amsterdam. He devoted most of his career to portraits, dabbling in occasional genre scenes with dramatic chiaroscuro. His ability to capture his subjects' expressions was equal to Rembrandt's, though he didn't explore their characters as much. Both masters used the same expressive, unpolished brush strokes and their styles went from bright exuberance in their early careers to dark and solemn later on. The 19th-century Impressionists also admired Hals' work. In fact, his *The Merry Drinker* (1628–30) in the Rijksmuseum's collection, with its bold brush strokes, could almost have been painted by an Impressionist.

### Group Portraits

Hals also specialised in beautiful group portraits in which the participants were depicted in almost natural poses, unlike the rigid line-ups produced by lesser contemporaries – though he wasn't as cavalier as Rembrandt in subordinating faces to the composition. A good example is the pair of paintings known collectively as *The Regents & the Regentesses of the Old Men's Alms House* (1664) in the Frans Hals Museum in Haarlem. The museum is a space that Hals knew intimately; he lived in the almshouse.

## Vermeer

The grand trio of 17th-century masters is completed by Johannes (also known as Jan) Vermeer (1632–75) of Delft. He produced only 35 meticulously crafted paintings in his career and died poor with 10 children; his baker accepted two paintings from his wife as payment for a debt of more than 600 guilders. Yet Vermeer mastered genre painting like no other artist. His paintings include historical and biblical scenes from his earlier career, his famous *View of Delft* (1661) in the Mauritshuis in Den Haag, and some tender portraits of unknown women, such as the stunningly beautiful *Girl with a Pearl Earring* (1666), also hanging in the Mauritshuis.

*Frans Hals devoted most of his career to portraits*

### Famous Works

Vermeer's work is known for serene light pouring through tall windows. The calm, spiritual effect is enhanced by dark blues, deep reds, warm yellows and supremely balanced composition. Good examples include the Rijksmuseum's *Kitchen Maid* (also known as *The Milkmaid,* 1658) and *Woman in Blue Reading a Letter* (1664), and, for his use of perspective, *The Love Letter* (1670).

*The Little Street* (1658) in the Rijksmuseum's collection is Vermeer's only street scene.

### Other Golden Age Painters

Around the middle of the century, the focus on mood and subtle play of light began to make way for the splendour of the baroque. Jacob van Ruysdael (c 1628–82) went for dramatic skies while Albert Cuyp (1620–91) painted Italianate landscapes. Van Ruysdael's pupil Meindert Hobbema preferred less heroic, more playful, scenes full of pretty bucolic detail. (Note that Cuyp, Hobbema and Ruysdael all have main streets named after them in the Old South and De Pijp districts, and many smaller streets here are named after other Dutch artists.)

The genre paintings of Jan Steen (1626–79) show the almost frivolous aspect of baroque. Steen was also a tavern keeper, and his depictions of domestic chaos led to the Dutch expression 'a Jan Steen household'. A good example is the animated revelry of *The Merry Family* (1668) in the Rijksmuseum; it shows adults having a good time around the dinner table, oblivious to the children in the foreground pouring themselves a drink.

**Great Dutch Paintings (and where to see them)**

*Night Watch, Rembrandt (Rijksmuseum)*

*Peter Denies Christ, Rembrandt (Rijksmuseum)*

*Self Portrait, Rembrandt (Rijksmuseum)*

*The Merry Drinker, Frans Hals (Rijksmuseum)*

*Kitchen Maid, Vermeer (Rijksmuseum)*

*Woman in Blue Reading a Letter, Vermeer (Rijksmuseum)*

*Wedding Portrait, Frans Hals (Rijksmuseum)*

## 18TH CENTURY

The Golden Age of Dutch painting ended almost as suddenly as it began when the French invaded the Low Countries in 1672. The economy collapsed and the market for paintings went south with it. Painters who stayed in business concentrated on 'safe' works that repeated earlier successes. In the 18th century they copied French styles, pandering to the fashion for anything French.

The results were competent but not groundbreaking. Cornelis Troost (1697–1750) was one of the best genre painters, and is sometimes compared to the British artist William Hogarth (1697–1764) for his satirical as well as sensitive portraits of ordinary people; Troost, too, introduced scenes of domestic revelry into his pastels.

Gerard de Lairesse (1640–1711) and Jacob de Wit (1695–1754) specialised in decorating the walls and ceilings of buildings – de Wit's trompe l'oeil decorations (painted illusions that look real) in the Bijbels Museum are worth seeing.

## 19TH CENTURY

The late 18th century and most of the 19th century produced little of note, save for the landscapes and seascapes of Johan Barthold Jongkind (1819–91) and the gritty, almost photographic Amsterdam scenes of George Hendrik Breitner (1857–1923). They appear to have inspired French Impressionists, many of whom visited Amsterdam.

Jongkind and Breitner reinvented 17th-century realism and influenced the Hague School of the last decades of the 19th century. Painters such as Hendrik Mesdag (1831–1915), Jozef Israels (1824–1911) and the three Maris brothers (Jacob, Matthijs and Willem) created landscapes, seascapes and genre works, including the impressive *Panorama Mesdag* (1881), a gigantic, 360-degree cylindrical painting of the seaside town of Scheveningen viewed from a dune, painted by Mesdag.

### Vincent Van Gogh

Without a doubt, the greatest 19th-century Dutch painter was Vincent van Gogh (1853–90), whose convulsive patterns and furious colours were in a world of their own and still defy comfortable categorisation (a post-Impressionist? A forerunner of expressionism?).

While the Dutch Masters were known for their dark, brooding paintings, it was Van Gogh who created an identity of suffering as an art form, with a morbid style all his own. Even today, he epitomises the epic struggle of the artist: the wrenching poverty; the lack of public acclaim; the reliance upon a patron – in this case his faithful brother, Theo; the mental illness; the untimely death by suicide. And of course, one of the most iconic images of an artist's self-destruction, which canonised him as the patron saint of spurned lovers everywhere is the severed ear, sent to a woman.

## The Artist's Legend: Myths & Facts

But is any of this actually *true*? Was Van Gogh's suffering, his trials and tribulations for art, actually as bold and colourful as the inimitable brushstrokes that even art neophytes around the world can recognise?

Well, the answer is: yes and no. Despite how legend would have it, the facts remain. He *did* cut off his ear, but only part of it. He *did* give it to a woman, but it was in a fit of despair to a prostitute he knew, not to a lover who had rejected him.

And he *did* actually sell his work during his lifetime – but only a single painting, *The Red Vineyard,* which now sits in Moscow. While in popular culture Van Gogh is often depicted as insane, he was in fact a depressive – contemporary medicine would probably diagnose him with bipolar disorder – who spent time in a psychiatric institution in Saint-Remy de Provence, where he kept a studio. Modern psychology makes a clear delineation between insanity and manic depression, and historians and doctors now believe Van Gogh suffered from this common illness, for which at the time there was no effective medicinal treatment (although some have countered that he suffered from epilepsy, lead paint poisoning, schizophrenia, or a host of other afflictions).

VINCENT VAN GOGH

For a moving window into the inner life of Vincent van Gogh, as well as a testimony to the extraordinary friendship and artistic connection he shared with his brother, Theo, read *Vincent Van Gogh: The Letters*. It contains all 902 letters to and from Van Gogh to his brother, friends, lovers, confidantes and fellow artists.

## Legacy of a Tortured Genius

Welcome to the stormy, torrid world of Vincent van Gogh, second only to Rembrandt in the lineage of Dutch artistic royalty. Who would have known, at his suicide in 1890, that the painter who once struggled to pay for basic food and art supplies would later sell a single painting (*A Portrait of Doctor Gachet*) at Christie's for $82.5 million? Probably no one.

Yet even among artists who become famous after their deaths, Van Gogh may be the most legendary – for his art, certainly, but also for his life. It takes a remarkable energy and focus to produce over 900 paintings and over 1100 drawings and sketches in less than a decade, and art historians muse that it may have been his very intensity – the relentless energy than verged on mania and cycled into melancholy and despair – that fuelled his imagination even as it led to his demise. While his paintings continue to inspire the world with their artistry, and remain, to many, the most groundbreaking works of the highly lauded Impressionist era, it is also the legacy of his exquisitely tortured genius that survives, and serves as a reminder of the terrible price that artists sometimes pay for their talent.

## Last Words

Even Van Gogh's rumoured last words ring with the kind of excruciating, melancholic beauty that his best paintings express. With Theo at his side, two days after he shot himself in the chest after a manic fit of painting, he is said to have uttered in French '*la tristesse durera toujours*' (the sadness will last forever).

## 20TH CENTURY

### De Stijl

De Stijl ('The Style') was a Dutch design movement that aimed to harmonise all the arts by bringing artistic expressions back to their essence. Its advocate was the magazine of the same name, first published in 1917 by Theo van Doesburg (1883–1931). Van Doesburg produced works similar to Mondrian's, though he dispensed with the thick, black lines and later tilted his rectangles at 45 degrees, departures serious enough for Mondrian to call off the friendship.

Throughout the 1920s and 1930s, De Stijl also attracted sculptors, poets, architects and designers. One of these was Gerrit Rietveld (1888–1964), designer of the Van Gogh Museum and several other buildings, but best known internationally for his furniture, such as the *Red Blue Chair* (1918) and his range of uncomfortable zigzag seats that, viewed side-on, formed a 'z' with a backrest.

#### Mondrian

One of the major proponents of De Stijl was Piet Mondrian (originally Mondriaan, 1872–1944), who initially painted in the Hague School tradition. After flirting with Cubism, he began working with bold rectangular patterns, using only the three primary colours (yellow, blue and red) set against the three neutrals (white, grey and black). He named this style 'neo-Plasticism' and viewed it as an undistorted expression of reality in pure form and pure colour. His *Composition in Red, Black, Blue, Yellow & Grey* (1920), in the Stedelijk Museum's collection, is an elaborate example.

Mondrian's later works were more stark (or 'pure') and became dynamic again when he moved to New York in 1940. The world's largest collection of his paintings resides in the Gemeentemuseum (Municipal Museum) in his native Den Haag.

### Van Gogh's Famous Five

- *Sunflowers (Van Gogh Museum)*
- *Wheatfield with Crows (Van Gogh Museum)*
- *Self Portrait with Felt Hat (Van Gogh Museum)*
- *Almond Blossom (Van Gogh Museum)*
- *The Bedroom (Van Gogh Museum)*

### MC Escher

One of the most remarkable graphic artists of the 20th century was Maurits Cornelis Escher (1902–72). His drawings, lithos and woodcuts of blatantly impossible images continue to fascinate mathematicians: a waterfall feeds itself; people go up and down a staircase that ends where it starts; a pair of hands draw each other. You can see his work at Escher in het Paleis in Den Haag.

### CoBrA

After WWII, artists rebelled against artistic conventions and vented their rage in abstract expressionism. In Amsterdam, Karel Appel (1921–2006) and Constant (Constant Nieuwenhuys, 1920–2005) drew on styles pioneered by Paul Klee and Joan Miró, and exploited bright colours and 'uncorrupted' children's art to produce lively works that leapt off the canvas. In Paris in 1945 they met up with the Danish Asger Jorn (1914–73) and the Belgian Corneille (Cornelis van Beverloo, 1922–2010), and together with several other artists and writers formed a group known as CoBrA (Copenhagen, Brussels, Amsterdam). It's been called the last great avant-garde movement.

Their first major exhibition, in the Stedelijk Museum in 1949, aroused a storm of protest (with comments such as 'my child paints like that too'). Still, the CoBrA artists exerted a strong influence in their respective countries, even after they disbanded in 1951. The Cobra Museum in Amstelveen displays a good range of their works, including colourful ceramics.

1

SIMON FOALE / LONELY PLANET IMAGES ©

2

4

ELLIOT DANIEL / LONELY PLANET IMAGES ©

**1. Street Art**
Amsterdam's streets can't keep a straight face.

**2. Cannabis College (p69)**
This nonprofit information centre educates visitors about recreational cannabis use.

**3. Rijksmuseum (p158)**
Rembrandt's *Night Watch* dominates Room 12 of the Netherlands' premier art museum.

**4. Café 't Smalle (p140)**
Set in a former *jenever* (Dutch gin) distillery, Café 't Smalle epitomises *gezelligheid* (conviviality).

KEN WELSH / ALAMY ©

WILL SALTER / LONELY PLANET IMAGES ©

JEAN-PIERRE LESCOURRET / LONELY PLANET IMAGES ©

JEAN-PIERRE LESCOURRET / LONELY PLANET IMAGES ©

JEAN-PIERRE LESCOURRET / LONELY PLANET IMAGES ©

**1. Kroketten (p38)**
Crumbed, deep-fried croquettes are a popular Dutch snack.

**2. Keizersgracht (p35)**
The Emperor's Canal was named as a nod to Holy Roman Emperor Maximilian I.

**3. House on Prinsengracht (p105)**
A familiar face and a welcoming hand on Prinsengracht, one of Amsterdam's liveliest canals.

**4. Cyclist in Spui (p64)**
Life's better on two wheels in Spui square.

# Canal Architecture

## Canal Rings

**The labyrinthine canals that create Amsterdam's fascinating landscape remain the spirit, soul and the physical history of the city, telling a thousand stories in the ripples of their serene waters.**

Try to imagine the city of Amsterdam *without* its iconic canals: it's nearly impossible. Actually, it would have been impossible to construct the city, as it looks today, without them. Far from being simply decorative or picturesque, or even just waterways for transport, the canals were necessary to drain and reclaim the waterlogged land. It is likely that none of the elegant houses on the Herengracht, for example, would have been constructed (and they would certainly not be still standing) had the canals not solved that essential problem of the modern city: keeping land and sea separate.

It helps to understand that much of the region is polder (land that once lay at the bottom of lakes or the sea). It was only reclaimed by building dykes across sea inlets and rivers, and pumping the water out with windmills (later with steam and diesel pumps).

The dawn of the 17th century brought one of Europe's greatest engineering and architectural marvels to Holland: the canal ring, an intricate network of waterways. The first of these, the Western Canal Ring, was built in the late 1600s. Of all the engineers and architects who contributed to the project, Hendrick de Keyser was perhaps the most definitive influence on this singular triumph of Amsterdam's Golden Age. A one-time sculptor who later became the town architect, De Keyser's work is celebrated for pioneering the Amsterdam Renaissance style of architecture.

In 2010, the entire 17th-century canal ring – including the Herengracht, Keizergracht and Prinsengracht – became the eighth Dutch treasure to land on the coveted Unesco World Heritage list. Many of De Keyser's buildings line these canals, most notably grand houses like the 1609 Huis aan de Drie Grachten (House on the Three Canals; Oudezijds Achterburgwal 249) which is notable for its steep gables, leaded glass windows and handsome shutters.

De Keyser also designed several of the city's best known Protestant churches, which all exemplify many of the signature features of canal architecture. Later, De Keyser's son Pieter famously designed the Huis Met de Hoofden, in which six carved heads of Classical deities dominate the facade.

To find fine examples of late 19th and early 20th century art nouveau, explore the residential areas near the Vondelpark.

**Right:** Amsterdam's distinctive canal architecture

# Canal Houses

## Gables

Among Amsterdam's great treasures are its magnificent gables – the roof-level facades that adorn the elegant houses along the canals. The gable hid the roof from public view, and helped to identify the house, until 1795, when the French occupiers introduced house numbers. Gables then became more of a fashion accessory.

There are four main types of gable: the simple **spout gable**, with diagonal outline and semicircular windows or shutters, that was used mainly for warehouses from the 1580s to the early 1700s; the **step gable**, a late-Gothic design favoured by Dutch Renaissance architects; the **neck gable**, also known as the bottle gable, a durable design introduced in the 1640s; and the **bell gable**, which appeared in the 1660s and became popular in the 18th century.

**Clockwise from top left**

**1.** Canal houses **2.** Carved wall tablet **3.** Bartolotti House

## Hoists & Houses That Tip

Many canal houses deliberately tip forward. Given the narrowness of staircases, owners needed an easy way to move large goods and furniture to the upper floors. The solution: a hoist built into the gable, to lift objects up and in through the windows. The tilt allowed loading without bumping into the house front. Some properties even have huge hoist-wheels in the attic with a rope and hook that run through the hoist beam.

The forward lean also makes the houses seem larger, which makes it easier to admire the facade and gable – a fortunate coincidence for everyone.

## Wall Tablets

Other house features include historic wall tablets. Before street numbers were introduced near the turn of the 19th century, many Amsterdam homes were identified by their wall tablets. These painted or carved stone plaques were practical decorations that earmarked the origin, religion or profession of the inhabitants.

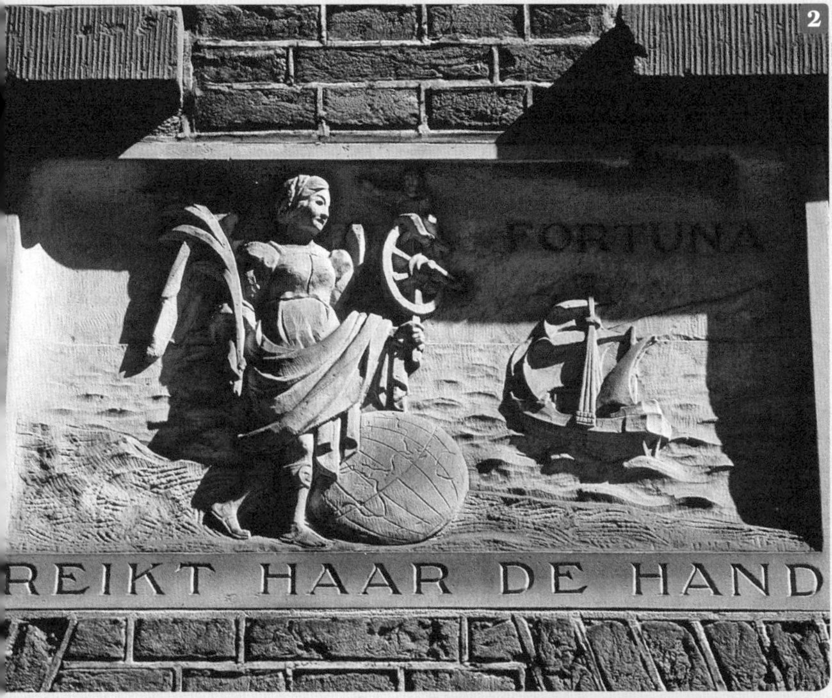

ELLIOT DANIEL / LONELY PLANET IMAGES ©

Beautiful examples of these stones are still found on many buildings along the main canals. Occupations are a frequent theme: tobacconists, milliners, merchants, skippers, undertakers and even grass-mowers are depicted.

The tablets also provide hints about the city's past. On the Singel canal, a stone depicting the scene of Eve tempting Adam with an apple hark back to a fruit market of yesteryear.

## MUST-SEE CANAL BUILDINGS

- Bartolotti House (Herengracht 170-172)
- Westerkerk
- Buildings along the Entrepotdok
- Huis aan de Drie Grachten (Oudezijds Achterburgwal 249)
- Bijbels Museum
- Museum Van Loon
- Felix Meritis Building
- Former milk factory (Prinsengracht 739-741)
- Huis Met de Hoofden

MARTIN MOOS / LONELY PLANET IMAGES ©

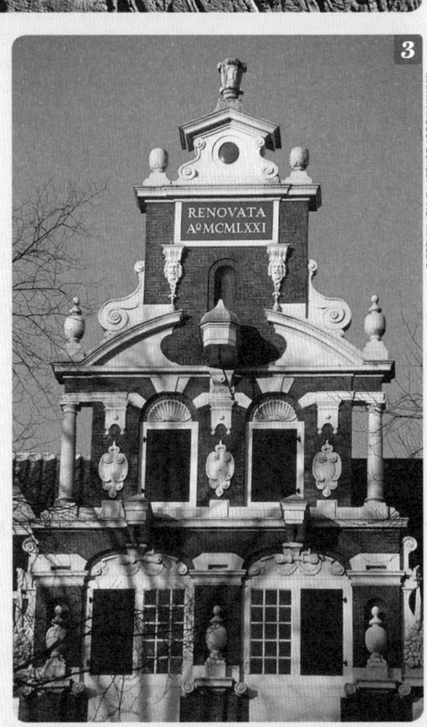

# Architecture in Amsterdam

**It is difficult not to be struck by Amsterdam's well-preserved beauty: the lovely canalscapes depicted in centuries-old paintings remain remarkably unchanged. Historian Geert Mak once described Amsterdam as 'a Cinderella under glass,' spared as it was from wartime destruction and ham-fisted developers. In fact, the comely old centre boasts no fewer than 7000 historical monuments, more humpback bridges than Venice and more trees per capita than Paris.**

## A CITY BUILT ON FREEDOM

Unlike many capitals, Amsterdam has few grand edifices to trumpet. There is hardly the space for a Louvre or a Westminster Abbey, which would be out of keeping with Calvinist modesty anyway. But you'll be pressed to find another city with such a wealth of residential architecture, and with an appeal that owes more to understated elegance than to power and pomp.

Amsterdam's beauty was built on freedoms – of trade, religion and aesthetics. Many of its gabled mansions and warehouses were erected by merchants in the Golden Age, with little meddling by city officials. Thus its leading citizens determined the look of the city, in what amounted to an early urban experiment.

Dutch architecture today is one of the country's most successful exports, with names such as Rem Koolhaas and Lars Spuybroek popping up on blueprints from Seattle to Beijing. Back home, rivalry can be intensely local as talents in Amsterdam and Rotterdam jostle for a spot in the architectural pantheon.

**Notable Buildings**

- *Oude Kerk (Old Church)*
- *Nieuwe Kerk (New Church)*
- *Royal Palace (Koninklijk Paleis)*
- *Amsterdam American Hotel*
- *Rijksmuseum*
- *NEMO*
- *Lloyd Hotel*
- *EYE Film Institute*
- *Muziekgebouw aan 't IJ*
- *Mint Hotel*
- *Centrale Bibliotheek Amsterdam*

## MIDDLE AGES

Around the year 1200, Amsterdam was a muddy little trading post on the Amstel river. The soft marshland couldn't support brick, so the earliest houses were made of timber, often with clay and thatched roofs (similar to ones still standing in Amsterdam-Noord today), but even these modest abodes would list into the soggy ground.

A fire burned down much of the city centre in the 15th century, and wood was sensibly outlawed as a main building material. There was plenty of clay to make brick, but this was too heavy, as was stone.

Engineers solved the problem by driving piles into the peat. Timber gave way to heavier brick, and thatched roofs were replaced by sturdier tile. Eventually brick and sandstone became de rigueur for most structures.

## DUTCH RENAISSANCE

As the Italian Renaissance filtered north, Dutch architects developed a rich ornamental style that merged the classical and the traditional, with their own brand of subtle humour. They inserted mock columns, known as pilasters, into facades and replaced old spout gables with step gables. Sculptures, columns and little obelisks suddenly appeared all over the Canal Ring. Red brick and horizontal bands of white were all the rage too.

Key commercial buildings include the **Greenland Warehouses** (Keizersgracht 40-44). Whale oil was a sought-after ingredient for soap, lamp oil and paint, and wells in these warehouses held 100,000L of the precious stuff. Nowadays they're chic apartments, but the facade is well maintained.

### De Keyser

Without a doubt, the best-known talent of this period was Hendrick de Keyser (1565–1621), the city sculptor. He worked with Hendrick Staets, a canal ring planner, and Cornelis Danckerts, the city bricklayer, to produce some of Amsterdam's finest masterpieces.

Every student of Dutch architecture knows the **Bartolotti House** (Herengracht 170-172), designed by De Keyser. He also put his stamp on three 'directional churches': the **Zuiderkerk** (Southern Church) and **Westerkerk** (Western Church), both Gothic in style, and the **Noorderkerk** (Northern Church), built for impoverished Jordaaners and laid out like a Greek cross inside – a veritable revolution at the time.

De Keyser also created the landmark **Munttoren** (Mint Tower; cnr Rokin & Singel). The national mint was moved here ahead of advancing French troops in 1673, but had little time to print any currency.

The **Rasphuis Gate** is another contribution from the prolific De Keyser. It's halfway along Heiligeweg, and once led to the Rasphuis, a model penitentiary where inmates would 'rasp' (scrape) Brazil wood for the dye industry.

De Keyser didn't limit himself to commercial, religious, or municipal projects; don't miss the gorgeous residences, such as the wonderful 1609 **Huis aan de Drie Grachten** (House on the Three Canals; Oudezijds Achterburgwal 249), a prime example of his artistry applied to residential architecture.



## DUTCH CLASSICISM

During the Golden Age of art in the 17th century, architects such as Jacob van Campen, and Philips Vingboons and his brother Justus decided to stick to Greek and Roman classical design, dropping many of De Keyser's playful decorations.

### OLDEST SURVIVING BUILDINGS

Only two early houses with timber facades have survived to this day. In a lovely courtyard near the Spui, the house at **Begijnhof 34** is the oldest preserved wooden house in the country, dating from 1465. The other specimen can be found at **Zeedijk 1** (home of the In 't Aepjen cafe, p78), from the mid-16th century.

The city's oldest surviving building is the **Oude Kerk** (Old Church, 1306), a fine specimen of Dutch brick Gothic style. The second oldest is the **Nieuwe Kerk** (New Church), a late-Gothic masterpiece from the early 15th century. You can clearly see how, over time, the Catholic choir and altar ceded ground to the Protestant pulpit. In both churches, notice the wooden roof frames.

Another classic of the era is the **Montelbaanstoren**, one of the city's signature buildings and a Rembrandt favourite. The octagonal steeple was designed by master architect Hendrick de Keyser to house a clock that's still in use today.

For a glimpse into the city's medieval seafaring past, visit its oldest monument, the evocatively named **Schreierstoren** (Tower of Tears; Prins Hendrikkade 94), located next to Centraal Station. It is rumoured to be the embarkation point for Henry Hudson's legendary journey to what became New Amsterdam – now known as New York City.

Influenced by Italian architects, the Dutch made facades look like temples and pilasters like columns. All revolved around clever deception. Neck gables with decorative scrolls came into fashion, often crowned by a temple-like roof. Garlands appeared under windows, and red brick, which was prone to crumbling, was hardened with dark paint.

The most impressive example of Dutch Classicism is Van Campen's **city hall** (now the Royal Palace). It was the largest city hall in Europe, and was given a precious shell of Bentham sandstone and a marble interior inspired by the Roman palaces.

*The facades of the Louis XIV style hung on until about 1750*

The Vingboons' designed the **Bijbels Museum** and the fine example at Keizersgracht 319. Don't miss Justus Vingboons' **Trippenhuis**: it's about as austere as it gets. It was built between 1660 and 1664 for the wealthy Trip brothers, who made their fortune in metals, artillery and ammunition. The most striking hallmarks are up at roof level – chimneys shaped like mortars.

Later in the 17th century, facades became plainer as the pendulum shifted to sumptuous interiors. Adriaan Dortsman, a mathematician by training, was a leader of this austere style. Dortsman's greatest hits include the **Ronde Lutherse Kerk** (Round Lutheran Church) and the **Museum Van Loon**.

## 18TH-CENTURY 'LOUIS STYLES'

As Holland's trading might faded, the wealthy fell back on fortunes amassed in the mercantile era. Many invested or turned to banking, and conducted business from their opulent homes. Traders no longer stored goods in the attic because they could afford warehouses elsewhere.

The Gallic culture craze proved a godsend for architect and designer Daniel Marot, a Huguenot refugee who introduced matching French interiors and exteriors to Amsterdam. Living areas were bathed in light that fell through sash windows on white stuccoed ceilings. As the elegant bell gable became a must, many architects opted for the next big thing: a horizontal cornice.

The dignified facades and statuary of the Louis XIV style hung on until about 1750. In rapid succession it was followed by Louis XV style – rococo rocks, swirls and waves – and Louis XVI designs, with pilasters and pillars making a comeback.

Standing in front of the late-Louis–style **Felix Meritis Building**, step back and note the enormous Corinthian half-columns, with a pomp that architect Jacob Otten Husly was skilled in imparting.

The **Maagdenhuis** (Spui 21), designed by city architect Abraham van der Hart, is a more sober brand of this classicism. Built in 1787 as a Catholic orphanage for girls, the building is now the administrative seat of the University of Amsterdam.

## 19TH-CENTURY NEOSTYLES

After the Napoleonic era, the Dutch economy stagnated, merchants closed their pocketbooks and fine architecture ground to a halt. Seen as safe and saleable, neoclassicism held sway until the more prosperous 1860s, when planners again felt free to rediscover the past.

The late 19th century was all about the neo-Gothic, harking back to the grand Gothic cathedrals, and the neo-Renaissance. It was around this time that Catholics regained their freedom to worship openly, and built churches like mad in neo-Gothic style.

A leading architect of the period was Pierre Cuypers, the man known for a skilful design blur on several neo-Gothic churches, something he had in common with CH Peters. Their contemporary, AC Bleijs, created some of the greatest commercial buildings of the era.

Pierre Cuypers designed two of Amsterdam's iconic buildings: **Centraal Station** and the **Rijksmuseum**, both of which display Gothic forms and Dutch Renaissance brickwork. A similar melange is CH Peters' General Post Office, now **Magna Plaza**. The ebullient neo-Renaissance facade of the **former milk factory** (Prinsengracht 739-741) was built in 1876 to a design by Eduard Cuypers (Pierre's nephew).

Bleijs designed the high-profile **St Nicolaaskerk** as well as the intimate 1881 **PC Hooft Store** (Keizersgracht 508). The latter, a Dutch Renaissance throwback with a Germanic tower, was built to commemorate the 300th birthday of the poet and playwright Pieter Cornelisz Hooft.

The facade of AL van Gendt's **Concertgebouw** is neoclassical, but its red brick and white sandstone are all Dutch Renaissance.

Around the turn of the century, the neo-Goths suddenly fell out of favour as art nouveau spread its curvy plant-like shapes across Europe. Art nouveau's influence can be seen in the former headquarters of Greenpeace International, still referred to as the **Greenpeace Building** (Keizersgracht 174-176). The towering edifice was built in 1905 for an insurance company, and its tiled facade shows a guardian angel that seems to be peddling a life policy. Other art nouveau structures are the **Amsterdam American Hotel** and the riotous **Pathé Tuschinskitheater**.



## BERLAGE & THE AMSTERDAM SCHOOL

The father of modern Dutch architecture was Hendrik Petrus Berlage (1856–1934). He criticised the lavish neostyles and their reliance on the past, instead favouring simplicity and a rational use of materials.

In Berlage's view, residential blocks were a holistic concept rather than a collection of individual homes. Not always popular with city elders, Berlage influenced what became known as the Amsterdam School and its leading exponents Michel de Klerk, Piet Kramer and Johan van der Mey.

The titans of the Amsterdam School designed buildings of 'Plan South,' an ambitious project mapped out by Berlage. Humble housing blocks became brick sculptures with curved corners, odd windows and rocket-shaped towers, to the marvel (or disgust) of traditionalists. It was a productive period that ushered in a new philosophy of city planning, given a boost by the 1928 Olympic Games held in Amsterdam.

The **Beurs van Berlage** displayed the master's ideals to the full, with exposed inner struts and striking but simple brick accents. Johan van der Mey's remarkable **Scheepvaarthuis** was the first building in the Amsterdam School style. It draws on the street layout to reproduce a ship's bow.

*A leading architect of the period was Pierre Cuypers*

De Klerk's **Het Schip** and Kramer's **de Dageraad** are like fairytale fortresses rendered in a Dutch version of art deco. Their eccentric details are charming, but the 'form over function' ethic meant these places were not always fantastic to live in.

## FUNCTIONALISM

As the Amsterdam School flourished, a new generation began to rebel against the movement's impractical and expensive methods. In 1927 they formed a group called 'de 8', influenced by the Bauhaus, Frank Lloyd Wright and Le Corbusier.

Architects such as Ben Merkelbach and Gerrit Rietveld believed that form should follow function and advocated steel, glass and concrete. The Committee of Aesthetics Control didn't agree, however, which is why you'll see little functionalism in the Canal Ring.

After WWII, entire suburbs such as the sprawling Bijlmermeer in Amsterdam-Zuidoost were designed along functionalist lines. By the late 1960s, however, resistance had grown against such impersonal, large-scale projects.

Rietveld left Amsterdam the **Van Gogh Museum**, where the minimalist, open space allows the artist's works to shine. You can also enjoy coffee inside his **M Café** at Metz Department Store (p113).

Aldo van Eyck's work also remains controversial, with critics arguing it looks out of place against the 17th- and 18th-century surrounds. His designs include the **Moederhuis** (Plantage Middenlaan 33), built for 'fallen women'.

## THE PRESENT

Since the 1970s, designers have lent a human scale to the suburbs by integrating low- and medium-rise apartments with shops, schools and offices. In the Plantage district, a must-see is the huge **Entrepotdok**. Sprawling half a kilometre along a former loading dock, the crusty shipping warehouses have been recast as desirable apartments, studios and commercial spaces. Nearby, the Eastern Docklands were full of derelict industrial buildings until the 1980s and early '90s, when they got a new lease on life.

Looking southeast from Centraal Station, you can't miss the green copper snout of **NEMO**, a science museum designed by Renzo Piano that resembles the prow of a ship. The cubelike glass shell of the **Muziekgebouw aan 't IJ** stands not far to the north, on the IJ waterfront. Clad in a voluptuous body of aluminium and glass, **ARCAM** (Architectuur Centrum Amsterdam) is a tribute to the city's architectural prowess.

The Eastern Docklands is home to an innovative community called **IJburg**, which has in the past few years become home to more than 10,000 residents on a string of artificial islands; about 45,000 residents are predicted to inhabit the islands by 2013. The curvaceous Enneüs Heerma Brug, dubbed Dolly Parton Bridge by locals, links it to the mainland. Other important Eastern Islands and Docklands areas include KNSM Island and Java Island, home to innovative residential projects as well as stylishly repurposed Docklands buildings. Most notably, the historic Lloyd Hotel started off as a hotel, but went through various incarnations as a Nazi prison and a juvenile facility, before it was re-imagined by a visionary bunch of Dutch artists, designers, and architects.

*Eastern Docklands is home to an innovative community called IJburg*

Exciting projects continue to sweep their way through the city centre. On the shores of the IJ just east of Centraal Station stands the **Oosterdokseiland**, a row of landmark buildings that includes the **Centrale Bibliotheek Amsterdam** and features a high-density mix of shops, restaurants, offices, apartments and a music conservatorium. An exciting new addition is the **Mint Hotel**, the city's largest hotel.

Northwest of Centraal Station and also on the IJ, you'll find the **Westerdokseiland**, a harbour that has been repurposed. On a former industrial estate across the IJ river, housing blocks and office towers are springing up at the Overhoeks development, where the architectural centrepiece is the **EYE Film Institute**.

# Music

**Oh Calvinism. One can't deny its effect on music. Example: the dour church elders began to allow organ music in churches in the 17th century, as it kept people out of the pubs. Since then, Amsterdam has contributed relatively little to the world's musical heritage. These days, the world's top acts perform here regularly, and local musicians excel in (modern) classical music, jazz and techno/dance. Sure, Dutch culture lacks a modern musical figurehead like Mick Jagger. A rock and roll hotbed it's not, yet Amsterdam remains an energised epicentre of converging musical traditions – yet another reason why this city is as cutting edge as it is classic.**

## CLASSICAL

The Netherlands has orchestras in cities throughout the country, but Amsterdam's Koninklijk Concertgebouw Orkest (Royal Concertgebouw Orchestra) outshines them all. In addition to having been called the world's best orchestra by British classical music authority Gramophone, the ensemble plays in the coveted, near-perfect acoustics of its winning concert hall, the Concertgebouw). The orchestra's director since 2004 is Mariss Jansons, whose long list of credentials includes the Pittsburgh Symphony. If you're looking to catch one of the top-flight soloists in the world, head here first. The orchestra also frequently performs abroad, matching works by famous composers with little-known gems of the modern era.

The Concertgebouw is only one of several venues in town for classical music. Chamber music plays in the Beurs van Berlage, and the city's extant and converted churches often host concerts.

As for Dutch home-grown talent, you can hardly do better than the mop-topped pianist Ronald Brautigam, who has performed around the country and all over the world. Violinist-violist Isabelle van Keulen founded her own chamber music festival in Delft, and brings in the crowds wherever she appears. The country's leading cellist is Pieter Wispelwey, the first cellist to ever receive the prestigious Netherlands Music prize for the most promising young musician in the country (1992). He's known for his fiery temperament and challenging repertoire.

### CROSS-CULTURAL BEATS

With nearly half of Amsterdam's population descending from other ethnic backgrounds, is it any wonder that this city is a vibrant epicentre for world music? From music inspired by the Caribbean beats of Suriname, the Dutch Antilles and other former Dutch colonies, to Cuban salsa, Dominican merengue and Argentinean tango, you'll can count on cross-continental grooves at these festivals and venues.

- **Badcuyp** Vibrant music cafe with offerings from jazz to salsa.
- **Bourbon Street Jazz & Blues Club** For blues, funk, soul and rock 'n' roll.
- **Bitterzoet** For a variety of music – sometimes live, somtimes a DJ.
- **Tropentheater** Music, film and performances from around the world.
- **Melkweg** Offers a diverse range of music.
- **Roots Festival** With world music, theatre, dance and film.

Pianist Wibi Soerjadi is one of the country's most successful classical musicians, famous for his sparkling interpretations of romantic works and his Javanese-prince looks. Soprano Charlotte Margiono is known for her interpretations of *The Marriage of Figaro* and *The Magic Flute*. Mezzo-soprano Jard van Nes has a giant reputation for her solo parts in Mahler's symphonies.

For 'old music' you shouldn't miss the Combattimento Consort Amsterdam, concentrating on the music of the 17th and 18th centuries (Bach, Vivaldi and Handel). The Amsterdam Baroque Orchestra (ABO) and Choir, conducted by Ton Koopman, tackled the enormous task of recording all existing cantatas of JS Bach. The ABO tours internationally, but when home can often be seen performing at the Concertgebouw.

The Netherlands Opera is based in the Stopera (officially called the Muziektheater), where it stages world-class performances, though its forays into experimental fare stir up the inevitable controversy.

If your taste run to modern classical and experimental music, Amsterdam's a perfect place to hear some of the best. Head to the Muziekgebouw aan 't IJ, a prime, acoustically-stunning venue for this kind of work. You may hear worthwhile Dutch performers including the Trio, Asko Ensemble, Ives Ensemble, Nederlands Kamerkoor, Nieuw Ensemble, Mondriaan Kwartet and Schönberg Quartet.

To see Dutch jazz legends for the price of a beer, head to Jazz Café Alto, the city's most intimate jazz cafe. See father and daughter Hans and Candy Dulfer, tenor and alto saxophonists, play their daring styles solo or together. Or marvel at trumpeter and Jordaan native Saskia Laroo's mix of jazz and dance.

## JAZZ

The Dutch jazz scene has produced some mainstream artists in recent years. Among gifted young chanteuses are Fleurine, Ilse Huizinga and the Suriname-born Denise Jannah, who records for Blue Note and is widely recognised as the country's best jazz singer. Jannah's repertoire consists of American standards with elements of Surinamese music.

Astrid Seriese and Carmen Gomez operate in the crossover field, where jazz verges on or blends with pop. Other leading jazzers are bass player Hein van de Geyn, guitarist Jesse van Ruller and pianist Michiel Borstlap, winner of the Thelonious Monk award. Borstlap was commissioned by the Emir of Qatar to write the world's first opera in Arabic.

Peter Guidi, an effervescent soloist on the flute is, set up the jazz program at the Muziekschool Amsterdam and leads its big band, Jazzmania.

*Boerenrock* (farmer's rock) is a Dutch genre that combines rock and pop with regional dialects and rural subject matter. *Levenslied* (song of life) is a type of Dutch pop music (sung to the accompaniment of traditional instruments such as the accordion) that speaks to love, death, and other sentimental topics.

## POP & ROCK

Ever heard of 'Nederpop?' It's the nickname for Dutch popular music that is usually sung in Dutch, though is also occasionally sung in English.

There's a better chance that you've heard older hits by Dutch bands, such as 'Radar Love' by Golden Earring, 'Venus' by Shocking Blue or 'Hocus Pocus' by Jan Akkerman's Focus. The highest-profile Dutch rock star, Herman Brood, captured punk hearts with *Herman Brood & His Wild Romance* album at the end of the '70s. Later, the Dutch became pioneers in club music, fusing techno and industrial into the dark, hyperactive beat that became known as 'gabber'.

The 1990s came on strong, with crossover indie rock icon Bettie Serveert touring internationally and proving to the world, once again, that the Netherlands knew how to rock and roll. Nowadays Amsterdam is the pop capital of the Netherlands, and talent is drawn to the city like moths to a flame, with plenty of rock-scene regulars, like The Death Letters and Go Back to the Zoo, some of whom tour internationally.

# Survival Guide

# Transport

## GETTING TO AMSTERDAM

### Air

Most people flying to Amsterdam arrive at **Schiphol International Airport** (AMS; www.schiphol.nl), 18km southwest of the city centre.

#### Travel to/from Schiphol International Airport

TRAIN

From 6am to 12.30am, trains run between the airport and Amsterdam's Centraal Station (€3.70 one way, 20 minutes, every 10 minutes). Trains run hourly in the wee hours. Nederlandse Spoorwegen (NS), aka Dutch Railways, operates the service. If you have coins, buy tickets from the machines in Schiphol Plaza's central court. If you only have euro bills, head past the machines to the ticket windows and purchase tickets from an agent for a €0.50 surcharge. Non-Dutch credit and ATM cards won't work.

BUS

- **Connexxion** (www.airporthotelshuttle.nl; one way/return €15.50/25) runs a shuttle bus (every 30 minutes 6am to 9pm) from the airport to several hotels; the list of participating properties and fares is on its website. Look for the Connexxion desk by Arrivals 4.
- Visitors staying by the Museumplein or Leidseplein can take bus 197 (one way €4, 30 minutes). It departs outside the main airport hall.

TAXI

A taxi to the city centre takes 20 to 30 minutes (longer in rush hour) and costs €40 to €50. The taxi stand is just outside the station hall to the left.

### Train

National and international trains arrive at Centraal Station, in Amsterdam's centre. There are good links with several European cities, including six daily trains from Frankfurt (four hours).

- The high-speed **Thalys** (www.thalys.com) runs from Paris (4½ hours) via Brussels nearly every 30 minutes between 6am and 9pm.
- **Eurostar** (www.eurostar.com) runs from London (5½ to seven hours) at least five times daily; it stops in Brussels, where you transfer onward.
- **Fyra** (www.fyra.com) operates the newest, fastest trains, reducing travel times from Amsterdam (via Schiphol airport and Rotterdam) to Brussels (1¾ hours) and Paris (three hours).
- For national train schedules and booking, see the Holland by Train website (www.ns.nl).
- For international booking and information, see the NS Hispeed website (www.nshispeed.nl).

#### Travel to/from Centraal Station

Centraal Station is in the city centre, and well connected to transport options onward.

TRAM

- Eleven of Amsterdam's 16 tram lines stop at Centraal Station, and then fan out to the rest of the city.
- For trams 4, 9, 16, 24 and 25, head far to the left (east) when you come out the station's main entrance.

TAXI

Taxis queue near the front entrance. They may refuse to take passengers short distances or may charge a flat fee of €10 to €15 for only a few kilometres. See if you can negotiate. If you can manage to take public transport to your hotel, it is by far the best option.

### Bus

Bus travel often is cheaper than train travel to Amsterdam.

**CLIMATE CHANGE & TRAVEL**

Every form of transport that relies on carbon-based fuel generates CO², the main cause of human-induced climate change. Modern travel is dependent on aeroplanes, which might use less fuel per kilometre per person than most cars but travel much greater distances. The altitude at which aircraft emit gases (including CO²) and particles also contributes to their climate change impact. Many websites offer 'carbon calculators' that allow people to estimate the carbon emissions generated by their journey and, for those who wish to do so, to offset the impact of the greenhouse gases emitted with contributions to portfolios of climate-friendly initiatives throughout the world. Lonely Planet offsets the carbon footprint of all staff and author travel.

- **Eurolines** (www.eurolines.com) connects the city with all major European capitals.

### Travel to/from Amstelstation

Buses arrive at Amstelstation, south of the centre, with an easy metro link to Centraal Station (about a 15-minute trip).

## Car

If you're arriving by car, it's best to leave your vehicle in a park-and-ride lot near the edge of town. A nominal parking fee (around €8 per 24 hours) also gets you free public transport tickets. For more info see www.bereikbaar.amsterdam.nl.

# GETTING AROUND

Central Amsterdam is relatively compact and best seen on foot or by bicycle.

The public transport system is a mix of tram, bus, metro and ferry. Visitors will find the trams the most useful option.

The excellent **Journey Planner** (www.9292ov.nl) calculates routes, costs and travel times, and will get you from door to door, wherever you're going in the city. It even offers a car versus public transport comparison.

## Tram, Bus, Metro & Night Bus

- The **Gemeentevervoerbedrijf** (GVB; www.gvb.nl) runs the public transport system.
- The **GVB information office** (Stationsplein 10; ⏲7am-9pm Mon-Fri, 10am-6pm Sat & Sun) is across the tram tracks from Centraal Station's main entrance, and attached to the VVV tourist office. The GVB information office is the prime place for visitors to pick up tickets, maps and the like.
- Fast, frequent trams operate between 6am and 12.30am. The metro and buses serve primarily outer districts. Nachtbussen (night buses, 1am to 6am, every hour) run after other transport stops. The routes radiate out from Centraal Station.

### Fares, Tickets & OV-chipkaarts

- Tickets are smartcards called the **OV-chipkaart** (www.ov-chipkaart.nl). Either purchase a re-usable one in advance at the GVB information office, or purchase a disposable one (€2.60, good for one hour) when you board.
- Some trams have conductors responsible for ticketing, while on others the drivers handle tickets. If transferring from another line, show your ticket to the conductor or driver as you board. Buses are more conventional, with drivers stamping the tickets as you board.
- When you enter and exit a bus, tram or metro, hold the card against a reader at the doors or station gates. The system then calculates your fare and deducts it from the card. Fares for the re-usable cards are much lower than the disposable ones (though you do have to pay an initial €7.50 fee; consider it if you're a repeat or long-stay visitor, as the card is valid for five years).
- You can also buy OV-chipcards for unlimited use for one or more days, and this often is the most convenient option.

### Travel Passes

- The GVB offers unlimited-ride passes for 1/2/3/4/5/6/7 days (€7/11.50/15.50/19.50/24/27.50/30), available at VVV offices, metro-station machines (valid for up to 72 hours only) and from tram conductors (valid for 24 hours only).
- The I Amsterdam Card (p259) also includes a travel pass.

## Bicycle

The vast majority of Amsterdammers (555,000 in fact) get around town on their *fietsen* (bikes). Cycling is such a big deal here, we've devoted an entire chapter to the pursuit; see p32 for details on rentals, tours and road rules.

## Boat

### Canal Bus

The **Canal Bus** (www.canal.nl) does several circuits between Centraal Station and the Rijksmuseum, offering a unique hop-on, hop-off service. For more information, as well as tour boat details, see p35.

### Ferry

Free ferries run to Amsterdam-Noord, departing from piers behind Centraal Station. The ride to Buiksloterweg is the most direct (five minutes) and runs 24 hours. Another boat runs to NDSM-werf (15 minutes) between 7am and midnight (1am on Saturday), and another goes to IJplein (6.30am to midnight). Bicycles are permitted.

## Taxi

➡ Find taxis at stands at Centraal Station, Leidseplein and a few hotels, or call one; **Taxicentrale Amsterdam** (TCA; ☎777 77 77) is the most reliable.

➡ Rates are roughly €3.50 plus €1.95 per km – a ride from the Leidseplein to the Dam is about €12.

➡ Drivers sometimes cannot change large bills (or claim they can't) and often don't know smaller streets.

➡ At taxi stands look for a pink ID card displayed in the window, which allows drivers to drive on tram lines, and shows the driver has passed a city knowledge exam; you needn't take the first car in the queue.

➡ Late at night, it's sometimes possible to negotiate a flat rate before starting out.

➡ A nice alternative when available are the open, three-wheeled scooters of **TukTuk Company** (www.tuktukcompany.nl, in Dutch; ⏲10pm-3am Fri & Sat) and **Bicycle Taxis** (www.fietstaxiamsterdam.nl, in Dutch); they often have lower rates, and can be flagged down in the street, especially near Leidseplein and Rembrandtplein.

## Train

➡ **NS** (www.ns.nl) runs the nation's rail service. Trains are frequent from Centraal Station and serve domestic destinations at regular intervals, sometimes eight times an hour.

➡ The main service centre to buy tickets for both national and international trains is on the station's west side. The left-luggage lockers (€5 per day) are on the east side.

### Domestic Tickets

➡ Tickets can be bought at the NS windows or ticketing machines.

➡ At Centraal Station, there are change machines at the entrance to the main Ticket Service Centre.

➡ To use the ticketing machines, find your destination on the alphabetical list of place names, enter the code into the machine, then choose 1st or 2nd class (there's little difference in comfort, but if the train is crowded there are usually more seats in 1st class). Then choose 'without discount' and the period of validity (ie 'today' or 'without date' for a future trip). For tickets without a date, be sure to validate the ticket in a yellow punch gadget near the platform before you board.

➡ Day-return tickets (aka *dagretour*) are 10% to 15% cheaper than two one-way tickets.

### International Tickets

➡ **NS Hispeed** (www.nshispeed.nl) has separate windows to buy international tickets,

### TRAIN TRIBULATIONS

Buying a train ticket is the hardest part of riding Dutch trains. Among the challenges:

➡ Only some ticket machines accept cash, and those are coins-only, so you need a pocketful of change.

➡ Ticket machines that accept plastic will not work with most non-Dutch credit and ATM cards.

➡ Ticket windows do not accept credit or ATM cards, although they will accept paper euros. Lines are often quite long and there is a surcharge for the often-unavoidable need to use a ticket window. There used to be one window at both Schiphol International Airport and Centraal Station that accepted credit cards, but the last we heard these had been closed.

➡ Discounted tickets for Hispeed and Fyra trains sold on the web require a Dutch credit card. The cheap fares can't be bought at ticket windows.

and there can be long queues. Upon entering, take a numbered ticket based on the kind of service you need: advance purchase, picking up a reserved ticket, or purchasing tickets for services departing within an hour. Pickups and immediate departures get higher priority. Don't even think of taking a number for other than what you're planning to buy – you'll be sent to the back of the queue.

- You can also purchase tickets by phone (☎0900 92 96, per minute €0.35, 8am to midnight), or by credit card online, but you must pick them up at Centraal Station's international ticket windows.
- Be sure to reserve in advance during peak periods.

## Car & Motorcycle

We absolutely recommend against having a car in Amsterdam, but if you must, read on.

### Parking

- Pay-and-display applies in the central zone from 9am to midnight Monday to Saturday, and noon to midnight on Sunday.
- Costs are around €5/29/21 per hour/day/evening in most of the city centre, and around €4/23/15 elsewhere within the Canal Ring. Prices ease as you move away from the centre.
- Parking garages include locations at Damrak, near Leidseplein, and under Museumplein and the Stopera, but they're often full and cost more than street parking.
- It's best to leave your vehicle in a park-and-ride lot near the edge of town. See www.bereikbaar.amsterdam.nl for details.

### Road Rules

- Drive on the right-hand side of the road.
- Seat belts are required for everyone in a vehicle.
- Children under 12 must ride in the back if there's room.
- Be alert for bicycles, and if you are trying to turn right, be aware that bikes have priority.
- Trams always have the right of way.
- In traffic circles (roundabouts), approaching vehicles have right of way, unless there are traffic signs indicating otherwise.
- The blood-alcohol limit when driving is 0.05%.

### Automobile Association

The **ANWB** (www.anwb.nl, in Dutch) is the Netherlands' auto association. Members of auto associations in their home countries (the AA, AAA, CAA etc) can get assistance, free maps, discounts and more.

### Rental

Requirements for renting a car in the Netherlands:

- Show a valid driving licence from your home country.
- Be at least 23 years of age (some companies levy a small surcharge – €10 or so – for drivers under 25).
- Have a major credit card.

All the big multinational rental companies are here; many have offices on Overtoom, near the Vondelpark. Rates start at around €30, but they change frequently, so call around. Rentals at Schiphol International Airport incur a surcharge. Companies include:

**Avis Autoverhuur** (www.avis.nl)

**easyCar** (www.easycar.nl)

**Europcar** (www.europcar.nl)

**Hertz** (www.hertz.nl)

**National Car Rental** (www.nationalcar-rental.com)

**Sixt** (www.e-sixt.nl, in Dutch)

## TOURS

For cycling tours, see p32. For boat tours, see p35. Our favourite walking tours include the following:

**Sandeman's New Amsterdam Tours** (www.newamsterdamtours.com; tours free, donations encouraged; ⏲11am & 1pm) Slick young guides lead an entertaining three-hour jaunt to the sights of the Medieval Centre and Red Light District. Meet at the VVV office (the white building) opposite Centraal Station, rain or shine.

**Prostitution Information Centre Red Light District Tour** (www.pic-amsterdam.com; Enge Kerksteeg 3; tours €15; ⏲5pm Sat) The Prostitution Information Centre offers fascinating one-hour tours of the Red Light District, where it explains the nitty-gritty of how the business works. Profits go to the centre; reservations are not necessary.

**Randy Roy's Redlight Tours** (☎06 4185 3288; www.randyroysredlighttours.com; tours €12.50; ⏲8pm Sun-Thu, 8pm & 10pm Fri & Sat) The darkest secrets of Mike Tyson, Quentin Tarantino and other celebs feature in this lively 1½-hour tour of the Red Light District. Meet in front of the Victoria Hotel (Damrak 1-5), opposite Centraal Station.

**Orange Bike** (☎528 99 90; www.orangebike.nl; Singel 233; tour €15; ⏲5pm Tue, Thu, Fri & Sun) Offers one walking tour – the highly informative, two-hour Cannabis Tour. Guides cater to the preferences of the group; for example, if people want to head to the less touristy areas and see more local coffeeshops, they will avoid the Red Light District.

**Mee in Mokum** (www.gildeamsterdam.nl; tours €5; ⏲11am Tue-Sun) One of the cheapest and often most intriguing tours, these are led by senior-citizen volunteers who often have personal recollections to add. The tours can be a bit hit or miss, depending on the guide, but are well worth the value. They depart from the cafe in the Amsterdam Museum.

**Urban Home and Garden Tours** (☎688 12 43; www.uhgt.nl; tours incl drink €30; ⏲10.30am Fri, 11.30am Sat, 12.30pm Sun mid-Apr–mid-Oct) These well-regarded tours look at Amsterdam dwellings from the perspective of home, garden and even gable. Visits include 18th century, 19th century and contemporary homes. Tours take 2½ to three hours. Reserve ahead – the meeting point for tours (near Rembrandtplein) will be revealed after you do. Call for last-minute bookings (⏲06 2168 1918).

**Drugs FAQ** (www.drugsfaq.nl; tours by donation; ⏲1.30 Mon, Tue, Thu & Fri) An informative look at Amsterdam's drug culture, both its myths and reality. The itinerary includes smart shops, a 'user room' (the tour doesn't go inside) and a look at fake drugs being sold on the street. Tours depart by the Oude Kerk.

# Directory A–Z

## Business Hours

The list below shows standard opening hours for businesses. Reviews throughout this book show specific hours only if they vary from these standards. Note, too, that hours can vary by season. Our listings depict peak-season operating hours.

**Banks** 9am-4pm Mon-Fri, some Sat morning.

**Cafes, pubs & coffeeshops** Open noon (exact hours vary); most close 1am Sun-Thu, 3am Fri & Sat.

**Clubs** Open around 10pm (exact hours vary); close 4am or 5am Fri & Sat (a few hours earlier on weekdays).

**General office hours** 8.30am-5pm Mon-Fri.

**Museums** 10am-5pm daily, some close Mon.

**Restaurants** Lunch 11am-2.30pm, dinner 6-10pm.

**Shops** Large stores: 9am or 10am to 6pm Mon-Sat, noon-6pm Sun. Smaller shops: 11am or noon to 6pm Tue-Sat, from 1pm Sun & Mon (if open at all). Many shops stay open late (to 9pm) Thu.

**Supermarkets** 8am-8pm, though some in the central city stay open until 9pm or 10pm.

### PRACTICALITIES

- Dutch-language newspapers include *De Telegraaf*, the Netherlands' biggest seller; and *Het Parool*, Amsterdam's afternoon paper, with the scoop on what's happening around town.
- Keep abreast of news back home via the *International Herald Tribune* or the *Guardian*, or weeklies such as the *Economist* or *Time*, all widely available on newsstands.
- The monthly, English-language magazine *Time Out Amsterdam* gives the scoop on the city scene. *Uitkrant* and *NL20* are free Dutch-language listings magazines you can pick up around town.
- The metric system is used for weights and measures.
- Amsterdam banned smoking in all bars and restaurants in 2008, but you'll find some establishments ignore the order, and people light up freely.

## Customs Regulations

For visitors from EU countries, limits only apply for excessive amounts. Log on to www.douane.nl for details.

Residents of non-EU countries are limited to the following:

**Alcohol** 1L of spirits, wine or beer.

**Coffee** 500g of coffee, or 200g of coffee extracts or coffee essences.

**Perfume** 50g of perfume and 250mL of eau de toilette.

**Tea** 100g of tea, or 40g of tea extracts or tea essences.

**Tobacco** 200 cigarettes or 250g of tobacco (shag or pipe tobacco) or 100 cigarillos or 50 cigars.

## Discount Cards

Visitors of various professions, including artists, journalists, museum conservators and teachers, may get discounts at some venues if they show accreditation.

Students regularly get a few euros off museum admission; bring ID.

Seniors over 65, and with partners of 60 or older, benefit from reductions on public transport, museum admissions, concerts and more. You may look younger, so bring your passport.

For more information on which discount cards provide fast-track entry to sights, see p31.

**Cultureel Jongeren Paspoort** (Cultural Youth Passport; www.cjp.nl; card €15) Big discounts to museums and cultural events nationwide for people under age 30.

**Holland Pass** (www.hollandpass.com; 2/5/7 attractions €25/40/50) Similar to the I Amsterdam Card but without the rush for usage; you can visit sights over a prolonged period. You buy a pass usable for two, five or seven attractions that you pick from 'tiers' (the most popular/expensive sights are top-tier). Buy from GWK Travelex offices and various hotels.

**I Amsterdam Card** (www.iamsterdam.com; per 24/48/72hr €39/49/59) Available at VVV offices and some hotels. Provides admission to many museums, canal boat trips, and discounts and freebies at shops, attractions and restaurants. Also includes a GVB transit pass.

**Museumkaart** (Museum Card; www.museumkaart.nl, in Dutch; adult/child €40/20, plus €5 for first-time registrants) Free entry to some 400 museums all over the country for one year. Purchase at museums ticket counters or at Uitburo ticket shops (p49).

## Electricity

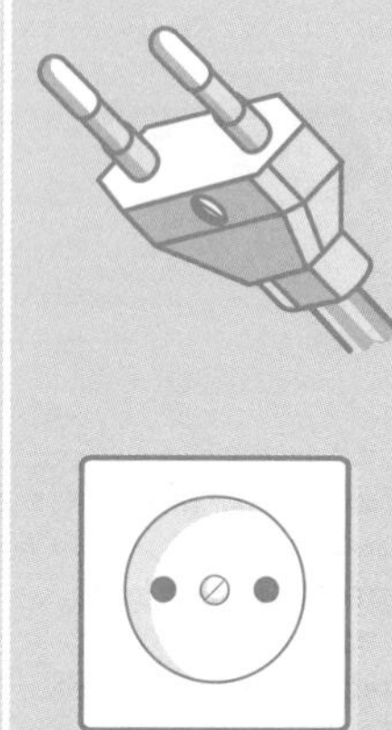


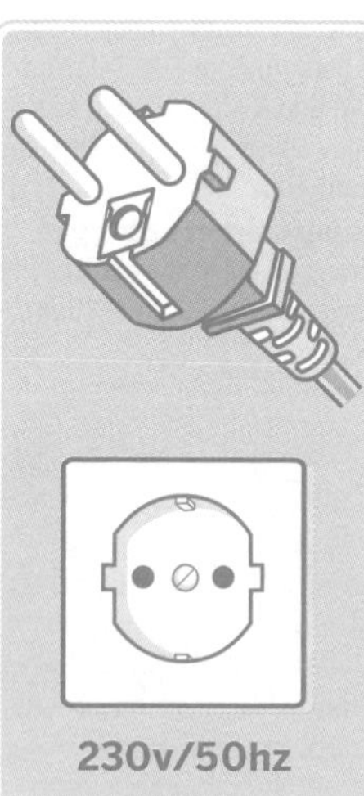


## Embassies & Consulates

Amsterdam is the country's capital but, confusingly, Den Haag is the seat of government. So the embassies (including those for Australia, Canada, New Zealand and Ireland) are in Den Haag, but Amsterdam has several consulates:

**France** (☎530 69 69; www.consulfrance-amsterdam.org; Vijzelgracht 2)

**Germany** (☎574 77 00; Honthorststraat 36-8)

**UK** (☎676 43 43; www.britain.nl; Koningslaan 44)

**USA** (☎575 53 09; http://amsterdam.usconsulate.gov; Museumplein 19)

## Emergency

Police, fire, ambulance: ☎112

## Internet Access

- Wi-fi is common in lodgings across the price spectrum; many places also have a computer on-site for you to use or will rent you a laptop.
- Several cafes offer free wi-fi, including all Coffee Company (www.coffeecompany.nl, in Dutch) branches.
- Many coffeeshops double as internet cafes.
- We've identified sleeping, eating and drinking listings that have wi-fi with a 🛜. We've denoted lodgings that offer internet terminals for guest use with a @.
- Outlets of the public library (Openbare Bibliotheek) offer free terminals and wi-fi.
- Internet cafes are scattered, though there's a cluster around Centraal Station. Expect to pay around €3 per hour.

**Centrale Bibliotheek Amsterdam** (p179) The stunning main library is chock full of terminals; it's near Centraal Station.

**Internet City** (Nieuwendijk 76; ⏰9am-midnight) More than 100 terminals; it's not far from the main coffeeshop drag.

## Legal Matters

The Amsterdam *politie* (police) are pretty relaxed and helpful unless you do something clearly wrong, such as chucking litter or smoking a joint right under their noses.

Police can hold offenders for up to six hours for questioning (plus another six hours if they can't establish your identity, or 24 hours if they consider the matter serious). You won't have the right to a phone call, but they'll notify your consulate. You're presumed innocent until proven guilty.

### ID Papers

Anyone over 14 years of age is required by law to carry ID. Foreigners should carry a passport or a photocopy of the relevant data pages; a driver's licence isn't sufficient.

### Drugs

- Technically, marijuana is illegal. However, possession of soft drugs (eg cannabis) up to 5g is tolerated. Larger amounts are subject to prosecution.
- Don't light up in an establishment other than a coffeeshop without checking that it's OK to do so.
- Hard drugs are treated as a serious crime.
- Never buy drugs of any kind on the street.

### Prostitution

Prostitution is legal in the Netherlands. The industry is protected by law, and prostitutes pay tax. Much of this open policy stems from a desire to undermine the role of pimps and the underworld in the sex industry.

In Amsterdam's Red Light District you have little to fear as the streets are well-policed, but the back alleys are more dubious.

## Medical Services

The Netherlands has reciprocal health arrangements with other EU countries and Australia. If you're an EU citizen, a European Health Insurance Card (EUIC), available from health centres (or, in the UK, post offices), covers you for most medical care. You still might have to pay on the spot, but you should be able to claim it back at home.

Citizens of other countries are advised to take out travel insurance; medical or dental treatment is less expensive than in North America but still costs enough.

For minor health concerns, see a local *drogist* (chemist) or *apotheek* (pharmacy, to fill prescriptions).

For more serious problems, go to the casualty ward of a *ziekenhuis* (hospital).

### Referrals

Contact the **Centrale Doktersdienst** (Central Doctors Service; ☎592 34 34; ⏲24hr) for doctor, dentist or pharmacy referrals.

### Emergency Rooms

Hospitals with 24-hour emergency facilities:

**Onze Lieve Vrouwe Gasthuis** (☎599 91 11; www.olvg.nl, in Dutch; 1e Oosterparkstraat 1) At Oosterpark, near the Tropenmuseum. It's the closest public hospital to the centre of town.

**VU Medisch Centrum** (☎444 44 44; www.vumc.com; De Boelelaan 1117, Amsterdam Buitenveldert) Hospital of the Vrije Universiteit (Free University).

### Pharmacies

Forget about buying flu tablets and antacids at supermarkets; for anything stronger than toothpaste you'll have to go to a pharmacy.

**Dam Apotheek** (☎624 43 31; Damstraat 2; ⏲8.30am-5.30pm Mon-Fri, 10am-5pm Sat, noon-5pm Sun) is conveniently located just off the Dam.

## Money

- The Netherlands uses the euro (€). Denominations of the currency are €5, €10, €20, €50, €100, €200 and €500 notes, and €0.01, €0.02, €0.05, €0.10, €0.20, €0.50, €1 and €2 coins (amounts under €1 are called cents).
- To check the latest exchange rates, visit www.xe.com.

### ATMs

Automatic teller machines can be found outside most banks, at the airport and at Centraal Station. Most accept credit cards such as Visa and MasterCard/Eurocard, as well as cash cards that access the Cirrus and Plus networks. Check with your home bank for service charges before leaving.

ATMs are not hard to find, but they often have queues or run out of cash on weekends.

### Changing Money

Generally your best bet for exchanging money is to use **GWK Travelex** (www.gwk.nl), with several branches around town:

**Centraal Station** (⏲8am-10pm Mon-Sat, 9am-10pm Sun)

**Damrak** (Damrak 1-5; ⏲8.15am-9.30pm Mon-Sat, 9am-7.45pm Sun)

**Leidseplein** (Leidseplein 31a; ⏲9.30am-5.30pm Mon-Sat, 1.30-5.30pm Sun)

**Schiphol International Airport** (⏲24hr)

### Credit Cards

All the major international credit cards are recognised, and most hotels and large stores accept them. But a fair number of shops, restaurants and other businesses (including Dutch Railways and supermarket chain Albert Heijn) do not accept credit cards, or accept only European cards with security chips.

Some establishments levy a 5% surcharge (or more) on credit cards to offset the commissions charged by card providers. Always check first.

For a backup plan against any security chip issue, consider getting the **Chip and PIN Cash Passport** (www.us.travelex.com/us/products/cash-passport), a preloaded debit MasterCard from Travelex that has the precious security chip embedded. You won't want to use the card much, as the exchange rates you get when you load it are pretty awful (read the regulations carefully). But it can be helpful to have in emergency situations when your home credit card won't work.

### PIN Cards

While in Amsterdam you'll notice people gleefully using 'PIN' cards everywhere, from shops to public telephones and cigarette vending machines. These direct-debit cards look like credit or bank cards with little gold-printed circuit chips on them, but they won't be of much use to visitors without a Dutch bank account.

### Tipping

Tipping is not essential, as restaurants, hotels, bars etc include a service charge on their bills. A little extra is always welcomed though, and common in certain instances.

- Hotel porters €1-2
- Restaurants round up, or 5-10%
- Taxis 5-10%

### Travellers Cheques

Travellers cheques are rare – you'll be hard-pressed to find a bank that will change them for you.

## Post

- **TNT Post** (www.tntpost.nl) handles the national mail service, which is fairly reliable and swift with deliveries. Post offices are generally open 9am to 5pm weekdays. You can buy stamps at newsagencies, supermarkets and souvenir shops.
- **Main post office** (Singel 250; ⏲9am-6pm Mon-Fri, 9am-noon Sat) Large and well-equipped.
- **Stopera post office** (Waterlooplein 10; ⏲9am-6pm Mon-Fri, 10am-2pm Sat) Convenient branch.

## Public Holidays

Many restaurants and other businesses close for two to six weeks in summer, usually in July or early August.

Banks, schools, offices and most shops close on these days:

**Nieuwjaarsdag** New Year's Day, 1 January.

**Goede Vrijdag** Good Friday, March/April.

**Eerste & Tweede Paasdag** Easter Sunday and Easter Monday, March/April.

**Koninginnedag** Queen's Day, 30 April.

**Bevrijdingsdag** Liberation Day, 5 May. This isn't a universal holiday; government workers have the day off but almost everyone else has to work.

**Hemelvaartsdag** Ascension Day, 17 May 2012, 9 May 2013.

**Eerste and Tweede Pinksterdag** Whit Sunday (Pentecost) and Whit Monday, 27 and 28 May 2012, 19 and 20 May 2013.

**Eerste and Tweede Kerstdag** Christmas Day and Boxing Day, 25 and 26 December.

## Telephone

- The Dutch phone network, **KPN** (www.kpn.com), is efficient, and prices are reasonable by European standards.
- Phone booths (both coin and card phones) are scattered around town.

### Mobile Phones

The Netherlands uses GSM 900/1800, compatible with the rest of Europe and Australia but not with the North American GSM 1900 (though some convertible phones work in both places). G3 phones such as iPhones will work fine – but beware of enormous roaming costs, especially for data.

Prepaid mobile phones are available at mobile-phone shops, starting from around €35 when on special. You can also buy SIM cards (from €5) for your own GSM mobile phone that will give you a Dutch telephone number. Look for Phone House, Orange, T-Mobile and Vodafone shops in major shopping areas, including along Rokin, Kalverstraat and Leidsestraat.

New prepaid phones generally come with a small amount of call time already stored. To top it up, purchase more minutes at one of the branded stores, newsagencies or supermarkets, and follow the instructions.

### Domestic & International Dialling

To ring abroad, dial ☎00 followed by the country code for your target country, the area code (you usually drop the leading 0 if there is one) and the subscriber number. The country code for calling into the Netherlands is ☎31. Drop the leading 0 on city codes if you're calling from outside the Netherlands (eg 20 for Amsterdam instead of 020). Do not dial the city code if you are in the area covered by it.

**Netherlands country code** ☎31

**Amsterdam city code** ☎020

**Free calls** ☎0800

**Mobile numbers** ☎06

**Paid information calls** ☎0900 Cost varies between €0.10 and €1.30 per minute.

### Costs

Calls are time-based, anytime and anywhere. Here is a rough guide to costs (note phones in cafes and hotels often charge more):

**National call to land line** €0.10 per 15 seconds.

**National call to mobile phone** €0.10 per nine seconds.

**International call to Britain** €0.058 per minute.

**International call to USA** €0.073 per minute.

Incoming calls to Dutch mobile phones are generally free to the recipient.

### Collect Calls & Operator Assistance

The following are free calls to place:

**Collect call** (collect gesprek; ☎domestic 0800 01 01, international 0800 04 10)

**Operator assistance** (☎0800 04 10)

### Internet Calls

Services such as **Skype** (www.skype.com) and **Google Voice** (www.google.com/voice) can make calling home quite cheap. Check the websites for details.

### Phonecards

- For public telephones, cards are available at post offices, train station counters, VVV and GWK offices, and tobacco shops for €5, €10 and €20.
- KPN's card is the most common but there are tonnes of competitors (Orange, T-Mobile and Vodaphone among them) that usually have better rates.
- Train stations have Telfort phone booths that require a Telfort card (available at GWK offices or ticket counters), although there should be KPN booths nearby.

## Time

Amsterdam is in the Central European time zone (same as Berlin and Paris), GMT/UTC plus one hour. Noon in Amsterdam is 11am in London, 6am in New York, 3am in San Francisco and 9pm in Sydney. For daylight savings time, clocks are put forward one hour at 2am on the last Sunday in March and back again at 3am on the last Sunday in October.

When telling the time, be aware that the Dutch use 'half' to indicate 'half before' the hour. If you say 'half eight' (8.30 in many forms of English), a Dutch person will take this to mean 7.30.

## Toilets

These are not a widespread facility on Dutch streets, apart from the redolent, free-standing public urinals for men in places such as the Red Light District. Many people duck into a cafe or department store. The standard fee for toilet attendants is €0.50.

## Tourist Information

The **VVV** (Vereniging voor Vreemdelingenverkeer; www.holland.com) is the Netherlands Tourism Board.

In Amsterdam, the VVV runs offices in conjunction with the **Amsterdam Tourism & Convention Board** (www.iamsterdam.com).

**VVV Main office** (Stationsplein 10; ⌚hotel bookings 9am-7pm, transport tickets & information 7am-9pm Mon-Fri, 10am-6pm Sat & Sun) Located in front of Centraal Station, and connected to the GVB transport office. It can help with just about anything: it sells the I Amsterdam discount card; theatre and museum tickets; a good city map (€2.50) and cycling maps. It also books hotel rooms (commission charged). Staff are always helpful, even if queues can be quite long; be sure to take a number when you walk in.

**VVV Leidseplein office** (Leidseplein 26; ⌚10am-7.30pm Mon-Fri, 10am-6pm Sat, noon-6pm Sun) Run in conjunction with the Uitburo ticket shop.

**Holland Tourist Information** (⌚7am-10pm) A VVV-run office at Schiphol International Airport.

## Travellers with Disabilities

- Travellers with reduced mobility will find Amsterdam moderately equipped to meet their needs.
- Most offices and museums have lifts and/or ramps and toilets for the disabled.
- Many budget and midrange hotels have limited accessibility, as they are in old buildings with steep stairs and no lifts.

- The city's many cobblestone streets are rough for wheelchairs.
- Restaurants tend to be on ground floors, though 'ground' sometimes includes a few steps.
- Tram lines 5 and 24 run wheelchair-accessible carriages. All buses are accessible, as are metro stations.
- For access details at entertainment venues and museums, contact the Uitburo (see p49) or the VVV (p263).
- More questions? Check the accessibility guide at **Accessible Amsterdam** (www.toegankelijkamsterdam.nl).

## Visas

Tourists from nearly 60 countries – including Australia, Canada, Israel, Japan, New Zealand, Singapore, South Korea, the USA and most of Europe – need only a valid passport to visit the Netherlands for up to three months. EU nationals can enter for three months with just their national identity card or a passport that expired less than five years ago.

Nationals of most other countries need a so-called Schengen visa, valid within the EU member states (except the UK and Ireland), plus Norway and Iceland, for 90 days within a six-month period.

Schengen visas are issued by Dutch embassies or consulates overseas and can take a while to process (up to two months). You'll need a passport valid until at least three months after your visit, and will have to prove you have sufficient funds for your stay and return journey.

The **Netherlands Foreign Affairs Ministry** (www.mfa.nl/en) lists consulates and embassies around the world. Visas and extensions are handled by the **Immigratie en Naturalisatiedienst** (Immigration & Naturalisation Service; ☎0900 123 45 61, per min €0.10; www.ind.nl). Study visas must be applied for via your college or university in the Netherlands.

## Women Travellers

In terms of safety, Amsterdam is probably as secure as it gets in the major cities of Europe. There's little street harassment, even in the Red Light District, although it's best to walk with a friend to minimise unwelcome attention.

The **Centrum voor Seksuele Gezondheid** (☎512 49 03; www.acsg.nl, in Dutch; Louwesweg 6; ⌚8.30am-4.30pm Mon-Fri) is a clinic at Slotervaart Hospital offering information and help with sexual problems and birth control, including the morning-after pill.

# Language

The official language of Amsterdam and the rest of the Netherlands is Dutch, which has around 20 million speakers worldwide. As a member of the Germanic language family, Dutch has many similarities with English.

The pronunciation of Dutch is fairly straightforward. The language does distinguish between long and short vowels, which can affect the meaning of words, for example, *man* (man) and *maan* (moon). Also note that aw is pronounced as in 'law', eu as the 'u' in 'nurse', ew as the 'ee' in 'see' (with rounded lips), oh as the 'o' in 'note', öy as the 'er y' (without the 'r') in 'her year', and uh as in 'ago'.

The consonants are pretty simple to pronounce too. Note that kh is a throaty sound, similar to the 'ch' in the Scottish *loch*, r is trilled – both may require a bit of practice – and zh is pronounced as the 's' in 'pleasure'. This said, if you read our coloured pronunciation guides as if they were English, you'll be understood just fine. The stressed syllables are indicated with italics.

Where relevant, both polite and informal options in Dutch are included, indicated with 'pol' and 'inf' respectively.

## BASICS

| | | |
|---|---|---|
| **Hello.** | *Dag./Hallo.* | dakh/ha·*loh* |
| **Goodbye.** | *Dag.* | dakh |
| **Yes./No.** | *Ja./Nee.* | yaa/ney |
| **Please.** | *Alstublieft.* (pol)<br>*Alsjeblieft.* (inf) | al·stew·*bleeft*<br>a·shuh·*bleeft* |
| **Thank you.** | *Dank u/je.* (pol/inf) | dangk ew/yuh |
| **You're welcome.** | *Graag gedaan.* | khraakh khuh·*daan* |
| **Excuse me.** | *Excuseer mij.* | eks·kew·*zeyr* mey |

**How are you?**
*Hoe gaat het met u/jou?* (pol/inf) — hoo khaat huht met ew/yaw

**Fine. And you?**
*Goed. En met u/jou?* (pol/inf) — khoot en met ew/yaw

**What's your name?**
*Hoe heet u/je?* (pol/inf) — hoo heyt ew/yuh

**My name is ...**
*Ik heet ...* — ik heyt ...

**Do you speak English?**
*Spreekt u Engels?* — spreykt ew *eng*·uhls

**I don't understand.**
*Ik begrijp het niet.* — ik buh·*khreyp* huht neet

## ACCOMMODATION

| | | |
|---|---|---|
| **Do you have a ... room?** | *Heeft u een ...?* | heyft ew uhn ... |
| **single** | *éénpersoons-kamer* | *eyn*·puhr·sohns·kaa·muhr |
| **double** | *tweepersoons-kamer met een dubbel bed* | *twey*·puhr·sohns·kaa·muhr met uhn *du*·buhl bet |
| **twin** | *tweepersoons-kamer met lits jumeaux* | *twey*·puhr·sohns·kaa·muhr met lee zhew·*moh* |

| | | |
|---|---|---|
| **How much is it per ...?** | *Hoeveel kost het per ...?* | hoo·*veyl* kost huht puhr ... |
| **night** | *nacht* | nakht |
| **person** | *persoon* | puhr·*sohn* |

**Is breakfast included?**
*Is het ontbijt inbegrepen?* — is huht ont·*beyt in*·buh·khrey·puhn

| | | |
|---|---|---|
| **bathroom** | *badkamer* | *bat*·kaa·muhr |
| **bed and breakfast** | *gasten-kamer* | *khas*·tuhn·kaa·muhr |
| **campsite** | *camping* | *kem*·ping |
| **guesthouse** | *pension* | pen·*syon* |
| **hotel** | *hotel* | hoh·*tel* |
| **window** | *raam* | raam |
| **youth hostel** | *jeugd-herberg* | *yeukht*·her·berkh |

### Signs

| | |
|---|---|
| **Ingang** | Entrance |
| **Uitgang** | Exit |
| **Open** | Open |
| **Gesloten** | Closed |
| **Inlichtingen** | Information |
| **Verboden** | Prohibited |
| **Toiletten** | Toilets |
| **Heren** | Men |
| **Dames** | Women |

## DIRECTIONS

**Where's the ...?**
*Waar is ...?* — waar is ...

**How far is it?**
*Hoe ver is het?* — hoo ver is huht

**What's the address?**
*Wat is het adres?* — wat is huht a·*dres*

**Can you please write it down?**
*Kunt u dat alstublieft opschrijven?* — kunt ew dat al·stew·*bleeft* *op*·skhrey·vuhn

**Can you show me (on the map)?**
*Kunt u het mij tonen (op de kaart)?* — kunt ew huht mey *toh*·nuhn (op duh kaart)

| | | |
|---|---|---|
| **at the corner** | *op de hoek* | op duh hook |
| **at the traffic lights** | *bij de verkeerslichten* | bey duh vuhr·*keyrs*·likh·tuhn |
| **behind** | *achter* | *akh*·tuhr |
| **in front of** | *voor* | vohr |
| **left** | *links* | lingks |
| **near (to)** | *dicht bij* | dikht bey |
| **next to** | *naast* | naast |
| **opposite** | *tegenover* | tey·khuhn·*oh*·vuhr |
| **straight ahead** | *rechtdoor* | rekh·*dohr* |
| **right** | *rechts* | rekhs |

## EATING & DRINKING

**What would you recommend?**
*Wat kan u aanbevelen?* — wat kan ew *aan*·buh·vey·luhn

**What's in that dish?**
*Wat zit er in dat gerecht?* — wat zit uhr in dat khuh·*rekht*

**I'd like the menu, please.**
*Ik wil graag een menu.* — ik wil khraakh uhn me·*new*

**Delicious!**
*Heerlijk/Lekker!* — *heyr*·luhk/*le*·kuhr

**Cheers!**
*Proost!* — prohst

**Please bring the bill.**
*Mag ik de rekening alstublieft?* — makh ik duh *rey*·kuh·ning al·stew·*bleeft*

| | | |
|---|---|---|
| **I'd like to reserve a table for ...** | *Ik wil graag een tafel voor ... reserveren.* | ik wil khraakh uhn *taa*·fuhl vohr ... rey·ser·*vey*·ruhn |
| **(two) people** | *(twee) personen* | (twey) puhr·*soh*·nuhn |
| **(eight) o'clock** | *(acht) uur* | (akht) ewr |

| | | |
|---|---|---|
| **I don't eat ...** | *Ik eet geen ...* | ik eyt kheyn ... |
| **eggs** | *eieren* | *ey*·yuh·ruhn |
| **fish** | *vis* | vis |
| **(red) meat** | *(rood) vlees* | (roht) vleys |
| **nuts** | *noten* | *noh*·tuhn |

### Key Words

| | | |
|---|---|---|
| **bar** | *bar* | bar |
| **bottle** | *fles* | fles |
| **breakfast** | *ontbijt* | ont·*beyt* |
| **cafe** | *café* | ka·*fey* |
| **cold** | *koud* | kawt |
| **dinner** | *avondmaal* | *aa*·vont·maal |
| **drink list** | *drankkaart* | *drang*·kaart |
| **fork** | *vork* | vork |
| **glass** | *glas* | khlas |
| **grocery store** | *kruidenier* | kröy·duh·*neer* |
| **hot** | *heet* | heyt |
| **knife** | *mes* | mes |
| **lunch** | *middagmaal* | *mi*·dakh·maal |
| **market** | *markt* | markt |
| **menu** | *menu* | me·*new* |
| **plate** | *bord* | bort |
| **pub** | *kroeg* | krookh |
| **restaurant** | *restaurant* | res·toh·*rant* |
| **spicy** | *pikant* | pee·*kant* |
| **spoon** | *lepel* | *ley*·puhl |
| **vegetarian (food)** | *vegetarisch* | vey·khey·*taa*·ris |
| **with** | *met* | met |
| **without** | *zonder* | *zon*·duhr |

### Meat & Fish

| | | |
|---|---|---|
| **beef** | *rundvlees* | *runt*·vleys |
| **chicken** | *kip* | kip |

| | | |
|---|---|---|
| **duck** | *eend* | eynt |
| **fish** | *vis* | vis |
| **herring** | *haring* | *haa*·ring |
| **lamb** | *lamsvlees* | *lams*·vleys |
| **lobster** | *kreeft* | kreyft |
| **meat** | *vlees* | vleys |
| **mussels** | *mosselen* | *mo*·suh·luhn |
| **oysters** | *oester* | *oos*·tuhr |
| **pork** | *varkensvlees* | *var*·kuhns·vleys |
| **prawn** | *steurgarnaal* | *steur*·khar·naal |
| **salmon** | *zalm* | zalm |
| **scallops** | *kammosselen* | *ka*·mo·suh·luhn |
| **shrimps** | *garnalen* | khar·*naa*·luhn |
| **squid** | *inktvis* | *ingkt*·vis |
| **trout** | *forel* | fo·*rel* |
| **tuna** | *tonijn* | toh·*neyn* |
| **turkey** | *kalkoen* | kal·*koon* |
| **veal** | *kalfsvlees* | *kalfs*·vleys |

## Fruit & Vegetables

| | | |
|---|---|---|
| **apple** | *appel* | *a*·puhl |
| **banana** | *banaan* | ba·*naan* |
| **beans** | *bonen* | *boh*·nuhm |
| **berries** | *bessen* | *be*·suhn |
| **cabbage** | *kool* | kohl |
| **capsicum** | *paprika* | *pa*·pree·ka |
| **carrot** | *wortel* | *wor*·tuhl |
| **cauliflower** | *bloemkool* | *bloom*·kohl |
| **cucumber** | *komkommer* | kom·*ko*·muhr |
| **fruit** | *fruit* | fröyt |
| **grapes** | *druiven* | *dröy*·vuhn |
| **lemon** | *citroen* | see·*troon* |
| **lentils** | *linzen* | *lin*·zuhn |
| **mushrooms** | *paddestoelen* | *pa*·duh·stoo·luhn |
| **nuts** | *noten* | *noh*·tuhn |
| **onions** | *uien* | *öy*·yuhn |
| **orange** | *sinaasappel* | see·*naas*·a·puhl |
| **peach** | *perzik* | *per*·zik |
| **peas** | *erwtjes* | *erw*·chus |
| **pineapple** | *ananas* | *a*·na·nas |
| **plums** | *pruimen* | *pröy*·muhn |
| **potatoes** | *aardappels* | *aart*·a·puhls |
| **spinach** | *spinazie* | spee·*naa*·zee |
| **tomatoes** | *tomaten* | toh·*maa*·tuhn |
| **vegetables** | *groenten* | *khroon*·tuhn |

### KEY PATTERNS

To get by in Dutch, mix and match these simple patterns with words of your choice:

**When's (the next bus)?**
*Hoe laat gaat (de volgende bus)?* — hoo laat khaat (duh *vol*·khun·duh bus)

**Where's (the station)?**
*Waar is (het station)?* — waar is (huht sta·*syon*)

**I'm looking for (a hotel).**
*Ik ben op zoek naar (een hotel).* — ik ben op zook naar (uhn hoh·*tel*)

**Do you have (a map)?**
*Heeft u (een kaart)?* — heyft ew (uhn kaart)

**Is there (a toilet)?**
*Is er (een toilet)?* — is uhr (uhn twa·*let*)

**I'd like (the menu).**
*Ik wil graag. (een menu)* — ik wil khraakh (uhn me·*new*)

**I'd like to (hire a car).**
*Ik wil graag (een auto huren).* — ik wil khraakh (uhn *aw*·toh *hew*·ruhn)

**Can I (enter)?**
*Kan ik (binnengaan)?* — kan ik (*bi*·nuhn·khaan)

**Could you please (help me)?**
*Kunt u alstublieft (helpen)?* — kunt ew al·stew·*bleeft* (*hel*·puhn)

**Do I have to (get a visa)?**
*Moet ik (een visum hebben)?* — moot ik (uhn *vee*·zum *he*·buhn)

## Other

| | | |
|---|---|---|
| **bread** | *brood* | broht |
| **butter** | *boter* | *boh*·tuhr |
| **cheese** | *kaas* | kaas |
| **eggs** | *eieren* | *ey*·yuh·ruhn |
| **honey** | *honing* | *hoh*·ning |
| **ice** | *ijs* | eys |
| **jam** | *jam* | zhem |
| **noodles** | *noedels* | *noo*·duhls |
| **oil** | *olie* | *oh*·lee |
| **pastry** | *gebak* | khuh·*bak* |
| **pepper** | *peper* | *pey*·puhr |
| **rice** | *rijst* | reyst |
| **salt** | *zout* | zawt |
| **soup** | *soep* | soop |
| **soy sauce** | *sojasaus* | *soh*·ya·saws |
| **sugar** | *suiker* | *söy*·kuhr |
| **vinegar** | *azijn* | a·*zeyn* |

## Drinks

| | | |
|---|---|---|
| **beer** | *bier* | beer |
| **coffee** | *koffie* | *ko*·fee |
| **juice** | *sap* | sap |
| **milk** | *melk* | melk |
| **red wine** | *rode wijn* | *roh*·duh weyn |
| **soft drink** | *frisdrank* | *fris*·drangk |
| **tea** | *thee* | tey |
| **water** | *water* | *waa*·tuhr |
| **white wine** | *witte wijn* | *wi*·tuh weyn |

# EMERGENCIES

**Help!**
*Help!* help

**Leave me alone!**
*Laat me met rust!* laat muh met rust

**I'm lost.**
*Ik ben verdwaald.* ik ben vuhr·*dwaalt*

**There's been an accident.**
*Er is een ongeluk gebeurd.* uhr is uhn *on*·khuh·luk khuh·*beurt*

**Call a doctor!**
*Bel een dokter!* bel uhn *dok*·tuhr

**Call the police!**
*Bel de politie!* bel duh poh·*leet*·see

**I'm sick.**
*Ik ben ziek.* ik ben zeek

**Where are the toilets?**
*Waar zijn de toiletten?* waar zeyn duh twa·*le*·tuhn

**I'm allergic to (antibiotics).**
*Ik ben allergisch voor (antibiotica).* ik ben a·*ler*·khees vohr (an·tee·bee·*yoh*·tee·ka)

# SHOPPING & SERVICES

**I'd like to buy ...**
*Ik wil graag ... kopen.* ik wil khraakh ... *koh*·puhn

**I'm just looking.**
*Ik kijk alleen maar.* ik keyk a·*leyn* maar

**Can I look at it?**
*Kan ik het even zien?* kan ik huht *ey*·vuhn zeen

**Do you have any others?**
*Heeft u nog andere?* heyft ew nokh *an*·duh·ruh

### Question Words

| | | |
|---|---|---|
| **How?** | *Hoe?* | hoo |
| **What?** | *Wat?* | wat |
| **When?** | *Wanneer?* | wa·*neyr* |
| **Where?** | *Waar?* | waar |
| **Who?** | *Wie?* | wee |
| **Why?** | *Waarom?* | waa·*rom* |

**How much is it?**
*Hoeveel kost het?* hoo·*veyl* kost huht

**That's too expensive.**
*Dat is te duur.* dat is tuh dewr

**Can you lower the price?**
*Kunt u wat van de prijs afdoen?* kunt ew wat van duh preys *af*·doon

**There's a mistake in the bill.**
*Er zit een fout in de rekening.* uhr zit uhn fawt in duh *rey*·kuh·ning

| | | |
|---|---|---|
| **ATM** | *pin-automaat* | *pin*·aw·toh·maat |
| **foreign exchange** | *wisselkantoor* | *wi*·suhl·kan·tohr |
| **post office** | *postkantoor* | *post*·kan·tohr |
| **shopping centre** | *winkel-centrum* | *wing*·kuhl·sen·trum |
| **tourist office** | *VVV* | vey·vey·*vey* |

# TIME & DATES

**What time is it?**
*Hoe laat is het?* hoo laat is huht

**It's (10) o'clock.**
*Het is (tien) uur.* huht is (teen) ewr

**Half past (10).**
*Half (elf).* half (elf)
(lit: half eleven)

| | | |
|---|---|---|
| **am (morning)** | *'s ochtends* | *sokh*·tuhns |
| **pm (afternoon)** | *'s middags* | *smi*·dakhs |
| **pm (evening)** | *'s avonds* | *saa*·vonts |

| | | |
|---|---|---|
| **yesterday** | *gisteren* | *khis*·tuh·ruhn |
| **today** | *vandaag* | van·*daakh* |
| **tomorrow** | *morgen* | *mor*·khuhn |

| | | |
|---|---|---|
| **Monday** | *maandag* | *maan*·dakh |
| **Tuesday** | *dinsdag* | *dins*·dakh |
| **Wednesday** | *woensdag* | *woons*·dakh |
| **Thursday** | *donderdag* | *don*·duhr·dakh |
| **Friday** | *vrijdag* | *vrey*·dakh |
| **Saturday** | *zaterdag* | *zaa*·tuhr·dakh |
| **Sunday** | *zondag* | *zon*·dakh |
| **January** | *januari* | ya·new·waa·ree |
| **February** | *februari* | fey·brew·waa·ree |
| **March** | *maart* | maart |
| **April** | *april* | a·*pril* |
| **May** | *mei* | mey |
| **June** | *juni* | *yew*·nee |
| **July** | *juli* | *yew*·lee |
| **August** | *augustus* | aw·*khus*·tus |

**Numbers**

| | | |
|---|---|---|
| 1 | *één* | eyn |
| 2 | *twee* | twey |
| 3 | *drie* | dree |
| 4 | *vier* | veer |
| 5 | *vijf* | veyf |
| 6 | *zes* | zes |
| 7 | *zeven* | *zey*·vuhn |
| 8 | *acht* | akht |
| 9 | *negen* | *ney*·khuhn |
| 10 | *tien* | teen |
| 20 | *twintig* | *twin*·tikh |
| 30 | *dertig* | *der*·tikh |
| 40 | *veertig* | *feyr*·tikh |
| 50 | *vijftig* | *feyf*·tikh |
| 60 | *zestig* | *ses*·tikh |
| 70 | *zeventig* | *sey*·vuhn·tikh |
| 80 | *tachtig* | *takh*·tikh |
| 90 | *negentig* | *ney*·khuhn·tikh |
| 100 | *honderd* | *hon*·duhrt |
| 1000 | *duizend* | *döy*·zuhnt |

| | | |
|---|---|---|
| **September** | *september* | sep·*tem*·buhr |
| **October** | *oktober* | ok·*toh*·buhr |
| **November** | *november* | noh·*vem*·buhr |
| **December** | *december* | dey·*sem*·buhr |

## TRANSPORT

### Public Transport

| | | |
|---|---|---|
| **Is this the ... to (the left bank)?** | *Is dit de ... naar (de linker-oever)?* | is dit duh ... naar (duh *ling*·kuhr·oo·vuhr) |
| **ferry** | *veerboot* | *veyr*·boht |
| **metro** | *metro* | *mey*·troh |
| **tram** | *tram* | trem |

| | | |
|---|---|---|
| **platform** | *perron* | pe·*ron* |
| **timetable** | *dienst-regeling* | *deenst*·rey·khuh·ling |

| | | |
|---|---|---|
| **When's the ... (bus)?** | *Hoe laat gaat de ... (bus)?* | hoo laat khaat duh ... (bus) |
| **first** | *eerste* | *eyr*·stuh |
| **last** | *laatste* | *laat*·stuh |
| **next** | *volgende* | *vol*·khun·duh |

**A ticket to ..., please.**
*Een kaartje naar ... graag.* — uhn *kaar*·chuh naar ... khraakh

**What time does it leave?**
*Hoe laat vertrekt het?* — hoo laat vuhr·*trekt* huht

**Does it stop at ...?**
*Stopt het in ...?* — stopt huht in ...

**What's the next stop?**
*Welk is de volgende halte?* — welk is duh *vol*·khuhn·duh *hal*·tuh

**I'd like to get off at ...**
*Ik wil graag in ... uitstappen.* — ik wil khraak in ... *öyt*·sta·puhn

**Is this taxi available?**
*Is deze taxi vrij?* — is *dey*·zuh *tak*·see vrey

**Please take me to ...**
*Breng me alstublieft naar ...* — breng muh al·stew·*bleeft* naar ...

### Cycling

| | | |
|---|---|---|
| **I'd like ...** | *Ik wil graag ...* | ik wil khraakh ... |
| **my bicycle repaired** | *mijn fiets laten herstellen* | meyn feets *laa*·tuhn her·*ste*·luhn |
| **to hire a bicycle** | *een fiets huren* | uhn feets *hew*·ruhn |

| | | |
|---|---|---|
| **I'd like to hire a ...** | *Ik wil graag een ... huren.* | ik wil khraakh uhn ... *hew*·ruhn |
| **basket** | *mandje* | *man*·chuh |
| **child seat** | *kinderzitje* | *kin*·duhr·zi·chuh |
| **helmet** | *helm* | helm |

**Do you have bicycle parking?**
*Heeft u parking voor fietsen?* — heyft ew *par*·king vohr *feet*·suhn

**Can we get there by bike?**
*Kunnen we er met de fiets heen?* — *ku*·nuhn wuh uhr met duh feets heyn

**I have a puncture.**
*Ik heb een lekke band.* — ik hep uhn *le*·kuh bant

| | | |
|---|---|---|
| **bicycle path** | *fietspad* | *feets*·pat |
| **bicycle pump** | *fietspomp* | feets·*pomp* |
| **bike repairman** | *fietsen-maker* | feet·suhn·*maa*·kuhr |
| **bicycle stand** | *fietsenrek* | feet·suhn·*rek* |

# GLOSSARY

**bibliotheek** – library

**bier** – beer

**biertje**– glass of beer

**bitterballen** – small, round meat croquettes

**broodje** – bread roll (with filling)

**bruin café** – brown cafe; traditional Dutch pub

**cafe** – pub, bar; also known as *kroeg*

**coffeeshop** (also spelt *koffieshop* in Dutch) – cafe authorised to sell cannabis

**CS** – Centraal Station

**dagmenu** – set menu

**dagschotel** – daily special in restaurants

**drop** – salted or sweet liquorice

**dwarsstraat** – street connecting two (former) canals

**eetcafé** – cafe serving meals

**fiets** – bicycle

**frites** – French fries

**gezellig** – convivial, cosy

**gezelligheid** – conviviality/cosiness

**gracht** – canal

**Grachtengordel** – Canal Ring

**GVB** – Gemeentevervoerbedrijf; Amsterdam municipal transport authority

**GWK** – Grenswisselkantoor; official currency exchanges

**hof** – courtyard

**hofje** – almshouse or series of buildings around a small courtyard, such as the Begijnhof

**jenever** – Dutch gin; also spelled *genever*

**kaas** – cheese

**kade** – quay

**kerk** – church

**koffiehuis** – coffee house (distinct from a *coffeeshop*)

**koninklijk** – royal

**kroketten** – croquettes

**markt** – town square, market

**NS** – Nederlandse Spoorwegen; national railway company

**OV-chipkaart** – fare card for Dutch public transit

**pannenkoeken** – pancakes

**paleis** – palace

**plein** – square

**proeflokaal** – tasting house

**Randstad** – literally 'rim city'; the urban agglomeration including Amsterdam, Utrecht, Rotterdam and Den Haag

**stadhuis** – town hall

**stamppot** – mashed pot with potatoes, another vegetable, bacon bits and smoked sausage

**stedelijk** – civic, municipal

**straat** – street

**strand** – beach

**stroopwafel** – syrup waffle

**toren** – tower

**VVV** – tourist office

**waag** – old weigh house

**De Wallen** – Red Light District

**zaal** – hall

# Behind the Scenes

## SEND US YOUR FEEDBACK

We love to hear from travellers – your comments keep us on our toes and help make our books better. Our well-travelled team reads every word on what you loved or loathed about this book. Although we cannot reply individually to postal submissions, we always guarantee that your feedback goes straight to the appropriate authors, in time for the next edition. Each person who sends us information is thanked in the next edition – and the most useful submissions are rewarded with a free book.

Visit **lonelyplanet.com/contact** to submit your updates and suggestions or to ask for help. Our award-winning website also features inspirational travel stories, news and discussions.

Note: We may edit, reproduce and incorporate your comments in Lonely Planet products such as guidebooks, websites and digital products, so let us know if you don't want your comments reproduced or your name acknowledged. For a copy of our privacy policy visit lonelyplanet.com/privacy.

## OUR READERS

**Many thanks to the travellers who used the last edition and wrote to us with helpful hints, useful advice and interesting anecdotes:**

Víctor Arráez, William Ballantine, Roos Blanken, Robin Brooks, Jordan Capeloto, Erik de Groot, Barbara Delissen, Evie Economou, Marion Eisele, Engin Ersoz, Ciara Fritsch, Liberato Gargiulo, Nienke Gritters Doublet, Marc Hedberg, Mark Holmes, Karel Houtsnip, Karin Jarmeby, Jitso Keizer, Sami Keskiaho, Janica Kleiman, Myriam Lepine, Daniel Musikant, Jan Peter Beekman, Inga Schnabel, Linda & Stephen Smullen, Ronald Soesan, Riël Timmermans, Marco Toscano, Fred van Gunst, Sonja van Minnen, Peter Vast, Lina Vieira, Aulene Wessel, Bernard Westerdijk, Géraldine Wójcik.

## AUTHOR THANKS

### Karla Zimmerman

Many thanks to Ernesto Diringuer, David Gorvett, Harriet Frost and Manon Zondervan from the Amsterdam Tourism and Convention Board for your knowledge and help on the ground. *Bedankt* to Ryan Ver Berkmoes for the train tribulations and then some. A big thanks also to co-author Sarah Chandler for the beery companionship in Amsterdam. Thanks most to Eric Markowitz, the world's best partner-for-life, who kept the home fires burning while I disappeared amid the windmills.

### Sarah Chandler

Karla Zimmerman, thanks for setting a spirited tone for this project: here's to another memorable evening at the Café Belgique. Jennifer Christensen, I owe you big time for luring me back to Amsterdam. To Bibi Spoelstra, thanks for absolutely everything. Matthijs Openneer, you rock: from Dutch lessons through watching *The Wire*, to teaching me how to properly appreciate FEBO. Finally, thanks to everyone at Quinto and Kingfisher – where I wrote parts of this manuscript – for instantly welcoming me like a regular.

## ACKNOWLEDGMENTS

Cover photograph: Prinsengracht, Amsterdam, Jon Arnold Images/AWL images. Many of the images in this guide are available for licensing from Lonely Planet Images: www.lonelyplanetimages.com.

## THIS BOOK

This 8th edition of *Amsterdam* was researched and written by Karla Zimmerman and Sarah Chandler. The 7th edition was researched and written by Karla Zimmerman, Caroline Sieg and Ryan Ver Berkmoes, with additional content by Jeremy Gray and Simon Sellars. The 6th edition was written by Jeremy Gray and the previous editions were written by Andrew Bender, Rob van Driesum and Nikki Hall. This guidebook was commissioned in Lonely Planet's London office, and produced by the following:

**Commissioning Editor** Jo Potts
**Coordinating Editor** Dianne Schallmeiner
**Coordinating Cartographer** Brendan Streager
**Coordinating Layout Designer** Jessica Rose
**Managing Editors** Annelies Mertens, Anna Metcalfe
**Managing Cartographer** Alison Lyall
**Managing Layout Designers** Chris Girdler, Jane Hart
**Assisting Editors** Elisa Arduca, Susie Ashworth, Joanne Newell, Elizabeth Swan
**Assisting Cartographer** Alex Leung
**Assisting Layout Designer** Paul Iacono
**Cover Designer** James Hardy
**Cover Research** Naomi Parker
**Internal Image Research** Aude Vauconsant
**Language Content** Laura Crawford, Annelies Mertens
**Thanks to** Janine Eberle, Ryan Evans, Mark Griffiths, Liz Heynes, Laura Jane, David Kemp, Indra Kilfoyle, Sonya Mithen, Wayne Murphy, Vivienne New, Susan Paterson,Trent Paton, Piers Pickard, Alison Ridgway, Averil Robertson, Lachlan Ross, Michael Ruff, Julie Sheridan, Amanda Sierp, Laura Stansfeld, John Taufa, Angela Tinson, Gerard Walker, Kate Whitfield, Clifton Wilkinson, Juan Winata

See also separate subindexes for:
EATING P279
DRINKING & NIGHTLIFE P280
ENTERTAINMENT P282
SHOPPING P282
SLEEPING P283

# Index



Sights p000
Map Pages **p000**
Photo Pages **p000**

## EATING

## DRINKING & NIGHTLIFE



Sights p000
Map Pages **p000**
Photo Pages **p000**

## ENTERTAINMENT

## SHOPPING



Sights p000
Map Pages **p000**
Photo Pages **p000**

# Amsterdam Maps

## Map Legend

### Sights
- Beach
- Buddhist
- Castle
- Christian
- Hindu
- Islamic
- Jewish
- Monument
- Museum/Gallery
- Ruin
- Winery/Vineyard
- Zoo
- Other Sight

### Eating
- Eating

### Drinking & Nightlife
- Drinking & Nightlife
- Cafe

### Entertainment
- Entertainment

### Shopping
- Shopping

### Sleeping
- Sleeping
- Camping

### Sports & Activities
- Diving/Snorkelling
- Canoeing/Kayaking
- Skiing
- Surfing
- Swimming/Pool
- Walking
- Windsurfing
- Other Sports & Activities

### Information
- Post Office
- Tourist Information

### Transport
- Airport
- Border Crossing
- Bus
- Cable Car/ Funicular
- Cycling
- Ferry
- Metro
- Monorail
- Parking
- S-Bahn
- Taxi
- Train/Railway
- Tram
- Tube Station
- U-Bahn
- Other Transport

### Routes
- Tollway
- Freeway
- Primary
- Secondary
- Tertiary
- Lane
- Unsealed Road
- Plaza/Mall
- Steps
- Tunnel
- Pedestrian Overpass
- Walking Tour
- Walking Tour Detour
- Path

### Boundaries
- International
- State/Province
- Disputed
- Regional/Suburb
- Marine Park
- Cliff
- Wall

### Geographic
- Hut/Shelter
- Lighthouse
- Lookout
- Mountain/Volcano
- Oasis
- Park
- Pass
- Picnic Area
- Waterfall

### Hydrography
- River/Creek
- Intermittent River
- Swamp/Mangrove
- Reef
- Canal
- Water
- Dry/Salt/ Intermittent Lake
- Glacier

### Areas
- Beach/Desert
- Cemetery (Christian)
- Cemetery (Other)
- Park/Forest
- Sportsground
- Sight (Building)
- Top Sight (Building)

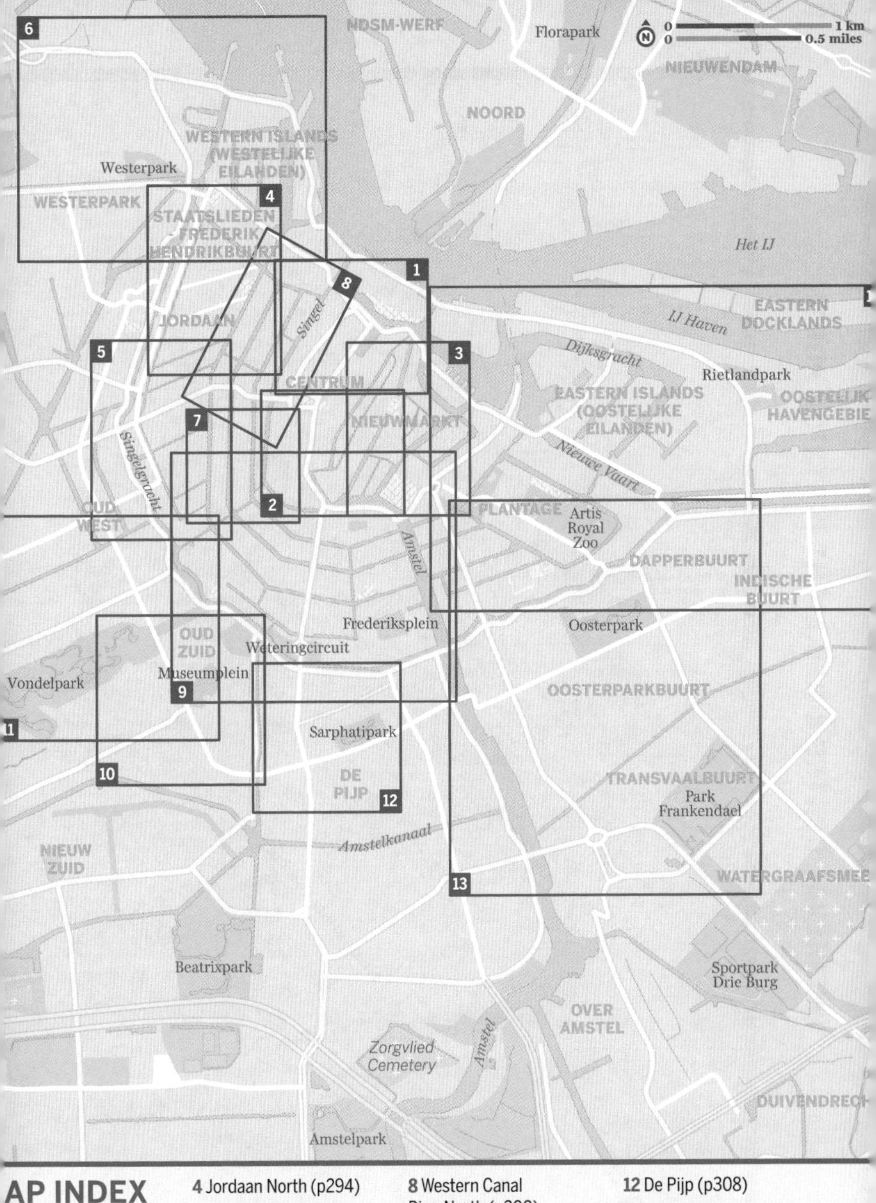

NDSM-WERF
Florapark
0 1 km
0 0.5 miles
NIEUWENDAM
NOORD
WESTERN ISLANDS (WESTELIJKE EILANDEN)
Westerpark
WESTERPARK
STAATSLIEDEN - FREDERIK HENDRIKBUURT
Het IJ
Singel
JORDAAN
IJ Haven
EASTERN DOCKLANDS
Dijksgracht
Rietlandpark
CENTRUM
EASTERN ISLANDS (OOSTELIJKE EILANDEN)
OOSTELIJK HAVENGEBIE
NIEUWMARKT
Singelgracht
Nieuwe Vaart
OUD WEST
PLANTAGE
Artis Royal Zoo
Amstel
DAPPERBUURT
INDISCHE BUURT
Frederiksplein
Oosterpark
OUD ZUID
Weteringcircuit
Vondelpark
Museumplein
OOSTERPARKBUURT
Sarphatipark
DE PIJP
TRANSVAALBUURT
Park Frankendael
Amstelkanaal
NIEUW ZUID
WATERGRAAFSMEE
Beatrixpark
Sportpark Drie Burg
OVER AMSTEL
Amstel
Zorgvlied Cemetery
DUIVENDRECH
Amstelpark


## AP INDEX

Key on p288

See map p298
See map p294
See map p300
See map p290
Haarlemmer Houttuinen
Haarlemmerstr
Buiten Brouwersstr
Herenmarkt
Binnen Vissersstr
Droogbak
Brouwersgracht
Keizersgr
Panaalst
Gouwenaarsst
Roommolenstr
Singel
Smakst
Engelsest
Nieuwendijk
Stromarkt
Herengr
Herengracht
Langestr
Koggestr
Teerketelsteeg
Spuistr
Korsjespoortsteeg
Nieuwezijdsarmst
Korte Kolkst
Oude Nieuwstr
Nieuwezijds Voorburgwal
Sint Jacobsstr
Nieuwezijds Kolk
Kolkst
Oude Brugst
Yellow Bike
Lijnbaansst
D van Hasseltsst
Mandenmakersst
Recycled Bicycles
Suikerbakkersst
Bergstr
Nieuwe Nieuwstr
Onze Lieve Vrouwest
St Geertruidenst
Mosterdpotst
St Nicolaasstr
Torensluis
't Hot
Beurspassage
Torenst
Molst
Gravenstr
Beursplein
Zoutst
Nieuwe Kerk
Eggertst
Damrak
Damrakst
Papenbrugst
Valkenst
CENTRUM
Mozes en Aäronstr

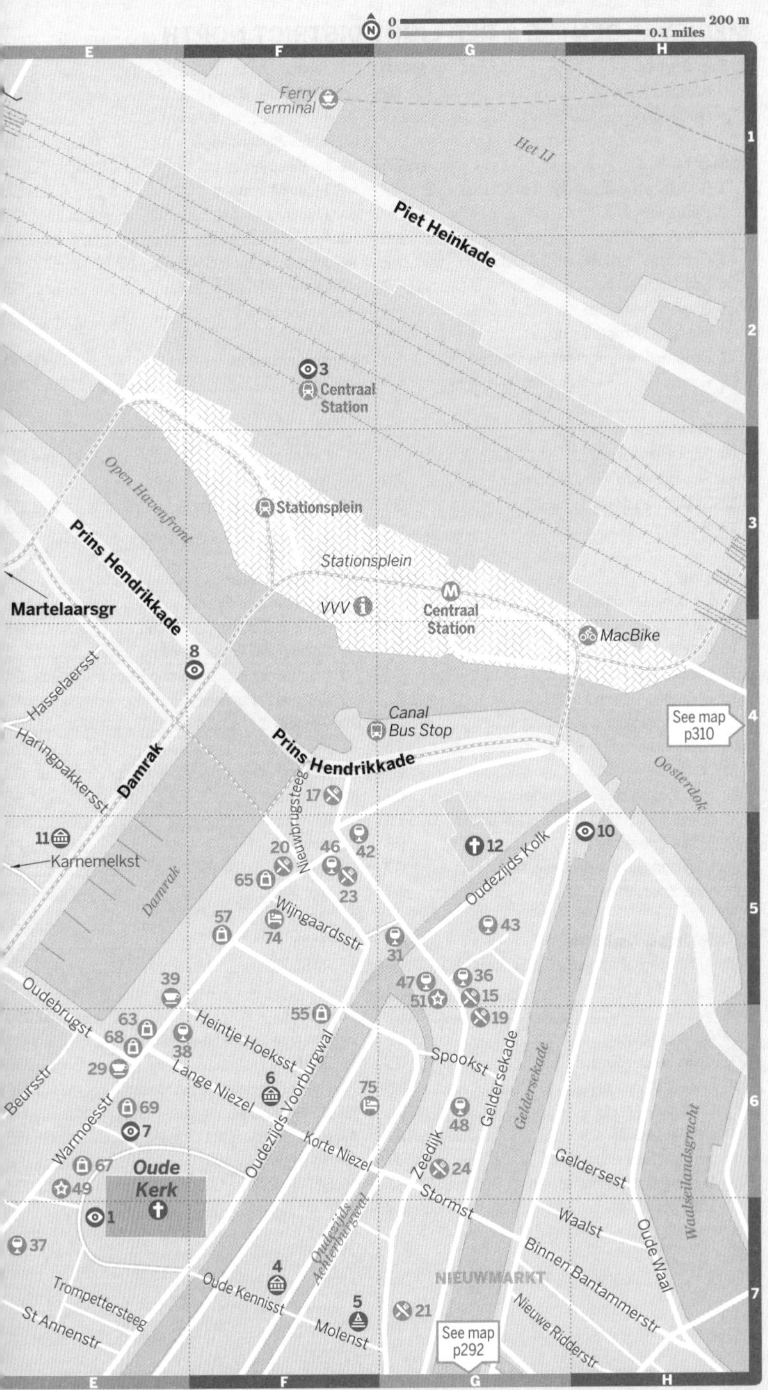

0 200 m
0 0.1 miles
E F G H
1 2 3 4 5 6 7
Ferry Terminal
Het IJ
Piet Heinkade
3
Centraal Station
Open Havenfront
Stationsplein
Stationsplein
VVV
Centraal Station
MacBike
Prins Hendrikkade
Martelaarsgr
8
Hasselaersst
Haringpakkersst
Damrak
Canal Bus Stop
See map p310
Prins Hendrikkade
Oosterdok
Nieuwbrugsteeg
17
11
Karnemelkst
20
46
42
12
10
Oudezijds Kolk
65
23
Damrak
57
Wijngaardsstr
74
31
43
39
47
36
51
15
Oudebrugst
55
19
63
68
Heintje Hoeksst
38
29
Lange Niezel
6
Oudezijds Voorburgwal
Spookst
Geldersekade
Geldersekade
Beursstr
75
69
48
7
Warmoesstr
Korte Niezel
Zeedijk
24
Geldersest
67
Oude Kerk
49
Waalseilandsgracht
Stormst
1
Oudezijds Achterburgwal
Waalst
Oude Waal
37
Binnen Bantammerstr
NIEUWMARKT
4
Trompettersteeg
Oude Kennisst
5
21
Nieuwe Ridderstr
Molenst
St Annenstr
See map p292

## MEDIEVAL CENTRE & RED LIGHT DISTRICT NORTH *Map on p286*

**Top Sights (p60)**

Nieuwe Kerk ... B7
Oude Kerk ... E7

**Sights (p63)**

1 Belle Statue & Golden Torso ... E7
2 Beurs van Berlage ... D6
3 Centraal Station ... F2
4 Erotic Museum ... F7
5 Guan Yin Shrine ... F7
6 Museum Amstelkring ... F6
7 Prostitution Information Centre ... E6
8 Randy Roy's Redlight Tours meeting point ... F4
9 Ronde Lutherse Kerk ... C3
10 Schreierstoren ... H5
11 Sexmuseum Amsterdam ... E5
12 St Nicolaaskerk ... G5
13 W139 ... D7

**Eating (p71)**

14 De Bakkerswinkel ... D7
15 De Bakkerswinkel ... G5
16 De Keuken van 1870 ... C4
17 Dwaze Zaken ... F4
18 Gebr Niemeijer ... D3
19 Hofje van Wijs ... G6
20 Kam Yin ... F5
21 Nam Kee ... G7
22 Rob Wigboldus Vishandel ... C7
23 'Skek ... F5
24 Thais Snackbar Bird ... G6
25 Van den Berg's Broodjesbar ... C7
26 Villa Zeezicht ... A7

**Drinking & Nightlife (p75)**

27 Akhnaton ... C5
28 B van B Café ... D6
29 Baba ... E6
30 Cafe Belgique ... C7
31 Café de Barderij ... G5
32 Café van Zuylen ... A6
33 Cuckoo's Nest ... D5
34 De Blauwe Parade ... A7
35 De Drie Fleschjes ... B7
36 De Engel van Amsterdam ... G5
37 Durty Nelly's ... E7
38 Getto ... E6
39 Hill Street Blues ... E5
40 Homegrown Fantasy ... B6
41 In de Wildeman ... D5
42 In 't Aepjen ... F5
43 Molly Malone's ... G5
44 Oporto ... C7
45 Prik ... A6
46 Proeflokaal de Ooievaar ... F5
47 Queen's Head ... G5
48 T Mandje ... G6

**Entertainment (p79)**

49 Argos ... E6
50 Bitterzoet ... C4
51 Casablanca ... G5
Casablanca Variété ... (see 51)
52 Web ... D5
53 Winston Kingdom ... D7

**Shopping (p80)**

54 Bols Le Cellier ... A6
55 Brouwerij de Prael ... F6
56 Chills & Thrills ... D3
57 Coca (Leaf Experience) ... F5
58 Condomerie Het Gulden Vlies ... D7
59 Female & Partners ... A6
60 Geels & Co ... D7
61 Hema ... C6
62 Hempworks ... D3
63 Himalaya ... E6
64 Innerspace ... A6
65 Kokopelli ... F5
66 Mark Raven Grafiek ... B7
McCarthy's ... (see 15)
67 Mr B ... E6
68 Nana ... E6
69 RoB ... E6

**Sleeping (p209)**

70 Aivengo Youth Hostel ... C4
71 Bellevue Hotel ... D3
72 Flying Pig Downtown Hostel ... D4
73 Hotel Brouwer ... B5
74 Hotel Luxer ... F5
75 Hotel the Crown ... F6
76 St Christopher's at the Winston ... D7

## MEDIEVAL CENTRE & RED LIGHT DISTRICT SOUTH *Map on p290*

Key on p289

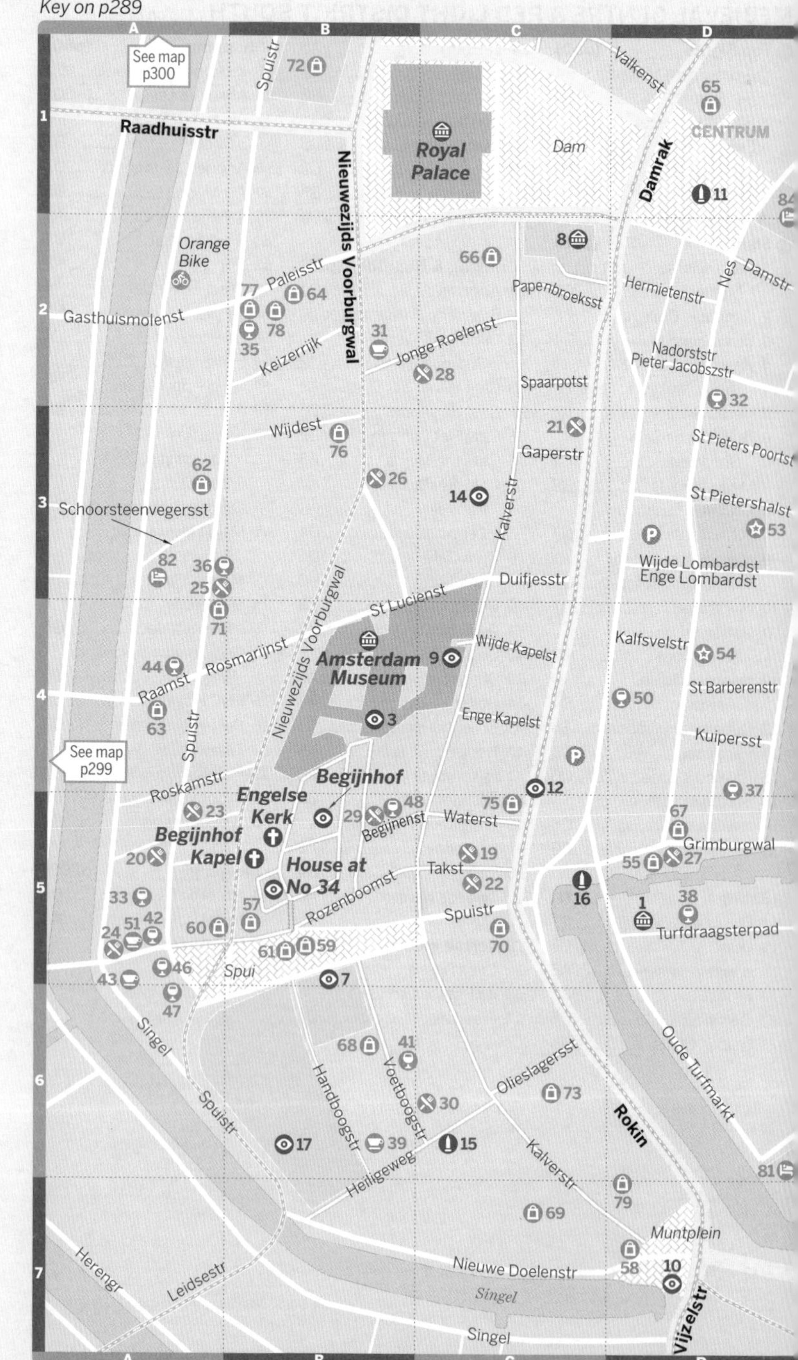

See map p300
See map p299
Raadhuisstr
Spuistr
Royal Palace
Dam
Valkenst
CENTRUM
Damrak
Nieuwezijds Voorburgwal
Orange Bike
Paleisstr
Gasthuismolenst
Keizerrijk
Jonge Roelenst
Papenbroeksst
Hermietenstr
Nes
Damstr
Nadorststr
Pieter Jacobszstr
Spaarpotst
Wijdest
Gaperstr
St Pieters Poortst
Schoorsteenvegersst
Kalverstr
St Pietershalst
Wijde Lombardst
Enge Lombardst
Duifjesstr
St Lucienst
Rosmarijnst
Raamst
Amsterdam Museum
Wijde Kapelst
Kalfsvelstr
St Barberenstr
Enge Kapelst
Kuipersst
Roskamstr
Begijnhof
Engelse Kerk
Begijnhof Kapel
House at No 34
Begijnenst
Waterst
Grimburgwal
Takst
Rozenboomst
Turfdraagsterpad
Spui
Singel
Handboogstr
Voetboogstr
Olieslagersst
Oude Turfmarkt
Rokin
Heiligeweg
Muntplein
Herengr
Leidsestr
Nieuwe Doelenstr
Vijzelstr
MEDIEVAL CENTRE & RED LIGHT DISTRICT SOUTH

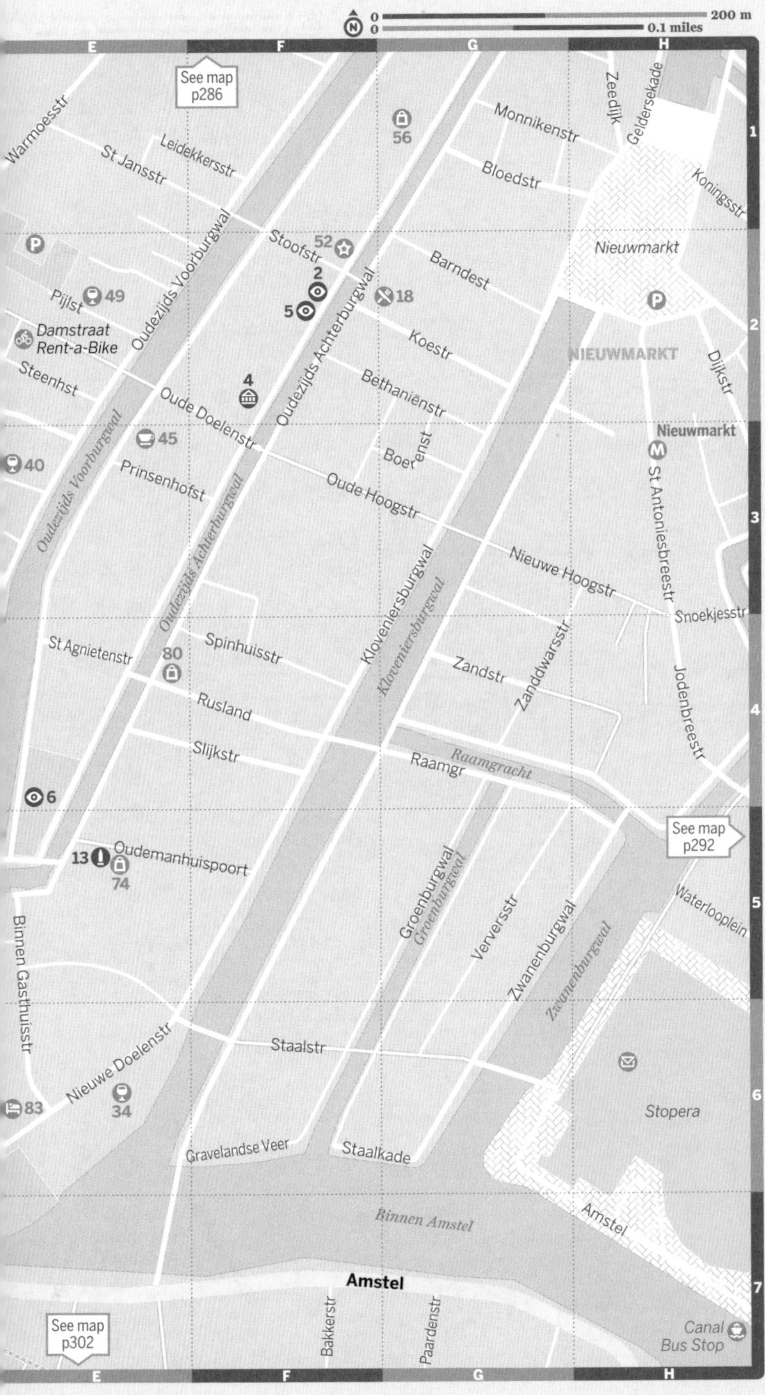

0 200 m
0 0.1 miles
See map p286
Warmoesstr
St Jansstr
Leidekkersstr
Monnikenstr
Bloedstr
Zeedijk
Geldersekade
Koningsstr
Nieuwmarkt
NIEUWMARKT
Stoofstr
Barndest
Pijlst
Damstraat Rent-a-Bike
Steenhst
Oudezijds Voorburgwal
Oudezijds Achterburgwal
Koestr
Bethaniënstr
Dijkstr
Oude Doelenstr
Boerenst
Prinsenhofst
Oude Hoogstr
St Antoniesbreestr
Nieuwe Hoogstr
Snoekjesstr
Kloveniersburgwal
St Agnietenstr
Spinhuisstr
Zandstr
Zanddwarsstr
Jodenbreestr
Rusland
Slijkstr
Raamgr
Raamgracht
See map p292
Oudemanhuispoort
Waterlooplein
Binnen Gasthuisstr
Groenburgwal
Verversstr
Zwanenburgwal
Staalstr
Nieuwe Doelenstr
Stopera
Gravelandse Veer
Staalkade
Binnen Amstel
Amstel
Bakkerstr
Paardenstr
Canal Bus Stop
See map p302

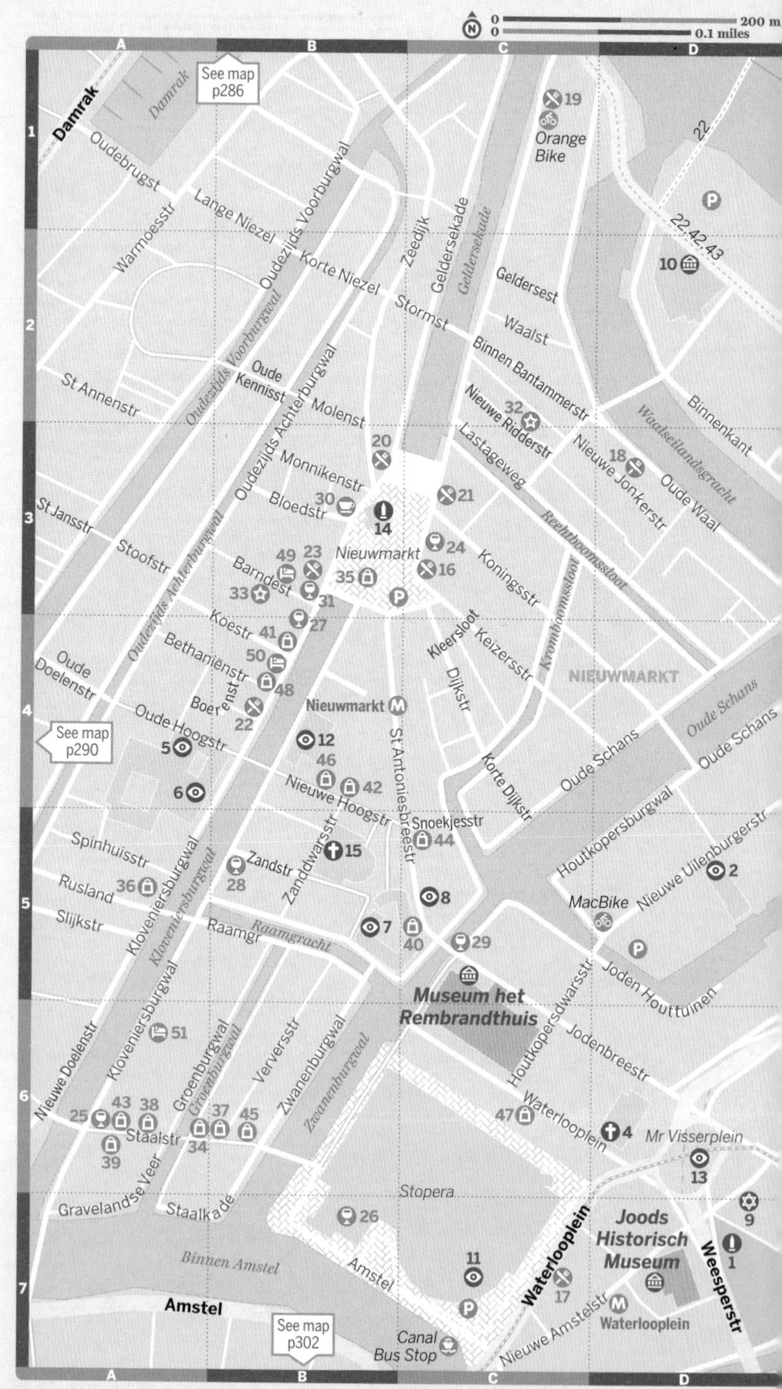

0 200 m
0 0.1 miles
See map p286
See map p290
See map p302
Damrak
Oudebrugst
Warmoesstr
Lange Niezel
Korte Niezel
Oudezijds Voorburgwal
Zeedijk
Geldersekade
Geldersest
Waalst
Stormst
Binnen Bantammerstr
Orange Bike
Oude Kennisst
Molenst
St Annenstr
Oudezijds Achterburgwal
Monnikenstr
Bloedstr
Nieuwe Ridderstr
Lastageweg
Nieuwe Jonkerstr
Oude Waal
Binnenkant
Waalseilandsgracht
Recht Boomssloot
Kromboomssloot
St Jansstr
Stoofstr
Barndest
Nieuwmarkt
Koningsstr
Koestr
Bethaniënstr
Kleersloot
Keizersstr
NIEUWMARKT
Oude Doelenstr
Oude Hoogstr
Nieuwmarkt
Dijkstr
St Antoniesbreestr
Oude Schans
Nieuwe Hoogstr
Korte Dijkstr
Snoekjesstr
Houtkopersburgwal
Nieuwe Uilenburgerstr
Spinhuisstr
Zandstr
Zanddwarsstr
Rusland
Slijkstr
Kloveniersburgwal
Raamgr
Raamgracht
MacBike
Joden Houttuinen
Museum het Rembrandthuis
Houtkopersdwarsstr
Jodenbreestr
Nieuwe Doelenstr
Groenburgwal
Verversstr
Zwanenburgwal
Staalstr
Waterlooplein
Mr Visserplein
Gravelandse Veer
Staalkade
Stopera
Binnen Amstel
Amstel
Joods Historisch Museum
Weesperstr
Nieuwe Amstelstr
Waterlooplein
Canal Bus Stop

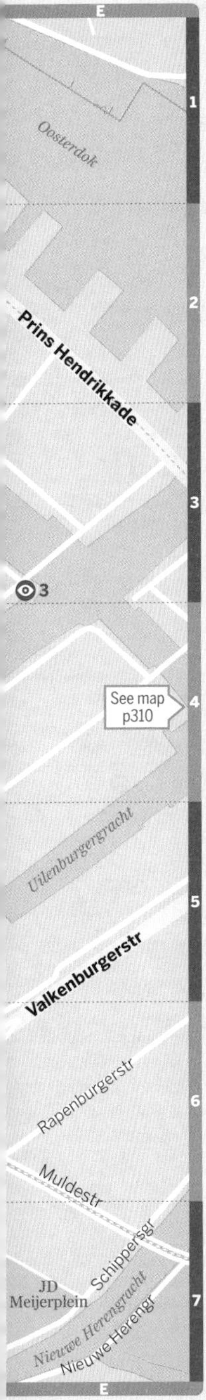

E

1

2

3

4

5

6

7

E

Oosterdok

Prins Hendrikkade

3

See map p310

Uilenburgergracht

Valkenburgerstr

Rapenburgerstr

Muldestr

Schippersgr

JD Meijerplein

Nieuwe Herengracht

Nieuwe Herengr

### Top Sights (p87)

Joods Historisch Museum ... D7
Museum het Rembrandthuis ... C5

### Sights (p88)

1 Dockworker statue ... D7
2 Gassan Diamonds ... D5
Kleine Trippenhuis ... (see 48)
3 Montelbaanstoren ... E3
4 Mozes en Aäronkerk ... D6
5 Narrow House ... A4
6 Oostindisch Huis ... A4
7 Pentagon Housing Estate ... B5
8 Pintohuis ... C5
9 Portuguese-Israelite Synagogue ... D7
10 Scheepvaarthuis ... D2
11 Stopera ... C7
12 Trippenhuis ... B4
13 TunFun ... D6
14 Waag ... B3
Waterlooplein Flea Market ... (see 47)
15 Zuiderkerk ... B5

### Eating (p91)

16 Café Bern ... C3
17 Tokoman ... C7
18 Hemelse Modder ... D3
19 Lastage ... C1
20 Latei ... B3
21 Nam Kee ... C3
22 Nyonya ... B4
23 Toko Joyce ... B3

### Drinking & Nightlife (p92)

24 Café Cuba ... C3
25 Café de Doelen ... A6
26 Café-Restaurant Dantzig ... B7
27 De Bekeerde Suster ... B4
28 De Engelbewaarder ... B5
29 De Sluyswacht ... C5
30 Hill Street Blues ... B3
31 Lokaal 't Loosje ... B3

### Entertainment (p93)

32 Amsterdams Marionetten Theater ... C2
33 Bethaniënklooster ... B3
Muziektheater ... (see 11)

### Shopping (p93)

34 & klevering ... A6
35 Antiques Market ... B3
Boerenmarkt ... (see 35)
36 Book Exchange ... A5
37 De Beestenwinkel ... B6
38 Droog ... A6
39 Filmantiquariaat Cine Qua Non ... A6
40 Henxs ... C5
41 Jacob Hooy & Co ... B4
42 Joe's Vliegerwinkel ... B4
43 Juggle ... A6
44 Knuffels ... C5
45 Puccini Bomboni ... B6
46 't Klompenhuisje ... B4
47 Waterlooplein Flea Market ... C6
48 Webers ... B4

### Sleeping (p210)

49 Christian Youth Hostel 'The Shelter City' ... B3
50 Misc Eat Drink Sleep ... B4
51 Stadsdoelen Youth Hostel ... A6

# JORDAAN NORTH

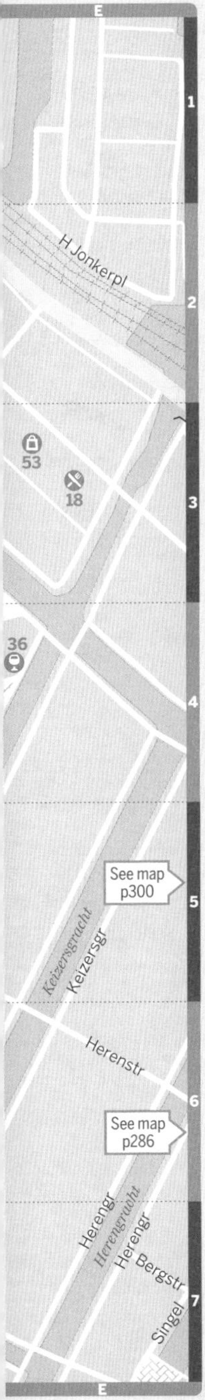

**Sights (p132)**

1 Amsterdam Tulip Museum ........ C6
2 Claes Claeszhofje ........ C6
3 Haarlemmerpoort ........ C1
4 Karthuizerhofje ........ C5
5 Lindenhofje ........ C4
6 Noorderkerk ........ D4
7 Noordermarkt ........ D4
8 Pianola Museum ........ C5
9 Suyckerhofje ........ C4

**Eating (p134)**

10 Bordewijk ........ D4
11 Burger's Patio ........ B6
12 Cinema Paradiso ........ B5
13 De Bolhoed ........ D5
14 De Pizza Bakkers ........ D2
15 Duende ........ D4
16 Hostaria ........ B6
17 Japanese Pancake World ........ B6
18 Jordino ........ E3
19 Koevoet ........ C4
20 La Oliva ........ C6
21 Small World Catering ........ D2
22 Toscanini ........ D4
23 Winkel ........ D5

**Drinking & Nightlife (p140)**

24 Café P 96 ........ C6
25 Café 't Monumentje ........ C5
26 Café 't Smalle ........ C6
27 Café Thijssen ........ D3
28 De Blaffende Vis ........ C5
29 De Prins ........ C7
30 De Reiger ........ C7
31 De Tuin ........ B6
32 De Twee Zwaantjes ........ C6
33 di'Vino Wijnbar ........ C5
34 Finch ........ D4
35 Het Papeneiland ........ D4
36 Proust ........ E4
37 Vesper Bar ........ D3

**Entertainment (p142)**

38 Movies ........ C1

**Shopping (p143)**

Boerenmarkt ........ (see 7)
39 Boutique Petticoat ........ C4
40 Callas 43 ........ D3
41 Cellarrich ........ D2
42 Discostars ........ D2
43 Het Oud-Hollandsch Snoepwinkeltje ........ B6
44 Lab 13 ........ C1
45 Lindengracht Market ........ C4
46 Mechanisch Speelgoed ........ C5
47 Moooi Gallery ........ B5
Noordermarkt ........ (see 7)
48 Nou Moe Stripwinkel ........ D4
49 Ook ........ C1
50 Op de Dijk ........ D2
51 Rock Archive ........ C6
52 Roode Bioscoop ........ C1
53 't Zonnetje ........ E3
54 Westermarkt ........ B5
55 Your Cup of T ........ D5

**Sleeping (p214)**

56 All Inn the Family B&B ........ B6
57 Hotel Acacia ........ B4

See map p300

See map p286

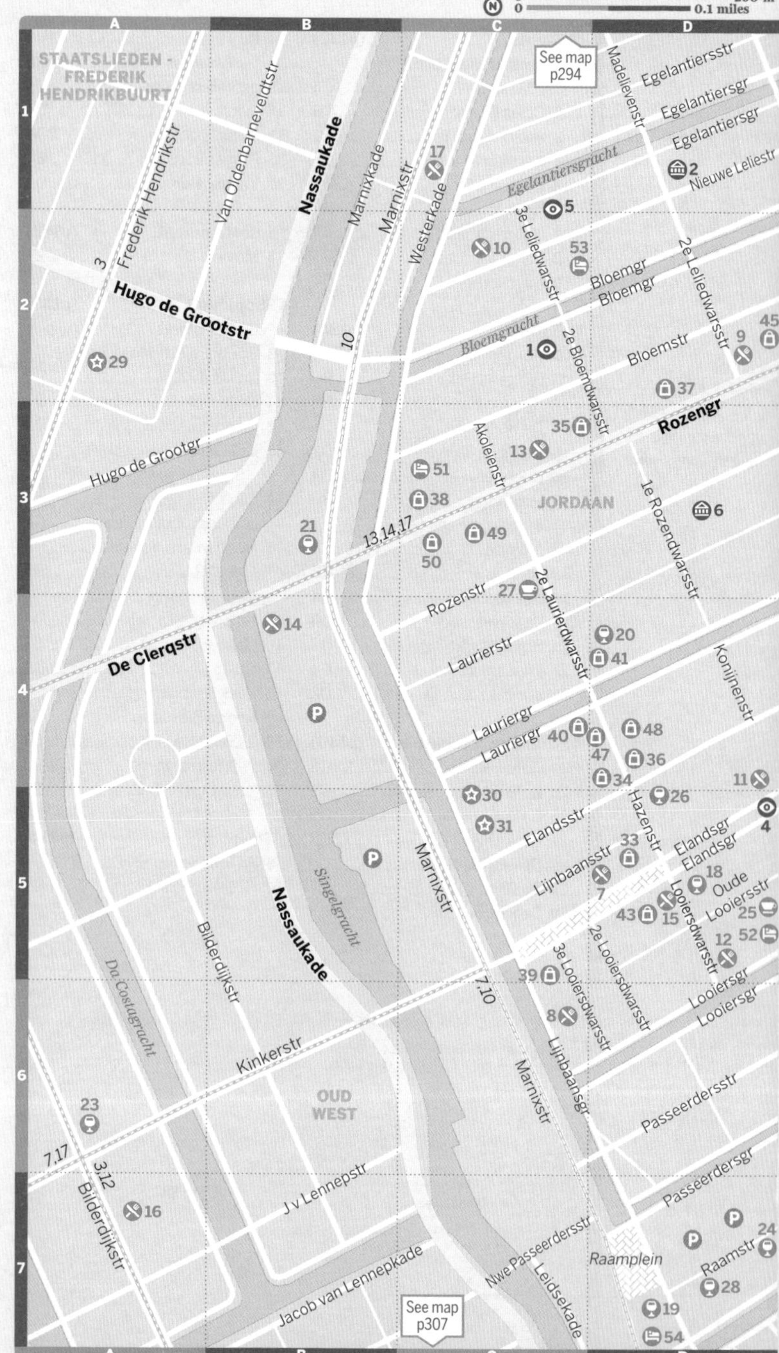

0 200 m
0 0.1 miles
See map p294
See map p307
STAATSLIEDEN - FREDERIK HENDRIKBUURT
JORDAAN
OUD WEST
Frederik Hendrikstr
Van Oldenbarneveldtstr
Nassaukade
Marnixkade
Marnixstr
Westerkade
Hugo de Grootstr
Hugo de Grootgr
De Clerqstr
Madelievenstr
Egelantiersstr
Egelantiersgr
Egelantiersgracht
Nieuwe Leliestr
3e Leliedwarsstr
2e Leliedwarsstr
Bloemgr
Bloemgracht
2e Bloemdwarsstr
Bloemstr
Rozengr
Akoleienstr
1e Rozendwarsstr
Rozenstr
2e Laurierdwarsstr
Lauriergr
Laurierstr
Konijnenstr
Elandsstr
Elandsgr
Lijnbaansstr
Hazenstr
Oude Looiersstr
Looiersdwarsstr
2e Looiersdwarsstr
3e Looiersdwarsstr
Looiersgr
Singelgracht
Bilderdijkstr
Da Costagracht
Kinkerstr
Lijnbaansgr
Passeerdersstr
Passeerdersgr
J v Lennepstr
Jacob van Lennepkade
Nwe Passeerdersstr
Leidsekade
Raamplein
Raamstr

E
1
2
3
4
5
6
7
Prinsengr
44
42
See map p300
Westermarkt
Raadhuisstr
32
Prinsengr
Keizersgr
Reestr
Prinsengracht
46
Berenstr
3
See map p299
Runstr
Prinsengr
Keizersgr
Keizersgracht
Molenpad
Leidsegr
Kerkstr
22
Prinsengr
E

### Sights (p132)

1 De Drie Hendricken ............ C2
2 Electric Lady Land ............ D1
3 Houseboat Museum ............ E5
4 Johnny Jordaanplein ............ D5
5 St Andrieshofje ............ C1
6 Stedelijk Museum Bureau Amsterdam ............ D3

### Eating (p134)

7 Balthazar's Keuken ............ D5
8 Brasserie Blazer ............ C6
9 Broodje Mokum ............ D2
10 De Vliegende Schotel ............ C2
11 Divan ............ D4
12 Festina Lente ............ D5
13 Manzano ............ C3
14 Moeders ............ B4
15 Pazzi ............ D5
16 Riaz ............ A7
17 Semhar ............ C1

### Drinking & Nightlife (p140)

18 Café de Jordaan ............ D5
19 Café de Koe ............ D7
20 Café de Laurierboom ............ D4
21 Café Soundgarden ............ B3
22 De Pieper ............ E7
23 De Trut ............ A6
24 G-Spot ............ D7
25 La Tertulia ............ D5
26 Saarein ............ D5
27 Sanementereng ............ C3
28 Thermos Day Sauna ............ D7

### Entertainment (p142)

29 De Nieuwe Anita ............ A2
30 Korsakoff ............ C5
31 Maloe Melo ............ C5

### Shopping (p143)

32 A Space Oddity ............ E3
33 Arnold Cornelis ............ D5
34 brown clothes ............ D4
35 Broer & Zus ............ C3
36 Chocolatl ............ D4
37 Christodoulou & Lamé ............ D2
38 De Kasstoor ............ C3
39 De Looier Antiques Market ............ C5
40 English Bookshop ............ C4
41 Eva Damave ............ D4
42 Galleria d'Arte Rinascimento ............ E2
43 Jefferson Hotel ............ D5
44 Josine Bokhoven ............ E2
45 Kitsch Kitchen ............ D2
46 La Savonnerie ............ E4
47 Olivaria ............ D4
48 Petsalon ............ D4
49 SPRMRKT ............ C3
50 Wonen 2000 ............ C3

### Sleeping (p214)

51 Christian Youth Hostel 'The Shelter Jordaan' ............ C3
52 Hotel Amsterdam Wiechmann ............ D5
53 Hotel van Onna ............ C2
54 International Budget Hostel ............ D7

# WESTERPARK & WESTERGASFABRIEK

**Sights** (p134)
- 1 Drieharingenbrug ... D3
- 2 Museum Het Schip ... B2
- Westergasfabriek ... (see 14)
- 3 Westerpark ... C3
- 4 Zandhoek ... E3

**Eating** (p139)
- 5 Marius ... D2
- 6 Raïnaraï ... A3
- 7 Restaurant PS ... D3

**Drinking & Nightlife** (p142)
- 8 Jet Lounge ... B4
- 9 Media Café ... B3
- 10 Westergasterras ... B3

**Entertainment** (p142)
- 11 Filmhuis Cavia ... A4
- 12 Het Ketelhuis ... B3
- 13 Pacific Parc ... B3
- 14 Westergasfabriek ... B3

**Shopping** (p143)
- 15 De Kunstfabriek ... B3

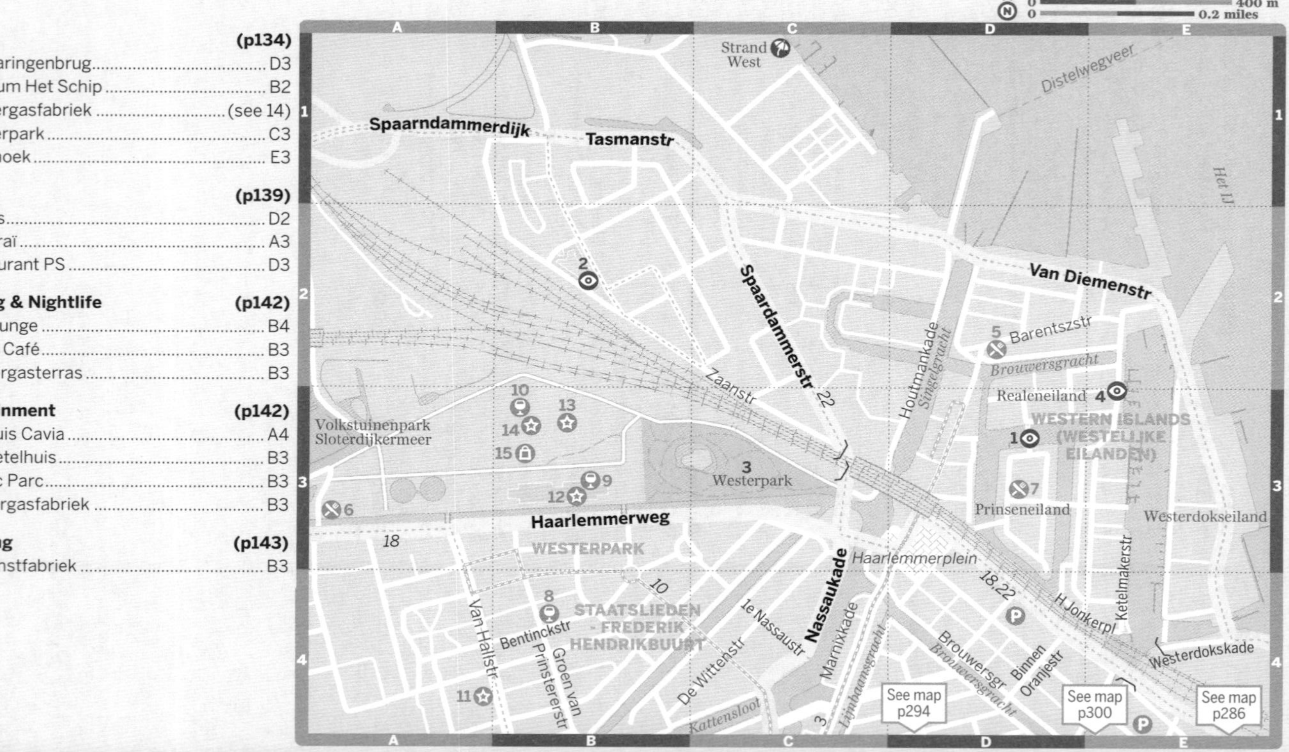

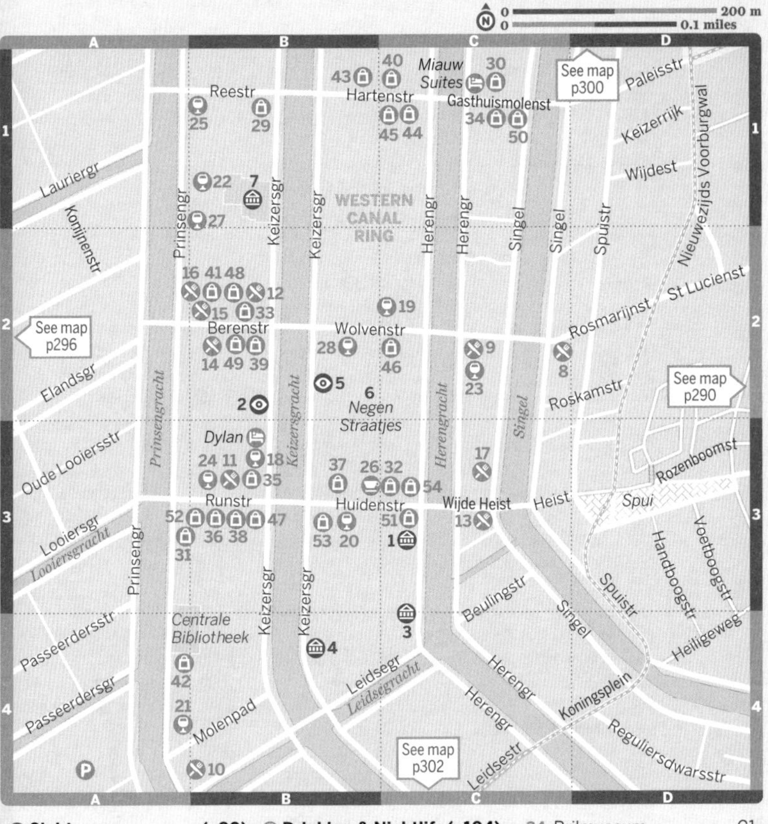


**Sights (p99)**
1 Bijbels Museum ............ C3
2 Felix Meritis Building ............ B2
3 Het Grachtenhuis ............ C4
4 Huis Marseille ............ B4
5 Keizersgracht 319 ............ B2
6 Negen Straatjes ............ B2
7 Netherlands Media Art Institute ............ B1

**Eating (p102)**
8 Broodje Bert ............ C2
9 Buffet van Odette ............ C2
10 Casa Perú ............ B4
11 Cilubang ............ B3
12 De Struisvogel ............ B2
13 Lef ............ C3
14 Lunchcafe Nielsen ............ B2
15 Mokka ............ B2
16 Pancakes! ............ B2
17 Singel 404 ............ C3

**Drinking & Nightlife (p104)**
18 Bar Barbou ............ B3
19 Brix Food 'n' Drinx ............ C2
20 Café de Pels ............ B3
21 Café Het Molenpad ............ A4
22 Café Restaurant van Puffelen ............ B1
23 De Admiraal ............ C2
24 De Doffer ............ B3
25 Koffiehuis 'De Hoek' ............ B1
26 Pâtisserie Pompadour ............ B3
27 Vyne ............ B1
28 Wolvenstraat 23 ............ B2

**Shopping (p106)**
29 Amsterdam Watch Company ............ B1
30 Antonia by Yvette ............ C1
31 Bakkerij Annee ............ A3
32 Beadies ............ C3
33 Boekie Woekie ............ B2
34 Brilmuseum ............ C1
35 Darling ............ B3
36 De Kaaskamer ............ B3
37 De Spiegelbeeld ............ B3
38 De Witte Tanden Winkel ............ B3
39 Episode ............ B2
40 Exota ............ C1
41 Fashion Flairs ............ B2
42 Frozen Fountain ............ A4
43 Gamekeeper ............ B1
44 Hester van Eeghen ............ C1
45 Lady Day ............ C1
46 Laura Dols ............ C2
47 Local Service ............ B3
48 Marlies Dekkers ............ B2
49 Mendo ............ B2
50 Nic Nic ............ C1
51 Scotch & Soda ............ C3
52 Skins Cosmetics ............ B3
53 Van Ravenstein ............ B3
54 Zipper ............ C3

Key on p301

# WESTERN CANAL RING NORTH

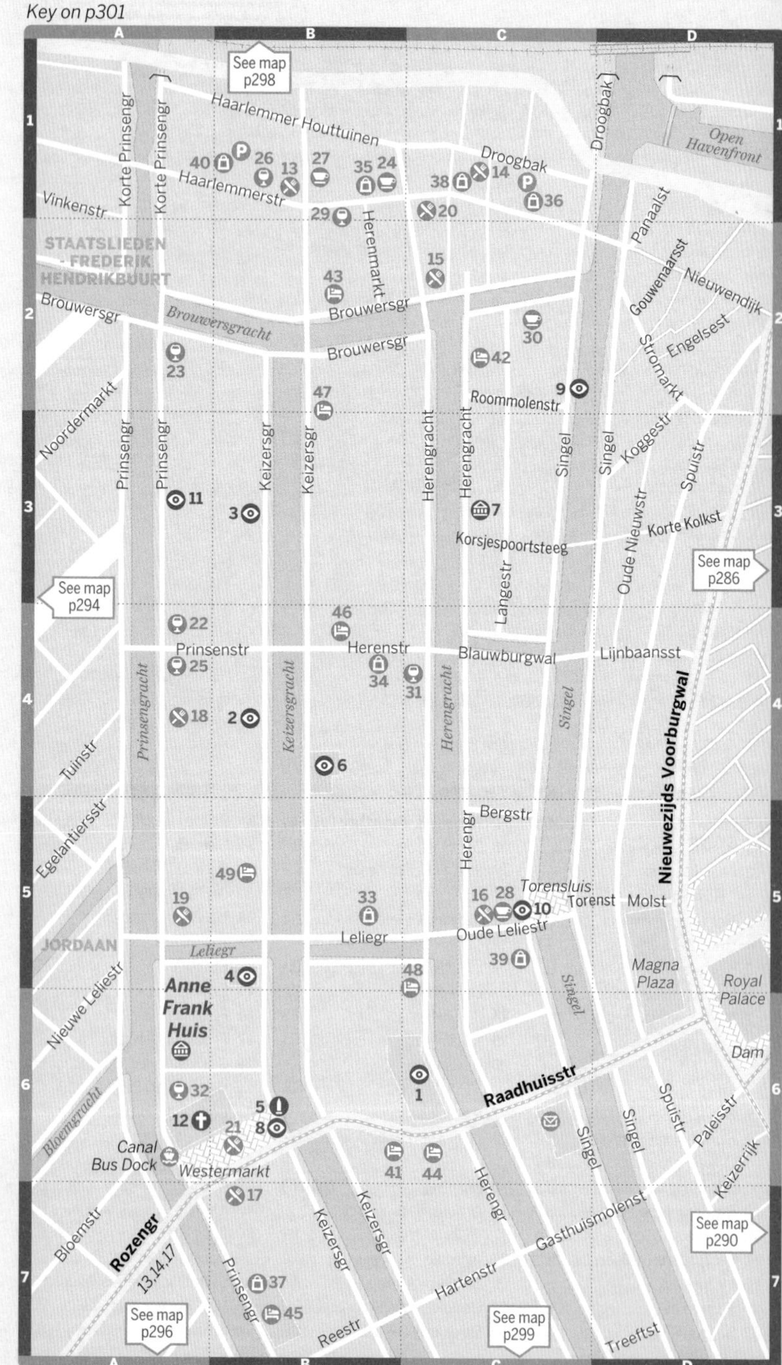

## WESTERN CANAL RING NORTH *Map on p300*

Key on p304

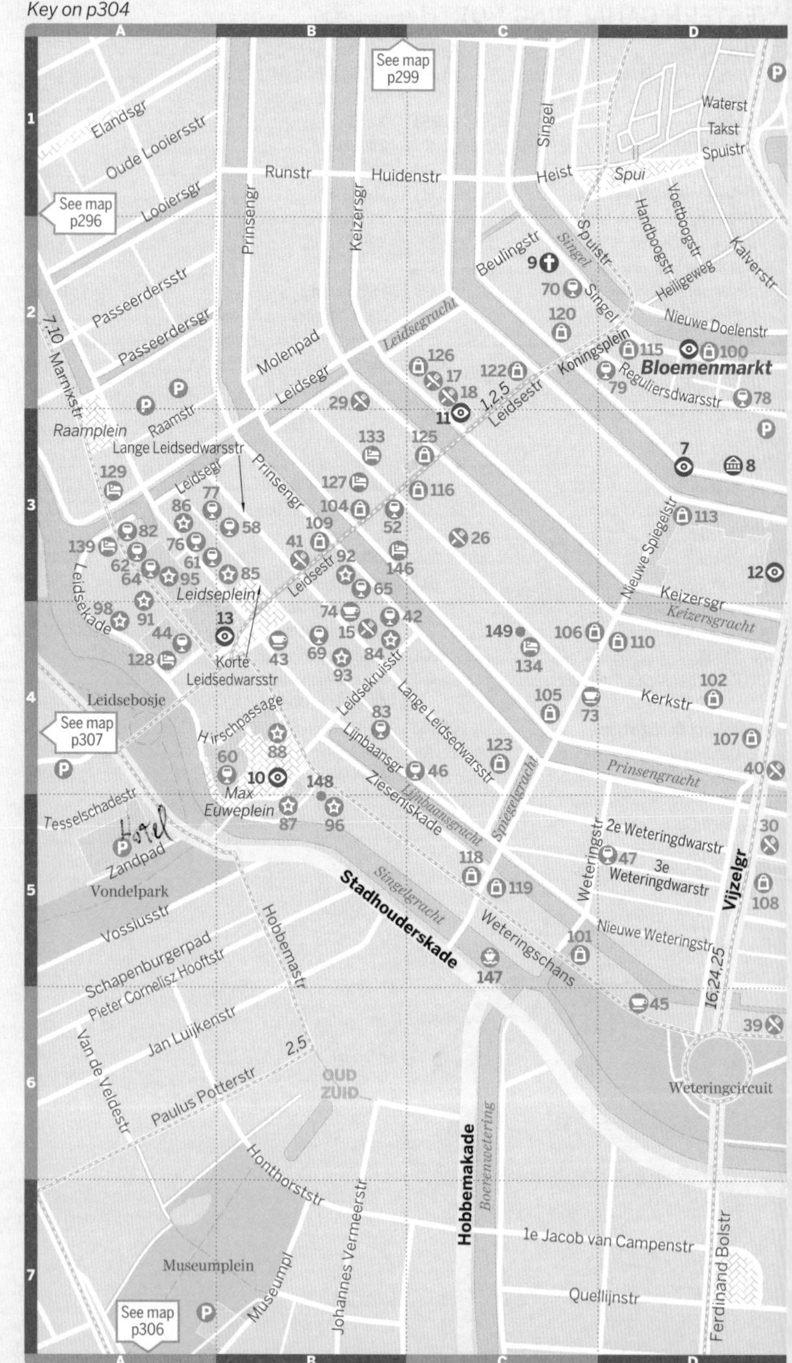

See map p299
See map p296
See map p307
See map p306
Elandsgr
Oude Looiersstr
Looiersgr
Runstr
Huidenstr
Prinsengr
Keizersgr
Singel
Heist
Spui
Waterst
Takst
Spuistr
Handboogstr
Voetboogstr
Kalverstr
Heiligeweg
Beulingstr
Nieuwe Doelenstr
Koningsplein
Bloemenmarkt
Reguliersdwarsstr
Leidsegracht
Leidsestr
Passeerdersstr
Passeerdersgr
Marnixstr
Molenpad
Leidsegr
Raamplein
Raamstr
Lange Leidsedwarsstr
Leidseplein
Leidsekade
Korte Leidsedwarsstr
Leidsebosje
Hirschpassage
Max Euweplein
Leidsekruisstr
Lijnbaansgr
Lijnbaansgracht
Zieseniskade
Spiegelgracht
Nieuwe Spiegelstr
Keizersgracht
Kerkstr
Prinsengracht
Tesselschadestr
Zandpad
Vondelpark
Vossiusstr
Schapenburgerpad
Pieter Cornelisz Hooftstr
Hobbemastr
Stadhouderskade
Singelgracht
Weteringschans
Weteringstr
2e Weteringdwarstr
3e Weteringdwarstr
Nieuwe Weteringstr
Vijzelgr
Weteringcircuit
Jan Luijkenstr
Van de Veldestr
Paulus Potterstr
OUD ZUID
Hobbemakade
Boerenwetering
Honthorststr
Johannes Vermeerstr
Museumpl
Museumplein
1e Jacob van Campenstr
Quellijnstr
Ferdinand Bolstr

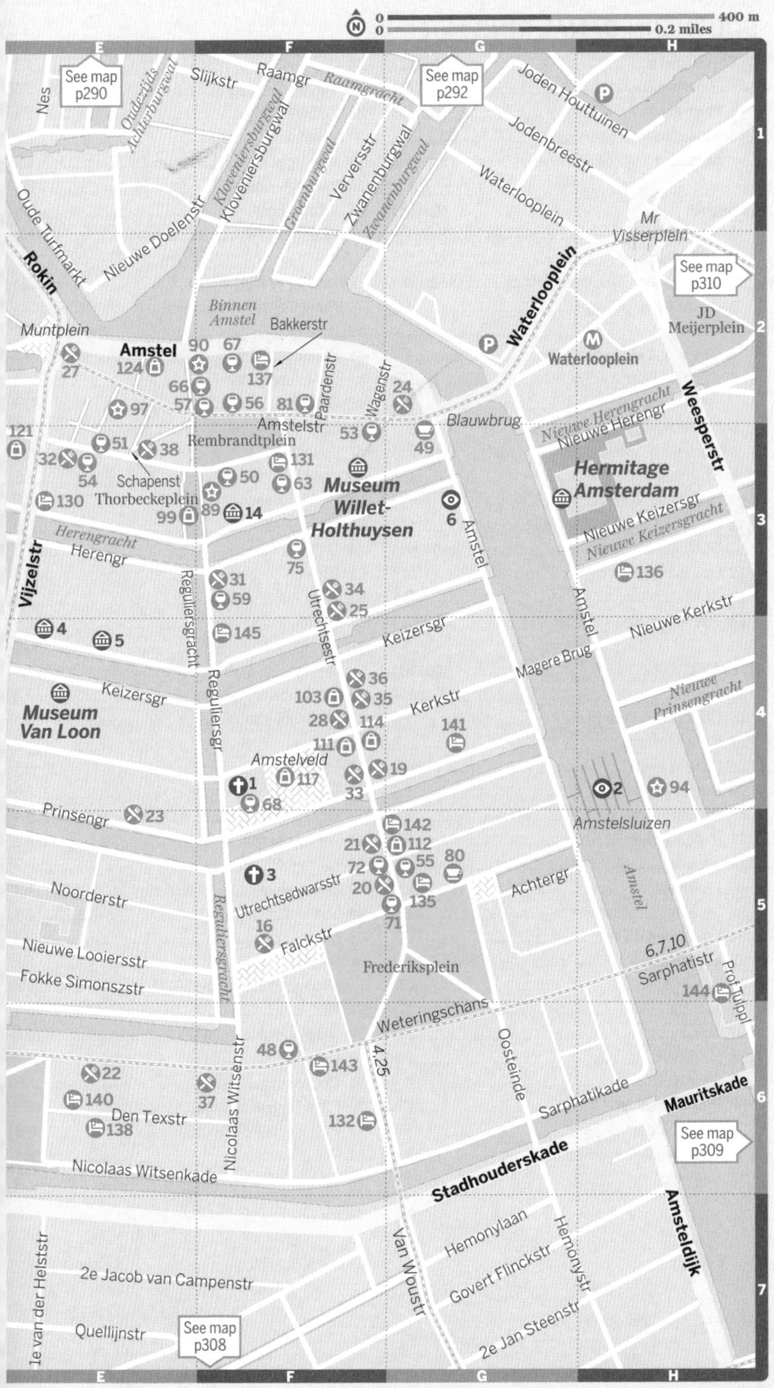
See map p290
See map p292
See map p310
See map p309
See map p308
Nes
Oudezijds Achterburgwal
Slijkstr
Raamgr
Raamgracht
Joden Houttuinen
Jodenbreestr
Waterlooplein
Kloveniersburgwal
Groenburgwal
Verversstr
Zwanenburgwal
Oude Turfmarkt
Rokin
Nieuwe Doelenstr
Mr Visserplein
Binnen Amstel
Bakkerstr
Muntplein
Amstel
Waterlooplein
JD Meijerplein
Paardenstr
Wagenstr
Amstelstr
Rembrandtplein
Blauwbrug
Nieuwe Herengracht
Nieuwe Herengr
Weesperstr
Schapenst
Thorbeckeplein
Museum Willet-Holthuysen
Hermitage Amsterdam
Nieuwe Keizersgr
Nieuwe Keizersgracht
Herengracht
Herengr
Vijzelstr
Reguliersgracht
Utrechtsestr
Keizersgr
Nieuwe Kerkstr
Magere Brug
Reguliersgr
Museum Van Loon
Kerkstr
Nieuwe Prinsengracht
Amstelveld
Prinsengr
Amstelsluizen
Noorderstr
Utrechtsedwarsstr
Achtergr
Falckstr
Nieuwe Looiersstr
Fokke Simonszstr
Frederiksplein
Sarphatistr
Prof Tulppl
Weteringschans
Oosteinde
Nicolaas Witsenstr
Den Texstr
Sarphatikade
Mauritskade
Stadhouderskade
Nicolaas Witsenkade
Amsteldijk
Hemonylaan
Hemonystr
Van Woustr
Govert Flinckstr
2e Jacob van Campenstr
1e van der Helststr
Quellijnstr
2e Jan Steenstr
400 m
0.2 miles

## SOUTHERN CANAL RING *Map on p302*

**Entertainment** **(p126)**



**Shopping** **(p127)**



**Sleeping** **(p211)**



**Transport**

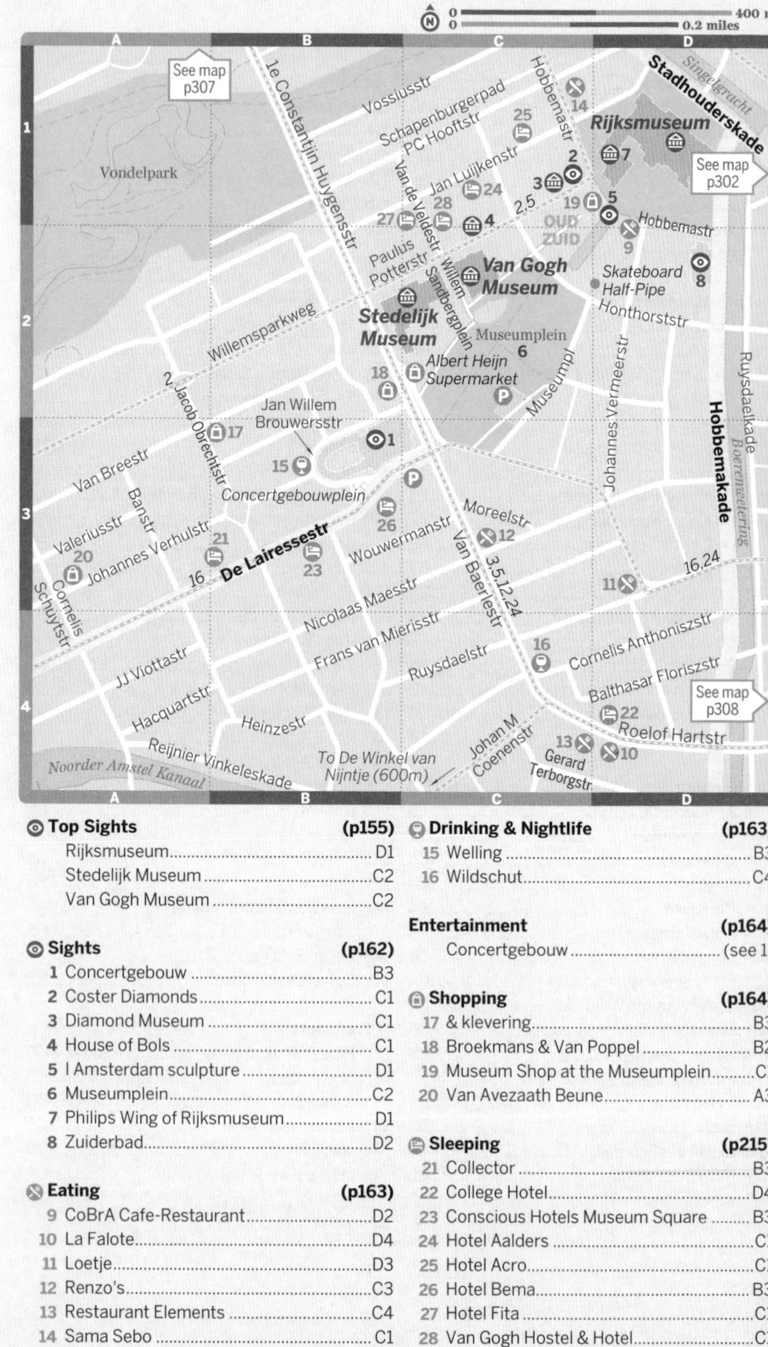


**Top Sights** (p155)
- Rijksmuseum ... D1
- Stedelijk Museum ... C2
- Van Gogh Museum ... C2

**Sights** (p162)
- 1 Concertgebouw ... B3
- 2 Coster Diamonds ... C1
- 3 Diamond Museum ... C1
- 4 House of Bols ... C1
- 5 I Amsterdam sculpture ... D1
- 6 Museumplein ... C2
- 7 Philips Wing of Rijksmuseum ... D1
- 8 Zuiderbad ... D2

**Eating** (p163)
- 9 CoBrA Cafe-Restaurant ... D2
- 10 La Falote ... D4
- 11 Loetje ... D3
- 12 Renzo's ... C3
- 13 Restaurant Elements ... C4
- 14 Sama Sebo ... C1

**Drinking & Nightlife** (p163)
- 15 Welling ... B3
- 16 Wildschut ... C4

**Entertainment** (p164)
- Concertgebouw ... (see 1)

**Shopping** (p164)
- 17 & klevering ... B3
- 18 Broekmans & Van Poppel ... B2
- 19 Museum Shop at the Museumplein ... C1
- 20 Van Avezaath Beune ... A3

**Sleeping** (p215)
- 21 Collector ... B3
- 22 College Hotel ... D4
- 23 Conscious Hotels Museum Square ... B3
- 24 Hotel Aalders ... C1
- 25 Hotel Acro ... C1
- 26 Hotel Bema ... B3
- 27 Hotel Fita ... C1
- 28 Van Gogh Hostel & Hotel ... C1

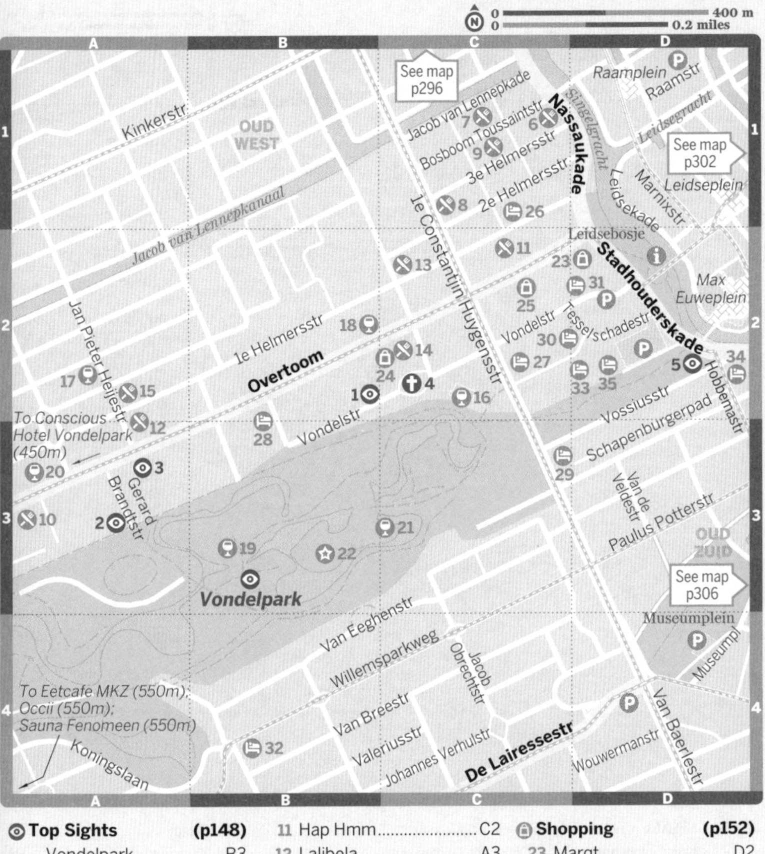


**Top Sights** (p148)
- Vondelpark ........ B3

**Sights** (p149)
- 1 Hollandsche Manege ........ B2
- 2 Orgelpark ........ A3
- 3 OT301 ........ A3
- 4 Vondelkerk ........ C2
- 5 Vondelpark Main Entrance ........ D2

**Eating** (p149)
- 6 Blue Pepper ........ C1
- 7 Café Touissant ........ C1
- 8 Café Westers ........ C1
- 9 De Italiaan ........ C1
- De Peper ........ (see 3)
- 10 Fondue & Fondue ........ A3
- 11 Hap Hmm ........ C2
- 12 Lalibela ........ A3
- 13 Lunchroom Wilhelmina ........ C2
- 14 Overtoom Groente en Fruit ........ C2
- 15 Paloma Blanca ........ A2

**Drinking & Nightlife** (p151)
- 16 Café Vertigo ........ C2
- 17 Golden Brown Bar ........ A2
- 18 Gollem's Proeflokaal ........ B2
- 19 Het Groot Melkhuis ........ B3
- 20 Parck ........ A3
- 21 't Blauwe Theehuis ........ C3

**Entertainment** (p152)
- 22 Openluchttheater ........ B3

**Shopping** (p152)
- 23 Marqt ........ D2
- 24 Pied à Terre ........ C2
- 25 Women's Outdoor World ........ C2

**Sleeping** (p214)
- 26 Flynt B&B ........ C1
- 27 Fusion Suites ........ C2
- 28 Hotel de Filosoof ........ B3
- 29 Hotel Piet Hein ........ C3
- 30 Hotel Roemer ........ C2
- 31 Hotel Vondel ........ D2
- 32 Hotel Zandbergen ........ B4
- 33 Owl Hotel ........ D2
- 34 Park Hotel ........ D2
- 35 Stayokay Amsterdam Vondelpark ........ D2

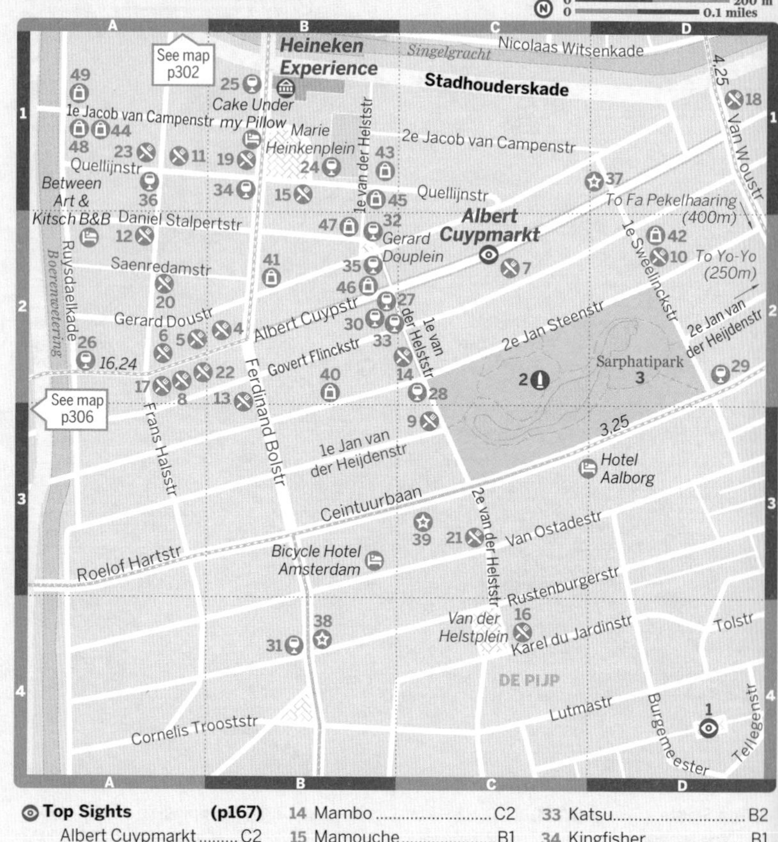


**Top Sights** (p167)
- Albert Cuypmarkt ........ C2
- Heineken Experience ..... B1

**Sights** (p167)
- 1 De Dageraad ........ D4
- 2 Sarphati Memorial ........ C2
- 3 Sarphatipark ........ D2

**Eating** (p167)
- 4 Albina ........ B2
- 5 Bakken Met Passie ........ A2
- 6 Balti House ........ A2
- 7 Bazar Amsterdam ........ C2
- 8 Burgermeester ........ A2
- 9 Café Volle Maan ........ C3
- 10 De Soepwinkel ........ D2
- 11 De Waaghals ........ A1
- 12 Eet Winkel Het Magazin ........ A2
- 13 Lunchroom Hannibal ........ B2
- 14 Mambo ........ C2
- 15 Mamouche ........ B1
- 16 Op de Tuin ........ C4
- 17 Orontes ........ A2
- 18 Roots ........ D1
- 19 Taart van m'n Tante ........ B1
- 20 Today's ........ A2
- 21 Wild Moa Pies ........ C3
- 22 Zagros ........ A2
- 23 Zen ........ A1

**Drinking & Nightlife** (p171)
- 24 Barça ........ B1
- 25 Café Berkhout ........ B1
- 26 Café Binnen Buiten ........ A2
- 27 Café de Groene Vlinder ........ B2
- 28 Café Krull ........ C2
- 29 Café Sarphaat ........ D2
- 30 Chocolate Bar ........ B2
- 31 Gambrinus ........ B4
- 32 Het Paardje ........ B2
- 33 Katsu ........ B2
- 34 Kingfisher ........ B1
- 35 Pilsvogel ........ B2
- 36 Quinto ........ A1

**Entertainment** (p173)
- 37 Badcuyp ........ D1
- 38 CC Muziekcafe ........ B4
- 39 Rialto Cinema ........ C3

**Shopping** (p173)
- 40 Bleecker ........ B2
- 41 Blonde ........ B2
- 42 De Emaillekeizer ........ D2
- 43 De Vredespijp ........ B1
- 44 Fietsfabriek ........ A1
- 45 Het is Liefde ........ B1
- 46 Noor ........ B2
- 47 Raak ........ B2
- 48 Stenelux ........ A1
- 49 Tiller Galerie ........ A1

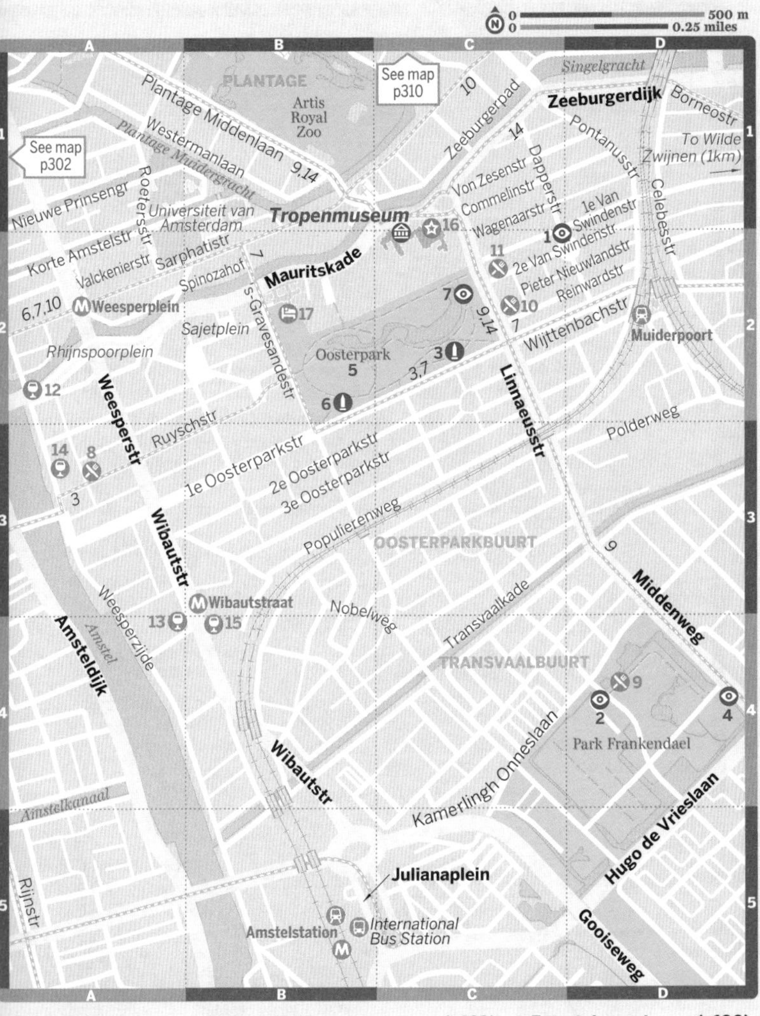


## Top Sights (p186)

Tropenmuseum ........... C2

## Sights (p186)

1 Dappermarkt ................ C2
2 De Pure Markt .............. D4
3 De Schreeuw ................ C2
4 Frankendael House....... D4
5 Oosterpark.................... B2
6 Slavery Memorial.......... B2
7 Spreeksteen ................. C2

## Eating (p189)

8 Cafe Ruys ...................... A3
9 De Kas ........................... D4
10 Pata Negra .................... C2
11 Roopram Roti ............... C2

## Drinking & Nightlife (p189)

12 Amstel Haven ................ A2
13 Canvas........................... A4
14 De Ysbreeker ................ A3
15 Trouw............................. B4

## Entertainment (p190)

16 Tropentheater ................C1

## Shopping

Dappermarkt .......... (see 1)

## Sleeping (p218)

17 Hotel Arena.................... B2

# PLANTAGE, EASTERN ISLANDS & EASTERN DOCKLANDS

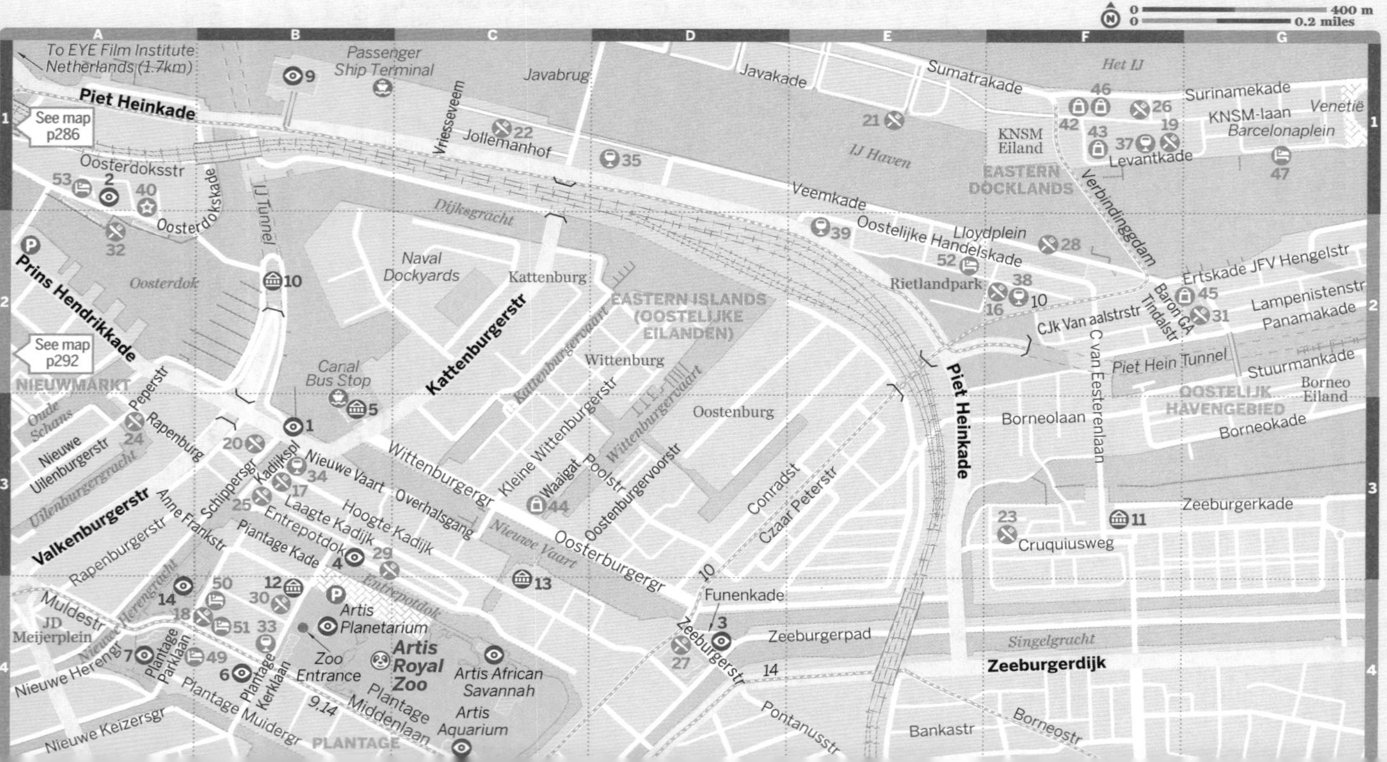

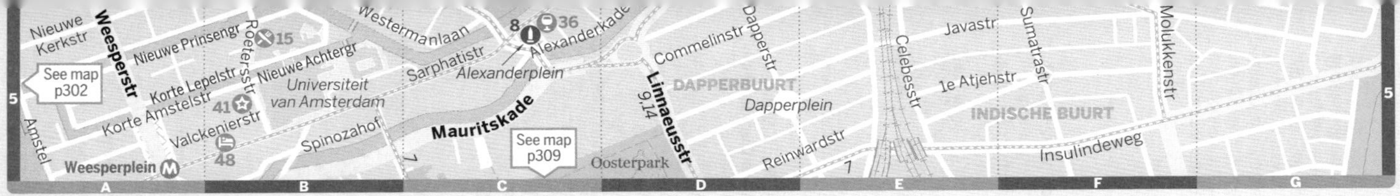

Nieuwe Kerkstr
Weesperstr
Nieuwe Prinsengr
Roetersstr
Nieuwe Achtergr
Westermanlaan
Sarphatistr
Alexanderplein
Alexanderkade
Commelinstr
Dapperstr
Celebesstr
Javastr
Sumatrastr
Molukkenstr
1e Atjehstr
DAPPERBUURT
Dapperplein
INDISCHE BUURT
Korte Lepelstr
Korte Amstelstr
Valckenierstr
Universiteit van Amsterdam
Spinozahof
Mauritskade
Linnaeusstr
9,14
Oosterpark
Reinwardstr
Insulindeweg
Amstel
Weesperplein
See map p302
See map p309
A B C D E F G

| **Top Sights** | **(p178)** |
|---|---|
| Artis Royal Zoo | B4 |

| **Sights** | **(p177)** |
|---|---|
| 1 ARCAM | B3 |
| 2 Centrale Bibliotheek Amsterdam | A1 |
| 3 De Gooyer Windmill | D4 |
| 4 Entrepotdok | B3 |
| 5 Het Scheepvaartmuseum | B3 |
| 6 Hollandsche Schouwburg | B4 |
| 7 Hortus Botanicus | A4 |
| 8 Muiderpoort | C5 |
| 9 Muziekgebouw aan 't IJ | B1 |
| 10 NEMO | B2 |
| 11 Persmuseum | F3 |
| 12 Verzetsmuseum | B4 |
| 13 Werfmuseum 't Kromhout | C4 |
| 14 Wertheimpark | A4 |

| **Eating** | **(p179)** |
|---|---|
| 15 Agora | B5 |
| 16 Café de Cantine | F2 |
| 17 Café Kadjik | B3 |
| 18 Café Smith en Voogt | B4 |
| 19 De Wereldbol | F1 |
| 20 Éenvistweevis | B3 |
| 21 Einde van de Wereld | E1 |
| 22 Fifteen | C1 |
| 23 Gare de l'Est | F3 |
| 24 Greetje | A3 |
| 25 Koffiehuis van den Volksbond | B3 |
| 26 Kompaszaal | F1 |
| 27 Langendijk Eetcafe | D4 |
| 28 Odessa | F2 |
| 29 Paerz | B3 |
| 30 Plancius | B4 |
| 31 Roos en Noor | G2 |
| 32 Sea Palace | A2 |

| **Drinking & Nightlife** | **(p182)** |
|---|---|
| Brouwerij 't IJ | (see 3) |
| 33 Café Koosje | B4 |
| 34 Café Orloff | B3 |
| 35 Café Pakhuis Wilhelmina | D1 |
| 36 De Groene Olifant | C5 |
| 37 Kanis & Meiland | F1 |
| 38 KHL | F2 |
| 39 Panama | E2 |
| Star Ferry | (see 9) |

| **Entertainment** | **(p182)** |
|---|---|
| Bimhuis | (see 9) |
| 40 Conservatorium van Amsterdam | A1 |
| 41 Kriterion | B5 |
| Muziekgebouw aan 't IJ | (see 9) |

| **Shopping** | **(p183)** |
|---|---|
| 42 Arrival/Departure | F1 |
| 43 De Ode | F1 |
| 44 Frank's Smokehouse | C3 |
| 45 JC Creations | G2 |
| 46 Loods 6 | F1 |

| **Sleeping** | **(p218)** |
|---|---|
| 47 Captain's Place | G1 |
| 48 Hotel Allure | B5 |
| 49 Hotel Hortus | B4 |
| 50 Hotel Parklane | B4 |
| 51 Hotel Rembrandt | B4 |
| 52 Lloyd Hotel | E2 |
| 53 Mint Hotel | A1 |

# Our Story

A beat-up old car, a few dollars in the pocket and a sense of adventure. In 1972 that's all Tony and Maureen Wheeler needed for the trip of a lifetime – across Europe and Asia overland to Australia. It took several months, and at the end – broke but inspired – they sat at their kitchen table writing and stapling together their first travel guide, *Across Asia on the Cheap*. Within a week they'd sold 1500 copies. Lonely Planet was born.

Today, Lonely Planet has offices in Melbourne, London and Oakland, with more than 600 staff and writers. We share Tony's belief that 'a great guidebook should do three things: inform, educate and amuse'.

# Our Writers

### Karla Zimmerman

**Coordinating Author: Medieval Centre & Red Light District, Nieuwmarkt, Old South, Oosterpark & South Amsterdam** During her Amsterdam travels, Karla admired art, bicycled crash-free, ate an embarrassing number of Droste chocolates and bent over to take her *jenever* (Dutch gin) like a local. She has been visiting Amsterdam since 1989, decades that have seen her trade space cakes for *stroopwafels* (syrup waffles), to a much more pleasant effect. Based in Chicago, Karla writes travel features for newspapers, books, magazines and websites. She has authored or co-authored several Lonely Planet guidebooks covering the USA, Canada, Caribbean and Europe. Karla also wrote Welcome to Amsterdam, What's New, Need to Know, Top Itineraries, If You Like, Museum Top Tips, By Bike, Canals and the Survival Guide chapters.

Read more about Karla at:
lonelyplanet.com/members/karlazimmerman

### Sarah Chandler

**Western Canal Ring, Southern Canal Ring, Jordaan & the West, Vondelpark & Around, De Pijp, Plantage, Eastern Islands & Eastern Docklands** Sarah fell in love with Amsterdam during university, though it was only later, as a local, that she mustered sufficient bravery to master the deceptively tricky Dutch art of cycling. When she's not frolicking in the Vondelpark, drinking *koffie verkeerd* (milky coffee) canalside at Café 't Smalle or indulging her cinematic obsessions at the Pathé Tuschinskitheater, Sarah works as a writer, actress and lecturer at Amsterdam University College. She loves calling one of her favourite neighbourhoods on earth – Amsterdam's Latin Quarter, De Pijp – home. Sarah also wrote Month by Month, With Kids, Like a Local, For Free, Day Trips and the Understand chapters.

Read more about Sarah at:
lonelyplanet.com/members/sarahchandler

**Published by Lonely Planet Publications Pty Ltd**
ABN 36 005 607 983
8th edition – Feb 2012
ISBN 978 174179 903 3

10 9 8 7 6 5 4 3 2 1
Printed in China